Gardner Murphy

Gardner Murphy

Integrating, Expanding and Humanizing Psychology

by

Lois Barclay Murphy

Lois Barclay Murphy

McFarland and Company, Inc., Publishers
Jefferson, North Carolina, and London

Frontispiece: **Gardner Murphy lecturing, about 1960.**

British Library Cataloguing-in-Publication data are available

Library of Congress Cataloguing-in-Publication Data

Murphy, Lois Barclay, 1902–
   Gardner Murphy : integrating, expanding and
humanizing psychology.
     p. cm.
   Bibliography: p. 375.
   Includes index.
   1. Murphy, Gardner, 1895–[1979].   2. Psychologists—
United States—Biography. I. Title.
BF109.M85M87 1990 150'.92 [B]   89-42740
ISBN 0-89950-443-4 (lib. bdg. : 50# alk. paper) ∞

Manufactured in the United States of America

McFarland & Company, Inc., Publishers
  Box 611, Jefferson, North Carolina 28640

For the students,
colleagues and friends
of Gardner Murphy
who have made this book
possible

Table of Contents

*Between pages 98 and 99 are 16 pages
of plates containing 37 photographs*

Preface : Purpose, Problems, and Solution

The approach of the twenty-first century has increased pressure to record the history of the twentieth, and a major contribution to history comes from biographies of those who lived it. For the young science of American psychology, we have accounts of the lives of William James, G. Stanley Hall, Edward Lee Thorndike, Kurt Lewin, Abraham Maslow, J. Banks Rhine, and those of Edward Tolman and Gordon Allport are being written. These are in addition to over a hundred short autobiographies in the seven volumes of the *History of Psychology in Autobiography*; three volumes of *The Psychologists;* and *Models of Achievement*. Gardner Murphy wrote three autobiographical chapters, one in each of the first two of the series mentioned above, and one in the *Journal of Parapsychology*. But after he died, some of his colleagues and former students wanted more and urged me to write a biography of him: "You know him better than anyone else does." I agreed naively, not knowing about the huge losses of archives: The psychology department at Columbia had discarded records in a house-cleaning effort—there was no documentation of his twenty years there as teacher and chairman of the college psychology program; letters to and from his mother during his two years in World War I have not been found and may have been discarded by her or lost at times of moving from one house to another, then to an apartment in New York; two four-drawer files belonging to Gardner were discarded by a superintendent of our townhouse when we moved from Bronxville to Topeka; important files from Gardner's years at Menninger were lost in a move from one building to another.

Neither Gardner nor I kept diaries and we were not yet in the era of taped conversations. My geriatric memory is poor and so is that of some crucial colleagues and friends. Moreover, physical limitations made it impossible for me to fly around for interviews as other biographers do now.

Consequently it has been necessary to limit this account of Gardner's work and life to sources actually available through letters and phone conversations with surviving colleagues, students, research assistants, friends, relatives and existing archives, Gardner's writing, and my own spotty memory. A detailed chronological account has been impossible. What was possible was an account of those of Gardner's contributions to psychology with which I was familiar and which his colleagues discussed. I see these in relation to his hopes and his vision of what psychology needed, as well as in relation to the context of his contributions in the Zeitgeist, his own evolution, and concurrent personal influences.

Robert Gittings has commented that after centuries of biographies shaped by the imagination, prejudices and voyeurism of their writers, biography has now reached an era of common sense and a commitment to accuracy. Pseudo-psychoanalytic speculations have had their day; logical interpretations based on evidence are essential. This makes sense to me. I cannot approach Gardner's vision of a complete account of a personal life as he developed it in his *Personality: A Biosocial Approach to Origins and Structure;* that would have involved in-depth biosocial studies at successive stages of his life. This is an overview which may stimulate others to explore roots of American psychology in the twentieth century.

Another problem confronted me: how to achieve the unity of theme expected in an account of a life when I am writing about a versatile man of wide interests, multiple commitments, changing moods, who veritably seemed to be a different person in different settings—the "sober as a judge" and too serious Yale student, as seen by his peers and some of his teachers there; the "happy man" and "enthusiast" seen by some friends in his middle years; the awesome teacher described over half a century by his students; the playful companion described by young friends; the sad scholar about whom a friend worried when Gardner was in his sixties; and the father who was always a source of joy as seen by his own children.

A thread of unity weaves through all of the great range of interests, commitments and moods: the intensity and sensitivity of his responsiveness to people, to nature, to the challenge of psychical research and the challenges of psychology in the changing social and technological world of his century. He was seen by some colleagues as a major integrator of the different trends in psychology at a time of fragmentation; by others as an enlarger of the scope of psychology when it was too limited; and by still others as a humanizer of psychology when it was forgetting the needs of human beings. Intensely committed to these efforts as he was, few of his peers saw the whole Gardner Murphy. I have tried to describe his dimensions and some of what he meant to his generation and what he bequeathed to the next one.

In addition to records and correspondence in archives, correspondence, interviews, and informal conversation with the following people have contributed facts and impressions of Gardner which made this book possible:

Ned Aiken, Cecile Anderson, Heinz Ansbacher, Dr. John Archibald,

Thelma Babbitt, Ruth Bachwig, Gordon Barclay, Leonard Beadle, Richard Benson, William Bevan, Evelyn Beyer, Barbara Biber, Warren Blanding, Peter Blos, Margaret Brenman, Jerome Bruner, Alice Bryan, Dr. Robert Carraway, M. Chari, Joseph Chassell, Irvin Child, Donald Cook, Lolafaye Coyne, Joan Criswell, Laura Dale, Marjory de Vries, Elizabeth des Cognets, Solomon Diamond, Rogelio Diaz-Guerrera, Thomas Dolgoff, Margaret E.B. DuBois, Philip H. DuBois, Joan Erikson, Sibylle Escalona, Lorenz Finison, Colin Frank, Kevin Frank, Riley Gardner, Ruth Gardner, A. Bartlett Giamatti, Alfred Glixman, Judith Greissman, Ernest Haggard, Gerald Haigh, Calvin Hall, Lucien Hanks, Eugene Hartley, Ruth Hartley, Anemona Hartocollis, Pitsa Hartocollis, Grace Heider, Melissa Hersh, Ernest Hilgard, Cotter Hirschberg, Robert Holt, Wayne Holtzman, Ann Holzman, Philip Holzman, Leonard Horwitz, Susan Irza, Mary Cover Jones, S. David Kahn, Catherine Karuba, Daniel Katz, Fred Keller, William Key, Prem Kirpal, Otto Klineberg, V.K. Kothurkar, Joseph Kovach, Stanley Krippner, Herbert Krugman, Louis G. Lane, Irving Lazar, Richard Lazarus, David Leary, Gerald Ledford, Morton Leeds, Bernard Levy, Ruth Levy, Jane Likert, Rensis Likert, Frank Lorimer, Petra Lorimer, Lester Luborsky, Ruth Luborsky, Helen M. Lynd, William McGill, Harold McNamara, Henry Margenau, Eli Marks, Margaret A. Marsh, Lois Jean Masters, Martha Mednick, Hyman Meltzer, Marilyn Meltzer, Catherine Menninger, Karl Menninger, Roy Menninger, Carmen Michael, Donald Michael, Mrs. H. Miller, Al G. Murphy, Leonard Murphy, Henry A. Murray, Henrietta Nechin, Herbert Nechin, Theodore Newcomb, Candy Newman, Dr. Cap Oliver, Robert Oliver, Dr. Sean O'Reilly, Karlis Osis, Drena Owens, Therese Perkins, Mary Perry, Larry Plotkin, Helen Poffenberger, John Popplestone, Harold Proshansky, Meyer Rabban, Ishak Ramzy, Jean Ray, J.B. Rhine, Lester Roach, Irwin Rosen, Max Rosenbaum, Arthur Rosenthal, Saul Rosenzweig, Gautam Sarabhai, S. Stansfeld Sargent, Gertrude Schmeidler, Saul Sells, Georgene Seward, John Seward, Irving Sheffel, Howard Shevrin, Carol Signorella, Dr. Harold Silver, Jerome Singer and mother, Colleen Small, Joy Small, Margaret Small, Brewster Smith, Marie Smith, Charles Solley, Robert Sommer, Donald Spence, Herbert Spohn, Ross Stagner, Bernard Steinzor, Ian Stevenson, Ernest Taves, Eugene Taylor, James Taylor, Montague Ullman, Amy Wallerstein, Judith Wallerstein, Nina Wallerstein, Robert Wallerstein, Ralph K. White, Rhea White, Marshall Williams, Gwen Zeichner, Louis Zurcher.

Among these, special help has been given in the critical reading of chapters by Joan Criswell, Lucien Hanks, Eugene Hartley, Ernest Hilgard, Cotter Hirschberg, Wayne Holtzman, Philip Holzman, William Key, Otto Klineberg, Joseph Kovach, Stanley Krippner, David Leary, Morton Leeds, Al G. Murphy, Leonard Murphy, S. Stansfeld Sargent, Gertrude Schmeidler, Saul Sells, Jerome Singer, Brewster Smith, Robert Sommer, Herbert Spohn, Ross Stagner, Ernest Taves, Eugene Taylor, Montague Ullman, Robert Wallerstein, Ralph K. White, Louis Zurcher.

    Al Murphy was a perennial source of information, memories, perspectives, insights, and he was also a helpful and sensitive critic of early drafts of chapters.

    Noelle Beatty was a most helpful editor, reducing the manuscript to a feasible size, cutting my overly generous repetitions of important events in Gardner's life, and introducing order when order was needed.

    Lucy Whittier was angelically patient as she typed revision after revision.

I / Orientation

1. Introducing Gardner Murphy, Psychologist, 1920–1972

The Gold Medal Award of the American Psychological Foundation, highest award in the profession, presented "in recognition of a distinguished and long-continued record of scientific and scholarly accomplishment" was granted to Gardner Murphy in 1972. Its citation read: "To Gardner Murphy — A peerless teacher, a felicitous writer, an eclectic psychologist of limitless range, he seeks to bring the whole of human experience to bear in understanding behavior."

Paradoxically this tribute focused on Gardner's style. Other awards recognized his contributions to the development of psychology as a young science in the twentieth century, a science that was torn between the hope to achieve recognition as a natural science with the prestige of physics and the pressure to study the nature of the mind, the activity and problems of human beings. Nineteenth-century psychology in Europe focused on laboratory research but in America William James and G. Stanley Hall — both of whom developed laboratories, to be sure — opened the door to a much wider range of topics in psychology. In fact, the flood of new problems produced a revolution and with it, conflicting views of what was properly included in psychology as a science.

If Helmholtz or Wilhelm Wundt or any other major psychologist of the nineteenth century could have looked at the program of a recent annual convention of the American Psychological Association, he would have been astonished, perhaps dismayed or overwhelmed. Forty-seven divisions within the Association? Papers on "How to Prevent a Nuclear War," "Human Diversity: Race, Culture, Class, and Ethnicity," and "Psychoanalysis Versus Psychotherapy"? These topics are indeed remote from the studies of sensation and reaction time which engrossed nineteenth-century psychology. One way to understand these changes is to review the life and work of one who actively participated in them, and was sensitive to the dramatic changes in the political,

3

economic and social life of the mid-twentieth century. Post–World War I anxieties in the twenties, the great Depression in the United States along with exacerbated racism and the shadow of Hitler in Europe in the thirties; World War II in the forties, with a short-lived alliance with the Soviet Union followed by inquisitional pursuit of people suspected of being Communists or Communist sympathizers; the Supreme Court decision in the fifties outlawing segregation of black students in separate schools; in the sixties the struggles for civil rights for blacks and President Johnson's "war against poverty" which revealed potentialities of the poor; his war in Vietnam that aroused nationwide protests — all of these prompted study by the social sciences, including social psychologists.

This was also an era of enrichment of science and the arts in America by creative scientists escaping from Hitler's totalitarianism and genocide; this group included psychologists and psychoanalysts — and natural scientists — physicists, chemists, and biologists. The influx contributed to a certain erosion of turf-protection in the scientific world as multidisciplinary conferences and projects helped scientists of different fields to communicate with each other and to appreciate the resulting hybridization, as Gardner referred to it later.

The transformation of American psychology is thus the product of a complex evolution shaped not only by the cultural changes but by the creativity of twentieth-century psychologists including Gardner Murphy. During the years from 1920 to 1972 he integrated the new with the old, expanded psychology as he maintained an endlessly hospitable mind to new, even taboo, approaches and concepts, carried on research that extended the range of accepted psychological problems, and passionately supported the principle that psychology should serve human needs.

Some experimental psychologists have questioned whether Gardner was a scientist in the true sense of the word. The Columbia University zoologist Theodosius Dobzhansky wrote in his superb volume, *Mankind Evolving,* "Science is cumulative knowledge." He emphasized the complementary needs for specialization and for synthesis in science. In the Daedalus volume, *The Making of Modern Science,* Edward Shils — fellow of Peterhouse, Cambridge University, and professor of sociology at the University of Chicago — summarized the several contributions characteristic of the development of a science: facts "rigorously demonstrated by commonly accepted procedures dealing with relatively reproducible observations"; theories bound to data; discussions of modification of previous hypotheses called for by the new data; syntheses and consolidation of existing research bringing order into a broad field; summaries in textbooks for students; articles which summarize the state of knowledge on a particular problem and furnish a hypothesis based on new observations; essays which refine and clarify particular ideas; theoretical treatises which present all the major concepts or variables relevant to the topic. He did not mention the historical survey which describes the succession of concepts supported by observation, research, integration of findings and inferences from them; reviews which place issues and research findings of the present in perspective. Gardner's contributions included all of these, over his more than half a century of teaching, research, writing, and lecturing in this country and around the world.

Observations of the accumulation of knowledge and the progress of theoretical formulations are best made by historians. Gardner Murphy's historical perspective enabled him to perceive relationships not seen by those who were constantly involved in day to day work in the laboratory. His classical education, which included a mastery of ancient Greek and studies of the history of philosophy, together with his deep commitment to an evolutionary view of human life and thought made it natural for him to see each concept in a specialized area in terms of the process which led to its emergence.

The task of the historian also requires an ability to perceive interrelationships between different lines of research and to identify common principles not recognized by the researchers themselves. Gardner's integrative drive (partly developed from his creative response to the contrasting ecologies, accents, and life styles of his beloved Northern and Southern relatives) contributed to this perceptiveness.

In Gardner's classroom teaching, in countless lectures, in his supervision of research, Gardner provided an historical orientation to the concepts and theories that were being discussed, or studied experimentally. Along with this ever-present historical view of psychological theories he pointed to connections between research findings in different areas which others had not noticed. This vertical and horizontal integration was his persistent and unique contribution to both young and mature psychologists of the midcentury.

His 1929 *Historical Introduction to Modern Psychology,* which had its last revision in 1972, attacked the issue of temporal integration by showing how philosophical and empirical origins had evolved to modern theories such as behaviorism and Gestalt. The integration across subspecialties progressed gradually. In 1931 he began to relate the structuralist psychology of Wundt and Titchener to new research on social processes. Shortly thereafter he began the integration of personality and clinical psychology with social and cognitive psychology. Gardner was also ingenious in devising new experimental procedures to uncover data relevant to his theoretical framework; e.g., using emotionally loaded learning tasks to replace the nonsense syllables of Ebbinghaus fame.

Gardner's move in 1952 to a post as director of research at the Menninger Foundation symbolized the final step in his work toward integrating the diverse "psychologies" of the time. From his early years in experimental psychology he had extended scientific methods and logic into social psychology; and he clarified the linkages between laboratory psychology and the psychology of personality. It was only natural, therefore, that he would seek to integrate clinical psychology with experimental, social, and personality psychology. At Menninger it was possible for him not only to reflect on problems facing the clinicians, but also to stimulate research linking diagnosis and therapy with scientific issues of perceiving, learning and remembering.

This move also provided flexibility of schedule which made it possible for him to communicate—through lectures and conferences—his seasoned perspectives and insights on human problems of the day.

Paradoxically, all of these contributions to psychology as it was institutionalized in the universities of the twentieth century were preceded and accompanied by Gardner's dedicated efforts on behalf of parapsychology, referred to in William James' papers and later as "psychical research." His determination to push the American Society for Psychical Research to a fully rigorous scientific level of work was an important factor in the improved status of psychical research in the scientific world.

Gardner had the courage to venture predictions about future developments in psychology. Because of his breadth of vision, he was asked on at least three occasions to offer extrapolations of the evolution of American psychology as he saw them. While "Psychology in the year 2000" cannot yet be tested for validity, it is obvious that his earlier predictions and at least components of that 1969 vision have already been confirmed.

Themes that meant most to Gardner, that he thought of as "really me," included the ideas of canalization, autism, Spencerian three-phase evolutionary theory, feedback, and his version of field theory. We find his biosocial concept of personality development generally accepted now. His concept of social psychology as an empirical science is taken for granted. His "holistic," comprehensive, systematic approach to personality has provided a foundation for further studies of personality. His leadership, with other leaders of the Society for Psychological Study of Social Issues helped to stimulate research on human problems, and his passionate support was crucial in the acceptance of the statement "The object of the APA shall be to advance psychology as a science and as a means of promoting human welfare," in the constitution of the American Psychological Association. In other words, his contribution to integrating, expanding and humanizing psychology is, I believe, his most enduring contribution to the development of psychology. This includes his insistence that all methods are needed, each for its appropriate problems, and that no source of psychological insight can be ignored.

To enumerate these contributions is not enough for understanding how they evolved. Real understanding can only come from an exploration of the roots of Gardner's basic drives, the experiences which nurtured his creativity, and the sequences of opportunities, demands and challenges which made his contributions possible. Without understanding the man he became, we cannot understand either the choices he made or the reasons for their impact on generations of students, their assimilation into the sinews of psychology, and their influence on contemporary life.

From Isaac Newton to Charles Darwin to Richard Leakey, early experiences of scientists have contributed to the emergence of ideas that shaped their contributions to the evolution of science. In psychology, William James is a familiar example of the interweaving of life experience and creative thinking; today the public demands the living context in which scientific progress takes place.

Gardner Murphy's lifelong curiosity and quest for reality, stimulated in early childhood, and his guiding theme, "plus ultra"—there is more beyond—both reflected and supported an extraordinarily open mind; his commitment to "integrating the new with the old" made him a unique generalist in psychology; his empathy for underdogs and sensitivity to young and old which won him the love of students and colleagues had roots both in his innate sensitivity and responsiveness and in his early development. All of these and other trends in his complex personality and wide ranging thought can best be understood in the context of his varied, sometimes conflicting early experiences.

Very little orientation to the changing intellectual and cultural climate of the time is provided in the autobiographies of psychologists in the *History of Psychology in Autobiography*; only the difficulty of finding work as a psychologist during the Depression, and the pull away from theology exerted by the influence of college science give hints of wider forces shaping their lives and their psychology.

In his own autobiography for the *History of Psychology in Autobiography* Gardner gave important clues to his motivations as a psychologist as he began his account with his discussion of his "uncertain identity," developing from conflicts between his Northern and Southern identifications, and between his locally distinguished grandfather and the plebeian name of his reformist father. At the end of his account he wrote, "Certainly Dewey was right that one's personality shapes one's philosophy," and he continued with the remark that an enduring and growing trait of his had been a "passionate need for inclusiveness." His own unpublished as well as published notes provide evidence of influences on his development.

Gardner's work was intimately interwoven with his life—his enthusiasms, his friendships, his family, his values and hopes for humanity, the intellectual and social developments of the century and his vision of the future.

My own experience and knowledge of his professional life was one-sided; a biography would have to share the experience of his students and his colleagues, their observations of his contributions to them and to the evolving science of psychology—and these should be shared directly in their own words.

Although Gardner was considered unique in his outstanding teaching and writing, he shared background influences, standards of achievement, values and interests with many others of his generation of psychologists and these contributed to their appreciation of him expressed in a long series of

honors. He was a psychologist's psychologist. One survey reported that he was
second only to Freud in the number of students he inspired to go into
psychology; and it was said that many of his students were major figures in the
who's who of psychology at midcentury. With his friends and students he was
at the center of some of the most important trends of the century in
psychology. The respect in which he was held is attested by Gardner's many
honors in addition to receiving the Gold Medal Award of the Psychological
Foundation: the presidency of the American Psychological Association and of
the Society for the Psychological Study of Social Issues, as well as the presidency
of several regional psychological associations, the Society for Psychical Research
(London) and the American Society for Psychical Research, honorary degrees
from the University of Hamburg and the City University of New York, election
to the New York Academy of Sciences and the American Academy of Arts and
Sciences.

Gardner was not only a scientist, teacher and writer. He was a warm, enthusiastic, richly experiencing man—devoted to his family, his friends and his
students and delighting in the arts and in nature. His sensory responsiveness
and resonance contributed to his view of humanity as isomorphic with the
universe, and evolving under the same laws. At heart he was a seeker, a
philosopher, and a humanitarian.

2. The Peerless Teacher

The New York years were teaching years as well as writing years, at summer sessions in addition to the September to June college terms. After he left New York for Topeka, Kansas, Gardner taught rarely—at the University of Kansas, at Kansas State University, and at the Menninger School of Psychiatry. When he retired from Menninger in 1967 he was a visiting professor at the George Washington University in D.C. until 1972.

Although Gardner and I discussed our joint interest in teaching, my busy life as homemaker, mother, wife, teacher at Sarah Lawrence College and researcher studying child personality afforded no margin of time for attending his courses. I did not know that his students held him in awe for I was not awed by him. The first glimpse of their experience of Gardner came to me in the opening chapter of the Festschrift given to him for his 65th birthday in 1960.

It is characteristic of GM to start his presentation promptly, drawing from his pocket some folded papers which he lays upon the desk (and rarely looks at), and to continue at a rapid-fire pace that ends with papers and watch, which has emerged during the period, back in his pocket, the last point being finished with a grammatically complete sentence that ends as the final bell rings.

His lectures most often develop a theme or provide a general frame of reference, rather than merely summarize data. In his presentations, GM has been known to draw upon Aristotle and Popeye, and in a single hour to use illustrative material from ancient Japanese art, medieval European agriculture, eighteenth-century English philosophy, contemporary New England home life, as well as from recently published and unpublished research by psychologists, physiologists, and geneticists. He is scrupulous in acknowledging the sources of his material and writes the references on the board with complete citations of publication data for journal articles.

The awe of the students for the teacher is usually crystallized when they discover that the "notes" taken out of GM's pocket at the beginning of a lecture are the back of an envelope on which two or three illegible words have been scrawled. After exposure to hour after hour of brilliant lectures, only to discover that all had been presented without any more prompting than a couple of cues

9

and that references were given from memory, students tend to be somewhat sub-
dued and respectful in his presence. This attitude has been neither sought nor
desired by "GM."

The lecture is not GM's only form of presentation. Sessions are interrupted
at times with dramatizations. In discussing social attitudes, he might quote from
Gilbert's *H.M.S. Pinafore* and posture "and this should be his customary at-ti-
tude" in a manner that is a faithful copy of the original illustration in the book.
In presenting the "volley-theory" of hearing to an introductory class, he might
tramp across the platform and induce members of the class to follow along, out
of time, to produce an idea of the action in the auditory nerve. And, of course,
he uses classroom experiments, demonstrations of tests and equipment and procedures, and occasional films. His ingenuity is so great, however, that many of
the classroom "demonstrations" are of a caliber comparable to much currently
published research.

The letters to me from his students, and the contributions to journals gave
more insight into Gardner as a teacher, at different times over the years.
Different sensitivities and interests of his former students give varying portraits
of Gardner, with varying samples of the intellectual diet and the kinds of support he offered them. A psychiatrist wrote:

> In 1926, as a sophomore in Columbia College, I took a course in abnormal
> psychology. The instructor, a pale young man of about 30, with dark glasses and
> thinning sandy-colored hair, would lounge on the edge of his desk as he led the
> class in informal discussions about what today would be termed altered states of
> consciousness. He was then, as later, an engaging talker with an easy, limpid style
> and a powerful command of his subject. Levels of awareness other than those of
> ordinary waking consciousness became a reality as classroom demonstrations of
> posthypnotic suggestions, automatic writing, and other evidences of dissociation
> (à la Bernheim and Janet) were given with the aid of student volunteers. There
> were also visits to "asylums for the insane." . . . His death was to me almost like
> a species becoming extinct. For there will not soon be another with such a rare
> combination of scholarly and literary gifts.

In the twenties and even the thirties, psychological concepts were not
generally understood. There was no *Psychology Today*, advice of psychologists
was not conveyed daily though the media, and many parents who did not
understand what psychology was protested the plans of their sons and
daughters to go into this strange, unknown field. Gardner became an "intellectual father" to some of these students. Others wrote that he was their "spiritual
father." A few had been orphaned or estranged from their natural parents.
Many who went away to college, leaving home and their parents, had endured
a loss that left a gap waiting to be filled. Some of them were freshmen at the
age of sixteen or seventeen and would complete the A.B. degree almost before
they were out of their teenage years. Perhaps the fact that his own father had
died when Gardner was seventeen made him intuitively sensitive to the needs

of such youths so that without conscious knowledge of their story he provided a warm support they experienced as fatherly:

> When I arrived at Columbia [in 1935] with the dust of the Idaho potato fields scarcely gone from my shoes [wrote one student 45 years later], there was much that I didn't know. Gardner sensed this and took me under his wing. He became my godfather in a general way, and specifically so in the intellectual sense. In our work together he taught me more about the design of experiments and the scientific method than I ever learned in the classroom.... Above all Gardner talked to me—wisely where my lack of knowledge was evident, patiently where exasperation might have been more appropriate. And he did put me to work.

Still others with a home tradition of culture were inspired by Gardner's way of finding psychological ideas in human experience of all times and places. A sensitive, creative, rather naive banker's son came to Columbia from Wisconsin; he wrote of his experience:

> Gardner was already a legend in 1931 when I entered his course in the history of psychology. An esteemed psychologist, summering in Madison, Wisconsin, had spent two hours telling me of Gardner's accomplishments and insisted that I work with him when I went to Columbia. Under that mastodon skeleton in Schermerhorn Hall, newly met psychology students had extolled him as a teacher during impromptu evaluations of the departmental faculty. When finally I first saw him in the class room, my image of the robust hero was shaken, as a pale, balding man of delicate health began reading through tinted glasses the class list. He then hurriedly wrote on the blackboard a dozen titles for reading and began talking about Aristotle.
>
> Since my testament had declared that psychology of importance had begun about 1860, I was startled again. What followed, however, turned out to be more fascinating and thought-provoking than any previous class room experience, at the same time more frustrating because it resisted being organized. Later we understood that Gardner was exposing us to the massive intellectual tradition of the West, complete with trends, countertrends, and independent illuminations, as it reflected on the content of psychology through the centuries. The panorama of soul, mind, consciousness, reason and other formulations appeared in a context from Plato to Freud. We reached for his *History of Psychology* to steady ourselves, yet all of us privately agreed that hearing surpassed reading this tale.
>
> The following year, I deliberately risked extending my confusion by registering for his social psychology. The immediate focus on contemporary research gave it utility for the coming "prelims," but soon we were straying into such foreign fields as sociology, anthropology, and economics, whose utility seemed quite marginal. My confusion mounted again as Gardner began dissecting current research for assumptions about the nature of man and society, tracing the descent of these concepts from Hobbes, Rousseau, Adam Smith and wherever else the trail might lead. His prose flowed from the inner gaze of a guru and with the grace of an artist who has embodied the sonata of this concert into his being. One day after class, in answer to my question, he explained why he never used notes, saying: "If there is something I can remember only by notes, how can I expect you to remember it on an examination?"

Gardner saw no point in just training us to pass examinations or just to become technically competent psychologists. He was exposing us to an enormous charting of knowledge pertinent to psychology, which, unlike the bounded literature of the classics, extended indefinitely into unexplored sources. Psychology existed everywhere, covered a fair section of time since the Cambrian period, and somehow extended with life beyond animals to plants. For him, ignorance, rather than being a vice, was the condition in which men lived but should strive to remedy. Only when students had moved into new sources off his chart, was his duty as a teacher fulfilled. These sources might be found in poetry or sculpture, written in cuneiform or mimed in silent drama.

Another message became clearer as we found him guiding our research. Then he was concerned with the still formless unknown to which all are at least partly blind, for we live most of our lives within structured familiarity. To fathom such an unknown, past sources of knowledge were only tangentially useful. At best they led to hunches, possibilities, directions of thought which might leap to the mind of a reader but left him mulling, possibly for years, before a researchable question could be formulated. Though Gardner expected much less from his candidates for the doctorate, many of us were uncertain. In conference after conference he demonstrated the technique of exploration, moving quickly over a simple statistical table to unveil its dreadful and baffling implications.

The experience often left me at sea, unsure whether my table met his standards or the whole tack needed to be sailed on another bearing. At the same time, bent on educating a student properly, he continued to urge us into broadening activities: a project to examine the psychology developing in the intellectual climate of Russia; some courses with the anthropologists just two flights above; an introduction to psychical researchers seeking the conditions that limit ESP. Though existing knowledge could not be encompassed by any man within his life span, Gardner saw that firm island surrounded by the indefinitely extending unknown, where orthodoxy, busily exhausting the vitality of its own formulations, proved no more serviceable than what were dubbed pseudosciences.

These higher imperatives channeled most of our intercourse. This ever frail man drove his personal frailties into the background; domestic life seldom crossed the avenue to Columbia. Yet he must have kept some track of his students when he complimented me one morning for having joined a student picket line. At one lunch he set me straight on the relation of the stock market to the depressed national economy; at another he dampened my thoughts of a postdoctoral year at Harvard. One of his weekends was generously devoted to revising the awkward prose of my dissertation. After a near debacle at my formal oral examination, he salvaged my degree in a half-hour defense and later explained, not his defense, but the nature of my blunder.

Ten years later, Gardner's lectures not only were fresh and inspiring but students were even more deeply moved by them; in 1982 a psychologist described most vividly the setting and his experience of the personality course at City College of New York in 1941:

The room was a large one in the main building accommodating about a hundred students in the audience of whom perhaps a third were "sitting in" (not registered for the course). Gardner always finished precisely as the bell rang, to the amazement of all.

This was followed by applause, mainly for the intellectual content and clarity but perhaps almost as much for the style. The students loved his voice, his unusual and gentle face, his old-fashioned clothes. He was discussed all the time by the psychology majors. They said G.M. meant "great man" and that his first name was really *God*.

On the last day of the course the students applauded as usual, and Gardner left very quickly as usual, but they crowded after him following through the halls, out the door, all across the campus, up to the entrance of Townsend Harris Hall, where the psychology department was located. They applauded all the way. I think all of the students who participated remember the event very well, and consider it a high point in whatever sense of dedication they attribute to their own intellectuality. They certainly never met anyone like Gardner before or since, and probably doubt that there ever was another like him anywhere.

In answer to my inquiry as to the reason for the intensity of enthusiasm of City College students for Gardner this writer explained that it was largely due to the fact that his democratic orientation offered an alternative to Marxism at a time when many students were drawn to Communist ideas and were tempted to join the Communist Party.

At Harvard in the wartime summer of 1942 Gardner gave a course in social psychology; one student described a different style and focus:

Gardner Murphy was not what I would call a dynamic teacher. He was dry and even a little austere, and had none of the platform presence of such Harvard greats of the time as Roger Merriman and Howard Mumford Jones. He walked back and forth almost constantly while talking; we used to comment that it was like watching a ping-pong game. This should have been distracting, but somehow it wasn't.

Although I was then in my third year in psychology at Harvard and had been exposed to some of the greats of the day like Allport, Boring, Murray, and White in psychology and Hocking in philosophy, when Gardner Murphy came into my academic life it was like being hit by a Mack truck. Here was a whole new perspective that I didn't even know existed, a discipline of the mind that was unlike anything I had ever been exposed to. And, for the first time, I was involved.

The class met every day, as I recall, and even now I remember how surprised I was each evening at the neatness and logic of the notes I had taken that morning without even being aware of it. For to me Gardner Murphy had a clarity of thought and expression that I have never seen matched since. For example, that summer I took a course in the history of primitive religions; Gardner Murphy taught me more about that subject in one or two class sessions than the eminent anthropologist was able to convey in all the weeks of the "religions" course!

There followed a rare description of Gardner's dramatic illustrations of a point:

There was a desk on the platform and a chair, and these were integral props for each class. Dr. Murphy would lean on them for brief moments, occasionally putting a foot up on the chair and, on one occasion, stepping rapidly onto and off the chair to demonstrate how a Schneider Index was obtained. If this seems irrelevant to social psychology, perhaps it was. But to me it was just one more evidence of the richness of Dr. Murphy's knowledge and the ability to impart it graphically.

Dr. Murphy always wore a dark suit with a vest that summer. He had a large gold pocket watch which he wore on a chain across his vest. One day he started the class session by taking the watch and chain and handing them to another undergraduate, Ben Barksdale, sitting in the front row.

"Barksdale," he said, "throw my watch out that window." He pointed to the open window at the front of the classroom. We were on the third floor of Emerson Hall in Harvard Yard and because this was before the day of air-conditioned classrooms the windows were open. Barksdale looked at Dr. Murphy, then at the watch, then back at Dr. Murphy. "Go ahead, Barksdale," Gardner Murphy said, "throw it out the window." Barksdale looked at the watch again, then at Dr. Murphy. He hesitated for a moment, then handed the watch back to Dr. Murphy and retreated to his seat.

Gardner Murphy turned to the class. "Our subject today is 'Suggestion,' and you've just seen a demonstration of why it so seldom works."

That was probably the height of drama for that particular course, and yet of all the courses I took before or have taken since there have been none that have taught me as much substantive information while opening vistas on worlds I never knew existed. This was my first introduction to Klineberg, Mead, Benedict, Myrdal, Malinowski, Boas, and a score of others. Although I had considered myself reasonably literate before then, I realized that this was the beginning of whatever genuine intellectual literacy I might ever achieve. Something had happened that had never happened before: I was getting excited by ideas. The only comparable experience I can recall is reading Norbert Wiener's *Cybernetics*: the experience is like a series of flashes of lightning. Things hitherto unseen and unknown are briefly illuminated in stark clarity.

A final observation on the social psychology course is that one of its byproducts was that it provided me a rationale for civil rights that has been at the heart of whatever involvement I have had in the movement since then.

A down-to-earth approach was described by a teacher recalling Gardner's 1948 course in social psychology at Columbia, with its "eloquent — never oratorical — fireworks" and the "vivid word-pictures of his illustrations and metaphors." He remembered

most vividly a class in which Gardner dealt with the impact of neighborhood and locale on the acquisition of attitudes, values and traits. He described in warm, human terms his own experience in a way that turned my thoughts to my own West Virginia steel-mill town setting. So when he asked the class to contribute I found myself the first to respond. I went to the blackboard and launched into a systematic description of the local environmental conditions which had had immense impact on me. I had always been subliminally aware, of course, but this class and his approval touched off a personal connection to a social-psychological issue which has always held paramount interest for me as I deal with developmental ideas.

A Princeton psychologist described the scene during the late forties at City College where Gardner's lectures had become legendary:

> Undergrads in many departments came to listen to his lectures on life (officially designated as personality theory in the class schedule). The auditorium was totally jammed every day; even floor sitting space was at a premium. The last lucky ones would get to stand in the doorway. I married the young lady who saved me a seat.
>
> Gardner Murphy (God Murphy for short to the undergrads) was an object of worship and respect. His bantering style earned him every student's love.
>
> But, to me at least, he also seemed formidable. The first time I spoke to him "in person" I left his cathedral-office with some very special positive feelings about him, and no memory of what had actually transpired. But I somehow knew that he had approved my use of a room for a funny little study on ESP I wanted to carry out—and was amused by it!

In 1943 on the occasion of the centenary of William James' birth, Gardner was invited to give a memorial lecture at Harvard. A psychoanalyst who was interested in parapsychology described the event:

> He spoke on "Parapsychology and Personality" in Emerson Hall. Given the keen competition for students' attention at Harvard in those days, an audience of 50 was considered to be a successful showing. That evening, over 400 listeners crowded the lecture hall. . . . His presentation, as always, was modest, matter of fact, never dogmatic, and never concealing the weaknesses or tentativeness of the material he was discussing. Yet his staggering grasp of the subject in its finest detail, his evenhanded, scholarly judgments, and his legendary skill of exposition, together with his exquisitely precise command of the English language, gave our small group the sense of having in our camp the finest intellect among his Harvard peers. Gardner met with a few of us later, and his openness, warmth, and capacity to listen patiently and sympathetically were immediately apparent.
>
> Gardner's appearance at Harvard that evening was only one of many occasions when he placed the full weight of his status and prestige behind young men like myself who otherwise might have been totally intimidated by the biases of our times, particularly when expressed so dogmatically by men of such power and renown as B.F. Skinner.

When Gardner was in his late sixties a psychologist took a course at the University of Kansas which stimulated him to new explorations.

> Your course in the history of psychology at KU in 1961 was the most rewarding experience of my academic career. You sent me scurrying through everything from *De Anima* and *Parva Naturalia* to *On Ghosts and Spyrits That Walk by Night*. And as a result of your very moving lecture on William James, I have enjoyed reading much of what he wrote, including the several volumes of his letters. You made me realize the breadth psychology has.

While most of his students described to me the impact on them of the range and variety of concepts, illustrations and sources presented in his lectures, his cultivated style and extraordinarily precise timing, a 1942 Harvard student, later a colleague at City College, thoughtfully analyzed the structure of his lectures, and their stimulus to the students:

> Murphy's lectures, even where he is most knowledgeable, never neglect the uninformed part of his audience. The perspective that he gives is wide. The broad issues that make the field worth studying are brought forth early, by lively examples and by general statements, so that the beginner's interest is excited — and from then on, the beginner is in there with him, and cares enough about the problem to be glad to learn some of its details. First he shows the vista; then he fills in the facts; always he points to the gaps where we need more facts for our thinking. Like Shakespeare, he persuades those who hear him to "piece out the imperfections with your thoughts." He leads his readers and listeners to explore.
>
> This quality became a legend among the students in his psychology classes at the City College of New York during the 1940s. Many were later to become distinguished psychologists, leaders in their own areas. Week after week, these bright students found his lectures so exciting that they formed the habit of meeting for coffee after every lecture he gave, because they needed to keep on thinking about the ideas he had been putting to them, and the new insights and exciting possibilities buzzing inside them. During the lecture there were so many facts which they had jotted into their notebooks, trying to keep up with Murphy's flow of ideas, that they had not had time to absorb the implications; they felt they had to share and examine it all together. And to anyone who has seen how other lectures end, with notebooks closed and students hurrying away or talking to each other about the personal affairs that were interrupted by the class hour, this need to keep on thinking about the lecture topic is a remarkable tribute to the way Murphy presented the technical problems he discussed.

A letter from a clinical psychologist of distinction who was in Gardner's Harvard course in 1942, summarized the enduring impact of Gardner's approach echoed by many of his students:

> For me, Gardner was one of the few people who could really encompass psychology, who seemed to know it all and could put it all together. I can't hope to be so inclusive, but I do have the ambition to achieve some similar synthesis, and his example is important to me there.... He was a master at integrating ideas rather than generating distinctively novel ones that might carry his stamp on them; in that way, he was something like David Rapaport, unlike though the two men were in so many ways. Both were great teachers, who deeply influenced their students by personal example. The fact that so many of us wanted to put together a *Festschrift* for Gardner vividly attests to this kind of influence: very few psychologists have been so honored by their students during their lifetime.
>
> He had the rare capacity to foster the independent growth of people, rather than draw them under his personal spell or make them his disciples. He didn't have ideas he was eager to ram down your throat, though he had lots of ideas; he always seemed genuinely interested in hearing your ideas, as many a magnetic teacher did not.

One of the last generation of Gardner's students, who first studied with Gardner as an undergraduate at George Washington University in 1970–71, wrote after Gardner died:

The G.M. I knew was aged, in obviously failing health but his mental faculties had not diminished ...; he continued to make contributions to the field even from his death bed and he never ceased to appreciate the experiences of life.... I learned about psychology from a mentor whose knowledge about the field was encyclopedic, whose perspective was vast and rich, and whose personal experiences alone were an education. More importantly, I learned some lessons about how to live from one of the finest human beings I have known. These lessons took on a special poignancy as it became clear that G.M. was facing life's final challenges.

In the spring of 1971 a frail old man stood at the front of the room in high-topped shoes. The weariness in the body contrasted with the alertness and bemusement in his eyes. Despite unmistakable signs of Parkinsonism, his style of lecturing was striking. He effortlessly spoke in polished prose with barely a glance at his notes. He spoke more clearly, more precisely, more beautifully than all but a few scholars could write. He brought every field of knowledge to bear on a chosen topic, with illustrations and quotations from the arts, philosophy and other social sciences without pretension. Yet he seemed humble almost beyond belief.

I remember thinking that here was a man who was fully developed both intellectually and emotionally, and that if psychology produced such men, then psychology must be worth pursuing. In the last class of the semester, the students expressed their appreciation to G.M. by presenting him with an illustrated biography of Beethoven, knowing that Beethoven was a favorite of his. I never saw such an expression of affection for their professor by any other class.

For the required paper on some aspect of the social and cultural determinants of personality I chose to write on the effects of Hindu religion and culture on the Indian personality, hoping that G.M. knew little about it. He was enthusiastic in support of my topic and helpful with suggestions about how to proceed. At the library I discovered that this was one of his interests, and I found his 1953 *In the Minds of Men*. I spent much of the summer writing a 100-page paper, with a cover letter apologizing for its lateness, and some ideas for related research.

When I took the paper to his office G.M. greeted me like an old friend, which felt like an honor I did not deserve. He asked if I would like to pursue the topic or some other one in an independent study during the next semester. Flattered, but not confident that I could measure up to his expectations, I said I would think about it and get back to him. Fortunately my pride overcame my fears and I decided to study mysticism; the next semester I continued with a field research on personality characteristics of deeply religious political activitsts. I probably read as much for those two courses as I did for all other undergraduate courses combined — not because he was a difficult taskmaster — he was not at all demanding. I think the key reasons were:

First, his joy in learning was infectious. He delighted in new ideas, in finding the larger context for a theory.

Second, he had a stronger faith in my abilities than I did. He subtly took it for granted that the directions I wished to pursue were worthwhile, and that I could master the reading. But he left all the key decisions up to me. He linked my ideas to those of others—for instance, saying at one point, "So you're a *Verstehende* psychologist." When I asked what that meant, he launched into a historical explanation that left me feeling that what I wanted to do was part of an old tradition in psychology.

Third, his assistance in research efforts included telephone calls to old friends who could help me locate subjects for my field research. He asked permission from the author of a copyrighted projective test for me to use it in my project.

When I wrote a noted clinical psychologist about my puzzlement as to why students referred to Gardner as "God" he responded:

> The tone of Gardner's voice, his total manner, expressed personal concern, compassion with humanity and concern with you as part of humanity, going far beyond the academic routine. He seemed above and removed from such routine, more spiritual, like some significant clergy. Furthermore, his great empathy seemed combined with first-hand knowledge of the meaning of suffering.

This innate ability to empathize was undoubtedly a large part of Gardner's extraordinary success as a teacher. He never stood on ceremony, never took an authoritarian stance. Instead he used various ways to put the student on a level with himself. A member of the CCNY psychology faculty wrote:

> Murphy's concern for each individual's special worth showed itself in small ways that set the tone for the larger ones. When a student came to speak with him Murphy would characteristically pull out two chairs so that he sat opposite the student rather than at or behind the desk. He arranged the space to make it a meeting of two human beings, not a meeting of the Professor ... with an outsider.... He was genuinely interested in everyone's hobbies, family, living arrangements, current pleasures and difficulties; he helped where he could; he remembered; he inquired later. He would often take lunch at a coffee shop across from the college rather than at the Faculty Dining Room, and typically would sit at a counter with a vacant seat beside him, making it easy for anyone to slip into the next seat and speak to him without appointment.

His support ranged from a gently tactful correction of spelling to putting a dissertation through the press so that a graduate student "gallivanting" in Europe during the summer could receive his Ph.D. in October instead of the following June. When a student's dissertation was on a topic outside the range of the department faculty, Gardner arranged for an appropriate expert to be added to the committee.

During World War II Gardner managed to have college credit given to his students for courses taken as a part of Army training. One former student wrote:

> I was deeply concerned over the fact that I lacked the B.A., being shy a few credits. G.M. took this matter into his own hands and when I completed an

Italian Area and Language course to the point of adequate fluency for the Army, he saw to it that I was awarded my degree in June 1944. For a G.I. who was never sure where his next assignment would end, this was a matter of profound satisfaction and gratitude.

Gardner encouraged another ethically anxious G.I. to accept the offer from City College to receive his B.A. on the basis of credits for Chinese language as "an ancient language" substitute for the Latin requirement. And all through the war he wrote to former students overseas—in certain instances "more often than my parents did." This kindness went beyond his students to wartime support of mothers. One mother wrote in 1976 about her experience in September 1943 when she went to City College to collect her son's diploma and those of two of his close friends, all of whom were in training:

> The war was on and you saw before you a mother whose only son and his dear friends and many other fine young sons were being trained to be sent into battle. My heart was full of pain and fear. However you gave me about an hour of your precious time and I never forgot your encouraging word.

Gardner had a large view of his students' training needs and confidently offered suggestions that at times seemed beyond realistic possibilities. In the early 1970s, a graduate student, married and with three children to support on a small salary, was astonished at Gardner's recommendations.

> He nonchalantly told me that I should visit with the leading researchers in biofeedback, and calmly outlined his proposed trip for me . . . to visit leaders in Denver, San Francisco, Los Angeles, and Topeka. My mouth fell open as he talked and . . . I tried to explain what a wonderful dream trip that sounded like, but there was no way it could become a reality. . . . He was untouched by my arguments—and I felt a little irritated with him, thinking his head was in the clouds. . . . But the seed had been planted, and a generous brother-in-law financed the trip, with a supplementary check from Gardner. That trip was tremendous. I met all the pioneers in biofeedback.

Gardner had a way of helping in a crisis. One student described an occasion when he was ill with a severe flu at the time of an examination. He asked a relative to call the department and to ask what should be done. Gardner replied, "just have him come in when he is well." When the student came in, still weak about a week later,

> With the ever-present kindness Professor Murphy led me to his office, . . . cleared off the desk and said, "Make yourself comfortable here." He presented the questions and an exam pad, and said, "I'll see you later." Off he went, leaving me undisturbed, to work on my last undergraduate exam alone, in the privacy of that special office . . . at ease. How grateful I was . . . after the anxiety of doing well in the course.

Georgene Seward wrote:

> There is no better example of Gardner's loving kindness than Gardner's unex-
> pected personal visit to John and me in New London, Conn., in 1939 to give us
> his emotional support when John developed a TB spot on his lung. When we
> thought our world was coming to an end, Gardner made it all seem possible and
> temporary. He left us with the feeling that "this too shall pass," which it did.
> Our gratitude can never be fully expressed!

Many of Gardner's spontaneous gestures of financial assistance to
destitute students were made during the Depression when he was teaching
evening classes and summer school to make ends meet on a salary of $4000 a
year. Gardner offered one young man a check with the comment, "You look
hungry. Repay this when you can." The student—by now a distinguished
leader in psychology—said he could not have got through the spring without
that help.

Gardner's professional generosity earned him the deepest respect of his
students; he never published under his own name work that had been done
under his direction—as many professors do. One former student, now a well-
known psychologist, recalled,

> On one examination I wrote at length on a single question—an option he per-
> mitted. In returning the blue-book, he asked if I would like to prepare the
> answer as an article, which he would recommend for publication, because he
> would like to cite it in the second edition of *Experimental Social Psychology,*
> then in preparation. Later it appeared in Moreno's journal, *Sociometry,* under
> the title "A Neglected Aspect of Motivation." We hear so often of professors who
> "steal" the ideas of their students. Gardner went out of his way to insure that
> I could get the fullest credit for this, and I have had few occasions for greater
> pride than the footnote, about 20 years later, in *Human Potentialities,* in which
> he included my name with five others (and each excepting mine that of a truly
> distinguished, universally recognized contributor) as having "contributed to his
> conception that human wants are directly related to the positive outgoing nature
> of man, and not only to his visceral tensions."

Gardner believed that a good teacher should stimulate students to new
levels of functioning. Many were surprised, challenged by his theme as some
of them put it, "You can be better than you are." His perception of his
students' potentialities awakened their own vision of what they might do.
"Who, me?" Theodore Newcomb thought when Gardner asked him to join
us in the 1937 revision of *Experimental Social Psychology.*

Gardner's receptivity to students' research undertakings, to new methods,
new ideas, and new problems freed his students to be creative. Margaret Brenman, now a revered and creative psychoanalyst at the Austen Riggs Center, was
a vivid, intense, eager and fascinating young student in the late thirties. Her
letter to me after Gardner died described his response to her original method:

When I realized that my personal and most precious contact with Gardner took place in the space of one year I am astonished because I consider him, along with Rapaport and Erikson, to be one of the most important both influences and mentors in my professional development. . . . When I was trying to do a masters in psychology at Columbia University and feeling terribly inadequate that I would not be acceptable to Woodworth or to Warden in his animal laboratory, Gardner took very seriously my proposal to use a method which Erik Erikson would now call the method of "disciplined subjectivity." Gardner accepted this as not only respectable, but extremely interesting. I told him I wanted to use the intensive in-depth interview and that my data would consist in the intensive study of the single case. I can well remember how thrilled I was and honored that Gardner invited me to visit you all in Bronxville to discuss my conceptual and methodological problems.

A colleague discussed Gardner's guidance of individuals in this way:

Always oriented towards the desirability of transforming promising insights into empirical demonstrations, GM is as receptive to discussions of qualitative data and crude analysis techniques as he is to the most sophisticated experimental designs and advanced applications of mathematics to data for which conventional statistical techniques seem inappropriate. When several students spent an afternoon rolling dice to test which of several extensions of probability theory was correct he sympathized, but he felt that it was unnecessary since they should have known enough mathematics. However, when a student who had embarked upon a pilot study checking some hypotheses of "schismogenesis" permitted himself to be diverted into a safer study that would involve fewer uncontrolled variables, Gardner Murphy was really disturbed. The "safe" study could be done by almost anyone, but few without the imagination, resourcefulness and social sensitivity GM detected in the particular researcher would venture into the trickier fields.

Invariably, however, GM is considerate of the reality pressures on students and contrives to help with very limited school research budgets, and sometimes with his own, to contribute to the costs of a study; or to hire the student to do work on a subsidized research so that he need not be diverted too far from psychology in his search for financial aid. He often has more confidence in his students than they have in themselves, and encourages them to borrow money to permit them to continue their education. Planning research within reality limits is also recognized, and adjusting designs to changing conditions is accepted. Yet the need for "good" research is never lost from sight. Where in his classroom teaching GM succeeds in having his students outdo themselves, so in his research guidance does he help them discover inner resources they have not known to exist. Approaching him for approval in cutting down the number of samples to be secured for a study or of subjects to be run in an experiment, students find themselves leaving the conference with renewed faith in the importance of their project and a self-proposed increase in their activity in order to establish properly the hypotheses they have advanced.

Gardner's respect for his students was not limited to a concern with their course work.

He appreciates the fact that a student's question about a point in psychology might actually represent a disguised inquiry about a member of his family; in like fashion is he sensitive to nuances in his relationships outside of classroom. What the student thinks is important, *is* important. There is never any condescension in discussing sports or social activities, and he is as ready to respond to such leads as he is to problems in current world events or philosophy or genetics or psychology. Students are people, and people are accorded an unfailing courtesy. The sorely tried student looks forward to the day when he can get GM to precede him through a doorway, and GM is kind enough to permit such a triumph occasionally, though customarily he would hold the door for his junior.

"Friends don't have titles," he once maintained to an assistant who was addressing some materials to be sent to Gardner's associates in other institutions; this is probably the context within which he answers his telephone: "Mr. Murphy speaking." He is a friend to his students though they scarcely dare aspire to such status. Concerned as he is with the professional development of his former students, personal affairs are equally important. Though he never pries, once the student introduces personal matters, GM is ever the friend inquiring about the health of a father or the progress of a romance, or, in time the development of a child.

Gardner seemed to have an endless capacity to excite students about psychology. At George Washington University where he taught until he was 77 years old after leaving the Menninger Foundation at the age of 72, this still went on. One of his students said to me, "All through high school and college, school was boring. . . . I just wasn't excited about anything until I got into Gardner Murphy's class and then I began to see the light, and I saw exciting possibilities. . . ." Gardner apparently evoked a combination of drive, investment, commitment and eagerness in this young man (now a psychologist) that had not emerged before.

The Evolution of an Approach to Teaching

In his autobiographical chapter for *The Psychologists,* Volume II, Gardner wrote, "There was no question that I was going to be a teacher." His mother had been a teacher and since his father's commitment was to education, the educational atmosphere he had breathed almost from birth probably made him even more acutely aware of the gifts of his own teachers, summarized in a letter to Elliott Joseph for a volume on teaching:

> . . . There were a half-dozen people who very profoundly touched my life, either through what they taught, or through the way they taught, or through the fundamental human warmth and depth of their personalities. . . . *Ralph Theller,* at Hotchkiss School, conveyed to me once, and for all, the meaning of beautiful English writing; there could be no greater debt. *Chauncey Tinker,* who taught me freshman English at Yale was absolutely electrifying. *Jack Adams,*

who taught sophomore English, was one of the most profoundly, and utterly lovable friends that ever taught, and I owe an inexpressibly deep tribute to him, both for what I learned to feel in English literature, and for what I learned about public speaking in the debating work, of which he was the coach. *Albert G. Keller,* who taught introductory anthropology, had a more profound impact upon my basic ways of thinking than anyone else in my life. *Harry Emerson Fosdick* taught a course at Union Seminary on "The Use of the Bible," which was the most brilliant exhibition of incredible power and skill as a teacher, that I have ever encountered. *Harry Elmer Barnes,* threw at a few of us at the *New School*, a brilliantly unified picture of the industrial society in which we live.

Whereas Gardner's students described the superb structure of his lectures and their wealth of ideas and allusions, Gardner's own writing reflects the sensuous pleasure ideas gave him. Along with that responsiveness was his vivid emotional resonance: "The teachers were great because they were intensely and passionately in love with their subjects . . . [and] fascinated by the capacity to share [their] multiple vision for generation after generation by fiery or by lyrical moments."

When we (Gardner and Lois) became college teachers we were both concerned with educational goals and approaches. Gardner wrote about the teachers' craft, while I wrote — with Henry Ladd — a book on emotional factors in learning. We discussed plans for courses, and when either of us was ill, the other was sometimes able to pinch-hit for the incapacitated one. I taught a course on "personality development in children" in the graduate clinical program which Gardner initiated at City College and we wrote a few joint papers. Our approaches differed, although both of us believed that active learning and involvement of the student were necessary. Gardner worked toward these goals by including references to experiences, interests, and metaphors relevant to the students' lives, while I began a course by asking students what questions were on their minds, questions they thought psychology might help to answer; this led to questions about heredity, environment, individual differences and other problems one would normally be approaching in a psychology course. Since Columbia classes were large, lectures were basic, supplemented by discussion groups. At Sarah Lawrence College in the thirties and forties small discussion groups and weekly individual conferences were typical. Gardner was deeply interested in the Sarah Lawrence approach and wrote, "The Sarah Lawrence world was extremely creative; a world of individualized work . . . there were no grades; there were simply standards of understanding and excellence. . . . I have never seen such educational morale in my life. . . ."

The experience of learning was so precious to Gardner that he even saw my everyday sharing observations, opinions, and experiences as my "teaching" him. Many years after our marriage he wrote, "it would be completely impossible to say anything meaningful about my subsequent path in psychology without indicating that this has been a dance of constant new steps being taught me by one who is herself deeply committed to the teaching world." "There were electrifying conversations . . . [and] she began to teach me some of the levels and forms of humanistic psychology in which I was weak, and she had a kind of objectivity and a kind of intellectual honesty which for me had been an unrealizable ideal." "It is self-evident to anyone who knows me that I have learned a great deal more psychology from Lois than from any other living person."

But through all of this it never occurred to me that I was "teaching" him—I merely thought that he was interested in my observations of the relation between personality and test results. The only point at which I might have felt that I was teaching him was in 1935 when he resisted my reading Rorschach's *Psychodiagnostik* to him. I felt that it was the most exciting and important psychology book I had ever encountered; he felt that he had heard enough about the Rorschach method when he listened to Samuel Beck's oral examination at Columbia. But I refused to give up, and insisted that he must read it with me. It was the most vigorous confrontation that we had in 53 years of our happy marriage. Once we got into it he was as enthralled as I was, and it was a major influence on his subsequent research.

In his paper "The Teacher's Craft," Gardner gave a more extensive account of his ideas about teaching:

> The delight in teaching and love of observing the teacher's craft came to me first of all through high school debating. It called for careful preparation in terms of large blocks of ideas in an intelligible order; it called for documentation (at first, of course, always through the World Almanac). . . . [O]ne learned to earmark the abysmal traps into which one's opponents had fallen or must fall, winding up with a clinching (and clenching) peroration.
>
> When I went on to "public speaking" at the Hotchkiss School where I talked about "Lee and Grant," I had been schooled with real devotion. Jack Adams (at Yale) carried me through from formal English essays to terse debating briefs, and while it was still the rule to memorize the major addresses, the rebuttals, which of course were the real clinchers, had to involve the capacity to "think on one's feet." This, in other words, was one kind of teaching in miniature; teaching in a one-evening performance, in which we taught and were taught by the necessities of the intrinsic logic of the problem on the one hand and the audience capacities and predilections on the other.

His teachers had given him "a sense of the delight in playing with ideas, trying to communicate them in vivid ways, and in reaching students or other audiences dynamically," so that they became aroused and involved. One way to involve students "is by phrasing abstract principles in terms of metaphors, similes or other images that are part of the student's own mental furniture" and another is to "use paradoxical questions." Chauncey Tinker at Yale gave him "a sense of how it is possible to stretch the scope of the student's mind and contribute to greater integration at the same time."

That training in college stood him in good stead when he reached Columbia after returning from World War I in 1919. R.S. Woodworth, then head of the psychology department, invited him to make a seminar presentation of his 1917 master's thesis at Harvard, a study of free association in psychotic and normal people. "There was no problem about laying out a 45-minute presentation using the blackboard and major headings. . . . Woodworth looked at me in a dreamy 'can't believe it' way when I ended my talk at exactly the 45-minute point." Gardner felt that it was that skill which led the department to entrust him immediately with beginning psychology classes in the "extension" division. At Columbia,

> Woodworth's graduate seminar was a remarkably successful object lesson in ongoing participation at a mature level. It [group discussion] was made famous by William H. Kilpatrick and it reached its really most magnificent level in the "topology" (Gestalt) conferences of Kurt Lewin. Kurt would gently set the stage, then sit to one side. As the speaker took the platform, Kurt would beam with joy as issues would get complex and controversial and break out into roars of glee when someone attacked his own position. This I am offering as an illustration of a teaching method in which there is no longer a polarization of teacher and taught; or indeed perhaps it would be better to say in which the teacher is being taught so much that his delight in a reciprocal relationship is the dominant feeling, that it is truly a group contribution, not a form of social ascendancy or dominance that makes up the heart of the communication process.

Gardner then asked "how do you know whether you have really accomplished what you set out to accomplish?" He felt that "if they're enjoying it they are probably getting more than if they are bored stiff." He credited his Grandpa King in Concord, Massachusetts, with being a model for making a wide variety of allusions.

> It was a Yankee habit which he had cultivated to a fantastic degree; and since I was always "reinforced" for farfetched allusions or analogies, I assumed that any old kind of farfetched allusions or analogies, whether literary or not, would bring commensurate reinforcements, and they always did. . . . It was a process which my mother's mother could quite rightly call "omnium gatherum," . . . which included everything I had ever learned at Worthington Hooker High School, or at Hotchkiss, at Yale or Harvard, or at Columbia, or for that matter while hiking in the Pyrenees, or reading Popeye aloud to my son.

After nearly forty years of teaching Gardner reflected on the dynamic process of releasing the potentialities of students. In his John Dewey lecture, *Freeing Intelligence Through Teaching* (1960), he dealt not with the craft but with the philosophical and psychological theoretical basis for his approach. With building blocks found in William James, Bergson, Dewey, Freud and especially Darwin and Einstein, he contructed his thesis that learning cannot be separated from motive, or the rational from the irrational. . . .

> Thoughtful men had asked persistently whether rationality may not be the child of irrationality.... Indeed, with Plato himself the creative force is love.... The rational may best continue to grow in the instinctive soil in which it was engendered, and, too clear and sterile a surgical separation of thought from its ancestral and parental roots in love and impulse may threaten its viability.

More concretely he related the earliest learning to the child's response to the mother:

> One could love not only the mother, the mother's voice, the tone of her voice, but tone in general. From this point of view the great task of education is to evoke an understanding love. Everything that is real comes soon to be invested with an active seeking love. Many a little child loves the shaft of the sunbeams through the nursery, the dew on the grass, the salty splash of the sea, and loses this as he grows up into the world of rationality. As Wordsworth said, "A sordid boon."

Gardner deeply believed in an instinctive craving for the world of understanding:

> The child is barely three when he bombards us with questions probing into realities he is newly discovering. He craves to discover, to think, and to find that things make sense ... the organism ... craves commerce with the reality which engulfs it ... there is ... an innate capacity for effective reality seeking and testing.

He did not believe in elaborate techniques:

> The teacher is carrying out no sleight of hand, no manipulation of displacements and sublimations, when he or she enriches, strengthens, catalyzes and gives new directions to the life of thought.... The fact that the teacher wishes to share understanding can enhance the process, but both he and the pupil turn their love and understanding not only towards one another but toward the rich real world.... The interpersonal relations of teacher and pupil and the pupil's potential response to the reality waiting to be discovered are two aspects of one learning process. The irrational and the rational are intimately blended in the teacher's communications, as they are in the intercommunications between the members of the group which is learning. The clarifying merges into the electrifying. Indeed the clarifying, just by being clarifying, can become electrifying.

He then went on to the role of the teacher:

> The teacher helps the child to discover for himself a reality which is then shared ... rather, realities which the child bumps into, hears, smells, fingers, looks at, manipulates, enjoys ... the excitement of such contact ... can ... guide it to the real. The child makes abstractions on the basis of his own direct, often unique experience. The role of the teacher will not be fulfilled by turning

over a thousand stones, but by enabling the child or youth to see in the stone which arouses his interest the history of this world, the evolution of its waters, atmospheres, soils and rocks, prying into deeper meanings "just because they are there."

We have seen that students did not feel pressure, demands, reproofs from Gardner: "If you know the motivation, you do not have to apply—cannot apply—external rewards and punishment . . . reinforcement, when effective, consists of allowing the motivation to pursue itself. . . ." This, he implied, leads to "the fulfillment of that discipline which lay in the task itself rather than in external authority."

Gardner expressed his lifelong belief that American education must find a way to "conserve the great tradition which comes down to us from Greece, from India, from Old Testament times, from a great many other rich materials; the conception of continuity and slow, steady accretion of strength as contrasted with the revolutionary."

Illustrating respect for tradition Gardner recalled "men in World War I who were risking their lives that American life might go on . . . who carried their Classics in a side pocket, to read a little Shakespeare in a moment of leisure. . . ." Tradition is an anchor against the storm, a source of security in the midst of confusion, an assurance of continuity. But still there is anxiety. He went on, however, to emphasize the need for flexibility. A society or educational system oversteeped in tradition too often resists necessary change. The proud Spanish conquerors left a tradition which could not maintain itself—because of the rigidity of the Spanish gentleman. To be too rich in a tradition means to be rigid. In America, for instance, the rigidities of Beacon Hill and the Harvard of Oliver Wendell Holmes made it "difficult for the Elliotts and the Conants to juggle . . . Harvard into confronting the Mid-Twentieth Century." His own contact with rigidities of the South confronted in a visit to Sewanee, led him to reflect on Erik Erikson's concept of identity, as presented in *Childhood and Society* and *Young Man Luther*. He made the point that

unless your own deep acceptance of yourself is stronger than your anchorage upon tradition, you can't respond to the great challenges. . . . Fulfillment of yourself . . . can come only from knowing that life is change, . . . a process of identification, not with one person nor one tradition, but with humanity at large in a process of endless self-discovery. Identity, then, the discovery of who one really is, can never be simply a discovery of one's place in a tradition. It . . . means the discovery of where you're tending, or where you might tend . . . of the inner resources by which one can leap forward to something new.

The core of Gardner's message was that "the teacher has got to be the kind of person who can inculcate a spirit of freedom to explore, to enjoy, to face both tradition and challenge."

II / The Child
Was Father to the Man

3. Forebears and Family: Identification and Conflict

Forebears and Gran'pa King

Forebears may have a determining influence on a growing child or have little influence aside from their varying genetic contributions to temperament, physical and mental characteristics as these unfold. Gardner Murphy was unique among his relatives in at least one way; no scientist is found in the list of over 200 forebears and family members which he assembled for an ontological study assigned by Yerkes at Harvard in his first year of graduate work.

The descendants of the Brewsters, Kings, Prides, Brighams and other lines of his mother's forebears were seen by Gardner as competent, energetic, honest, reliable, friendly, generous people. Some of them were leading citizens in their communities; his maternal great-grandfather was a temperance reformer and an abolitionist. His mother's paternal aunt, and his mother's mother were teachers who "took a deep interest in their pupils." There were successful farmers in the eighteenth and nineteenth centuries, a sea captain, and several physicians, and, far back, the lay religious leader Elder Brewster of the *Mayflower*. We hear of neither geniuses nor rogues on his mother's side of the family. Nor did any individual foreshadow Gardner's distinguished career as a psychologist with a philosophical orientation.

Gardner felt that a characteristic of his "near kin" was a general nervousness and irritability. On his mother's side, he also mentioned a hasty "slap-dash" quality—not characteristic, however, of his maternal grandmother. "I certainly have my share of it," he added, but his cousin Margaret Babbitt was "the most slap-dashy of us all." Industry, reliability and unselfishness were at the same time characteristic traits on both sides of his mother's heritage.

In his autobiographical *Study of Myself,* written at Harvard when he was 21, Gardner constructed a table on which he rated his ten nearest relatives on willpower, self-control, honesty and altruism. He used a ten-point scale with five as average; honesty was simply rated as positive. Of thirty ratings, none were below five and only four ratings of five were given. In short, he considered his close relatives to be above average on those character traits. "Of course, admiration for my parents is beyond any possible expression.... The utter unselfishness of both is without doubt the moral trait that makes the greatest appeal to me." Aside from his parents he admired most his maternal grandmother: "Her cheerfulness, her sympathy, her broadmindedness and her altruism ... made the biggest impression on me."

As to the religious stance of his forebears, aside from his deeply religious parents, and his maternal great-grandfather who was a clergyman, Gardner knew only that the earlier ones were of "New England settler stock and were therefore probably very religious," but, he felt, not extremely puritanical. Looking at his forebears as representatives of the serious, responsible New England of centuries past we see Gardner as a child of that culture with its deep commitments to goodness, with righteousness balanced by humor.

In a later autobiography written in his seventies, Gardner described his heritage as "a very confusing conglomerate of northern European stocks and families that came by way of Ireland, England and Scotland, and—far enough back—many other European stocks." His impression was that the families for generations back were companionable people, loving informal and intimate social activity. "There is frequent evidence of close affection and friendship throughout the ancestral record.... [T]he ancestors seem to have been respected, often loved, members of their communities, ... but clubs, lodges, etc. have been of little or no importance." We have no real evidence that his remote forebears meant much to Gardner—he did not talk about them.

Grandparents on his mother's side were, by contrast, dear and vivid, and their presence was a vital force in Gardner's childhood. Most important was Gran'pa King, a lineal descendant of Elder Brewster, and a devoted companion of Emerson in their work for the Concord Library. After Emerson died in 1882 George King became chairman of the Library Committee. Always "Gran'pa King" to Gardner, he was a man of literary culture, wit, and faithful citizenship—the man whose free-wheeling allusions to Shakespeare, Milton, the Bible and other classics were reflected in Gardner's teaching and writing.

George Augustus King, elected to the Concord Social Circle in 1885, and also a member of the prestigious Saturday Club of Boston, was born in Charlestown, Rhode Island; his mother was the daughter of Captain Absalom Pride, master of a full-rigged ship, who had married Huldah Brewster, a lineal descendant of Elder William Brewster of the *Mayflower*. Gran'pa King's father was a country doctor descended from Elder Thomas King who arrived from England in 1635 and joined the followers of John Lothrop, the founders of the first Congregational Society of America. Gardner's greatgrandfather, Dr. King, wrote three books, one of which had the title "Quakery Unmasked." Except for one journalist, he is the only author among Gardner's forebears.

George attended schools in Rhode Island and Massachusetts — but as the seventh of eleven children his college education could not be financed by his father. He sailed to Charleston, South Carolina, at the age of 17, intending to teach. On shipboard, he studied Whately's *Principles of Logic,* the beginning of a continuous process of self-education and of a lifelong love of books. Following a short period of teaching, he returned to Massachusetts to become a lawyer and after studying law on his own, he entered the office of a judge of probate until he was admitted to the bar in 1857 at the age of 23.

He soon acquired a reputation for integrity and his impressive and sincere manner made him an effective advocate. In 1864 the governor of Massachusetts appointed him to a committee to adjudicate questions of title of the Dartmouth tribe of Indians to lands in the towns of Dartmouth and Westport, and in 1869 at the age of 35 he was elected to the Massachusetts Senate. Foresighted and eloquent in stating his views on controversial issues, he attracted considerable attention and in 1868 was appointed a member of the Board of Overseers of the Massachusetts Agricultural College of which Louis Agassiz was also a member; the two became warm friends. He rapidly gained wide respect for his energy and good judgment. Along with his many public efforts, he carried cases of needy individuals, such as that of a woman whose husband had divorced her and had contributed nothing to her support. She lost her suit, but George King generously assumed the costs imposed by the court in order to save the woman "this last drop in her cup of bitterness."

Having lived on the Cape until 1870, he moved to Concord in 1871 at the age of 37. He immediately devoted himself to the community; he was elected to the School Committee in 1875, and four times was moderator of the town meeting. In 1875 he was a member of the committee on the centennial celebration, and also of the Monument Committee, which had charge of the erection of the Minuteman memorial at the North Bridge. The sculptor, Daniel Chester French had been a member of his Sunday school class, and George King was greatly pleased when the town chose his pupil's design for the monument.

In addition to all of these civic activities, he gave his best thought for 46 years to expanding the Concord Library's nucleus. At the time of his death in 1919, the modest collection of 6400 volumes, "hardly more than will be found in many household collections of books," had increased to 48,379, most of which he had read or looked through himself. Mark Twain's *Huckleberry Finn* was considered "too vulgar" and he rejected it. He added "excellent editions of all the principal Greek and Roman classics, as well as what is best in the abundant wealth of English literature," along with books in German, French and Spanish and the "best histories of our own country and especially of New England, and more particularly of Massachusetts and Concord." Due to the "low moral tone of imaginative literature — both English and American" — fewer novels were added. His constant aim was to have a library worthy of the traditions of the town. "None will deny that he was one of the greatest benefactors of the library," wrote his biographer in the fifth volume of *The Memoirs of Members of the Social Circle in Concord,* which concluded, "This man loved books, and he knew what was in them. He was a man of culture, reflection, and appreciation of letters."

This grandfather was closer to Gardner during his boyhood than his own absent father, if only because of his presence, his library, and Gardner's delight in his adroit quotations from the classics and from Shakespeare and other English poets. George King was not a religious man; his interests were literary, rather than philosophical. He cannot be said to have been one of the Concord transcendentalists. When he was about seventy, he decided to learn French, and without any instructor became a good enough French scholar so that when Gardner sent newspapers from France during the Great War he read them with considerable facility. He also enjoyed music — it was his little phonograph and his records of the Scottish singer Harry Lauder and of Caruso that Gardner loved to take down to the dock on the Concord River and play for himself.

Gardner's description of his grandfather reflects the sensitivity to his grandfather's moods he had felt since boyhood. "He adored his three daughters — and I intensely approved his feelings — and he felt unhappy with a rather unaffectionate and unresponsive son.... He had been, as a young man, intensely romantic, yearning and eager for the kind of literary intensities that Shakespeare and Burns evoked in him. He knew the classics of English literature thoroughly, and quoted ... stretches of sublime — or poking much fun — ridiculous verses, partly because 'something snapped when he was a boy,' and partly because he never had the fame to which he aspired. Although he was a leading citizen he could not experience the adulation that went to the great Concord families of historical and literary fame. He was very eager about new things in the United States and in the world, assuming, however, that the old rules of life would apply in the frontier. He fought the first World War with an old man's bitter intensity. The Allies were absolutely right, and the Germans absolutely wrong." He died in 1919 after the Allies had won.

"He had an extraordinary capacity for quoting, in the most dramatic possible way, a line or a series of lines that would throw everything into a new perspective. The tenderness for his own daughters was extended very, very fully to the son whom he acquired when his daughter Maud came back from San Antonio, Texas, to be married to Edgar Gardner Murphy in August, 1891. Her husband's death in 1913 was a tragic blow which George King did not absorb." Another symbol from his last years was his warmth and excitement when Gardner started learning the violin in 1913. When he scratched out "Annie Laurie," Gardner remembered the joy of his grandfather's chuckle, almost amid tears, "Why, that's 'Annie Laurie'!" But the classics touched him most deeply. "He apparently regarded Thoreau as something of a bluffer and poked fun, as did other Concordians, at the 'life in the woods' which permitted him to 'come and get a loaf of bread from his mother,' and let Emerson pay his taxes.

"He was, of course, a staunch and intense admirer of Lincoln, and through all his life, from the Civil War onwards, a devout Republican. He believed in all the sturdy virtues of the East Massachusetts settlers, and the doctrine of making your way by infinite struggle and infinite hardihood." Gardner added that he was a grand old wonderful figure whom they all loved to hear talk about his boyhood or go on and on about Concord doings or "poetry." There was often a pathetic and nostalgic note—from later years he remembered "Youth is a blunder, manhood a struggle, old age a regret" (Disraeli) and he continued to comment on the tragedy of life. Gardner had no memories of discipline, or of puritanical admonishments from his grandfather. Although he was estranged from his beautiful wife in the later years—they communicated through his youngest daughter Louise, who lived with them—Gardner's grandparents apparently had no harsh words or arguments. That estrangement may have been another source of Gran'pa King's sadness.

Despite his deep early identification, Gardner felt that as a young man he could not wholly identify with an old man whose work was far off in the mid–nineteenth century, who was failing in strength and essentially a person to be loved and be proud of. In his mid-teens, Gardner ran into a few things that rather repelled him; particularly his grandfather's great conservatism or general Republican reactionary outlook, but this was part of the "politics" of life; "we were essentially the same at the primitive feeling level." Certainly, Gardner felt, as for himself he identified "at least sometimes, as much with Gran'ma and with Aunt Louise, and at least twenty times as much with mother."

It was his grandparents' home at 88 Main Street in Concord, not far from the library, to which Gardner took me on a visit during one of our New England summers. Although it would have been easy to visit his early home in Kingston on one of our explorations in the Catskill Mountains of New York, or to have stopped in Chillicothe, his Ohio birthplace, on one of our cross-country drives to the west, Gardner never suggested it. Nor did he ever suggest that we visit the Montgomery, Alabama, home of his Southern preschool years. It was Gran'pa King's home that was his anchor, the setting of his happiest memories, the symbol of continuity in his childhood and youth, the place where he felt most at home, and where he had a sense of belonging. When Gardner wrote of the "pure culture of Concord," he surely had in mind the culture of his grandfather as well as the Emerson tradition. It was Concord that Gardner considered his home town. His ashes were interred at his request in the King family plot on a high ridge in the Sleepy Hollow Cemetery.

Gardner's Mother: Maud King Murphy

Gran'pa King's love of books, civic leadership, warm affection, and intensity provided an ideal masculine role model for his loving grandson, and his home was a haven for other relatives who visited—including his grandchildren

George and Margaret Babbitt, children of his eldest daughter, Gardner's Aunt Minnie. Aunt Louise, George King's youngest daughter, lived at home until her death from diabetes. While the extended family was important to Gardner, it was his mother, he wrote, who had the most influence on his life. In fact, she was almost constantly available to him, with a continuity of presence unbroken except by Gardner's absence in World War I and his travels.

The stability of Gran'pa King's home in Concord—his mother's hometown—and of his mother's presence contrasted sharply with the discontinuities of setting, climate, lifestyle, and speech patterns Gardner encountered as a boy in a series of moves from North to South to North again. During the period when Gardner was seven to thirteen years old, his father's base was Montgomery, Alabama, while his mother went North with her sons—for two years in Concord at first. Gardner therefore did not have to compete with his father for time with his mother—she was a guiding, stimulating and controlling presence. In view of her pride in her King family, and in her brilliant husband, it seems probable that some of the energy with which she nurtured her sons may have been motivated by a hope to produce men the equal of her father and of her husband. In Gardner's case, efforts may have increased because of her doubts that he would be a success. Her doubts are reflected in such comments as "no original combinations of words," in her notes on his early vocabulary, and in expressions of distress and judgments of his inadequacy in some ordinary physical activities. The only criticism of his older brother, DuBose, that I encountered was her remark that when he made his chocolate creams he always made them exactly the same way, implying a lack of experimenting or originality, or a tendency to follow rules.

Gardner and his brother were deeply devoted to their brilliant self-sacrificing mother; DuBose wrote in one letter that she was "perfect," and he hoped to find a wife like her. And at the end of his book *Approaches to Personality* Gardner quoted the old song "I want a girl just like the girl that married dear old dad." She read to him from his earliest years and guided his reading after he learned to read for himself. She also introduced him to birds. She taught him to sing ("do-re-mi") when his teacher reported that he seemed to be tone deaf, and she also taught him to play simple melodies on the piano. Music and birds became sustaining lifetime interests, along with geography and languages. What she gave him in childhood not only enriched his life for three-quarters of a century, but was also a foundation for his lifetime devotion to her. Her friends were equally devoted to her and considered her a wonderful, brilliant woman with wide-ranging interests in music, literature, politics and events of the time. After her husband died we experienced her as unsmiling; her wit was generally at the expense of someone else and she was rarely enthusiastic. She judged a visit by its "success," not in terms of pleasure. She assumed that it was her right to impose her standards on the young.

Maud, the second of four King children, grew up in Concord, Massachusetts, after her early childhood in Barnstable, on Cape Cod. Like her older sister Minnie she attended Vassar College. After Maud graduated, Vassar received a request from the superintendent of schools in San Antonio, Texas, asking if any Vassar graduate was interested in a teaching position in the public schools of that city. She accepted eagerly, much to the surprise and shock of her family, who, however, did not forbid her to go.

This adventure led to her marriage to a Southerner, at first another shock to Concord; in San Antonio she met and became engaged to a young Episcopal priest, Edgar Gardner Murphy, who resided in the select boarding house run by his mother. Edgar and Maud were married in Concord the following year. Her father loved the brilliant young Edgar after he came to know him.

Maud was proud of her New England heritage; her pride of family led to her disapproval of a series of her nephew George's potential brides. Cousin Louise, Maud's brother's daughter, wrote me that Aunt Maud considered them not good enough for their family; after he finally married, his wife told me that George said Maud was a "shrew." With both of her daughters-in-law she was intrusive and domineering. Margaret Floy Washburn, her classmate at Vassar, commented to me, "Oh yes, I remember that aggressive blonde girl." Gardner's closest friend, Frank Lorimer, remembered that when he visited Gardner, his mother insisted that they should always come down to breakfast fully dressed, in shirts and ties. No casual, informal dress was acceptable. And Frank, as well as others, remarked that she was "a formidable woman."

Her challenging and critical comments had a devastating effect on her sensitive and pretty Southern daughter-in-law; when Mother Murphy commented, "Why do you waste time and money wrapping up Christmas packages like that?" Alice felt demeaned and broke down. Making things pretty and attractive was her pride and joy, and to have this ridiculed was an overwhelming blow. After a couple of years of "Darling child" letters to me, filled with unsought and inappropriate advice, I protested that I was "nobody's darling *child*," and she did then address me by my name. She also wrote that Gardner—then 33 or 34 years old—had said he wished she would treat him as an equal (meaning, as an adult), "but how can I when I am 30 years older?" One might see her aggressiveness as one aspect of an outgoing vigorous nature which was also expressed in possessive affection in letters to Gardner as well as to me: "Darling precious child" she was still writing to him years after he married at the age of 31. My family had been treating me with respect as an adult since college days and I was shocked at her approach.

I also protested sharply another time: when our son was 15 months old he was learning to use a spoon to eat his breakfast oatmeal. When he spilled a bit, she slapped his hand. I said, "If you have to slap my baby you can do it when he's at your house, but not when he's at home." I was too angry to think clearly enough to explain that slapping his hand in the midst of a learning process could discourage his learning to use his hands.

She commented that she had never slapped her children "after they were old enough to remember," then told how she slapped Gardner's hand when he was a baby, reaching through the slats of his crib to touch her when she was trying to rest. In an account of DuBose's childhood she remarked that perhaps she had emphasized obedience too much, "but obedience is convenient." She also told of the surprise of a Montgomery neighbor at DuBose's six-year-old self-control in never leaving the unfenced front lawn. "But I told him not to," Mrs. Murphy had replied—making it clear that her sons knew they must obey such rules. That her strictness was not typical of the community is implied in her neighbor's surprise. With both boys so well-behaved before the age of six the socialization pressures were evidently very consistent. On Sundays, bicycles were not used and the children played quietly "as was appropriate."

There are few direct records of her methods of discipline, but Gardner wrote in his Harvard autobiography that scoldings hurt him most of all. He also said that he could not bear being put in a closed closet and that an intense fear of confinement had resulted from this—even to the sense of confinement when a football player landed on top of him.

Four years older than her husband, it seems likely that she took it for granted that it was her responsibility to take care of proprieties and the habits that gentility required at the turn of the century. Gardner remarked, "The mother is the center of the home." I could not understand how a person could be genuinely loving and so punitive at the same time. But there is no doubt that she gave her sons devoted attention, stimulation, and guidance. He and DuBose were good boys, and they became good men.

Gardner's mother was seen differently by different persons: adored by her sons and her dearest friends, a neighbor who bought 88 Main Street after George King died in 1919 found her "cold and businesslike," controlling, dominating and aggressive unlike other Concord women. Gardner commented that she "tossed off" (put down) the Concord authors with the exception of Emerson. Hawthorne was not mentioned at all, and she was annoyed at Louisa May Alcott for basing a minor character in one of her books on herself.

Maud's pretty and brilliant elder sister, Minnie, became a successful lecturer on Emerson after graduating from Vassar. But Maud did not talk about her when she discussed other members of the family. In view of her mother's gentle ways and the warmth of her father, we wonder about the source of Maud's aggressive controlling style. Could it have developed from competition with her prettier sister? Why was she so aggressive at Vassar? Her sister Minnie had preceded her there; did Maud feel under pressure to make a name for herself equal to that of her sister? Why did Maud put down most Concord authors? Why was she such a strict disciplinarian to her sons, so controlling, dominating, intrusive into the lives of her adult sons and daughters-in-law, so infantilizing? It seems that she had an overwhelming need to maintain superiority. When this was granted, she did not need to be dominating.

Rigid puritanical attitudes toward sex were typical in New England, and Gardner's mother's standards, strict as they were, were brittle, even devastating in this area. In 1919–20 when her sons and their friends returned from World War I and explored friendships with girls, Gardner's mother told them it was "wrong to touch a person of the other sex before they were engaged"; after Gardner and I were married she told me, "Sex is just for having children." In 1936 when her small grandson asked why a nude statue in the Metropolitan Museum had a fig leaf she said hurriedly, "Hush, we don't talk about that."

In contrast to the relative financial comfort Gardner's mother experienced in her parents' home, she was, and felt, "poor" as a minister's wife. Commenting on the Puritan motto "Use it up, wear it out, make it do" she added, "Do without," and felt that their lifestyle was one of conspicuous nonconsumption. The fact that her closest friends from Concord days, the Smiths and the Blanchards and Emily Shepard, were well-to-do, as was her sister-in-law in San Antonio, along with the fact that her sons needed scholarships and financial help from relatives for their college education, added to her "poor-mouthing." Actually, when I visited Concord in 1926–29, she was maintaining a household for her mother that included a nurse-companion for Gran'ma King, a housekeeper-cook, and a part-time laundress. This household was supported by the modest estate left by Gran'pa King, and some contribution from her brother, George, along with her pension from Andrew Carnegie that was continued after her husband's death in 1913, and some royalties from his books. Aside from selling two poems to Harper's Monthly magazine, revising Edgar's star book, and writing a concise biography describing his work, she did not undertake gainful work after the age of 48, when her husband died. And there is no evidence of civic activities in Concord although she was only in her fifties when her father died in 1919. At that time she sold 88 Main Street and moved to a smaller setting in one-half of the "Block House." In view of her intelligence and literary gifts, her limited activity is a puzzle, and was distressing to Gardner, who wished that his brilliant mother would "use her brains."

Since Gardner's Gran'pa King had held distinguished positions in the town and state and Gardner's father's advice was sought by leaders of his time including Andrew Carnegie and President Theodore Roosevelt, his mother may well have had doubts as to whether Gardner would ever equal these men. Her remarks to me that she "had always hoped Gardner would marry a beautiful rich girl" and — after he was elected president of the American Psychological Association — that "He would never have achieved so much had it not been for you," implied earlier doubts. DuBose's athletic and social success in contrast to Gardner's youthful ineptitudes evidently added to a certain lack of confidence in their mother's view of Gardner.

Gardner's extended description of his mother emphasized her fatigability, irritability, devotion and self-sacrifice along with her breadth of vision, sanity of judgment, common sense, sense of values — her literary, scientific and philosophic knowledge and interest coupled with a power of original thinking in those fields. It is possible that her failure to do more writing or carry on activities outside her home with her parents was due to her fatigue, which must have increased in the years when she cared for her sick husband, and indeed, may have masked a depression after his death. The financially rewarding literary work of Louisa May Alcott, and the legend of the famous Margaret Fuller, stood as strong precedents for women's literary and social work — although most women of Concord were homemakers, as were her friends.

DuBose and Gardner were both so deeply impressed by, and grateful for, the unusually rich cultural foundation given them by their stimulating mother, that they were blind to her aggressive, controlling, critical behavior to her daughters-in-law. Gardner wrenched himself out of the puritan restrictions and also out of Protestant theology, and he later carefully avoided telling her about activities of which he knew she would disapprove. At the same time he remained dependent on her emotional support even after he had a family of his own. She lived to be 92, and died of pneumonia in 1957.

Most of us have cultivated "stimulus barriers," which Freud and others postulated in the effort to understand why a two-month-old baby is not overwhelmed by the complexities of his surroundings. We pay attention to what we choose to attend to, and, to maintain our sanity, we become adept at shutting our ears, eyes, and other sense organs, in order to avoid being invaded by more stimuli than we can deal with. Gardner did not lack a selective capacity — it was aimed at excluding what was negative, and including as much as possible of what was good, beautiful, endearing — as if he had assimilated in infancy Keats' *Ode on a Grecian Urn:* "'Beauty is truth, truth beauty,' — that is all ye know on earth, and all ye need to know." The aggressive qualities of his mother did not fit the image that he wanted to maintain. Maud's extreme puritanism, demand for order and obedience, tactlessness, forthrightness, self-assurance and pride of family as well as her hope that Gardner would marry well reflected the image of women in Amory's *The Proper Bostonians.* That is, even if her mother and other women of Concord were less aggressive and more gracious, a culture pattern existed that seemed right for her.

Although Gardner wrote repeatedly of his closeness to his mother, he said that he never saw any evidence of an oedipal problem. By this he evidently meant that he did not feel aware of competition with his father, nor was he aware of hostility toward him. Actually, since his father was away from the family so much from 1902 to 1908, when Gardner was seven to thirteen, and since when Gardner was nine years old he was out of school for a year and taught by his mother, the mother-son closeness was, if not enforced, at least supported by the circumstances of their lives. Leaving home to go to France in World War I, and to Columbia University after he returned presented no conflict apparently. It is strange that we have neither Gardner's letters to his mother nor hers to him during this time, although his World War I letters to his dear Cousin Catharine in New Haven were saved. His emotional tie to his mother did not prevent his intellectual independence, or limit his freedom in planning his career, or in his search for a wife.

It seems clear that Gardner's conscious identifications were primarily with his New England family and its cultural setting, especially his mother and Gran'pa King, her father. But his gentle, affectionate, creative personality seemed to me like more that of his father.

Gardner's Father: Edgar Gardner Murphy

Physically, Gardner's parents presented a striking, if not unusual, contrast. His father was tall, slender, dark-haired and brown-eyed, with a serious, intent, thoughtful gaze. His mother, blonde, blue-eyed, of barely average height, had a determined, tense stance. Intellectually, however, they had much in common: Edgar Gardner Murphy always insisted that his wife was more than his equal.

Edgar was the gentle parent, pouring out his affection for the younger son he adored, and for his first son, DuBose, who resembled him physically. Gardner's build and coloring were those of his mother, although his emotional intensity resembled that of his father. There is no record of paternal discipline comparable to Gardner's memories of his mother's punishments and scoldings, but his father did exert control, and was intensely interested in his son's education, especially his written work.

Edgar Gardner Murphy was an Episcopal priest during Gardner's first six years. We do not know whether little Gardner listened to his father's eloquent sermons in Montgomery, Alabama, as I listened to my own father's resonant voice — and then "preached sermons" from the landing of the stairs in our house when I was four and five years old. From what Gardner became and from the extensive records of the sort of man his father was, we can infer the son's identification; Edgar was gentle, warm, tactful, passionately concerned about human rights, justice, and the needs of children. He was also eloquent, persuasive, inspiring, and gifted with an infectious sense of humor. Are these the roots for Gardner's devotion to liberal political causes? While Gran'pa King was a generous socially sensitive lawyer and a leading citizen, he was not a vigorous fighter for reform programs. Gardner does not discuss, in his autobiographical writings, the influence on him of his father's pioneering work on behalf of southern education, voting rights, and child labor laws. But when I read his mother's careful account of Edgar's work, I had a déjà vu experience — the quality of devotion, the passionate intensity of his efforts, the capacity to inspire others all reminded me of Gardner. It seems likely that Gardner was imprinted at an early age with his father's intense commitment to social causes before the years in Concord when he was breathing the atmosphere of his grandfather's more traditional intellectual circle.

Gardner commented on the contrast between the extensive records of his mother's New England forebears and the dearth of information about those of his father. We know only that his father, Edgar, was born in Fort Smith, Arkansas, and that his father's mother, Janie Gardner Murphy, was a brave woman who left Fort Smith with her sister and her little son and daughter for San Antonio in the hope of recovering from "consumption," after her husband left the family. She did recover and established an elite boarding house to support her family. She later saved enough money to contribute $1000 to the education of each of her grandsons.

Evidently Gardner did not know that his plucky grandmother, Janie, was the daughter of John Gardner and his first wife, who owned a plantation in Fort Smith. Janie's daughter, Gardner's Aunt Ethel, was a beautiful woman of distinguished appearance and southern grace. Gardner did not keep in close touch with his wealthy Southern cousins. Despite his lack of attachment to the South, his Southern father was a source of quiet pride and identification, and he treasured early correspondence with his father.

Edgar was five years old when his father left the family. In San Antonio without the presence of a father, young Edgar was deeply responsive to the "personable young rector" of St. Mark's Episcopal Church, the Reverend Walter Richardson, who often dropped in to join the group of young people gathered at Mrs. Murphy's pleasant boarding house for games, food and conversation. Edgar was soon persuaded to join the church choir, then other activities of the church, and was confirmed. When still in his teens he decided to become a priest, with Richardson's encouragement. His excellent high school record enabled him to gain a scholarship at the University of the South in Sewanee, Tennessee. There he was profoundly influenced by the Reverend William Porcher DuBose, later dean of St. Luke's School of Theology, which he had helped to organize. They became close friends and it was he for whom Edgar and Maud's first son was named. After graduation from Sewanee, Edgar went to New York for a year's additional training at the General Theological Seminary and served as Sunday lay assistant at the Church of the Incarnation. While there he listened to the visiting Rev. Phillips Brooks of Boston whose eloquent style of lecturing he imitated. At the end of that academic year he returned to Texas to begin his own ministry at a little mission, St. Paul's, near Fort Sam Houston and was ordained as deacon in August 1890. He soon became deeply attracted to the brilliant young teacher Maud King, who was also living at his mother's boarding house. After their marriage on August 31, 1891, in Concord, they returned to San Antonio, where he was assistant to the minister at St. Mark's Episcopal church and minister-in-charge of a little church near the army post. Early in 1892 an alarming illness, later diagnosed as heart disease, interrupted his work for several months. After his recovery in 1893 he accepted an appointment as minister of Christ Church at Laredo, Texas.

There Edgar was shocked and religiously outraged by the lynching of a

Negro in a nearby town. "To Murphy . . . the mad lawlessness of the mob was a dreadful challenge to Christianity and to all our claims to civilization," wrote Gardner. He and a few men who shared his feeling issued a call for a mass meeting in Laredo. Although he was only in his early twenties, Edgar had an incredible capacity for leadership; the mayor, district attorney and district judge were the first to sign their names to the following set of resolutions he formulated in 1893:

> Whereas the news of the torture of the negro Smith by the people of Paris, Texas, has come to our ears and has been duly verified, we, citizens of Laredo in the County of Webb and the State of Texas, in mass meeting assembled, wish to place upon record our condemnation of the hideous vengeance which the men of Lamar County have visited upon their wretched victim. Although we are aware of the fact that there are some in this community who will take no part with us, we deem it to be a duty to our great and beloved State and to the entire South to utter and to publish our detestation of a punishment so unnaturally and incomparably barbarous. Therefore, be it Resolved—
>
> *Resolved, I,* That while we would not palliate in the slightest degree the crime for which the negro died, and while many of us do not regret that he should have received a speedy and shameful death, we can, nevertheless, see no justification of a penalty which made an orgy of torture and a festival of agony.
>
> *Resolved, II,* That in our judgment, such a penalty, by eliciting the sympathy of the civilized world rather in behalf of the criminal than in behalf of his victim cannot help the South either in the control of its negro population or in the solution of what is the greatest criminal problem which has ever been given into the charge of any people.
>
> *Resolved, III,* That in our opinion, satisfaction is thoroughly futile and inadequate in the punishment of such a crime. The idea that there *can* be any satisfaction for a crime so unnatural, unutterably despicable, as that which the negro had committed is entirely false. The truth that Vengeance is God's is not the rebuke but the absolute assurance of justice.
>
> *Resolved, IV,* That we call upon those in every community of the State, who sympathize with us in the condemnation of this outrage upon the honor of our Southland, to gather in general assembly and to rebuke with us an exhibition of popular ferocity and of social madness which has never been equalled in the history of any land or time or people. Such a deed is the challenge of the popular conscience. We cannot be guilty of the complicity of silence. We cannot be inactive if we would. The honor of the nation, the good fame of the State, the obligations of religious loyalty and of civic pride, demand the utterance and the publication of our protest.

While that was the beginning of his commitment to work constructively on the "race problem," he was not able to get actively involved until the turn of the century when he returned to the South after three years as a priest in Episcopal churches in Chillicothe, Ohio, and in Kingston, New York.

Edgar moved to Montgomery, Alabama, in 1899 as priest at St. John's church. Later that year, he called together a "company of representative and distinguished men, for the frank, open discussion of . . . that which was known as the Race Problem." This group formed the Southern Society with the purpose of "Promotion of the Study of Race Conditions and Problems in the South." This distinguished group planned to educate the public "as to the facts of the situation and a better understanding of the remedies for existing evils." The Society's first action in January 1900 was to call a Conference on Race Relations to meet in Montgomery in May. Montgomery, Mobile and Birmingham papers supported the plans and the *Atlanta Constitution* printed a warmly sympathetic editorial. "Throughout the South, city newspapers and little papers in the country towns took the plan seriously. From some cities of the North came an unexpected and cordial sympathy. . . ."

Outstanding friends and supporters from New York and Philadelphia became involved in planning the great conference sponsored by the Southern Society in Montgomery in the spring of 1900. H.A. Herbert, former secretary of the navy in Cleveland's cabinet, Mayor Waddell of Wilmington, N.C., J.T. Graves of Atlanta, and ex–Governor McCorkle of West Virginia all participated in the conference, speaking to large attentive audiences, sometimes with old-fashioned oratory, sometimes fortified with statistics. The *Proceedings* of the conference, edited by Edgar Gardner Murphy, became a permanent contribution to the study of race relations.

After this stimulating meeting Edgar was invited to speak at a major church congress in Providence, and at an engagement in New York where he acquired important new friends such as Andrew Carnegie, who contributed $50,000 for a library in Montgomery, and later, an annuity after illness forced Edgar to retire. Another new friend was George Foster Peabody, who assisted him in providing a building for the Young Men's Christian Association.

Early in 1900 he was invited to the dedication of a new building at Tuskegee where, in an impromptu speech, he asserted that the thinking men of the South knew that "any civilization that bases itself on the despising of character . . . carries at its own heart the element of its self-destruction." And turning to the black student body before him, he said that the Declaration of Independence was at first a prophecy and the Emancipation Proclamation represented but a liberty in the document. They must attain and utilize a "freedom of accomplishment" and advance the whole conception of emancipation. There was tumultuous response.

In the course of these efforts he became acquainted with Booker T. Washington, whom he invited to the rectory for an evening discussion. He did not invite him to come for a meal, feeling that in the heated atmosphere at the turn of the century social integration could hurt the progress of efforts to improve Negro-white relationships. The little boys did not meet him.

Edgar also became involved politically in 1901, insisting that "the absolute supremacy of intelligence and property . . . shall be evenly and equally applicable in theory and in fact, to white and black. . . ." He wrote frequently to the newspapers attacking the widespread tendency to disfranchise Negroes, and, although the new Alabama State Constitution was disappointing to him, he felt that a framework had been erected in which progress was possible.

Edgar soon came to feel that he could carry on this work better if he resigned from his Montgomery church, which he did in 1901. He then became passionately involved in working for legislation to prohibit children under twelve from working in the mills. His efforts were at first centered in Alabama; later he initiated the National Child Labor Committee dedicated to stimulating child labor regulation in all the states.

The "greatest speech against child labor ever delivered in America was an impromptu address he made before the National Conference of Charities and Corrections in 1903." This address is still considered memorable in the struggle to remedy the conditions of working children.

In 1901 he had been appointed executive secretary of the Southern Education Board (started as an outgrowth of lectures given by Robert C. Ogden in both South and North) and was also vice president of the Conference for Education in the South. He edited the reports of the sixth, seventh and eighth sessions of that conference, and also the official reports of the Conferences on Race Problems of the South. In these activities he met and worked with major reformers—Jane Addams, Florence Kelley, Booker T. Washington and others. Edgar's extraordinary creative energy is like that of other fatherless men.

Gardner was five years old at the time of the 1900 conference in Montgomery, and during his childhood years when the family was separated from 1902 to 1908 he knew that his father was doing important work. It is likely that in his earliest years Gardner consciously or unconsciously absorbed the image of a father who was writing articles and books and giving speeches. This exposure must have contributed to his acceptance of writing as part of life's daily activities—one eats, sleeps, works, plays, writes. Despite his frailness and recurrent heart attacks, Gardner's father had extraordinary energy and capacity to inspire. It is tempting to believe that Gardner was impressed by these efforts, this energy, and this impact on the South and that this awareness contributed to his own social and civil rights commitments, to his peace efforts and to the intensity of his work as a social psychologist and parapsychologist. During all the years that I knew Gardner he never mentioned any of the outstanding people with whom his father had worked, but the idea of being of service, "doing good," and accomplishing something important had become deeply rooted in his mind by the time he reached adolescence.

His father's social gifts and very wide range of friends also made a deep impression on Gardner, who, by comparison felt that he was socially inept and had few friends. But the fact that his father was a leader, and a pioneer, and was both nationally and internationally minded probably added to Gardner's assumption that he also could be a leader. His father's "profound conception of democracy" must have been absorbed by Gardner as well, and this could have contributed to his lifetime emphasis on the potentialities of humanity.

In December 1907, when Gardner was twelve, his father became seriously ill with a flare-up of heart disease while attending a planning conference of the Southern Education Board at Old Point Comfort, Virginia. This time his wife rushed down to his side, and after a few weeks he recovered sufficiently to return to New York. But he realized that his health problem would interfere with continued work. On January 28, 1908, he sent a letter of resignation, but carried on until May in order to see an important conference to completion.

This resignation must have been an extremely anxious time for both parents—with no income in sight and no money saved from Edgar's modest salary. It is inconceivable that the boys would have been unaware of the stress of their father's failing health, his necessary retirement, and uncertain future. It was in this context that the combined influence of an intensely religious maid and a teenage friend made profound impact on Gardner and led to his deep adolescent immersion in religion.

Gardner's father continued writing after leaving the Southern Education Board. In *The Basis of Ascendancy,* published in 1909, he advocated improvements in education, which he believed would contribute to improvements in race relations. The book did not support complete equality between Negroes and whites and met with some criticism and controversy that proved stressful to its author. Edgar Gardner Murphy was a radical reformer of his time, but he did not glimpse the level of change that would be under way after the 1954 school desegregation decisions, nor Martin Luther King's dream of total freedom for blacks.

Gardner's adult appreciation of his father was conveyed in a letter to Daniel Levine in 1960:

> I think his basic determination to work in educational and social reforms was humanitarian. He was intensely aware of the gross misery, poverty, ignorance, which were the post–Civil War lot of the Southern family, and particularly the Southern child. I think it was a big heart more than anything else. There was also an intellectual aspect to it. He felt that Christianity, if it meant anything, had to be practical and sound in its human relations. His reason for leaving the Church was that he got so deep in educational and philanthropic, and indeed political, issues having to do with child labor and the development of educational facilities for both white and Negro children, that he felt he could battle this out better, and be respected as an equal more effectively, if he was a layman. I do not think he felt any "limitation within the church" nor did he "feel laymen would respect his views more if he were not a minister." The ministry, however, is a little bit removed from the tough battle line of everyday life. . . .
>
> While it is in general true that his books and articles on social problems are cast entirely in secular terms, you will find a sprinkling of deeply religious ideas in many of the pamphlets and the verses he wrote in the defense of the child, attacks on the Alabama mill system, and many other things of the early part of the century. While he was intensely devoted to the needs of children and a terrific fighter, he believed in using conservative methods.
>
> He was infinitely gentle, firm, strong, did not have . . . fanaticism. He was intense

in his devotion to rectitude of life. There was some sternness in this, but it was not at all violent nor was it Calvinistic. He was an intense dedicated reformer.

His irritability, probably caused by his constant pain and misery, was often unbearable to young Gardner, who sometimes felt bitter, but this feeling was healed by "the most remarkably earnest love which I always knew he felt for me, as for the rest of us."

Gardner wrote that his father's health broke down from 1904 onwards with recurrent attacks of his heart disease. "When I was nine years old he was fighting a losing battle but went on writing and lecturing, and after he had to retire in 1908 he saw many people at the [New Haven] house, and in the last few years in the New York apartment. The struggle against exploitation and misery had to be replaced to some degree, however, in the very last years, with the struggle just to keep alive." Still there were "family humor, whimsy and fun; and the more intense language of love and devotion would not have seemed appropriate to my mother to convey in her biography of her husband."

Gardner's description of his father as a "man of remarkable energy, capacity and personality, admired and loved by an enormous number of warm friends, and a leader in many great movements to which he gave his life" was documented by an account from the archives of the state of Alabama. Edgar Gardner Murphy published five books, two of them dealing with problems of the South. A pamphlet, "Alabama's First Question" did much in the campaign for local taxation for public schools. Many public addresses had had wide influence, as did the National Conference on Race Problems and Conditions in the South. He also wrote many papers published in Southern newspapers and national journals. In addition to this effort on behalf of education and race problems, his campaign for anti–child-labor legislation as chairman of the Alabama Child Labor Committee resulted in a law in 1903 and a better law in 1907.

Gardner experienced his father as uniquely heroic — "often in intermittent or continuous pain, always weak and half-sick, he pushed through great enterprises. . . . Keen of mind, with a quick sense of humor and a broad sanity of perspective, he won the admiration of the public men with whom he worked, and of countless personal friends."

Gardner's father died at the age of 43, the June before Gardner reached his eighteenth birthday, at the end of his freshman year at Yale. The last months had been "terrible"; Gardner said he tried to help but couldn't do much. Still, Gardner had not realized that death was to come so soon. In none of his autobiographical writings does he describe the private funeral in St. Agnes' Chapel in New York City or the public funeral in Trinity Church, Concord. His father was buried in Sleepy Hollow Cemetery in the King family plot. Nor did Gardner mention the memorial services in New York at St. Mark's in the Bouwerie, and in the Ethical Culture Society Auditorium when the secretary of the National Child Labor Committee noted, "Mr. Murphy deserves to be honored as one of the rarest and finest personalities that have in recent times appeared in American public life." His writing and speaking were compared to Jefferson's and Madison's in their statesmanlike quality. Felix Adler, founder of the Ethical Culture Society and cofounder of the National Child Labor Committee said he had found in Edgar Gardner Murphy "something of the quality of the religious seer."

Gardner must have attended these services with his mother and brother. Since their father and his work were so separated from the boys' growing up, it is possible that these meetings provided the first opportunity for the boys to see and meet some of the national leaders with whom their father had worked. Their deeply felt eulogies meant much to Gardner's mother, who recorded some of their words in her loving biography of her husband.

Gardner and His Brother, DuBose

The influence of the adults in Gardner's family was on the whole consistent: his grandfather's love of books, his grandmother's cheerful stoicism, his mother's broad culture and the interests she stimulated in Gardner, along with her strict and punitive discipline, his father's adoration of him and his image of his father as a man dedicated to reform. But the impact of Gardner's relation with his brother was very different at different stages of their development.

When Gardner was a baby, his two-and-a-half-year-old brother had been protective, liking to hold him in bed, with his arm around him, "so he won't tummel out." They were companions playing together with neighbors in Montgomery according to their mother's records of an incident in which they were found with empty beer bottles playing "drunken men." She also recollected pillow fights which she was sure that DuBose initiated even though they ended with his tantrums.

DuBose was imaginative, playing "grocy-man with pensu' behind his ear" and imitating other adult roles in his preschool years. We do not know to what extent Gardner participated in all this—he does not mention it in any of his autobiographies. But from Gardner's endless playfulness as an adult—in charades and games at home, at Holderness parties, and on our visit to the Children's Park in Tashkent in 1960 as well as in many other settings, it is tempting to assume that early dramatic play gave a foundation for his later spontaneity in games with children.

In San Antonio, where they lived for a year in 1901 when Gardner was six and DuBose was eight, and in Concord, there were occasional ballgames with DuBose and with their cousins George and Margaret Babbitt. After reading *Two Arrows* written by W.O. Stoddard, Gardner and DuBose played "hunting mountain lions." When DuBose was with his playmates outside of the family, however, he excluded Gardner. Their relationship was similar to the one between William and Henry James: rejecting his younger brother, William bragged, "I play with boys who curse and swear!" Gardner felt left out, and began as a young boy to feel "isolated" despite the presence of playmates. At the age of 21 he wrote: "My relations with my brother consisted of periodic oscillation from a good-tempered compatibility to a strong irritation and antagonism . . . there were periods when I was quite frequently 'mad at' him. In general I was not particularly devoted to him, I am sorry to say, and was very easily incensed at him."

DuBose was better coordinated, more athletic, more socially at ease, and Gardner increasingly felt that he was not a social success like his brother. There is no evidence of happy closeness with DuBose, but the boys shared household chores from Concord days until their departure to Hotchkiss. Gardner's delights and "crazes" were his alone. DuBose was a year ahead at Yale, active in college organizations and a fraternity member. Classmates of Gardner's wrote to me that "there was more rivalry than love" between the brothers; apparently DuBose did not give any support to Gardner as he entered Yale.

Following graduation from Yale, when DuBose was studying to become an Episcopal priest (as his father had been until DuBose was nine) Gardner was becoming deeply committed to a scientific view of the world. Their conceptions of faith came into painful conflict. Gardner wrote a long anguished letter to DuBose explaining his commitment to scientific *truth,* which he felt excluded the dogmas of Protestant theology, and the rituals of the church. The gulf between the brothers deepened, but they maintained a relationship based on family loyalty and responsibility. Repercussions of the deep persistent feelings of isolation that had been reinforced by, if not initiated by, DuBose's boyish exclusion of Gardner from his own gang may have contributed to Gardner's sensitivity as a college teacher to the shyness and insecurity of some young students, and also to his avoidance of competitive and aggressive peers.

It seems probable that academic competition between the boys was also intense, judging from the lists of prizes won by both, but as children this was not evident. While DuBose learned to read at the age of five, Gardner was infatuated with numbers: he was not at all interested in reading or in academic learning until the age of seven. Then when he did discover books his response does not appear to have been in any way related to DuBose's achievement—he was wildly excited about the books themselves. This excitement apparently did not evoke a sense of the achievement possibilities in school. He remembers being tardy, careless, uninterested, not concerned about marks in the early grades. However, after his mother's tutoring in Branford helped him to enter the sixth grade in New Haven, he ended the year second from the top in his class and more ambition developed. After that he was first in his class, and continued this level of achievement at Hotchkiss. The opportunity for academic success may have attracted him in view of his sense of athletic and social inferiority to his brother. In his "Study of Myself" he wrote that he was probably

more ambitious and more original than DuBose, while his brother was "a better mixer" socially, more "sane," and more efficient. He added that DuBose
was cheerful, "takes life as it comes and enjoys it"—while he (Gardner) was
"apt to worry, grow restless, and become unhappy." He also saw affinities; he
and his brother had similar scholarly interests, tastes in literature and music,
and the same enthusiasms, for instance, for baseball. There was at least one
continuing shared interest—their mutual admiration for Arthur Rubinstein;
DuBose gave Gardner Rubinstein records on at least two occasions.

Gardner felt that he was probably more independent—and his subsequent career confirmed his intellectual independence. DuBose was a little
more independent of their mother, as he made his home in the South. Gardner did not mention a major difference that impressed me—DuBose's style and
moods remained stable within a rather narrow range. By contrast, Gardner
could be delightfully spontaneous and playful, or serious to the point of
dryness; witty and humorous, or anxiously oversensitive to confrontation.
Gardner's range of responsiveness was unusually broad, and as a man he was
more passionately committed than his brother to causes of peace and justice,
the rights of women, and hungry children. DuBose was deeply appreciated by
the congregations of his churches. As far as I am aware, there is no evidence
of open conflict or destructiveness between the brothers; rather, they maintained a mutually loyal relationship without intimacy.

Shortly after World War I, Gardner and DuBose seemed to tacitly agree
to go their separate ways—as far as their basic personal relationship was concerned. This was made easier by the fact that they were separated geograph-
ically; their personal visits were few and far between.

The nature of DuBose's relationship with Gardner in the early years could
not have been detected by anyone who watched them together later. On
DuBose's New York visits, the tone was one of mutual cordiality; if anything,
Gardner was somewhat more self-assured. A baseball game that Gardner and
our son, Al, attended with DuBose in the forties was a happy occasion.

Gardner was devoted to his brother's children, Leonard and Alice Gardner
Murphy, and kept in close touch with them after DuBose died in 1959. He had
also wanted to assist DuBose in finding adequate psychiatric help for his
vulnerable wife, Alice, who broke down at each of Maud's visits, then became
permanently hospitalized. But DuBose felt that the psychiatric resources in the
South were adequate and he also felt that Alice felt too insecure about Northerners to attempt a visit to a Northern center.

During the 1950s Gardner was generous and concerned with DuBose's
medical problems (when a colonic tumor developed) and his support to
DuBose's children. He talked of DuBose's last illness with reserve, and one had
the feeling that he did not want to tell more than necessary. Gardner bore his
brother's death stoically, although his realization that he was the last survivor
of his immediate family left at times a bleak expression on his face.

4. Gardner's First Six Years in North and South

The years between Gardner's birth in 1895 and his 1919 entrance to Columbia University to work toward his Ph.D. included a series of very different phases; during his first six years the family was united, with his father in charge of one church after another in widely different regions. During the next six years, from 1902 to 1908, his mother and her two sons were in Northern towns of Concord, Massachusetts, and Branford and New Haven, Connecticut, while Gardner's father was travelling in the South as executive secretary of the Southern Education Board. When ill health forced Edgar Murphy to retire he rejoined the family in New Haven and they were all together from 1908 to 1910, after which the two youths went to Hotchkiss School and their parents moved to New York. Gardner's father died there in June, 1913, at the end of Gardner's first year at Yale. Three more years at Yale, a year at Harvard for his master's degree in psychology, and two years in Europe in World War I transpired before he entered Columbia. Gardner lived in seven different towns and cities before he entered Yale, and the discontinuities in the large environment, as well as in his family life, provided many a challenge to a sensitive growing boy struggling to achieve a continuity of self—an identity. Even in his first six years he lived in four different cities; this period preceded the two years in Concord that were so crucial to the integration of that sense of himself.

The atmosphere of the home at the time Gardner was born was affected by his parents' experiences in the previous three or four years. After their marriage in August, 1891, they returned to San Antonio, moving to Laredo, Texas, in 1893. During that year their first child was born on July 21. They named him DuBose after Dr. DuBose, Edgar Murphy's revered mentor at Sewanee. All of the family were so often ill in the South Texas climate, however, that they accepted a call from St. Paul's Church in Chillicothe, Ohio, hoping that the northerly location would be better for their health. Gardner was born there on July 8, 1895, to a mother still almost constantly ill with the

51

same chills and fever she had had in Texas. His father worked strenuously both to give St. Paul's cultivated congregation elegant sermons (which were soon published as a book with the title *The Larger Life*), and to establish another church in a section of the city where no church had existed. The Murphys made many good friends in the city, but Edgar also had recurrent attacks of fever and weakness.

The baby Gardner was born in a setting of warm welcome by his frail parents who were, however, often too fatigued and unwell to give much attention to their little boys. They had to be left with their devoted nurse-helper, Mamie Studer, when their parents were resting or occupied with church responsibilities. It is also probable that Maud did not suggest or permit her husband to share care-giving activities with their babies; from Maud's distress at the responsibilities her son DuBose had to assume as a father of a baby whose mother was not well, it sems obvious that shared infant care was not a concept with which she was comfortable.

We have no account of the home where Gardner was born, but it was usual for an established parish to have an ample parish house for the minister's family. Gardner's lifelong love of art may have had its roots in his early months as he gazed at pictures on the wall (which later he told me were the only important things in the house); a large old print of the Sistine Madonna which I saw in his mother's house in 1925 was probably one of the early pictures. An early photo of him as a little toddler leaning against a magnificent old tree provides an image of one setting where he could have watched the "golden sunlight" streaming down through the leaves, as he recalled in later years; such experiences could have laid down beginnings of his lifelong love of forests. And the ill health of his parents which often prevented the close attention the baby craved could have meant long periods of time during which such sensory delights were his chief satisfactions.

His parents had hoped for a little girl, and had selected the name Lelia Gardner (after Edgar's aunt) before the baby was born. When the little boy appeared, he was named Gardner. His mother kept very few notes on this baby in contrast to her warm, vivid and empathic account of DuBose's earliest years. She told me that her milk gave out when Gardner was two months old and he was then given cow's milk. She also told me about slapping Gardner's hand when he tried to reach through the crib slats to touch her as she rested. It does not appear that his attachment to his mother was reduced by this punishment — he never gave up reaching out for contact, not only with her but with friends. Still, this early distancing may have contributed to his deep and recurrent sensitivity to feelings of being left out and isolated, which were reinforced by childhood experiences with peers. Although he had some playmates and companions from the age of four through his college years, "middle level" friends did not satisfy his craving for intimacy and closeness. (That his mother was not playful seems probable from this incident: one time when I was on the floor playing with my toddler son she asked, "Why are you doing that?" Apparently *playing* with a baby was beyond her comprehension.)

There are no accounts of interesting or appealing qualities about this second little boy, who may indeed have been more quiet and less interesting than his active, imaginative older brother. In fact, comparison between the two seemed to slant his mother's memory toward Gardner's deficiencies: she told me that he did not begin to read until he was seven years old, that he had so much trouble with other boys when he was nine that she took him out of school and tutored him at home, and that when she visited him at Camp Algonquin when he was 13 he was so awkward in putting on his shirt that she felt he was not adequate to the camp experience and did not send him the following year, although he desperately wanted to return. Her comments about his limitations would not have raised so many questions in our minds if they had been balanced by memories of his appealing qualities as a child, but it was "Cousin Catharine" who sent us a picture of "that dear little boy."

With intellectual parents concerned about and active in the community, and a mother who had been a teacher before marriage, as well as a talkative brother, baby Gardner must have heard a great deal of talk around him, as well as talk addressed to him. How important language was to his mother is apparent in the brief notes she made about him which included an analysis of his eighteen-month-old vocabulary; in contrast, she left no records of what he enjoyed, was excited or disturbed about, what consoled him, the development of laughter, or any description of the sort of baby he was. His mother records Gardner's words as accurately pronounced, while DuBose used childish approximations: "Teet-tar" (streetcar), he had the table-bell to "tamp" (stamp), "hannle" (handle), "so many dus' [dust] around here."

In a tiny dim snapshot of Gardner as a toddler we see an appealing, blond, softly curly haired little one in a watchful attitude. Whether Gardner was playful as a baby, we have no record. If not, where did his spontaneity and playfulness even with babies come from? Sticking out his tongue, making faces to evoke their laughter, playing little games, Gardner was a joy-giving father to our babies even when they were very young.

The sibling rivalry between DuBose and Gardner that persisted through college may have been fed by DuBose's awareness that his father who "loved both of his sons, adored Gardner," as their mother told me. Maud may also have had some jealousy of her husband's adoration of little Gardner while she was so fascinated with DuBose; such feelings could have contributed to the ambivalence about her second son. But she was dutifully careful to give her boys equal attention, gifts, care.

Gardner wrote that as a very young child he liked all suitable food, was happy, affectionate, not especially fearful, very interested in animals and in all bottles; with "continual *new* interests, intense in *small* possessions. Not imitative; original interests." Evidently these items are recalled from comments by relatives since he also said he did not remember *himself* in any setting before Montgomery when he was four and five years old. Gardner's own memories — colorful, dramatic images of what he saw — not of what he did, nor of anyone of his family, start at the age of three when they moved to Kingston, New York. What he remembered of their home there was the fireplace, the bellows nearby and a cat lying on the hearth. The astonishing glow and dance of the wood fire were evidently imprinted deeply and meaningfully. (And he described his delight at the age of six, seeing his fire chief Uncle Billy Tobin leap over the picket fence in front of his house, dashing to a fire in San Antonio.)

Over our years together Gardner enjoyed and was expert at making the fires in the fireplaces of our successive homes and for picnics. The fire-making and controlling were always Gardner's job and he enjoyed it. He loved Wagner's "fire music," and often described a vivid, stimulating person as fiery, not meaning aggressive but exciting. To be "full of fire" was to pour out interesting ideas. His name for me was "Loki" (after the Norse fire god), a response to the stimulus he felt from me, but enlarged by his own romantic fantasy. His own brilliant lecturing and writing were warm with leaps of thought through time, history, literature, and the cosmos — as if the movement of flames in the fireplace had energized and freed his mind for leaping associations as a very young child. Gardner describes sensory experiences in his early years more vividly than he describes any people, writing of the "vividness, warmth, snapping electrical vitality of the childhood memories that come back to me whenever I ask them to. . . . The brilliant golden sunshine that plays through the leaves, and lights from the mosses in a fairyland forest which I encountered in Massachusetts and Tennessee and Alabama. . . ." He thought this sensory world was important in his work: "My love of psychology is first a love of experience as it comes through senses, affects, complex association patterns and memory or creative fantasy."

After one year in Kingston, the family moved to Montgomery, Alabama. Gardner's memories of the next years are rich and vivid with clear images of people, of nature, and of things that excited him. The Montgomery home was largely dominated by females — Mamie Studer had come South with them at first, and there was an old Negro woman, a former slave, to whom they were devoted. A visit to Concord "was very important in establishing identification with Gran'ma King, Aunt Minnie and Aunt Louise" as well as with Gran'pa King. Gran'ma King came down for a long visit, and she and Gardner "were devoted to one another." He spoke of identifying with her patience and cheerfulness when he knew her later in Concord. He remembered feeling that he was "the child of my mama and papa" and "very deeply belonged to the immediate group," with "a simple pride in the family as a whole."

For the first time there were neighboring playmates, who wondered what language the little Northerners talked, and Gardner was puzzled — perhaps he already felt "alien" as he did at later moves — when the Southern boys talked of "chucking rocks" while the Murphy boys spoke of "throwing stones." The contrast between the South to which his father belonged and the North of his mother was already laying a foundation for an identity conflict.

In his mother's story of life with DuBose, Gardner was included as she described an occasional Sunday afternoon trip to the railway depot half a mile from their house, to watch the freight train that would roll down the track. Gardner loved trains, both real ones, and Turner's great painting, *Rain, Steam and Speed.* She also mentioned reading to the little boys Hawthorne's *Tanglewood Tales* and Kipling's *Just-So Stories,* of which the lonely White Seal was Gardner's favorite, he later told me.

The impression she gave of her handling of DuBose made clear her expectation that he would always respect limits, and he usually did. However, once when he was bored and restless in the Sunday School class of which she was in charge, she sent him to the next room to quiet down; but he did not remain—he used the five cents given to him for the Sunday School collection to take a streetcar home. She said there were no hard words on either side, and there seldom were. This, if accurate, contrasts with Gardner's memories of unfair discipline, which led to a "drawing away from the grownup world." His mother also told me that he often protested "T'ain't fair."

Gardner was very intense indeed about "not being bossed." Once he refused to be photographed and his mother asked him just to "stand next to DuBose while his picture is taken." He did but when he saw the picture of himself standing next to his brother, he protested, "You play no twicks on me!" Gardner wrote later that it was in Montgomery that he developed a clear consciousness of self; he remembered himself as serious-minded and thoughtful at that time, but he did not mention how much he was absorbing from his parents' intense discussions of race problems and child labor in the South. (I do remember how concerned I was—at the age of five—about the deprived, neglected children I saw on the streets in south Chicago and how Jane Addams who was helping poor children became my idol.)

He also remembered "the enormous tooting of whistles which welcomed the new century on the night of December 31, 1899–January 1, 1900." That is the only memory of sounds, which is surprising in view of his later deep response to music. His interests at that four- to five-year-old stage were extremely keen, and he was especially excited about numbers after Gran'ma King brought him a calendar with red numbers on it. Oddly enough, for a little boy who was to grow into a man who loved, acquired, read, wrote and edited books in his adult life, he did not have an early interest in books, letters or learning to read.

Gardner's mother had been reading to DuBose from the time he was two. Perhaps books to Gardner were what someone read *to* you—you didn't need to bother with them yourself. Or perhaps the books his mother read, geared to DuBose's level, were beyond Gardner's level in his early years. There was no hint in his or her memory of his first six years of the excitement about books that later developed "like wild-fire" and continued throughout his lifetime. His mother told me that if she asked him to run an errand he would go happily if she gave him an address in numbers, but not if she simply gave him the names of the person or shop involved. This interest never left him. One of his last books was *From Pythagoras to Freud,* and one of his major theoretical articles was "Organism and Quantity."

The age of four and five is generally a time of high imagination, emotion, fear, curiosity, and creativity, and Gardner's intense temperament made it inevitable that he would have vivid experiences in all of these areas. He remembered distinctly several terrors of that time — especially fears of confinement, of the dark, of strange people and places, of being left alone under unusual conditions, and of the unknown. But as he grew older he liked to explore new countries, and his approach to science was especially to press beyond the barriers around the known into the unknown.

Experiences with puzzling realities evidently occurred at the age of five or six as well; they are not located in Montgomery or San Antonio in his accounts, but must have occurred in one of those cities. The little brothers had two large tin animals, Horsie and Doggie. One day Gardner found the two halves of Doggie fallen apart and he was shocked. Where was Doggie's soul, what was he? To the imaginative child Doggie was a person, with a soul; now what was he?

About the same time Gardner had been told that a "devil's spade" was buried in the ground behind their house. He dug up the earth at the place indicated and found a little toy spade. Later his mother told him that a fairy would put a dime under his pillow if he left his first baby tooth there when it came out. And there were other fairy stories. All of these experiences left a deep impression and were not only remembered, but evidently became the roots of his reflectiveness, speculation, and lifelong concern with the nature of reality.

There is a striking contrast between Gardner's report of his impression that he was not fearful in Kingston, but that he had many terrors in Montgomery, and was very intense emotionally. We may wonder whether anxiety was evoked by tensions he sensed around the discussions of his father's rapidly developing involvements in efforts to improve race relations, his father's decision to resign from his Episcopal priesthood — a drastic move which must have been discussed at home — and by the decision for Maud to go to Concord with her two boys. We know from longitudinal studies how disturbed children of that age may become when they are told about such major changes. The fact that they would be returning to Concord where they had visited would ease the change, but still they were to leave their father behind. One can only wonder whether the fear of the unknown was not a reflection of what Gardner was overhearing or being told.

Gardner was sensitive to emotional exchanges between parents: "As long as my father was in good health there was no quarreling or almost no quarreling at all" — in contrast to "the way in which Uncle Eugene Babbitt [his mother's brother-in-law] held aloof and was disagreeable." Granted that Edgar Murphy was irritable when he was ill, we can only wonder about the role of his aggressive wife — wonderful as she was and deeply as they loved each other — in provoking or not preventing provocation of her sick husband. The fact that Gardner mentions this problem in discussing Montgomery implies that the momentous issues under discussion were seldom the subject of irritable argument at that time, in contrast to the later years of his father's illness. Any raised voices, sharp remarks, or irritable arguments could, however, have contributed to the anxiety of a sensitive young boy and could have made him vulnerable to other fears.

An alert and sensitive child may assimilate attitudes, values, and concerns of the larger environment. Although radio, television, and the current profusion of weekly magazines and newspapers were not bringing the world to the ears and eyes of a child at that time, still there was talk, especially in politically and socially interested families as both of ours were. What was going on in Gardner's early years that might have seeped into his consciousness through overheard conversations among grownups, or that might have been reflected in his father's sermons is not told directly, but we do know that in addition to conversation about the problems with which his father was concerned, he probably heard about his mother's and grandmother's trip to Tuskegee, Booker T. Washington's institute to train black students. He may have heard about the visit to his father of that great Negro leader and the plans for, and excitement about the success of, the momentous Montgomery Conference held in 1900 to discuss race problems. It is interesting that he commented in the "Study of Myself" that at that time, as he believed, he more nearly resembled his father than his mother. This may imply his empathy with his father's concern about Negroes.

The 1900 Conference on Race Problems led to invitations for Edgar to speak in New York, Washington and Boston; it was in this period that Gardner's father met influential people of the time: Lyman Abbott, Walter Hines Page, Andrew Carnegie and George Foster Peabody. Gardner never mentioned to us the repeated absences of his father or the outstanding men and women who had been impressed by him. After his 1903 address on Child Labor as a National Problem, the noted Jane Addams, who had appeared on the same program, offered her congratulations and friendship — and Edgar felt that meeting her had been worth the effort of the speech. By 1901 Edgar's sense of acceptance by the leaders was strong enough for him to write to President Roosevelt in behalf of Thomas G. Jones' appointment to a federal judgeship and to persuade Booker T. Washington to add his support. The appointment was made. Edgar's disapproval of the Beveridge bill excluding from interstate commerce products from all plants employing children under fourteen evoked the President's appreciation. "Your letter came at just the right time. There is no one whose judgment on such a matter would more affect me than yours," Roosevelt wrote in 1907. (Edgar consistently disapproved *federal* control of child labor.)

Something of these experiences and of his father's ease in dealing with contemporary leaders could have contributed to Gardner's freedom in making contact with established leaders of his own time. An example is his successful initiative shortly after the end of World War I to persuade John Dewey to help him raise funds to feed starving Russian children. Whether he was in this country or in others around the world, as in conferring with Nehru, he was at ease with leaders, with a naturalness that seemed to have deep roots. We do not know whether Irene Ashley, the American Federation of Labor representative, came to the Murphy home in 1900 when she brought her report on the condition of child mill-workers in the South. Whether she did or not, the fact that their father became so concerned about child labor could not have been lost on the boys. It was the National Child Labor Committee, not the problems of the South, that received Gardner's attention for many years of his adult life.

Gardner's conscious memories of Montgomery were focused on his immediate family. He felt that while his parents were affectionate and sympathetic they did not realize "how much difference it would have made to me had I felt free to tell what was going on in my mind. I always felt that I was babied, treated as less mature than I was, not given credit for the intelligence I possessed. . . . But my parents understood me much better than most parents understand their children, and were most remarkably devoted to me."

Gardner was six when the family went to San Antonio to live near Edgar's mother in 1901 before going to Concord in 1902. Although his father's sister Ethel's family was also in that Texas city, Gardner never said much about them. In San Antonio, Gardner said, he played alone most of the time; DuBose at that stage "seemed remote," and Ethel's two children, Edgar and "Daughter" were younger than Gardner. He remembered the beautiful little stone "Anchor blocks" he and DuBose used occasionally to construct a village complete with a population, which he regarded as a great achievement. Although he went to kindergarten during this period, he recalled nothing of it. Later, he thought of himself during his first six years as a happy child; warm and colorful memories transcended the frustrations and anxieties of that time.

Joyous, enthusiastic, warm, generous and full of love of the universe, Gardner was an optimistic, happy man. Some recollections of his mother about child-rearing, specifically related to Gardner's brother but undoubtedly relevant to little Gardner may throw some light on his happy disposition. "Aunt Emily" Shepard, one of their mother's dearest friends in Concord (which they visited one summer during the Southern years), taught children "to use a cheerful tone when they ask for what they want." She added later that DuBose learned not to "fuss" — it was no fun; he got what he wanted better in other ways. And it was recorded that when he was glum Aunt Emily urged, "Run outdoors and find a happy-boy smile." DuBose could "go behind some curtain or into some corner and there by magic 'find a smile.'" Their mother also recorded of DuBose that at the age of two "he had a cheerful way of doing as he was told." And he knew that "tears were not profitable" and after a disappointment returned to his normal ways of finding fun in everything. Aunt Emily's approach was undoubtedly used with Gardner as well, and must have consolidated the happy moods he spontaneously experienced. His optimism could have had deeper roots — when one source of milk gave out, there was more. When they left Kingston, they found new delights in Montgomery.... When they left the South for Concord, that was best of all.

It was in the San Antonio year that the family went on occasional picnics — sometimes Uncle Billy "went hunting but he did not actually do much hunting." On the way home from one such picnic a hungry, brown, floppy-eared dog followed them, and Gardner tells how unfair he thought it was for the family to feed their own dog and refuse to feed the stray. But when Gardner asked his mother whether he could spend his weekly allowance of a dime in any way that he wished, she agreed. He used it to buy food for the dog. In one autobiography he saw this as the beginning of his lifelong concern for underdogs, but did not suggest that it was related to his own feeling, throughout his growing up, of being an underdog in relation to his more skillful, more athletic, more socially successful older brother. Nor did he connect his feeling for underdogs with his father's passionate concern for Negroes in the South, which developed after he was horrified by that lynching. Gardner was six years old at the time of the episode with the hungry dog. What is impressive here is his challenge to the adult authorities and conventions, in the context of his sympathy for the neglected, rejected hungry dog. It is certainly important that his effort to alleviate that hunger was not prevented by his mother and he may in the end have received praise from someone in the entourage for his generosity. Certainly, his generosity increased, to the extent of not safeguarding his own needs throughout his life.

In 1901 his father decided that he could be more effective in his efforts to improve education — for blacks and whites both — in the South, if he withdrew from the ministry; there was no less loyalty to Christianity but as Dr. DuBose wrote, he was becoming "the philosopher, the statesman, the prophet of the coming social revolution." This was another major decision which must have been discussed in letters or on visits, and which must have been absorbed by the boys. Gardner was six years old; he was no longer an Episcopal minister's son; he was the son of a leader in a national organization, a man who was fighting to make the world better.

We know that even at the age of three or four some children try to clarify for themselves the patterns and sequences of their experiences. Conceptualizing a structure of their lives is an urgent need, as if they want to make sense out of the complexity and change. They internalize their experiences and try to integrate them into a whole. For such children a persistent drive to integrate may acquire what Gordon Allport, after Woodworth, called "functional autonomy," an acquired motive as important as the basic motives rooted in sensory needs.

Did this happen with Gardner? We do not have childhood projective tests, his drawings, nor pictures of his play constructions. But we do have that memory of constructing a village, we know what he went through as a child, and we see the drive to integration repeatedly expressed in his writings, and in his teaching with his hospitality to the old and the new—and with his commitment to both tradition and challenge.

5. Growing Up in Emerson's Concord

Gardner was seven years old when his mother took her two sons to Concord, Massachusetts, to be near Gran'pa and Gran'ma King. There Gardner would pass by the homes of Emerson, Thoreau, Hawthorne, and the Alcotts and picnic on Walden Pond. Maud's move with the two young boys was explained by them—in their memorial booklet for her—in terms of the good schools in Concord. In her biography of her husband there is no mention of the discussions which must have led to this plan; no mention of reasons for leaving her husband's base in Montgomery, or for not settling in or near New York where his central office was; no mention of the strain on Edgar's frail health that would be involved in long trips to visit them; no mention of what the lack of sustained contact with their father would mean to the growing boys. We do not know whether Montgomery schools in 1902 were really inadequate, whether Maud had misgivings about the boys' growing up in a racist atmosphere, whether she feared reprisals for her husband's controversial efforts, nor even whether her husband urged this move. Nor is there any record of the boys' feelings about this move after several previous ones, or about leaving their father behind. We do know that Gardner had not established roots or friendships in Montgomery or in San Antonio. The greetings of his loving grandparents must have warmed the change, despite the shock of leaving his father.

During Gardner's crucially important developmental years, from age seven to thirteen, he and DuBose had an absentee father; passionately committed to his struggles on behalf of Southern education and of child labor laws, Edgar visited rarely. As executive secretary of the Southern Education Board he did make periodic visits to New York City for conferences. Sometimes he combined these with stops in Concord. Although his sons grew up on their mother's image of their heroic, brilliant father, the boys had no opportunity for firsthand acquaintance with their father's work and very little opportunity to know him as the head of the family. It was their mother who held that role.

When he did visit for holidays Edgar brought gifts; Gardner told me how much it meant to him that his frail, busy father went to great trouble to bring him a miniature steam engine that made real steam — a toy for which Gardner had longed. It was such gestures that conveyed the devotion Gardner felt from his father and that bridged the geographical gulf between them.

An absentee, but adoring, father left Gardner with few concrete memories, and perhaps some ambivalence, since he never quoted his father and he described only a few episodes of companionship at a rare baseball game or vaudeville show. Life with a distant father punctuated by a few joint experiences contrasted sharply to the sense of pervasive presence or continuity that he felt with his grandfather during those two years in Concord and during summers afterward, and the constant presence of his mother. It was his mother who read to him — books like *At the Back of the North Wind, King Arthur and Knights of the Round Table* and other children's classics — and who carefully supervised his own reading. She was the disciplinarian who taught her children the proprieties, manners, and standard of decency supposed to characterize "well brought up" children.

Life in Concord was very different from the previous pattern of home life. Not only was there no father's daily presence in the home, there was no Mamie Studer to do the household work and cooking. The boys stoked the furnace, shovelled snow, ran errands and took care of their own rooms. Life was centered in home, school and Sunday school — and their grandparents' home. There is no record of the boys visiting other children's homes in Concord.

Although Gardner and his brother and mother lived in a modest house on Belknap Street, they spent much time with, and felt part of, his mother's family — all of whom loved this affectionate little boy, whose build and blond coloring were like that of his Concord relatives. DuBose, by contrast, was dark, thin and tall like his father — a fact that doubtless contributed to his continued Southern identification. Gran'pa King's love for his three daughters, and in turn their affection for Maud's warm-hearted, enthusiastic younger son with his "crazes" must have intensified Gardner's response to them. It was the larger family, including his cousins George and Margaret along with the aunts and uncles, which gave him the intense feeling of "really belonging, . . . just as much as if my father had not come from San Antonio." In addition to the King family, "Aunt Emily" encouraged the boys with her own special child-rearing device — "Find a happy-boy smile." To be cheerful was a basic value inculcated from the earliest years.

The series of previous moves had evidently given Gardner an early sense of alienation, which sensitized him to the new and cherished feeling of belonging. And the love of so many female relatives left a lifelong sensitivity to women; as a man he was more than an ideological feminist — he was naturally supportive, understanding and appreciative of the potentialities of women.

The feeling of belonging in his mother's family and the joy of his father's occasional visits were, however, shadowed by his feeling of ambiguity about his identity—his sense of being a maverick—as he described it in an autobiography and in interviews. From the age of seven to nine, when children are becoming acutely conscious of differences of many kinds, and when they are also becoming conscious of status, both inferior and superior, Gardner found himself in a dual situation. While he belonged to his mother's family whose Boston lawyer father identified him with the old New England Protestant business and professional families, his surname Murphy placed him "smack in the middle of 'Texas,'" the area across the tracks in Concord where lived the Irish immigrants who worked with their hands, not their brains. He omitted to add that his Southern father—invisible to other boys—had come, in fact, from the real Texas, with only a remote Irish background.

Actually, his aristocratic denial of status (while quietly assuming it) had strong roots in Texas as well as Concord. The easy, aristocratic bearing of both his father and his aunt Ethel Tobin, the high standards and the financial success of his grandmother's boarding house, and the family history of plantation life, all testify to a consciousness of family status that persisted through financial limitations. When his parents went to Bad Nauheim in the hope of help with Edgar's heart problems they could not afford first class tickets. Edgar remarked that even if they could not afford first class quarters they could *be* "first class." He never compromised this standard. Edgar's approach to improved education and the betterment of race relations had a quality of Christian noblesse oblige that was in contrast to Jane Addams' dedication to helping the poor by living *with* them (different in turn from "living *like* the poor," as Gardner and some of his friends advocated in the early twenties).

Young Gardner did not reject the Irish, or other workers; he integrated his feeling about them with his feeling about his King heritage. He felt that he belonged both with the elite and with the underdogs, and throughout his life he identified and was at ease with both. That is, he was at ease with leaders who shared his values, and who were not pretentious "stuffed shirts," or aggressive competitors. He was always eager to encourage the young to "be better than you are," and to assist, especially, minority group students to find opportunities worthy of their potential. Gardner's determination at the age of six to feed a hungry dog gives another dimension to his feeling for the underprivileged.

But why, with his Concord grandfather among the elite, did he identify himself with the minority group merely because of his Irish name? His brother, DuBose, did nothing of the sort. In an interview with Montague Ullman at the age of 71, Gardner again told how isolated he felt during his childhood and youth when his brother excluded him. Perhaps these feelings of isolation merged with the underdog feeling, and minority-group identity, and the feeling of being different implied in his statement that mavericks were his "kind of people."

Compensating in part for these feelings of conflict in identity, rejection and insecurity was the deep feeling of belonging in his grandparents' home surrounded by their acceptance and love, and the companionship of cousins, of whom George Babbitt was a favorite. Although he never said as much, I think the conflicts combined with the sense of belongingness may have helped him to forge an independent identity, gradually to wrench himself away from the puritan ways of his mother, and to bypass the coercive trends that transiently dominated social, political and intellectual patterns over his lifetime. He not only seemed unique to his students but maintained unassailable integrity in his political and intellectual life.

When Gardner wrote that he grew up "in the pure culture of Concord" — where he lived only from the age of seven to nine years, but where he spent many summers through the years of his childhood and adolescence — what was his actual experience? The famous Concord authors of the mid-nineteenth century had long since died, but they still lived in the minds and hearts of Concord. One of the teachers in the school the boys attended lived with "Miss Ellen," Emerson's daughter, through whom the culture of the Emerson family continued to be conveyed to the school. Emerson's son and grandson were also there, along with Frederick Alcott Pratt, nephew of Louisa May Alcott, to reinforce the tradition of respect for their distinguished forebears. And Gardner's grandfather had been a member of the select Social Circle — a group of men elected for life, not on the basis of wealth or fame (Emerson and Judge Hoar were the only famous members) but on the basis of citizenship. The Social Circle members were leaders who took a prominent part in town meetings, held town offices and were admired "both for their common sense and their oratory." They strongly influenced the thought and action of the town and held the trust of their neighbors. They were men of public spirit — the "good old New England public spirit," by which the members of a community help to support its communal life. The unique "characters" of the town were cherished. Dr. Josiah Bartlett "was the finest specimen of an old fashioned doctor ... one who carried in his mind and heart the history, the antecedents, and the wants of the whole town, and who, by long service and genuine sympathy had become the trusted friend, counselor and helper of a great multitude in all classes and conditions.... His character was founded in his honesty: of speech, of action, particularly in money matters, in his sense of right, ... in his faithfulness to his professional duties, no matter what the weather or his own ill-health." Judge Hoar was "keen in his understanding, brilliant in his wit," and two other members "had the tendency to sainthood."

Gardner was acquainted with Edward Waldo Emerson, son of Ralph Waldo Emerson; Edward's memoir recounts the series of ministers in his genealogy. Ralph Waldo Emerson was for a time a minister. Edward was "born in a town where the old ideals and simple living were prized...." He was "surrounded by loving care, and went to academy and college almost as a matter of course." His mother was "deeply religious and spiritually minded.... Her purity and elevation and nobility of character were a precious privilege for her children to see." She read the Bible and sang hymns with her children. Edward spoke of the "impossibility of evil speaking or thinking." The young Edward Emerson had begun the study of Latin when he was about eight, and Greek when he was twelve. He became a doctor who said, "Keeping at least an outward show of cheerfulness . . . helps to form a habit of philosophic cheer under stormy skies." To be cheerful was a value we find reflected over and over again both in descriptions of people and in Maud's record of child-rearing emphases.

When failing health and an inheritance from his father led Edward Emerson to give up the rigors of medicine as a profession he turned to both painting and lecturing on art, as well as editing his father's writings, and writing memoirs of his father and of Thoreau. He loved his summer home near Monadnock, a mountain in southern New Hampshire where Gardner's mother and grandmother sometimes spent their vacations. "His was an ideal family life. He was a companion to his children and read aloud to his wife in the evenings." He always looked on the best side of people, his conversation was never humdrum, his wit and humor were "never satirical, but lively and playful." He was never cross nor irritable, nor did he get depressed, except when he was ill. He was rarely angry. Much of this description of Edward Emerson could describe Gardner as a man. Gardner knew this gentle man and others of similar warmth, conscientiousness and devotion.

It was always to the fact and feel of Concord that he returned when he wanted to reminisce about the happiest things he remembered in his childhood. It seems clear that "the pure culture of Concord" was embodied in the fine-grained people to whom Gardner was exposed there, and from whom he absorbed the warmth, humor, integrity, and consistency in "living his values" described by his students.

Margaret Lothrop's charming little book, *The Wayside*, conveys the atmosphere of Concord as she tells of the family life of the Alcotts, who lived in the spacious old house before her own family bought it. Much of this family life style was characteristic of the family experience of Gardner's growing up as well as of our life together. Reading together, charades, writing verses to commemorate birthdays or other events, humor and lively conversation, tutoring of the children by one or the other parent, or both, as well as participating in household chores and gardening were part of everyday life.

The Lothrops' friends included Emerson, Thoreau, Longfellow and Whittier; education focused on literature, the Greek and Latin classics, history, and languages, especially German. (Gardner's mother was at home with French as well as German and she learned Greek with her sons.) Over and over again Margaret Lothrop refers to the gentle character of most of this group of family-loving men, especially Hawthorne and Emerson and the deep and stable love and devotion between husband and wife. Social concern was also strong in Concord; escaping slaves had been successfully protected and hidden. Robert Owen, the idealistic innovator of a socialist community, was a guest.

When Gardner said that Concord was his "home town," he meant that his roots were there. Chillicothe, his birthplace, meant nothing to him. There were no memorabilia, no pictures of the home or church there, no other items to keep an image of Chillicothe alive. In contrast, there are pictures of Gardner on his grandfather's dock on the Concord River with his mother and DuBose, and another on the step with his little dog.

When Gardner lived there, nature—trees, rivers, hills—was his joy and comfort. Besides the beautiful quiet-flowing Concord River there was an enormous range of animal and plant life, which formed a steady backdrop for Gardner's years there. Walden was not just Thoreau's world and creed of living with nature, it was Gardner's retreat and playground as well and canoeing on the Concord River, bordered by majestic trees, was a favorite recreation. Trees and ponds were a source of comfort and strength to the end of his life—each of our homes after we left New York City was surrounded by trees and usually near water.

Gardner's feelings about his Concord roots were partly related to what he felt was its physical beauty. He said, "I love the place very intensely and that pattern of the small New England village as *the* place for human beings to live; and this was very much intensified by the beautiful Concord River. The Kings' acre went from the house, walking down the lawn about a hundred yards to the river. Countless times we went canoeing, . . . that time and later years." Books about Concord and the Concord River convey the love of townspeople for their picturesque river "with its numerous landings at the foot of the gardens that slope down to the water." Each family had its boats and Gardner's love of canoeing lasted until ill health in his last years made canoeing no longer possible. The sculptor Daniel Chester French and his ornithologist friend Will Brewster had reunions on the river for many years, and there were floats and meetings for water sports as well as so many picnics that Concord came to be known as "Picnic Town." Gardner loved the beautiful river, which was celebrated by his mother in a poem published in the *Atlantic Monthly*.

What distinguished Concord from other New England towns was its historical as well as its intellectual heritage. It was here that the first important battle of the Revolutionary War was fought. It was here also that the philosophy which became known as Transcendentalism came to its fullest flower. Transcendentalists were, according to Perry Miller, "Children of the Puritan Past who, having been emancipated by Unitarianism from New England's original Calvinism, found a new religious expression in forms derived from romantic literature and from the philosophical ideas of Germany." Miller says, "We may . . . see in the Transcendentalists not so much a collection of exotic ideologies as the first outcry of the heart against the materialistic pressures of a business civilization." Emerson's Transcendentalism was his creative answer to the stifling Calvinism and cold Unitarianism of New England.

There were family discussions about the Alcotts, about Thoreau, about Emerson as persons, but the influence of Concord extended beyond the books of Concord authors. William James came to lecture: he was actively interested in the medium Mrs. Piper, whose lawyer was Gran'pa King. And when he was sixteen, Gardner discovered in his grandfather's library Sir William Barrett's book on psychical research, which planted seeds that bore fruit in Gardner's later work in that field.

Gardner's remembrances of Concord remained bathed in a sunny light, but even a casual reading of representative Concord authors shows that perhaps that world was not so pure nor lit with sunshine as these memories would indicate. The Transcendental outlook was not shared by all Concordians. The Unitarians, who formed the central core of the Concord establishment, "viewed Transcendentalism critically; at the same time they viewed their Puritan heritage as being outmoded, while they still retained much of its philosophical and moral rigidity."

There was a dark side to Emerson, who is quoted: "Tis strange that it is not in vogue to commit hara-kiri, as the Japanese do at sixty. Nature is so insulting in her hints and notices, does not pull you by the sleeve, but pulls out your teeth, tears off your hair in patches, steals your eyesight, twists your face into an ugly mask; and all this at the same time that she is moulding the new figures around you into wonderful beauty, which, of course, is only making your plight worse." But Gardner did not absorb the negative aspects of Concord thinking; he always emphasized the good and the optimistic.

The shift from Montgomery to Concord was a shift from the atmosphere of zeal — reform, the struggle to improve race relations and to reduce the exploitation of children in the mills — to the Concord atmosphere of tradition, culture, and legendary creativity. The move also marked Gardner's shift from rejection of books and learning to eager excitement about books. Gardner's humanitarianism was developed over a lifetime in which he combined his enthusiasm for books and for the culture of the arts with efforts to contribute to democratic change.

While the ecology, traditions and culture of Concord with which he identified provided a permanent foundation for a sense of goodness and beauty in Gardner's life, the world of boys contributed confusion and conflict. His puritanical mother was horrified when she learned of his small boy sexual discoveries, with her husband too far away to give perspective. After a painful confrontation with his mother about bad words Gardner became "even more of a good boy" than he had been before, with increasing closeness to his mother, and identification in that he was "seeing through her eyes and using her as a touchstone of reality."

At the same time that Gardner was absorbing the love of his mother's family, the beauty of Concord, and his mother's vigorous upbringing, he was developing two interests that were important for the rest of his life. He entered school there, and soon was entranced with a little book which introduced Kate: "This is Kate, Kate can read!" And soon Gardner was reading "like a house afire." He kept his Kate book all his life, along with *Two Arrows* by W.O. Stoddard. His Aunt Ethel sent him a beautiful Hiawatha book and Gardner exclaimed "I love my Hiawatha book more than anything else in the world except you, Mother!" Once captured, he progressed rapidly in school, skipping a grade—although he said later that until he was in New Haven, he was careless, "slapdash" and tardy. He never talked about his elementary school teachers in Concord, nor did he discuss any aspect of the school program or its life.

After his mother taught him a few rudiments of piano-playing he discovered that he could play by ear, after a fashion. Singing and playing the piano exuberantly were, along with enjoying his grandparents' Victrola, the beginning of a lifelong love of music.

Gardner's musical interests developed from the music popular in Concord during his growing-up years. Beethoven, Handel, Schubert, Haydn, and Mozart were part of the New England landscape, and there exists a memory of James Russell Lowell dancing quadrilles, discussing with his partner the relative merits of Beethoven's Fifth and Sixth symphonies. The late nineteenth century and the early years of the twentieth century were part of a do-it-yourself musical culture; the phonograph had just become a household resource at the time of Gardner's growing up. Home piano-playing was much more common than it is now, and the practice was for pianists and string players to get together at intervals and sight-read quartets and trios. All of the women of Gardner's family played their Steinway upright piano, using books of "arrangements" of excerpts from operas and concertos as well as sonatas. Gardner enjoyed Gran'pa King's records of popular songs, Sousa marches and operatic excerpts, which he played to his heart's content on the phonograph he took down to the dock at the riverside.

In addition to serious music, the popular music of the day was sung in private homes to the accompaniments of piano and harmonium. Gardner later enjoyed playing by ear both songs he liked to sing and segments of music he heard at concerts and operas. He acquired a collection of symphonies, concertos, and operas that were a major source of joy to the end of his life. He also composed a few deeply moving pieces for me and for his dear friend Frank Lorimer.

Gardner always felt that he changed dramatically when he was seven— whether it was due to the shock of leaving his father, coming back North, identification with his mother's family, or his sexual discoveries, repressions, acceptance of guilt (over "evil thoughts"), or simply conceptual and verbal maturing, he did not know. Learning to read and discovering music when he was seven were exciting and probably contributed to the sense of change, after which he felt a lifetime continuity in his sense of self.

It was at this time that Gardner became acutely conscious of right and wrong, and of good and evil. To express anger was wrong, and "evil thoughts" had to be repressed in order to meet his mother's standards. In retrospect, he felt that from other boys' points of view, his goody-goody ways were obnoxious. But there must have been other good boys in Concord. In view of his mother's account of DuBose's temper tantrums, it is interesting that Gardner's conscience and control in this respect as well as in others were so severe. DuBose may not have been so easily hurt by their mother's scoldings at that time, but he became less flexible as an adult.

Gardner later struggled out of the straitjacket of the Victorian Puritanism of his mother and the absolutist morality characteristic of it, but he never gave up what he absorbed from, and warmly identified with, the Transcendentalism of Emerson and the "pure culture" of Concord. Gentleness, kindness, generosity, modesty, independent thinking, productivity and devotion to the values of truth, beauty and goodness were all part of this. Deeply interested in mysticism, he was not a mystic; he was too critically, rationally, scientific to open himself to mystical experience. The closest he came to it was his deep intellectual conviction of human isomorphism with the universe.

He remembered sitting on the doorstep with his cousin Margaret at the age of seven remarking that "if you looked at seven years from one point of view it seemed like just a moment of time, but if you looked at it from another point of view seven years was a long time." He felt that he was not a child any more, he was thinking like a grownup — everything before was little-boy stuff. This sudden maturing, he felt, increased his identification with his mother, and with the Kings, and with the literary figures Emerson, Robert Louis Stevenson, and Longfellow whom he adored.

The literary self paralleled the development of some limited athletic skills, partly through games of baseball and football, partly through occasional battle games with his brother and cousin George as they absorbed King Arthur stories. His heroes at that time were Hector, Robin Hood, Sir Pelleas the Gentle Knight, and the Indian boy Two Arrows in the Stoddard story. He read countless books about boys' clubs, groups, and teams such as the "Fairport Nine." While he often felt excluded from DuBose's gang, rejected as "a little kid" the big ones did not want to play with, he was expanding a world of his own.

Certainly Gardner's sense of continuity of self from the age of seven involved even more than the reflectiveness he was aware of developing then. His joy in nature (with memories back to Montgomery at the age of four) and delight in sensory experience in front of the Kingston fireplace and also in infantile experiences; his love of books which began at seven, reinforced by his mother's early reading out loud; his deep ethical sense and the strong conscience that developed at seven; his inhibition of anger; his search for intimacy and his affection toward people of both sexes in his large family and also to others; the complexity of his dual elite-underdog sense of identity and his caring for minorities; his seriousness and sense of duty—all of these characteristics established at an early age continued through his long life.

Still, there was room for changes as he himself recorded in his "Study of Myself," and in interviews toward the end of his life. He saw himself as "quite nervous and high strung," and thought that he had a "morbid imagination," and a "sensitive and high-strung temperament." But, "I did not have a reputation for high temper simply because I knew I ought not to 'get mad' and repressed the emotion." He meant "suppressed" since he continued, "I was certainly deep in feeling" . . . "I was, I think, revengeful as a small child, but of course I knew it was wrong when I acquired a moral point of view (at seven) and repressed it as far as possible. I was self-centered and morbidly introspective for a child." He attributed his excessive goody-goodyness in part to his training in the first years, and in part to his seriousness.

For no other period of Gardner's growing years do we have such a deeply felt, and richly delineated account of his experience as in the Concord years: the town and what it meant to him, its beauty, traditions, memories and residues of former glory and its present gentility, his own delight in nature, his mother's family, and his love for them, their wit, their music; his mother's nurturance, control and discipline, her puritan taboos and literary delights; his swift engagement with and love of beautiful and absorbing books; his struggles as a boy with satisfactions and frustrations in the world of boys; his sense of change within himself to a level of thinking like a grownup and the identity conflicts resulting partly from the interaction between his reflectiveness and self-awareness on the one hand and the external facts of an ever present mother and absent father, Northern mother and Southern father, elite extended family but a blue-collar ethnic name, as well as the conflict between being a good boy and being a regular boy like the others—active, impulsive, noisy, free.

Gardner's childhood years, from 1895 to 1910, covering the turn of the century, the end of the Victorian era, and the peak of the reform movement, were years of idealistic optimism in America. The period of realism in literature, and of Freudian uncovering of sex conflicts, guilt, and aggressive drives was on a distant horizon, not yet visible in Concord, which was still bathed in Emersonian values and benevolence. "Aunt Emily's" suggestion to "run around the block and find a happy-boy smile" was a way of stimulating a pattern of cheerful self-control and developing techniques of helping oneself to evoke and maintain a cheerful mood. To be cheerful was an obligation at the time of the "See no evil, hear no evil, speak no evil" motto. This pervasively value-laden atmosphere, breathed in a setting of love and belongingness was absorbed so deeply by Gardner, and supported so consistently by his own temperamental enthusiasm, that it remained a foundation for the joyous, happy life style that we saw in the Gardner we knew at home. It also underlay his lifetime pattern of scotomatizing negative aspects of people he loved, especially his mother.

In the years before World War I there was no radio, no television to fill a child's life with images and sounds of violence, or Walt Disney fantasies, or endless commercials urging children to pressure their mothers to buy new exciting toys or sugary breakfast foods. The few toys were more passionately cherished, like Gardner's tin "doggie," and when they broke, the disaster was heartbreaking; children didn't take it for granted that whenever a toy was broken it could be quickly replaced with another. Commitment, deep investment, while rooted in the earliest attachment to mother and to father, spread to the adored toys, then to friends, and finally to the one who became a lifelong partner. In contrast to the modern dispersal of attention and emotional response over the wide range of stimuli provided by contemporary radio and television, the mobility provided by automobiles, buses and planes, and the endless flow of new exciting commercial products, Gardner's feelings remained focused on his family, the home and activities in the home. Attachments were intense, and communication in conversation and in letters was cultivated. While all of the Concord atmosphere of creativity and high thinking was being absorbed into Gardner's tissues, it was Gran'pa King himself, his wit, his humorous mingling of Shakespeare with breakfast or dinner—"Is there a distant prospect of Eton?"—that reinforced the freedom and spontaneity of Gardner's mind. While there was much with which he could not identify, he absorbed the rich playful use of literary allusions and puns which enlivened his grandfather's daily conversations.

6. Branford and New Haven : Troubled Adolescence

The family was in Concord for only two and a half years, when Gardner was seven to nine years old; they then moved to Branford, Connecticut, where they could more easily see Edgar on his visits to his New York headquarters. Why they did not move to New York City or a nearby suburb is never discussed in any of Gardner's accounts or in any extant letters. If, when his father became executive secretary of the Southern Education Board, the family had moved to New York, the boys would have seen much more of their father, less of their mother's family, and they would have had a very different childhood experience. Possibly the main reason for this move was that Branford was less expensive than living in New York or one of its suburbs—finances were very limited.

As it was, Branford was not satisfactory—"There weren't our kind of people there," Gardner wrote; the boys in his fifth grade class were very rough and he could not cope with bullies. Having skipped a grade, he was a year younger and the teacher was inadequate. Gardner's mother took him out of school; in retrospect, he felt that she would not have done this if the Branford school situation had not been really "terrible." He was scared and confused and his mother saw that although leaving school was bad, staying in school would have been worse. It was in that year at home that she taught him geography and French, and gave him a foundation for a knowledge of birds; the warmth of his relation with his mother and sense of relief at leaving the unbearable school situation doubtless contributed to his lifetime passionate love of travel, languages and birds.

None of the settings in which Gardner grew up was free from some degree of conflict, alienation, and frustration, even in as satisfying a community as Concord. But in terms of relationships with other boys and school, Branford was traumatic. In Concord he had developed a conscience, an intense sense of right and wrong, and he had committed himself to being a good boy. And

Gardner was no fighter; he felt that it was wrong to show anger. He had no conspicuous athletic skills which might give him prestige in a group of boys his own age, although he enjoyed baseball; in short, he was ill-equipped to get along with the rough and tough boys of Branford.

In contrast to the almost ideal world of Concord, the move to Branford was a disaster; the town was unattractive, the population was not like what he had known earlier, and there were no relatives. His father was still in the South and could not help him. The loss of familiar surroundings was threatening. He felt alien, and was "pretty largely alone. . . . The kids weren't the kind of kids" he had known in Concord. He felt isolated, strange, and as his sensitivity to rejection deepened he began to feel abnormal and inadequate. Recurrent experiences of being the new boy in well established neighborhoods, when moves were not as common as they are now, added to his alienation; fortunately his mother realized that Gardner needed a more adequate setting and they left Branford after one year.

His rescue from the frightening world of tough boys deepened his closeness to his mother and his appreciation of her commitment and devotion to him. We do not know whether alternatives other than removal from school and the peer group were possible — we have to assume that there was no other school available and no other class at his grade, that it was not realistic to expect his teacher or principal to be more supportive. In good schools today, a parent can consult with the teacher and sometimes work out a plan to help a child's adjustment.

There was, as far as we know, no male figure in Branford to give support or stimulation; indeed, Gardner was stranded for masculine companionship of any age. It is inconceivable that he did not long for his father's presence that year. But although he spoke of resenting some of his mother's unfair punishments he never complained, in autobiographies or to us, of the lack of his father at times when he needed a father's help. Apparently he took it for granted that his father's important work had priority over everything else.

Gardner made rapid academic progress with his mother's tutoring, and easily entered the sixth grade when the family moved again the following year to New Haven. But his sensitivity to isolation — already rooted in the earlier experiences of rejection by his brother's friends — was deepened to the point that he felt isolated and socially inadequate years afterward, even when he actually had playmates and friends in New Haven, and at Hotchkiss and Yale.

There is no record of how DuBose fared in Branford; since he was apparently more of a fighter in addition to being more athletic, we can assume that he managed to get along. At any rate, he was not taken out of school. The fact that Gardner could not cope with school must have added to his sense of inferiority to his brother — a deep sense perhaps underlying his comment to me in 1926 that he felt inferior to the suitor I had rejected when I married him, and also to my distinguished father.

Still, the foundation his mother gave him in French and geography added intense interest in languages and the possibilities of travel. His mother taught him how to recognize birds by their colors and shapes and song. On our walks through New Hampshire woods, chickadees would flock onto low pine branches as he approached, as if knowing that he cherished them. And we counted species—in the forties and fifties at our New Hampshire cottage we easily found 30 to 40 different species; we both loved the hermit and wood thrushes' songs in our own woods, and the exquisite white-throated sparrows' song high in the ravine on Mount Washington. When we could no longer climb the mountains or even hike in our own woods, Gardner's ear was always acutely alert to the song of a bluebird or a song-sparrow or a mockingbird in the surrounds of our Washington, D.C., home. On his 82nd birthday at our New Hampshire retreat, *Birchlea*, a rose-breasted grosbeak sat on a vine about ten feet from Gardner's chair on the porch and sang, as it were, a birthday song for twenty minutes—a "peak experience." While the peer group problems left scars that were never wholly dissolved, the new learnings brought lifetime dividends.

Gardner must have felt enormously relieved when the family left the alien Branford for New Haven to live in the house his father's "Cousin Will" Elkin had bought, planning ahead for his retirement from his position as director of the Yale Observatory. Cousin Catharine, who loved "that dear little boy" was there; a good school where Gardner entered sixth grade was close to their house. He could feel at home there, although he never thought of it as his home town despite the fact that he lived in New Haven much longer than he lived in Concord. He never loved New Haven as he loved Concord.

Gardner played football as center, with the "Ellums," and began to feel adequacy as one of the boys—until his father prohibited further participation in that game because of its dangers. (Gardner had already knocked out a front tooth at the age of eight, and he broke a leg when he was ten.) He wept in despair, but his father was firm and the obedient boy sadly yielded to the restriction; presumably he could still play baseball but he was not as competent as he was in football. Years later, he felt that his father had made a mistake—that football had helped him to begin to overcome his sense of isolation and inadequacy to other boys.

In the summer of 1909, he went to Camp Algonquin on Squam Lake, in New Hampshire. He loved the lake, the mountains they climbed, the forests around the lake and he wanted desperately to return the next year. But his mother felt that he was so awkward he was not up to the company of the other boys; she did not allow him to return. He never forgot Squam Lake and the mountains of New Hampshire; after we were married, that was where he wanted to go for vacations, and the little house we eventually designed for a hillside spot near the lake was a joy for over a quarter of a century.

His mother's refusal to let him return to camp was, along with his father's taboo against football, a major disappointment. Still he was accepted in "Burgee's gang" and according to his account of that period in his Harvard "Study of Myself," he made a number of friends; a Yale classmate who had been a member of the same group of New Haven boys wrote me that he considered Gardner a regular one of his playmates. But the traumatic experience in Branford had apparently hurt him so deeply that he did not fully trust his acceptance by the other boys. He was sensitive to being teased. At the same time, the Irish and German boys probably regarded him as a snob, he felt, "certainly as a person to be viewed at a distance." At the age of 71, in his interview with Dr. Ullman, he described his low status in this gang where Burgee was able to beat up everyone else, and the hierarchy was defined by each boy's ability to fight; he felt that he was at the bottom of that hierarchy.

In some other ways the New Haven years were good — with nearby East Rock wooded cliff for climbing and hiking and watching birds. There was more interesting school work and teachers liked the well-brought-up boy. He was not only free of the severe anxieties of Branford, he really felt at home, and became a Yale fan. The years from the age of ten to fifteen in New Haven were the longest stretch of time he lived in any town; during the last three of those years the family was together, after his father retired in 1908 from the Southern Education Board because of ill health.

But at the difficult age of thirteen, the pressures of adolescence were intensified by his very emotional nature and by the anxieties reinforced by the recurring illnesses of his father. His inner life became "morbid" according to his own accounts of that stage; he was "fanatically religious," "ascetic," preoccupied with "holy words" (he would bow his head when he heard them) and overstimulated by Moody and Sankey emotional religious revivals, which he attended with a friend. At the same time, he was aware of what he was doing, and when he realized that his parents were disturbed by the head-bowing he gave it up. During the years when Gardner was thirteen to fifteen his parents were inevitably preoccupied with his father's illnesses, with financial problems and with anxieties about the future. And there were arguments (even "quarrels") disturbing to Gardner.

Although Gardner thought of himself as "morbid," there is no evidence that anyone else considered him other than an unusually serious boy. Certainly his father's illnesses, and his parents' irritability under so much stress and anxiety must have weighed upon the sensitive, devoted boy who was struggling with the typical physical and social problems of adolescence, aggravated as they were by his disturbing experience in Branford, his frustrations in not being allowed to play football or to return to camp, and his feeling of inferiority — athletically and socially — to his older brother.

Despite the anxieties, he did well in school, ending his first year in New Haven second from the top of his class; from that time on, he was second to none. In New Haven High School, school became really interesting for the first time. Earlier, although he was "very good at spelling, geography and history," he was "not much interested in school work." "School was simply a bore." But in high school the great majority of his studies constantly interested him; he did so well that he was granted scholarships for Hotchkiss preparatory school in Lakeville, Connecticut, for his last two years before he went to Yale. High school debating gave him an activity in which he could be competent, and introduced him to politics and to "the arts of persuasion."

It was when he was thirteen years old that his father gave him the *Scientific American,* to which he then subscribed for the rest of his life. He "went wild" about Henry Norris Russell's articles on the skies — another of what the family called "Gardner's crazes"; "the star interest was very deep and full of delight" and he explored knowledge about the motions of the heavenly bodies in *Popular Astronomy* as well.

At the same time, in freshman year in high school he began studying Latin and Greek (along with English, algebra and ancient history). He became so fascinated with languages that he made up "a sort of ideal language, based on very extreme simplification of vowel and consonant sounds and the way they are combined."

In 1910 his father took the whole family to Bad Nauheim where his health had previously been helped by Dr. Schott. After a brief and delightful visit in England and the Netherlands they settled down for two months in the resort. While there Gardner enjoyed talking with boys at the tennis court and picked up a speaking knowledge of German. He enjoyed the lovely old town with music and his good relations with the boys. And he learned some of the things he could do to help care for his father.

During these years of great family stress, but also mutual devotion between parents and sons, sibling rivalry, and Gardner's heartbroken acceptance of his father's restriction of football and his mother's refusal to let him return to camp, we see an impressive contrast between his vulnerability — reflected in his anxious, disturbed inner life — and his ceaseless efforts to be one of the boys at the same time that he was successfully meeting the demands of school teachers, and responding to his family's standards and his father's needs for support and companionship. Balancing his vulnerability was strength. He never withdrew from peer relationships after Branford; he did not rebel at home. How could a sensitive boy rebel against such devoted, greatly stressed parents?

7. Hotchkiss : "Scholarship Boy"

Before Gardner left for Hotchkiss preparatory school he had moved six times through very different communities in the North and South, with very contrasting balances of support and stress. In addition to the discontinuities and complexities that contributed to problems of identity, he had struggled with conflicts between his mother's puritan demands for obedience and conformity on the one hand, and his longings to be accepted by the peer group as one of the boys on the other hand—a struggle between being "a good boy" and wanting to be free and spontaneous.

A close friendship in New Haven with an evangelical Lutheran boy who, along with a Swedish maid, introduced him to the Moody and Sankey type of emotionally intense revival religion, evidently developed at the time his mother was in Virginia caring for Gardner's father during a severe illness. It is likely that this friendship helped to meet Gardner's deep longing for intimacy and shared closeness. Going to school at Hotchkiss, then, meant leaving his New Haven friends and the satisfactions they had brought him.

Hotchkiss was another strange new setting, another stressful experience for this sensitive boy who had entered the junior year when groups were well established. Again he was a new boy, without athletic or social skills to ease his entrance to the peer group. Moreover, he was a scholarship boy, assigned to wait on tables and wash dishes in the kitchen; his position was different from that of the rich boys in that elite school. However, his roommate, Malcolm Baber, wrote me that he and Gardner were similar in their athletic deficiencies and their academic strengths. Malcolm became a loyal friend, to whom Gardner wrote regularly from France in World War I; and when Gardner was desperately ill in the last years of his life, "Babe" kept in touch, sending generous checks "for something to give Gardner pleasure." But his companionship at Hotchkiss did not meet Gardner's longing for intimacy. In addition, he was "girl-hungry" in that all-male environment—such a contrast with the female dominated worlds of earlier years, and also a contrast with his coeducational high school in New Haven.

In this rather emotionally barren setting Gardner threw himself into his studies with an intense feeling that he needed to earn and maintain his scholarship for another year. In contrast to his early casualness about studies, he overworked, as he said later; he won honors, with many prizes. Hotchkiss gloated over the scholastic achievement Gardner demonstrated in the College Board Examinations taken in June 1912. He ranked first in eight different subjects: Latin grammar, advanced prose composition, Greek grammar, elementary prose composition in Greek, Xenophon, prose composition, Greek sight translation of prose, and elementary algebra.

Gardner never mentioned to us the many prizes and honors he won at Hotchkiss and Yale. We discovered some of them when we found beautiful leather-bound books including a volume of Shelley's poetry; and, finally, after he died, we found reports in newspaper clippings which had been kept by his mother.

Hotchkiss had a happy custom of cancelling class and other schedules when a graduate won an important prize:

SCHOOL ENJOYS HOLIDAY
GARDNER MURPHY '12 WINS HONORS AT YALE

According to the usual custom now for several years the school is given a day of recreation, omitting the regular schedules, whenever some important prize is won by a Hotchkiss graduate in college. Therefore on Tuesday morning, October eighth, a holiday was announced in recognition of the winning of the High Chamberlain Prize at Yale University, for which Gardner Murphy of the class of 1912, and a graduate of the Hartford High School divided the first honors, the prize being the income of one thousand dollars awarded annually to that member of the Freshman class who has passed the best examination in Greek required for admission.

For this reason was the holiday granted, together with the fact that Murphy received honorable mention in the Samuel Henry Galpin Latin Prize which is awarded under the same conditions as the Chamberlain Prize.

Murphy is greatly to be congratulated upon his success in Greek and Latin, in which subjects he received several prizes at the end of Upper Middle and Senior years in school. It is certain that the school enjoyed to the fullest extent the pleasures and privileges of a whole day exempt from text book labors. The added fact that the day was one of those cloudless bracing days of autumn, when the foliage is noticeable for its many colors, did much for making the day a memorable one.

And his parents shared his "glory" with pride.

In his 1966 interview with Ullman, Gardner did not mention the school holiday and referred to the prizes as "minor." But in 1912 after years of feeling inadequate, inferior to his brother, at the bottom of the peer group, this recognition must have been an important reassurance, for when he entered Yale he tried out for the freshman glee club, dramatics and the debating team.

In addition to Greek, Latin, and English, Gardner had two years of German at Hotchkiss, building on his speaking knowledge acquired at Bad Nauheim. He also took courses in physics and advanced algebra; later he said that he wished he had gone further with mathematics.

At Hotchkiss he encountered "the first of a few really great teachers," Ralph Theller—"an incredible teacher" of English composition. He would assign three or four short essays a week—book reviews or "little whimsies that we developed, and would give you a grade of 76 or 77 because you had missed a point you might have made, or because you were fuzzy or a little confused in the articulation between two sentences. And he would spend an hour talking about Tolstoi and why it was important not only to read English English but to read translations. He also coached public speaking." Gardner felt forever indebted to Ralph Theller for his training in writing and speaking; he gave an "oration" that pleased his father deeply. Although Gardner expressed unbounded admiration for certain great teachers at Yale and in New York, he never described in such detail what made them great. In short, Gardner was not only very successful academically at Hotchkiss, but he was inspired with a vision of what great teaching could be, and he was sensitized to what a great teacher can mean to a student.

Parallel with his hard work at studies, he was preoccupied with religion and was active in school religious meetings and duties. He thought at times about being a missionary, and also became interested in medicine, with the idea that he might be able to help his sick father. But neither of these fantasies became a commitment. Socially he still felt out of things, he was "not a part of the inner group" although he had a reasonable number of "fringe friends." Probably Gardner's grandfather's inner circle status and the fact that his father had distinguished friends gave him a sense of pressure to be socially as well as academically successful.

In contrast to his deep love for Concord and his sense of being at home in New Haven, Gardner never reflected any warmth about the two Hotchkiss years; one gets the feeling that they simply had to be lived through, as a bridge to Yale. Intensely loving letters from his father during these years encouraged, stimulated and appreciated his efforts, especially in writing, and his parents' pride in his academic achievements seems to have been much greater than his own.

There are no surviving letters from Gardner to his father—letters which may have been written daily from Hotchkiss and Yale in view of his father's disappointment when no letter came and his joy when he received a letter, and also his request for a daily letter. Some of his father's letters to him at Hotchkiss convey directly the quality of his father's feeling for him, his pride, support, faith, stimulus and implicit demand for the highest standard in writing, along with his outpouring love:

My Dear Gardner:

You dear dear *Son:* you *know* how glad your old daddy is at that fine record with the oration. I always *knew* you could do it! You boys both have it in you to be *clear strong helpful* writers; and the power to *do* it helps the power to appreciate it (and 'tother way round, too) and being able to *appreciate* is a lasting and ever increasing joy. But it requires good true work— taking pains—as well as "the impulse which like a fountain" etc. and so many fellows forget *that*. They write *cleverly* at the start and getting satisfied with themselves they are found, at the end, still writing *cleverly;* but never writing with the grip and mastery that evidence the highest qualities of style. Oh! it is so worth while, such a *pleasure*, to work the *best* of oneself *into* one's work. And then it's always an added happiness (a happiness that unfortunately doesn't always come to us) when others whose judgment is worth while *see* and appreciate our *best*. And so we do lovingly rejoice with you; but we are chiefly glad because you are glad and are happy—and my arms are round you with the lovingest hug, and—well *you* know, you *Precious*! God guide you and bless you!

Your Father, E.G.M.

This combination of ardent love, praise and stimulus to achievement must have contributed to Gardner's need for achievement and recognition. The assertion of faith in his son's potentialities and achievements is reminiscent of Gardner's capacity to inspire students with his communication to them of potentialities they did not realize they had.

We know very little else about Gardner's experience with his ill father; one letter from his father gives us a glimpse of Gardner's devotion. This letter, also sent to Gardner at Hotchkiss, was written when his father's health was failing at a rate that made him especially sensitive to the loving support of his son:

My dear Son:

I wonder if you can know how greatly your little visit cheered and helped me? You were so patient and loving and helpful every minute of the time! You are growing up out of "*little*-boyhood" and are getting to be a young man; and you are a pride and joy to your father. God guide you and keep you through all the years—my own son!

Edgar Gardner Murphy

Hotchkiss confirmed and consolidated Gardner's intellectual capacities, his talent in and mastery of languages, especially the classics, his writing and speaking skill. Superficial friendships did not satisfy him; he longed for a level of intimacy in which feelings and thoughts could be shared.

8. Yale : Death of Gardner's Father : Discovering Truth

After his two years of absorption in Greek, Latin, and English at Hotchkiss, Gardner entered Yale in 1912, at the age of seventeen, with a narrow and intense scholarly preoccupation. His father, so very skillful in his work with groups in the church, and in his wide educational and social efforts, and with many friendships among vigorous creative men, had struggled hard to understand him, not realizing how the many moves and the lack of a sustained peer group and stable friendships had led to Gardner's feelings of isolation. By the time Gardner entered Yale his father was too ill to be of much support.

But Gardner's situation at Yale was different from that at Hotchkiss; he was no longer the scholarship boy required to spend two hours a day on kitchen work. To be sure he was still poor in a college of predominantly rich students, but there were others in the same boat. Gardner was still intensely religious and during his freshman year he worked in the Yale Mission. There were others who were religious and in fact, he had friends who planned to go into the ministry.

Yale was not the strange new place Hotchkiss had been. The years in New Haven living in the Elkins' house and his father's honorary degree from Yale had made it the natural place to go to college. There would still be his favorite East Rock to explore and Cousin Catharine and Cousin Will to provide a sense of at-homeness when his parents were living in New York. He roomed again with Malcolm Baber and had other interesting and intelligent roommates — among them Donald Quarles (later Deputy Secretary of Defense).

Memories of his relationships vary — at one time Gardner recalled many friends; at another time he said that he had "middle-level friends" but no intimate ones. His lack of athletic skill and social ease still worried him, since DuBose, in a class ahead of him, was elected to a fraternity and to offices in various college organizations.

Gardner sang second bass in the freshman Glee Club. He was rejected for the freshman debating team but was part of the team for his remaining years at Yale. Some of his academic work became more of a delight than any he had known before — especially his course in English literature with Chauncey Tinker — not only a brilliant and unforgettable teacher, but one who appreciated Gardner's intellectual independence. Gardner often referred to Tinker's capacity to make English literature "simply glow," and whenever he spoke of this gifted teacher it was with a special light in his eyes and with a sense of an inspiring force that never left him. "I never saw such craftsmanship as he had — a tremendous capacity to make things real; more than real — just three-dimensional — overwhelming." His presentation of Shakespeare's *Henry IV* plays was vividly dramatic, and his discussions of nineteenth-century poetry must have been eloquent, judging by Gardner's excited enthusiasm. The class read Dickens' *Great Expectations* which meant so much to him that when we were married, ten years after his senior year at Yale, it was one of the first books he wanted us to read aloud to each other. And Shelley, Keats and Wordsworth were so precious to him that his discovery of my love for those poets created an instant bond.

Gardner felt loved by John Chester ("Jack") Adams, another inspiring professor of English literature. With him, he found a feeling for the English language and for naturalness and directness of presentation; this was especially important because Gardner had been exposed to the formality of his father's style. Adams trained the members of the debating club to plan to use their time — not a minute more or a minute less. This was a superb preparation for public speaking. But Jack Adams was more than a dedicated teacher — he was a devoted friend.

Gardner's father died on June 23, 1913. After the burial Gardner remained in Concord with his mother and in this time of loss and grief they drew closer together. Maud felt a responsibility to care for her aging parents — her younger sister Louise who had lived with them had died from diabetes. Gardner was again with his admired Gran'pa King and his cheerful, stoical, affectionate grandmother, in his beloved "home town." That family base must have been a comfort and there were the pleasures of canoeing with Sally Bartlett, the young librarian, on the Concord River, and playing favorite records again down on the dock.

Neither grief nor pride was ever directly expressed by Gardner in writing or talking about his father's work and death. In his interview with Montague Ullman he described his experience during the year at Yale following his father's death. He was lonely and gloomy, and felt left out when he was not invited to join a fraternity. He had a lot of inflammation and pain in his eyes; the best ophthalmologist in New Haven recommended that he give up the glasses he had worn since his earlier eye examination. But studying was torture without his glasses and his studies "tumbled" — after a straight-A record his freshman year that won him a scholarship paying fifty dollars a year through college. Evidently by the second term he returned to using his eyeglasses, but considerable discomfort continued until in 1927 Dr. Marlowe in Syracuse demonstrated and corrected a muscular imbalance that had caused the problem.

The first term of the second year was especially gloomy. Beginning baldness also appeared. But he emphasized that he felt aware of a profound change that year and the following one. He remembered that shortly after his father's funeral a friend of his father's said, "For the aged, death is a signal of the end—for the young it's a challenge to new life." Gardner recalled that he had "some sort of half-mystical idea" that he could "do something important which in a sense would be carrying on my father's struggle." He also felt that he gained a remoteness from the growth period, a detachment, "certainly a lot of intellectual maturing [was] going on." His physical growth had been completed at seventeen.

Gardner said in that interview that a "metamorphosis" occurred after his father's death. He became more intellectually mature; he grew closer to his mother who had lost her 43-year-old brilliant and beloved husband. He also made a vigorous effort to correct what he thought were his faults of being scatter-brained and irresponsible. After recalling his "metamorphosis," he remembered a continuity in self-feeling at a deeper level: "I became myself at the age of seven . . . I had a feeling of unbroken continuity . . . I began to think of myself as reflecting about myself . . . I haven't changed. . . . My capacity to praise and blame myself remain intact. . . . The involved [in activity] self can change many times in a day—but the detached self somewhat less."

Reflecting further on his "metamorphosis" after his father's death, he said that frequent visits to Concord to visit his mother and her family led to further "recentering." He saw his earlier self as "enormously confused, clumsy, scatter-brained, irresponsible. . . . Nobody could count on me except in a very narrow round of academic activities. . . . I made up my mind in Junior year at Yale that I couldn't respect myself any more on this basis—and I began to keep a regular series of checks and balances, keep a notebook. . . ." The notebook became the "little black date-book" for which Gardner was so noted, crowded with memoranda and appointments all his adult life. He made "understandings based on punctual discharges of duties, . . . the academic world generalized more."

This Benjamin Franklin type of self-imposed control sounds rather grim, but it did not interfere with his "enormous joy" in the Greek that he learned at that time—the rhythms of Aeschylus' *Persians* as they changed with the succeeding phases of the drama and his awareness of a "tremendous idea . . . represented with tremendous intensity of language." He continued, "Of course the feeling of the Greek drama was one of glory in the midst of tragedy."

Gardner concentrated on this special Greek learning in order to apply for the Winthrop Prize of $200, which he won and used for a trip across the United

States to the San Diego World's Fair, to San Francisco, through the Rockies on the way, and to Grand Canyon on the return trip. Grand Canyon was one of the "greatest experiences" of his life, if not *the* greatest. He did not directly connect the glory of Aeschylus and of this trip with his father's tragic death, but the related feelings seem obvious.

Gardner had not yet found his life's work at the time of his father's death; he had not yet questioned his father's Episcopal theology; he had not yet found an intimate friend at Yale. His father's death was a shock — for, although he was aware of the seriousness of his father's illness, the possibility of an early death had not seemed real to him.

In the fall he had found the warm response of Jack Adams, who became in part a father surrogate to be loved and enjoyed. Jack Adams took him sailing and, in his letter to support Gardner's application for a Rhodes Scholarship, commented on how companionable he had found Gardner. In later years Gardner talked more about Jack Adams than he talked of his own father. Adams' appreciation of and stimulus to Gardner were evidently crucial in Gardner's coming to terms with that loss; he responded to new ideas and to their implications. Anthropology, Darwinism, and psychology challenged his theological beliefs over the next two years; his "faith was eroded," in the context of his emerging deep commitment to science. Still, he felt the central concepts of mind and soul independent of the body, or philosophical dualism, might have validity. How could he confirm this? Could psychical research, to which he had been introduced through Sir William Barrett's book *Psychical Research,* provide evidence? If so, the belief at the heart of Christianity — the immortality of the soul — might survive the process of erosion. He asked his professor of psychology what college courses might provide a foundation for work in psychical research and he was told that psychology would be important; his commitment to psychology began in this way. It is possible that a hope to confirm the survival of his father contributed to the deepening of his commitment to psychical reserach, at the same time that he was struggling, with agony, to emancipate himself from his father's theology.

Only later, in his endless defense of causes concerned with righting wrongs — civil rights, feeding starving Russian children and other children around the world, helping students during the Depression, and aiding refugees escaping Hitler or Communism — do we see evidence of identification with his father's life-long commitment to meeting human needs. It was this side of his father's work — his commitment to helping people — with which Gardner profoundly identified.

We can surmise that the death of his father freed Gardner to think independently about his religious and scientific beliefs and reinforced a need to keep his father alive, proving the possibility of survival and living his Christian values. Several different influences converged to transfer Gardner's religious passion to science, especially psychology and psychical research.

During the long years of his growing up when so much of the time he felt isolated from other boys, sensory experiences of nature and music had filled his solitude with delight in color, rhythm, and sound. Introspective as he had grown, he was more aware of "the mind" than other boys. He "loved all that stuff about the mind," but it was after his father's death that he developed a commitment to psychical research, in a sense following on the heels of William James, with James' respect for the medium, Mrs. Piper, and interest in telepathy, clairvoyance and the rest. Gardner was interested in psychology both in its own right and as a foundation for work in psychical research. Psychology became his major field of study.

He discovered psychology courses naively: in his freshman year when a classmate told him that one of the things he could take in his sophomore year was logic/psychology, Gardner asked, "What's that?" The student replied, "In the fall term you study logic; in the spring term, psychology." Gardner remembered asking, "What's the difference?" And when he was told that logic tells you about the rules of correct reasoning while psychology is a sort of study of people and how they think and feel, Gardner said, "I guess I want that." The logic course seemed stupid to him but psychology was well taught with William James' *Briefer Course* and Pillsbury's textbook. This introduction to James was the beginning of a lifelong devotion to him; later Gardner read James' monumental two-volume *Principles of Psychology* and his letters, and he wrote about James extensively.

His laboratory training in experimental psychology was more than a means to an end. "There are your facts, Gardner, go after them," said the instructor, Horace English, who became a lifelong friend. Empirical science gradually absorbed much of the intensity of commitment that had been given to evangelical religion, although a final confrontation between theology and truth did not take place until the year after Yale, at Harvard. "Truth" won the battle, but the certainty of Gardner's religious conviction had been gradually weakening during his Yale years.

Gardner's interest in academic studies had broadened in college. After he had mastered Greek and Latin and acquired a speaking knowledge of German and French as well, he took a course in Japanese in his junior year "because it was a different language from any he had studied." He thought for a time that he might work on the psychology of language—he felt that his interest was primarily aesthetic, not far from his interest in art and music. But his interests in sociology, philosophy, religion and biology, all of which contributed to his interest in psychology, won out. He continued to be enough interested in languages to work on Russian before we went to the Soviet Union and he picked up a good deal of Italian before we went to Italy; but after Yale he never focused on languages again. Other courses that meant a great deal to Gardner—and provided new vistas of knowledge that contributed to a changed world outlook—included an extraordinary introduction to anthropology taught by A.G. Keller. His dramatic Darwinian evolutionary viewpoint led Gardner to an interest in social science with economic and political aspects, and it also contributed to the challenge to his religious orthodoxy. Anthropology became his minor, and zoology, magnificently taught by L.L. Woodruff, opened still more vistas. One can see here the seeds of what was gradually integrated with Gardner's biosocial approach to personality, first expressed in our 1931 *Experimental Social Psychology,* and fully developed in his 1947 magnum opus, *Personality: A Biosocial Approach to Origins and Structure.*

After he became a psychologist concerned with the interaction of the organism and the environment, he regretted deeply having had only one year of inorganic chemistry. When he gave up the idea of a medical career, he thought of being a brain specialist so that he could prove the independence of personality from brain mechanics, in line with a demonstration of the transcendence of personality over mechanistic concepts in a book called *Brain and Personality,* by a certain Dr. Thompson.

In senior year Gardner was delighted when he was elected to the scientific society Sigma Xi; this was salve to his hurt feelings after losing a debate with Harvard senior year, and never being elected to a fraternity at Yale. The fact that his brother was not only elected to a fraternity but had also held offices in several societies added to those disappointments.

Yale, from his first year there, was intellectually exciting, nourishing, challenging, a new universe of thought and expression, very different from the passive learning of high school and of Hotchkiss, much as he had loved Greek and much as he had appreciated Ralph Theller's discipline in writing. At Yale there were new ideas, questions, issues to be thought about.

The intellectual and spiritual world of Gardner's parents was a world of absolutes, of concepts of right and wrong that could not be argued. Until his adolescent years Gardner's religious faith, absorbed from his family and their world, had been neither modified nor challenged. In his grandfather's library, to be sure, he had discovered a book, *Faiths of the World,* which introduced him to the fact that the Christianity in which he had grown up was not the only religion—but that was a purely intellectual fact. It did not consciously undermine his beliefs. The sense of fellowship in the Moody and Sankey revivals meant most to him in that period when he longed for intimacy, and still felt incompletely accepted by peers. In the Yale Mission undoubtedly this same emotional appeal was intense.

At his grandfather's dinner table there were intellectual discussions of philosophical and psychological topics, and also of the issue of inheritance of acquired characteristics argued by Lamarck and Darwin. The reflective, serious, and curious boy that Gardner was, heard and remembered some of this but at the time these ideas did not consciously confront his intensely felt religious beliefs. However, they may have prepared the soil which nourished seeds planted when he went to Yale. In his years there, Yale with its anthropology and psychology, its deeper education in evolution, its emphasis on science as the only path to truth, and Professor Tinker's account of the impact of Columbus' discovery of the New World in 1492 pushed hard against the structure of absolutes. *Ne plus ultra* as applied to the Pillars of Hercules at the edge of the Atlantic had to yield to *plus ultra*. "Plus Ultra" (or, "there is more beyond"), with its implication of endless new discoveries, became so central to Gardner's feeling that he used it for the title of one of his autobiographies.

The fact that among the papers he wrote at Yale Gardner preserved his study on Jeanne d'Arc implies that this sensitive, carefully researched and documented account of Jeanne's childhood meant more to him than other reports written for his courses there. He concluded that Jeanne's visions were real. This deep interest continued when he went to France in 1917 with the Yale Mobile Hospital and on a few days' leave, visited her home. (He also went to Lourdes, and to London to visit the Society for Psychical Research.) His deep interest in Jeanne d'Arc reflected his emotional response to a heroic woman leader as well as his commitment to study psychical events of different sorts; he came back with several mementoes of that visit, small silver medals containing the image of Jeanne d'Arc.

Another paper, an address written in the spring of his senior year at Yale, foreshadowed his lifelong dedication to efforts for peace: its title was "The Larger Neutrality." America was not yet involved in the war against the aggression by Kaiser Wilhelm, World War I. He wrote

> We are all by nature partisans. Our prejudice almost precludes the possibility of a comprehensive sympathy for all who need that sympathy. But there is another reason for the shallowness and bitterness of our opinions regarding the European war.... We find it much easier to say that "Germany has gone mad" than to study with genuine honesty the intricate causes of the war.... Because a great nation has broken her national faith, we have seen fit to attack her civilization, her achievements, her masses of men and women.

He then analyzed the range of attitudes toward the war among Americans, the danger of a gradually growing impatience and gradually increasing bitterness. He believed that if our nation can found its desire for peace upon the principles for which America stands, principles of honor and service, we shall have a safeguard which is adequate in preserving peace as long as peace can possibly be maintained. He felt that the most serious aspect of the entrance of the United States into the war would be its acceptance of the philosophy of revenge,

> so pitifully masquerading as honor. ... Talk about national honor is a thin disguise for the desire to get even with those at whose hands we have suffered or to cover up a supposed loss of prestige. ... Such a desire is inherently selfish. One of the greatest services of America consists in showing the world that a great

nation may stand above the petty resentments ... may preserve friendships in
spite of injuries....

He asked his Yale audience to "combine the fiercest enmity toward war
with the greatest solicitude for its victims." Reviewing the progress of the
previous decade in international exchange and collaboration in science, letters,
commerce, industry—how "mind has borrowed from mind, how nations have
influenced one another in the very fundamentals of civilization"—he stated
that the salvation of the spirit of cooperation depended largely upon America.

> The only attitude which is consistent with our American ideals is one of the
> broadest and most comprehensive sympathy with every nation. We must not re-
> nounce the spiritual kinship which we bear to every one of the great belligerents.
> It is at once the privilege and the duty of America to keep open the channels of
> spiritual communication with her neighbors, to consecrate herself to the task of
> friend, to show the world that the occasions which might lead others to war can
> be forgiven without violating national honor.... She must consecrate herself to
> a higher patriotism which shall mean not the petty ethnocentrism of a self-willed
> people, but a devotion to the world and to the future, to the principles upon
> which international understanding and peace must always rest.

In these two papers written in his college years before he reached the age
of 21, we see values that persisted through Gardner's lifetime—heroism,
respect for all people, sympathy, forgiveness, cooperation, mutual understanding, devotion, moral idealism, honor—as against the petty, the selfish,
the vengeful. It was as if the crisis of the war had mobilized and consolidated
the ideals that had flowed together from church, from Concord life, from his
father's dedication to human rights, a dedication supported by his mother.

In his senior year at Yale, Gardner and Frank Lorimer discovered each
other, and Gardner found the intimacy he had longed for in a friendship that
endured through his long life. Frank was the son of a Baptist minister in Maine
and had the rugged directness and the appearance of physical strength of a
backwoodsman. Gardner idealized him, thought of him as Whitmanesque
and romantically felt that Frank should be a poet. Tall and dark haired like
DuBose, Frank became a loving brother who was not competitive. There was
an intimate sharing of views about life. Frank understood Gardner's struggles
to emancipate himself from the Puritan straitjacket of his mother's concept of
proprieties. At the same time, Frank appreciated her literary sophistication and
broad culture. To Frank, Gardner poured out his thoughts about theology and
ideals.

During Gardner's graduate year at Harvard, when Frank was studying
theology at Newton, they saw each other from time to time, corresponded, and
became very close. It was to Frank that Gardner confided his concerns about
the two major decisions he had to make—the decision about his life-work and

"the wife decision." And it was to Frank that he poured out his frustrations and despair during the war, his longing to "do a man's part," his grief at the killing on the World War I front.

Gardner graduated from Yale a changed youth, no longer the hasty, careless boy but a young man with a goal in life, with an intimate friend for which he had longed, with an image of the kind of father-figure he would become for his future students, with a commitment to the pursuit of truth and with an ecstatic conviction that there *is* more beyond — "plus ultra." He had been sent to Hotchkiss and Yale as a family commitment. He now made his own choice to go to Harvard for graduate work. From that point on he was always goal-oriented.

The death of a father, like the death of a leader in battle, can stimulate the son to pick up the torch and carry on. It leaves the son with a responsibility, a sense of becoming part of an older generation with a goal to be met. When the death is unexpected, the shock is greater, and it may be relieved by a deeper identification with the father's goals and values. In his "Study of Myself" Gardner said that he was probably more ambitious than his brother; DuBose had been athletically, socially and academically successful and although Yale acquaintances felt that he was very competitive, we do not know of any grand visions of achievement comparable to Gardner's hope to prove the independence of mind and soul from the brain, and therefore prove the reality of survival and the essence of Christianity. After graduation from Yale and especially after Gardner's year at Harvard the brothers went their different ways — DuBose completed training for the Episcopal ministry, following in his father's early footsteps. Gardner continued with psychology and psychical research and, in time, activities applying psychology to basic human problems of human conflict, war and peace — with the humanitarian commitment of his father's most passionate years.

9. Harvard : Humanistic Psychology

In the spring of his senior year at Yale, when Gardner was considering his next step on the way to becoming a psychologist he went down to New York to explore the Columbia University psychology department. Despite his deep commitment to the experimental method as *the* scientific method the laboratory there gave him a very negative impression—he found the place rather bleak "what with its pickled brains and charts"; the catalogues and the whole picture of physiological psychology were not what he wanted at that time. When he visited Harvard, he found a different atmosphere. There was more of a "philosophically and humanistically"—a culturally oriented— approach. That decision to go to Harvard for graduate work foreshadowed the kind of psychologist he would become and the kind of influence he would have on psychology. He had a rewarding year there in 1916–17 after a summer in which he spent five solid weeks reading the history of philosophy at Harvard's Widener Library "all day every day." He read Bakewell's *Source Book in Ancient Philosophy* and a systematic text; he was so moved by the concepts of the Greek philosophers that he accumulated a collection of books, both primary sources and discussions, especially of Plato. (In later years every room in the house had copies of Plato in the bookcase.) His realization of the importance of early philosophy for the history of psychological concepts led to further reading in the history of psychology, especially volume III of Brett. It is obvious that his thorough grounding in Greek at Hotchkiss and Yale had provided a superb background for his interest in Greek philosophy; an indelible impression was made on him then and later by Heraclitus, Socrates, Epicurus and the Pythagoreans, and through his lifetime of teaching and writing he introduced his discussions of psychological and ethical issues with a reference to one or more of these early thinkers.

At Harvard he "got a good mix of philosophy, psychology and parapsychology with such delicious extras as Parker's course, the Structure and Function of Central Nervous Organs, and George Foote Moore's delightful History of Religions." He learned much in a "Study of Myself" in Yerkes' course on ontogenetic psychology: "he urged us to bring in absolutely everything that we could find out about our past." There were also courses with Münsterberg, with Langfeld and with E.B. Holt, courses which Gardner considered good but not brilliant. His exciting Chauncey Tinker at Yale had created such a standard that apparently Gardner was a little disappointed not to find comparable inspiration at Harvard, and at Harvard there was no professor who offered the friendly companionship Gardner had cherished with Jack Adams at Yale (although Yerkes was interested in Gardner and kept in touch with him, writing of his dismay at Gardner's shift to the Menninger Foundation in 1952).

The combination of philosophy courses, history of religions, and physiological psychology supported the erosion of Gardner's theological faith and in March 1917, "with much writhing" he made "a sharp clean cut" that severed himself from his father's Episcopal trinitarian beliefs. The struggle and pain of this were reflected in letters to Frank Lorimer, and to his brother, who was completing his training for the Episcopal priesthood. Gardner's commitment, he explained at length, was to *truth* and he could not accept the Episcopal doctrines as truth. But his ethical and humanitarian commitment became deeper than ever, and later he took courses at Union Theological Seminary, where modern historical criticism of Biblical literature, combined with a strong emphasis on the brotherhood of man, eased the break. While he never accepted the ritual of "This is my body . . . and blood" in visits to Episcopal churches with his brother's son, he was at home at meetings of the Friends (Quaker) congregations and ecumenical community churches. Unlike the psychologist, Leonard Carmichael, and the anthropologist, Margaret Mead, he was never able to accept the church ritual symbolically.

The family had kept a Harvard philosophy examination Gardner took, which demonstrates the attention given to religion, and Gardner kept his paper on Confucius and Christianity. He defended Christianity as a source of general principles adaptable to changing conditions, in contrast to the precepts of Confucius which are not, he felt, relevant to the modern needs of China. To the end of his life Gardner consciously remained a "Christian," notwithstanding his rejection of theological concepts; it was the ethics and love of Jesus to which he was whole-souled in commitment.

The suffering attending his major break with the religious faith of his father was eased by a major development in his interest in psychical research. The psychologist L.T. Troland was also on the Harvard faculty, and as Gardner studied with him he was introduced to scientific literature in psychical research; Troland invited Gardner to assist him in an experiment. Harry Helson, another graduate student—himself destined to become a distinguished psychologist—had had firsthand experiences with mediums and poltergeist events; and George Estabrooks also participated in the work with Troland. That Harvard year, then, deepened Gardner's intellectual commitments to a philosophical and humanistic orientation to psychology, and to the practicality of participating in psychical research.

But there was a deeper commitment to values which he had selectively absorbed from his religious upbringing and his Harvard study; his formal statement of this commitment was made in 1956 in a unique book, *This Is My Faith*, edited by Stewart C. Cole. This volume included essays discussing the personal faith of 25 "representative Americans"; the group included Albert Einstein, Harvard philosopher Ernest Hocking, William H. Kilpatrick, who was the most famous educator of that time, Ordway Tead, a noted economist and member of the National Commission for UNESCO, and Gardner Murphy among others. The editor of the book posed five questions of which the first was "In the Judeo-Christian religions ... what religious values ... do you think should be emphasized in contemporary thought and practise?"

Almost half of these thinkers emphasized some form of expression of the principle of love, as in "Love thy neighbor as thyself." Among this group was Gardner Murphy, who developed this theme most ardently as he asserted the value of love, both given and received. He added scientific support, referring to the concepts of two major child psychiatrists of the time: René Spitz pointed out that children may die for lack of love and David M. Levy wrote on "affect hunger." Gardner asserted that love is an absolutely fundamental central experience rooted in human tissues. He found other religious groups with an emphasis on love and rejected the assumption that this was unique to the Judeo-Christian tradition.

Beyond this, he felt that other things were profoundly worthy of love — the sea, stars, dogs, robins. "Love spills over, it does not draw sharp lines." And, he believed, that in a certain sense it can be the love of the all — "the fulfillment of man is achieved both through loving many individual persons and things and also loving the allness, the totality of the world." He felt that in the evolution of life within the world there has been an increasingly rich capacity for appreciation, resonance and love, and he thought that this was a trend which the universe produces not accidentally but by virtue of its very nature. He saw this trend as basic to the communications over distance without direct sensory contact studied in parapsychology and he noted that modern physicists are more open to the study of these trans-space, trans-time, transpersonal events than are most psychologists, bound as they are to an outmoded level of physical science.

Questions on Gardner's examinations at Harvard tell us more about the unique foundation he gained for his development as a psychologist. Questions on the final exam in Aesthetics include "Discuss the relation of pleasure to beauty"; "Trace the origin of the art impulse and its relation to the play impulse both in the individual and the race"; "Describe fully and criticize the theory of empathy ..."; and "How is the Freudian theory applied in literature and the drama?" A final examination in Philosophy 3 included these two questions: "Describe and criticize the Pragmatic conception of *truth*" and "What should a young man's attitude be as he faces the universe and plans out his own career?" And a final exam in Philosophy 18 asked, "Discuss the relations of science and religion in the nineteenth century, and show how their relation affected the development of philosophy" and "What is Bergson's view of instinct?"

Courses such as these, which earned Gardner his master's degree in psychology, bridged his classical education, his avid reading in philosophy the previous summer, and the more focussed training in psychology he was to receive at Columbia University; he never lost the Harvard breadth and human perspective.

10. World War I : Its Influence on Gardner

World War I erupted in Europe during the summer of 1914, after Gardner's sophomore year at Yale. In his autobiographies he did not mention this, but that paper written at Yale in 1916 expressed his concerns; his boyhood summers in Bad Nauheim had given him a deep affection for things German, especially music. He had played with boys who could have been soldiers in the Kaiser's army.

In 1915 Gardner's team won their debate with the Princeton team on the issue of an increase in the army and navy. Effectively he summarized that the American navy and army were an adequate defense against foreign aggression, that a sudden increase in the navy and army would make us a military nation more reconciled to war and would also invite hostile preparations against us. In that Yale paper, "A Larger Neutrality" he had reviewed the breadth of American sympathies and bonds and President Wilson's proclamation. He concluded with a moving discussion of American ideals, and "a larger patriotism." He hoped America would remain neutral.

But the United States declared war on April 6, 1917; a conscription law was passed May 18. After he received his M.A. in June 1917 at Harvard, Gardner enlisted in the Yale Mobile Hospital Unit. Following training, the unit embarked on August 23 with the American Expeditionary Force. Neither in any extant letters nor in any autobiographical papers did he describe that voyage, a vivid account of which was written by another member of the unit: Enlisted men were in the steerage eating breakfasts of oatmeal dotted with maggots; lunches of horse meat, potatoes, and hard tack, and suppers of rice, hard tack and tea. As the ship approached the Irish Sea it was struck by a torpedo which, however, caused no major damage. After docking at Liverpool they boarded a train for Southampton and that night crossed the channel; following a couple of days at a dismal rest camp they went across France on a slow freight train which carried the famous sign "Huit chevaux ou quarante hommes." They spent six months at Limoges, which Gardner found frustrating, wishing he could accomplish something to serve his country.

Completely committed now to the war to save democracy, the war to end wars, he optimistically expected to beat the Germans in a year-and-a-half. After he was assigned to run the YMCA canteen, making purchases, organizing stock, tending store, cleaning the rest room, he was considerably happier. Finally they moved up to the front and established the mobile hospital. His classmate Marshall Williams has recounted that they were obliged to wash in kerosene and even launder their clothes in it in order to keep the lice under control. But in his own letters to his Yale friends Malcolm Baber and Frank Lorimer, Gardner never described a day's work. Instead, he wrote of his pleasure in getting acquainted with French and the French people, whose cheerfulness "in the face of all they have undergone and their marvellous democracy and good-fellowship" he had admired. He visited the home of Jeanne d'Arc, preserved almost as it was in her time, with the moving addition of "the Stars and Stripes" side by side with the tricolor in Jeanne's church. A friend of Gardner's told me that he was happiest on days off when they hiked in the French countryside singing along the road. And he was delighted with visits to and from his cousin Edgar Tobin, "one of the most successful American aviators" who did "some magnificent acrobatics." His brother, DuBose, on horseback, also visited him unexpectedly. In a casual, newsy way Gardner wrote Malcolm Baber that he had seen a dozen Yale acquaintances; later he wrote of his shock at the deaths of those killed in the last six weeks of the fighting including two very good friends who "had gone through hell during the summer only to be picked off so near the end."

Gardner was commissioned a second lieutenant, Corps of Interpreters, U.S. Army, as of November 16, 1918, but he was immediately assigned to intelligence work and was "comfortably situated in a magnificent billet with a fine little French family, with all the luxuries of home . . . not hounded by any more coercion from outside." From there he was sent to Coblenz, where he billeted with Frau Grunert, a friendly hausfrau to whom he wrote letters for years afterward with the warmth he had felt for Germans since his boyhood.

In Germany he was interested "in Boche psychology." He wrote to Baber, "You would think they would have at least sense enough to stop praising the Hohenzollerns in public. The birth of the German democracy needs a few extra midwives." He was thinking about returning to graduate work; not returning to school would be "mental suicide."

His military record included no involvement in any "battles, engagements, skirmishes"; his war service earned him three gold chevrons. According to the Army record of May 31, 1919, he was "relieved from further duty" and, on July 7, 1919, he received his honorable discharge.

After we were married Gardner did not want to discuss the war or the Mobile Hospital, and, consequently, this part of his life remained private. His medical experience proved valuable in family emergencies as, for example, when his cousin George Babbitt developed blood poisoning in his right arm, Gardner realized how serious it was and quickly took him to a hospital, where his life was saved, although the arm was amputated at the elbow.

Although we never discussed those difficult months, Gardner and I did enjoy singing some of the World War I songs together, especially the humorous and love songs:

There's a long, long trail awinding
Into the land of my dreams . . .
To the day when I'll be going
Down that long, long trail with you.

How deep Gardner's feelings about World War I were can be judged from his lifelong concern with peace and international relations related to the maintenance of peace. His first research after he became a member of the Columbia University faculty was a study of political and international attitudes; he was chosen by his colleagues in the Society for Psychological Study of Social Issues (SPSSI) to prepare a book on war and peace; he gave lectures on such topics as "Can Research Prevent War?" and "Political Invention as a Strategy Against War"; he was on committees working on postwar planning during World War II; he gave financial and direct moral support to legislators such as senators Hubert Humphrey and George McGovern and he protested the Vietnam War.

In 1944 Gardner received a letter from the Harvard philosopher William Ernest Hocking expressing appreciation for his speech on a "Just and Durable Peace." Hocking commented on the lack of an adequately strong public opinion to support the League of Nations—a lack he felt was due to the fact that the wide world was too big for most Americans to get excited about. "However what you said about the great masses being willing to make sacrifices for what they consider a good world order is solid stuff on the other side." He stated that he wanted to receive anything Gardner's group (SPSSI) distributed to the public.

At the time of the Cuban crisis in 1962 an ecumenical group of major Protestant, Catholic and Jewish leaders telegraphed Gardner an urgent request to meet with their group on October 28 in Washington, D.C., to seek ways to "broaden awareness of further approaches for resolving the Cuban crisis, providing evidence to the President that devoted Americans will support him in imaginative efforts to alleviate the present danger to national and international security."

In 1961 the *Bulletin of the Atomic Scientists* published Gardner's paper "What Can the Behavioral Sciences Contribute toward World Survival?" This paper was based on a lecture given to the Los Angeles Society of Clinical Psychologists. Anxious about the world crisis, Gardner shared his conviction that atomic horrors had been talked about so much that "we have actually gotten passive, hopeless, resigned to our doom, to the point where we are nearly paralyzed and behavior sciences are not being mobilized for the prevention of catastrophe."

Gardner believed that serious research should be undertaken by social scientists to retrieve fear-laden desires and impulses and avoid colossal diplomatic errors in a world that enormous technical skills had rendered increasingly dangerous. With the support of the nuclear scientist Leo Szilard, he stated that achieving an international agreement for total disarmament was basically a psychological problem. His suggestions included global studies of the nature of war; research into the causes of World War I, including the growth of the armaments industry and of propaganda skills, and the intensities of Fascist and Nazi ideology leading to World War II; and studies of contemporary dictators and totalitarianism in regard to the push toward aggrandizement and war. Finally, world leaders needed to develop a sharper perception of the relation between military arms and high-level economic and political decision-making processes contributing to the upheavals in the Middle East and in Eastern Asia. Studies using the interdisciplinary skills emerging in the Center for International Studies at the Massachusetts Institute of Technology under Ithiel Pool dealt with the ways in which communication among top-level military, scientific, and social science leaders affects national destiny. Ithiel Pool himself discussed the extraordinary way public opinion, acting through top leaders, can influence public policy. Gardner felt that with the newly rich expansion of modern information theory, cybernetics and computers, international exchanges of information even with potential enemies might enable each national government to perceive the unity of human knowledge so that the "great Frankenstein monster" of the machine which plans war might, instead, plan peace.

After consideration of the ideological conflict between capitalist democracy and Marxism, Gardner stated his belief that analysis and research could develop a plan for world order that preserved cultural diversity and the next year he encouraged communication among leaders at the decision-making level in China, the Soviet Union, the United States. He warned, however, that psychology had fallen behind in crucial ways, that we know vastly more about communication than about power or about the structure of decisions in terms of the historical flow of the period in which they are made.

Gardner constantly tried to integrate modern scientific thinking with his own reflections on the possible contribution of psychology. He found hope in models developed by David Katz, Irving Janis and Harold Guetzkow to test conceptions relevant to world order; in the use of opinion analysts in regard to the world diplomatic struggle; in the meetings of junior diplomats under the aegis of the American Friends Service Committee to exchange ideas with each other and even across the Iron Curtain; and in new steps in communication between Soviet and American business and political leaders. He begged behavioral scientists to give concentrated attention to the effort to understand the intricacies of the power system within each national group and to the common threads that connect the power elite in various nations. Understanding among nations could lead to the unified acts that mean peace for humanity.

Gardner and Lois Murphy singing at a party in Topeka in about 1962; he enjoyed singing together more than anything except mountain climbing.

Gardner's mother, Maud King Murphy, at graduation from Vasser in 1888 and at age 73 in about 1938; GM in San Antonio, summer 1896, one year old.

GM's father Edgar Gardner Murphy *(left);* "Grandpa King"; GM in 1900, 5 years old.

Gardner *(right)* at age 4 with brother Dubose, 6; GM in Concord, about age 9.

Gardner at about age 11, with bow and arrow and with bat; GM, about 8 years old, with his mother on Grandpa King's dock on the Concord River.

Above: Gardner *(standing),* at about 9, with Dubose, about 11, on Grandpa King's dock, about 1904; GM at Columbia in 1922, and in 1940.

Opposite: a brotherly contrast — Dubose *(left)* in 1910 and GM at Yale in 1916; Lois Murphy with Al and Midge, 1936.

Gardner at Arapahoe, 1941, and with Al in about 1941.

Gardner as the Little King
in a family charade, Bronxville, N.Y., about 1940,
and telling a story to 6-year-
old Midge, about 1938.

Gardner with eldest granddaughter Colleen, age 2, in 1953, and with son Al at Birch-lea, about 1949.

Lois and Gardner, about 1966, in the White Mountains, N.H., and GM with Midge and youngest granddaughter Dawn, at Birchlea, about 1963.

Helen Ross *(left),* Anna Freud and
GM in Topeka, about 1962; *left to
right,* Piaget, GM, Riley Gardner, I.
Ramzy at Menninger Foundation,
about 1960; Pars Ram, at UNESCO
project in India, 1950.

Otto Klineberg, about 1930 at Columbia; and Jean and Karl Menninger, Robert and Judith Wallerstein *(lower left);* and Ruth and Lester Luborsky, all about 1961.

Larry and Mary Frank at Cloverly, about 1940; GM and Margaret Mead on the Franks' veranda at Cloverly, 1964.

Gardner Murphy at about age 77, after Parkinsonism had developed. *Overleaf:* Gardner and Lois Murphy, 68 and 61, in Topeka (photo by Philip Holzman).

III / The New York Years

11. Columbia University : Gardner Becomes a Psychologist

When Gardner returned from Europe and the bloodbath of World War I in July 1919, he was immediately caught up in an era of dramatic social change and challenge to the mores and values of the prewar era. His own strong interest in the political and social problems of the times did not, however, interfere with an intense concentration on plans for graduate work, and his search for "the wife." He visited his mother and grandmother but felt no need to live with them. Still in military uniform, he went to Columbia in July to discuss his plans with the head of the psychology department, Professor Robert S. Woodworth. "Woody," as his students called him, was intrigued to meet a soldier who wanted to become a psychologist, and was a helpful guide in Gardner's path to the Ph.D.

A post–World War I Zeitgeist had permeated the intellectual world of the east that exerted a major force on Gardner's development as a man and as a scientist. Intellectual, cultural, and social experiences did not come in separate packages; they were inextricably intertwined. In the 1920s, women bobbed their hair, kept their own names after marriage, and began to smoke and drink in public as signals that they were "modern." Serious people, extricating themselves from their Victorian puritanism, discussed Havelock Ellis' ideas of free love and trial marriage, and read van de Velde's 1928 book *Ideal Marriage* for its illuminating discussions of sex. Passage of the Nineteenth Amendment granting women the right to vote reinforced Gardner's deep commitment to women's rights and fulfillment, expressed both in his support of women students and in his vision of a productive wife who would "use her brains."

There was deep concern among intellectuals about the Sacco-Vanzetti case, about the frightening revival of Ku Klux Klan violence against Negroes, and about increasingly confrontational labor conflicts. As one of Gardner's friends later wrote me, discussions "were not light-hearted." She felt that Gardner, especially, did not have much "joie-de-vivre." But those mind-stretching conversations dealing with contemporary issues that had not been part of his Yale and Harvard education were important for the direction his development as a psychologist would take over time.

When Gardner started graduate work, he lived for a few years with his friends Frank Lorimer and Frank's wife, Faith Williams; their home was the manse belonging to the Harlem Baptist Church where Frank was the pastor. Joseph Chassell, a Union Theological Seminary student, later a psychiatrist and psychoanalyst, lived there as well with his wife, Ruth Boardman. Years later Joe recalled the first time he "saw the newly mustered out pair of 'Yalies' in the Union Theological Seminary Book Store, especially the tall blonde some-what sardonic Gardner with his round gold-rimmed glasses." We *never* saw a sardonic Gardner!

Ruth Boardman introduced Gardner to her vigorous Barnard College roommate, Margaret Mead. Having known her before she went to Samoa to study adolescents there (and to prove that she could do field studies as well as a man), Gardner shared the widespread enthusiasm about her book *Coming of Age in Samoa* that gave her instant fame and, with her next book, *Growing up in New Guinea,* provided an impetus to the "culture and personality" movement in social science.

Gardner's social life was more satisfying than ever before; he rarely spoke of having a sense of isolation after 1919. With the Lorimers and the Chassells he belonged to a companionable "gang" of graduate students in the social sciences at Columbia who gathered for supper at the Russian Tea Room for long political discussions, and explored picnic spots along the Hudson. "Bunch," a member of the gang, wrote me in the 1980s that she enjoyed Gardner's ability to "spout poetry at length" and to sing all the words of all the songs they loved to sing on their picnics across the Hudson. (After Gardner and I began our own hikes and picnics in 1924–25 he taught me the songs they had sung so often, and we sang together for fifty years.) Satisfying as the companionship in the gang evidently was for Gardner he did not keep in close touch with any of that group except Frank and Faith who remained lifelong intimate friends.

Developing precious friendships was important to Gardner but he had more on his mind. In the later years of our marriage he told me that he had decided to go to Columbia instead of Harvard or Yale because he thought that in New York he would be more likely to find the girl he wanted to marry. As it turned out, it was not Gardner's search for a possible wife that brought us together. In the fall of 1924 Ruth Munroe, one of my closest friends at Vassar and my housemate in New York, was taking the history of psychology course Gardner was by that time teaching. I paid little attention to her accounts of the interesting discussions she had with him after class and I was unresponsive when she insisted that she wanted to bring him to tea. I was studying at Union Theological Seminary, with a focus on comparative religion; this involved work on the religions of India. With the idea of getting an M.A. at Teachers' College, Columbia, I also took a four-hour course there with W.H. Kilpatrick, famous for his development of John Dewey's ideas. I took no other courses at Columbia or elsewhere. Union and the brilliant teachers there absorbed my interest and energy and I was not interested in marriage at that time. I did not have time for her fascinating psychology teacher, I thought. I was also struggling to disengage myself from a friendship with a gifted and sophisticated Union student who had turned into a passionate suitor. Since I did not love him I was neither flattered nor pleased when he said that I had passed all of his tests (!). Ruth said I was an ass not to marry him, but when she accepted the fact that I found him too possessive and aggressive she decided (without my realizing it) that Gardner would be fine for me. She did bring him to our apartment for tea one afternoon and Gardner recalled "electrical conversations." His mother later told me that he wrote her about Lois, an interesting girl he had met at Ruth Munroe's apartment, "but she always runs off to type her papers for Union."

I was, however, thrilled with his moving recitations of Greek verses from Aeschylus' *Persians* in a resonant rhythmic voice. Our mutual attraction was not primarily physical at first; it was a meeting of minds and hearts that created a deep mutuality. Gardner's closest friend, Frank Lorimer, remarked after Gardner died, "That little Vassar Phi Bete from Cincinnati gave Gardner energy and strength and he was happier than he had ever been in his life." Years later Gardner wrote that with Lois

> a new kind of world began ... we explored many things in heaven and earth.... Her interest in education, in clinical psychology and in comparative religion, deeply reinforced my own, and we began a sharing of intellectual, aesthetic, philosophical and other concerns like music, mountains and travel which has never diminished.... Her interest in psychical research, as a challenging pioneer field, was a primary factor in maintaining my own morale.

I shared other areas of his old world as well, for I had been a member of the Socialist Club at Vassar; I had studied labor problems in my economics courses and was as concerned with the issues of the time as were the members of the "gang." At Vassar although my major was in economics I had the equivalent of majors in psychology and in English prose and poetry, as well as advanced courses in French and an exciting course in music that built on my previous musical training. In my explorations of the Vassar library I had discovered *Human Personality and Its Survival of Bodily Death* (1903), by the eminent psychical researchers F.W.H. Myers. To my surprise, Gardner also valued this work.

My physical difference from Gardner's blonde King family, with my olive skin (on which my mother's friends had commented disparagingly since the other Barclay children had peaches and cream coloring) was a problem for him until he decided romantically that I was his "nut-brown maiden." The intellectual, aesthetic, spiritual resonance transcended the problems. We were married in 1926, and, a year later, President MacCracken, the "godfather" of the new experiment in education in Bronxville, Sarah Lawrence College, recommended me for the faculty to teach comparative religion.

Although Gardner never put it this way, I think he was released by a sense of belonging, by my uncritical acceptance, by my spontaneous delight in his recitations of poetry, by our singing together. His sense of togetherness and freedom contributed to his responsiveness to experiences and ideas new to him. My "influence" was my bringing a new world of real-life observations—of children especially—which was fascinating to him. He responded to it eagerly; I never had to argue about the implications.

Meanwhile Gardner had settled down to work toward his Ph.D. He enjoyed the brilliant teaching of Hollingworth as well as that of Woodworth and he appreciated the warm support of A.T. Poffenberger. Hollingworth's abnormal psychology was considered by Gardner to be one of the great offerings at Columbia; Hollingworth believed in sharp and clear descriptions which they had to dig out of the best available literature and to which he added in his own lectures. He taught primarily by reference to experimental materials, especially those of the school of E. Kraepelin. In this course Gardner acquired a working knowledge of the main obvious clinical findings in the field and some introduction to theory. Though Hollingworth was by no means sympathetic to psychoanalysis, he did, nevertheless, direct the students to much of the literature and this helped spark Gardner's deep interest in psychoanalytic theory. Hollingworth was notable for the crystal clarity of his concept of redintegration (when one psychological pattern is followed by another, there is established a tendency for any ingredient in the earlier pattern to precipitate the latter). Gardner was also impressed by his theory of the psychophysical continuum (there is no mental world and no physical world; you can make a contiuum from the most purely mental to the most purely physical).

He also took Poffenberger's systematic psychology, and other courses at Columbia. A.T. Poffenberger, next to Woodworth in seniority, was a quiet, gentle man, more involved than Woodworth in American Psychological Association activities; he became personally fond of his student. When Gardner died, "Poff's" daughter Helen wrote me a warm letter, telling how much her father had valued Gardner and how she herself had been in awe of him. Poffenberger was also a sensitive artist with the camera, and each year until he died, his Christmas cards, with uniquely exquisite nature photographs, were a joy. It was Poffenberger to whom the younger New York psychologists turned for support during the Depression in their efforts to help unemployed psychologists.

Gardner felt he was lucky to study with Robert S. Woodworth—a psychologist's psychologist, gentle, whimsical, warm, almost quaint in his workman's laced up boots, and indifferent to appearance. Woodworth wrote about schools of psychology, but was not one to develop a school of his own. He was a generalist, an eclectic in the most integrated sense of the word and, although Gardner never referred to him as a model, certainly "Woody's" support and warmth contributed to Gardner's productivity and confirmed his own integrative eclecticism. Like Woodworth, Gardner was never one to participate in the battles of the psychologists in the 1920s and '30s which were interrupted by World War II and, unfortunately for the process of integrating psychology, renewed in the 1950s and '60s.

Woodworth's course was a broad and balanced survey of the whole of experimental psychology insofar as it could be taught four hours a week for a year in 1919–20. It was based on Ladd and Woodworth, *Elements of Physiological Psychology*. Although Gardner's psychology courses at Yale had given him a good start, he did not consider any of them "great teaching." And although his M.A. professors at Harvard had been helpful, he still did not consider them outstanding. But at Columbia, he found greatness in Woodworth:

> The first great teaching I ever experienced in psychology was not from a systematist, nor indeed barely from an experimenter. Entering the classroom in a frowsy, unpressed old suit, Woodworth would make his way, obviously unprepared, to the blackboard, not quite sure how far the class had moved or what the topic was for the day. He would mumble, then stop dead, fail to find the phrase that he wanted, turn and look at the class in a helpless sort of way, go back to the blackboard and utter some inimitable word of insight or whimsy which would go down in our notebooks to be remembered in the decades that followed. In order to explain, for example, why the nervous system in some primitive forms is on the ventral side, but later finds its way on the back, indeed on the backbone, Woodworth said he had it worked out that one of the tunicates was standing on his end and fell over. Or, having described the place of the red nucleus in the brain, he would come to a point for recapitulation and refer, with a smile, to the "little Bolshevist nucleus." He did not know why Aristotle thought that the function of the brain was to cool the fluids unless perhaps it was connected with the fact that Aristotle's thinking was not so hot (years before the slang "hot" began to be used as we use it today). It was in this very class that Woodworth recited the following, which has been credited to dozens of people:

> Psychology was the science of the soul; it lost its soul, then it lost
> its mind (turning, and with a flourish, and with a long pause),
> now it has lost consciousness.

The course consisted of long and solid sequences of factual chunks, evidence being tossed on one side, then on the other, and a tentative conclusion drawn. Dogmatic statements of the following sort were to be heard: "Well now I should think that perhaps there might be a fair amount of evidence in favor of that theory, but then, you know, there are some things against it. In fact, you might say that the evidence against it is just as strong (long pause) perhaps." The course exemplified the general principle that you don't have to be a teacher or know anything about teaching, or do any planning, provided that you are absolutely full of your subject, that you love it and love to communicate it, and that you have some eager beavers in front of you who want what you have to offer. Woodworth fulfilled absolutely all requirements, and to be with him was a great experience.

Two other Woodworthian items: "You've got to learn the nervous system," he said, "the way a monkey learns a forest—in three dimensions." In referring to a German philosopher, he said, "he was the most deep-down-divingest, the most long-under-stayingest, and the most up-mud-bringingest I ever saw."

He made the physiological psychology of 1919 come alive. This, of course, he had already prepared for in his revision of the *Elements of Physiological Psychology,* but had kept up. He saw where psychology was and what it was likely to become. He went on doing this, of course, for another 40 years, including his 1938 *Experimental Psychology,* his 1947 revision with Harold Schlosberg, his many achievements as experimenter, and later achievements as a systematist.

He was also sort of a center of gravity, a sort of general touchstone, a middle-of-the-road, typical wise, mature, thoughtful and creative representative of the psychology of the period between the two world wars. It was very characteristic of him that when he was offered the APA gold medal for his achievements, he decided to talk about the generation of psychologists of whom he was one member, not at all noting his own contributions but noting the spirit and the achievements of that generation which carried the message from Wundt, Galton, Titchener, on into the period of technical psychology which has reached its flowering in this period since World War II.

Woodworth's quiet warmth and interest in his students are reflected in a letter to Harold Jones a few weeks after he had begun his work at the University of California, developing the Institute for Child Welfare Research in 1928:

We are missing you every day; you have left quite a hole. Of course, Gardner's being away at the same time makes the gap in our phalanx wider still.... Klineberg brought back some interesting results from West Virginia and from Haskell Institute on tests of white and Indian children. His conclusions were that differences in speed of reaction were a very important factor in producing race differences in performance tests, and that the differences in speed of reaction could be more reasonably attributed to environment than to native constitution. ... [H]is dissertation was put into good shape, and he defended it nobly, and now he is off to Europe on his National Research Council (NRC) Fellowship.

Along with Woodworth's balanced, quiet, humorous perspective in psychology, and his often vague manner, he was perceptively aware of his colleagues and students and their families—without ever developing intimate relationships.

Gardner's doctoral dissertation was a study of types of word association in dementia praecox, manic depressive, and normal persons; he said at one time that "it wasn't worth publishing, but it was published," and it has been quoted many times. In the work for this he joined Dr. F.L. Wells on his rounds at McLean Hospital in Waverly, Massachusetts, for two months. He observed interviews with different kinds of patients and assisted in the laboratory. He also gave six Stanford-Binet tests, learned a little about ratings, "and a very tiny little bit of statistics on my own."

While Woodworth guided his mastery of psychology, Gardner was energetically educating himself in broader terms. In his evenings he "went right through William James' *Principles of Psychology* from beginning to end." At the same time he enrolled in a course with James Harvey Robinson on the history of the human mind and another on modern industrialism with Harry Elmer Barnes at the New School for Social Research. He also took courses at Union Theological Seminary, where "the work included some of the greatest teaching of my life," notably Fosdick's course on the use of the Bible and Scott's on the life of Christ. These theologians probably appealed to Gardner so intensely not only for the brilliance of their presentation but also because their realism and use of historical criticism provided a perspective that eased the strain from the erosion of his traditional Episcopal faith at Yale. Fosdick and Scott supported Christian values, and the significance and inspiration of the life of Jesus. Scott was a leading promulgator of "the social gospel," which displaced traditional theology.

Gardner's teaching schedule evolved gradually after he began his second year at Columbia. Woodworth was amazed at his first seminar presentation, which was beautifully organized and terminated exactly at the end of the allotted time. Woodworth's recommendation led to an offer to teach elements of psychology in the Extension Division in 1920, later known as General Studies. In 1923, after receiving his Ph.D. he began to teach the history of psychology; his account of this was as follows:

> I discovered the history of psychology essentially through finding that I was going after everything in the genetic method, and there wasn't any course at Columbia in the history of psychology, so it was an obvious thing I could do. I read Brett, Volume III, during the spring and summer of 1923; in fact, I read him on the boat coming back from Europe in 1923. I threw ideas together from obvious sources, like the materials I'd had with Woodworth, various odds and ends from the history of religion, and so on, and began teaching the course, I think, in the fall of '23, knowing very little indeed about it, but getting a good deal of integration into it by 1925.

One day at the Faculty Club, H.L. Hollingworth remarked, "Now you've done the work of pulling all this material together, why don't you write a book?" Gardner was surprised and delighted. There was at that time no suitable text for students; G.S. Brett's three-volume *History of Psychology* "was a useful survey of a philosopher's psychology" but not a very clear indication of how modern psychology came into being—"it was the growth of modern psychology that I wanted to emphasize." His lectures were stenotyped, then read to him by three devoted Columbia students because Gardner was having painful difficulties with his eyes; when a new ophthalmologist restored his ability to read, he was able to correct his galleys. The International Library of Psychology in London published Gardner's *Historical Introduction to Modern Psychology* in January 1929. Boring's *History of Experimental Psychology* came out later that year with several references to Gardner's book; with different orientations, the two books "never competed in any serious sense." Both went through successive editions, and both have been "bibles" for graduate students for over half a century.

That Gardner was able to be productive is amazing, since in addition to his eye problem he was extremely fatigable after a severe illness in the spring of 1925—only later diagnosed as encephalitic influenza. A cot in his office provided rest after a lecture, and a short walk brought him to our nearby apartment for lunch and more rest. Finally, in 1934, Dr. William Hay's sanitarium, with a month's detoxification routine and special diet, restored Gardner's health. Meantime he had decided to "bluff it out"; we married in 1926, produced a baby son in 1930 and acquired a baby girl in 1932. More stenotyped lectures produced five books by 1935. Their royalties paid for medical expenses, babies and summer travel.

The first paragraphs of Gardner's first book reflect the ease with which his hospitable mind welcomed the wide range of psychological problems on which experimental research was being carried out, and the equal ease with which he saw roots of contemporary concepts in the ideas of past philosophers.

> From colour-theories to defence-mechanisms, from the functions of a white rat's vibrissae to the mystic's sense of unutterable revelation, from imaginary playmates to partial correlation—wherein lies that unity of subject matter which leads us to speak, compactly enough, of "contemporary psychology"? From behaviourism or *Gestalt* psychology to psychoanalysis or the objective measurement of character, the eye wanders over an interminable range of experiments, measurements, hypotheses, dogmas, disconnected facts, and systematic theories. In a sense it is true to say that through all this vast melange the very birth-cry of the infant science is still resounding. In another sense psychology is as old as occidental civilization, and all these seething multitudes of investigations and opinions spring from an inconceivably rich and variegated history. The complexity of contemporary psychology suggests that its understanding may well require the use of that *genetic* method which it has itself repeatedly demanded in recent years. Whatever difficulties there may be in finding unity in the various psychological disciplines, there is at least one unity to which we may cling for orientation and perspective, for appreciation and synthesis; and this is the tranquil unity of history.

The centuries since Descartes and Hobbes have woven together the psychology of antiquity and the physical science of the Renaissance, the nineteenth-century triumphs of biological science and the twentieth-century genius for measurement, while a multitude of social forces, as well as strokes of individual genius, have shown unities of method and conception underlying all the problems of psychology, and indeed of life itself. For what is experimental psychology if not an embodiment of the notion of a fundamental unity between psychology and physiology, and what is behaviourism if not an attempt to make that unity more complete; what is psychoanalysis if not an insistence on the fundamental unity of normal and abnormal, and of conscious and unconscious motives; what is the *Gestalt* psychology if not an emphasis upon those Aristotelian "forms" which contribute the patterns both of the things of the physical world and of the data of immediate experience?

Gardner's books varied in the nature and durability of their influence. Paradoxically, his first book, the *Historical Introduction to Modern Psychology,* in print for over 50 years with the second edition in 1949 and the third edition, with coauthor Joseph Kovach, in 1972, was the most enduring. I believe several qualities contributed to this impact: it was the first history written at a level of clarity and grace that undergraduates could appreciate; its vertical integration of contemporary issues with those of preceding centuries — even to the ideas of the ancient Greek thinkers (in the second edition); its horizontal integration, relating psychologists' theories to those developing in related disciplines such as biology, sociology, anthropology and even physics and chemistry; its evocative analogies with images from literature and the arts and, increasingly in successive editions, its use of everyday experiences in the manner of William James. The historical depth gave students a sense of participation in an important tradition — a feeling that counteracted the uneasiness created by the conflicts, fragmentation, and insecurities resulting from inconsistent outcomes of experimental work as well as from the fierce criticisms of schools by members of another school. Gardner provided a perspective in which all methods were worthy of respect and there was room for very different concepts. The student did not need to reject introspection when experimental work on behavior became popular; Adler's ideas of organic inferiority could be accepted without rejecting Freud's concept of the unconscious. From the first edition Gardner presented a contemporary international perspective, as with the addition of a chapter by Heinrich Klüver on German psychology in the first edition and a chapter on Soviet psychology in the third edition. The pattern of teaching a course, then writing a book based on that course continued.

In 1924 when Woodworth gave up his evening graduate class in social psychology he asked Gardner whether he would be interested in taking it. And he was. From 1924 to 1929 he "dealt with a more or less systematic picture of hereditary and acquired components in social behavior, including the usual thing on suggestion, imitation, and sympathy, the self, the group, etc., and during the spring dealt with individual differences in social attributes." His development in that decade into a "social psychologist" needs a chapter for itself.

Gardner accepted a full time appointment in 1925–26 as an instructor, teaching the introductory course, general psychology, in addition to the course on history of psychology and the graduate course on social psychology in the evening. His closest friend in the department at that time was Harold E. Jones, the departmental representative (i.e., chairman) for undergraduates, who taught courses in developmental and in experimental psychology. In 1928, Harold and Mary Cover Jones went to the University of California to establish the Institute of Child Welfare Research, and Gardner was made representative for undergraduate work in psychology. He continued in this capacity until 1940, when he left Columbia for the City College of New York as chairman of the new psychology department. From 1928 to 1930 Gardner shared the introductory psychology course with Mortimer Adler and Prescott Lecky.

By 1929–30, when Gardner was appointed assistant professor, three instructors had been added to deal with the large number of students registering for the beginning course in psychology. In 1930–31 John Seward, a graduate of the Columbia psychology department who had studied with Gardner, was appointed to teach experimental psychology, freeing Gardner to add a course in the psychology of religion.

In the catalog for 1930–31 Gardner described Psychology 1 and 2 in a way that conveyed his commitment to humanizing psychology and rejecting the traditional approach to the discussion of the nervous system and mental faculties in introductory psychology courses.

> An introductory lecture course with class demonstrations of experimental techniques upon which scientific psychology rests. Much of the material of the course is treated from a genetic biographical standpoint. The first semester I study the developing individual from infancy through adolescence. The second semester, I trace the course of a number of adult lives in the light of their heredity and developmental history. In the course, I especially emphasize man's social behavior and relations between psychology and the social sciences. A prerequisite is Contemporary Civilization.

Gardner's conception of what students needed in this introduction to psychology was an orientation to human life. By 1933 the students for this course had so increased in number that two sections were listed in the catalogue.

Throughout the thirties Columbia offered the introductory course, Henry Garrett's course in tests, Poffenberger's course in applied psychology, Carl Warden's courses in comparative psychology, and Gardner's history of psychology. Gardner added more courses each year; often these additions were taught by psychologists brought from outside of Columbia. Of these new instructors, he was closest to Otto Klineberg, whose creativity and enthusiasm were so congenial to his own. John Seward, with his wife, Georgene, who had studied with Gardner, also remained friends after they left for California.

Along with being the representative of the undergraduate psychology department, teaching extension courses, and, in one year, summer courses at Columbia, Gardner was supervising dissertations of doctoral students in the graduate division of the psychology department. Fifteen of these dissertations were published in the Archives of Psychology between 1934 and 1940.

Unfortunately, limited storage facilities led to the destruction of the department's "dead files." In consequence we cannot now document the faculty routines that added to the pressures on Gardner's time and energy reserves, and also gave him varied experiences in administration. There were departmental committees, faculty meetings and committees, Psychology Society (departmental) meetings with guest lecturers, a regular half-day annually for a review of qualifications of students for Phi Beta Kappa, and a host of formal and informal occasions. There was a presentation to the Social Science Research Council (SSRC) on historiography, as well as service as the American Psychological Association representative to the SSRC; there was the meeting Gardner called of selected individuals from different disciplines and specializations to share sources in professional literature that were not obvious to others. There were the innumerable conferences with professionals from various parts of the United States and other countries who came especially or who found themselves in New York and who wanted to exchange information and ideas with Gardner and to get his critique of their work. His "little black book" crowded with appointments kept him oriented to the demands of each day.

Illustrative of some of the campus pressures on Gardner's time is the recollection of one who was a freshman in 1928–29. This student's academic adviser felt inadequate to provide guidance for one with a career objective to join the Foreign Service of the United States. In consequence, an appointment was arranged for the student to consult with Gardner, who devoted a complete afternoon to a conference exploring the student's career goals and the kind of training that might be most useful, and outlining some constructive steps that might be taken. As departmental representative, Gardner was called upon to counsel with psychology majors, and to approve programs for registration if they departed from customary guidelines.

The administrative atmosphere at Columbia University in the thirties has been described by E.J. Shoben in his book *Lionel Trilling*: There were remarkably few Jews at Columbia at that time — "Isadore Rabi, the Nobelist in physics, Meyer Schapiro, an art historian whose scholarly eminence was unsurpassed, Irwin Edman and Felix Adler, philosophers whose intellectual achievements were reinforced by advantageous friendships in society." There were no Jews in the English department until Trilling determined to break the barrier and succeeded by getting W.W. Norton to publish his dissertation on

Matthew Arnold. He sent the book to President Nicholas Murray Butler, who invited him to a formal dinner at the president's mansion with the provost, dean, and chairman of the English department. After a discussion there in which he said, "At Columbia, we recognize merit, not race," Butler himself, invoking his "summer powers," appointed Lionel Trilling an assistant professor of English. There were a number of gifted Jewish students in the psychology department, despite Garrett's view that "we should not take Jewish students because they would not be able to get a job." There were no black members of the faculty; Kenneth B. Clark, one of Gardner's students, was the first black student to obtain a Ph.D. in psychology. When his gifted wife, Mamie Clark, obtained her Ph.D. in psychology, Professor Garrett commented, "now you'll go home [the South] to teach." Gardner and I were disheartened by or even shocked by the prejudice among some of the faculty.

The ethos at Columbia was "publish or perish," and publish Gardner did, at an astonishing rate. After his *Historical Introduction to Modern Psychology* in 1929 (and, 60 years later, still in print in its third edition with Joseph Kovach), came *The Outline of Abnormal Psychology* and, in 1931 *Experimental Social Psychology,* which was recognized by the Nicholas Murray Butler medal. In 1932, he published *Approaches to Personality* with F. Jensen. An introductory textbook, *General Psychology,* in 1933 was followed in 1935 by a *Briefer General Psychology.* The rapid development of research led to the second edition of *Experimental Social Psychology* in 1937 with Theodore Newcomb. Then Gardner's longitudinal study, with Rensis Likert, *Public Opinion and the Individual* was published in 1938.

But all of this did not bring the promotion that peers and students thought he deserved. Gardner felt that as chairman of the undergraduate division of the psychology department he had a secondary status despite graduate teaching and directing many dissertation studies (in 1939, on 22 dissertation committees). Respected internationally as well as nationally, he was restless at the burdens which left no time for his own research, and at his low salary ($4000 a year) since he was helping to support his mother as well as his own family.

Students were puzzled and speculated—was he being held down because of his interest in parapsychology? Or was it his tolerance of students drawn to Marxism during the Depression and his permitting students to cut class for peace demonstrations, they wondered. That Gardner was both loved and respected by many students was recalled by a leading psychologist, Saul Sells, who added: "He was considered a champion of the underdog and a protector of the oppressed. He was viewed as soft toward some whose politics were radical (possibly Marxist) but I never heard anyone accuse him either of being a Marxist or of endorsing Marxism."

President William McGill wrote me, on September 18, 1979, that when he arrived at Columbia in 1956 he was curious about what had gone on "in the heyday" of the psychology department during the 1920s and '30s. He talked to nine psychologists, some of whom (such as "Woody" Woodworth) had been there then, and others who were still members of the department. The consensus was that an intense struggle for ascendancy was going on between the clinical, social, and experimental wings of the department and that experimental won. McGill felt that Gardner's situation had nothing to do with his interest in parapsychology or his support of students' peace activities.

The Columbia psychology department enjoyed considerable academic status and proved to be advantageous for Gardner's development. Along with teaching and supervising dissertations, he produced texts later characterized by psychologists Calvin Hall and Gardner Lindzey as among "the most vital and influential movements in modern psychology ... his work had few critics because it has been built into the sinews of psychology." From the Columbia base, he established himself in professional organizations, started editing a psychology series for Harper & Brothers, helped launch J.L. Moreno by reviewing for professional publication *Who Shall Survive?* and served as the founding editor of the journal *Sociometry*. Most important for the development of psychology between the two world wars was the emergence of his identity as a social psychologist who stimulated a flood of empirical studies on important human problems.

12. Taking Social Psychology Out of the Armchair

In view of the intensity of Gardner's interest in philosophy, history, evolution and especially the history of ideas, one would hardly expect him to become known as a social psychologist, but that is how he was viewed for much of his professional life. To be sure, he "loved all that stuff about the mind" and teaching the history of psychology was not only filling a gap in psychology offerings at Columbia, it was an opportunity to teach what he loved. But when Woodworth offered him the social psychology course he did not hesitate to take on that responsibility. There had been no social psychology at Yale when Gardner was a student there but he had studied sociology with the great W.G. Sumner and respected him. His training in experimental method in psychology as the truly scientific method had also made a deep impression on him.

The endless discussions of social problems with his friends in "the gang" from 1919 to 1923 had led him to study contemporary social issues scientifically. This was reinforced when he met Robert and Helen Lynd in Florence, Italy, in the summer of 1923. Robert was a sociologist, and Helen was a social historian; together they were dreaming up a pioneer anthropological or social science study of an American community. Gardner later visited them in Muncie, Indiana, and was excited by their firsthand study of contemporary mores and community life, which became the famous book *Middletown*.

When he met me in the fall of 1924, he explored my ideas, interests and experiences. I shared what I had learned about children in the Cincinnati Psychological Laboratory of the Board of Education (it would be called a clinic today), as well as observations of the warmhearted women in the factory where I worked in the summer of 1920 in order to get some experience of what it was like to be a laborer. (My task was to punch holes in clock-faces—a task so unbearably boring that I deliberately broke my needle occasionally in order to have the respite of walking up to the foreman's desk to get another one.) The women factory workers, taking me to be a high school girl on vacation, were endlessly kind to me. This experience reinforced my interest in the needs and rights of labor, and in problems of economic and social conflict. I was planning to take a course in economics in the coming term and I felt very ignorant about the industrial world and its problems.

I had also made a study of a training school for delinquent girls for my senior honors thesis at Vassar; in the spring of 1923 I had spent two weeks taking the place of a matron who had been gagged by three girls who stole her keys and escaped. Gardner was interested in all of my ideas and experiences as I shared what I had learned of the lives of the delinquent girls. Some of them were appealing, naive victims of Puritanical fathers and judges. Most were sullen and resentful at the punitive, depriving atmosphere of the place. My experiences and his visit with the Lynds opened Gardner's eyes to aspects of life and human problems with which he had not had much, if any, contact.

In addition to these various influences supporting his concern with social problems, Floyd Allport's *Social Psychology* appeared in 1924. Gardner was interested in it, in part because he had met Allport at Harvard and had been moved by Allport's friendliness when he met him again in France during World War I. Later, Allport invited Gardner to teach social psychology at Syracuse University in the summer of 1927. Allport's book, with its examples of his own experiments, in addition to the Lynds' study, gave Gardner a stimulating glimpse of a scientific—that is, empirical—approach for social psychology. At college (1919–23) I had not been exposed to any research in the field of social psychology, and Gardner's approach seemed innovative, exciting and important. Margaret Floy Washburn's course in social psychology at Vassar was built on the works of Tarde, LeBon, Veblen, Ross, and McDougall, along with books on the family (she advised us to marry and have children). She also included the psychology of religion (James' *Varieties of Religious Experience,* and others). In the world of psychology in New York of the twenties these classics were regarded ambivalently; certain concepts were familiarly bandied about, such as Veblen's "conspicuous consumption" (and we were happy not to be guilty of that). But those who were ambitious to be taken seriously as scientists looked down their noses at "armchair theorizing"—it could not be considered scientific. (Eugene Hartley told me that when Muzafer Sherif came to Columbia in the early thirties he was amazed that Hartley would discuss social psychology so freely—you could not do that at Harvard.) Gardner now envisioned a wholly scientific social psychology that would hold its own with accepted branches of the discipline.

In this atmosphere the idea of *Experimental Social Psychology* was born. Gardner had also been deeply impressed by Hugh Hartshorne and Mark May's Yale studies of honesty, deceit and character, and he invited May to be a coauthor of the book. At first Mark agreed; then he decided that he was too busy to do justice to the task. Gardner then asked me to work on the data on the children. (This was the spring of 1929, the end of the first year of Sarah

Lawrence College and my first year of teaching. I had been one of a group among the faculty who took the democratic constitution of the new college seriously and argued for faculty participation in administration. I was fired on the ground that I was not a good teacher, but with the rumor that I was considered the ringleader of a group of troublemakers. The president was fired in turn by the trustees for poor financial management and her successor invited me back; I returned in the fall of 1930. This gave me the year to work on my part of *Experimental Social Psychology* and also to produce our son, Alpen.) We worked on the book as coauthors in 1929 and 1930, with bibliographical help from S.S. Sargent and Philip DuBois; the fat volume appeared on library shelves in 1931.

That book has been considered to be a pioneering, even "landmark" book and received the prestigious Nicholas Murray Butler award in recognition of its contribution. Otto Klineberg, who worked with us on charts and bibliography for the next edition (1937); and Theodore Newcomb, who collaborated as coauthor; Eugene Hartley, who was a student of Gardner's; Rensis Likert, Gardner's first dissertation student; Stansfeld Sargent; and Muzafer Sherif, another dissertation student, all became distinguished social psychologists who developed their own independent approaches to social psychology. All of them produced texts that were widely used. Gardner never wanted a "school," or group of followers—he wanted to stimulate his students and support their independent development. They were heirs to his vision of a wholly empirical social psychology.

In Part I of *Experimental Social Psychology*, "Basic Principles," Gardner first discussed the place of social psychology among the social sciences. The next chapter on biology of motives confronts "the complicated biological and social facts" that he felt were not adequately dealt with in brief formulations of instinct and learning. Not unlike James, he objected to oversimplification; he kept his eye resolutely on the complexity of behavior, even in babies. He pointed out that when one says that some babies get angry when they are hungry, hunger and anger are each treated as units, but

> hunger and anger are complicated . . . what may appear to casual observation as a single pattern response, to be designated in common parlance by one word, is a complicated cluster of responses. Similarly, what we may casually speak of as one response because of some superficial continuity may go through a series of stages in the individual organism, necessitating the recognition of quite distinct responses at different times . . . it would be better to describe in each case just what happened.

It is in this 1931 volume that Gardner first struggled with the issue of the relation between the organism and the environment, which he clarified for himself long before his 1947 biosocial approach to personality. In 1924 Leonard Carmichael had published his challenging paper "Heredity and Environment:

Are They Antithetical?" His position was this: there never is a time when the environment fails to act upon the chromosomes. (This was years before the evidence that smoking and drugs taken by pregnant mothers can produce defects in their infants.) Gardner's response to Carmichael's position at that time was to point to statistical evidence of individual differences. And he added, "the business of science consists in isolating aspects of things, whether these aspects ever isolate themselves spontaneously or not." He did not feel that Z.Y. Kuo's evidence "that kittens can be made to kill a rat, to love it, to hate it, to fear it, or to play with it; it depends on the life history of the kitten," eliminates the importance of heredity. Those were the days when J.B. Watson was claiming that by conditioning he could train any one of a dozen healthy well-formed infants "to become any type of specialist I might select—doctor, lawyer, artist, merchant-chief and yes, even beggar-man and thief, regardless of his talents, penchants, tendencies, abilities, vocations and race of his ancestors." To counteract this extreme position Gardner held the fort for heredity, although conceding the contribution of environment. Watson's view neglected both innate differences and the spontaneous creativity, sympathy and coping initiatives that many of us observed in children—and that stimulated me, over time, to demonstrate these tendencies. Gardner emphasized the importance of canalization (development of tastes) in addition to conditioning (as discussed by Watson and others). There is still a need to demonstrate individual differences from birth in sensory preferences and interests which, in some children, lead to lifelong investments, as with child musicians, and very early scientific absorptions of men who become scientists.

In 1929 and '30 when we were preparing *Experimental Social Psychology,* Gardner and I were influenced by several trends in the social sciences, including psychology. We had attended Ruth Benedict's course in anthropology and had talked with Margaret Mead when she returned from Samoa; we knew Harold and Mary Jones and Harold's work on the galvanic skin response of infants. I knew Helen Thompson Woolley's emphasis on the need to look at the whole child from my work at the Psychology Laboratory of the Board of Education in Cincinnati; we knew some psychoanalysts through John Levy; we were well exposed to the generally accepted assumption at that time that the I.Q. was a measure of inherited intelligence, to Gordon Allport's discussions of traits, as well as to Gesell's assumption of genetic control of development of the child. Against these, May and Hartshorne had demonstrated striking environmental influences on character.

It was Gardner with his talent for integration who saw clearly that *both biology* (that is, heredity and the current state of the organism) *and environment,* that is, the culture, the family interactions and the immediate social and material situation, contributed to social behavior. "The social is literally an aspect of the biological." "The learning of an activity from another human being is just as biological a fact as any to be found in nature." "The knee-jerk is to a considerable degree affected by the relation between the subject and the examiner." He recognized his debt to Carmichael's view that heredity and environment cannot really be distinguished and contrasted, that there never is a time when the environment fails to act upon the chromosomes.

This integrative approach to the biological and environmental forces (both broadly as well as specifically conceived) contributing to social behavior was developed in subsequent writing and found its most influential expression in Gardner's *Personality: A Biosocial Approach to Origins and Structure* (1947).

Traditionally, social psychologists had been concerned with the nature of motivation. Gardner never presented a taxonomy, or list, of motives. William McDougall had seen motives in terms of a number of instincts—curiosity, flight, pugnacity, and so on—which were associated with specific emotions. "Lists of human motives are at least as old as Aristotle's *Rhetoric*," Gardner wrote, "but there is no instance in history in which the passion for listing or making inventories of human motives enjoyed such popularity as in the decade which followed McDougall's book (1908). Thorndike's *Original Nature of Man* (1913) and Woodworth's *Dynamic Psychology* (1928) are typical . . . in the same era sociologists, economists and educators . . . made up new lists of their own. (Veblen's *Instinct of Workmanship* (1914) and Trotter's *Instincts of the Herd in Peace and War* (1916) are typical of that group.)"

Gardner recorded the erosion of the instinct trend, beginning with 1919 and Knight Dunlap's contention that adult action-patterns cannot be dissected into elementary instinctive components. While he never joined the list-makers, Gardner's emphasis on the organic basis of behavior persisted and he continued to see tissue needs as the source of motives. If we illustrate the contrast between McDougall and Watson with the motive of flight, we see that Watson viewed flight as a response conditioned by specific experiences while McDougall viewed it as part of a repertoire of motives. Gardner objected to both, with his insistence on the simultaneous organic and experiential basis for motives.

He did not consider our *Experimental Social Psychology* to be in any way final or definitive. He simply felt that in view of the incredible pace at which experimental studies were being carried on—studies of infants and children, of phenomena such as social facilitation and suggestibility, and the measurement of social traits—it was high time for a volume suggesting what social psychology "is and what it may become," that is, an empirical science.

In *Experimental Social Psychology* we were not presenting a system, although Gardner was clear about his commitment to what he called a "biosocial" approach. The book served as a catalyst, or, as S. Stansfeld Sargent wrote in *Problems in Social Psychology* (1952), a "methodological rallying point for psychologists." Later, Brewster Smith—an outstanding social psychologist of the post–World War II generation—wrote that he read *Experimental Social*

Psychology "from cover to cover" and "encouraged by the Murphys' text" he delved into Sherif's *Psychology of Social Norms* (1936) along with Klineberg's (1940) "classic interdisciplinary text." By 1940–41, in Smith's first year of graduate study at Harvard, his special fields had become personality and social psychology.

Ross Stagner commented that *Experimental Social Psychology* was valuable mainly for drawing together in one volume a widely dispersed set of references. Gardner, however, regretted the haste with which we had produced the book, remarking to Stagner, "It stinketh of the paste-pot," meaning that many papers allegedly relating to the same phenomena were set side by side with little exploration of their theoretical and methodological bases or errors. Still, on other occasions, he recognized the impact described by Sargent and by E.R. Hilgard, who wrote me that *Experimental Social Psychology* "brought social psychology into the mainstream of an experimental psychology in the same direction, but with more substantial substance than Floyd Allport's earlier book."

Fay Berger Karpf's *American Social Psychology* (1932), an authoritative history of the early years of social psychology, considered *Experimental Social Psychology* to be an imposing survey of the field, going a long way in the direction of an inductive scientific approach. She predicted correctly that "other treatments of the subject from this standpoint are bound to follow." In the 1980s we see over 30 texts in social psychology, with psychology still opposing its methods to those of sociology, as it began to do in the thirties. Sociologists—for instance, Maurice R. Davie in *Refugees in America* (1947)—utilize both quantitative methods in surveys and sensitive observations of refugees in interviews; but a marriage of psychological analysis with such a careful sociological approach could have thrown more light on factors involved in the contrasts between child refugees who made outstanding adjustments to their new country and those who could not adjust.

The impact of Gardner's early work and writing in social psychology is also reflected in a paper by S. Stansfeld Sargent (1952). He wrote that sociologists had worked out a fairly consistent approach to social psychology, emphasizing uniformities of behavior within the group rather than variations in the social behavior of its members: "Sociologists have focussed upon the *interaction* rather than the *individuals*." Psychologists by contrast, he commented, had a less consistent approach. "It is difficult to pin down a central theme in the writings of McDougall, Floyd Allport, Gault, Dunlap, Kantor, and Murchison, the last five of whom wrote in the 1920s." Sargent observed that after the 1931 Murphy and Murphy *Experimental Social Psychology,* something approximating a psychological approach could be seen—"it centered about the individual who stimulates and is stimulated by others—his innate tendencies and his learning, his perception, emotions, motives and attitudes." By 1952, Sargent noted, a chapter on biological and social factors in behavior (which

Gardner had discussed in 1931) as well as emotion in perceiving and remembering (on which Gardner had worked in 1940–43) were included in many books.
"Furthermore," Sargent asserted, "social psychology is of necessity interdisciplinary in character," and "a broad systematic interpretation of human social
behavior" is "a kind of field interpretation in which the nature and structure
of the social situation *and* the personality trends of the participants *and* the
interactional processes are all important." Gardner made the same point in his
teaching and in our chapter "The Influence of Social Situations upon the Behavior of Children," in Carl Murchison's 1935 *Handbook of Social Psychology*.

At the same time that he was dreaming of the volume on experimental
social psychology, Gardner accepted the offer of $3600 from the Columbia
University Council for Research in the Social Sciences to undertake research on
student attitudes. This study occupied his attention for several years after the
Experimental Social Psychology was published.

Gardner was not a hands-on laboratory technician; he had gone to Harvard for his M.A. in 1917 because he preferred a humanistic atmosphere to the
laboratory settings at Columbia. But now the opportunity to teach social
psychology and then to undertake research and to supervise social
psychological studies of doctoral candidates provided a good fit to his interests
as well as to his values — his drive to make a contribution not only to psychology
but to the understanding of human problems. The problems on his mind, as
on the minds of others concerned with postwar issues, were those of international relations, labor and race relations. Tests of many kinds were mush-
rooming — tests of temperament, character, and attitudes; these suggested
techniques for a study of political attitudes and their origins. The social
psychology assignment was in this context a lucky opportunity at that stage of
Gardner's development as a psychologist. He could work on issues that mat-
tered to him. When his first graduate student, Rensis Likert, told Gardner that
he wanted to do his dissertation research with him, Gardner invited him to
work on the attitudes study — a proposal equally appealing to Likert.

"Social psychology" is an umbrella term, covering a wide range of social
functions, interactions, relationships at the behavior level, the motivational
and attitude level, and the genetic level. Gardner focussed on socialization,
starting with that early research with Rensis Libert: how does a person acquire
attitudes? How important are such influences as socialization by parents and
peers, personal experience, majority opinion, facts and objective evidence?

In a letter to me in 1980 Likert described their research as it started in
1929: "We collected data from more than 600 students in nine different colleges or universities. At the University of Michigan and Columbia we obtained
groups of students who each gave nine hours of their time completing ques-
tionnaires, responding to interviews, etc. The questions dealt with political,
economic, religious and international issues and attitudes toward Negroes."
Necessity is the mother of invention and since IBM machine runs comparing

each student's response on one question to that on every other question were not economically feasible for all 600 students, Likert devised a way to analyze the data to test the generality or specificity of attitudes. This led to his method for scaling attitudes, which replaced the previously much used Thurstone Method and the Guttman Method, and became the most widely used method for scaling attitudes. The development of his original method became Likert's dissertation, which was published in 1932 as *A Technique for the Measurement of Attitudes.* This early work with Gardner was the beginning of Likert's lifework on public opinion research and led to his establishment in 1946 of the Bureau of Program Surveys at Ann Arbor. This group was joined by Kurt Lewin's Research Center for Group Dynamics to comprise the Institute for Social Research in Ann Arbor.

Gardner spent a good deal of time from 1932 to 1938 writing up the extensive longitudinal material he and Likert had collected. *Public Opinion and the Individual,* with Likert as coauthor, was published in 1938. Gardner's summary reflects his persistent convictions about research. He believed that the most serious defect of the study was the failure to achieve a full integration of quantitative and qualitative data. "Not only were autobiographical materials inadequately exploited, but we found ourselves insufficiently prepared to make the best use of the data obtained on personalities of parents and students' reading habits." Quantitative methods were not ready when they realized that the most important variables to be followed up were of this rather intangible or personal sort. He recommended that the next step in attitude research should involve gathering better diary, interview and other biographical material.

His second recommendation was directed toward interdisciplinary cooperation: "Sociologists, child psychologists, psychiatrists and historians will be needed in the development of a technique really adequate for the study of the genesis of personal attitudes on public issues."

Influenced by Gardner's study with Likert, Theodore Newcomb carried on a unique longitudinal study of attitudes of Bennington College students from 1935 to 1939, with later follow-ups. The focus was on changes in attitudes during a period of dramatic and controversial social change in the United States. Where Gardner and Rensis Likert had studied the relation of students' attitudes in 1929 to 1934 to their backgrounds and personality, Newcomb's study demonstrated the flexibility of attitudes and described changes relating to current influences in students' college lives that led them in a direction away from their parents' convictions. Ted documented the continuing process of socialization as freshmen were influenced by their perception of the attitudes of upperclassmen and faculty and by a desire to be approved by both. When his second study of freshmen in 1959 to 1960 demonstrated that the liberal stance of the college reinforced the predominantly liberal orientation of a student, the power of the college environment became clear. Follow-up studies showed that attitudes developed or reinforced in the college not only influenced the students' self-images but also guided their choice of environments after college, with the result that college influences tended to persist. The extraordinary Newcomb series of studies, then, used techniques of studying attitudes not merely to measure current student opinions at a given time, but also to add knowledge about the impact of life in a cohesive college community upon the values of the students through college and years later; these studies demonstrated the value of longitudinal studies of socialization.

Our research on sympathetic behavior in young children (as Gardner said, 10 percent his and 90 percent mine) began in 1932, and I soon found differences in the behavior of the same child in different environmental settings. In the summer of 1933, when we were hoping that some months in Ouray, Colorado—free of all outside pressures—would improve Gardner's health, we worked together on an article reviewing evidence for the effects of different situations on the social behavior of children. And of course we were delighted by Lewin, Lippitt and White's Iowa experiment showing changes in the behavior of children handled by different leadership styles; Ronald Lippitt and Ralph White rotated roles as democratic and autocratic leaders to rule out personality effects. But extreme environmentalism evoked a vigorous protest; it would take time before the overlap of organism and environment could be seen in perspective.

In 1925 a stimulating young student who had a medical degree, then studied anthropology with Boas before he decided to go into psychology, was urged by another student to take a course with Gardner Murphy. He attended the history of psychology course and was enthralled by the eloquence of Gardner's lectures, the breadth of his knowledge, and the range of concepts and facts that he brought into discussion of any issue. During the thirties he worked closely with Gardner in social psychology. This was Otto Klineberg, whose own range from medical, anthropological, and psychological to musical and artistic interests led to a special resonance and attachment and cherished collaboration. And Otto Klineberg's classical studies of the relation of environment to intelligence test scores provided not only another dimension to the organism and social environment discussion—but a major step toward progress in civil rights. At that time, influenced by the results of intelligence tests in World War I, the idea of innate intellectual inferiority of blacks was generally accepted and deeply merged with the prevalent racial prejudice of the period.

Otto was not only thoroughly grounded in the scientific data pointing to the impact of culture on personality, but he was also uniquely perceptive and open to recognizing the ground-breaking implications of his own research findings. In the summer of 1926 he gave intelligence tests to Yakima Indian children on the West Coast and was intrigued by the fact that they ignored directives to work as fast as they could. Because of the time-limited criterion of test success their scores were lower than those of white children, *but they were more accurate.* Klineberg realized that the Indian children were working by their own cultural standards of precision, and that evaluating their "intelligence" by the different cultural standards of white children made no sense.

He then wondered what environmental differences might be affecting the intelligence scores of black children, whose tested I.Q.'s were lower than those of white children. Going to New Orleans, he tested 64 children there, dividing them into groups according to the length of time they had been attending city schools instead of the less adequate rural schools. He found that the I.Q.'s actually improved in relation to the length of time the children had attended the urban schools.

This was a major breakthrough, an exciting challenge to the concept of a static, heredity-determined intelligence test score, and further, a seminal contribution to the understanding of cultural influences on personality. More than a decade after Klineberg's Yakima study, Harold Skeels and Marie Skodak, at the University of Iowa, demonstrated impressive changes in I.Q. in children moved from a sterile, confining, unstimulating orphanage to an institution where they were loved, played with, and stimulated. And in time, the work of Nancy Bayley, of Lester Sontag, and of Alice Moriarty extended the understanding of many factors influencing the level and the stability of I.Q. The suggestion that the I.Q. was neither stable nor determined solely by heredity (including biological race differences) was viewed by the diehards in psychology as heresy.

Otto's findings were exciting to us for many reasons, in addition to Gardner's concern with organism-environment interaction. Our own values led us to be responsive to the new data and our revised *Experimental Social Psychology* with Newcomb (1937) included references to all of Klineberg's work up to that time. In short, Otto was providing scientific evidence to support both Gardner's evolving biosocial theory and the values with which we had been brought up. Klineberg's further studies of race differences, brought together in a book with that title, were suggested and sponsored by Gardner. In response to this work certain major psychologists, such as Florence Goodenough, revised their views of intelligence test scores but others were not convinced. Fortunately Anne Anastasi, a leading psychologist, president of the American Psychological Association in 1972 and recipient of many honors, made extensive and favorable use of Klineberg's findings in her classic volume, *Differential Psychology* (1937). Although controversy continued, the iron curtain around the I.Q. had been penetrated.

Eli Marks, another of Gardner's students who had participated in the Murphy-Likert study of attitudes, was one of nine students who carried out dissertation studies under the direction of Otto Klineberg as part of Klineberg's subsequent reports on Negro intelligence and selective migration, published in 1935. After he received his Ph.D. Marks went to Fisk University and as assistant professor from 1935 to 1942, carried out a study of skin color judgments of Negro college students.

Following Klineberg's successful challenge to the prevalent belief in the intellectual inferiority of Negroes, a series of important doctoral studies examined attitudes toward Negroes, and their own views of themselves. E.L. Horowitz's study, "The Development of Attitude toward the Negro" (1936) was followed by Ruth Horowitz's pioneer investigation of self-identification in nursery-school children (1939) and Joan Criswell's sociometric study of racial cleavage in Negro-white school children (1937). These studies were followed in turn by K.B. and M.K. Clark's studies of skin color and segregation as factors in racial identification, and the development of consciousness of self and the emergence of racial identification in preschool Negro children. The Clarks acknowledged that one of the techniques used in a subsequent study was a modification of Ruth Horowitz's method of studying self-identification. Evidence from this series of studies in the twenties and thirties strengthened the brief (to which Kenneth B. Clark contributed) for the Supreme Court hearing that led to the 1954 desegregation decision. Klineberg presented his account of this development at the 1986 fiftieth anniversary of the Society for Psychological Study of Social Issues (see chapter 13). Klineberg and Eugene Horowitz both contributed studies on Negroes used by Gunnar Myrdal in his monumental *An American Dilemma*, which appealed to the American conscience: the constitutional assertion of equality in all human beings with its implication of equal sharing in all of the basic rights was daily denied in American prohibitions against Negro equality in vehicles, schools, and public facilities, as these prohibitions reflected the general assumption of Negro inferiority.

Muzafer Sherif's arrival at Columbia and support from Gardner marked the beginning of another creative career in social psychology. At first Sherif used the autokinetic phenomenon (the perception of movement of a static spot of light in a dark enclosure) to demonstrate the influence of others' stated perceptions. From this he went on to other innovative studies of which the Robbers' Cave experiment is probably the most famous. With his collaborators, Sherif set up two groups of boys in separate competitive camps. After hostility had developed between the groups, an emergency was created that required cooperation between the groups. As a consequence of working together to deal with the problem, the hostility evaporated.

Gardner was delighted when Muzafer Sherif developed both laboratory and field studies to demonstrate basic psychological laws, thus beginning to contribute "hard data" that could qualify social psychology as a truly scientific discipline. Gardner's study of socialization of attitudes with Likert, Newcomb's longitudinal studies of attitudes, Klineberg's studies documenting cultural factors in the I.Q. and the series following the Horowitzes' studies of Negro children, along with Sherif's ground-breaking experiments were, I believe, the social psychological investigations that meant most to Gardner, that made the greatest contribution to social psychology of the pre–World War II era, and also that had the most enduring impact on social psychology.

Shortly after the first edition of *Experimental Social Psychology* and in part as a consequence of its publication, several important, even exciting books appeared, all of them landmarks in their fields: Allport and Vernon's *Studies of Expressive Movement,* Susan Isaacs' *Social Development in Young Children,* Moreno's *Who Shall Survive?,* Bridges' *Social and Emotional Development of the Preschool Child,* Piaget's *Moral Judgment of the Child,* and, of course, Sherif's *Psychology of Social Norms.* This stunning group of volumes presented new perspectives and opened doors to new research approaches. For instance, Piaget broke ground in the area of the cultural relativity of moral judgment; this was followed by Eugene Lerner's studies of sociocentrism in children. There were also many new statistical studies of social attitudes and adult personality. All of this made the first edition of *Experimental Social Psychology* obsolete. It had accomplished its purpose of establishing an empirical social psychology.

The emphasis of the new edition was to be on the process of individual socialization, and Theodore Newcomb joined us to prepare the section on measurement of the adult personality and attitudes. Gardner's first chapter in the new edition reviewed, more concisely than in the 1931 volume, the history of concepts in social psychology, and the emergence of an awareness that social psychology was more than a problem in individual psychology. An anti-instinct movement had been followed by the introduction of urges, impulses, drives, into the psychologist's vocabulary, but Gardner did not feel that the instinct problem had been settled: the work of McDougall had brought "a new emphasis upon the dynamic aspects of both individual and social psychology."

Paralleling the decline of the instinct doctrine was the extension of anthropological studies of culture "with relatively little dependence upon assumptions as to the original nature of man." Social psychologists took over this concept "of a highly plastic human nature shaped almost entirely by the culture which acts upon it." Gardner was always concerned with universal laws, laws applying to all cultures. These laws had to do with the transmission of culture or learning of a culture, and he felt that laws relating to suggestion and social facilitation probably "hold good among oriental as well as among occidental peoples, and among the primitive as well as among the advanced." "Whether any of our laws are really fundamental and necessary laws, . . . can be determined only by experiment . . . [and field study]." In other words, he was concerned not primarily with descriptive accounts of specific aspects of social behavior but with explanatory principles that would contribute understanding of the dynamics of social development and social behavior. This concern with basic laws and with dynamics reflects both his historical training and his early interest in psychoanalysis, which is focussed on dynamic concepts.

In the mid-thirties, at the time of writing the second edition of *Experimental Social Psychology,* Gardner noted that the experimental method had not created a unified and systematic social psychology. The "data are like a few pieces from some great jigsaw puzzle; there is no possibility of glimpsing the whole." He saw the various research trends as isolated and lonely "fingers into the sea" — separate, uncoordinated zones of research.

While studies of specific aspects of social behavior of children such as aggression, sympathy, and cooperation, had been carried out here and abroad, it took Gardner's historical and theoretical orientation to introduce the concept of socialization. This was a logical step from his early view of the overlap of the organism and the environment, and his inference that much of social behavior must be learned. Thus he wrote a long chapter (nearly 100 pages) in the 1937 edition of *Experimental Social Psychology* on "The Learning Process in Social Situations." Reflecting his love of birds, he began the chapter not with a description of any learning process in children but with experiments that demonstrated how a sparrow reared in a nest of canaries gradually approached a canary song — giving evidence of "a capacity which ordinarily makes possible the indoctrination of each new generation into the ways of its parents." In the first edition he had not gone so far. In the second edition he documented many examples of conditioning to everyday signals in daily social life, and the ways in which a conditioned response becomes a motive.

He went on to deal with the question of how to explain the failure to learn: the process of meeting new situations moment by moment involves blocking of biologically weak responses by those which are strong. This is the principle of dominance as defined by Gregory Razran; Gardner summarized the process in this way: "When two separate responses tend to be aroused by two distinct situations, the effect of the situations is not the independent production of the two responses, but the reinforcement of the biologically dominant response and in time the disappearance of the other." (At times the response is a compromise.) "New habits are not plastered on piecemeal, they are assimilated into the dominant pattern." In childhood, "except for overwhelming new experiences, such as . . . a death in the family, . . . the old is for the most part dominant over the new. . . . This is why personality, despite its complexity, inevitably tends to unity and continuity."

Gardner proceeded to analyze the classic problem of suggestibility and its relation to prestige of the suggesting person, then imitation, and sympathy — all in terms of experimental data. In this way he brought classic armchair concepts into empirical social psychology. But he also included psychoanalytic concepts of identification, introjection, trauma and reaction formation, with their emphasis on the role and strength of emotion supplementing the conditioned response principle — and, in the case of identification, providing a major clue to the process of becoming like one's ideal or parents . . . and of taking over the culture of the group.

But Gardner saw that conditioning did not suffice as an explanatory principle, it oversimplified complex events. He was impressed by the importance of familiarity, what we are used to, and he used the term "canalization" to refer to the process by which tastes are developed. Canalization describes the way in which the first, or unconditioned, stimulus remains the adequate one because it is satisfying in itself; no substitute stimulus is involved as in conditioning. In a conditioning experiment the dog responds to the bell that announces meat. The bell is not satisfying in itself and the response to it fades out if meat is not forthcoming. The response to meat is canalized, not conditioned — the meat is satisfying in itself and the response to it does not fade out. "There is enormously less conditioning and more canalization in social life than most writers have recognized," Gardner wrote in this chapter. One might add that neither mother nor apple pie is satisfying as a result of conditioning — that term has been overused. If the apple pie is delicious we want it the next time it is available, not because consuming it has been rewarded by something else.

It is canalization, Gardner felt, that leads to "the ethnocentrism of the anthropologist as well as the attachment of a dog to its familiar owner," and that accounts for fixations, for favorite toys, and for all cases of persisting direct satisfiers for a drive. At the same time that he insisted that canalization and conditioning must be recognized as separate principles, he suggested that they are both aspects of a general physiological principle. In his volume *Personality* (1947) he discussed canalization at greater length.

Gardner considered *values* to involve a complicated process of fixation; the value world of a given organism in the world of objects to which it is fixated. "We do not need the concept of sublimation to explain a taste for music, poetry, gossip, religion, poker or politics." "The degree of *urgency* involved in a value when one wants lamb chops and alligator pears and when one wants Stravinsky may be the same. Granted that the taste for Stravinsky is acquired, so are all other tastes." The concept of the set toward the object he saw as essential: "We value much which we cannot now have and a good deal which we shall never have. Value is a statement of preparation for a response."

In discussing conflict and integration of values, Gardner commented that "values may be integrated insofar as the organism finds a positive relation among them," but "other values however are lost while one is being pursued. Conflict of values arises when the same activity which leads toward one makes the achievement of another more difficult."

The 1937 edition of *Experimental Social Psychology* so far eclipsed the first edition that it has often been referred to as *the* groundbreaking volume both by people who evidently were unaware that the 1931 pioneer volume existed, and others who were aware of it. It is ironic that the interruption of World War II constructed such a barrier between prewar and postwar research that many students have remained unaware of the prodigiously creative period of the thirties.

After *Experimental Social Psychology* (1937) Gardner never wrote another social psychology text. He started the ball rolling in 1931, and the momentum increased. In that stream of social psychology textbooks that publishers were now glad to produce were volumes by several young social psychologists who had had a glimpse of how to make a book as they assisted or cooperated with Gardner in the late twenties and early thirties: Eugene Hartley, Otto Klineberg, Theodore Newcomb and S. Stansfeld Sargent. Muzafer Sherif, with his wife, Carolyn, produced a stream of their own; a copy of most of these was sent to Gardner inscribed with generous expressions of gratitude to him for his support. Muzafer's frustrations at Harvard had sensitized him to the precious experience of being appreciated. He felt especially grateful to Gardner for stimulating him to write the *Psychology of Social Norms* and arranging for its publication by Harper's. Other innovative social psychologies appeared — such as J.F. Brown's *Psychology and the Social Order.* By 1970 over 1100 social psychology books were indexed at the Library of Congress.

Gardner continued to write on specific topics — notably social motivation, in Gardner Lindzey's 1954 *Handbook of Social Psychology;* and he wrote many papers on the psychology of peace, of ethics, and of family life. His books *Human Nature and Enduring Peace* (1945) and *In the Minds of Men* (1953), which recounted the research findings in studies of conflict in India, were both appreciated in the book review sections of the *New York Times.* What he cared about most was making science contribute to the solution of human problems; he pointed a direction but never claimed to have found final solutions. His work as a founder and president of the Society for the Psychological Study of Social Issues provided a channel through which he could express his commitment.

In a letter to Calvin Hall in 1954 Gardner shared his current feeling that the studies he sponsored in the thirties and the *Experimental Social Psychology* were probably his most important contributions to psychology. In the 1980s Richard Evans commented in his book *The Making of Social Psychology* that he placed the chapter on Gardner Murphy first because it was Gardner who initiated the development of empirical social psychology. For those who share that view, he created a science, or we might say he created a bridge to a vast new territory of scientifically rigorous empirical studies of social influences, processes, and social experience. Beyond this, his biosocial view expressed in 1931 gradually permeated psychology; the endless arguments about heredity versus environment of the first quarter of the century were no longer scientifically defensible.

Gardner's chapter on social motivation in Gardner Lindzey's 1954 *Handbook of Social Psychology* is one of the richest, most down-reaching, outward-stretching papers he ever wrote. It is biological, anthropological, sociological, historical; it moves from the simplest sources of drive energy in the tissues to the most complex ethical, religious and political motives, often with vivid down-to-earth illustrations along with literary and philosophical allusions. It deals with motivation in general, simple physical motives as well as higher order social motives, always with a focus on the question where do the motives come from?

He began the chapter with a statement of his purpose: "We shall attempt here a theory of the raw material of human nature: its primitive mainsprings of social action and social awareness, the elaboration of which under social influences gives the social individual." In other words, just as a quarter-century earlier in the first *Experimental Social Psychology* (1931) he was oriented to the problem of socialization, in this later, classic statement, he was concerned with the origins and development of social motivation.

By the time Gardner began to write this long chapter he had seen more than enough lists of motives. "Under W. McDougall's influence, E.L. Thorndike (1913) listed nearly a hundred mainsprings of action, R.S. Woodworth (1918) over fifty," while W.I. Thomas (1923) listed only four wishes, such as those for new experience and for security, and H.A. Murray (1938) listed some thirty needs, most of which were social.

Gardner felt that list-making would not be as productive as an analysis of the "push," or élan — to use Bergson's term — that provides the energy used in all drives, including the social motives. This energy must come from all of the tissues of the organism, and to make this explicit, he himself did list visceral, activity, and sensory drives, and, in addition, emergency responses. Sexual and maternal drives were included in the group of visceral drives, and were the only directly social ones included. Insofar as the "impulse to cope with and to master the environment" is directed to people, social drives of leadership, aggression, deference, superiority (to use some of Murray's list) could be involved.

Gardner's first three groups included drives in which internal stimulation plays a major part in initiating response, while in emergency responses the stimulation for a response is likely to be a sudden disturbance in equilibrium resulting from outside stimulation. He added "etc." to each group in order "to remind ourselves that there are many more known drives than it is useful to catalog. We are abstracting from a complex and fluid matrix, and there are doubtless many drives waiting to be identified and described."

Just as basic as the tissue-based drives he outlined is the "inherent human tendency toward development or complication of these drives in a particular manner." The tendency to form conditioned responses, to cathect or invest or canalize — the tendency to associate, to give structure, to remember or to forget — "all these are dynamic forms of activity which come with the human package." There are second order elaborations. The development of human motives such as the desire to communicate and to be understood "are expressions of the way in which elementary motive patterns are elaborated into action patterns." The drives are socialized in accordance with the pressures and models of the individual culture.

If we argue that Murray's "affiliation" need, or need for companionship and social contact, is very basic, Gardner would point to the complex sensory and activity needs which contribute to this. Actually we do not have an adequate experiment to test whether all of the sensory, activity, feedback or dyadic stimulation involved in companionship can be satisfied by other than animate objects, although a child's teddy bear or doll comes close. For myself, I do not believe that an infant can be socialized without interplay with a responsive human being—and Harlow's little monkeys were unable to consummate heterosexual relationships when brought up on the tactually soft inanimate mother. (Later he found that peer group play was crucial.) In Gardner's list, which includes sex and maternal drives, "etc.," the "etc." should include a need to be nurtured—not just touched, fed, cleaned, and stimulated, but a need to be responded to, enjoyed, smiled at and played with. This is, to be sure, a "complex higher order" need, but one which is not met in foundling nurseries where only basic sensory and activity drives are provided for. Just as higher order cognitive functions of integration and problem-solving involve more than sensation and reflex action, higher order drives must be recognized in their own right.

Although Gardner emphasized the tissue-based organic source of motivation, he readily included the anthropologists' emphasis upon the shaping of motives in different cultures, especially following Boas and the "American Historical School" of anthropology, although he protested their neglect of attention to the sources of energy. At the same time he felt that Ruth Benedict's and other anthropologists' emphasis upon the role of social experience rather than social action prepared the way for acceptance of the role of perception, as in the work of Sherif (1936). He held that perceptual patterns are molded in different ways in different cultures and different group settings. Gestalt influence, especially through Kurt Lewin's field theory, and study of the life space of individuals stimulated attention to the immediate influence of the participant in a social situation. While psychiatry and psychoanalysis continued to emphasize drives and the social context, the latter was seen by learning theorists as providing the major determinants of personality. Gardner saw that this theory was supported by the concept that activity could become the source for further activity as John Dewey proposed, and that, as Woodworth put it, a mechanism may become a drive. Furthermore, G.W. Allport's conception of "functional autonomy" stipulated that purposeful activities may continue to be carried out for their own sake without being reinforced by the original motive. Still, Gardner noted that the relation of drive to mechanism had not been adequately clarified for certain psychologists, although he himself felt that both aspects could be included: "Social behavior becomes a socially patterned release of inherent energies."

This is the hub of the wide-circling concept, which we cannot follow in detail here. As an example of one type of elaboration of social patterns and motivations we can first quote his discussion of ramifications of food needs:

"The need for gratification or titillation of the senses of smell, taste, touch, . . . and the web of associations between food needs and the need for company, make it forever impossible to explain etiquette, the food style, the ceremonial aspects of the "date" and the banquet, the social meaning of eating with one's own group (excluding the person of lower status), all of which are intelligible only by considering the fusion of many tendencies." He gave other examples of the integration of social motives, along with sensory and activity motives: "When we have heard magnificent music we are likely to be more sensitive to friendly relationships, to be more in love. . . ."

He continued with a discussion of social motivation and the learning process, with its conditioning, reinforcement, canalization or cathexis, and the relation of canalization to "cultural lag," the weaving of associations between the different motives in the form of integrated wholes. Then, in discussing complex motives, he reviewed the implications of Karl Marx's discussion of motives of different social strata, Tawney's *Religion and the Rise of Capitalism,* the Calvinistic pressure to do right in the eyes of God, and Max Weber's contrast between the Protestant and the Catholic ethics, including the support of business and success in the former. He also took up the contribution of psychoanalysis as family psychology and the conflict between tendencies resolved by the principle of dominance.

His discussion of motivation in relation to the self led to a discussion of gain, power, and prestige in which he reviewed the infant's grasp of objects in the early weeks and the development of attachments to cherished objects which, as William James noted, became parts of the self, and which enhance prestige, as in Veblen's "conspicuous consumption." From this, he dealt with the question as to whether all motivation is "selfish," and finally returned to his guiding principle of the interplay of characteristics of organism with the environment in discussing individuality in motivation: ". . . each individual emerges with a very complex pattern of individualized personality characteristics. . . ."

Gardner concluded that social motivation is not something available in a Sears, Roebuck mail-order form to all members of the human species. "Moreover . . . symbolic ways of living modify the motive system more in one individual than in another." He felt that our understanding of motivation would remain incomplete until adequate attention had been given to the problem of integrating the biological and the social concepts, both empirically and theoretically.

Gardner's contribution to the development of empirical social psychology is recognized in some postwar volumes, usually by authors who themselves began to be productive in the thirties. In 1961 a symposium at Columbia, when an interdisciplinary department of social psychology was inaugurated, saw him as the founder of social psychology there. On that occasion, Otto Klineberg noted that the new department of social psychology was the first of its kind, and its inauguration represented a coming of age and, by implication, a finding of its identity, after a long period of uncertainty about its rightful place among the social sciences. Fifteen other papers were presented, among them Henry W. Riecken's "Research Developments in the Social Sciences." After quoting Gordon Allport's statement that the core of social psychology is the "attempt to understand and explain how the thought, feeling and behavior of individuals are influenced by the actual, imagined or implied presence of other human beings," Riecken discussed contributions of social psychology to other sciences, "namely in the development and refinement of techniques for collecting data systematically." Perhaps the most prominent contribution, he continued, "has been the study of attitudes and opinions, together with the concomitant technology of scale construction and the analysis of panel data. The use of attitude scales and opinion surveys is now widespread in almost all of the social sciences." He also commented that "some of the popular topics in social psychology a decade ago are still alive today—for example, leadership; socialization; the perception of people . . . the measurement of opinions and attitudes and changes in them, and social effects on cognitive processes." These are not the only ones he mentioned, but it is interesting to reflect that these are precisely the topics that Gardner was initiating, or exploring with his graduate students in the thirties.

Gardner's own paper, *The Future of Social Psychology in Historical Perspective,* began as usual with a gesture to history: "The little five-toed eohippus probably did not think of himself as the forefather of a Kentucky Derby winner, nor did Anton Mesmer think of himself as an ancestor of social psychology." He saw that the pedigree charts were complex and that the history of social psychology was a matter of determination by cultural context, that is, ingrained value and attitude patterns, shared and transmitted like the other treasures of culture. In a certain sense, he suggested, every new idea expresses the readiness for impregnation on the part of a vital mother who, with her own genes, potentiates the ancestral vigor of another mode of thought, coming to terms with her own. Then, vividly reviewing a wide range of personalities of the nineteenth century who had provided seeds for a new science in the simultaneous appearance of books on crowd psychology in the 1890s with the findings of the clinicians developing hypnosis, he stated that what remained to be done to create a social psychology was to coin a term to give the new enterprise a name—and this was done by Edward A. Ross and a few months later by William McDougall. But it remained to make this new science systematically experimental, with a system of interrelated ideas and methods. In order to gain respect from established experimentalists, social psychologists accommodated to their canons and in doing so, often worked on petty problems. Creative people like Lewin, Sherif and Moreno ignored the standard patterns. The contrast between these two orientations suggested to Gardner the different processes of the inchworm who keeps his rear end on the ground while he surveys the possibilities ahead, and the hoptoad who leaps into a new region. "Actually when Lois and I were working on the first edition of *Experimental Social Psychology* we found that the inchworms had been busy at many different points . . . but there was no overall conceptual scheme at all." He continued to describe how the inchworm procedures lead to piecemeal assemblies of material; and the hoptoad methods set up new conceptualizations far afield. He pointed out that the hoptoad methods result in premature systematization.

Gardner felt that we do not know enough about basic laws at work to attempt extrapolation or prediction; sudden new unexpected forces knock the extrapolation curve into a cocked hat. "Usually this is because of a sudden 'step function,' a quantum principle, in which the little shimmering spots of new discovery leap suddenly into a bright new light." He felt that underneath a new step function many hidden factors were at work, which in their combination manage to trigger the shift from one level to another. Typically, Gardner draws a historical comparison: "the long-haired Achaeans, swash-buckling pirates from the Danube basin, interacting both biologically and culturally with the dark, reflective, earthbound people of the Peloponnesus and the Mediterranean islands created the brilliant flash which we know as Greek civilization." He used this example in order to emphasize that the hybridization principle gives us much which sheer extrapolation cannot allow, and that the hybridization process, represented by the encounter of Darwinism with psychopathology, was the first step in engendering social psychology. Then he contrasted the influence of modern physics with its problems of continuity and discontinuity and of absolutism versus relativism in space and time, with the influence of demands during World War II for applications of psychological techniques to morale studies, public opinion analyses, international relations, problems arising from race and class, and suspicions and antagonisms. Observing that substantial and fruitful applications acted back upon the original mother science which made them possible, he added that those of us who thought two decades ago that we were social psychologists have found that there can be no longer a general social psychologist; "there is small-group research in mental hospitals, there is Güttman scaling for attitudes."

But he was not advocating passive submission to the winds of change, noting that we "can define more sharply the values which we hope will be fulfilled by the development of social psychology." Gardner admitted that in his early work in social psychology he underplayed a number of large empirical movements which were not founded upon experimentation and overplayed many small and unimportant experiments in the hope of gaining respect for social psychology as an experimental science. He believed that empirical studies of the value systems of social psychologists could be a way to bypass blind spots. He also challenged the process of assigning prestige solely to abstract cognitive achievements. "Perhaps a rich resonance to human needs . . . could play a large part in the leavening of the development of both percepts and skills in social psychology and perhaps . . . the discovery that our science makes human beings more like neighbors and less like strangers would bring into sharp relief some affective relationships which could be used both in applied social psychology and in the redefinition of forgotten relationships."

Finally, Gardner ventured a prediction that social psychology will move in a direction determined by three primary forces: prevailing value concepts about the human sciences, the prestige standards which reward psychologists with advancement, and the urgent practical requirements given by domestic and international politics. He felt these forces were so formidable that the chances were slim for another giant—like a Darwin or Einstein or Freud—to bring a creative vision that would lead to a new kind of social science. He feared that social psychology would become more and more technical, and limited. But creativity could be encouraged by providing for hybridization with training in a wide diversity of ways of thinking, including physical sciences, economics, political science, philosophy and fine arts, and opportunities to know something about people in various natural settings, "and to have both objective interpretation of and empathic contact with them." He urged that the student be allowed to choose unrealistic problems. "We must hold up to [the student] the images of the laughed-at . . . scientists of other times" who were in time recognized as creative leaders in an important new development. In a more confident moment he asserted that in between long silent periods, people with high creativity will appear who will shake and wrench the structure of social psychology, and will develop modes of empirical attack upon social problems which are not derived from any of the existing methods.

He pleaded for avoidance of the rigidity that can result from the desire for respect toward our field as a science.

> Social psychology can do a lot of good in a troubled world. It seems to me that I remember something about sorrow and pity playing a part in the work of the great psychiatrist, Pinel, and something about sympathy playing a major role in the life of Kurt Lewin. With the world repeatedly tottering, with no hiding place from the destruction which hangs in the high skies or in the depths of the sea, we need not be ashamed if we emphasize that understanding the human predicament with a sense of tragedy as well as with a need for power and prestige may play a vital part in the final escape from terror.

This prescient statement was written before the Cuban missile crisis, the Vietnam War, the civil rights struggles with their tragedies, and the murders of the Kennedys and of Martin Luther King.

13. Making Psychology Work on Human Problems : SPSSI

The creation of a new organization, institution, or structure typically takes place in an atmosphere of eagerness and hope for the achievements it is expected to bring into reality. But it is impossible to describe the intensity of the spirit and vitality of this atmosphere in the early years of the Society for the Psychological Study of Social Issues (SPSSI). We can only review the forces that brought it into being in 1936, and some of the early steps in its development, along with the relation of SPSSI to Gardner's basic values.

Psychology for Gardner was always the science which could help to solve human problems and contribute to man's understanding of his place in the universe. A variety of his efforts were motivated by this conviction: his early study, with Rensis Likert, of the relation between public opinion and the life history of the individual; his focus on basic issues in social psychology and personality; his research emphasis on reality-testing and on outgrowing self-deception. He described himself as a seeker. But at heart he was a healer of the ills of society, and his deep commitment to the Society for Psychological Study of Social Issues was an expression of that commitment.

As we review the steps that led to the founding of this spirited little organization we need to glance at some of the forces that prepared the way for it. The success of the revolution in Russia had given hope for change, but the immediate stimulus was the great Depression, which sensitized many psychologists to the suffering of the millions of unemployed workers. In New York men were selling apples—or anything easily marketable—on street corners, and some were living in "box houses," large packing boxes. Hundreds of psychologists were unemployed, and some men whose businesses failed committed suicide or abandoned their families.

Gardner was a child when Jane Addams created a new center in Chicago—her famous Hull House—to educate and inspire poor children and their families. Edgar Gardner Murphy, Gardner's father, left his Episcopal priesthood in the South when he became executive secretary of the Southern Education Board, dedicating his life to the improvement of race relations through better education for both whites and Negroes. He also initiated the National Child Labor Committee to work for laws prohibiting the employment of young children in the mills.

Many of the early leaders of SPSSI had grown up in this reformist period. Famous muckrakers Lincoln Steffens and Ida Tarbell had helped to develop their intense consciousness of and protests against the evils of American society — especially the exploitation of labor in the coal mines and the steel mills. Their belief in progress was fortified by the development of labor unions, which fought for better working conditions and better pay, along with increased recognition that children should be in school, not working in mills. Earnest parents echoed maxims such as "Help to make the world better." As youths they had been drafted for World War I and became caught up in the whole-souled commitment to "make the world safe for democracy." Some of their youngsters were now going to "progressive schools" that emphasized early foundations for good social relations, and support for creativity. (Years later, when an aggressive teacher in Bombay accusingly challenged me with the question "Why don't your American teachers follow Madame Montessori?" I commented, "Madame Montessori is your Goddess, John Dewey is our God.")

In other words, their confidence in social change was rooted in many factors. The drive to "make the world better" was energized by deep Judeo-Christian ethical values. The religious families of the Allports, the Murphys, the Newcombs and the Quaker Tolmans, among others, were humanitarian, not radical. The promise of progress implied in the theory of evolution learned in college, the visions of a good life that fired the experiments of Robert Owen and other visionaries, and the success of some labor unions in winning a decent wage for their members all supported dreams of positive social change.

In New York of the twenties Goodwin Watson, Theodore Newcomb, and Gardner and I were attending the lectures of Ernest Scott on "the social gospel" of the brotherhood of man, and of Harry F. Ward on the Christian ethic, at Union Theological Seminary. The National Council of churches, a liberal Protestant organization, as well as specific groups such as the Methodist Federation for Social Service (of which Harry Ward and my father, Wade Crawford Barclay, were leaders) based their political and social policies on the credo of "the brotherhood of man."

In the SPSSI's fiftieth anniversary issue of the *Journal of Social Issues* (June 1986) E.R. Hilgard briefly reviewed related organizations active during the thirties: the Student Christian Movement, the World Student Christian Federation, and the student YMCAs and YWCAs (of which two later presidents of SPSSI, Rensis Likert and E.R. Hilgard, were presidents while they were undergraduates at the universities of Michigan and Illinois). Concerns about poverty, race prejudice, and peace were central to the work of these organizations.

Hilgard also described the role of the liberal National Council on Religion in Higher Education, which provided Kent Fellowships for able college graduates to study at certain liberal divinity schools and also to work in other fields such as philosophy. Among SPSSI presidents, Likert, D. Cartwright and Hilgard had been Kent Fellows and maintained continued friendships with other Kent Fellows. They formed a network of individuals with deep social concerns, many of whom became influential in other organizations. Although Gardner had not been a Kent Fellow he found kindred spirits in this group, which was also linked to such members of the Teachers College faculty as George Hartmann and Goodwin Watson. For all of these young psychologists the social philosophy of liberalism or progressivism was also fortified by the literature of social criticism of the time and the socialistic politics of LaFollette as well as liberal magazines like *The Nation* and *The New Republic.* The Depression stimulated some liberals to become radical out of their disappointment with democracy.

Gardner and I were both concerned about the widespread unemployment in the thirties. I was taking Sarah Lawrence College psychology students into New York to see the packing-box shacks in which men were living, to a loft where a club of unemployed men met, and to Harlem to see the miserable living conditions in apartments, where huge rats were wallowing in garbage in the courtyard. I shared all these experiences with Gardner, describing what we saw on our trips. Young psychologists were among the unemployed during the Depression and felt strongly that something had to be done about the situation.

In Chicago, a brilliant young psychologist, Isadore Krechevsky (later, David Krech) began to relate his failure to get an academic job not only to the difficult times, but also to an unenlightened society. He joined a new organization, New America, founded in 1934 by the leftist Harry F. Ward, by then retired from his ministry. Other members were Selden Rodman, an activist in John Dewey's League for Independent Political Action, and Goodwin Watson, a student of Dewey's as well as Ward's.

The psychologist Ross Stagner was also unemployed in Chicago at the time and he, with Krech and others, circulated a petition asking the American Psychological Association (APA) to respond to the unemployment. This led the APA to appoint a Committee on Standard Requirements for the Ph.D. in Psychology, which discussed the desirability of finding ways of "straining out weak brothers and sisters" (who do not have an adequate background in the natural sciences). A new concern about the possibility "that professional psychological service can make increasing contributions to community life" was included in the instructions to the committee chairman, A.T. Poffenberger, in 1934, but he reported that the committee did not touch this task, believing that "to tamper too much with the laws of supply and demand even in psychology may be a precarious business." Younger psychologists in New York

formed the Psychologists League protesting this view, and agitated for federal
support for unemployed psychologists through the Works Progress Administration (WPA). The League continued through the thirties to agitate for
expansion of WPA employment for psychologists, publishing a series of proposals for the greater employment of psychologists in the schools, courts,
clinics, and institutions.

After extended efforts at the 1935 Midwestern Psychological Association
meetings, more petitions were sent out, again asking the APA to respond to
the unemployment situation. By the time of the 1936 APA convention, with
the persistent efforts of the Psychologists League, the New America
psychologists, and the Association of Consulting Psychologists, a resolution
was passed commissioning a joint committee of those organizations to consider
the feasibility of working out ways and means of increasing the opportunities
for psychological service in education, social service, business and industry.
Meantime, Krech and two other New America psychologists at the University
of Chicago placed an ad in the *American Guardian,* asking psychologists to respond who were interested in the "important contemporary problems of social
and economic change."

At the 1936 APA convention at Dartmouth College in Hanover, New
Hampshire, the movement jelled. Ross Stagner chaired a meeting at which the
Society for the Psychological Study of Social Issues (SPSSI) was founded; Good-
win Watson was elected chairman and David Krech, secretary-treasurer. Gard-
ner was the second chairman. The initial Council of SPSSI included Gardner,
Gordon Allport, E.R. Hilgard and Edward Tolman, who were known as lib-
erals, along with a number of radicals—George Hartmann, Horace English,
Ross Stagner, Leonard Doob, and J.F. Brown, an avowed independent Marxist.
The founding of SPSSI was of great importance to a large and growing group
of psychologists.

According to Hilgard, "Gardner's efforts at keeping the Society objective
are noted by citing the fact that he (with Ted Newcomb) had later deleted from
the Industrial Psychology Yearbook a polemic against Communism from the
socialist standpoint by George Hartmann." The stress that many APA members
had suffered was combined at this meeting with the reformist spirit to create
an organization that enabled psychologists to contribute to human welfare by
bringing relevant scientific research and analytical thinking to bear on issues
such as how to deal with the causes of war, industrial conflict, social injustice,
and the defense of intellectual freedom.

Shortly after our 1932 visit to Germany to adopt a delightful baby girl
from an orphanage in Cologne, Hitler came into power. We were worried
about the comments of some of our friends there, that Hitler was "doing some
good things for Germany." Gardner saw clearly that Hitler was an evil man,
and we felt forebodings, although I doubt that we realized until later that all
of Europe and the United States as well would be embroiled in the coming war.

World War I had left Gardner with a passionate commitment to peace. Daniel Katz, another leader in SPSSI, wrote me that he thought it was Gardner who stimulated the formation of an SPSSI committee on war and peace. When this committee abandoned its book, as a result of problems resulting from the entrance of the United States into the war after Pearl Harbor and of disagreements between its members, Gardner was asked to take responsibility for a book on peace.

Since Gardner's book, *Human Nature and Enduring Peace,* was prepared at the request of SPSSI after the collapse of the first plan for a book on the psychology of peace and war, it is important to look at what happened to the earlier effort. A committee chaired by Ross Stagner included J.F. Brown, Ralph K. White and Ralph Gundlach. Their book was conceived as a synthesis — to be prepared by the committee — of views on war and peace of outstanding authorities in the fields of political science, economics, history and sociology. Other chapters would compare opinions of such experts on the causation of war with the opinions of people at different economic levels and in different occupations. Questions of nationalism, diplomatic policies and economic relationships would be a major concern, and it was also believed necessary to evaluate the roles of such motives as the desire for excitement, for glory, and for adventure. The issues of motivation for peace, why peace movements have failed, and why international propaganda has been unsuccessful would also need attention. Following this would be a study of the process of conversion of aggressive nationalism into specific kinds of militaristic activity. The psychology of wartime, including war neurosis and morale breakdown, the effects of war — including revolution and depression associated with the end of war — would constitute another section.

Hilgard and Newcomb agree that after that book was abandoned, "Gardner was selected to do the yearbook *Human Nature and Enduring Peace* to represent the mainstream liberalism of SPSSI as against its radicalism, while also reflecting the respect with which he was held in the psychology of personality and in social psychology." His writing was respected, as was his liberal stance, which rejected the dictatorship of Communism as well as that of Hitler, consistently defended the need for protection of human rights, justice, and political democracy, and stressed cooperation among nations as well as between labor and management.

There were 53 collaborators in the *Human Nature and Enduring Peace* book planned by Gardner. He decided to direct specific questions to this large group of psychologists and social scientists, requesting answers of 100 to 500 words. Approximately half of the group were friends or acquaintances known through Gardner's activities in the American Psychological Association. Others included writers on issues related to war and peace. Under the pressure of concern created by the war, all of those who were asked to respond cooperated. Gardner organized the contributions, wrote comments on many of them, inserted transition passages and, in addition, wrote the first six chapters and three of the last five, "though in his modesty he does not designate their authorship," as Hilgard commented.

He consulted the original committee at times, but the large task of making a book out of these varied, mostly short pieces, was done by him alone between 1941 and 1944. Eugene L. Hartley, Edwin B. Newman and Ralph K. White were appointed to serve as the Committee of Editorial Review; Ernest R. Hilgard, chairman, wrote the preface, which reviewed the principles of scientific inquiry governing publication of yearbooks of the Society for the Psychological Study of Social Issues. Katz emphasized that to his knowledge "there were none of the hassles in the production of *Human Nature and Enduring Peace* such as those often associated with a large cooperative venture."

Gardner's initial chapters dealt with "the 'raw material' of which war is made," frustration as a cause of war, the struggle for gain, power, and prestige, the loaded world-view, and strategy against war. He addressed questions on "obstacles to peace" to psychologists and social scientists qualified to discuss problems of Germany, Japan, and other trouble-spots. Other questions directed at a possible positive program dealt with issues of world order, world-minded education, the practicality of democracy, the role of the churches, public opinion and world order, and the "moral equivalent of war." Gardner's three chapters in the final part described a continuing program toward world order. He also worked on the final chapter, which contained "The Psychologists' Manifesto," a statement on human nature and peace presenting ten basic principles that should be considered in planning the peace. Sixty percent of the nearly 4000 psychologists to whom the statement was sent with an appeal for signatures responded, and, of these, 99 percent concurred and signed the Manifesto. This statement was prepared in the summer of 1944 by a group, many of whom had contributed to the book, so that the Manifesto presents the essence of the findings of the book.

HUMAN NATURE AND THE PEACE
A STATEMENT BY PSYCHOLOGISTS

Humanity's demand for lasting peace leads us as students of human nature to assert ten pertinent and basic principles which should be considered in planning the peace. Neglect of them may breed new wars, no matter how well-intentioned our political leaders may be.

1. *War can be avoided: War is not born in men; it is built into men.*
   No race, nation, or social group is inevitably warlike. The frustrations and conflicting interests which lie at the root of aggressive wars can be reduced and redirected by social engineering. Men can realize their ambitions within the framework of human co-operation and can direct their aggressions against those natural obstacles that thwart them in the attainment of their goals.

2. *In planning for permanent peace, the coming generation should be the primary focus of attention.*

Children are plastic; they will readily accept symbols of unity and an international way of thinking in which imperialism, prejudice, insecurity, and ignorance are minimized. In appealing to older people, chief stress should be laid upon economic, political, and educational plans that are appropriate to a *new* generation; for older people, as a rule, desire above all else, better conditions and opportunities for their children.

3. *Racial, national, and group hatreds can to a considerable degree, be controlled.*

Through education and experience people can learn that their prejudiced ideas about the English, the Russians, the Japanese, Catholics, Jews, Negroes, are misleading or altogether false. They can learn that members of one racial, national, or cultural group are basically similar to those of other groups, and have similar problems, hopes, aspirations, and needs. Prejudice is a matter of attitudes, and attitudes are to a considerable extent a matter of training and information.

4. *Condescension toward "inferior" groups destroys our chances for a lasting peace.*

The white man must be freed of his concept of the "white man's burden." The English-speaking peoples are only a tenth of the world's population; those of white skin only a third. The great dark-skinned populations of Asia and Africa, which are already moving toward a greater independence in their own affairs, hold the ultimate key to a stable peace. The time has come for a more equal participation of all branches of the human family in a plan for collective security.

5. *Liberated and enemy peoples must participate in planning their own destiny.*

Complete outside authority imposed on liberated and enemy peoples without any participation by them will not be accepted and will lead only to further disruptions of the peace. The common people of all countries must not only feel that their political and economic future holds genuine hope for themselves and for their children, but must also feel that they themselves have the responsibility for its achievement.

6. *The confusion of defeated people will call for clarity and consistency in the application of rewards and punishments.*

Reconstruction will not be possible so long as the German and Japanese people are confused as to their status. A clear-cut and easily understood definition of war-guilt is essential. Consistent severity toward those who are judged guilty, and consistent official friendliness toward democratic elements, is a necessary policy.

7. *If properly administered, relief and rehabilitation can lead to self-reliance and co-operation; if improperly, to resentment and hatred.*

Unless liberated people (and enemy people) are given an opportunity to work in a self-respecting manner for the food and relief they receive, they are likely to harbor bitterness and resentment, since our bounty will be regarded by them as unearned charity, dollar imperialism, or bribery. No people can long tolerate such injuries to self-respect.

8. *The root-desires of the common people of all lands are the safest guide to framing a peace.*

Disrespect for the common man is characteristic of fascism and of all forms of tyranny. The man in the street does not claim to understand the complexities of economics and politics, but he is clear as to the general directions in which he wishes to progress. His will can be studied (by adaptations of the

public-opinion poll). His expressed aspirations should even now be a major
guide to policy.
   9. *The trend of human relationships is toward ever wider units of collective
      security.*
      From the caveman to the twentieth century, human beings have formed larger
      and larger working and living groups. Families merged into clans, clans into
      states, and states into nations. The United States are not forty-eight threats to
      each other's safety; they work together. At the present moment the majority
      of our people regard the time as ripe for regional and world organization and
      believe that the initiative should be taken by the United States of America.
  10. *Commitments now may prevent post-war apathy and reaction.*
      Unless binding commitments are made and initial steps taken now, people
      may have a tendency after the war to turn away from international problems
      and to become preoccupied once again with narrower interests. This regres-
      sion to a new post-war provincialism would breed the conditions for a new
      world war. Now is the time to prevent this backward step, and to assert
      through binding action that increased unity among the people of the world
      is the goal we intend to attain.

   The procedure Gardner followed in working on *Human Nature and Enduring Peace* was in line with his January 1938 comments as chairman: "The
main activities now in progress relate to the preparation of the Yearbooks....
[The Yearbook Committees] expect to be given not only moral support, but
active collaboration from all who can give the time. *The collaboration of social
scientists other than psychologists is clearly imperative* if the work is to be
thoroughly adequate from the point of view of history, sociology, economics,
government, etc...." (italics added). Gardner's multidisciplinary orientation,
already clear in his teaching, was crucially important for his own yearbook. And,
basic to his commitment, he added he felt that questions of scientific research
and questions of action relevant to the world scene were equally important.
   He commented on the interesting and significant studies of motives,
values, interests, and attitudes that are not published promptly or at all, and
the value of prompt publication to prevent others from getting into blind
alleys. "Following Watson's address on 'Orientation' last September, we have
wondered how we could avoid getting caught in the morasses of the petty,
trivial and ephemeral, and to catch from one another the big insights which
will give us a really formidable mass of trenchant ideas and vital applications."
His emphasis on cooperation may have facilitated the cooperative work of
various groups in wartime research.
   In line with some of these suggestions, reports of ongoing studies were included in the SPSSI Bulletin of January 1938. Gardner described studies by doctoral candidates at Columbia whom he was supervising and also the long-term
study he was conducting with Rensis Likert. Eleven other studies of attitudes
dealt with relationships of students' attitudes to parents, changes in attitudes
during college, differences in attitudes of students in liberal arts, science and
commerce programs, as well as a study of attitude formation.

Daniel Katz wrote me that Gardner "was a leading spirit in planning SPSSI volumes on *Social Change* and on *Persistence to Change* — volumes which were abandoned with the outbreak of war." Katz also remembered sitting in SPSSI Council meetings exchanging guilty glances with Ruth Tolman as Gardner made suggestions about "What should be done to reach the goals to which we had given lip service. In the early days Gardner, Krech and Goodwin Watson represented the spirit of SPSSI and blazed the trail for the rest of us. Gardner contributed at three levels: on an ideological plane in formulating the ideals of equity and social justice; at the intellectual level of analysis and program planning, and at the pragmatic level of activities for implementing programs."

Katz also recalled Gardner's "wisdom about social change in the thirties when revolutionary doctrines were popular. His insights into the nature of Stalinism were on target long before most liberals knew what was going on." Clearly Gardner's leadership in SPSSI was a potent force stimulating the study of political and social attitudes in the late thirties and in the following years. "He was perceived by many of the SPSSI members as the very model of a social psychologist, and our confidence in his judgment was confirmed in the gentle way he went about smoothing out disputes as well as suggesting constructive approaches to problems of making SPSSI optimally effective," wrote Ross Stagner.

The first meeting at which research papers on social issues could be read and discussed was at the APA convention in Columbus in 1938. This was SPSSI's first public appearance and the revered chairman of the psychology department at Columbia and 1914 APA president, Robert S. Woodworth, was chairman of that meeting. Among the seven papers read were: Ross Stagner's "Analysis of Public Opinion and the Prevention of War," S.S. Sargent's "Emotional Stereotypes in the *Chicago Tribune* — A Study of Newspaper Propaganda Arousing Standardized Emotional Reactions In Readers" and O.H. Mowrer's "Authoritarianism vs. Self-Government in the Management of Children's Aggressive (Anti-social) Reaction as Preparation for Citizenship in a Democracy."

While Gardner had urged that SPSSI members work on important problems, it was not clear how social psychological findings could be effectively applied. The four planned yearbooks were aimed at a general audience and in 1945 the *Journal of Social Issues* was established with a policy of devoting each issue to a single social problem. The *Journal* helped to educate the public. In a few cases, findings were used in governmental hearings, as when the studies of desegregation were made available for use by the Supreme Court. Some members of SPSSI have had contacts with Congress; for instance, during the Vietnam War Ralph White's SPSSI-sponsored study of perceptual factors contributing to that war was circulated by Senator William Fulbright to all members of the Senate Foreign Relations Committee.

When Otto Klineberg became executive secretary of SPSSI he consulted with private agencies, governmental bureaus, and the United Nations. Conferences were held at the 1952 APA convention in Washington, D.C., to provide opportunities for representatives of several federal agencies and social psychologists to discuss possible contributions of psychology to current government problems. In the sixties, I, along with Susan W. Grey and other SPSSI members, participated in planning and implementing Head Start and Parent-Child Centers; I presented an account of Head Start functioning to a congressional committee hearing in 1969, in addition to preparing 10 booklets, *Caring for Children,* for use in Head Start.

In other words, Gardner's hope and push as the second chairman of SPSSI, to see scientific studies contribute to the solution of social problems and to see SPSSI members working on such problems, has been to some degree fulfilled. His contribution to the goals of SPSSI was recognized by the Kurt Lewin Memorial Award in 1953 (following George Brock Chisholm, Edward C. Tolman, Gordon Allport, Tavistock Institute of Human Relations, and Gunnar Myrdal; Margaret Mead and Otto Klineberg received the award later).

A core group of psychologists who were also liberals or progressives were active in related organizations during the late thirties and forties. Gardner and Gordon Allport of Harvard, together with Barbara Burks of the University of California, helped to bring refugees from Nazism to the United States and to find positions for them. Edward Tolman, Gordon Allport and Gardner were friends who worked together during this period as officers of the American Psychological Association. Undoubtedly the established leaders of this group, their close rapport with each other contributed strength to the new organizations concerned with putting psychology to work in the service of human needs. "In SPSSI Gardner was clearly a leader because of his compassion for people who were suffering during the depression years . . . without being identified with 'radical' movements," according to E.R. Hilgard.

Influenced by Gardner's World War I background, and our glimpse of Hitler's intentions on our 1932 trip to Germany, we viewed the 1940 German blitzkrieg across the low countries as handwriting on the wall. My brother, Gordon Barclay, did not wait for Pearl Harbor—he enlisted, soon becoming an adjutant general, while the rest of us worried. Gardner's own efforts were focussed on SPSSI and his work on *Human Nature and Enduring Peace,* looking to the future. He also made at least one speech at a War Bond rally, and as some of his students wrote me, kept in close touch with them when they were overseas. The SPSSI responded to the times by creating the Committee for National Morale, which helped to define roles for social psychologists in the campaign for war preparedness and undertook to develop a national morale "consciousness" among social psychologists. Gordon Allport introduced Goodwin Watson's volume *Civilian Morale* in the first chapter with the observation that not until the summer of 1940 did "morale" become "the theme of countless lectures, conferences, articles."

In the early years of SPSSI, democratic liberals worked side by side with their more radical colleagues. Although Gardner was never a "fellow-traveller" participating in any Communist activity, this cooperative stance probably helped to make him suspect, along with other liberal psychologists. E.R. Hilgard wrote, "These charges of 'suspicious organizations' against Gardner were ridiculous. I later suffered some of the same charges that led temporarily to my dismissal from the National Advisory Mental Health Council."

It is odd that people did not realize that the presence of strong liberal democrats in an organization along with radical psychologists could have the effect of limiting the influence of the latter. An example is the conflict that developed over that first war/peace book written by a committee that included two Stalinists and two anti–Stalinists. "Some of the debates were hot and heavy," wrote Ross Stagner, and the four had to work through the areas of difference until they could find points on which they agreed. There is no evidence that the anti–Stalinists were dominated by the Stalinists. The possibility that anti–Stalinists could hold their own against Stalinists, or in-fluence them, apparently never occurred to the guardians of our national security who later withdrew Gardner's security clearance. Gardner's passion for fairness and democracy included a deep respect not only for free speech but for freedom of thought. While he inspired students with his democratic alter-native to Marxism, certain superficial similarities between some of his philosophical-value formulations and some of those of the extreme left (who deceptively tried to protect themselves) may have contributed to suspicions of security-minded officials in the tense, anxious period of World War II. When Georgene Seward's loyalty was questioned and specific reference was made to her relationship to Gardner, she replied that he could never have adopted Communism because he would never let anyone do his thinking for him.

In view of the danger to the constitutional foundation for democracy, Gardner's security problem needs to be reviewed here. When E.R. Hilgard resigned as of August 31, 1943, as SPSSI representative on the Emergency Com-mittee in Psychology of the National Research Council (NRC), Gardner was ap-pointed to succeed him. On March 28, 1944, Karl M. Dallenbach, chairman of the NRC, wrote to Theodore Newcomb, secretary of SPSSI, that at the last meeting of the Emergency Committee it was voted that SPSSI be notified

> that because of failure of continuation of clearance of its nominee, the Emergency Committee is recommending to the National Research Council that Dr. Gardner Murphy's appointment be rescinded . . . [and that SPSSI be] urged to nominate another of its members to serve on the Emergency Committee. . . . The Emergency Committee wishes to go on record that its action does not mean that it concurs in the procedures which seem to make the action necessary. . . . It was with deep regret that the Emergency Committee took it. Dr. Murphy was present when the action was taken and he concurred in it.

Gardner was president of the American Psychological Association at that time.

Since Gardner's liberal and democratic stance and loyal devotion to efforts toward achieving peace were known to many SPSSI members and probably to the Emergency Committee, Dr. Dallenbach assumed that SPSSI would not want to accept this announcement. He added, "Your immediate reaction will probably be not to do that (nominate another member) but I hope that after due consideration you will. If you do not you will only be hurting your colleagues.... The Emergency Committee needs the representative of your society and the point of view your Society represents. If we do not have your representative on the Emergency Committee psychology will be the loser." Rensis Likert was appointed to take the place vacated by Gardner. Apparently there was no opportunity for a hearing in which Gardner's loyal stance could easily be vindicated by scores of witnesses, and, since the activities of the FBI were secret, there was no way to know on what basis Gardner was considered a security risk.

Ten years later when a friend wrote him about her difficulty in being allowed clearance, Gardner wrote,

> As Otto Klineberg remarked the other day, a list of the people who can't be cleared would be practically equivalent to a list of Who's Who in American Social Science.... I didn't in fact do any work for the American Committee for Protection of the Foreign Born [which he apparently thought was a factor in the denial of his clearance]. I just gave them a check in response to a specific appeal.... The only hope for an honest person is full light on the facts. That was what I tried to say in a recent letter to the *American Psychologist*.... Sanford tells me that the letters they printed, attacking me from the right and attacking me from the left, were all they received.... There is a legal issue surely, and the Civil Liberties people must surely know what lines of legal redress are open.... I was told at Montreal that Boring was heading a new APA committee looking into defense of psychologists and I have written him asking if there is something to report.

A postscript on that friend's letter mentioned that "You probably know that you are one of the 'bad men' on the S.A. list, along with John Seward, Edward Tolman and others. Any trainee who has had work with any of you has to give an account of himself to the Loyalty Board. Any consultant who has had such contact, is even worse off because he is never given a chance even to do that...."

Not long after this exchange Senator Joseph McCarthy was shamed on live television for his appalling behavior and the McCarthy era was over. But the effects were felt for a decade—the decade of the passivity of college students who seemed to be anxious not to get involved in controversial problems.

After Gardner's death, the Freedom of Information Act made it possible for me to ask what the FBI record on Gardner included. I was told immediately that there was a record on me and my father as well. The record on Gardner included a report on recommendations he had written for colleagues suspected or known to be Communists, and his support for a large number of what the FBI considered suspicious organizations. Gardner's commitment to freedom of speech and of thought was so deep that he never mentioned possible or known Communist affiliations; his recommendations focussed on the scientific integrity and teaching skill of the psychologist about whom he was writing. He repeatedly told me that he tried to avoid support of Communist front organizations (but it was sometimes hard to be certain about an organization's affiliations).

According to the FBI record, Lois Murphy was one of the leaders of Sarah Lawrence College who was either a starry-eyed idealist or a Communist. My father, Wade Crawford Barclay, was under suspicion because he was the leader of a cooperative grocery store in Evanston; a member of the board of the cooperative was believed to be a Communist.

Many of the early SPSSI leaders were confident that science in the form of social psychology research could bring about social reforms. They were as passionate, determined and convinced of their cause as the radicals of the American Communist Party were convinced of theirs. Daniel Katz commented that "Gardner and Krech were both committed to the belief that the discovery of truth through research could get us out of the social dark ages." Research was just as feasible on significant social problems as on the trivial questions with which so many psychologists were occupied.

Katz also noted that Gardner believed it was not enough to look at a single issue that involved the application of social psychology. "It was necessary to dig deep into social processes to get at basic causes." When Katz was named chairman of a committee to prepare a volume on *Resistance to Social Change,* Gardner suggested contributors from a broad spectrum of the social sciences.

It is not unusual for innovative ventures to be ridiculed at first and SPSSI was not exempt from this treatment. Daniel Katz recalled that in the early days SPSSI was a small group of so-called "dedicated damn fools" and there was little competition for roles when, for instance, yearbooks were in preparation. People volunteered or were asked to take on an assignment because of their known interests. Most committees were special purpose committees.

Beginning with concerns about unemployment and labor relations, race relations and prejudice, and war and peace, SPSSI developed eventually into an organization of over 2500 members concerned about human rights, liberties, needs and adaptations. Among the committees authorized by the SPSSI Council for 1943–44 and reported in the February 1944 issue of the SPSSI *Bulletin* was the Post-war Planning Committee, with Gardner Murphy as chairman. Georgene H. Seward was chairman of the SPSSI Committee on Roles of Men and Women in Postwar Society and the Committee on Postwar Planning for Women of the NCWP (National Council of Women Psychologists). Areas of research and analysis have included problems of minorities, women, youth, the aging, and religious and political deviants, and such issues as justice, morals in government, protection of human subjects in research, among many others. Individual members have also been activists in various ways, within and beyond SPSSI. The SPSSI is an expression of concerns that have roots in the needs of the times and in the values of its members, and it is part of a broader trend in which both SPSSI members and other progressives try to meet those needs. In addition to planning socially significant studies and having a direct impact on some governmental decisions, SPSSI is a catalyst, generating an atmosphere in which additional organizations emerge, such as organizations supporting peace efforts, arms control, and a freeze on nuclear weapons.

The Society for the Psychological Study of Social Issues, then, constitutes a dedicated group of psychologists and social scientists who implement principles of concern for human rights and liberties in their living and working situations, and also politically. It is by no means the only organization with this commitment to basic democratic values. The democratic structures of Sarah Lawrence College and Antioch College, the movement in church organizations to accept women as priests, and of course the activist racial and feminist groups all share the movement toward actualization of the American principles of recognition of human rights and liberties, but SPSSI's contribution is distinctive. As a scientific group, SPSSI mobilizes facts about socially relevant areas, and it was through SPSSI that Gardner came closest to a fulfillment of his hope that psychology would contribute to human welfare.

When Gardner received SPSSI's Kurt Lewin Memorial Award in 1953, he gave an address on "Human Potentialities," which Arthur Rosenthal, publisher of Basic Books, urged him to develop into a book by the same title. The book was published in 1958, and was distilled by Norman Cousins of the *Saturday Review* into an article, "A Cosmic Christmas Carol."

In addition to his deep commitment to the SPSSI, Gardner responded to supported efforts to obtain justice for victims of questionable court decisions. He supported efforts to promote peaceful solutions of international and other conflicts, and contributed articles to papers committed to meeting social needs, such as "The Psychological Basis of Democracy" in the *Social Questions Bulletin,* an organ of the Methodist Federation for Social Service.

Gardner's article stated, "With our forefathers on this continent, democracy was a faith. . . . Neither [Jefferson] nor the generation which broke through the Alleghenies into the Great Plains made any explicit use of science in their task of group living." After briefly commenting on the influence of evolutionary theory and on theories of Robert Owen, Saint-Simon, and Marx, he wrote that "thoughtful Americans . . . began to wonder whether the scientific method . . . might not . . . offer a basis for sounder forms of social living." The article then reviewed studies showing the effectiveness of cooperation — eight "boys organized as teams turned out much more and better work than the same boys did on an individualistic basis."

He went on to discuss studies of group thinking, committee work, and social interaction which demonstrated for him that definite laws of cooperative interaction could be defined: "in the group many more ideas arise; constructive criticisms come from the group which never occur to one criticising his own work; and greater flexibility of attack on problems is permitted than can be obtained in individual work." He described the World War II study of Kurt Lewin with Margaret Mead which showed that groups presented the wartime problem of utilizing nonpreferred cuts of meat actually carried out the group decision to make the sacrifice after democratically led discussions, whereas the active response to formal factual lectures was slight. Similarly, group decisions among factory workers resulted in gains in level of production not matched by individual pleading or exhortation.

Gardner cited other studies indicating that democratic leadership contributes to good working levels and good morale: Moreno's studies of the positive effects of congenial group structures in the New York Training School for Girls illustrated his belief in the importance of the scientific contribution to the success of democracy. Among these scientific contributions are the attitudes and opinion studies which led to the clarification of demands of many Americans — as shown now in the demand for a stop to the arms race. In conclusion, he stated that psychological research has begun to show the intense practicality of democracy. The article documents the intensity of Gardner's own commitment to the use of science to make democracy increasingly successful.

Before SPSSI was organized, Braly and Katz (1932) worked on the issue of social stereotypes, and Otto Klineberg carried on pioneer studies of cultural factors affecting intelligence test performance. His 1935 *Race Differences,* written at Gardner's urging and included in his Harper's series, undercut traditional rationales for discrimination against blacks. As noted, several of Gardner's students, including the Horowitzes, the Clarks, and Joan Criswell, all published papers on effects of discrimination and prejudice on children's social behavior and the self-image of black children. In 1945, the first two numbers of the *Journal of Social Issues* were devoted to racial and religious prejudice.

In the sixties, although Gardner was no longer on the Council of SPSSI, he was still providing guidance via correspondence to those who were carrying active responsibilities. To Dr. Isador Chein at New York University, then president of SPSSI, he wrote on August 14, 1962, "I . . . am full of a topic which I believe is important for SPSSI — in fact, of very great urgency indeed." The problem was concerned with Henry Garrett's letter in the *American Psychologist* on the evidence for lower I.Q.'s in blacks than in whites. That letter protested the September 1961 resolution of SPSSI taking exception to a paper Garrett had published earlier that year. In that paper, Garrett had listed five sources which he believed had contributed to the equalitarian view of race differences, but which showed — he thought convincingly — "that Negro-white differences in mental tests are so regular and persistent as strongly to suggest a genetic basis."

Gardner wrote that Otto Klineberg's chapter on race differences in a new book soon to be published would be by far the best way for Chein to answer Henry Garrett.

> It is a well-balanced factual picture of research.... I believe that it is just desperately important for SPSSI to write for the *American Psychologist* a full, clear, fair, honest, and not too high and mighty, reply indicating where the social science position actually lies and avoiding the ad hominem arguments in the strictest possible way. Frankly I thought that the ill temper and the tone of 'now let me teach you something' which appeared both in Henry's [Garrett's] and in your [Chein's] letters were not going to help us at all in reference to the serious issue of making this a factual matter.... Certainly the matter of acknowledging the points that he makes that tell effectively against premature conclusions along equalitarian lines should be given as full consideration as everything else.... [O]ur claims are essentially two—first, that the individual factor is of such massive importance and the group differences so extremely obscure that we would do well to base public policy as far as possible upon the ways of nurturing individual competence, ... second, that ultimate questions of integration and so on ... can be fought out as citizenship problems in terms of a value system which we will explicitly state. ... [I urge you to] see to it that some sort of fair, objective and complete rejoinder to Garrett is prepared where all psychologists could see it, feeling that here is a factual issue in which the social science people really know their stuff and can keep their tempers, and meet honestly all the issues that are still unclear.

It was this persistent pressure for fairness and scientific objectivity that led to the feeling among some members of SPSSI "that SPSSI is the superego of the American Psychological Association but Gardner Murphy is the superego of SPSSI," and also to the feeling of many who wrote me that "Gardner was my ego-ideal."

Gardner's influence in SPSSI was enormously strong because in addition to his formal involvement he was eloquent in expressing a perception opposed to a prevalent view and deeply committed to critical principles about which not everyone was convinced. Ralph K. White has written that 1946 was a time when American gratitude for the Soviet contribution to the struggle against Hitler was fast eroding as the Soviet army took and kept most of eastern Europe. Americans felt that the Soviets were embarking in earnest on the program of world conquest proclaimed in the Communist Manifesto. Ralph White shared that view.

Then, at the 1946 conference of the American Psychological Association, Gardner spoke to a packed auditorium with this message:

> Put yourself in the Russians' place. Suppose our country, the United States, had just been bled white by a great war on our own soil. Suppose an invader had

conquered all of the United States west of the Mississippi, all of the South and at one time had gone almost to Washington. Suppose that after years of desperate struggle we had managed to throw them out. Wouldn't we be tempted to make sure that in another such war the Mexicans and Canadians would not be against us?

Most Americans, White continued, were ignoring this fact; no one else had the insight and the guts to empathize with our potential enemy. This made such a profound impression on Ralph White that it deeply influenced his thinking from that time on; Gardner's emphasis on empathy was "the essence" of White's chapter on the Soviet people's image of themselves, and of us, in the landmark book *International Behavior,* edited by H. Kelman, and of White's 1983 book, *Fearful Warriors: A Psychological Profile of U.S.-Soviet Relations,* as well as his articles on similar themes. A new organization of political psychology grew out of the increasing empathic awareness that developed in the next few years.

Another example of Gardner's direct influence on the side of human values was recalled by Ted Newcomb.

> [In] a typical, and unforgetable, event in New York over a 48-hour session in what was then the Pennsylvania Hotel, the clinical members of APA, together with some nonmembers were threatening to create a rival organization. Forty-odd APA members were invited to what turned out to be a critical decision. Until then the purposes of APA were described as follows: "The object of the APA shall be to advance psychology as a science." Gardner argued eloquently, passionately and effectively, that we should add the phrase "and as a means of promoting human welfare." The latter phrase remains, today, exactly in his wording. He was not the only one to advocate this, but it was he who turned the tide.

At the fiftieth anniversary of the founding of the Society for Psychological Study of Social Issues, in 1986, Otto Klineberg reflected on the role of SPSSI in the 1954 desegregation decision of the Supreme Court. He was in Paris at the time, a member of the secretariat of UNESCO, and on the day after the decision, as the local representative of the social sciences, he received dozens of calls of congratulation from UNESCO colleagues — who may not have known of his personal contributions nearly a quarter of a century earlier. Klineberg felt that SPSSI helped to provide an atmosphere of acceptance among social scientists. More specifically, psychologists who testified at the trials preceding the Supreme Court decision "included at least six former presidents of SPSSI [including Gardner] as well as others who participated in SPSSI activities." Klineberg was involved when he was consulted by a member of the Legal Defense Fund about the possible use of social science material, and he reported Kenneth Clark's analysis of relevant research presented at the 1950 White House Conference on Children. "This lawyer, R.L. Carter, and Judge Thurgood Marshall contacted Clark, and what followed is history."

The fact that seeds for understanding the effects of racism that were nurtured by Gardner and his students in the 1930s have contributed to progress toward justice and equality is illustrated by Otto Klineberg's summary of important publications not only by SPSSI members but also by nonpsychologists. Klineberg's chapter on race and psychology, published in the UNESCO *Courier* in 1977 and translated into 15 languages, received international publicity. In that chapter he mentioned that programs planned to teach specific skills, problem-solving and thinking have had a substantially positive influence on the performance of disadvantaged children. The success of educated middle-class blacks is visible on every television network, although black ghettos still perpetuate malnutrition in mothers, and premature babies at risk for compromised development. National organizations, private and government funded, are at work to correct this. In 1975, members of SPSSI continued their involvement in this area. Responding to the series of publications on the inferiority of blacks by A.R. Jensen, they wrote and published *Genetic Destiny: Scientific Controversy and Social Conflict* as their answer to Jensen's position.

Klineberg felt that in psychological terms, the study of race relations was related to international relations; both "use the dehumanization of the 'enemy'" to justify their actions. Nonpsychologists are now using psychological reports in their own writing about both race and international relations. For example, in 1900 Richard Kluger—a former journalist and editor—published *Simple Justice: The History of Brown v. the Board of Education and Black America's Struggle for Equality,* in which he included a complete account of the testimony presented by psychologists and other social scientists that prepared the way for the Supreme Court hearings. These publications are evidence of the process of diffusion in which Gardner placed his hope for progress.

14. Creating a Psychology Department at City College

Brief accounts of Gardner's work typically state that he was chairman of the psychology department at the City College of New York from 1940 to 1952. This is true as far as it goes, but it does not convey the actual experience of that time. His presence enhanced the status of City College and made an unexpected contribution to the graduate student population in psychology, and he initiated a distinguished graduate program in clinical psychology at City College. The new position also gave him more opportunity for research, writing, outside lectures and work at the American Society for Psychical Research as well as the Society for Psychological Study of Social Issues and the American Psychological Association.

John Peatman, an assistant professor in the joint philosophy-psychology department at City College, was instrumental in the move from Columbia. He occasionally took a train at the 125th Street Station going home to Larchmont when Gardner was taking a parallel train going home to Bronxville, and they met on the platform. Gardner found the young psychologist congenial and in the course of their conversations, Peatman became aware that Gardner was heavily burdened. In his eleventh year as an assistant professor and chairman of the Columbia College division, he was teaching and supervising dissertations in the Graduate division as well. In the winter of 1940 Peatman asked Gardner whether he would come to City College if a full professorship could be worked out for him. Gardner said that he would consider it.

A change was then under way at City College; the psychologists were discontented in the philosophy department, which then included psychology. The decrease in the number of philosophy students resulted in the assignment of philosophers to teach the elementary psychology courses. Peatman led the way to separate psychology from philosophy and to make psychology an independent department, and his suggestion that they import Gardner as chairman was enthusiastically received.

At the same time appointment of a new philosophy professor, Bertrand Russell, had been given a unanimous recommendation from the department and the president, and had been approved by the Board of Education. But Bertrand Russell's appointment was rescinded by the New York Supreme Court. Bishop Manning of New York, who was a member of the Board of Higher Education, had protested the appointment, citing Russell's "scandalous" book *Marriage and Morals*. Moreover, a taxpayer had brought a suit before the court; she was fearful that Russell would seduce a daughter. Mayor LaGuardia simply voided the budget line. Gardner wrote a letter of protest, "but LaGuardia didn't even see fit to answer me." Gardner's courage in defending free speech was to create trouble for him later, but his work at City College began in an atmosphere warm with excitement at the establishment of the psychology department with the internationally distinguished chairman they were so delighted to have.

Advantages for Gardner in moving to another college in New York City, instead of accepting an appointment in other institutions which had offered invitations, were that our two children could remain in their superb Bronxville school and we could remain in our much enjoyed ample home in Bronxville. It was large enough for visits from friends and members of each of our families; it welcomed frequent visits by his widowed mother who was emotionally very dependent on him. I could retain my happy position at Sarah Lawrence College, which Gardner appreciated and enjoyed almost as much as I did. And last, but not least, we would still be in reach of the museums, concerts and operas in New York, which meant a great deal to us.

The only transitory doubt Gardner expressed had to do with the status of City College, little known at that time outside of New York. Gardner himself was widely respected in the profession and deeply committed to the development of psychology as a science; he wondered momentarily whether this move would diminish his influence. I assured him that his status was part of him and would go with him. Actually, according to many psychologists, his presence there immediately raised the status of CCNY. At that time he was in his third year as a member of the Council of the American Psychological Association; and by 1944 he was president of the Association, after his 1941–1942 presidency of the Eastern Psychological Association. He had already been president of the Society for Psychological Study of Social Issues (1938–39) and his leadership in that group continued along with his preparation of the third yearbook of the Society. His problems during the forties were not those of status but of security risks, since his liberal stance and peace activities led to suspicions by the FBI.

After Gardner became chairman of the department, the program expanded; courses in experimental psychology and physiological psychology as well as Gardner's yearlong sequence in developmental psychology and personality were added. Gardner "tried to develop a department with a broad scope, with support for every kind of psychology and every kind of systematic method that could be used." And he consciously tried to develop "respect for individuality in teaching, to encourage publishable research, and quality as a psychologist."

The result was stunning both for City College and for psychology in this country; more City College students went into psychology professionally than those of any other psychology department in the United States. Of Gardner's first group of honors students, Roy Schafer, Leo Postman and Harold Proshansky made distinguished contributions to psychology, and Herbert Spohn later became director of research at the Menninger Foundation, occupying Gardner's chair in the eighties.

As the number of students increased, new members of the CCNY psychology faculty were added, and a strong, effective department developed. In his original negotiations with the college administration Gardner had stipulated that he would need $10,000 to set up a suitable laboratory for experimental psychology and this was readily granted. He gave Joseph Barmack the responsibility for the laboratory, and provided support without pressure.

Gardner himself undertook — in his honors seminar — experiments on the influence of drive on perception and memory. He had been excited by Nevitt Sanford's study of the influence of need on perception, in which experimental subjects deprived of food for varying lengths of time had interpreted ambiguous pictures in terms of food; the longer the deprivation, the greater the tendency to find food in the pictures. That gave Gardner an idea he tried out with Robert Levine as experimenter. Drawings of food objects, household utensils like brooms, and meaningless geometrical designs were presented behind a ground-glass screen which showed only a vague contour behind it. Levine found that the longer the subjects had been without a meal, the more the subjects thought they saw things good to eat. This led to a variety of ideas for studying the influence of affect on perception. In another experiment, with Harold Proshansky, it appeared that simple lines appeared longer when small rewards were handed out. This suggested that the organization of the perceptual field — the tendency to emphasize one aspect of what is seen and to relegate the rest to the background — could be studied experimentally. A simple test for this process was made by drawing a curving line through a circle in such a way as to produce two interlocking faces, crude as they were. The faces were separated, and shown to the student subject one at a time; a little money was handed to the student as he looked at one face and taken away as he looked at the other. When the faces were combined so that the subject could see either one, the rewarded face was usually seen. This implied that the individual tends to perceive what has been gratifying and to shut out that which has been associated with the disagreeable.

Leo Postman participated in these studies and continued further experimentation with Jerome Bruner; they focussed on the relation of value to perception and developed more sophisticated methods. In addition they called this type of research the New Look at perception—a new look which Gardner always insisted began with Nevitt Sanford's study of the influence of food-deprivation on perception. In the fifties, Gardner continued this line of investigation, which he now viewed as the problem of perceptual learning.

Barmack remembered that early in 1942 Gardner first submitted a request to the CCNY president for a master's degree program, and repeated the request later in that year, and again a year later with the justification that World War II had created an acute shortage of psychologists in the military services and in civilian life. In June of 1944 the Board of Higher Education authorized a limited amount of graduate work and in 1945, Bruno Klopfer offered a series of courses on the Rorschach; in 1946 two courses by the internationally known organismic neurologist Kurt Goldstein, were added. At the same time, the Education Committee of the New York Psychoanalytic Institute agreed to a year's course in psychoanalytic theory by our friends Ernst Kris and René Spitz, and I gave a full year course in normal personality development.

In 1946 a full M.A. program in clinical psychology was initiated. Forty students applied and six were accepted for matriculation. The group applying included 14 students with Ph.D.'s, one M.D., one Ed.D. and others who already had an M.A. degree. It attracted students from around the world and members of teaching staffs of Princeton, Delaware, New York University, Rochester and other institutions. The program operated on a financially self-sustaining basis, with small fees. The distinguished faculty were more interested in sharing their disciplines in this pioneer clinical program than in getting high salaries—their primary source of income was elsewhere.

Morale was high within that teaching group and also in the college; some of the undergraduate faculty participated in research with thesis candidates, since the part-time faculty of the program could not undertake this added responsibility.

Modest as always, Gardner gave the entire credit for this program to Barmack, who handled the administration of it; the original effort and the involvement of our friends as faculty were Gardner's no small contribution, and Barmack felt that "there really is no way of representing adequately the power and importance of Gardner Murphy's contribution to the development of the department," including the honors seminars attended by both faculty and students. Of the people who received Ph.D.'s in psychology in the United States in 1949, the largest number had received undergraduate training at CCNY and this position was maintained into the 1970s. In other words, a momentum developed which continued.

Gardner was the first to credit the special situation of City College. At that time many major universities and medical schools had small quotas for Jewish students. City College in Gardner's day accepted students on a merit basis only. As a public institution, City College offered free tuition, making expenses low at a time when first a depression, then rising inflation created financial difficulties for students. As a result an extraordinary number of highly gifted students applied, students who accepted a great deal of hard work and were well prepared for doctoral studies. Gardner's presence at this crucial time of transition and opportunity ignited fires of enthusiasm that produced an outstanding department. He was conspicuous for awarding credit for their successes to his students and faculty. "He rarely admitted that kudos was due him," according to Ross Stagner.

In interviews with Larry Nyman years after Gardner had left, colleagues reminisced about their own feelings in regard to Gardner's presence at City College. Milton Smith had been a psychologist in the philosophy department at CCNY before 1940. He felt that "getting Gardner to City College was one of the luckiest things that ever happened to the department. Gardner was a genius and a lovely person. He inspired loads of brilliant students to come to City College and take courses with him." Barmack was also excited that Gardner gave him the responsibility to develop the laboratories. Part of Gardner's energizing talent lay in his trust in people and his expectations of them. He delegated authority to members of the department relevantly and in a way that stimulated and gratified them.

Kenneth B. Clark, the only black member of the department, felt more than comfortable on the City College staff— "there was a lot of fun, excitement . . . my colleagues were nice people." He found himself "a part of a group of wonderful, warm, very intelligent, very serious, but by no means pedantically serious, people with humor." "They didn't seem to be suffering from the usual professional and personal insecurities that made people competitive or bitchy. I wasn't even aware [of the fact that] I was the only black member of the department."

Clark's first appointment at City College was followed by an invitation to start a department of psychology at Hampton Institute. After Pearl Harbor, he was appointed to the Office of War Information. Because of the lack of government protection for him in the assigned field work in the South, he left the OWI and returned to City College in 1943, where he remained except for one year. He transferred to Queens College in 1946 but found the staff too competitive with too much bickering, and asked Gardner to take him back. "I have to come back. I feel much more comfortable here."

Clark's feeling about the department was echoed by Gertrude Schmeidler, who was invited by Gardner to City College in 1945.

> Its spirit was so different from most other places. . . . There was very much of an "all-for-one and one-for-all" kind of feeling there, non-competitive, friendly, fostered by Gardner's being Chairman, because what he did was try to look out for each individual's interest. . . . [I]nstead of competition, there was a feeling that you were being nurtured and encouraged, pushed to advance in your own most desired direction. Decisions that have been cut and dried at other institutions, such as the formal requirements for majors or for honors work, and the

courses to be offered, were made only after carefully considering various individual students' strengths and weaknesses. When the decision was at variance with existent rules, Murphy was always ready to battle the administration for what would best help the growth of any student. Recognition of special needs became a congenial Department objective.

This pattern of treating students as individuals was basic to the Sarah Lawrence College program and Gardner had been impressed by my reports on it.

Schmeidler also said that he had the same concern for individual staff members, and a remarkable gift for evaluating the skills of each; he would use his own skill first to encourage the development of the potential he saw and then to facilitate its recognition by others. "For one, a clever teacher, he would arrange a publisher's contract for a workbook to make the good teaching ideas available professionally. For another, a clinician, he would arrange entree to psychoanalytic groups and training. For others there were research grants or the opportunity for committee work which would lead to higher professional status." For all there were introductions to those who would stimulate and advance them, and to unexplored areas within or close to psychology that would tie in with their interests. "Each of his colleagues found unexpected and promising directions of growth. This flourishing atmosphere carried over into their teaching and their courses grew each year instead of merely being repeated. Their own excitement about being in a developing field carried over to their students."

In contrast to some departments in other universities there was a notable absence of defensive competitiveness and back biting. Since each member of the department was encouraged and supported there was no need to be envious of anyone else. The morale of the department was high and friendliness was pervasive. Gardner's informality and ready appreciation of the others provided a contagious model.

Gardner employed his City College secretary Henrietta Boettinger to help in his writing during the forties. She remembers taking notes on his history of psychology evening course at the New School for Social Research, and transcribing them; from this evolved his second edition of the *Historical Introduction to Modern Psychology* in 1949. He also dictated sections of his personality book. "He could dictate for three solid hours, barely taking time to catch a breath, from a few notes on a sheet of paper. He could say a great deal in a short time." Even when they were traveling uptown from the New School on 12th Street he would start dictating on the subway—"he could not waste a second." Quoting from Japanese poetry, discussing Indian art, or giving esoteric references, he used graduate students to verify his references and help with his bibliography, she added.

While Gardner felt that there were no great rifts in the City College department comparable to the hostility, however cool, between Warden and

Garrett at Columbia, there were annoyances due to the wartime situation which required many short-range decisions and rescheduling of classes. In general, everyone was on at least one committee and usually the department accepted committee recommendations. The wartime draft affected the student body and the kinds of courses that needed to be offered. There were discussions of how much they could afford to give to war research—some war-related projects did not win a very cordial response.

There were also tensions fanned by the Rapp-Coudert investigations into loyalty which were going on when Gardner went to City College. Promotions were withheld, for instance, from Max Hertzman because he had been seen by informers (who were repentant Communists) at meetings of a secret leftist group. Gardner's position, in writing recommendations, was to report solely on the level of teaching and scientific work without regard to the politics of the psychologist. His support of the leftist R. Tryon, of the University of California, on the ground of his excellent scientific work was cited in FBI records. A psychologist like W. Neff who was openly and obviously a leftist and was fired was met by strong waves of both support and rejection. Gardner sensed residues of this when he lectured at City College in the sixties and again in 1969–70. He was told that some students had never recovered from the assaults on radicalism from 1938 to the early fifties; they feared that the attacks could recur.

During the forties the entire staff was doing outside work, which Gardner neither encouraged nor discouraged. He recognized the impact of inflation on the faculty families and understood their needs. When there were difficulties in getting salary increases he and the dean agreed that four associate professors should be promoted to full professorships, thus automatically increasing their salaries.

With almost a free hand at City College, and total support from Dean Gottschall and President Wright, Gardner developed the department along lines in which he believed. He repeatedly expressed appreciation of the dean and the president—who were "so generous to me and to the department." He felt that the seven hours of teaching along with his administrative respon-sibilities, which included membership on numerous college committees, was a "ridiculously small load." It made possible a substantial amount of time to work on parapsychology at the American Society for Psychical Research and to work on American Psychological Association responsibilities, as well as to devote to his writing. The major contributions in that decade were *Human Nature and Enduring Peace* (1945), *Personality: A Biosocial Approach to Origins and Structure* (1947), and the second edition of the *Historical In-troduction to Modern Psychology* (1949). His book *In the Minds of Men* (1953) reported for the general reader the results of research projects he stimulated on his UNESCO assignment in India in 1950. It was written while he was at City College and published the year after he left. Both of us taught courses at the

William Alanson White Institute of Psychiatry and Gardner taught his social psychology course at Columbia when Otto Klineberg was away.

In the early seventies Nyman conducted a series of brilliant interviews with members of the City College Psychology Department, many of whom had been there when Gardner was chairman; these give a rich picture of the department and the qualities of his leadership. Nyman summarized in a 1983 letter to me his own impression:

> Gardner seemed to have a natural talent for bringing the most 'unexpected' types and views together—and not in a narrow superficial conforming sense—but more with the flair of a great orchestral conductor who gives quiet signals of encouragement to each instrumentalist.
>
> Gardner was an amazing person—in many ways—I have seldom known a person who was able to tie the most complex and diverse ideas together and make them appear to have been inevitably linked. His contributions to the department and college were of such significance (let alone to psychology as a whole) that no one could overstate his role. Gardner's modesty, genuineness, measure a man who knew how to share his talents with his colleagues and students. He made certain positive assumptions about people and the world that he touched. He seemed to assume that people do things well because that is the nature of man—particularly, the academic and scholarly man—I think that some of his modesty evolved with a shyness; other aspects of his modesty were natural ramifications of the nature of events and man. He let his contributions literally speak for themselves and seemed to enjoy and encourage his colleagues' efforts by making sure that they received public acknowledgment.

Larry Plotkin, another member of the City College psychology department, added, "no psychologist trained between 1940 and 1970 was uninfluenced by Gardner's contributions. His lectures held generations of students spellbound."

Although Gardner's twelve years at City College had been extraordinarily productive for the College and for psychology in general, he was profoundly disappointed at his inability to develop a doctoral program which—in early discussions with the president and the dean—he understood they had approved for the future. In 1948, after the master's program had received such wide recognition, he applied to President Wright, who pointed out that the authority for a Ph.D. program had to come from the State Board of Regents. He was reluctant to initiate a request at that time because the Division of Teacher Education was currently undergoing fiscal expansion. Two years later Gardner approached Harry Gideonse who was chairman of the psychology department at Brooklyn College; he thought it might work to apply for two clinical Ph.D. programs, one at City College and one at Brooklyn. This effort failed as well at that time.

Moreover, with the end of the war and the enormous need for clinical help for veterans, returning students preferred to go into clinical psychology and

Gardner could not develop his research seminar again. He began to realize that to try to do serious advanced research there was unrealistic. Finally, he began to consider bids from other institutions, but the overture from the Menninger Foundation—for Gardner to be director of the Research Department—had the most appeal because, and only because, of the research opportunity which he craved. The spring of 1952 was his last semester at City College.

Not only did Gardner have unpressured time to write at City College and time to support experimenters in psychical research, he had the enthusiastic support of the College administration, and a responsive and gifted staff who were also productive. How much the situation there meant to him became clear when in the late fifties he responded warmly to the efforts of his successor as chairman of the department, John Peatman, to develop a Research Institute with Gardner to return as director. The department, the dean and the president all wanted to make this possible, as is clear from correspondence between 1956 and 1960. But the State Board of Education rejected the plan, saying that it would be unfair to the other colleges in the large New York City College system to give City College such an Institute. Some years later a Ph.D. program was actually developed; if this had been possible while Gardner was there, he would not have left City College.

Gardner's feelings about his years at CCNY were expressed in his 1960 letter to Peatman after receiving the Festschrift prepared by Peatman and Eugene Hartley, in the year of his 65th birthday:

> I . . . have thought again with a great deal of satisfaction of our years of personal and professional association and sharing. . . . Naturally, anyone would be grateful for so much warm congratulation on a period of life in which his efforts met with tangible success and with a deep sense of inner gratification in something well worth while done through sharing with his friends. That keystone structure in my life, that experience of helping to build a department and initiate some new educational scientific efforts, will always be very precious to me.

15. New Influences from Europe and New England

It is impossible to think about the years at Columbia University without thinking about the intellectual ferment going on in psychology in the 1930s, although not all psychologists were concerned with this. No other period in American psychology was marked by such dramatic developments as the twenty years before World War II; this was especially true of the intellectual world of the East Coast. Titchener's introspectionism had been superseded by behaviorism, with J.B. Watson as its most aggressive protagonist. The pervasive atmosphere of social change marked by the achievement of votes for women at the end of World War I, the anxieties following the Versailles Treaty, then the Depression, and Hitler's bewildering rise to power, contributed to the widespread readiness to respond to new intellectual stimulation.

The twenties had added to Gardner's "middle of the road" approach new trends in psychoanalysis, anthropology and social sciences. The friendships of the twenties with their intellectual explorations prepared him for further mind-stretching encounters in the thirties, which he saw as a time of tremendous transitions in psychology: "We enjoyed the new in its relation to the old, and the personal in relation to the impersonal." Here we will sketch some of the new intellectual encounters that contributed to Gardner's evolving conception of personality, which he later set forth in lectures on that subject and in his impressive *Personality: A Biosocial Approach to Origins and Structure*.

After Hitler came to power, we met some of the gifted psychoanalysts and Gestalt psychologists within days or even hours after their arrival. Only by sharing Gardner's comments on, along with my memories of, some of these encounters can I convey the intellectual exhilaration of those days, and something of what the creative thinking of the thirties meant to Gardner. He recalled first of all, his earlier contact with Heinrich Klüver, a German psychologist.

> When working on the first edition of the *Historical Introduction to Modern Psychology*, it became evident that the newer developments in German

psychology could not adequately be handled. In particular, the Gestalt movement could not be properly surveyed with a degree of coverage and a kind of skill which the topic manifestly required. Heinrich Klüver, who was then giving intensive research attention to eidetic imagery, proved to be just what we wanted. He was a German scholar with the typical intensive training, both in history and in languages and laboratory sciences as well as philosophy, which would supply the perspective. He took on the job, preparing the appendix to be found in that first edition.

Gardner was overwhelmed by his scholarship and grateful for his contribution.

> We have kept in touch off and on through the years. His exactness as a laboratory scientist was frequently punctuated by gay or caustic little forays in the direction of humor. One of our visits was an occasion of visiting his laboratory at the University of Chicago. Noting the three things for which he thought he might be remembered, all of them were contributions to the histologists' skills in the staining of tissues. It was delightful to know stain-maker and value-theorist rolled up in the same man.

We had both read Charlotte Bühler's accounts of her research on children when we were working on the first edition of *Experimental Social Psychology,* and we were excited at the opportunity to meet her at Barnard in 1931 just before our book went to press. When Gardner congratulated her on her book on small children she replied, "Which one?" He said it was the *Sociological and Psychological Studies of the First Year of Life* and before very long we worked out a good modus vivendi. This was continued at one long conversation in our walk-up apartment on West 121st Street, was maintained by correspondence between Vienna and New York, and then after the years of the Nazi regime in Germany and its final invasion of Austria when she returned to New York there was an attempt to renew acquaintance in the later thirties. "The prima donna atmosphere of that great researcher became embittered somewhat through the experiences in Vienna, and particularly by the difficulty of getting accepted in New York. Attempts to help her to understand what she was up against in an analytically-oriented New York practice of psychiatry and psychology were not very successful." She could not understand why she was not instantly granted all the prerogatives she had enjoyed in Vienna. "But Loees, in Vienna, I had seexty assistants," she complained. She rejected my account of the Rorschach approach. Later, however, when I had administered a Rorschach to her, although she remarked, "I like wallpaper designs better," she seemed to see possibilities. It was interesting later to discover her giving instruction and doing research in Rorschach and later establishing herself as a clinical psychologist in Los Angeles.

One of the most stimulating of the psychologists who came from Germany at the time of Hitler's rise to power was Kurt Lewin. Since he arrived in New York shortly after *Experimental Social Psychology* was published in 1931, it was natural for us to be excited about his approaches to social psychology, and Gardner wrote:

"Kurt Lewin cut a meteoric flight through our experience of personality and social psychology research in the decade from 1932 until his death in 1947." Gardner met him at the Columbia Faculty Club in 1932, as he arrived on our shores from a Germany in which the provincial elections were all already going Nazi; and as he established himself at Stanford, at Cornell, and at Iowa, his studies of dynamics, especially of family and small-group dynamics, made us see what kinds of new methods could be productive in experimental social psychology and what kind of leadership was going to remake the practical psychology of both school and industrial plant.

> His field theory, though far from clearly worked out then or later, was a massive inspiration to us, and we have often felt that our own systematic efforts were close to his. We had the privilege of twice attending the meetings of the dynamic psychologists, or the "topologists" as they were often called, once at Harvard and once at Cornell.

In an interview with Alfred Marrow, Gardner discussed his response to Lewin at length; the topology group assembled by Lewin included other friends of ours, and, as Gardner remembered,

> When Margaret Mead, Edward Tolman, Kurt Koffka, and Erik Erikson, with their quite different approaches, joined in, everything that was said and each response to it would stimulate a new idea. There was no atmosphere of attacking and rejecting, and there was none of the painful conflict often present in discussions of theoretical differences. . . . While the papers were being delivered, Lewin sat quietly in the back of the room, sometimes appearing to be only half listening. But once the discussion began, he was his usual animated self, bursting with ideas, comments, criticisms and encouragement. He was always in good humor; he particularly enjoyed having people disagree with him.

Gardner was "completely captivated by the very charm and convenience, both of the broad conceptualization and of the graphic representations." He continued,

> In fact, in my first efforts to describe my own version of field theory, in a paper which appeared in the *Journal of Social Forces*, embodying what I had offered at the American Psychological Association in 1936, I used planes, surfaces, and subdivided areas in the manner of Kurt. I did not feel that the conception of "psychological space" (or, as Stern put it, "personal space") was well worked out and Kurt and I once had a hot argument as to whether some of his diagrams gave us a sociological picture of persons interacting in a group or whether somehow the life space of each of the persons involved could be adequately represented in this manner.

In the same interview Gardner also remarked to Marrow that one of the most common objections to Lewin's work was that

> he was concerned with present cross-sections of behavior, not with the history of how they came into being. The other main objections were that he had not really shown the nonutility of the reductions of wholes into definable units, that he had neglected individual differences, and that he had not shown that the topological (or any kind of graphic) portrayal of functions was more serviceable than the current verbal and conventional mathematical methods.

Gardner believed that Lewin could certainly have replied to all this: "Look at the new experiments and results which in point of fact did come from the new approach." To this Gardner would have added, "not the new methods alone, and not the specific individual alone, but the field relation of these two — and indeed their relations to the twentieth-century world and to the psychology prevalent in the world — is what gave field theory the vitality and the productiveness it achieved."

Psychologists, as Gardner recalled, "began everywhere to talk about aspiration level in the spirit of Kurt's pupil Hoppe, and the Zeigarnik effect related to memory for completed and uncompleted tasks." It became clear to Gardner that "Lewinian psychology was rapidly elevated to a position of great importance."

We also remembered an especially memorable interchange between Lewin and Harry Murray before the blackboard in Cambridge in 1936. Lewin had been mapping field forces and Murray had been wondering whether qualitative variations among different kinds of forces could be represented. "How do you," said Murray, with chalk in hand, "mark these for qualitative distinctions?"

> "Why, we just use different colored chalks," said Lewin, with those inimitable long fluttering and giggling laughs that endeared him to all who surrounded him. The laugh was often the more welcome if it was at his own expense, and here he subtly enjoyed the chance to press home his advantage, showing that he had not really missed in his field theory the reality of qualitative variations among forces. In our frequent warm personal meetings with him during the 1930s and after the outbreak of the war, he shared with us the intensity of his conviction that social psychology must move into daily community and political reality.

It was after a "topology" conference that Kurt earnestly advised me to give up my interest in psychoanalysis; I did not feel that there was a conflict between Lewinian and psychoanalytic thought. I continued our interest in Kurt's work and I continued to learn more psychoanalysis, and of course Gardner supported my determination.

Gardner tried valiantly to promote Lewin for a position at the New School

of Social Research in New York. But Lewin, the innovator, was too heretical
for Köhler. Köhler's counsel was followed, and in spite of the efforts of Horace
Kallen and Gardner, Lewin was not invited to join the New School faculty.

Not all of our encounters with the émigrés led to close friendships, but
we had a memorable if brief time with another leading German psychologist,
William Stern. We met him almost literally as he got off the boat after Hitler's
rise in 1933. Gardner wrote:

> He had already created a new field, the psychology of testimony, around the
> turn of the century; he had systematically elaborated an applied psychology; he
> had been one of the first and best observers of children, and he had created both
> a philosophy of personalism and a psychological system, personalistics, in which
> each event was seen as the expression of the unique person. Those of us con-
> cerned with the field of psychology of personality could never say quite enough
> regarding this conception of the individual as the true center for all psychological
> processes, a view developed more adequately in this country by Gordon W.
> Allport than by anybody else.
>
> Stern had the presence, the range, the skill, and the power of a great
> psychologist as he talked to us there at the King's Crown Hotel in the Columbia
> neighborhood of New York. As extraordinary accident would have it, Max Wer-
> theimer, a founder of Gestalt psychology, was there too, and under the same cir-
> cumstances. Seldom have we heard anything like the dialogue between the two
> giants—Stern showing the role of the incomplete, the ragged, the confused, the
> empirical reflection of incomplete, flexible, or ever-changing personality, while
> Wertheimer was pleading for the recognition of order, law, principle, the struc-
> tural and functional unity which science must claim.
>
> "But," said Stern, "is there not a place for lack of order or for disorder, as well
> as for order? Is there not un-Gestalt as well as Gestalt?" "Yes," Wertheimer ad-
> mitted, and from that time on as the conversation unrolled we felt that Wer-
> theimer had met his match in the ultimate logic of the directions in which
> psychology must move. It seemed just as likely that the matrix, the ever-flowing
> wellspring from which psychological realities spring, is itself truly un-Gestalt,
> not so very far indeed from what Freud called *Id*, and that range, heights, and
> depths of scientific psychology are an important but not the sole kinds of
> psychology worthy of pursuit.

Continuing to describe the Gestalt group, Gardner wrote:

> Wolfgang Köhler made the rounds of the American universities when the
> Gestalt movement was young in this country right after the First World War, and
> it was a delight to see him in action at Harvard and to keep in touch with him
> later at the University of California, at the Brussels International Congress of
> Psychology, and in between. Our closest contact was the occasion of his giving
> a lecture at City College reporting his new findings on direct currents in the brain
> as related to figural after-effects. City College was especially honored by being
> given this presentation at this time, and we always took it as a personal act of
> generosity.

Rudolf Arnheim, another German Gestalt psychologist, showed up at City College about December 1940, shortly after Gardner moved there, wanting to find a place in an academic department of psychology. We soon found that we had a good deal in common, especially an interest in painting and poetry, in which his highly creative studies always fascinated both of us. His obvious maturity, charm, range of aesthetic and cultural interests, and his practically perfect English, made him easy to place among the many refugees who were coming our way. Partly through my effort, Rudi became a member of the Sarah Lawrence College faculty, and Gardner recommended him for the faculty for the New School for Social Research. We were intensely excited about his book, *Art and Visual Perception* (University of California Press, 1964) which we devoured shortly after it appeared, and from which Gardner drew material. We spent a very memorable day with Rudi in 1946 when we were beginning to plan our summer place, Birchlea, in Ashland, New Hampshire. Rudi drove with us and with my sister, Gwen, through the Franconia Notch, and as we rode we compared ideas about poetry and sang folk songs. Gardner never forgot the sound and sight of the swinging of Rudi's axe as we cleared out the little private roadway into Birchlea, and we shall never forget his intimate ease as a member of our summer family. Years later, Rudi gave a memorable lecture in honor of Gardner in the series at the Graduate Center of City College of New York.

Not as quickly recognized as Charlotte Bühler but over time even more influential was the child psychologist in Geneva, Jean Piaget. His generous greeting to us on visits to Harvard and Columbia in 1936 was followed by much correspondence when our dear friends, Barbara Burks and Eugene Lerner, studied with him in Geneva shortly thereafter. We saw him with delight at two international congresses, and in 1961 had the unique privilege of a three-weeks' visit from him as a Sloan Professor at the Menninger Foundation.

> Alternating between extremely difficult intellectual interchanges, complicated by our imperfect grasp of French and relieved by delightful moments of wandering with us around our nearby Lake Shawnee while he looked for tiny flowers and mosses, and sharing our enthusiasm for the wild rice from Minnesota which turned out to be one of his favorite delicacies at our table (vive le riz sauvage!), we learned something about the man which is precious to us. It was his long discussions with our colleague, Riley Gardner, which taught us to begin to understand the complexities of his theory of attention and, in particular, of centration and the points at which an American psychology of individual differences might eke out and extend this generalized conception of psychological dynamics.

Though Gardner had known about the Rorschach method for personality analysis from the time of Samuel Beck's doctoral dissertation at Columbia in 1932, we were not well acquainted with its promise until I met Anna Hartoch in 1934 with her imaginative regard for every trace of individuality in the record. Soon afterward we met Bruno Klopfer who worked on standardization in the methods of scoring and educating the American public on the potential of the Rorschach. Gardner wrote,

> Klopfer we think of in terms of his capacity to make quantitative sense out of each separate aspect of response to the inkblots, while Hartoch's memory means to us more the sensitive capacity to conceive of a total ongoing personality pattern in which the separate integrative operations contribute to the design of a personality as a whole.

Anna Hartoch was the Rorschach specialist on Carolyn Zachry's *Adolescent Study* with which Sarah Lawrence was cooperating. As part of getting acquainted with the power of the Rorschach technique several of the faculty volunteered for Rorschachs and I participated. After being deeply impressed by Hartoch's accurate comments, I decided to include Rorschach records on preschool children, beginning with two-year-olds. We reviewed records over five years with one child in a joint pair of papers, one in which I summarized the child as he was seen in our nursery school, and one in which Hartoch presented his Rorschach records and her interpretation.

Getting to know Anna Hartoch well naturally led to our acquaintance with her husband Ernst Schachtel, the most creative and thoughtful Rorschach analyst in this country. At dinner with them we met the analyst Frieda Fromm-Reichman, whose patience and deep understanding of mentally ill patients was a model for others' work. That evening we enjoyed another side of her as she chuckled, "I came away from Aspen drunk on music." We knew how she felt.

We both knew the analyst Erik Erikson for his brilliant studies of the play technique used with Yale freshmen in the early thirties and for his memorable studies of zones and modes of taking in and giving out as paradigms of psychic operations. I first met him in New York in 1935 at Carolyn Zachry's adolescent study seminar and was deeply moved by his extraordinary perceptiveness. I was also impressed by the potentialities of the miniature-life toy method of play for studying normal children; that meeting with Erikson inspired my subsequent work on child personality.

We had our first prolonged conversation with him after he had studied children at the University of California in the late summer of 1938. We saw him again and had a long talk about submarine crew psychology and about the state of the war just as Bataan was captured at the beginning of 1942. In the 1947 summer session at Berkeley we had the delight of visiting the Eriksons' place at Orinda, singing folksongs to Joan Erikson's guitar, splashing in the huge pool, and watching their daughter's nine-year-old joy in her donkey.

Soon we went over the draft of what was to be *Childhood and Society* (1950), about which Erik was diffident but about which we were enthusiastic and rightly confident. His conception of psychosocial development richly documented in that book added a new dimension parallel to the Freudian view of psychosexual development. Erikson's concepts of identity and his devotion to the problems of youth contributed new depth to the study of child development; his thinking met the needs of youth with such sympathy that his name became a household word. (Gardner tried valiantly to get Harper's to accept this book, but the general editor did not appreciate it. Norton accepted it and has since enjoyed the privilege of publishing the Eriksons' many seminal contributions to psychoanalytic thought, clinical work, and creative activities.)

Gardner recalled his impressions over the years:

> Erikson's gentleness and diffidence, the little quiet expressions of humor, did not prepare one for the very firm definitions of principles which appeared in the speech and writings of later days, nor such acts of incisive courage as his refusal to take the California Loyalty Oath, and his resulting move from California back to the East.

We visited the Eriksons about 1954 in Stockbridge, and again about 1957; and we shared the very wet top of Mt. Washington with them in 1959. We had a long and extraordinary visit in his office at Harvard in September 1961, planning the selection of psychoanalytic materials to be used in the *World of the Mind*.

We felt that his perspectives on children would lead to a major contribution in a study of children in India and shared this hope with our friends the Sarabhais, who invited him to come to Ahmedabad. Once there he was moved by the influence of Gandhi in that city, and he used the opportunity to interview every living person who had known Gandhi, gathering material for his classic study, *Gandhi's Truth* (1968).

Later we visited the Eriksons at Cotuit on Cape Cod, and when Gardner was in our Holderness "home hospital" in 1976 they stopped in while they were on a visit to their friends Peter and Merta Blos. Exchange of papers, manuscripts, and books kept us in close touch across the miles, while the broadcast of Erikson's Jefferson Lecture in Washington brought his voice into our home when Gardner was incapacitated and we could not attend.

Joan's colorful visualization of interwoven developing psychosocial strengths provided a fresh and unforgettable form to their view of the life cycle, while her creative use of freely chosen activities in a program for disturbed young people demonstrated the healing and growth-supporting power of activity that is individually meaningful. Their joint work is in the tradition of the Curies and a few other couples of rare mutuality and dedication.

In addition to our initial inspiring contact with Erikson and our ensuing friendship with Joan, we met their friend Peter Blos, who was also working on the adolescent study with Carolyn Zachry. His contributions to the understanding of disturbed adolescents, and his profound studies of pre-oedipal father-son relationships and of Freud's relation with his own father are major contributions extending the tradition of classical psychoanalysis.

With his wife Merta he renovated for summers a farmhouse in New Hampshire a few miles from our home, and there the Blos musical parties were a precious addition to our convivial gatherings. Peter's sensitive appreciation of and resonance to Gardner, to his passion for bluebirds, and his transcendence over incapacitation, made him another very special friend and a unique support to me after Gardner died.

Two other analysts cooperating with the Zachry study in the thirties were Erich Fromm and Fritz Redl. Fromm gave seminars on reactions to authority — passive, cooperative, or resistant. I found him orderly but rather ponderous. In striking contrast was the ebullient Fritz Redl, overflowing with good spirits — sometimes a little maudlin — and endlessly courageous in his effort to understand and to help the most severely destructive boys.

René Spitz was another warm, sensitive, humane analyst whose movies of grief-stricken babies, and papers on anaclitic depression and hospitalism contributed to a stream of research on young children's reactions to separation from their mothers. At a time when I was focussing on preschool children's responses to new experiences he urged me to study infants' reactions to strangeness but I was too involved in the studies with the children to add a new study. I had observed wide individual differences in babies' differentiation of a strange woman from mother; for instance, at four months, one baby was piteously disappointed when he realized that a woman about the same size was not his mother. And in longitudinal records examples of even younger infants' "stranger anxiety" could be found. Spitz agreed that the varying perceptual maturities of infants contributed to their awarenesses of difference.

David Rapaport became a close friend not long after arriving here as a refugee from Hungary and from the world over which the Nazi shadow was darkening. Gardner helped him a little with his first book published in this country, *Emotions and Memory*; and supported his efforts to establish himself in Kansas as a clinical psychologist. Gardner's student, Roy Schafer, learned much from him there, and after we went to the Menninger Foundation in 1952 we found a group of vigorous and insightful clinical psychologists who had all been trained by Rapaport in the middle and later 1940s. We kept up our contact with his hard-driving thought and his world of enthusiasm and sentiment as we visited him in Stockbridge and in New Hampshire, finding always that there was a profound comprehension of psychoanalytic theory, and a capacity for disciplined thought that we have seldom encountered. His passionate love of poetic beauty was evident when he would, on request, recite Hungarian — or Greek — verse for us, or when he would tell us with glowing eyes of the joy of early dawn blueberry-picking when the sheen, the almost invisible dew is glistening in the early morning sun. Rapaport's sudden death from a heart attack in 1959 was a major loss to psychology as well as to his friends.

Our contacts with other European psychoanalysts included some of the pioneers in ego theory. John Levy, Ruth Monroe's husband, the analyst, died of nephritis in the late thirties, and after a few years Ruth Munroe married Bela Mittelmann, an experienced and creative analyst, who shared insights and perspectives on ego theory with us, especially during their summers at the 200-year-old Cape Cod cottage in New Hampshire which Ruth and John had bought in 1932 and brought back to life. Gardner had found Ruth Munroe a stimulating student and wrote:

> Her endless receptiveness and sensitivity, her creative flair for research, combined with her marriage to an analyst to make us aware in an easy daily way of many realities which could scarcely be derived as well from books. Her familiarity with French and with German philosophy and general literature, and her excitement in encountering Gardner's ideas about the history of psychology, made it natural to share all sorts of ideas with her and led to a much fuller understanding of the original things she was doing with the Rorschach method and later her extraordinary perspective in achieving a comparative vision of the various psychoanalytic schools.

Ruth joined the Sarah Lawrence faculty and while there carried out an important study demonstrating that predictions of college success on the basis of Rorschach records were more successful than predictions made on the basis of ACE's. Later she taught the course on the Rorschach method in the City College Graduate Clinical Program. All through the years until her death she remained a close friend, with visits summer after summer when her family and ours were both in New Hampshire only a few miles apart.

At dinner with Ruth and Bela in New York we met Heinz and Dora Hartmann — Heinz with grace and humor beyond what we expected from his sober writings. Even more than his *Ego and the Problem of Adaptation*, his paper on "Mutual Influences of Ego and Id" and other papers with Ernst Kris and R. Loewenstein provided concepts crucial to our evolving ideas about personality and about children's ways of coping with stress. We became more acquainted with Marianne and Ernst Kris on a visit to their Connecticut country home, surrounded by woods with a brook running through it. It was on this visit that I described to Marianne some recent observations of a very young baby's persistent goal-oriented activity in pursuit of an object despite repeated failure; she invited me to join their Yale group studying infants but our Murphy family life made this impractical.

Gardner was also stimulated by another analyst in the thirties:

> The name of the analyst A.H. Kardiner brings back the summer of 1939 when he and we and our two small children sat on the porch of a little rented house on Squam Lake, New Hampshire and discussed *The Individual and His Society* which had just appeared. It was, we thought, a great book, marking a massive contribution of psychoanalytic theory to the problem of character types, specifi-

cally to the differentiation of that which all members of a cultural group share
to that which is more distinctively individual within them. The molding of the
individual biological predispositions into a "basic personality structure" which
belongs to all those nurtured in the same manner, this conception of primary and
secondary institutional influences and the attempt to tease out from anthropological material the actual stuff which goes into the molding of the central
or basic personality was developed further in 1945 and in other later papers.

In the same period we were stimulated by developments in American
psychology when psychologists from other universities came to New York for
conferences or committee meetings, and when we visited the Harvard Clinic
and the Yale Child Study Center, or when we attended interdisciplinary
conferences.

Gardner met John Dewey in a smoking car on the Long Island Railroad
in the summer of 1921, as he later described: "The gentle, slouching, roll-your-
own smoker offered only simple and casual acquaintanceship, not enthusiasm
and not pomp and circumstance, just a casual discussion of heredity, learning,
schooling, and the political tides of the day." Gardner had read enough Dewey
to keep the conversation going. Soon he drafted Dewey to be chairman of a
committee collecting clothes and food to be sent to Russia through the Famine
Relief Agency. He saw Dewey off and on for all of the New York period, "at-
taching to this slight, quiet little man the vast admiration earned by a great
leader of the epoch." I had "been brought up" on Dewey in the first decade
of this century, when my father studied with him at the University of Chicago.
My father and mother discussed Dewey and James, and some of their ideas,
at the dinner table when I was nine and ten, a little pitcher with big ears, listening, impressed me.

After Harold Jones left Columbia in 1928 to become director of the new
Institute of Child Welfare Research at the University of California in Berkeley
we kept in touch, and Harold invited Gardner to teach the summer session — in
1938 and 1947. In the latter summer I worked up case studies of four preadoles-
cents from their folders containing physical, social and psychological scores and
ratings to demonstrate the need for an integrated view of individual children.
I had been especially impressed with Harold's study of infants' galvanic skin
responses; he found that quiet infants had stronger reactions than active infants. I was also deeply interested in the dramatic changes some children made
as they traversed the transition years into adolescence.

On these Berkeley summers we also talked with Jean Macfarlane, whose
guidance study of 200 Oakland children interested both of us; Jean shared her
vivid and insightful accounts of the development and changes in some of the
children when we met over the years at APA conferences. We have always felt
sad that her rich observations and deep understanding of the children never
led to a comprehensive integrative report. My own developmental studies owe
much to those under her direction at Berkeley.

Extremely important to both of us was Lawrence K. Frank, as Gardner wrote:

> Of the many people who have been far-ranging seekers and integrators of biological and social science materials related to personality and education, the first in our time and also the most indomitably non-sectarian and cross-cultural was Lawrence K. Frank. Larry was at the General Education Board when we first knew him in the 1920s, integrating all kinds of research that had a bearing on education. He was at the Josiah Macy, Jr., Foundation during the decade of the 1930s, and through the financial resources of that institution supported our research on personality of young children in the Sarah Lawrence College Nursery School. It was he who constantly pushed for research on "personality and culture," conducted seminars at Yale and at his home, Cloverly, in Holderness, New Hampshire, wrote countless articles reflecting the modern spirit, the "climate of opinion," and the modalities of reciprocity between individual biological organism and cultural press, guidance, and molding. It was largely because Larry had a summer place at White Oak Pond, Holderness, New Hampshire, that we spent summers there and finally built our home there in 1947. Larry and Mary and their seven children, and more grandchildren, have been major forces in both our personal and our professional lives. It was Larry, for example, who was constantly pointing out implications of fresh medical and biological research for problems in learning theory, personality formation, and the clinical and educational meanings of specific behaviors.

It was Larry, looking at my data on children's anxious responses to pictures, who developed the conception of projective methods expressed in his 1939 paper on that subject; my 1938 paper with Ruth Horowitz described more concretely the variety of projective methods useful for studying child personality.

It was Larry's hospitality that meant many visits with Margaret Mead and Gregory Bateson, Rhoda Metraux, and other social scientists. These personal settings offered opportunities for intimate exchanges not possible in the interdisciplinary conferences he financed through the Josiah Macy, Jr., Foundation. Those meetings brought together pediatricians, psychoanalysts, psychologists and anthropologists who learned to communicate with each other and to be receptive to contributions of different methods and theories to the study of problems of human development.

In 1928–29, we both took Ruth Benedict's course on primitive religions. It was essentially a seminar and discussion of a few primary sources, including her own work, with a comparison of historical, psychological, evolutionary, and other broad approaches in which emphasis was naturally placed upon the historical and cross-cultural approach. She was, as always, gentle, generous, shy, nervous, winsome, deeply convinced of the validity of her historical emphasis, but insecure in the presentation. We knew Ruth off and on all through the 1930s, congratulated her on *Patterns of Culture,* shared with her in peace meetings, and heard her accounts of the personality studies in Japan, to which she was devoted during World War II and which became preparatory to her *The Chrysanthemum and the Sword.*

The path from Ruth Benedict goes, of course, to Franz Boas, whom we deeply admired. Gardner had talked to him in 1921 or thereabouts regarding anthropology courses and had made so bold in 1923 as to ask Boas, and also Dr. Frank Goddard at the American Museum of Natural History, to help him investigate a medium who purported to communicate in American Indian languages. Boas' great scorn for mediums was certainly justified by the outcome in this instance. Boas sat on various Ph.D. committees in psychology of which Gardner was a member and had also been a familiar figure at the time of the Benedict course on primitive religions. Boas' conception of the role of culture in relation to the development of intellect, as expressed for example in *The Mind of Primitive Man,* and his broad cross-cultural conception of human nature, made a major impact upon us both in the late 1920s and early 1930s. Gardner recalled

> His tragic face, scarred and mutilated by a Heidelberg duel, combined with his erect posture and his almost running gait as he walked, made him as memorable physically as he was intellectually. In terms of the impact of the social sciences upon psychology in the nineteen thirties he was, we think, the greatest figure of that era. Certainly, the Benedict and Mead contributions must be seen in the light of the overarching influence of such a man.

A kindred spirit, like Gardner in the William James tradition, was Gordon W. Allport. He was just leaving Dartmouth for Harvard when Gardner met him at the Hanover conference on personality and culture, in 1930, and they saw one another off and on during the next decade, talking about Gordon's work in Gestalt psychology. The Allport-Vernon *Studies in Expressive Movement* awakened Gardner to the importance of the experimental approach to personality, and the book was featured in the revision of *Experimental Social Psychology,* 1937. "The day in 1939, when Gordon visited the Murphy family in our Bronxville home was ever memorable through the warm exchanges and through Gordon's thoughtfulness about the children beforehand by bringing them a box of chocolates. How seldom it was, we realized, that our hard-hitting intellectual friends foresaw the likely response of the children." They said at the time that he was their favorite visitor, but they also remembered Eugene Lerner's warm interest in them and Abe Maslow's bedtime stories when he visited us while he was teaching at Brooklyn College.

Gardner and Gordon Allport talked largely about experimental work in social psychology and about the newly arrived waves of psychologists from Central Europe, one of whom—Werner Wolff—had done such significant work that they shared in bringing out his book on the *Psychology of Expression* in 1943. Gordon Allport was warm and gentle, but tough in his judgments, writing to us "Let us give help in every possible way to the creative refugees who have something to offer; let us find a place for them; let us struggle to help Wertheimer, Stern, Werner, and all who can be placed where they need to be; for those inadequately trained or with just 'fruity' ideas we must not confuse issues." Allport and Gardner worked with Barbara Burks to find academic positions for the émigrés. They also worked on the Committee of the Social Science Research Council on cooperative and competitive habits. There were other delightful meetings, such as the one at Brandeis in the summer of 1956 and several extravagantly generous letters from Gordon to Gardner regarding his writing.

The psychiatrist Adolph Meyer and Gardner also met at the personality and culture conference at Hanover in 1930 and had a warm and intimate talk at the meetings of the Social Science Research Council in 1936; we both talked with him at the 1946 Bar Harbor conference.

> His gentle, steady, broad, positive conviction about the habit factor in psychosis and about the psycho-biologic unity, the indivisible oneness of the living system impressed us both as we read him and as we talked to him. His steady dignity and very, very gentle, warm fugitive smile were especially real when he asked if we could help him to get his scattered writings into a single volume. As it happened, the task fell to others more competent than ourselves, but the inspiration and the sense of unity with his approach have been lasting.

As experimental social psychology was taking shape, the child psychiatrist David M. Levy was extraordinarily productive.

> His studies of sibling rivalry and maternal over-protection were models for the quantitative use of clinical data focused in terms of clearly defined problems in personality development. His studies of maternal endocrine predispositions as related to maternal feelings, and his studies of sucking and of weaning in both human and animal infants, and the comparative vision which led to the studies of aggression in relation to restricted environment, were all exciting. We found him equally inspiring in personal conversation, with a vigorous insistence upon experimental demonstration of clinically derived principles and with a freshness and subtlety that was rare in experimental psychology. We shared with him, at Bar Harbor in 1946, the problems of heredity and environment in the growth of personality.

It was there, on a walk in the woods with Gardner, who was excited by the birds, that David commented, "Gardner, you *are* an enthusiast."

We met the psychoanalyst Harry Murray on a visit to the Harvard Clinic in 1935 or 1936, and on the occasion of the extraordinary dialogue between Murray and Lewin mentioned above. We were delighted to discover the rich and flexible personality system that Murray devised in *Explorations in Personality* (1938).

While others thought of him simply as a clinician who had developed the Thematic Apperception Test, we thought of him as a warm and generous philosopher of human nature with a medical background, deep familiarity with both Freud and Jung, wide and deep understanding of experimental psychology and a great gift for leading young men and women into productive clinical psychology. We kept on discovering Murray at APA meetings and, in reading his extraordinary productions, including both the *Assessment of Men* and the vivid little article "Dyadic Studies of Personal Creativeness." We found him so to speak, all over the world; there is no place in the geographic spread of psychology over the face of the earth that Murray and the Thematic Apperception Test are not known.

Harry Murray drove up from Cambridge twice to visit us in New Hampshire; he also came to see Gardner during his final illness in Washington, D.C., and he was a devotedly helpful and inspiring friend to me.

Gardner was as deeply responsive to biologists as he was to the anthropologists, analysts, and new voices in social psychology. He wrote:

It was through the good will of J.P. Scott, working with the grand old man, Robert M. Yerkes, that we were introduced to the extraordinary conference on behavior and genetics, held at the Roscoe B. Jackson Memorial Center in Bar Harbor, Maine, in the summer of 1946. We had always believed deeply in the importance of genetics and of the pressing problem of the way in which genetic potentialities are shaped or potentiated by specific family and community environmental forces, but the actual encountering of a group of geneticists and a group of genetically-minded psychologists, psychiatrists, and other biologically-oriented research persons was an astonishing eye-opener. Scott and his group taught us literally in a few hours to see new dimensions in the experimental analysis of genetic components in personality. It was worth much to us also to have the fatherly warmth of Yerkes (with whom Gardner had had a course in 1916–17) and feel that though we were social psychologists we had a place in a biological setting.

As a seeker, a man eager to integrate more and more insights into the understanding of man and his place in the universe, Gardner came of age, and had his training and exposure to new psychological concepts, at just the right time. New York before World War I could not have offered a fraction of the intellectual delicacies available just before World War II, and after World War II the tidal wave had subsided.

16. The Humanist at Home

The New York years, especially from 1930 when our son, Al, was born, to 1950 when he was drafted for the Korean War, were our family years. The twenties had been Gardner's years of searching for a wife, and creating our marriage. Beginning with his visit to our apartment at Ruth Munroe's invitation, conversations Gardner described as "electric" — sometimes on hikes along the Palisades — led to our awareness of mutual interests.

Gardner described his memory of those hikes in an unpublished story, "Dyadic Thought and Work":

> It did not take Gardner and Lois long to discover one another because the nucleus of intellectual idealism that pulsated through the colleges made sharing Greek philosophy, Pauline theology, Eastern religions, Shakespearean drama, Wordsworth's and Whitman's poetry as satisfying as shared music or art or strolls along the Hudson.... When Lois described the joy of listening to Beethoven's Seventh Symphony, Gardner knew how she felt and when Gardner talked about Shelley, Lois had been there before.... Lois' excitement about Moffatt's and Foakes-Jackson's courses in history gave Gardner a realization that she loved intellectual history as much as he did.... [These interests] all became fused.

A later account also conveys feelings aroused in him by our discovery of each other:

> ... when Ruth Munroe invited me over, I met her roommate, Lois Barclay, a student at Union Seminary, with whom a new kind of world began ... we began a sharing of intellectual, esthetic, philosophical and other concerns like music, mountains, and travel, which has never diminished.... Her interest in psychical research, as a challenging pioneer field was a primary factor in maintaining my own morale.

Our time together was interrupted in the spring of 1925 by his severe attack of influenza. It left him weak; he had to give up his plan to go to Chicago the summer of 1925, when I was studying at the Divinity School of the University of Chicago. Later he told me that my letters had done much to consolidate his feelings. I was writing about my experience in Chicago—for example:

> Except for an occasional gaiety (like the opera *Aïda*) I am really studying now. Exegesis and lots of verse by verse stuff. St. Paul's theology in Romans carries on the mystical thread of last term and is rather fascinating. He is a most amazing person, such tremendous daring, incomprehensible conceptions so vigorously and unequivocatingly set forth.
>
> A Dr. Cadbury from Harvard who used to be a Quaker is blasting the "social gospel." Very stimulating and rather charming man. By the time one gets through the divinity school there isn't much religion left. With theology fallen into an ignominious heap, mysticism psychoanalyzed into disgrace, and the social gospel evaporated, pray what is left except a curio of the past. Lucky for us that we are interested in curios or we'd have to retreat, or return to psychology in spite of our feud with statistics.

In the fall of 1925 I was teaching in Baltimore in order to earn money to pay for another year of graduate study. Gardner came down several times and we explored the woods at Roland Park; when we stopped to rest he played his harmonica. He taught me to recognize birds I had not known. He recited poetry he loved, and we read to each other. He asked questions like, "Do you think a mystical experience brings new knowledge?" I said that I thought it was an emotional experience that intensified and illuminated insights and beliefs but did not produce new ones.

When I finally went up to New York, staying with Ruth, now married to the psychoanalyst John Levy, Gardner took me to *Aïda* at the Metropolitan Opera House, and we explored museums. Our feelings about music, wilderness, birds, poetry, art, contributed to a deep sense of intimacy. He became my best friend; his humor and love of music and poetry were irresistible. Still, he was professionally established and I was a naive graduate student seven years younger as well as seven inches shorter. I thought our relationship was a wonderful friendship. But on January 10, 1926, he exploded, "What *is* the *matter* with you? I want to talk about whether we might get married!" I was startled, and stars flew around my brain. Gardner felt that marriage should be sharing. And he emphasized that he wanted his wife to use her brains—not to spend more than twenty minutes a day on housework!

But Gardner faced potential problems—our tempos were different—I was slow, he was quick thinking. He even wrote that I did not have genius (!) but I responded, "I agree that I am no genius, but a Vassar Phi Bete and magna cum laude is not a moron either." I think that spunky response showed him that however modest I might be, I did respect myself.

I did not at that time or later—until I received the flood of letters from his students after his death—know that they considered him the Great Man,

God Murphy. He was simply the most lovable man I had met, companionable, responsive, sharing, fun to be with, as well as idealistic and courageous.

After we were married life went on much as it had in the preceding months. Gardner was eager to hear me read poems from the Rig Veda and other Indian literature. And I enjoyed reading to him, when his eyes were troublesome, some of the books he had cherished most; *Great Expectations* was a favorite Dickens novel which he wanted to share with me. Gardner's capacity to "spout poetry at length," as Bunch Alexander wrote me, including nonsense verses of Edward Lear, Gelett Burgess and Lewis Carroll, was one of his endearing qualities. Thus I became acquainted with the Yonghy-Bonghy Bo, The Walrus and the Carpenter and other friends from the nonsense tradition. In a deeply serious mood he read me Masefield's poems on the Self.

When Gardner's friend Frank Lorimer said that I had given Gardner something no one else ever had—strength, energy; and he was happier than he had ever been in his life—I wondered what that something was that was beyond what his family and friends had given him. They had all given him love and stimulation.

Why did he call me Loki—the name of the Norse fire god? And why did he write of electrical conversations? I can only guess that he was fired, electrified, by finding that I knew F.W.H. Myers, Walter Prince and William James as well as Shelley and Wordsworth and Blake, who all meant so much to him, and that I had thought about and had written papers on mysticism at Vassar and Union, and that I knew enough Greek to wax rhapsodic when he quoted verses from Aeschylus' *Persians.*

In one letter he wrote of a sense of "belonging," something that he had felt in Concord in his grandfather's family, after feeling isolated earlier. In New York, with so many friends who enjoyed his brilliance, warmth and humor, evidently that sense of belonging had not emerged until he met me. He did not use the term "soul-mate," a cliché of an earlier time, but something like that was what he felt. And along with that a sense of total acceptance; I did not have the doubts about him that his mother had reflected—with all that she also gave him.

At the same time, the fact that he *was* older than I was—in contrast to his position as the youngest of his family—and that he would be able to support and to encourage me, probably contributed to his sense of strength in contrast to the weakness he felt in comparison with his brother. And despite his continued closeness to his mother and need for her approval, my uncritical, unpressuring acceptance probably contributed to the release of energy.

His sense of being older is reflected in one letter in which he compared me to a "wunderkind" (wonder child) he had met. There was an element of Pygmalion—in his fantasy of making me into the kind of wife he thought he wanted—as he told a close friend toward the end of his life—"but after a couple of years I realized that she was just going to be herself." He protested my "downgrading myself," "eating humble pie," and I explained that however good any of my achievements were, they never reached my image of what was possible—each book could have been better, I continued to feel.

After we were married, music was increasingly important to us; Gardner had always loved the outdoors but music meant as much to him as the colors and sounds and forms of nature. While he was not an accomplished player on any instrument, nor even a sophisticated listener, music was a comfort in times of stress, a source of added depth in any relationship in which music was shared, and even a lifesaver at a time of critical illness. My own musical background, delight in music and modest ability to play the piano and to sing with Gardner was a joy to him.

Gardner taught me to "fake a tenor" for Yale songs and World War I songs. We sang "All in all to one another" from *Iolanthe*, Negro spirituals, the old Stephen Foster songs, as well as German, French and Scottish folk songs. Once in his last year he asked me to sing "The Castle on the River Nile" for one of our favorite nurses and when she remarked that I had a nice voice he commented, "To a man, his wife's voice is the most beautiful sound in the world."

Gardner had a wide-ranging repertory of popular songs from 1880 to 1930 which he sang on automobile trips and summer sings in New Hampshire, and when his children became interested in current popular music, he enjoyed such rhythmic favorites of the 1940s as "Chattanooga Choo-Choo," and "I've Got a Gal in Kalamazoo." He also enjoyed musical comedies, especially *The Sound of Music, Oklahoma, Carousel,* and *Annie Get Your Gun.* One of Gardner's older and lasting favorites was Robert Burns' "My luv is like a red, red rose, that's newly sprung in June, My luv is like a melody that's sweetly played in tune."

Both of our children had good voices and I sang to them as babies; we all sang together as they were growing up. Al became a Gilbert and Sullivan specialist, singing the Sergeant of Police, and the Mikado in high school, and many other Gilbert and Sullivan roles in off-Broadway productions. In 1975 when Gardner's life was hanging in the balance and the Key West Memorial Hospital medical staff felt that he could not survive, the doctors let me stay with him in the intensive care unit, where I held him and quietly sang love songs we had sung together after we were married. I felt that my songs could reach some level of consciousness even when he could not respond. When he was ready for discharge, a supervisor of nurses said to him, "She saved your life," pointing to me. We had sung on mountain tops, made love to the sound of Beethoven and Schubert; music had woven a bond that grew stronger with the years and sustained his fragile heart when life was ebbing. Later, when an excessive shot of valium knocked him unconscious again, it was Al's voice singing a favorite Gilbert and Sullivan song which stirred Gardner's response.

In his books, especially in *Encounter with Reality,* Gardner wrote repeatedly about the importance of sensory delights—visual and auditory. He remembered the exciting tooting of whistles in Montgomery at the celebration of the new century.

His mother taught him rudimentary harmony which enabled him to play by ear many piano classics, folksongs, and popular songs. When he heard for the first time a new symphony or song performed at a concert hall he would play it at home, recognizably well, although not quite accurately. As a piano player he said of himself, "I am 95 percent autodidact." He had also learned to play on the violin arrangements of such things as the minuettes from Mozart's E-flat symphony and a Mozart divertimento; but his violin-playing was less impressive than that of his piano.

As long as we were in and near New York we revelled in the operas at the Metropolitan Opera House from the family circle high over the balcony or standing room if we could not afford even the cheapest seats. And there were concerts at Carnegie Hall, Town Hall, Macmillan Theater near Columbia, and Lewisohn Stadium. We took the children to hear *Lohengrin* when they were nine and seven years old. Gardner would go to any opera where he could hear the ringing voice of Melchior. We heard all sixteen Beethoven quartets, all of his symphonies and trios.

Concerts at Carnegie Hall in the twenties and thirties were usually under the baton of Toscanini or Stokowski. Forever after, whenever we heard another conductor, Toscanini's precision and eloquence echoed in the background, and involuntarily we measured others by them although we respected and enjoyed Szell, Ormandy, Beecham, Mitropoulos, Koussevitzky and later, on television, Solti and Mehta.

Baby Al was entranced with music; he was never bored or frustrated as long as a record was on the phonograph. He enjoyed most in early months a rhythmic Czecho-Slovak dance song. He early developed a message, asking for music by blowing in the direction of the phonograph as he had seen us blow a bit of dust off a record before putting it on the player. His first word was "muz," at eight months. At three he cried one day after his grandmother responded to his request for a Beethoven symphony; she had selected the fifth symphony. When she asked why he was crying he whimpered, "I wanted the *sixth* symphony." He continued to be a music lover, worked with a musicologist for a while and acquired a library of records, then cassettes. And he was always alert to the musical preferences of Gardner and me. He was never satisfied with his skill on an instrument—piano or clarinet, but with good pitch and a resonant bass voice as an adult he enjoyed singing in Gilbert and Sullivan operettas for many years.

After Gardner wrote that "a new world" began with Lois, I was puzzled—a new world? Gradually I realized what he had felt. He had been teased, criticized, ridiculed and even rejected for his interest in psychical research by even his best friends as well as by colleagues; some of them "forgave" him.

Woodworth and Poffenberger tolerated his deviance, but understanding and support in New York for this deep commitment were a new experience. There is a poignant tone in his comment that "her support did much to bolster my morale."

Another clue to the meaning of his new world is seen in a comparison of his handwriting in letters to his mother and to me—the former was tight, small, cramped, while his handwriting in letters to me was free-flowing, open, impulsive. Marriage brought a new freedom, although he continued to need the closeness to his mother—as she needed to stay close to him—at the same time that he was stimulated by my understanding response to him.

Gardner's "new world" also included my two brothers and two sisters. Since Gordon and Gwen were in the New York area much of the time as adults, they were especially close. Gardner was warmed by the love of this group of Barclays.

There may have been more in Gardner's "new world." What it meant to him is suggested by his close friend Frank Lorimer's remark that before his marriage Gardner did not have the enthusiasm, spontaneity and joy that were the Gardner we knew. Many of his friends commented that he was a happy man. The "new world" released a new Gardner. And we never saw the awesome, erudite lecturer his students recalled.

Gardner's definition of marriage was sharing, and he said he wanted to share everything—he never made me a "golf widow," or for that matter, a vacation widow. Our shared delights were not occasional occurrences—they were a part of every day. They included music on piano, harmonica, guitar, or in singing; watching the changing patterns of the seasons marked in stages of leaves and in the ways of birds in different seasons—exuberant singing in the nesting and mating season; excited swirling, flocking in recurring circles like a magnificent ballet while organizing for migration. Gardner not only knew dozens of birds in the East, he could recognize them by their songs and other vocal signals. He introduced me to the "teach-teach" remarks of the ovenbird, the poignant Peabody-Peabody-Peabody of the white-throated sparrow, the versatile arias of the mockingbird, the lyrical song of the Baltimore oriole, and many more. He could hear the delicate notes of a bluebird long before I could see it. This was true in the early months of our mutual discovery and throughout our life to the last years of his illness. The songs of woodthrushes were an evening joy over our many years in New Hampshire. To "birders," even amateurs like us, the world of birds is stimulating, often awe-inspiring, exhilarating. While to a nonbirder, birds may seem a trivial aspect of a marriage, our enjoyment of, interest in and love of birds were a mutually shared delight.

Gardner longed to take me to Grand Canyon. In the summer of 1931 when he was teaching in Los Angeles he wrote me daily, desperately wanting a few days together at Grand Canyon on the way East. He was bone tired and needed restoration for body and soul. I was concerned about baby Al; he had been comfortable with me while visiting my family in Evanston but at the age of 13 months would he be able to tolerate staying with a neighbor nurse and her child while I was away for a week? I yielded to Gardner's entreaties, and Grand Canyon was glorious, majestic beyond human imagination with endless murals of subtly changing tones of pomegranate reds, persimmon, copper, and deep violet shadows. I found myself melting into it all with an intense sense of oneness with the universe and with Gardner.

Gardner was also at home in the skies—Cousin Will Elkin was director of the Yale Observatory and Gardner had become interested in astronomy, then stimulated his frail father—by then retired from the Southern Education Board—to study the skies with him. This led to his father's *Beginners' Star Book* and to Gardner's lifetime interest in stars, planets, spiral nebulae and the new discoveries about them in recent years. Wherever we went—he would comment on the constellations visible at that hour in that longitude and latitude. Along with his relationships with birds, and animals, this must have contributed to his feeling "part of the universe."

Our feelings about forests, mountains and lakes were equally intense and with these enthusiasms shared from the beginning of our relationship, the scope of sharing expanded rapidly as we explored music, literature, hiking and climbing, along with canoeing. But equally important was our shared respect for psychology and for the importance of research on psychical problems such as telepathy, clairvoyance, telekinesis and others. Gardner's feeling about sharing is implied in his statement on one curriculum vitae, written after his retirement from the Menninger Foundation: "In many of the activities listed, Lois Barclay Murphy has been my major collaborator, and in many cases, we have worked together on the same problems, especially in the field of child psychology and personality." It was Gardner's commitment to sharing that created the mutuality, the "twoness" that our friends described.

Gardner always felt close to his New England roots; New Hampshire, from 1932, and from 1947 our own Birchlea, provided continuity in our lives for nearly half a century. Not only the world of mountains, forests, lakes, birds, stars and aurora borealis, but friends so close that we were all part of one big family gathered in the Holderness area by Larry Frank who urged Ruth Munroe and John Levy, the Lynds, Murphys, Blos's, the Hartleys, and Margaret Mead, to buy, rent or build summer homes near his Cloverly. This created a congenial group with common interests and shared enjoyment of the White Oak Pond vistas, with its islands, its water lilies, its sunlit water and violet evening shadows.

Larry Frank was not only an intellectual giant who could discuss cybernetics with Norbert Wiener, Gestalt theory with Gardner, anthropology with Margaret Mead and child development with me, he knew the names of every wild flower along the roadside and the best secluded picnic spots at the edge of a river.

Larry's beautiful wife Mary, an educational psychologist, coordinated with grace and strength all of the activities of the household and its social life. In addition to cocktails and tea every afternoon, she put on parties for groups of 20 or 25 and dinners for the large family and its guests, as well as managing the endless housework involved for a large family. And along with all of this she arranged dazzling bouquets both for Cloverly and for neighbors. She was loved by the whole colony. The Cloverly parties were of two major kinds — parties with singing, charades and games in the house, and corn or "wiener" roasts at the stone oven on the edge of the Pond. At the sing parties Gardner played the piano, and amused the group with his lively rendering of "The Shocking and Amazing Table Manners of the Crowned Heads of Europe."

In addition to the singing, Gardner participated zestfully in the charades, which included all ages from the youngest child to the oldest adult. The words to be guessed ranged from relatively simple ones which the children could enjoy to Margaret Mead's complex terms like entropy which posed a problem even for the adults both to act and to recognize.

One summer an impromptu circus was held at the home of Ruth Munroe; Tim Munroe and Al were clowns, and worked up an act which ended with them falling off a very large rubber ball.

The late afternoon often found Gardner and me canoeing on serene White Oak Pond although the stillness was occasionally interrupted by the noise of a motorboat and the backwash of waves lapping at the boat; loons made their plaintive sounds late in the evening on the pond. We often paddled to the swamp where the graceful great blue herons, talkative blackbirds, silent bitterns and elegant cedar waxwings lived. When little Al was with us in a canoe he exclaimed with delight, "A frog on a lilypad!" amazed at the story-book image coming to life. In the early evenings sunsets were reflected on the quiet surface of the lake.

An occasional treat for all of us was an all-morning ride on the boat which delivered the mail to Squam Lake residents. This "mail boat ride" was a favorite of Al's; the combination of fast travel and summer breezes was irresistible. Gardner's pleasure was limited by his sensitivity to glare on the water; he protected his eyes with a broad-brimmed hat and focussed on the wooded shore.

Holderness provided a quiet place to write and to play, and a good balance between the isolation needed for work and communication between people. In addition to the group of summer residents there were occasional distinguished visitors who stayed at the Asquam House. The philosopher Irwin Edman spent a summer in the mid-forties working on his book *Philosopher's Quest,* from which he read aloud the Plato chapter and the Schopenhauer chapter to those who were interested. Our guests sometimes stayed at a motel or inn on the lake.

We also had our own enterprises and projects. Al's was an annual 18-mile hike to Laconia. Frequently—although not always—Gardner was there at 6 p.m. with the car to drive him back. Once Al attempted the 36-mile round trip and suffered badly swollen feet and severe nausea.

In 1947 after many years of renting large old houses for summer we built Birchlea, our echo of a Frank Lloyd Wright design; a 22-foot-wide panel of glass brought us the birches for which it was named, a vista of lake and forested hills beyond, and the sea of ferns which grew among the pines around the house. An eleven foot floor-to-ceiling fireplace wall was built of rocks pulled from the site of the house by an old expert mason who lovingly fingered and turned each one to gauge where it would fit. A wide overhang protected Gardner's eyes from the morning sun. A sixteen-foot-square deck with three walls of sliding glass panels brought the outdoors even closer on damp days, and hanging bird feeders lured chickadees, nuthatches and goldfinches close to us.

Gardner loved Birchlea so much that when he recovered consciousness after the weeks of struggle for his life in the Key West hospital he said mournfully, "I'll never get to Birchlea again," but I assured him that we would go up there and we did have four more summers in Birchlea.

I think the years of longing for an "intimate friend" and of feeling isolated, as well as the years of dreaming about the wife he wanted so urgently led to a sense of fulfillment that overflowed, merging the actual marriage into his dream. While his stimulus and endless support brought out capacities that I did not know I had, leading to achievement that I had never anticipated, his imagination both enlarged my achievement and absorbed it into his own.

An important part of Gardner's structure for family life was his insistence on two weeks a year with me alone. Those two-week vacations, usually in the White Mountains, were always honeymoons. One summer Constance Warren, the president of Sarah Lawrence College, offered us her home on the old farm near North Waterford, Maine—a heritage from her grandfather, with its handmade wood tools from the nineteenth century, a forest beyond the meadows, and not too far from the White Mountains where we climbed every summer in New Hampshire until the mid-1960s.

We both enjoyed mountain-climbing and we climbed mountains not only in New England but in Colorado, Japan, India, and hills in the Caribbean. Gardner loved the great view at the summit of Mount Washington when we could see all the way to the Atlantic Ocean on fair days, and sixty miles in every direction—that was literally a *plus ultra* experience. One of my favorite trails on Mount Washington was Glen Boulder trail, with its wealth of tiny ferns, mosses, berries along the way; we both enjoyed Ammonoosuc trail as it followed the brook up to the Lake of the Clouds hut, where we spent the night a couple of times. One morning in August 1945 we awoke to the news of the Hiroshima bomb—we had wondered what was going on the previous evening when President Conant of Harvard was abruptly summoned from dinner at the Ravine House where we were all staying. At first, Gardner felt that many lives were saved by the fact that the bomb made an invasion unnecessary; but soon he reflected on the appalling implications of these bombs with their capacity to demolish whole cities.

We were lucky to enjoy the same people—Ted Newcomb was my friend at Union Theological Seminary before I knew Gardner and later when Gardner and I became acquainted, I suggested that he watch out for an opportunity to get to know Ted. They became devoted friends. After Ted married his beautiful Mary Shipherd we were a foursome visiting back and forth for the rest of our lives. Helen and Robert Lynd, Gardner's close friends from 1923, and their friend Larry Frank who married Mary Hughes in 1939 were like family especially after we joined them in Holderness, and their children are like beloved grandchildren to me now. Other much loved couples in our foursomes were Otto and Selma Klineberg, Phil and Ann Holzman, Grace and Fritz Heider, Robert and Judy Wallerstein, Pitsa and Peter Hartocollis, as well as Ruth Munroe and John Levy from the first year Gardner and I knew each other, Eugene and Ruth Hartley, and Erik and Joan Erikson to whom we both owed so much inspiration.

Among some of the foursomes, the children became fond of us too; Nina Wallerstein, Anemona Hartocollis and Wendy Hartley visited Gardner in his last illness and Amy Wallerstein wrote about how he had always been a grandfather to her. These warm, enduring friendships were equally nurturing to Gardner and me.

Gardner felt fulfilled by our sharing of these enthusiasms for friends, nature, and music. I think his only disappointment was that I did not feel that I could be a political activist, with the children, the household, his mother, my parents and siblings, my teaching and research. And I was not willing to sacrifice any of those priorities for memberships in organizations that would involve attendance at meetings and committee obligations. So I did not join the American Psychological Association or the Teachers' Union. I do not now feel that I could have done more.

In all of my research, I collected, conceptualized and coded the data along with my assistants; I was much more a "hands-on" researcher than Gardner was and I could never have done the original work that he appreciated so much if I had not had this direct contact with children's behavior, working in my own exploratory fashion instead of using precoded ratings and leaving the work to assistants. My research areas and my methods were different from those accepted at that time; but Gardner always supported my independent ideas.

Gardner enjoyed our children. In an autobiography he wrote: "Our son, Al, was born in 1930, and our daughter, Midge, coming to us in 1932, gave another rich dimension to life—Al through his incredible clarity of perception and expression, his unlimited devotion to high standards in literature and music, and his Olympian sense of humor, and Midge for her robust directness, her earthy healthiness, her creativity, and her enthusiasm, gaiety and warmth." As a twenty-year-old he had written

> I feel the utmost responsibility for my possible children, and insofar as I can be of influence in such matters, for all unborn children. I am a very convinced eugenicist. . . . I want to let my ideas mature . . . in regard to the specific methods of child care and education. I want to know exactly how to give my children the best training I can give them. . . . My mental and moral traits ought to help me to be a kind, devoted, painstaking father, and to give my children a genuinely good upbringing. . . . A few children well attended to in physical and mental care are of more value to society than many allowed to "tumble up."

Those thoughtful comments did not hint of his great pleasure in children.

Gardner enjoyed our children's conversation; there was never a complaint that "Dad won't listen to me" as we heard in some other families. He was a companionable father, alert to the children's interests and needs, *not* preoccupied with training his children, gently corrective at times and never punitive; he did not repeat his mother's disciplinary patterns. He had ingenious ways of helping a child to overcome fear. For instance, when little Al resisted getting into the tub—he never liked water—Gardner brought a little "fireboat" that would squirt water to quench a tiny burning clump of paper. This made the tub-bath interesting. He gave Al a toy steam engine that made real steam like the one Gardner's father had given him. He was sensitive to childlike excitements: in Ouray, Colorado, when three-year-old Al was fascinated with the cascades of white water in the little "Un-com-pah-gre river," and with its name as well, Gardner frequently took him to stand at the railing on the low bridge and watch the water tumbling over rocks.

Al's first memory of his father was the image of him putting a record on the phonograph "for me to dance by." Another early memory recalled rides in the taxi with "Tony Vidella" in New York. When the children were two and four years old we held them up to the window looking down to the courtyard to hear the "Sole Mio man" sing operatic arias and Italian folk songs to the accompaniment of his accordion. Sharing also included the children in our own interests.

One January Gardner explained to him that a big calendar with pictures of trains was for a new year, 1935! Al was to be five years old that June. Gardner brought him a small bird book with a yellow cover and a picture of a Baltimore oriole on the cover, and a book of airplanes "with entrancing names like Sikorsky Amphibian," Al recalled. Gardner also brought him little booklets from the American Museum of Natural History, with 3-D pictures to look at with a 3-D glass. Some nights when Gardner returned late after an evening lecture he would leave a surprise under the children's pillows. On evenings at home he read King Arthur books to Al and Oz books to Midge. He bought other books that Al remembered liking, especially one about an Indian boy. Al recalled that Gardner "would always get me anything I liked. When I said I liked the *Eroica* symphony, he got it for me." And Al remembered that when he wishfully commented that he never got any mail, Gardner suggested that he "write" a letter to himself and mail it, and get it from the postman the following day. Al did so and was delighted when the mail came the following day with a "letter" for him.

As the children grew into middle childhood Gardner continued to be sensitive to their interests. In Berkeley in 1938, Gardner took the children on the ferry to the San Francisco Fleishhacker zoo; there they rode on the midget railroad. Gardner was not only thoughtful about providing experiences that the children would enjoy, he was responsive to their own ideas. For instance, they thought it was great fun to scamper over the benches that circled under eucalyptus trees on the University campus, around and around.

He also played elementary baseball and chess with Al, who said that he did not feel competitive with his father — he felt that Gardner was on his side. Al commented that he felt that he was living in the same world with his father — there was no generation gap of the kind we see today. "There was a lot of communication, sharing political ideas and feelings, including Gardner's negative judgments of Stalin, and his comments about race prejudice in Bronxville. Gardner's own prejudice was against stuffed shirts, and once when Al was walking along Broadway in New York with his father, he asked Gardner what a stuffed shirt was. Just then, pompous Nicholas Murray Butler walked by and Gardner said, "That's one."

By the time Al was nine years old, Gardner took him to major league baseball games, and we all went together to operas on Saturday afternoons — *Lohengrin, Il Trovatore,* and all of Wagner's Ring cycle. We saw Helen Hayes in the play *Harriet.* Wanting the children to be acquainted with our magnificent nation we took them on cross-country drives when Gardner was teaching in summer sessions at the University of California and Colorado. On one such trip we stopped at Niagara Falls where six-year-old Al, leaning over a railing, felt the spray from the falls as it splashed on his face; he exclaimed in awe "Some of Niagara Falls is falling on me!" One can never guess what experience will be special to a child.

As we spoke of driving through Kansas, Midge protested and threatened to get out of the car — she was not going to risk being blown away in a cyclone as Dorothy of Oz was! Gardner did not ridicule her; we could not guarantee there would be no storm in Kansas so he drove through Nebraska. On that return trip we stopped at Grand Canyon where the children stood breathless on the South rim, their taut immobile bodies eloquently reflecting feelings they could not put into words. We also visited my sister Eloise's home in Albuquerque where they became acquainted with real Indians at a nearby reservation. Another return trip included the mysterious geysers at Yellowstone, and a grizzly bear that pursued our car as we drove out of the park. Midge remembered Gardner's wonderful dragon-stories on those long drives, and Gardner and I remembered Al's hilarious imitations of radio programs.

When Al was 13 Gardner took him to a Yankees–Red Sox game; Gardner's principal spectator-sport interest was baseball; he never took Al to hockey, horse racing, tennis, or golf tournaments. He did not even pay much attention to Yale football. On occasion, he would get alumni tickets to the Yale–Harvard football game for Al to use taking various friends to New Haven. He never watched boxing (and never denounced the thuggery at the base of boxing — one person trying to knock the other unconscious — or the corruption of it — fixed fights). Apparently he saw some fencing in college (he once explained to Al the difference between foil, épée, and sabre). His eyes were extremely sensitive to bright sunlight and reflections so beaches gave him no pleasure and he never took the children to them, although in California he enjoyed the rocky shore at Point Lobos near Carmel.

Gardner shared the care of the children's medical problems. When Midge at three developed a boil on one buttock, Gardner took her to the doctor, carefully explaining, "The doctor will make it well, I will stay with you," and she repeated slowly, "Doctor will make it well and you will stay with me." And when he took her to the doctor for prescribed x-ray treatment of her severe ear infection, he stayed with her and gave her her favorite cream cheese sandwich as a reward for staying so very quiet during the treatment.

Al came down with pneumonia late in August 1942, and was ill for about three weeks. Gardner came into his room early every evening to talk briefly, and to listen to "Make Believe Ballroom," a popular-music radio program from 5:30 to 7:30. One evening they listened with great amusement to the first New York broadcast of "Der Fuehrer's Face" by Spike Jones and his City Slickers. Al felt that Gardner had a conflict about this; he enjoyed the song, but he seemed to have a lifelong habit of categorizing "serious" and "funny." It was inappropriate to say or do anything "funny" about "serious" topics such as Hitler, war, death, racism, physical deformity, and a few other topics. While Al convalesced from the pneumonia Gardner often played chess with him. After Al recuperated and before he went back to school, Gardner played "catch" with him very quietly in the side yard, not strenuously — just enough to help him get his strength back.

Although Gardner was not a punitive father he was frank with his disapproval — for instance, of the "fascinating G-man bubble gum cards" which Gardner said were in bad taste. And Al remembered Gardner's diatribes about the Hearst press. Al also remembered tensions about eating when Gardner insisted that he eat everything on his plate.

Gardner did not put pressure on the children to achieve in school but he was delighted when Al as an eighth grader won the junior high school spelling championship; the eighth grade was excited because it was the first time that someone other than a ninth grader had won. (Al himself wondered about the feelings of poor spellers who were required to compete as part of the English program but who must, Al felt, have been embarrassed.)

At the American Psychological Association memorial service for Gardner, Harold Proshansky, president of the Graduate Division of the City University of New York, commented that Gardner "lived his values." He certainly tried to, but it was not easy. He had felt that if we really cared about the poor we should live like the poor. But after a year of trying this, with an impoverished diet, and a musty little apartment I decided that if I was going to do anything worthwhile I would have to take care of my physical needs, and avoid allergies as much as possible. Then, with children, needs for play space, safety, and a clean environment took us out of the city, to Colonial Heights in Yonkers. At first, we were satisfied that the children were in a democratic Yonkers city school but the regime was so rigid that Al did not thrive and our doctor recommended that we transfer him to Bronxville School, one of the best public schools in the United States. After the first day there, six-year-old Al said, "This teacher understands children better than the other one, I want to stay here until I'm seventeen!" And he did. In order to avoid a car trip to and from school each day, we moved to Bronxville, a beautiful village populated by a large majority of very conservative people; fathers were businessmen, typically Wall Street stockbrokers, who read the finance news of the *New York Times* on the train to New York while Gardner read the editorials. By the age of nine or ten, appropriate children were invited to the snobbish dancing school, which Al rejected, after which Midge was not invited. As the 1944 presidential election approached, Al came home one day with his huge Roosevelt button carefully pinned on the inside of his jacket "because the other kids tried to smash it."

We had bought, for $17,000 at the Depression price, a ten-room timber and stucco house with two-thirds of an acre of land which provided the only unlandscaped play space in the neighborhood. The big house became an extended family center, where my sister Eloise, and four-year-old Margo, spent a month when Eloise's husband was in the Air Force in World War II and my brother Gordon and his wife and son spent a month during a change of jobs. Gardner's mother visited weekends, and friends could be informally entertained. The setting was remembered by Midge especially as a wonderful place in which to grow up, but of course the value conflicts for Gardner were intense. I was involved in the excellent progessive school with its gifted teachers and did not feel so uncomfortable at the relative lack of politically and socially congenial neighbors.

As Midge grew into the junior high school stage, the fact that she had not been in the dancing school crowd was a social handicap, and she unhappily felt left out. We decided that it was important for her to be in a school with values consistent with our own, and we enrolled her in a Friends boarding school at Woodstock, Vermont, where she was at ease with the group. We had never intended to send our children to any private school, but solving one value conflict led to that one. I believe these experiences contributed to Gardner's hope to do research on value conflicts; he might have found that they are very hard to avoid in our heterogeneous competitive society.

Although Gardner was very tolerant of children's limits and individual notions, he was very firm about the structure of family life: breakfast at 7:30 a.m., supper at 6 p.m., children off to bed at 8 p.m. so that we could have "grownup time" to ourselves for talking, reading, planning. The children did not protest; they had their own solutions for this period when they did not yet feel sleepy—listening to a little radio, reading comics, and in Midge's case drawing pictures on the window with toothpaste!

Stimulated by Al, Gardner played in a postal chess section sponsored by the magazine *Chess Review*. He won all six games in his section to finish first, but time pressures discouraged him from entering again. Al also selected movies that he felt were worthwhile for his parents to see in 1947, such as *Great Expectations* and *Miracle on 34th St.*

The "Gilbert and Sullivan phase" began in 1947 with our trips to see productions in New York's Greenwich Village and Al's role as the Sergeant of Police in the Bronxville High School production of *The Pirates of Penzance;* the next year he had the role of the Mikado in that musical, the first of over 30 times he was cast in that role in productions of the Columbia-Barnard and other Gilbert and Sullivan groups. In addition to attending Al's performances, Gardner wrote to England for recordings of *Ruddigore* and *Princess Ida* which could not be obtained in this country.

In the fall of 1948 Al started college at Columbia, and did not see much of Gardner, but later in the year Al took his father to a musical satire about Harry Truman. That spring Al, always perceptive about his father's moods, felt that Gardner was stimulated by the discussions of the UNESCO project, which he actually began to prepare for later that year before leaving for six months in India in August 1950.

Gardner's sharing and support of Al's chess, Gilbert and Sullivan and reading interests laid a foundation for lifetime satisfactions, as my sharing of Midge's mothering of an endless sequence of kittens laid a foundation for her lifelong nurturing as a mother, grandmother and nurse. Neither Al nor Midge followed in their parents' footsteps in the academic world; they each developed as caring human beings with their independent life styles. They both loved their sharing, supportive father dearly and felt no need for hostile rebellions as they went their own ways.

After Gardner died, when the minister conducting the memorial service called upon them for memories, Al said, "There was always joy," and Midge recalled, "He was the only one who could tell a story lasting for the whole drive from New York to New Hampshire."

17. Developing a Theory of Personality

Gardner's *Personality* (1947) is regarded by many as his most important contribution to psychology. Without doubt it represents his most original integrative effort, as it brings together from many disciplines data and concepts on how personality grows, providing "a map of the territory" to encourage the explorations of psychological travelers.

The evolution of this book, from 1931 to 1947, was interrupted by demands imposed during the Depression and World War II, some of which I have already discussed. The development of his theory of personality followed a very different course from that of his work as a historian of psychology and as a social psychologist; his nascent interest in personality is apparent in his study—begun in 1929 with Rensis Likert—of the relation of political attitudes to the experience of the individual. The biosocial orientation, which began to emerge in *Experimental Social Psychology* (1931), had roots in his deep interest in evolution. His approach contrasted with the concept of a genetically fixed I.Q. and other fixed traits which had been dominant through the first quarter of this century and, in fact, was slow to give way to the concept that both heredity and environment were dynamically involved from the moment of conception. His book *Personality* illuminates his belief that "everything is biological and everything is social"; he specifically did not believe that the two are "inextricably interwoven": he disagreed with "that unfortunate kind of dualism" and felt that situations play a very important controlling role in all biological events, including conception and growth.

The pace of the development of Gardner's conception is apparent in his decision to include three chapters on personality in *General Psychology* (1933), which he built from his Columbia introductory course; that book testified to his determination to include personality along with traditional psychological problems. The three chapters dealt with the development, measurement and theory of personality—including both empirical research and psychoanalytic concepts. These chapters were in addition to discussions of personality on seven different pages, and in a final chapter on schools. In short, personality occupied over one-sixth of a book th it covered the usual range of psychological problems — the senses, perception, feelings, emotions, motives, learning, memory, thought, dreaming, and hereditary and environmental factors. In these chapters he used observations of children — our own, and those of others; he allowed for, but did not grant much dignity to, observation as a scientific method, although elsewhere he recognized the contribution of observation to anthropology and to other sciences. But his earnest defense of the experimental method as the approach guaranteeing the greatest accuracy did not interfere with his recognition of the contribution of psychoanalysis and field studies to the understanding of personality.

Most discussions of personality through the thirties and into the forties were concerned with traits, expressive patterns, behavior deviations; H.A. Murray's studies, carried out in the Harvard Clinic, and J. McV. Hunt's *Personality and the Behavior Disorders* dealt with both normal and deviant expressions of personality. On the whole, the approaches were concerned with individual uniqueness. Clearly Gardner's nomothetic approach to the origins and structure of all personality, a systematic view of basic aspects of personality, had not been preempted by any of the discussions of personality of that period.

During the latter part of the decade of the 1930s Gardner was completing his *Public Opinion and the Individual* (1938) with Rensis Likert, and he was burdened with the supervision of many doctoral studies at Columbia. Our reading of Rorschach's *Psychodiagnostik,* our visit to H.A. Murray's group at Harvard, Nevitt Sanford's study of the influence of need on perception along with our excitement about Erikson's work, and my research on personality of young children at our Sarah Lawrence Nursery School, had made him restless and eager to do his own research and to get on with *his* book on personality.

In the summer of 1931 Gardner had worked on the *Approaches to Personality,* with critical help from my psychologist brother, Gordon Barclay; F. Jensen contributed three psychoanalytic chapters, and one was written by John Levy. This book grouped the major systems with implications for personality.

Considering his *Historical Introduction to Modern Psychology,* his anthology of papers on *Abnormal Psychology,* and our *Experimental Social Psychology,* it may not be surprising that Gardner wanted to bring together the dominant systems that had implications for personality theory as he saw it at that time: the Titchenerian conception of sensations, images and feelings, along with association and attention; and the behaviorist approach which our friend Mary Cover Jones as a student of John B. Watson's, its promulgator, had made vivid to him. Although he saw the defects of behaviorism's neglect of problems of the inner life and its narrow conception of learning, Gardner felt that the contribution of the concept of conditioning to the study of behavior was basic. Moreover his work on Pavlov's studies in the course of writing the

Historical Introduction predisposed him to be hospitable to the concept of conditioning. The atomism of these two approaches, the sensationist and the behavioristic, in no way kept him from becoming excited about the Gestalt way of thinking as he encountered it with Köhler and Koffka after hearing C.K. Ogden's discussion at an APA conference in 1922.

The conception of *Approaches to Personality* was daring in the twenties since the analysts were not at that time talking to the academic psychologists, and most of the latter were negative, not to say hostile, to the "unscientific" ideas put forth by psychoanalysts. Gardner and I were not acquainted with *any* major academic psychologists who treated psychoanalysis with respect. Margaret Floy Washburn, president of the American Psychological Association when I was at Vassar, warned us not to read Freud; she was typical of the establishment at that time, although earlier, William James had thought that Freud was making an important contribution. It is not surprising that Gardner received few plaudits for that pioneering venture.

How original Gardner's approach was can also be seen from the fact that there had been no course in personality at Columbia, Yale, or Vassar during the years from 1912 to 1923 when we were in college. Books whose titles contained the term personality tended to deal with aberrations.

This was the period when tests for temperament, emotions, and other aspects of personality were mutiplying like dandelions, often with the optimistic assumption that data collected in a laboratory offered a reliable index to stable, persistent aspects of mental and personality functioning. The contributions of physique and of environment were discussed separately in these papers as was the problem of types and also specific traits such as extroversion-introversion, radicalism-conservatism, and originality. Studies of endocrine glands and the autonomic nervous system also heralded an increasing interest in personality. In 1921 Gordon Allport, then Allport and Philip G. Vernon in 1930, published surveys of the field of personality study, defining it broadly to include character, temperament, attitude and emotions; the 1930 article covered 327 titles, chiefly articles reporting research. Over one-fourth of these represented German studies; half a dozen were French. Allport was especially influenced by W. Stern, the personologist with whom he studied in Germany.

Among the studies of character, Hartshorne and May's *Studies in Deceit,* their *Studies in Service and Self-Control* and, with F. Shuttleworth, *Studies in the Organization of Character* are probably most relevant to present-day issues. The environment was credited with shaping the mind and behavior, but there was little recognition of variability in different situations or with different internal conditions. Allport and Vernon noted the limitations of many studies but felt that with so much research "the outlook for a future systematic psychology of personality is bright indeed." In this survey Allport and Vernon noted A.P. Weiss' view of traits as instances of "biosocial equivalence" in his chapter "The Biosocial Standpoint in Psychology" in *Psychologies of 1930.*

Gardner read the Allport and Vernon survey carefully and was impressed by Weiss' thinking. The implications of the concept "biosocial" were to occupy Gardner for the decade of the thirties as he developed his own comprehensive conception of the roots and structure of personality.

At the time *Experimental Social Psychology* (1931) went to press Gardner had not yet committed to a subdiscipline of psychology. As he wrote later:

> In 1931, at the age of 36, I had begun a career in psychology, but I had not found an area of specific psychological research to which I was willing to make a commitment. During that summer when Lois and I were in the Grand Canyon of Arizona, it came to me that I wanted to spend my life studying human personality.... The black cliffs and deep blue shadows of the Canyon were symbolic to me of the intense sensory richness of the inner world, a world which I believed could be more effectively observed, investigated, described, and understood. Actually, such a conception had flashed upon me in less complete earlier forms from college years onward, but it was Lois at my side and the Canyon above, as we followed its upward graded trails, that gave this vision of personality its commanding appeal. I remember, as I attended a music service at St. Paul's Chapel, Columbia University that fall, saying to myself: "So it's to be personality, isn't it; that's what I shall do, isn't it?" As the months went by, this incomplete and indistinct resolution became more articulate by relating to the work in social psychology which Lois and I were already doing, and by relating to the family world of our little son, and to the research world of Columbia University with its friendship with Robert and Helen Lynd, Otto and Selma Klineberg, and Ted and Mary Newcomb. The strands woven together never were really sharply distinguishable one from another, and are certainly not accurately distinguishable today.

Why did that Grand Canyon visit lead to this focus and the drive to integrate his thinking about personality? That experience was intense with memories of his previous discovery of Grand Canyon on his cross-country trip sixteen years earlier, combined with an emotional and integrative "reunion with Loki" (me) after the summer's separation when he was teaching in Los Angeles. The dramatic external stimulation of the vast beauty of the canyon evidently evoked a sense of the scope of personality along with a deepened awareness of the importance of internal experience. He never analyzed the connection between that 1931 Grand Canyon experience and his new conception of personality, but he repeatedly recalled this integrative moment of vision and commitment.

Why did he mention my presence at that moment? Gardner saw the twenties as "the period of the child guidance clinics," the "pro- and anti–Watson, the pro- and anti–Freud ideas, and the crucible in which the new ideas of childhood were being heated, fused, poured out, stirred again, and repeatedly made into a center for a point of view about personality." In the late twenties he had given much thought to his focus as a psychologist. Our close friendship with Ruth Munroe and her psychoanalyst husband John Levy and my own earlier experience in the Psychological Laboratory of the Board of Education in Cincinnati interested him deeply. He wrote, "Lois' background in child and clinical psychology made a huge impact on me.... She was constantly seeing personality issues of which I was astonishingly unaware."

These had grown out of my work in 1921–24 under Helen Thompson Woolley, and then Mabel Fernald, two creative psychologists who emphasized the need to see "the whole child." The child's performance on the intelligence test could be influenced, they believed, by rapport with the examiner and ease in the testing situation, anxiety about school difficulties, interest or lack of interest in the tests, ability to concentrate, ambition to do well and many other aspects of the child's response. We were expected to include in our reports as complete a picture of the child's functioning as we could provide—a demand which influenced all of my own subsequent work, and my discussions with Gardner. He commented,

> Lois' work, together with that of Eugene Lerner [ego blocking tests], Benjamin Spock, then a young pediatrician, L. Joseph Stone [sensory and aggression tests], and their colleagues at Sarah Lawrence [Trude Schmidl-Waehner working with children's painting and Anna Hartoch working with me on children's Rorschachs] ... embodying her kind of sensitive study of the whole individual child became primary in the development of my empirically grounded field theory of personality.

When Gardner wrote that I brought up many issues about personality that he had not thought of I did not ask him what he had in mind. I now remember some of the issues that I discussed with him as I worked on my project on sympathy in young children in the early thirties. Gordon Allport had been writing on traits as if they were stable. I was impressed by the variability in the children's behavior and I devoted one whole summer in 1934 to charting variations in the behavior of individual children over days and weeks. I also began to see that the behavior of a child varied from one year to the next in different situations. There was a dramatic change in "Betsy's" behavior when she was shifted from a group in which she was the youngest and smallest—and least sympathetic, least cooperative and least aggressive—to a group in which she was one of the oldest and tallest; all of her behavior ratings went up when she was no longer lowest in the hierarchy. We also read Arthur Jersild's paper on changes in behavior from nursery school to kindergarten, and studies demonstrating changes in behavior after young children had been taught skills that gave them an edge over others. Some of these findings contributed to Gardner's field theory that personality is not determined solely by organic factors or by the environment—it is formed by the overlap of these.

But what was behind the intensity of his response to my observations on children and to the psychoanalytic interests of some of our friends in spite of the fact that behaviorism had such a stranglehold on psychology and the psychological establishment was so hostile to Freud? The roots of his interest in personality are reflected in his responses to art, literature, and above all to friends and colleagues. He felt, for instance, that Rembrandt's ability to convey a personality made him the greatest painter in the world; a fine print of a moving self-portrait hung on Gardner's study wall for many years, then in the living room of our home after he retired. And he was always more interested in the personalities than in the plots of novels—he responded deeply to the tenderness of Joe Gargery when we read *Great Expectations*. He was as interested in the personalities of his students, colleagues, his own teachers, and other scientists as he was in their ideas. At a philosophical level, Gardner's persistent concern with the question of the nature of man, and of man's place in the universe was at the root of the conception of personality that he finally developed.

In direct and indirect ways Gardner's thinking and writing reflected the influence of William James: every edition of the *Historical Introduction to Modern Psychology* contained a chapter devoted to William James alone. This was true of no other psychologist discussed in that book; most chapters were identified by concepts or trends.

Gardner's research on and discussions of the relation of affect and perception are recognized as one of his great contributions to psychology and basic in his conception of personality. His early assimilation of James contributed to his response to Rorschach's, Bartlett's, Murray's, Freud's and Rapaport's discussions of affect and needs in relation to cognitive processes. Although "feeling" had no sharply definable meaning for James, dozens of "feelings" appear in connection with James' discussion of instinct, emotion, "and indeed, the rational processes." But James' discussion of the will was most important of all as we can see in Gardner's 1971 "William James on the Will." Like James, Gardner was deeply interested in J.M. Charcot and P. Janet, with their studies of hysteria, hypnotism and dissociation, and especially their discussions of subconscious or unconscious mental life. This early orientation to the subconscious, along with F.W.H. Myers' conception of it, contributed to Gardner's early response to Freud's theories of the unconscious years before mainstream psychology had absorbed psychoanalytic thinking. But beyond the stimulus to Gardner's thinking, the comprehensiveness of James' *Principles* was undoubtedly a support for Gardner's own vision of a volume on personality.

Along with his deep feeling for James, we must remember Gardner's fascination with the history of philosophy and its concerns with the heart, soul, and mind of man. Moreover, this interest in the history of philosophy— supported as it was by his intensive classical education in Greek and Latin— made it impossible for him to board the behaviorist bandwagon led by Pavlov and J.B. Watson. His psychological roots were nourished in too rich a soil; Gardner couldn't let James down—nor Plato, Aristotle, Pythagoras or other mentors of his inner life. The latter included, along with Emerson, poets like Whitman and Masefield. In one piece of autobiography Gardner wrote:

> One other poetic message has been life-blood to me: John Masefield's series
> of sonnets on the self, beginning "Here in the self is all that man can know /
> Of beauty, all the wonder, all the power," and including the one that begins "If
> I could get within this changing I." This vision of man's resonance to the world
> is what I think psychology is all about.

All of these influences gave direction and force to Gardner's effort to find
a place for the self in psychology. His historical background, our psychoanalytic
friends, and my clinical experience contributed substance to his emerging view
that psychology should be concerned with personality, as well as with behavior
and environmental influences.

His personality theory took shape at first within his sense of himself, like
James, as an evolutionist. At Yale he had been deeply impressed by Darwin
and Spencer, then later by Heinz Werner's evolutionary approach to development. At Harvard he had worked conscientiously on Yerkes' ontology course,
which involved a study of one's own heredity and the environment which contributed to one's personality. Woodworth's physiological psychology at Columbia had introduced him to Sherrington's *The Integrative Action of the
Nervous System* (1906). Both of us were stimulated by Kretschmer's *Physique
and Character* (1925). These many influences determined the development of
what Gardner called the "organic" approach, which came into the center of his
thinking in the mid-thirties reinforced by Kurt Goldstein's *The Organism*
(1935).

Meantime, anthropological studies by Margaret Mead, by Ruth Benedict
and by their mentor Franz Boas, among others, were forcing a recognition of
the ways in which a culture shapes personality. And our own study of the influence of different situations on child personality, growing out of data in my
sympathy study, along with Hartshorne and May's documentation of the
character changes of children in different situations, forced a sharper formulation of the role of the environment. Gardner's diagram of personality as the
overlap between organism and environment crystallized his biosocial view of
the origin of personality.

During the thirties specific aspects of personality were seen in cross-
sectional, or functional, and psychopathological terms. After Kurt Lewin's *A
Dynamic Theory of Personality* appeared in 1935, studies of and books on personality proliferated. Important monographs and articles now focussed on personality. Dissertations and other studies multiplied in the forties along with
studies of emotion (or affect), expressive patterns, character, and specific personality tendencies such as dominance, prejudice, authoritarianism. Even rats'
emotional reactions were worthy of study. Both physiological and social factors
in personality came into focus in Mittelmann and Wolff's studies of emotion
and skin temperature, and Theodore Newcomb's *Personality and Social
Change*. All of these, and others, dealt with specific aspects of personality, and

although a developmental approach was not uncommon, no one else was searching for the roots and the soil from which personality takes shape.

Gardner first taught a course in personality in 1935 but of that course we have no record; we can only assume that it was a beginning which led to the course so famous at City College. We know that he had already made a commitment to his concept of personality as the overlap between organism and environment, and as part of this, the recognition of the influence of the earliest conditions in which the embryo is developing. Although the influence of alcohol and drugs was not yet documented, he became convinced that the principles of early canalization, habit, and the effect of dominance as it played a part in resolving conflicts shaped early development. In the late thirties he was steadily integrating a wide range of multidisciplinary studies into a comprehensive theory.

The spring of 1940 found Gardner enjoying a sabbatical semester with no obligations at the end of his Columbia years; he used the first months of that time to prepare for the City College of New York and we went to New Hampshire early in June where he could write in peace. We stayed in the "Longfellow Cottage" on Shepard Hill above Squam Lake; it was a wide two-storied house with a massive front door brought from the house of the famous minister Phillips Brooks — generous rooms always cool in the shade of towering white pines. A huge lawn, a tennis court and a croquet court 100 feet up a little slope beyond the woods belonged to the Asquam House where Gardner's mother and grandmother had stayed while he was at Camp Algonquin when he was 13. A "Whittier tree" at the edge of the path to those courts was remembered in Holderness as a tree under which Whittier sat while writing his poems.

It was in this relaxed, literary setting that Gardner settled down for nearly four months to work on his big idea for a comprehensive, basic book on the roots of personality. There was no telephone to interrupt the flow of ideas. The children sensed that he was busy and did not bother him when he was writing in his second floor study, away from household activities. In the afternoons, when he had written enough, he joined them in outdoor play as he did on weekends during the rest of the year — playing ball — "One-a-cat," Pussy wants a Corner, croquet, or tennis. His awareness of children and their growing is reflected in that book more than in any other book he ever wrote.

Half a mile away were the Franks at Cloverly on White Oak Pond, and the Lynds at Innisfeld at the crest of a slope overlooking that lake. Their children joined ours for games, rowboating and swimming in the lake and all of them joined Ruth Munroe's children to create a unique "circus" with stunts and dancing. And there were explorations with the children, trips to Polar Caves, the Lost River, and mailboat rides on Squam Lake. Margaret Mead and Gregory Bateson with baby Catherine were near us in a house I found for them on the shore of Squam Lake. They worked on their Bali films with time out for stimulating discussions on the Franks' long porch overlooking the garden and lake.

We can recall that on the occasion of his first visit to Columbia University in 1916, Gardner had been dismayed at the lack of evidence of concern with people — psychology there smelled of the laboratory, not of human life, and he had gone to Harvard for his master's degree. Now at the end of twenty years at Columbia his hope was to show the implications for personality of basic psychological principles.

The months at Longfellow Cottage made a good start on the book, but he needed more time. From mid-September his administrative work and teaching at City College, his increasing involvement with the American Society for Psychical Research, the Society for Psychological Study of Social Issues, and the Council of the American Psychological Association, interrupted his work on the *Personality*. Nineteen forty-one brought America into the war with new responsibilities in addition to Gardner's work on the yearbook for SPSSI; he had little time to continue work on *Personality* until *Human Nature and Enduring Peace* was in press. And in 1944 he was president of the American Psychological Association. But meantime he had been teaching the exciting personality course at City College as his students recalled for us. In 1945 and 1946 he was finally able to complete the volume.

The long years of the thirties had given time for development of a clear architectural structure for his wide range of concepts. While some details have to be modified in the light of research in subsequent years, that structure is sound; a half-century after his first course in personality at Columbia, his book is cited as a classic, and its basic concepts are part of American psychology. It was reprinted in 1966. Gardner was firm in his conviction that it belonged to its own point in time and he never wanted to revise it. He had other plans in mind, such as *Encounter with Reality* (1968).

The first chapter of Gardner's *Personality*, "The Approach," with several pages about William James, stated that "his life history will set us on our way"; Gardner used his sympathetic understanding of James' family background as a means to explore the development of personality. He asked whether the energy of James' robust, hard-driving, financially successful grandfather could be related to the lifelong quest of William's father, and the intense struggle "with the ultimates of mind, heart and universe" carried on by William himself. Keeping heredity in mind, Gardner noted the tenderness and liberality toward their children of all three — grandfather, father and son — and also the exuberant love of life and search for its meaning which characterized William's father. The complexity and constant change of environment and schools (from New York to Albany to Europe and back and forth) which Henry provided for his children may have contributed to the complexity, the unfinished quality, the pluralism of William James' work, Gardner thought. Intense new experiences along the way accompanied such things as the microscope his father gave fifteen-year-old William, who then became interested in anatomy.

He described the devotion of William James' mother to her husband and her children, and implied that William and young Henry may have gained their unusual receptivity of mind and aesthetic sensibility from her as well as from the world of literature, art, music, conversation and travel made available by their father's inheritance.

Here Gardner raised questions about what heredity can and cannot do, about early tastes, values, attitudes toward life and the role of identification with a loving father and a brilliantly perceptive mother. Further, he asked, "whence the unbearable fatigue and physical inadequacy in Harvard, which also disqualified James for military service; whence the eye trouble, indigestion, backaches, nervousness?" Gardner wondered whether these were "a unique personal expression of something for which heredity provided a base, to which the many changes of place, food, physical and social atmosphere offer a clue." He suggested that James' range of intense response—as in his early desire to be a painter, his later pursuit of a medical degree through thick and thin, his luxuriating in German philosophy, his English friendships—had such a range of intensity that his fragile organism had simply to pay a price.

Gardner's devotion and identification are reflected not only in the fact that a large print of a portrait of William James hung in his office but also in his struggle to understand the complexity of this beloved leader—in whom he may have seen some parts of himself—notably the wide range of intense responses, the determined drive to productivity, the aching body. There is an echo of his own temperament as he described James' love for new things, the changing and the creative, the strenuous and the heroic rather than the safe and sane; and in his description of James' "integration of the evolutionary and the progressive with the healing touch of personal freedom." He saw James as tremendously self-disciplined, mastering huge masses of technical material.

Turning to the relation of man to environment, Gardner wondered how the influences of America, of Harvard, of his security-giving wife, Alice Gibbens, and their children, the fame brought by his books, were all integrated into the mature James. Gardner doubted whether any cross-section of an individual life at one point in time could ever reveal the whole personality; we must look at the changing, growing, self-renewing processes of personality evolution. In each decade the James we saw "came from all that he had been before and from the new situation as advancing years brought a sense of what remained to be done."

With all of his mastery of the literature on James, Gardner felt aware that much was not known. In order to have a full picture of a personality, he felt, the threads from biology, from clinical experience, and from the social sciences need to be brought together, and this is what he tried to do in his own great book.

The fact that Gardner did not select a clinical case to open his discussion of personality emphasizes his determination to document the complexity of known factors as well as his conviction of the importance of unavailable knowledge about the origin and structure of an effective, creative, though vulnerable, personality. In the short space he allowed for the account of James' personality he did not attempt to use all that was known — for instance the rivalry that confused the mutual appreciation of the two brilliant brothers, William and Henry, and the anxiety which probably developed in a natural concern for the two younger brothers in the Army. These are obvious; what is not clear is William James' basic organic constitution with the strengths that made his achievements possible and the weaknesses that led to so much pain.

In this warm, sensitive appreciation, Gardner reflected his own identification with James and foreshadowed not only the complexity of the book he was writing but also the book's reflection of the range of Gardner's experiences. The first chapter orients the reader to his use of the term personality: he did not make a catalogue of certain human variabilities, but rather, tried to discover the nature of personality in general, "as one might try to discover the nature of trees in general." A case study of a particular person will be richer when the writer is fully aware of the laws governing the organized totality of a person. The psychologist must "look at individual persons under all the lights and through all the glasses that he can find." What this involves is suggested in his statement: "Personality study is an art and an engineering enterprise as well as a science, and at the present stage in its development, the three often flow together and refuse to be separated."

One has merely to peruse the index to *Personality* to see why some students said his course comprised the majority of their college education; his lectures on personality were called a "course on life." For example, Bach is followed by two Bacons — Francis Bacon of centuries ago and a Bacon of more recent years. W.K. Clifford who introduced "ejective consciousness" in 1879, is followed by Stanley Cobb, the psychiatrist; C.E. Coghill, the biologist; Coleridge, the poet; Confucius, of ancient Chinese history; C.H. Cooley (*Social Organization*, 1911); Copernicus, who revolutionized our orientation to the solar system; and W. Craig (with his doves). The "D"'s include Salvador Dalí and Charles Darwin. In addition to the authors we knew personally, Gardner was drawing on a vast range of scientists, writers, poets, and artists as he illuminated his concepts. The more than 500 creative people named in the index included 25 philosophers, 50 poets and novelists, and numerous artists, composers and politicians as well as biologists, psychologists and social scientists.

As some have complained, there is "not a single live person" in the book — that is, there are no case vignettes of a whole child or adult. But still, he described real people in action; for instance, De Quincey "made frantic attempts . . . to convey [the drug] experience to his fellows," and Salvador Dalí "attempted to get at the subjectivity rather than the objectivity of the world" and some people "follow St. Francis in loving the creatures of field and stream and 'our brother the sun' as well as their fellow human beings." A discussion of the self includes a reference to cartoons like those of William Steig's "About People" with their masks and false fronts. Discussions of concepts were enlivened with vivid allusions to human experience. It is no wonder that students eager for enlightenment hurried to the library to extend their acquaintance with the arresting characters of these famous creative personalities. And no wonder that some psychologists grumbled about such far-ranging associations when Gardner connected psychological principles with life and literature, art, and other sciences. Gardner's far-ranging associations came easily to him and were never forced. The minds of many scientists are furnished with well-organized files in which concepts and data are neatly arranged. Gardner's mind resembled an immense landscape laced with streams along which ideas flowed or rippled, with no barriers of time or category. Personality, to him, was everywhere and anywhere that human life could be found.

It is in the context of his awareness of how little is really known about the biology of James' inheritance that Gardner began the development of his theory in his section on "Organic Foundations." At the time he was developing his conception of the organic basis of personality—in the thirties—much that is known today was not known. It was believed, for instance, that nicotine and alcohol did not pass through the placenta. The full implications of the principle that the fetal environment and the genes of the embryo interact from the beginning were not realized even by Gardner.

Early in Part I Gardner stated his basic premise:

> Just as there is no biological process which is today completely independent of the conditions of life, so there is no social process except in and between the individual tissues of persons. Human evolution, then, as it goes on, yielding new biotypes, new personal potentialities, not only reflects, but in subtle and obscure fashion plays a part in guiding the more dramatic and obvious changes in social forms.

Typically, he then called upon the imagination and insight of the reader to explore the implications of the innate qualities of the organism and its special potentialities.

> Let us ask ourselves, says Clarence Day, what civilization would be like if the great cats, the lions, leopards, jaguars had invented it; if the great overreaching cerebral hemispheres had been superimposed upon the carnivorous ferocity of William Blake's *Tiger*. Civilization could be sublime in the manner of Assyrian art, gentle in the manner of kittens' play, but culture would express feline rather than simian needs. What, for example, shall we say about the right of free speech? Watch the simians in the field, forest or zoo, as they chatter. For the great cats, the right of free speech would yield to the right of personal combat.... Or turn, as did Swift, to a civilization built by the equines. What are the loyalties, the securities which this herd-minded, this intensely social race

would demand? Can one believe, any more than could Gulliver, that the equines would be capable of the chicaneries and brutalities of which the simians are perennially guilty.... There is a common fund of drive, of nervous exploratory activity, of easy fear and rage, of persistence, devotion, and brutality which lies deep in the tissues.

Gardner was constantly weaving together general principles; at the same time, he was constantly attentive to individuality. Traits are always in some measure the responses of specific tissues to specific environmental stimulation. What "is biological is at the same time social." The chapter "The Individual Constitution" illustrates differences in thresholds for sensory stimulation and also affective aspects of sensory responses, such as preferences for different colors, qualities and and intensity of light, sounds, touch. In addition to differences in activity he considered differences in endocrine glands, especially the thyroid and parathyroid whose excess or deficiency may predispose to emotional instability, and the pituitary, which is so important for growth and for sexual maturation. Individual differences in gonads help to determine differences in sexual maturation and in thresholds for both inner and outer sexual stimulation. Differences in endocrine balance are related to psychosomatic problems.

While Gardner recognized innate differences in these and other systems (cardiovascular, central and autonomic nervous systems, and so on) he also found room for effects of cultural influences at every point; "in all cultures stresses are at work ... and the general continuous load or strain upon the organism ... must be understood if the secondary load or strain of a specific environmental demand is to be appraised."

Over and above the specific contributions of specific tissue systems, with their thresholds, latencies, periodicities and after-discharges, Gardner emphasized "interorgan generalities," pacemaking or time-determining factors, as well as patterned interrelations that depend upon the dominance of one system over another. No tissue alone can determine any trait in a direct manner; individual personality traits are surface indicators of complex dynamic interrelations.

The organism requires nourishment; how is this basic need met? In the eighth chapter, on "Canalization," we find the most extended statement of this concept in Gardner's writings. Children "develop, when hungry, not a demand for food in general, but a demand for what they are used to," peanuts or whale blubber in different parts of the world. "So, too, over the face of the earth, children enjoy rhythms; the need is satisfied by different kinds of rhythms," games and music.

Gardner felt that Janet's term *canalization* aptly described the process that leads to specific tastes and preferences. He clarified the relation between canalization and conditioning by reminding the reader of Sherrington's distinction between preparatory and consummatory responses. The dog salivates when he hears the tuning fork that was presented with or before food. But he cannot eat and digest the tuning fork, and the tuning fork cannot end his hunger. Salivation is a preparatory response. Moreover, the connection between a substitute stimulus and a preparatory response does not last indefinitely if the tuning fork's sound is not followed by food. But canalizations endure: "in canalization we are dealing not merely with a signal that prepares for eating," but with a consummatory response (one that satisfies). When the stimulus is intrinsically satisfying, the canalized taste is not subject to extinction as is a conditioned response. A given taste leaves room for many more new tastes can be built up, and there is considerable transfer of generalization. Liking Turner's paintings makes it easy to enjoy Sung Dynasty paintings with their delicate nuances and wide horizons. Two of the major clues to personality seem to be "the specific ways in which canalized patterns are implanted in children by any society, and the study of the individual differences in content and form which such canalizations may assume in any society—in all types of motivation."

Freud's terms cathexis and fixation are also discussed in this context. The first of these refers to the canalization process, but it may lead to fixation, a type of canalization which "may act positively to make the individual unaware of some of his other canalizations" and may limit his contacts with the world. "It thus interferes with growth."

Canalization is not limited to objects in the external world; self-canalization may become a clue to the entire individual structure of canalizations. "If I pride myself on my love of Beethoven I may turn up my nose at all modern music." The adolescent's picture of himself is sufficient to block the expression of some childish tastes, although he may regress at times of reunion with those he knew in childhood—"the canalizations are not lost, they are overlaid by new activities."

> The strength of an individual canalization [Gardner continued], will depend on the initial strength of the general need from which the canalized need springs, the intensity of the gratification given by the canalized object, the developmental stage, and the frequency of such gratification.... In cultures in which the mother is a steady companion of the child, her face and voice, her touch, ... later the games or story telling which she provides are satisfiers that weave a broader texture of happiness.... But he loves her face, her voice, her footstep long before there is a whole mother. The experiences fuse into a wholeness because they often come together ... if these early satisfiers were bound tightly together so that mother was too completely satisfying, ... a later associate or lover must "have everything."

Similarly, after being "long in city pent" one must "go down to the sea again." Ulysses is "a part of all that he has met." The degree of satisfaction given by an experience is of cardinal importance. The concept of canalization is basic to an understanding of the vast amount of shaping and learning that does not require conditioning, or external rewards. This discussion of canalization is followed by even more extended discussions of conditioning and the hierarchy of conditionings.

A different way of engaging the reflection of the reader is seen in Gardner's approach to perception in the chapter "The Perceiver." He comments on Western man's ambivalence about his senses:

> Although everyone knows that it is brutish to rely on one's senses and that the clear light of reason puts the senses in their place, the ultimate test of sanity and adjustment is nevertheless to have sense, common or otherwise. The paradox has led us to contrast the senses with sense; a man comes to his senses as he reflects and discovers that his senses have been misleading him.

This is just one of the points at which he dealt with ambivalence or contradictions by confronting both sides of the issue. In this chapter he integrated different views of perception. The fact that his title for the chapter is "The Perceiver" rather than "Perception" reflects his fidelity to the conviction that it is always a *person* who is perceiving—a person with needs, expectancies, biases, which act selectively on the panorama of the environment to focus on that object—or that view of an object—that satisfies those needs. In the chapter on "Autism" he demonstrated with his City College experiments ways in which reward and punishment shape the perceiver's bias in the process of perceptual learning—an important contribution which was viewed by some as the initiation of the "new look" in perception.

In contrast with those who confine their study of personality to emotion, expressive patterns, characteristic behavior, and specific motives, Gardner included much of the inner life of imagination and thought, dreaming, and creativeness as well as perception. Mood and belief are looked at in relation to imagined processes. "Personality is first of all a drive system and this determines a person's way of thinking and believing." In order to illustrate the dynamics involved here he described his youthful heroine Jeanne d'Arc, whose village home he had visited during days off duty in World War I nearly thirty years earlier. Loving the Virgin, she prayed and prayed, the more when other children taunted her—prayed with an intensity which led first to ecstasy, then to hearing a voice, finally the voice she believed was St. Michael's. He told her to rescue the king. Soon two saints came to her and during her trial she told the judge that she had seen them "in exactly the same way I see you." The affect had brought the images.

In a similar way Gardner described the feelings of Blake, absorbed in the evangelism of Bunyan and the mysticism of Boehme, until his images became as vivid to him as those of Jeanne d'Arc had been to her. He put them down in engravings and verse exactly as he had seen them. Nietzsche's sister recounted that her brother said that he simply put down what the spirits said. Gardner implied that the origins of creativity can be found in all of us—in our deep longings, wishes, fantasies, and daydreams.

Continuing his discussion of the dynamic relation between affect and fantasy, Gardner asserted that thought is likewise a tension-expressing process. "The tension initiates the original activity . . . the wants evolve, however, as the activity goes on, and the images and processes involved may be valuable in their own right, so that it is *fun* to think." One thing leads to another and curiosity becomes a driving force.

> Each new thought or fantasy process establishes new structures in the mind of the thinker; in other words, one learns to think. . . . There is no one way to think, no one 'art of thinking,' no one thought craft that every craftsman can acquire. Rather, there are various types of logical thinking, various types of constructive and analytical thinking, each of which . . . (leads) to the acquisition of specific skills and hence to the increasing rigidity of the thinker's mind. Darwin at sixty could no longer read Shakespeare. . . . [T]he individual capacity for concentrated endeavor is actually greatest in those for whom the short-circuiting of all other activities is possible.

In his chapter on "The Dreamer," Gardner seems to plead with the reader to see what the competitive industrialized world, even with its devotion to progress, has forced us to overlook. This book

> is the work of an American who has listened like the rest to the pioneers and entrepreneurs, to the big doings of Paul Bunyan and Henry Ford, to Horatio Alger's success stories, to the be-not-weary-in-well-doing of the Lions Clubs, to all the excellent cultural molding-of-selfhood doctrines, to the group altruism of Jane Addams and John Dewey, to all that is up to date, socially-minded and progressive. All these influences and most of the books on personality by psychologists are so top-heavy with sociality that the little self is timidly hidden under the mass. But there is a private world and within this, a private, private world, a world of dreams, in and for oneself. When it is discovered, when its richness, strength and individuality are studied as objects of value for science and for art, there will be a psychology of personality more worthy of the name.

Dreaming, Gardner felt, is the realization of a biological function for which there is a need; it occurs because universal and important activities are expressed in and through it. Yet dreaming—exquisite, rich, beautiful, terrible, insane, furious, trivial, ineffable, silly, ravishing world that it creates—is often treated as a "nothing but" world; it is "nothing but a repetition of or preparation for waking experience." A description by De Quincey illustrates how magnificent a dream can be and prepares for the statement that each dream shows personal idiosyncrasies, motivation, and structural properties—there are great individual differences in the artistry of dreams. Although he does not say so, we get the impression that Gardner enjoyed dreams, his own and those of other people, as the most untrammeled expression of imagination.

It is here that his admiration of Freud is most intense: "Among all the flashes of genius in Freud's work, none is more compelling than the distinction between the latent and the manifest dream, for this provides the one necessary clue to the relation between the physiological world and the psychical world. The latent dream is the tension system." There are many alternatives for discharge of the tension. "The *dream work* is the process by which the tensions, in their facilitation and conflict, actualize, through the familiar autistic mechanism and figure-ground relationships, a perceptual whole." The dream is also a clue to the "architecture of our minds."

Without disagreeing with Freud's assertion that sexual references may always be found in dreams, Gardner emphasized the contribution of many or all other drives—sensory, activity and expecially ego needs. Any of these may mask any of the others. Their complexity means that there is no final interpretation for any dream, and major analysts, Stekel, Horney and others, continue to find "better" ways of interpreting. Gardner felt that "dreaming along with the dreamer," taking a "round trip ticket to a place far from the demands of waking existence" is necessary to capture the dream's intent. One part of the personality may take another part for a ride; a witty dream may be a take-off on oneself. "The Puritan and the Messiah are looked upon by the dreamer as his good old self, somewhat glorified and yet not quite as glorified as he expected. As he wakes he breaks into a laugh...."

Gardner recognized that the dreamer seems to be the artist freed of many of his temporal, local cultural constraints. His normal imaginative processes are broadened, enriched, and deepened. At the same time dreams do occasionally solve important problems. This occurred in a dream of the archaeologist H.V. Hilprecht, who had unsuccessfully struggled to decipher a cuneiform inscription on a broken clay tablet. The dream told how two pieces could be fitted together, after which the inscription could be deciphered. As soon as he found the fragments and put them together "the truth of the dream was demonstrated." In other instances, as with Coleridge's *Kubla Khan*, a dream may produce a creative work of value. Gardner felt that the apparent effortlessness of these productions may mean that more of the self is involved in the creation than is possible amid distractions of waking life.

Apart from the creative contributions of dreams, "most dreams have a lush or lavish quality which unambiguously bespeaks greater psychic freedom and creativeness." Here we assume Gardner was speaking of his own experience.

We have already seen, in the chapter on "The Dreamer," Gardner's deep interest in the concept of the self. The self was not a popular topic in the psychology of the early twentieth century, or for that matter, in Herbart's and

Helmholtz's day. Associations, and conditioning, seemed to take place independent of a self. But James Baldwin, William James, and McDougall discussed the *social* self, and James discussed an empirical *me*. For Gardner the self is a thing perceived as well as conceived, and it is responded to by oneself. One corrects, defends, enjoys oneself.

Recognition of the self by the self comes gradually as the baby observes its hands, hears its voice, experiences inner comforts and discomforts. As the different components of experience occur simultaneously and interact, they come to make up a perceived whole. Mother (and other people) serve as an anchoring point for a gradually developing self pattern perceived largely by analogy with the form of the mother. As Gardner discussed the origin and evolution of the self, and then oriented psychoanalytic concepts from Freud, Adler, Jung and others in relation to the self, we find some of his most original integration of concepts. Compensation for inferiority is an effort by the self on behalf of itself; defense mechanisms defend a self.

Although Gardner regarded Freud as the greatest genius in psychology in the twentieth century, he was critical of Freud's rejection of Adler, whose concept of compensation for organ inferiority is so relevant to understanding personality in the competitive culture of the west. A whole chapter develops this theme, as a "wide-spread biological principle." There is a perpetual struggle to make the actual self as much as possible like the ideal self. Demosthenes' conquest of stammering and achievement of oratorical power were so great that they fired the military to march successfully against Philip of Macedon's attack on Athens; Demosthenes became a hero. The weak, asthmatic Theodore Roosevelt, ridiculed by other boys, determined to develop muscle and skill and at Harvard he also mastered literary form. He pursued successive careers in the police and the military, and then became president of the United States. With other examples Gardner illustrated the need for approval by others as a validation of self-approval.

Mastery in many areas may lead to feelings of dominance, but a totally new situation for which a dominant person is unprepared may evoke insecurity; a sense of competence in familiar situations is not proof against *all* assaults. Adler's concept of "the style of life" also receives careful discussion. Gardner felt that Adler's thinking made sense; it is the injured self, the shamed, humiliated, beaten member of the community whose self-respect, whose status, whose sense of his own worth has been challenged so vigorously from without that he has learned to challenge it himself and is unable to feel self-pride. One has to look at ego development in the culture in order to understand vulnerability to inferiority feelings.

Gardner discussed psychoanalytic mechanisms—that is, mechanisms studied by psychoanalysts at length; he criticized certain popularized concepts, especially that of extroversion-introversion. Noting that in the distribution of a large sample of people we find real introverts and extroverts only at the extremes, he commented that most of us are extroverted part of the time, and introverted part of the time; it is therefore not useful to classify people into these types. Extroversion and introversion are aspects of the functioning of a self.

All through the book, an awareness of cultural differences recognizes the relativity of generalizations about personality. Still, the chapter "The Evolution of the Self" echoes patterns of competitive Western cultures with their pressures toward achieving status, power and possessions. To be sure, we see the "pecking order" in the barnyard and in the jungle. But much learning is experienced by the baby whose every new achievement brings applause, a feeling of importance and stimulation to new achievements.

In this book on personality there is a dearth of tycoons, pirates, Mafia godfathers, corrupting politicians, as well as serial murderers; even for the sake of extending science Gardner did not consort with rascals. In the half-century that we were together, he mentioned two "evil men," Hitler in World War II and Richard Nixon subsequently. Not that Gordon Allport, "Harry" Murray, or other students of personality were more comprehensive — the easily available college and high school students provided most of the subjects for research, and Gardner's mind was peopled with members of the fraternity of the arts, literature and philosophy.

He made clear at the start that he was not a clinician, and we do not find examples of schizophrenics, psychopaths or even illustrations of psychotic or hysterical episodes, although he discussed processes involved in mental illness. He did include people with multiple personalities as they were studied by Walter Prince and others. In the predominant bias toward discussion of average and of creative people he reflected the psychology of the twentieth century; it had not yet focussed on personalities of criminals or corrupt politicians.

Much of *Personality* is written in a cool light of theory with the grand aim of integrating all of the research data and concepts he found relevant to the understanding of the development of personality. But the heart of the book, I believe, is in the series of chapters in the section on "Personal Outlook," and those in the section on "The Self"; these include almost a third of the book. One does not have to make an effort to read between the lines to find where his own identifications in psychology lie, or to find the roots in his own experience, canalizations, and observations that give rise to his hypotheses. When he talked about the man who loves Beethoven but not modern music he was talking about himself. When he discussed the child's struggle to cope with his love for the loving mother and his anger at the punishing mother (and love usually wins out) he was also talking about himself. When he referred to the little girl who said that she can't fight with her brother unless she "has the pants on" he has in mind his daughter. Thoughtful observations of friends and other persons seen in social settings likewise provide grist for his mill.

Even more than the rest of the book, these pages need to be read with empathy and intuition and sensitivity; when they are experienced, not just summarized, they can release a stream of associations in the reader's mind that will evoke further hypotheses as well as awareness of the relativity of those presented here.

In Part Five, "Wholeness," Gardner developed his concept of the structure of personality, evolved from his reflections on Spencer's and then Heinz Werner's developmental stages: from undifferentiated to differentiated, to an integrated or organized structure. Extending that three-stage view of mental development to personality, Gardner looked for global dispositions that would characterize all the cells of one's body, such as speed of conduction within the nervous system, thresholds, rhythms, latent times, and after-discharges of tension. He expected to find general motor dispositions such as speed, strength, and endurance; sensory dispositions such as acuity and imagery; and affective dispositions such as intensity, evenness or volatility. (More than a decade later, in the 1959 study *Prediction and Outcome,* Escalona and Heider found that prediction was most successful on just such variables.)

Differentiated variables, Gardner stated, depend on the global variables. A person's style of walking and style of handwriting may share similar qualities of vigor or speed. He quoted Rounds' finding that speed in certain intelligence tests correlated with speed in the Achilles tendon reflex. But correspondence of traits could be due to conditioning as well as to the presence of a general disposition. The tendency to draw, write and move in large rather than small areas was found by Allport and Vernon to be a general tendency. But we know people like Margaret Mead whose writing was minuscule, in order to get as many of her anthropological notes on one page as possible, while her gestures were large. Here motives can modify initial tendencies to be expansive or contractible. Such tendencies are third level dispositions in Allport-Vernon's system, where congruence of apparently different tendencies is implied in the purpose — in each case — to be effective. Differentiation is the second stage and congruence is the third. These different levels or systems continue to exist in each individual, and even simultaneously: timidity or anxiety may be a general trait, a specific fear may become generalized to related stimuli; caution may be cultivated as a safe policy. And traits may be used as tools. We cannot deal here with Gardner's extensive discussion of organization of traits, but it is important to note that he saw second stage traits as emerging from first stage dispositions by virtue of specific local modes of interaction with the environment while third stage traits are not predictable from first stage traits. As systems become more complex they exhibit new functions.

The final section, Part Six, "Individual and Group," deals with group membership, economic determinism, social roles and ethos — chapters much appreciated by sociologists. In dramatic contrast to the diagrams and geometrical conceptualizations of the discussion of personality structure, the chapter "History as the Proving Ground" sweeps breathlessly through the sequences in Western civilization, illustrating the relationship between the dominant military, religious and economic forces in successive eras and analyzing the personalities of well-known men and women. Drawing upon literature, architecture and art, and the reflections of major thinkers of our time, the chapter is vivid and convincing: personalities are shaped by the compelling forces of each period.

The "Family as Mediator of Culture" discusses anthropological and sociological studies of the family as the immediate world of security, and presents family roles as models for many relationships in other groups, and as features of character structure. Because of extensive research in this area, the topic of the authoritarian personality is dealt with at length.

Situationism then leads to Gardner's formulation of field theory, which has its background in Clerk-Maxwell's equations for electromagnetic fields and Spemann's work in experimental embryology. Mother and infant are involved in a single field. Although Gardner ackowledged his debt to Kurt Lewin, his own development of field theory is different from that of Lewin. According to Gardner, the organism selects from the situation and the situation selects from the organism. He used the illustration of my experience at the New York Training School for girls; when I first was an observer, then spent a spring vacation there as a substitute matron, the institution was managed by a punitive superintendent amd the girls were sullen and hostile. A new and humane superintendent changed the atmosphere, providing attractive materials for the girls to make their own dresses, a beauty shop, job training, and easing of restrictions. The girls became more relaxed, cooperative and friendly. "We cannot define the organism operationally, in such a way as to obtain predictive power for behavior, except in reference to the situation." (One could also give examples from some patients who are negatively assessed by a series of examiners felt to be distant and cold, then seen positively as they respond to a therapist experienced as warm and caring.)

In a challenging chapter, "The Fitness of Culture for Personality," Gardner described the struggle between the individual and the norm, the aggressiveness with which, with "powerful and ever-repeated blows" from the culture, molding takes place. Taboos and restrictions are conveyed in a variety of ways, from signals conveyed by facial expressions to corporal punishment. The individual is molded by being sensitized to a particular system of signals. Not only are value systems canalized and conditioned and the impulses guided, but the ethos or feeling tone is shaped by cultural processes. However, culture meets the needs of people with varying degrees of success, and it is by not accepting culture as it is that new cultures are made.

In this context Gardner commented on the positive aspects of American culture, which recognize the importance of the individual and of individual responsibility and initiative and the concept that regard for the individual's welfare is the supreme test of a society. Along with this is the recognition of the richness contributed by individual differences, although this is inadequately developed since our society "neglects aspects of individuality which are not directly related to the success pattern of our era." Beyond these characteristics is the concept of freedom, "the right to do, read, talk, think as we wish," including freedom of inquiry into what makes nature or mankind tick. "Socrates and Roger Bacon did not enjoy this freedom." Gardner also felt that a major strength of our culture is the ardent belief in the continuity of progress. "A World's Fair staged during a Depression year may be named a Century of Progress and no one will blink." "Progress" includes science and technology and also social progress, provided it is not "radical."

In contrast to these basic strengths Gardner saw as cultural liabilities the American fear of economic insecurity, uncertainty of affection, and inordinate admiration of status and prestige, which leads to ego strain. In Americans, pathological insecurity is sometimes accompanied by the relative loss of group identification, and is increased by mobility from one locale to another, job instability, dissolution of the large family group and a high divorce rate. Value conflicts add other severe threats to our society. At the time when he was writing, recent preoccupation with World War II dominated the scene so that the domestic violence that emerged later was not foreseen.

The conception of identification with the group in the Soviet Union is seen as a major asset; so also is freedom from economic insecurity. Parallel with economic security are art, music, drama, literature. But pervasive coercion restricts the values a person wishes to satisfy, opportunities to explore, and even the identifications one wishes to make. Identification with Trotsky became a sin — unity is achieved through fratricide. Coercion may even constrict science. Gardner believed that both societies would change in years ahead. Culture as well as personality could change.

Always remembering the guides of former times, Gardner recalled a warning by Robert Boyle in *The Skeptical Chymist* (1677).

> He answered their [chemists of the time] assertion that they had shaken off superstition and found the high road to knowledge; he offered essentially a commentary on the dangers of premature enthusiasm. He saw that the chemists had established no firm basis . . . for a new science. . . . [O]nly when one realizes how little he knows can a sound beginning be made on the task of science.

Psychology, Gardner felt, was in about the same position today as chemistry was in Boyle's time, three centuries ago. Psychoanalysis, psychometric methods and cross-cultural studies of personality have developed within this century, and all of them "to the skeptic, full of untested assumptions." Neither in content nor in method, he asserted, have we solved the essential problem of the starting point from which a psychology could be written. A more serious difficulty is our uncertainty as to the nature of man and his place in the cosmos.

Like other living things, man has evolved by virtue of very complex principles about which the biochemists, the biologists and the field naturalists are still far from clear. We do not know "to what extent the principles operating within man are identical to the general principles which operate elsewhere in the universe." The relation of mind, feeling and purpose to the world of physics is almost as obscure as it was in the sixth century B.C.

After a long discussion of the conflicts involved between the need for self-realization and the equally strong wish to be part of the group (whether as expressed in, say, Christianity or in Marxism), Gardner suggested that eventually the scientific method will be ready to integrate with other insights of an intuitive or poetic sort to meet human needs. He felt that new modes of attack would emerge. There is no more "reason to believe that the methods of the mid-twentieth century are final . . . than to believe that Galileo's method and results were final." He implied that just as eighteenth century rationalism could not predict Darwinism, or the French psychiatry of 1880 predict psychoanalysis, we cannot predict the next steps in the development of psychology. The birth of new knowledge can only occur after a recognition of the limitations of the whole present system of conceptions. His skepticism was balanced by optimism that this development lay ahead.

The stream of stimulating contacts with Europeans, psychologists and social scientists came on the heels of Gardner's 1931 commitment to the study of personality, and the pages of this book are peopled with them. He wrote in his preface to the 1966 reprinting nearly 20 years after it first appeared, "The book belongs in the stream of time just where it is." He recognized that the dramatic changes in both Western and Eastern culture in the decades after World War II, and the important developments in genetics, and in developmental and cognitive research, would call for some major restatements of the facts illustrating the biosocial development of personality. But he felt that his *approach* to a formulation of its origins and structure could still be used as a framework for a revision. This he did not want to undertake — he had other plans in mind, and at 71, his years for writing might be short.

In addition to weaving into one tapestry a wide range of concepts from different fields of study — biology, biochemistry, sociology, aesthetics, philosophy and psychoanalysis, Gardner illuminated many chapters with our observations and experiences with children, as well as with vignettes from our studies. *Personality* integrates this vast panorama with perspective, wisdom, and empathy for human beings, along with flashes of shrewd and sardonic humor.

At the same time the book reflects the limitations of psychology in the first half of the twentieth century. The index includes anxiety, but not courage (where would research on courage be found?); insecurity but not competence, trust, or confidence; sensitivity but not coping and mastery; trauma but not resilience; jealousy but not tolerance; narcissism but not generativity. The fact that Gardner does include both empathy and sympathy as well as tact, cooperation, curiosity, integration, and love, points to his values and his concern with positive and socially valuable aspects of personality. But a new book written in 1970 after Erikson's discussions of trust, autonomy, initiative, intimacy and generativity; Robert White's analysis of competence; our Topeka studies of coping; and his own work on perception of reality—all would have extended his warm appreciation of socially constructive personality development. *Personality: A Biosocial Approach to Origins and Structure* needs to be seen as a milestone in the long road to an as yet incomplete theory of personality. In Gardner's *Personality* as in his City College course, which the students called his "course in life," we see his integration of his life experience along with the integration of contributions from the social sciences and from literature.

18. The Scientific Problem of Parapsychology

On the morning of the day that Gardner died of a coronary occlusion at 8 p.m. his friend and coauthor, Morton Leeds told him that proofs of their last book, *The Paranormal and the Normal,* had come. We had been working over it week by week during the four years of his transcendence over pain and frustration in our "home hospital," when he could not write and could speak through his tracheotomy only with difficulty. His first commitment to parapsychology had begun about 66 years earlier at Yale when he asked his psychology professor, Dr. Angier, whether psychology would be a good background for psychical research—the answer was "yes." Gardner wrote about the development of his work in psychical research in "Notes for a Parapsychological Autobiography," tracing his interest back to events in his childhood in Concord, Massachusetts.

Paradoxically, Gardner initiated his lifework as a psychologist as a foundation for work in the field of psychical research. As a parapsychologist he was midwife, administrator, theoretician, critic, and communicator; to a lesser degree he was an experimentalist in his own right, but it is fair to say that none of his research in parapsychology equalled the achievement of his landmark work in social psychology. At the same time he made a major impact on the field through his moral and financial support of young investigators, his leadership and demand for the highest scientific standards at a time when standards were being compromised, and his brilliant and expert defense of psychical research at certain crucial times when it was being attacked.

Long before Gardner, at age sixteen, discovered Sir William Barrett's book, *Psychical Research,* and even before the development of his intense religious feelings—when he was a boy of four or five in fact—an experience helped to shape memories that focussed the childhood wonder and curiosity of that imaginative little boy. Gardner himself connected this challenging childhood experience with his preoccupation with the question of souls. When his precious tin Doggie fell apart he was shocked and anxious: where was Doggie, what happened to his soul? Intense, sensitive and reflective, he never forgot that incident; it evidently contributed to a perennial wondering and ultimately to his passionate quest. The theme, *plus ultra,* "there is more beyond," must have reinforced this quest. The home atmosphere, the culture of Concord, the early experiences, Sir William Barrett's crucial book, and Gardner's intensity all contributed to the meshing of belief, question, and the impulse to search for the answer, which fed his lifelong commitment.

The soul and immortality were matters of passionate belief in the nineteenth and early twentieth centuries. (I remember how, during my first weeks at Vassar College in the fall of 1919, we got into heated discussions of the soul. I was attracted to Ruth Munroe who exclaimed, "If *anyone* has a soul, dogs have souls!") It is hard for adults today to appreciate the passion of religious feelings in the young of the early twentieth century, although we can remind ourselves of the recent upsurge of response to Zen Buddhism, Sufism, Yoga, transcendental meditation and even evangelical right-wing Protestantism under the impact of the intellectualism of modern liberal religion. Gardner wrote that his evangelical convictions supported a continued interest in psychical research. "The obvious positivistic or behavioristic attitude of the psychology department at Yale simply proved to me how ignorant they were." Although Gardner did not mention it, the loss of his brilliant and adored father just as he completed his freshman year at Yale may have added a poignant depth to his intense hope that the soul could have an afterlife, as Frank Lorimer suggested.

Gardner's deep interest in psychical research never wavered, but it was expressed in different ways at different stages of his life. Curiosity stimulated by the dinner table conversations in his Concord grandfather's home fed the sixteen-year-old boy's preoccupation with the soul; "the quickened flame never abated," he wrote in 1957. Richard Hodgsons's investigations of Mrs. Piper's mediumship in Concord were widely respected by Gardner's family and by others. In short, the atmosphere in which Gardner's early interest took root was free from the ridicule and hostility that met psychical research in New York and the East generally in the twenties and the thirties, and from the indifference Gardner encountered from 1912 on at Yale. Although his introduction to scientific concepts there, including the theory of evolution, undermined his intense evangelical theology, it did not erode his commitment to study the relation between mind or personality and brain, the question to which he hoped psychical research could give an answer.

Harvard was more hospitable to his interest than Yale had been; in fact, the psychologist L.T. Troland responded to Gardner's interest by inviting him to be an assistant in a small experimental study and suggested more reading in the field, focussing on the literature on telepathy. That was the year when the materialistic world view first encountered at Yale—especially in A.G.

Keller's course in anthropology—finally demolished Gardner's wavering faith as it had been shaped by his Episcopal heritage and by his adolescent exposures to evangelical religion. The scientific approach to psychical phenomena was, however, consistent with the respect for science which had been nourished at Yale, and which Gardner now deeply shared. At the same time that he was introduced to an experimental approach to psychical research, he worked on the philosophical issue of mind-body theory, and wrote a long paper (for E.B. Holt's course in the philosophy of nature) stating the case for a mind-body dualism—that is, for the independence of mind from brain. This issue continued to absorb him for the rest of his life.

During his time in France in World War I another experience affected him—a visit to the mysterious faith healings at Lourdes, some of which were certified by a qualified physician. Fifty years before the American studies of mental control of blood pressure, pain, and other physical conditions, these healings were seen as another form of psychical event. More important for his orientation to the range of these phenomena was his excursion to London and the office of the Society for Psychical Research (SPR) in the same period. Gardner joined the (SPR), thus consolidating his commitment to the field and making a place for himself in a group dedicated with utmost seriousness to intensive study of psychical events. It was a respectable group—its leaders included scholars of the stature of Henry Sidgwick, Sir William Barrett and F.W.H. Myers, a classical scholar whose work was admired by William James. Contributors to the *Proceedings* of the (SPR) included Oliver Lodge, the eminent English physicist, and Professor Richet, a French physiologist and Nobel prize winner.

At this stage, when young Gardner's intellectual and emotional commitments were bombarded by the assaults of the academic skeptics in America, the support of this distinguished organization fueled that "quickened flame." After he returned to the United States Gardner diligently pursued an excellent program of reading outlined by the Society for Psychical Research secretary. In fact, his feeling about the Society was so strong that in 1921 he asked the famed English psychologist at Harvard, William McDougall, whether there would be any chance of obtaining employment at the (SPR) on a permanent basis. "With all the ardent intensity of youth I had found what I believed in," he wrote many years later. It was the British investigations into the question of the survival of the soul after death from 1882 to the World War I period that filled the gulf left by the loss of his passionate evangelical faith.

Gardner was preoccupied with the issue of survival through the early years of his involvement in psychical research. "I was, of course," he wrote in 1956, "during all this time, trying to decide whether I believed that the evidence for survival was strong enough to warrant conviction." He went back to London in June of 1921—in the midst of his graduate work at Columbia—to explore further evidence in unpublished items and to talk with the officers of the

Society there. He recalled later that he was "slightly more pro than con." He saw "as no one but a psychologist can see" the impossibility of a personality without a body, of thought without a cerebral cortex. At the same time he could not resist the force of evidence of some of the apparitions that conveyed a sense of the "pressure of the surviving individual to make real his presence to the living." But Gardner himself never mentioned and I believe never had any experience of such an apparition of any of his dear ones after death—not his father who died in 1913 nor his grandfather who died in 1919, nor his mother who died in 1957. Still, this lack of confirmation by personal experience did not deter him from pursuing all the available evidence.

His interest was not, however, confined to the issue of survival. After his experiments in 1916–17 with Troland he accepted a stipend from the Richard Hodgson Fund and commuted weekly from 1922 to 1925 doing telepathy experiments at Harvard while teaching psychology at Columbia. Harry Helson and George Estabrooks worked with him on these experiments. He was close to the helpful Dr. Walter Franklin Prince, while the aging Dr. J.H. Hyslop and Dr. Elwood Worcester also gave him useful suggestions. On the way to the Warsaw Psychical Research Congress in the late summer of 1923 he met René Warcollier, the gifted French chemist, with whom he carried out a series of transatlantic telepathic experiments. This was his situation in the winter of 1924–25 when we first met.

Unfortunately, the weakness that persisted after Gardner's acute encephalitic flu in the spring of 1925 made further commuting to Harvard impossible; he could barely keep up his Columbia teaching. After we were married in the fall of 1926—still concerned with the survival problem—he read me the cross-correspondences seen in records of single and related messages conveyed by independent mediums. At the same time we carried on some informal telepathy (or clairvoyance) experiments with a friend who lived across the Hudson. In New York we attempted to receive what was "sent" from New Jersey; we had no success in the telepathy experiments but several times I had images of events that occurred the same day. At that time Gardner considered these to be evidences of telepathy or clairvoyance.

What impressed me most, however, during the late twenties and the thirties was Gardner's shock at the preposterous frauds perpetrated by the medium "Margery" who claimed to produce ectoplasm by paranormal means. Intense distress at the support given her by the American Society for Psychical Research and his feeling that the American Society's standards had deteriorated disgracefully, led him to participate in a "palace revolution." In 1941 Gardner became the director of research, determined to reestablish the scientific integrity of the Society. I think the effect of Margery's corruption of the American Society turned him away from work with mediums for the rest of his life. But he did not lose interest in the problem of survival; he responded positively to

Ian Stevenson's careful studies of cases suggesting reincarnation. Gardner in 1945 wrote three discriminating papers on survival and he included extensive material on survival in his 1961 book, *The Challenge of Psychical Research.*

Although he had no energy for active work in psychical research during the years between 1925 and 1934, when the encephalitic flu left him debilitated, his interest did not lag and he continued reading, with an implicit commitment to continue his work in that field when it became possible. I felt so certain of this that when the young biologist J.B. Rhine knocked at the door of our apartment one day in the fall of 1927 — when Gardner was in bed with a bad case of bronchitis — asking whether Gardner was committed to psychical research, I told him that he was. I explained Gardner's current situation and his expectation of returning to active work in the field. The rest of Rhine's story is well known — his widely publicized experiments in extrasensory perception, and his ingenuity in developing simple experimental procedures which could be used by others. His work gave tremendous impetus to a scientific approach to psychical research. Excited by Rhine's 1934 report, Gardner went down to Duke University to visit Rhine's laboratory. From that time on Gardner was actively involved in psychical research at many levels.

René Warcollier responded to Gardner's eagerness about his work after their transatlantic experiments from 1923 to 1925 and invited us to accompany his family to the French village of Pont Aven in the summer of 1929. The fortnight in that peaceful retreat gave time for long daily discussions and cemented a warm friendship, leading to Gardner's assistance in facilitating American publication of two of Warcollier's books: *Experimental Telepathy,* in 1938, and *Mind to Mind,* in 1948. In contrast to the tidy (and to me, boring) little figures on Rhine's cards, Warcollier's targets were interesting. In his introduction to *Mind to Mind,* Gardner commented that the "raw stuff" — of dreams and waking telepathic experiences — offers more for the study of dynamics in parapsychological functioning than does the process of choosing from mechanically sequenced cards in a deck, or the symbols on Rhine's cards. But it is very dfficult to exclude coincidence, and to arrive at statistically acceptable evaluations of free material such as that produced in Warcollier's experiments.

Gardner developed a multifaceted role in the American Society for Psychical Research and also in the Parapsychology Foundation. Using part of the royalties from his books he contributed to the financial support of two young psychical researchers, Gaither Pratt and Joseph L. Woodruff, whom he housed at Columbia to the bemusement of the friendly and tolerant senior psychologists Woodworth and Poffenberger. Certain other members of the psychology staff were anything *but* tolerant. Gardner again accepted the Hodgson stipend on the understanding that he could assign it to others.

During the same year (1935–36) that Gardner financed Gaither Pratt's first year at Columbia another gifted young scientist came to Gardner's door —

Ernest Taves. Gardner invited him to help on current psychical research and financed this by the Hodgson Fund and by the National Youth Administration, one of Roosevelt's imaginative ways of coping with the disastrous unemployment during the Depression. This began several years of Taves' work in parapsychology. Laura Dale became his research partner and he also had important contacts with Gaither Pratt and J.B. Rhine. The "Taves machine" was an important technical invention to facilitate the experimental work.

Gardner's role with Ernest Taves, Gaither Pratt, Joseph Woodruff, Laura Dale, S. David Kahn, and others carrying on studies in the psychical research area was active in different ways—from participation in their research, to financing their work in New York; guiding, stimulating and supporting their efforts when he was not participating in experiments. The American Society for Psychical Research flourished during the periods when Gardner was shaping it "like a gardener who loved his plants" as Karlis Osis wrote. "As far as I was concerned, Murphy was the Society," Osis once remarked.

By 1941, when Gardner became a member of the Board of Trustees of the ASPR as well as chairman of its Research Committee, he had acquired extensive administrative expertise as well as experience in supervising the research of Ph.D. candidates and in inspiring research ideas. All of this skill was now committed to lifting the work of the ASPR to a level of unassailable integrity. His election to the governing council of the American Psychological Association, and then to the presidency of that organization in 1943, and also of the SPR (London) in 1949, lent authority to the ASPR and contributed to the feeling that Gardner was the center of the Society. In addition, Laura Dale's meticulous and expert editing of the ASPR *Journal* added to the Society's prestige.

George H. Hyslop, a neurologist and son of the longtime president of the ASPR, James Hyslop, was now president. Gardner became vice president and helped to guide and implement the Society's policies. During the forties he spent six mornings a week at the offices of the ASPR, conferring, reading, writing and participating in all the work of the Society from budget allocations to research to publication policies of the *Journal*. Along with other relevant experience in the thirties, the fact that he had become editor of Harper's psychology series and had published six books of his own had given him an impressive editorial expertise.

On Saturdays in the forties, as Taves and Ullman recalled, there were lively sessions trying out innovative experiments with variable outcomes. Sometimes the results were positive, but rarely could they be replicated.

After Hyslop's death, when Gardner became president of the ASPR (in 1962), lecture attendance increased from 40 or 50 to 200, and membership increased steadily to over 2000 from the earlier plateau of about 800. According to Karlis Osis' historical account, this was a time when burgeoning interest in ESP and experiments in life styles contributed to a new enthusiasm in the

ASPR. Transcontinental experiments were undertaken and a day-long ASPR forum was held that attracted faculty members and researchers from 34 institutions. The staff was energized to develop a membership campaign, an executive secretary was appointed, the library was updated and improved with a new cataloging system, and a *Newsletter* was launched. These expanded activites were carried on by a gifted and devoted staff of parttime and fulltime employess.

Although results of parapsychological experiments in which Gardner participated were not as impressive as those of his experiments at City College which launched an important new approach to the study of perception, he found deep satisfaction in being part of the effort to move psychical research to acceptance as a credible science. It was especially gratifying to him to watch the innovative work of Gertrude Schmeidler who had been stimulated by his psychical research course at Harvard in the summer of 1942. Her pioneer studies of the influence of subjects' attitudes (favorable or unfavorable to ESP) initiated a new drive toward studying conditions favorable to success.

A grant of $100,000 from the Ittleson Foundation financed studies of the relation between creativity and extrasensory perception. Gardner administered this with allocations to several investigators such as Frank Barron at the University of California and Karlis Osis at the American Society for Psychical Research. With Gardner's aid, Montague Ullman, a psychiatrist, established a Dream Laboratory at the Maimonides Mental Health Center in Brooklyn; Stanley Krippner, a psychologist who had assisted Gardner earlier, became the director. Their work on telepathy in dreams was so impressive to Gardner that he contributed to the financial support of the laboratory; some of their important findings are described in their book, with Alan Vaughan, *Dream Telepathy* (1973). Both Ullman and Krippner remained close to Gardner, visiting him devotedly during Gardner's long illness in our "home hospital" in the 1970s. With Alice Moriarty, Gardner also carried on a study with children; they found dissociation to be a factor common to creativity and extrasensory perception in these children.

In addition to Gardner's generative relationship to those who worked at the ASPR he brought stimulating friends to the Board of Trustees, of whom Margaret Mead was one of the most helpful. Karlis Osis reported that she was "especially insightful," exposing deficiencies in the experimental methods of the 1940s as when she argued that the approach must be a study of the nature of what occurs in its whole setting, not just a search for the paranormal element in an unspecified context. This view reinforced Gardner's statements regarding the field in which paranormal (and other) events take place. Osis added that Mead also urged a study of why and when there is a loss of paranormal ability, and she recommended anthropological comparisons as well as studies of motivation.

A direct effect of Gardner's development as a psychologist specializing in the areas of social psychology, personality, and perception was his encouragement of the integration into parapsychology of relevant principles from psychology. His persistent demand for a comprehensive study of the field or context in which psi (any paranormal event) occurs is only one example. Another is seen in his student Donald Cook's description of Gardner's detailed guidance of Cook's study of psi in hypnotized subjects as compared with those in the normal state. Gardner asked Cook down-to-earth questions: How would he select his subjects and how would he ascertain their hypnotizability? How would he handle individual differences? What methods of statistical analysis would he use? And so on. Later, when Cook attended Gardner's 1945 lectures in parapsychology at the New School, Gardner discussed the trance medium (such as Mrs. Piper) as a deviant personality from the perspective of cultural anthropology, "behaving in accordance with a conflicting set of role demands whether or not the 'phenomena' produced were veridical.... The intent and actual performance of the medium had to be seen as the result of larger forces."

Gardner did not encourage competitive feelings between the ASPR and the Parapsychology Foundation established in 1951 by the medium Eileen Garrett. He was the Foundation's research consultant and gave the opening address at the Parapsychology Foundation's First International Conference in Utrecht in August 1953. Eileen Coly, president of the Foundation when Gardner died, wrote, "...we can say of Gardner Murphy as he said of William James, that what gave him the permanent place which he holds in psychical research is ... the courage and energy with which he stressed the importance of these inquiries ... [and] his insistence that an organized type of research enterprise must be set up, with continuity over the years."

After Gardner moved to Topeka, Kansas, as director of the Research Department of the Menninger Foundation from 1952 to 1967 he could no longer spend long hours at the ASPR. However, professional conferences in the East, discussions at the National Institute of Mental Health, pertaining to his Topeka research, and other professional demands brought him to New York approximately once a month and whenever he was near enough he stopped in for a visit to the ASPR, of which he was president from 1962 to 1971. He tried unsuccessfully to persuade his friend, the Yale physicist Henry Margenau, to join the Board, but on November 20, 1965, at the Barbizon-Plaza Hotel, Margenau did give an important address in an ASPR forum on extrasensory perception: "ESP in the Framework of Modern Science."

Gardner had a way of keeping in touch with his Menninger research group when he was away from Topeka, and his presence was always felt at the ASPR as well, even though he could not spend much time there. He continued to read parapsychology reports; his writing on problems in psychical research flowed at an even more rapid pace.

Over the years Gardner invested a considerable amount of time in fund-raising efforts. For instance, I recall the hours he spent in carefully preparing his testimony for the hearing on allocation of money from an estate willed to an organization devoted to discovering evidence of life after death (the Kidd estate). His effort succeeded in obtaining a large sum for research at the ASPR when the competition for the money was intense.

At least as important as his moral and financial support was his influence as a bridge to the psychological establishment. Most memorable was a symposium at the 1938 annual convention of the American Psychological Association in Columbus, Ohio. A young critic hoped to drive the final nail into Rhine's work. Rhine himself described the occasion as one in which he anticipated a public showdown as to what psychologists were thinking about parapsychology. J.L. Kennedy undertook the attack on the Duke experiments along with two other critics, while Rhine, Gardner, and one other psychologist were the defenders. The confrontation had received extensive advance publicity, which guaranteed a huge audience. The Yale psychologist Irvin Child, who attended that 1938 symposium, commented:

> Rhine's manner struck me as that of a beleagured hero, showing the strain of knowing from experience that irrational elements would be at least as conspicuous as rational elements in the attack he expected to receive.... Gardner Murphy seemed to me ... a sort of referee attempting to keep the controversy cool. He exposed the irrelevance of some of the critical attack on parapsychologists' findings, without himself taking any strong position on what interpretation should be placed on the findings ... [keeping] to his chosen path of strict rationality.

Rhine later recalled that the atmosphere was "the most extremely tense" that he had ever experienced in a public meeting. He wrote that "Murphy marshalled the evidence and arguments with a skill I have never seen equaled," and indicated his satisfaction at the outcome by noting that "the applause was eloquently indicative of the judgment as to who won the debate."

Another important development in acceptance of psychical research as a legitimate field for investigation was indirectly due to Gardner's influence. Conversations about psychical research with our friend Margaret Mead led to her election to the Board of Trustees of the ASPR and convinced her that the Parapsychological Association ought to be accepted as an affiliate in the American Association for the Advancement of Science (AAAS). Her effort on behalf of this move succeeded in 1969.

Gardner's writing on parapsychology included several major types of contribution: First, as with his writing on psychology he shared his appreciation of historical contributors to the field, especially William James and F.W.H. Myers. Next, he presented samples of data that he considered challenging. Third, he discussed in depth issues such as survival, with a critical analysis of positive and negative aspects of relevant evidence. Fourth, he formulated scientific principles that had to be respected in order for psychical research to be accepted in the world of science. And finally, he discussed theoretical problems that had to be solved in order to bring coherence to the data that seemed to defy accepted concepts of time and space.

A few of the writings closest to Gardner's heart deserve discussion here.

The influence of the psychologist and philosopher William James was so great that Gardner, with Robert O. Ballou, produced a book, *William James on Psychical Research* in 1960. We know that James was actively interested in "mental healing" and even tested the claims of the practitioners with visits to a "mind-cure doctress." "I sit down beside her and presently drop asleep, while she disentangles the snarls out of my mind.... I am now unconsciously to myself, much better than when I first went, etc.... Meanwhile what boots it to be made unconsciously better, yet all the while consciously to lie awake o' nights as I still do?" Thus James wrote to his sister in 1887 at the age of 45. Gardner commented that the fact that the "mind-cure doctress" did him little or no good did not diminish James' interest in what he considered the important experiment she was conducting; James believed in its potential value to therapy and to the task of learning more about the human mind and personality. He vigorously opposed the bills which Massachusetts legislators designed to stop the practice of mental healing by requiring medical licenses. In other words, although Gardner himself found the Concord ambiance tolerant, even supportive, in his youth, William James suffered disapproval by his medical colleagues, some of whom, according to his son, never forgave him.

In 1894 James explained the difference between diseases of the mind (for which mental cures are important) and organic diseases; he felt that the *facts* of successful healing by hypnotists, mind-curers, Christian scientists and others should be studied. "Anything that interferes with the multiplication of such facts, and with our freest opportunity of observing and studying them, will, I believe, be a public calamity." He went on to comment that "they are proving by the most brilliant new results that the therapeutic relation may be what we can at present describe only as a relation of one person to another person and they are ... resisting ... any legislation that would hamper the free play of personal force and affinity by arbitrarily imposed conditions."

At the same time that James defended the genuine and effective mind-healers, he was alert to and devastating in his criticism of "rapacious humbugs." This conflict was under way just as the physician Sigmund Freud was about to abandon the use of hypnosis for the development of the psychoanalytic method. Gardner wrote that to James, mental healing, psychical research and religion were related manifestations of "vastly important and little-understood areas of the human mind and its powers, which must be investigated...." Shortly after the founding of the Society for Psychical Research in London, James played a leading part in forming an American society, which became for a time the American branch of the London Society, and was then replaced by the present American Society for Psychical Research.

Gardner's language was not as dramatic as that of William James but what he wrote about James reflects an unconscious identification with the latter's courage, balanced support and criticism of psychical research and his efforts on its behalf.

The first day Gardner and I met we discovered our joint fascination with the writer and student of classics F.W.H. Myers, author of *Human Personality and Its Survival of Bodily Death*. In his 75th year, Gardner gave a lecture on Frederic Myers and the subliminal self—an eloquent expression of his empathy with the emotional development and early struggles of that creative man. The young Frederic Myers, born in 1843, was an eager, idealistic son of a clergyman who was plunged into doubts stirred by his reading of Darwin's *Origin of the Species*. The theory of evolution, with its implications for an understanding of human development, presented a major challenge to the religious doctrines of that culturally intense period.

The importance of Myers' early childhood experiences is conveyed in an autobiographical fragment. Once, Gardner wrote, he came upon a little mole that had "lost its life under the wheels of a cart." He comforted himself with the thought that its soul would go to heaven. When his mother explained "that the poor creature had no soul and would not live again, Frederic burst into tears of helpless despair." The pity which he felt for animals echoes Gardner's account of his concern as a five-year-old for the loss of his tin Doggie.

The vividness of Gardner's picture of Myers in the late nineteenth century age of turmoil and challenge is reminiscent of the turmoil in Gardner's mind as a Yale student encountering the scientific challenge to his Episcopal theology. Young Myers, like young Gardner, found himself in a world that was taking religious comfort away from mankind; this led to "a desperate need to persuade himself that there could be a life . . . beyond death." Myers at Cambridge, like Gardner at Yale, studying Latin and Greek, developed a deep attachment to "the great classical tradition"; and Myers at Cambridge in the early 1860s, like Gardner at Harvard in the summer of 1916, embraced Plato's "earnest confrontation of the problem of the nature of man, the nature of the soul, the possibility of conscious existence independent of the body and the sense that the first evidence for survival lies in the spiritual qualities of man." For Myers, as for Gardner, the classical philosophers offered a bridge from the Anglicanism of their fathers to the rationalism of science. In addition, both Gardner and Myers were deeply interested, as was William James, in faith healings and in H. Bernheim's use of hypnotism to cure physical ills termed hysterical. Evidence was suggesting that the mind could influence the body—pointing to a richer conception of human nature.

The spiritualist world in Myers' days at Cambridge in the 1860s included discussions of clairvoyance, telepathy, precognition, retrocognition, poltergeists and hauntings, as well as messages from the deceased conveyed through mediums. In time Myers made close friendships with gifted members of the

Society for Psychical Research such as Henry and Eleanor Sidgwick, Edmund Gurney, Richard Hodgson, Oliver Lodge and William James. We can imagine the intense dedication of this group and its stimulus for the creative, reflective mind of Frederic Myers as he sought to see the relation of psychical phenomena to the world of sleep and dreams, and to the world of imagination and creativity. In the context of evolutionary thought there must be a hierarchy of phenomena with genius at the top. It could have been this hierarchical view that led to the concept of a subconscious or subliminal mind—below the level of awareness. Myers wrote, as Gardner quoted in his lecture,

> I hold ... that this subliminal consciousness ... may embrace a far wider range both of physiological and of psychical activity than is open to supraliminal consciousness.... I believe telepathic and clairvoyant impressions ... to be habitually received ... by aid of adits and operations peculiar to the subliminal self.... And I believe that some of these impressions ... do in some sense transcend the limitations of time as well as of space....

Frederic Myers' book continued to have a cherished place in Gardner's inner circle of guides in the study of psychical research. It was even more important, I believe, than his friendship with Walter Prince of the Boston Society for Psychical Research.

Myers began to write his great two-volume *Human Personality and Its Survival of Bodily Death* in 1882, the year of the founding of the Society for Psychical Research. That book combined all of the psychical phenomena in a conception of human communication in relation to human personality that included memory, imagination, dreams, genius and the experiences of hypnosis. Gardner's comprehensive conception of personality echoes the comprehensiveness of Myers' volumes. In Gardner's last book, with Morton Leeds, *The Paranormal and the Normal,* there are more references to F.W.H. Myers than to any other author except Charles Tart, a contemporary psychologist whose major book on altered states of consciousness as well as work in parapsychology was of deep interest to Gardner.

Gardner's concern with evidence for survival of personality continued through his lifetime. We say "concern," because he was never completely convinced by his intensive studies of the evidence. In 1945 his booklet, *Three Papers on the Survival Problem,* was published by the ASPR.

The first paper, entitled "An Outline of Survival Evidence," patiently reviews, in its 32 pages, a range of examples of apparitions and of statements purporting to come from the deceased through the most famous mediums. These are analyzed, conceptualized and classified into half a dozen types, each type involving one medium. Gardner also discussed other mediumistic reports produced by the cooperation of two or more mediums, or by cooperation between communicators and still another group in which proxy sitters visited the medium on behalf of a distant person who wished to have messages from the deceased. The examples of sitters' experiences with a medium included:

1. Communication of facts not known to the medium but known to the sitter.
2. Communication of facts not known to the sitter.
3. Communication of facts to which no single living person has access.
4. Communication of facts not known to any living person.
5. Cases in which there is no intrusion by an unexpected communicator. (That is, no intrusion by someone different from the deceased person with whom the sitter wished to communicate.)
6. Cases in which the same communicator makes himself known through various sensitives by using the same message or phase or symbol.

In this paper Gardner dealt with two questions: whether the sensitive was telepathically gaining information from the sitter's mind or from some related person, and whether the medium was making relevant inferences from observations of the sitter or of his or her remarks.

Although Gardner was impressed by the material he had gathered, he was still sufficiently skeptical to contribute a second paper, "Difficulties Confronting the Survival Hypothesis." In this he discussed forcefully the biological difficulty presented by the fact that mind and personality as we know them are dependent upon a body with a nervous system, sense organs and muscles. What could mind and personality be without their physical bases? In addition, personality as we know it is an expression of a particular group of relationships on the planet. If it were transferred into utterly different circumstances, would it still be the personality that we know?

He noted that the "sensitive" sometimes refers to personalities who never existed. Such as Adam Bede and other fictitious personalities who purport to communicate directly. For example, G. Stanley Hall, an investigator in 1909, asked for "a niece Bessie Beals" who never existed but who was produced at several sittings. When Hall finally stated that there was no Bessie Beals, the communicator (Hodgson) maintained her reality. Gardner commented that the trance consciousness was adept in its myth-making fantasy, and asked, "How, then, is it that such an abundance of evidential communications have in fact been given?" He quoted the example of a deceased former chauffeur, supposedly helped by a deceased nephew to communicate through a medium. The remarks included evidential material, some of which was known to the sitter, while other details were not known but were later corroborated. Gardner believed that "appropriate" material is apparently picked up telepathically. In the context of this discussion he made clear his acceptance of telepathy. He also commented that the sensitive might be "the vehicle of precognitive powers," as well as of retrocognitive powers, defined by Myers as "super-normally acquired knowledge of the past."

Gardner's final comments on the mass of mediumistic records of communications from the deceased were that as a scientist he could not find any easy way to conceive of a soul as a spiritual entity independent of the living system known to biology, psychiatry, and psychology. Still, he felt that three types of evidence—apparitions, some dreams, and many mediumistic performances—could not be swept aside because the initiative, the directing force, the purpose of the communication seems plainly to come from no living individual, however fragmentary, dissociated or subconscious the vehicle appears to be. He felt that he could not as a psychologist find a "naturalistic" or "normal" way of handling this material.

"To me, the evidence cannot be by-passed, nor on the other hand the conviction be achieved. . . . I linger because I cannot cross the stream. We need far more evidence; we need a new perspective; perhaps we need more courageous minds." This was Gardner's conclusion at the age of 66, in *The Challenge of Psychical Research,* a primer of parapsychology (1961). While Rhine's writings from 1934 on reached a wider public than did Gardner's, Gardner's leadership and prestige as an internationally known psychologist helped to give parapsychology dignity and credibility. That book, *The Challenge of Psychical Research,* presents evidence, not conclusions. Gardner reminds the reader of the repeated struggles and conflicts which have developed around every revolutionary scientific finding that has disturbed the accepted world view. He always saw the present in the context of history, and history meant the observations of Aristotle and Pythagoras' followers as well as the nineteenth century forebears of modern parapsychology. This long perspective, with its implication that the problems and the facts of psychical research would not go away, gave a context and a push toward future progress. He included sample reports of a variety of psychical phenomena: spontaneous cases with careful authentication, telepathy and clairvoyance experiments, precognition, psychokinesis, and records of mediumistic communications relevant to survival of personality after death. These do not include the whole range of psychical phenomena, but he felt that they represented the evidence that offered the most urgent challenge.

Gardner saw psychical research not as an exotic, occult, or deviant field of events, but as part of psychology, to be carried on with the same absolute standards of precision and protection against faulty methods, errors in recording, and self-deception in arriving at conclusions that were required by science generally. He was deeply concerned about incompetent and unethical experimenters, and of course he was very disturbed about frauds which he had earlier seen for himself in observing Margery's mediumship and had suspected in the case of certain other popular exhibitors of psychic powers.

In line with this view he emphasized the necessity for repeatable experiments, in the sense that someone other than the experimenter who initiated a given experiment could duplicate the conditions, the procedures, and the results. He, therefore, reviewed the relevant states that had been found to contribute to success in experimental work: acceptance of the reality of telepathy, clairvoyance, and the like states of mind involving dissociation; passivity with an intent focus on the target; physiological conditions which favor such states, including fever, delirium, parturition, and conditions induced by some drugs and alcohol. He believed that it should be possible to cultivate these conditions and to train people to function paranormally.

He shared with the reader the difficulties attending the effort to meet scientific standards. In chemistry, when two different chemicals are combined the result is always the same, "not just sometimes"; but replications of psychical research experiments do not achieve this absolute regularity—at times the expected outcome occurs, at other times it does not; this is due to the enormous complexity of the interaction in parapsychology. Gardner saw that all the factors had to be replicated; the cultural attitude, the beliefs and assumptions of both the experimenter and the people who were being tested, their feelings about each other, the emotional intensity of their involvements, their physiological states (of well-being, fatigue, and so on), their motivations (curiosity, need to gain recognition, or to please), their positive or negative orientation in general, their capacities for single-minded concentration in a relaxed state, and many others. Just as temperature, humidity or pollution may affect certain chemical reactions, there are many favorable and unfavorable factors likely to influence success in a telepathy or clairvoyance experiment. The difficulty of replicating such a complex collection of conditions plays a part in the variations in results of experiments with different subjects and different experimenters. But it took years for different experimenters to focus on each of these factors; Schmeidler's sheep-goat experiments became famous for their demonstrations that people who believed in ESP would typically score higher than those who did not believe telepathy and clairvoyance were possible. This led to the exploration of other factors affecting performance.

In addition to discussing the problem of replication, Gardner reviewed problems of accuracy in recording results, which can be compromised by unconscious self-deception as well as occasional errors. The presence of two independent recorders has often been arranged to prevent or compensate for such mistakes. Since, at best, the positive scores usually exceed chance results by a relatively small figure, absolute accuracy is crucial, of course.

The intensity of Gardner's commitment to unassailable integrity and rigor in psychical research methods and in the interpretation of findings led to his own very cautious conclusions:

> We are dealing with the first steps that lead up to the gateway of science; not with a single step within the hall beyond those gateways. We have no science of parapsychology; no theoretical system tightly and beautifully organized...; no solid beams of repeatedly confirmed findings, reproducible by a careful experimenter who can exactly follow the specifications, sure of the general trend of the results he will get. Parapsychology is important as a challenge.

Gardner's deep concern for dependable repeatability stayed with him to the end of his life. During his last years he remarked, "I'd give every honor I've ever had for one repeatable experiment." One month short of his 75th birthday he presented a paper on "The Problem of Repeatability in Psychical Research" at the symposium "A New Look at Extrasensory Perception," at the University of California, Los Angeles. In this article his historical perspective reached further into the past than his earlier references to Galileo and Copernicus or even Pythagoras:

> The belief that Nature is orderly has grown upon us since Chaldean shepherds watched the stars and Stonehenge architects pointed their shafts at the returning sun. Among the ways of knowing — the poetic, the prophetic, the mystic, the heuristic — the ways of science have grown upon us . . . since Newton and Darwin, Planck and Einstein. And in every sphere of knowledge called scientific the generalized realities, the scientific laws to which a uniform and specific method has given rise, become the firm foundation for a society ever more insistent regarding the ultimate regularity of the events among which man must thread his way to an inscrutable future.

Gardner continued to express his trust in scientific laws as he wrote, "Among the life sciences laws are at least as fundamental as they are in the physical sciences." At the same time he admitted the occurrence of "strays," unclassifiable events which have no rationale. He insisted on the joint necessity of replication and of rationale as requirements for commanding scientific attention. If there is no rationale, if the event does not fit the accepted view of reality, the replication is doubly necessary. He often reminded his readers of J.B. Conant's emphasis on the fact that no event is ever accepted as science until it falls into an ordered and accepted system, and here he reminded the reader that parapsychology is very far from fitting into a coherent system that could replace nineteenth century physics. Only with consistency of results under defined conditions and an ordered system of ideas can parapsychology become a science.

He then asked, as he did in other discussions, "Do we have laws comprising generalizations about the conditions under which extrasensory perception occurs — laws like the conservation of energy. . . ?" His first suggested law is that of motivation — "Motivation is one of those things that works when it works." That is, fatigue in prolonged efforts can reduce the effect of the wish for a successful result. Second, he referred to the intensity of the affect involved in the target material, or the feeling about the experiment or the experimenter, or the partners in the experiment, but he was concerned that no attempt had been made "to see just where the affect played its part." Affective aspects of the experiment are differentiated from the general attitude toward the ESP experiment, its setting or the experimenter, and, at that time, no one had set up a multivariate design "in which the various attitudinal and affective factors can be combined with some confidence that a particular experiment will succeed."

Gardner felt that these factors accounted for relatively little of the success in ESP, and that it was necessary to make intensive studies of those persons who ranked high in a group of subjects in order to find other factors that might weigh more heavily. Beyond this, he felt that use of altered states of consciousness and biofeedback technique for studying the inner psychophysiological world could produce both more voluntary control and more systematic descriptions of the inner world of psychic functioning. He was excited about the possibility that "in certain parts of the EEG spectrum there may be regions specially favorable for the reception of paranormal messages." He made a plea for a taxonomy of psychological states, including the physiological factors involved in them, to help throw light on defensive processes which inhibit paranormal functioning. And he pointed to the need for studies of the pattern or system in interrelated aspects of life, and "the deep reciprocities between our inner life and the social world of physical and cultural ecology beyond which lies the world of energies not yet guessed." In this area he felt that we are about at the level of the world of 1600, "long before Newton." And even if we were to discover the kind of laws that he envisioned, there would still be bewildering individual differences which lie partly in the depths of molecular ecology and genetics and partly in unique ecological relationships between persons and certain fields as yet unguessed.

Gardner finished his paper on repeatability by charging researchers to be reasonably full and clear as to what the components in the successful method actually are, then replicate with a complex multivariate design to see the component and interactive aspects of the replicated successful outcome; then replicate to disentangle generic results and individual results related to the biology and ecology of a single individual. Finally, he urged them to combine factors that appear to be responsible for their success, until they get something that is intelligible as well as repeatable — something rational that can be conceptualized both for itself and in its relation to other scientific conceptualizable principles. Only then would they be ready to build a model, a theory of parapsychology.

In the same decade of the sixties when Gardner was writing about the requirements parapsychology had to meet he was also writing about the relation of creativity to extrasensory perception. The journal, *Fields Within Fields...* *Within Fields,* published his paper on "The Inside and the Outside of Creativity." Musing on man's long history of observation and description of the outside world with microscopes, sound-recording instruments, and mathematical calculations, he wondered what has led to the new demand to study the work of creative individuals who are preoccupied with the world of inner experience. Despite the fact that other life sciences have been developing a science of ecology, of the environment, Gardner noted that the study of creativity has so far focussed only on the inner factors related to creativity. Using rich illustrations of the impact of drastic changes in man's ecology—whether in terms of the ice age, tidal wave, or drought—upon the opportunities and challenges faced by man, he insisted on the need for "a sophisticated study of the total world in which creativity appears." His emphasis upon the ecology of creativity echoed his plea for the study of the total field in which psi occurs.

Gardner's contribution to parapsychology paralleled his response to psychology—always setting new facts, new problems in the perspective of the history of science and of thought while at the same time organizing and integrating new findings in relation to the need for a new system and also to improvements in models for research. In other words, his thinking constantly moved in both directions—back and forth from psychology to psychical research. Underneath his work in both disciplines was his basic concern with the relation of man to the world.

In parapsychology as in psychology, Gardner had an uncanny way of anticipating future trends. He supported biofeedback when it had barely hatched into the psychological world as he encouraged studies of subliminal perception and autokinetic effects at the Menninger Foundation. Newness and change created no conflict for him—they were to be incorporated in the tide of scientific progress, a tide whose depths reached back to Aristotle and whose waves reached into the future. In the field of parapsychology it was as if Frederic Myers, William James, Eleanor Sidgwick and other British and European scholars were always present in his mind, companions-in-arms.

Gardner's scorn of the trivial, whether trivial aspects of housekeeping on which he did not want me to waste time, or trivialities of shopping and other everyday matters, extended to his attitude toward research. Just as he bemoaned the tendency to carry on trivial studies in social psychology, he warned against trivial bits of psychical research. He encouraged investigators to get to fundamental issues, leading toward the definition of laws that are really laws.

Irvin Child's summary of Gardner's continuing influence emphasized his persistence in the pursuit of science in the field of parapsychology, "undistracted by dogma," his willingness to suspend judgment, and his role as "a source of the scholarly knowledge which can help direct future research." Child also emphasized the importance of Gardner's view that psi phenomena did not occur in isolation, they occur in people, and are intertwined with the whole sequence of cognitive-affective events within the people involved.

Another of the major parapsychologists since the third quarter of the century, Rex Stanford, considered that Gardner's central role in the reorganization of the "decadent" American Society for Psychical Research brought that group into a position of major influence in modern parapsychology. His vision inspired the younger workers to transcend the constraints of the laboratory and his boldness in seeing parapsychology in relation to the meaning of science pushed them to ask, as he did, How does the pattern of findings point beyond itself? "His mind generated penetrating suggestions, and many of the ideas he expressed [from the 1940s on] are close to the forefront of research today. . . . We find them in work on internal states and psi, in psychophysiological studies of ESP and even in the recent burst of interest in psi-mediated experimenter effects." Stanford's own work recognized the importance of a shift in the EEG characteristics from before to during the ESP task—a factor that Gardner had discussed years earlier. Stanford recalled how Gardner could toss out seminal suggestions "with the abandon of a child in a blackberry patch throwing handfuls of the goodies to his friends"—thus conveying the delight and exhilaration evoked by Gardner's generosity in sharing his ideas.

Karlis Osis added a note about one of Gardner's deeply ingrained convictions about research: "He felt that one of the keys to successful research was not to be in love with one's own ideas, but rather to care deeply about reality." Osis recalled a rare instance of Gardner's impatience, when he advised Osis not to focus so intently on his own pet ideas and not to expect the subjects to verify his grand hypotheses.

In 1924, when I first met Gardner, psychical research was a taboo topic in New York—psychologists and social scientists were anxious to demonstrate their sophistication and scientific integrity by ridiculing every area in the field—mediumistic activity most of all, but also experimental studies of telepathy and of clairvoyance. Gardner's friends who knew of his interest thought he was a little "touched" and certainly had unstable judgment; not one of them accepted the possibility that there was anything worth investigating. Even his closest friends shared this feeling, and made derogatory references to his "interest in the occult." In New York he was, as it were, in a rejected minority group. The resulting loneliness, and his sensitivity to the ridicule and criticism he received from his friends, meant that my support did much to strengthen his morale.

Over the years the acumen and brilliance of his presentations of psychical research aroused interest among some psychologists, and at least he gained respect from noted diehard opponents such as E.G. Boring, with whom he carried on extensive correspondence. In the 1980s, when there are dozens of courses in parapsychology in American universities, and Soviet scientists as well as American are investigating problems in the field, it is hard to realize what it was like sixty years ago.

Gardner's contribution in the field of parapsychology, as in psychology, generally, was integrative. He saw problems in the context of the long history of science, which is perennially equipped with blinders to screen out new data that do not fit into the accepted view of reality. The need for this was obvious in the twenties and thirties when the exposure of the fraud of the Margery case reinforced the hostility to psychical research already so deeply entrenched. It was Gardner's historical perspective combined with his scientific expertise that made possible his effective defense of psychical research.

Gardner's involvement in psychical research spanned his entire adult life and his commitment went to the heart of his devotion to the task of enlarging the scope of science, and to his deep concern with the relation between the mental and the physical, and the place of man in the universe. In the decades of the sixties and the seventies, Thomas Kuhn's emphasis on the importance of anomalous data for the reformation of science helped to bring Gardner's contribution into modern physics and philosophy.

Gardner's passionate commitment to science was so profound that he refused help from psychic healers when he was in the Neurological Institute of the National Institutes of Health for five months' experimentation with treatment for his Parkinsonism. To accept help from the healers would contaminate the experimental efforts at NIH, he felt. Gardner was always aware that his explorations of parapsychology had not satisfied his scientific goals. All of his knowledge, wisdom and generative ideas had not succeeded in producing a repeatable experiment that alone would lead to an adequate rationale or theory of parapsychology, and further, lead to a solution of the mind-body problem. He was a seeker to the end of his life; frustration never destroyed hope.

IV / A Wider World

19. India and the UNESCO
Study of Tensions

Gardner had not travelled to India before 1950 nor had he known personally any of the psychologists and social scientists in the universities there. Why was he selected for an investigation of the reasons for the current tensions and those that led to the violence and riots after India gained independence from Britain? He was known to have a gift for inspiring, stimulating and supporting serious research by others, especially including research relevant to human problems, and he had a reputation for fairness, wisdom and vision in confronting human problems. He was knowledgeable about Indian religions: he had read a book, *Faiths of the World* as an adolescent, being curious about other religions than his own, and at Harvard he had that course in the history of religions. After we were married, I introduced him to poems of the *Rig Veda,* and to the *Upanishads,* the *Bhagavad Gita* and other writings by religious leaders of India. Of course we had been deeply interested in Gandhi and his adoption of Thoreau's principle of civil disobedience as a nonviolent method of accomplishing social change. In addition we had read enough to be knowledgeable about Indian history.

Otto Klineberg, a former colleague at Columbia University, was acting head of the Department of Social Sciences of UNESCO. When the Ministry of Education of the Government of India asked UNESCO in March 1949, to provide a consultant for six months in India organizing research teams to explore reasons for social tensions, Klineberg invited Gardner to undertake the task, knowing of our interest in India. Gardner's study with Rensis Likert, *Public Opinion and the Individual,* his supervision of attitude studies by students, his leadership in social psychology and in the Society for Psychological Study of Social Issues all provided relevant experience. Gardner agreed to go in the summer of 1950 to stay through the fall semester.

Coincidentally, Gautam Sarabhai, a cultivated and civic-minded businessman, was looking for a consultant to help plan an institute in Ahmedabad

239

to help children with their problems; his wife, Kamalini, had already estab-
lished a small modern school there for children from three to ten years of age.
Gautam, who had friends in art circles in New York and elsewhere, asked Kurt
Roesch, an artist teaching at Sarah Lawrence College, for suggestions about
people who might be helpful, and Kurt recommended me. It happened that
Kamalini had heard me lecture at Bank Street College and she approved the
choice. I took the semester off from teaching at Sarah Lawrence to go with
Gardner and the Murphys flew together to India in August 1950, the first of
three trips there.

During the next six months we had many interesting encounters with
nonacademic people at village and city levels as well as with the professional
group. Scientists seem to us much the same around the world—members of
an international subculture. It was when we met policemen, airport managers,
village head-men, bearers, ayahs (children's nurses) that we found the endearing empathy, humor, and immediacy of relating that has been so appealing
to Western visitors. Rarely did we encounter hostility or even suspicion. We
did not take time off for the usual tourist excursions to Maharajah's palaces;
our time was chiefly spent with middle-class people, the backbone of India.

We arrived at the New Delhi airport on the evening of August 6. New
Delhi hotels were accustomed to Western delegates and tourists, and were
clean, comfortable, and equipped with good restaurants. We slept well and
joined the conference of administrators from the Ministry of Education, professors and other social scientists from universities in India—a conference in
preparation for which Gardner had done a tremendous amount of work in the
months preceding our trip. He had had long intimate interviews with available
Indians in the New York area, and with American experts on India—some of
them teaching on the East Coast, others on their way to the West, some of
them on periods of furlough and soon to return to India. Among these was
a brilliant psychologist and lay analyst, deeply concerned with problems of Indian character structure and with the capacity of India to understand and to
control her own development. This was Pars Ram, a Brahmin Hindu; he had
been teaching for over twenty years at the Forman Christian College in Lahore,
which was in Pakistan after partition. Forced to move to India, he became head
of the Department of Psychology at the East Punjab Universtiy. He was, at the
time, a UNESCO Fellow to the United States. A deep friendship with both of
us developed rapidly; he generously gave Gardner many hours, conveying his
conception of a planning activity which would include major Indian social
science scholars in a comprehensive study of social tensions. Pars Ram felt that
there should be a leisurely meeting in which they could think through ways
of coordinating their efforts, and in which they could develop research plans.
This led to the proposal for a four-day conference in New Delhi as soon as we
arrived. It was Pars Ram's experience and wisdom which made possible the impressive productivity of a mere six months' consultation in India.

Another major contributor to Gardner's preparations was Professor C.N. Vakil, director of the School of Economics and Sociology at the University of Bombay, who had been trained at the London School of Economics. He happened to be in New York for a few days before returing to India from some work in Puerto Rico. Businesslike, practical, efficient, with well-organized ideas which he shared at a rapid-fire pace, he added substance to Gardner's general concept of the study and the planning conference. He had specific ideas about what could be done in Bombay (and actually, at the time we reached there, he had a very competent research team ready to go to work).

In addition to these and many other individual discussions, Gardner enjoyed a two-day conference at the South Asia Regional Studies Center of the University of Pennsylvania in May 1950, financed by the Social Science Research Council. The chairman, Professor W. Norman Brown, and members of his staff went over preliminary questions Gardner had formulated regarding the nature of the social tension problem in India, and they offered practical suggestions as to how to proceed.

Following suggestions from Pars Ram, and from Dr. Richard Lambert who had carried on research in India, Gardner wrote to a large number of leading psychologists and other social scientists at Indian universities describing the UNESCO assignment. He received replies from several leaders who felt able to undertake research. Professor B.S. Guha of Calcutta, director of the Department of Anthropology of the Government of India, Professor H.P. Maiti of the Institute of Psychological Research and Service of Patna University, Professor Kali Prasad of Lucknow University, and Kamla Chowdry, a social psychologist with a Ph.D. from the University of Michigan — then involved in a study of industrial attitudes of mill workers — along with Pars Ram and Vakil, proved to be the leaders of the six research teams that were initially developed. These leaders, in some cases accompanied by their research associates, along with several representatives of the Ministry of Education, and other leaders in research such as Sohan Lal of the Ministry of Defense, Bandyopadhyay representing the UNESCO field office at Delhi University, Dorothy Spencer representing the United States Department of State, and Richard Lambert of the University of Pennsylvania, were all at the conferences, at which I took notes.

Tara Chand, Secretary of the Ministry, an impressive, very clear headed administrator, opened the conference stating his hope that the UNESCO project under Gardner's leadership would contribute more understanding of the forces contributing to tensions; he stayed with the conference, exercising a useful direction without dominating or inhibiting the group. The atmosphere was spontaneous and democratic, remarkably without heat or argument. The members of the group were warmly cordial to "the Murphys" and we were delighted with their eagerness about the task. Well oriented by his preparatory discussions, Gardner supported the group members and helped to integrate their various comments about sources of tension and what needed to be studied. Ideas flowed freely, not always in logical sequence, since some persons were knowledgeable about specific problems they wished to discuss while others were more concerned about other problems.

The theme of tensions between Muslims and Hindus recurred throughout the four days, as well as the problems of intercaste tensions, especially those involving the Harijans ("Untouchables"), conflicts between refugees from East and West Pakistan and residents of the areas into which they fled; tensions between mill owners and union members, and tensions between aboriginals and city dwellers. Different members of the conference, coming from different areas in India, had different perspectives: for example, Kali Prasad described Lucknow as a low tension area because of the effective and benign rule of the Muslims over a long period.

When methods of research were discussed it was agreed that the primary method would have to be the interview, and that the historical background of tension in each region of study would be considered, along with the economic and sociological picture which would contribute to an understanding of the dynamics of tension. The interviewers were to be graduate students or young staff members working as assistants to the team leaders at each university; they would be using carefully prepared questions formulated in the native language of the group being studied. All of the teams except the ATIRA team in Ahmedabad were to be financed by the UNESCO fund of $20,000 (or about 100,000 rupees in Indian money). This sum was also expected to cover Gardner's round trip and living expenses in India while my round trip and living expenses in Ahmedabad were financed by the Sarabhais, with whom I spent many weeks during the six month period. I accompanied Gardner to the universities of Aligarh, Lucknow, Patna, Calcutta and Bombay, participating in observations and discussions and giving talks in each of those areas; but I did not go with him to the South Indian cities of Madras, Bangalore and Poona. The Indians did not let us limit ourselves to research contacts; everywhere we went we were overwhelmed with hospitality and requests for speeches about psychology and child development. It was the experience of living in India for six months that put the problems in perspective and showed us the strengths of India.

Any observant visitor, whether he goes for travel, or on a "mission," or as a member of a Government program, will be likely to find himself the observed, even more than the observer. Searching eyes will watch his face, his actions, his moods, wanting to know, "What does he think of us?" Lecturing to some twenty groups within a few months, I was repeatedly asked, "What are your impressions of us?" And when I spoke of the ingenuity, the hospitality, the beautiful faces, the creativity in arts which I saw everywhere, they said, thoughtfully, "Then you aren't prejudiced against us, like Katharine Mayo, in *Mother India*?" Others sometimes asked, "And what about the gloomy side of our life?" When I asked one of the ministers of education why the Indians found it hard to accept appreciation, or were surprised at being appreciated, he said, "Well, we've been used to many of the British telling us we were no good, for a long time." Everyone knew the country was poor. Everyone felt overwhelmed with problems too big to solve. The naive outsider who tried to point out these problems was not telling anyone anything at all. He was merely "saying such an undisputed thing in such a solemn way," as Oliver Wendell Holmes put it. An infinite number of ways of stalling, preventing any response to criticism, was used.

The Indians feel suspicious of superficiality. For India could not possibly have survived on problems alone. India knows that where we count our life in America in a few hundred years, she counts hers in thousands, and that there is little ground for optimism that Western cultures will succeed in surviving half as long. If India has something to learn about making life more healthy, well-fed and comfortable, so has the West something to learn about how to live together and survive. But Indians do not tell the West what it could learn from them. The East is there, ancient, proud, uncomfortable, but surviving. Westerners have to ask, and look, and find out for themselves some of the things to be learned. We found that the Indians were not secretive, nor uncommunicative. They loved to talk and any Westerner who was ready to listen could learn a great deal fast.

In city after city, people asked us to visit their homes, "requested," invited and coerced us to give lectures, to join discussions and meetings. Our faintest wish immediately turned into reality, so that one friend took us to a movie in Delhi the first week, another arranged for a concert of Indian music by an outstanding zitherist and a singer; another took me to an art school to see the work of students, and another to the home of a young artist who was doing bold, original work quite different from the traditional patterns; another arranged for me to visit a class of South Indian dancing; others arranged invitations to homes of a wide variety of people, including a farmer ("Come and meet my two wives, the remarkable thing about them is that they don't quarrel"), a cotton merchant, various vice-chancellors (India is full of them, because the vice-chancellors changed every two years at many universities), teachers, dignitaries like Sri Ranavati and Sri Mansani with government posts, labor leaders, mothers with babies. We learned to eat with our fingers with the help of dry *chappatis,* sit cross-legged on the floor at meals, and meetings, squat on Indian hole-in-the-floor toilets, bathe by pouring a jug of water over ourselves in a corner of a tiled floor with a "sluice" draining off the water in one corner. People tell you their life history and details of married life almost as casually as we talk about the weather, and, incidentally, expect you to tell them what you talked about in your analysis and what problems you have had with your children.

In Delhi we met mostly intellectuals and government people — chiefly from northern India, Punjab, Uttar Pradesh and Bengal—educated either at Forman Christian College, or Calcutta, or at Oxford or Cambridge. Those who were educated in England often seemed negative, pessimistic and impotent, feeling that Indian problems were insuperable. The Formanites were generally active and optimistic. The Oxford group seemed blind to the strengths of the good villages, which I explored alone when I had a couple of hours to myself. Village houses were often lovely, like the best adobe villages in New Mexico, neat and clean, with beautiful brass utensils soft yellow from years of polishing. Women everywhere had an eye for colors, and bold, original, artistic ideas about combining them. I saw bullocks, gay with blue and white beads around their horns, and bells tinkling merrily around their necks; they were typical of the unexpectedly gay touches one finds in India such as decorated doors on Public Service Commission buses. I found lovely crafts, each in its own locality, but hard to find anywhere else in India. And I felt aware of this lack of all-India consciousness, everyone just living in his own little province or town or village, not knowing about the rest.

At the Gandhi ashram at Wardha a very interesting young chemist was experimenting on the use of cow dung for fuel-gas, the remainder to be used for fertilizer. He was also developing techniques for using human excrement for fertilizer through having movable outhouses which could be placed over trenches for limited periods, then shifted to other areas.

There were many other important and very different kinds of experiments in improving village life and agriculture, that were initiated by central and local governments as well as by missionary and Gandhi groups. We visited some of these experiments at Allahabad and Etawah. But they did not seem to know as much about each other as we do—no one had money to get around and visit what the others were doing. And the press did not have much to say about these things, as for instance the *New York Times* does in its Sunday education and other sections. Seeing "adult education" in a circle of 40 males, from 10 to 50 years of age, trying to read a big chart of Hindu words and letters by the light of one kerosene lantern, while jackals cry and dogs bark, jogged our views of possibilities.

India had millions of refugees after partition, and many of them were living in misery. But there was also the creative new refugee city, Faridabad, half an hour from Delhi, developed along cooperative lines from start to finish—cooperative housing, cooperative industry and stores, cooperative farms. We have to contrast here the piecemeal way in which we Americans set up a new housing unit, without regard to all the other aspects of life which make the new unit a slum.

Many aspects of India impressed us. We knew about the veiled Moslem women in purdah, who had no freedom to move about freely; we had not been told about the fact that there were some 200 women in legislatures all over India, many more than there were in the United States. Nor had we been told about the fact that women were accepted in medical school and law school without difficulty; in many medical schools 50 percent of the students were women. We knew about caste, yet did not know that there were Untouchables in the Indian Congress.

The United States has achieved miracles in reducing the death rate among babies and children and in preventing the diseases that cripple them; yet American children cry, suck their thumbs, wet their beds, have temper tantrums and many other problems that were rare in India at that time.

We enjoyed the conversations with three psychoanalytically trained and stimulating psychologists, Pars Ram, Maiti, and Bhandari. Pars Ram was a delight to talk with about anything. For instance, I was commenting on some lovely photographs; while they were beautiful, I did not like the fact that the architecture overshadowed the people; for me the people of India had been more important than the architecture. To this he replied, "But there is an alternative: the people can emerge from the architecture; in some areas the people and the architecture and the land are all in harmony." At times he was in these moods of appreciation of India, at other times he was sardonic, as when he commented that one main effect of the malarial climate was to eliminate the distinction between reality and fantasy. At still other times he was sharply critical of what he felt was the dependent character of the people of India, related to excessively prolonged suckling and infantilization of the children.

Politically the picture was hard to appraise; people were anxious about Pakistan and Kashmir problems; the Fascist wing was less of a threat and the Communist group stronger than formerly, with people feeling that the Communists were "just opportunists taking advantage of the communal (Muslim-Hindu) difficulties right now." Most widespread seemed to be student timidity, a feeling of frustration with the inadequacy of their education, a lack of leadership among the young generally, and economic anxiety.

The wide range of opportunities to get acquainted with people— intellectuals, government officials, teachers, villagers—contributed perspective to both Gardner's work and mine. Probably most important was the firsthand experience of the tolerance, wisdom and creativity characteristic of so many Indians in different roles, an experience which gave both of us an unassailable confidence in the strengths of the Indian people and an optimistic view of India's future, shadowed though it was in the early years of independence, by the many conflicts between religious and economic groups.

Gardner's monthly reports to the Indian Ministry of Education gave brief summaries of his work. He described, for example, being met in Bombay by Professor Vakil and his colleague Dr. Desai who had already organized a large staff of collaborators for the local research study. An advisory committee of 20 persons including professors in the University of Bombay and in the famous Tata Institute, along with other psychologists and social scientists had been formed. The first draft of an interview had been prepared; this focussed on

attitudes of the main communities toward one another and toward government policies. Some 25 postgraduate students of the schools of economics and
of sociology together with four students from the Tata Institute were ready to
get started on the research.

Gardner met with the advisory committee and the students each day for
long conferences on research methods, problems of sampling of persons to be
interviewed and problems of treatment of the data, as well as discussion of improvements needed in the interview schedule. It was decided that the revised
schedule would be used in a preliminary study of 30 individuals, and after this
the schedule would be revised again for use with the main sample, which
would consist of 75 men from each of three groups: the Hindu longtime
residents, the Hindu refugees mainly from Sind, and the Muslims. In addition
a smaller number of women would be interviewed. Ration cards were chosen
as the most suitable device for obaining a random sample of males from those
groups.

After discussion it was decided that three kinds of questions would be
used: those which permit a definite categorical answer so that data could be
treated statistically; questions whose answers would be coded so as to allow for
quantitative treatment; and questions whose answers required full qualitative
study. The main study was to be carried out during the students' October
vacation.

It was also decided that after this main study, there should be an intensive
study of 30 persons; this was designed to yield detailed information on the relation of attitude to individual personality. Those to be studied were to include
leaders, eccentrics or deviants, and average people from each of the three
groups. After the interviews the intensive cases would be interviewed by one
of the psychiatrists who had volunteered to participate and, finally, by a
psychoanalyst who would look for deeper factors.

The methods were designed to give administrators data of practical value,
and the Home Secretary, Morarji Desai, was eager to read the interviews in
their entirety. Gardner found that public opinion developed in Bombay as a
result of press notices and other informal writing was altogether positive.

In Bombay as in the other centers Gardner was asked to give lectures and
conduct seminars in addition to his intensive discussions with the group undertaking the tension studies. Elsewhere he also found plans for the research to
be well under way, chiefly needing detailed consultations to polish the procedures. At those centers where I joined Gardner — Aligarh, Lucknow,
Wardha — I was also asked to lecture.

Interest in the tension studies spread to other universities and where
Gardner encountered creative plans, as at Poona, for projects not originally included in the discussions at the August conference in New Delhi, he successfully pleaded for government support of them as part of the UNESCO group
of studies, although the funds had already been fully allocated.

At Aligarh Professor Pars Ram's team planned to undertake action research aimed to reduce tension by discovering group goals which the different communities could share. Tension level before and after such work would be studied along with a control group where no action research had been carried out.

In each setting Gardner supported the plan under way and used the consultations to improve the procedures of the research study and the analysis of data.

The psychologists reported that after the partition of Pakistan and India the most chaotically violent riots had involved Muslim and Hindu butchering, raping and pillaging. Since the Indian government was most concerned about the Muslim-Hindu tensions, Gardner gave special attention to this area of conflict. He spent two to three weeks with each research team, generally returning for a second visit after the first one. He reviewed the plans for the interviews, the selection of subjects and on his second visits discussed analysis of the data with the teams. Paradoxically, when we visited the Muslim University of Aligarh, whose benign, urbane and erudite vice-chancellor was Zakir Hussain, later president of India, we ourselves saw little evidence of tension as compared with certain encounters in Bombay. But Pars Ram's study in Aligarh uncovered hostile and anxious rumors of plans for riots in late February and March. This did not occur, but it was possible to record the sequence of exaggerations of a small conflict when a few Hindu boys assaulted a few Muslim boys for the latters' alleged misbehavior. From the first report of this small event, the story became: "Muslims were assaulted by the Hindus with a view to demoralize the Muslims" and then "there is an organized agency to uproot the Muslims." It appeared that there was a Muslim tendency to interpret all such events as deliberately planned to annihilate them. Lacking resources for an adequate study of the actual handicaps or the treatment of the Muslims, the research focussed on the frame of reference of the Muslims and the factors that determined it. An important factor was the Muslim Indian-language press, particularly the Urdu press which delighted in dilating upon Muslim grievances. "The literate Muslim accepts with faith and confidence the attitude toward the problems recommended by his newspaper and he transmits the same interpretation to his illiterate client," Gardner commented. What happens to Muslims in Hyderabad or Bihar is generalized to an overall picture of the plight of Muslims.

Actually, the Hindus and the Muslims were each suspicious of the other. Some Muslims felt hurt at being called Muslims instead of Indians—in their civic and economic life they wanted to be accepted as Indians along with the rest of the population. Distrust of Muslims also developed from the failure of many Muslims leaving India to pay bills owed to Hindus. However, a widespread opinion among Muslims was that they were in no danger of being exterminated or expelled from India—this phase would pass, they felt. They wanted specific complaints to be dealt with appropriately. This was true, along with the fact that some Muslims felt they were rejected by non–Muslims; this feeling was expressed more often by the middle and upper class strata of the Muslim group. Handicaps in earning a livelihood contributed to a feeling of insecurity in addition to the anxiety about Hindu acceptance and their right to live in India. Some working class Muslims felt that work was offered to Harijans and denied to their group.

Pars Ram's study in Aligarh was the most intensive: 50 Hindu and 50 Muslim males were interviewed in depth over a period of a year. The study was published as *A UNESCO Study of Social Tensions in Aligarh 1951–2* and Gardner considered it to be the best contribution among the UNESCO studies. Widespread insecurity was found among the Muslims in Aligarh as well as in Bombay; an intense persecutory trend, together with stereotypes of Muslims and Hindus expressed in their attitudes toward one another was accentuated by the press. Each group read the press in its own language; Hindus rarely read Muslim news sources, nor did Muslims read Hindu papers.

As a matter of fact, some Hindus were deeply prejudiced against Muslims, saying they were dirty, they were bigots and unfair to minorities under their rule, they preferred to remain aloof from Hindus. There were striking differences in the time perspective of Muslims and Hindus. In response to the question "If you had the power, what would you do about communal strife?" the Hindu response was typically "We've had these problems a long time, and it will be a long time before we are through with them." The typical Muslim response was "The police can stop it tomorrow if they want to."

Gardner suggested that the difference in time perspective might be due to the vast span of time conceived by Hindu cosmology, as contrasted with the dynamic or explosive nature of Muslim history. Or the difference might be due to the high anxiety level of the Muslims. He also noted that the Hindus were blind to the little incidents of discrimination to which the Muslims refer (and which were exaggerated over time).

About half of the Hindus believed that Pakistani agents interested in the migration of Muslim artisans to Pakistan deliberately brought about conflicts; and that Muslims in debt to Hindus or awaiting trial in courts, staged riots to make escape easier. But 40 percent of the Hindus regarded the riots as comparable to ordinary street quarrels. Nearly three-quarters of the Muslims interviewed in one area believed the riots were part of a government policy to drive the Muslims out; all of the Muslims thought the Hindus staged occasional riots to threaten the Muslims; many recounted the story of the Hindu who told Muslims, "Your days are numbered. This year Holi [holiday] will be celebrated with the Muslim blood." But the majority of Hindus did not know that Hindus played any part in fomenting riots, believing that Muslim hooligans were the troublemakers; they saw their own group as nonviolent.

In low-tension Lucknow, most Hindus — and Muslims as well — stated that as children they played together, and they accepted members of the opposite groups both in dining together and as intimate friends. The educated Muslim groups accepted all groups mentioned in the questionnaire — Christian, Harijan, Hindu, Punjabi, Sikh, even the Sindis who were in the forefront of the refugee problem. In this area the educated Muslims were extraordinarily tolerant of other groups. But more than half of the Hindus believed that relationships between the Lucknow communities were adversely affected by the influx of refugees, believing that the refugees were less cultured, were uncouth and discourteous.

Despite the general level of tolerance in Lucknow, most Muslims stated that they would not pass through a Hindu locality; and both Hindus and refugees would not pass through a Muslim locality. "One simply plays safe."

When they commented on what they liked or disliked about Muslims, most of the Hindus responded favorably to their belief in one God, their simple marriage ceremony, brotherliness, group prayers, widow marriages and loyalty. Hindus disliked Muslims' beef-eating, prayers five times a day, unsatisfactory personal hygiene, wearing beards, fanaticism and cruelty, opposition to other religions, purdah (seclusion of women), the burka (veil), conversion, divorce, and marriage with near relatives.

A majority of the Muslims believed that attitudes of Hindus had stiffened against the Muslims since the partition and they were especially afraid of the power of the Mahasabha and were insecure about the future of their children. Muslims resented the tendency of Hindu bands to play music in front of mosques, and the Hindus' interference with their eating of beef. Muslims felt that playing music before a mosque was baiting them. Muslims in Bombay felt the Hindus were trying to dominate their lives. The primary complaint of the Muslims was that the majority (Hindus) were interfering with their ways. In addition, higher Indian castes tended to keep their distance from Muslims who, on their side, preferred contact with high caste Hindus. The Hindus' distancing means that in many areas such as Aligarh a Hindu might never have been acquainted with a Muslim.

At the time of partition, with hostility boiling over, hundreds of thousands of Hindus fled East and West Pakistan hoping to reach safety, but thousands were caught, raped, slaughtered on the way. The loosening of controlling structures with consequent outpouring of aggression was like the horrors of North Vietnam's murderous assaults on South Vietnamese and Cambodians in recent years after the end of the Vietnam War except that further extension of power and acquisition of more territory was not involved. For those who succeeded in reaching a safe area in India, near Patna, Bombay or New Delhi, there was only a temporary, superficial welcome, if that. Those refugees who tried to set up shops or to get jobs competed with established workers who were making only a marginal living and were angry at being undersold. Those who were sheltered in refugee camps were suffering from inadequate food and water, cramped and filthy living quarters, insect bites, no arrangements for washing clothes, "terrible" latrines — and the bitterness of having had to leave all their possessions, their homes, their businesses, shops, and jobs, and finding no hope of rebuilding a decent life. The government helped at first but the problems were overwhelming. The tensions led to quarreling among the refugees themselves. They blamed the government for inadequate help. A few camps were adequately equipped — one of which we visited near Delhi. Self-help efforts to build adequate homes and cooperative businesses were successful there, but the government could not cope with all of the needs across the nation.

In Ahmedabad, Kamla Chowdry was in charge of the ATIRA study of tensions of the mill-workers. Gautam Sarabhai owned the Calico mill and wanted to improve the conditions of work. Modern machinery was installed with no problem, but the workers refused to use the hygienic bubble fountains installed for them. "It isn't human to lap up water that way — that's the way animals drink." But after two hours of more rationalizations, the workers admitted that the trouble was that the Harijans would be drinking from the same fountains. The fountains had to be given up and tumblers provided — those could permit discrimination!

With Muslims and Hindus working in the same setting it was significant that dissatisfaction was generally greater among Muslims than among Hindus both in respect to the physical conditions of the task and in respect to other aspects of the work. It seemed possible that dissatisfaction arising in relation to certain unfavorable aspects of the job spread to other aspects. Or attitudes toward work could be contaminated by attitudes about their situation in the community. Workers were dissatisfied with wages which were in fact just enough to make ends meet with no margin to provide for the future or for emergencies. Most workers were in debt. Most of the workers hoped that their children would not go into mill work. "Any other job than mill work!" A considerable amount of hostility to supervisors and jobbers who were responsible for the general flow of production was observed; this appeared among those at the bottom of the wage ladder. Muslims were usually weavers and there was little hostility to them in the mills. There were differences between mills, and there was much appreciation for the good working conditions in the Calico mill. During the years of the 1950s when we visited India three times, Ahmedabad was relatively free of riots; tensions existed but they did not lead to violence.

The six month UNESCO study was focused on an exploration of attitudes and experiences contributing to tensions; there were insufficient funds to undertake many experiments in reducing the tensions. However we visited certain experiments that were under way, including the Etawah project in Uttar Pradesh, between New Delhi and Calcutta. This project was under the guidance of Albert Mayer, a creative American architect and town planner;

Indian-trained agricultural workers demonstrated ways in which new seed, new ways of irrigation, fertilization and the like could produce a larger yield. Short-term goals were set so that achievements could be measured. The success of the Etawah project in 100 villages led to the addition of 300 more villages. The Ford Foundation supported over a dozen Etawah-like projects in different parts of India, with the addition of social science studies of changes in village life resulting from improved productivity. It was the hope that improved conditions of living could in turn reduce some of the tensions resulting from multiple day by day frustration.

After completing his report to UNESCO, Arthur Rosenthal, publisher of Basic Books, invited Gardner to write a book for the general public. This became *In the Minds of Men*; it described the tension patterns and also Gardner's view of the strengths of India as we had seen them in our explorations.

Professor V.K. Kothurkar of Poona University wrote me after Gardner's death,

> In his death, Indian psychology has lost one of its great sympathizers and a true friend. In 1950, on invitation from the Government of India as UNESCO consultant, Dr. Murphy addressed a small gathering of psychologists from all over India and in one big push, as it were, lifted a whole generation of leading Indian social scientists to a distinctly higher level of functioning. He gave a highly significant new direction to Indian social psychology. So massive was his direct and indirect impact that almost all social scientists in this part of the world left the barren, arid group-mind general-will speculations and gainfully turned to more fruitful and vital empirical social studies.

Gordon Allport, reviewing *In the Minds of Men,* said,

> Probably for the first time in history a social psychologist, employing in addition to his own gifted perceptions the tools of modern social science, has attempted to analyze the interlocking tensions of a great nation.... He compares prejudice in India and in the United States, thus helping to formulate the uniform laws that in any country underlie the deterioration of human relationships. He points to the remedial forces at work in India and in so doing marks the path where cures are to be found in any society.
>
> Especially striking to me is Murphy's achievement of a judicious balance between detail and pattern, e.g. between scientific analysis and political realities, between local fact and a sensitive understanding of the whole scene.

Allport added that the accomplishment was both a model for future international investigations by social scientists and a wholesome stencil for training in international relations.

20. Menninger : Moving to Topeka

Gardner returned from India in February 1951. He spent the spring semester teaching at City College and working on his report for UNESCO. His work on the book for the general public, *In the Minds of Men*, suggested by Arthur Rosenthal of Basic Books, occupied him for the summer of 1951 and his available time during the academic year of 1951–2.

The lack of research interest at the College was especially frustrating after his year of working with senior social scientists in India. He was restless, and ready for a change which would allow him to pursue his studies of the influence of affect on perceptual learning. There were overtures from universities in northern areas with bitter winters but since both of us were vulnerable to respiratory infections we rejected these proposals.

That same year changes were under way at the Menninger Foundation in Topeka, Kansas, which we knew was a distinguished hospital and center for psychiatric treatment and training. An officer of the Foundation, Dr. William C. Menninger — always known as "Dr. Will" — was undertaking a fund-raising effort and he wanted to expand research there. The first director of research, the distinguished David Rapaport, along with senior analysts Robert Knight and Margaret Brenman, had left in order to develop a new program at the Riggs psychiatric center in Stockbridge, Massachusetts. Rapaport's successor, Sibylle Escalona, and a leading research clinical psychologist, George Klein, were also planning to leave. In order to fill the gap left by the loss of these outstanding clinicians, Dr. Will felt that he needed to bring a distinguished "name" as the new director of research.

Although Gardner was not a psychiatrist, he was well known to psychiatrists and psychoanalysts in the East. In addition, his research on affect and perception was, George Klein thought, the original "New Look" in perception, and related to research under way at the Foundation. Escalona felt that my research on child personality could be continued with further studies of the children she and Mary Leitch had observed as infants. The Medical Committee responsible for recommending a new research director, and "Dr. Karl," the older brother of Dr. Will (and regarded within the Foundation as its real "boss") approved Klein and Escalona's recommendation that Gardner be considered for the new appointment. Gardner told Dr. Will that he would not consider the appointment unless there was an appropriate place for me, so the discussions continued in terms of a joint appointment. Dr. Will then invited us to visit the Foundation.

We went to Topeka in the fall, the most beautiful season in Kansas, and met a most congenial group: Lewis Robbins, Donald Watterson, Paul Bergman, psychoanalysts; and several clinical psychologists, including two of Gardner's former students, Philip Holzman and Martin Mayman. We both had conferences with Dr. Will. After we returned to New York, Gardner had a conference there with Dr. Will and Dr. Karl. When we had talked over our impressions, we decided to accept the invitation and move to Topeka. I was loath to leave Sarah Lawrence College, which had been such an ideal setting for my teaching and research, and where I had deeply satisfying friends, but Gardner's need for a research setting was intense and I felt that it was his turn to have the setting that he needed.

It was agreed with Dr. Will that Gardner would have time and assistance for his own basic research while at the same time he would be the responsible administrator for the research department as a whole. Seven thousand dollars was to be made available for two research assistants for Gardner. Dr. Will also approved my plan to study normal children's ways of coping with everyday problems, and he said "I'll pick up the tab." He accepted our provision that we have two summer months at our New Hampshire home for writing and integrating our research. (The usual pattern allowed one month's vacation each year for senior staff.)

In a memorandum prepared during discussions of the move with Dr. Will, Gardner had described four areas of interest which had grown out of "a dozen years of thought and research on the problem of the way in which personality serves to predispose toward one or another way of perceiving the environment."

The first concerned the way in which personality controls the accent or point of emphasis in the perceptual field. In any complex situation, whether in travel, shopping or moving to a new town, the interests and attachments of the individual spontaneously select and focus on certain stimuli while others are ignored. In Europe I see cathedrals, my sister sees castles. This became the study of the influence of affect on perceptual learning.

Second was "the problem of freeing oneself of perceptual distortions which have arisen in the service of personal needs." This of course could be stated as the problem of finding ways to improve reality testing—a major goal of much psychotherapy. The need for a sense of superiority, for instance, may lead to perceiving other ethnic groups as inferior to one's own group. These studies of perceptual learning and reality testing provided the focus for most of Gardner's own research during the years in Topeka.

Third, Gardner noted his hope to collaborate with Gertrude Schmeidler and others both in and outside of the Foundation "to clarify to some degree the relations of paranormal to normal perception with special reference to the factors of motivation [need-fulfillment] involved." Schmeidler had demonstrated in empirical studies that positive attitudes toward extrasensory perception were related to success. Many other attitudes — anxiety or fear of the unknown or affection for the experimenter — might influence the results of experiments. In the sixties Gardner was able to facilitate studies in this area and to a small degree conduct research or extrasensory perception in relation to creativity in children.

The fourth area was that of value conflicts, which he felt had much to do with mental health. A quarter of a century earlier, Hartshorne and May had studied the effects of conflicting home, school, and neighborhood environment on the character development of children. Gardner wanted to explore the effect of the value conflicts arising from such experiences and their relation to personality integration and to mental health. (Gardner's hope for a study of value conflicts was never fulfilled.)

To Gardner it was obvious that since clinicians are concerned with the issue of how realistic a patient's thinking is, the study of how perception — including distortions of perception — develops was fundamental. Principles dealing with the question of how perceptual patterns are acquired, or learned, were, therefore, important for psychiatry, even more basic, perhaps, than other issues of cognitive style being studied at the Foundation.

Going from the academic world — in which he had grown up and been nurtured through half a century — to the world of psychiatry involved a greater shift than Gardner had anticipated in view of his many friends back East who were analysts and psychiatrists.

It was a boon to have Sibylle Escalona's advice, orientation and support in the early years. Gardner found her "very sensitive and helpful in relation to my immediate problems." She repeatedly directed him to take all questions to Dr. Will and since it was he who had carried on negotiations with us, we assumed that he had the authority for appointments and directives. Dr. Karl was listed at that time as Director of Education in Psychiatry. What we did not know was that it was Dr. Karl who, a decade earlier, had added a scientific research arm by bringing David Rapaport to the Foundation. After Gardner's death, Dr. Karl told me that he had felt left out (of the planning for our appointments). Evidently this feeling contributed to the often strained realtionship between Gardner and Karl during Gardner's fifteen years in Topeka.

Very important for our mid-life adjustment to this new setting was the task of finding a satisfying home setting. In going to Kansas, Gardner was leaving a familiar world of intimate friends, family, and colleagues, for an area new to him, without his cherished mountains or evergreens — and a new group of colleagues in a field tangential to his own profession. Much as he wanted the research opportunity, doubts may have gnawed at him; he had memories of earlier moves to new towns where he felt isolated, and lonely. It was in a lecture in the spring before leaving New York that he said, "After all, it's a lonely world, it's a lonely culture we live in, it's a competitive culture in which a lot of people get isolated. The burden of the analysts Erich Fromm, Karen Horney, Harry Stack Sullivan . . . is that a primary factor in our disturbance is our loneliness." This is a unique statement, unparalleled in all of Gardner's writing, although it echoes his autobiographical accounts of childhood feelings of isolation. Gardner continued,

> If this be true, a primary factor in mental health is discovering the outreaching tendencies. However completely . . . isolated or withdrawn or hostile or frightened our individual may seem to be, there may be ways of reaching deep down and finding a hand which reaches toward us . . . part of our job is to discover this self healing which lies in . . . the demand for health, the demand for social reciprocity which lies very deeply within every patient.

This, of course, is a statement of the optimistic faith in human beings that was basic to Gardner's approach.

In order to help Gardner feel more at home and to have an attractive, hospitable setting that would facilitate his reaching out for friendships in the new environment, I insisted that we look for "our kind of place" to live. After systematically exploring Topeka we found exactly what we needed: three wooded acres with a stream bisecting them, a small log and stone house with a terraced slope up to the road; an elegant elm, a little plum tree and climbing roses covering the wall around the upper terrace. There were no evergreens, but Austrian pines flourished in Kansas and over time we planted sixteen of them. Attached to the two-car garage there was also a little guest house, which provided a welcome setting for visiting grandchildren and their parents, and for other visitors. This was a happy place for children of our friends to visit, and for me to have parties for the children in the coping study and for the children of the Head Start center with which I worked as a consultant. They ran, they climbed the hill at the south end of the woods, they hunted for crawfish in the creek. Several members of Gardner's staff and young clinicians shared vivid memories of the informal parties we had for them. One of the most memorable was a "sing-party" for young visiting Mexican psychologists.

It was a setting of charm for us and for Menninger visitors. Aldous Huxley, who was said to be "legally blind," leaning against the screen of the back porch where he could listen to the water burbling over the rock-bed of the creek, and smell the fragrance of the garden, said "I love this spot." And Anna Freud—at a lunch on the expanded glass-panelled deck we added after Aldous Huxley's remark—commented, "This reminds me of my own country place in Sussex." A.R. Luria from Moscow, Piaget from Geneva, friends from India, and from different parts of this country enjoyed their visits at "Deer Cliff" as the place had been called. Gardner never wrote again of feelings of loneliness.

We often drove out to the country Sunday afternoons to discover new vistas or lakes, and new places for long walks, or we explored nearby Lake Shawnee in a rented rowboat.

Topeka had its share of nationally known groups and also had a strong tradition of do-it-yourself music and theatre. We attended productions of Topeka Civic Theatre, a community group, and Gardner appeared in two of its productions, which included, among a variety of programs, a semistaged reading of John Steinbeck's *Of Mice and Men* when our son Al was a director of some of the Civic Theatre's plays. In Kansas City we enjoyed the superb Nelson Art Gallery.

There were not only losses and finding ways of coping with them; there were opportunities we had not envisioned. Menninger staff were encouraged to attend professional conferences in the United States and abroad, and to give lectures to a wide variety of audiences. Both of us accepted invitations to speak to professional groups at different universities and institutes in addition to our addresses at professional meetings. Our life in the Topeka years had a different sort of richness from the family life that had meant so much to Gardner before we went to Topeka.

The first months were spent getting acquainted with the various activities of the Foundation, sitting in on seminars and conferences, attending Dr. Karl's stimulating colloquia, and for Gardner, getting oriented to research under way in the Foundation while he began work on his perceptual learning project with two young assistants, Douglas Jackson and Melvin Weiner; Donald Spence, a graduate student at the University of Kansas, was also an early member of Gardner's group.

For the first year and a half I was on parttime while I completed the two-volume *Personality in Young Children*; on Menninger time I conducted conferences preparing for the coping project, and worked with the Children's Service senior staff on preliminary formulations for a book on the *evaluation of emotionally disturbed children*. The Children's Service accepted me warmly; Povl Toussieng, in charge of diagnosis, and Walter Kass, the chief psychologist in the Children's Service, both volunteered to work with me on the study of normal children's coping. Since Gardner was so sensitive to my research interests he was delighted at these developments and repeatedly wrote to professional friends that Kansas and the Menninger Foundation were good for me.

Over time, I undertook a few therapy cases including a severely brain damaged, educationally retarded, and emotionally disturbed twelve year old girl. (Since I had had no neurological training I was anxious about this case but my commonsense reinforcement of coping resources together with insights from my supervisor, Dr. Hirschberg, along with the girl's own courage and energy helped her to make good progress.)

I also attended Rudolph Ekstein's case seminar on therapy with schizophrenic children, an important learning experience.

My acceptance as a special research candidate for psychoanalytic training in the Topeka Psychoanalytic Institute was important to my research on early childhood. There I was lucky to be assigned to an analyst trained in London with Winnicott and Anna Freud, the most creative child analysts in the profession. This opened doors to understanding the inner life of infants and children, and in addition brought help from other child analysts who were interested in our coping study.

The Topeka Psychoanalytic Institute included a cosmopolitan group of analysts from Europe and London—among them Ishak Ramzy, Hermann van der Waals, Otto Fleischmann, Nellie Tibout, and Rudolf Ekstein, all of whom became intellectually congenial friends. The Fleischmanns, the Van der Waals, and Nellie Tibout visited us in Holderness. The Van der Waals' home was a small museum of modern paintings.

From 1952 to 1968, Gardner published eight papers dealing with his research; most of the reports on the successive research studies carried out by his young assistants were published under their names alone at Gardner's request—he did not believe in taking credit for work carried out by his staff.

During those sixteen years he wrote over 20 reviews, forewords and introductions for books by authors who valued the perspective within which Gardner would present their work; in addition, there were over 40 chapters in symposia for which their editors solicited contributions from well-known scientists. Twenty-two papers on mental health and on education were published, usually, after they had been presented as invited lectures, and a dozen papers on theory developed Gardner's reflections on broader issues of human life. Three dozen papers on psychical research dealt with methodological and theoretical problems in that field.

That was a stage of Gardner's life—from the age of 57 to 73— when even more than in the preceding years he brought a long view, often a philosophical level of perspective and integration to each new intellectual encounter; he became a social philosopher, while remaining the humanistic scientist he had always been.

In 1953 the Kurt Lewin Award stimulated Gardner's moving lecture on human potentialities. During the following three years the deterioration of his mother's health led to her death on May 10, 1957, while his brother's colonic tumor also proved fatal. The end of these lives—the last of his immediate family—may have contributed to his reflections on life and death in articles such as "The Boundaries Between the Person and the World," "The Enigma of Human Nature," both in 1956; "The Third Human Nature," 1957: and a discussion in *The Meaning of Death,* edited by Herman Feifel (1959). His continued thinking about man's place in the universe led to his "The Search for Person-World Isomorphism" (1965) and "The Nature of Man" in the same year.

Gardner had had a lifelong concern with peace and war and this found expression in such essays as "Nuclear Dementia" in *The Nation,* 1950, "Face Those Atomic Fears," in 1958, "Psychological Aspects of the Cold War," 1962; "A Psychologist Views the Nuclear Crisis," 1962, and "Political Invention as a Strategy Against War," in 1965.

Sputnik excited the world in 1957 and Gardner's "Facing the Realities of the Space Age" appeared in 1959. His "Testing the Limits of Man" was published in 1961 and "Where Is the Human Race Going?" the same year. Just as — when he moved from the South to Concord at the age of seven — he had reflected on variations in the sense of time, new changes in his life situation stimulated reflections on life.

21. Developing Menninger Research in the 1950s

After Gardner arrived in Topeka in September 1952 he poured his energy into the Menninger Foundation, conferring with staff members, attending group conferences, and lectures, corresponding with David Rapaport, George Klein, Robert Holt, and Sibylle Escalona—major figures in the research and clinical work of the Foundation in the late forties. With Lewis Robbins he made a survey of the current and potential research interests of the Foundation staff.

This survey identified all ongoing investigations and also all of the research interests of members of the Foundation who had not been able to carry out their ideas because of lack of time and funding. Over a dozen staff members—psychiatrists, psychologists, social workers, and a nurse supervisor—were interested in undertaking a wide variety of projects. At the same time, two projects were being carried on outside of the working schedule: R. Gardner and Martin Mayman were working on a study on "Recognition of Organicity from the Psychological Examination" and Ekstein was investigating "Altered Ego States" in children.

Ongoing research supported by the Menninger Foundation included a modest psychotherapy research project initiated by Paul Bergman, carried out parttime by nine therapists. Bergman divided his time between the project and other studies in psychotherapy. Bergman's innovative project was undertaking to evaluate psychoanalytic methods currently in use in the Foundation hospital, and also to try other approaches not approved at that time. After comparing clinical observations with psychological test findings during the course of therapy, the department of Adult Psychiatry set up a Committee on Evaluation of Psychotherapy with, at first, Donald Watterson as chairman, then adding Robbins as co-chairman. Small working groups dealt with the techniques of psychotherapy, factors in the patient, factors in the therapist relevant to prognosis in psychotherapy, ways of using psychological tests, improvement of a health rating scale, and follow-ups and controls. Watterson developed a termination interview and the social workers developed a follow-up project.

Four hours a week were allotted to Nellie Tibout to collaborate with my coping project which focused on preschool children.

In the hospital, Irving Kartus and Herbert Schlesinger were studying the interaction of physician and patients to whom sedative drugs were given. Another study by Derek Miller and Keith Bryant was concerned with the meaning of prescriptions for the handling of in-patients by hospital personnel and the ways in which patients interpret the prescriptions.

Robert Wallerstein and Joseph Satten were planning a study of the problems of the psychological treatment of alcoholism, including the motivation for treatment, and the meaning and consequences of offering antabuse to the alcoholic patient.

Doctors Wallerstein, Watterson and Holzman were working on plans for a joint psychiatric-psychological study of patients with a thyroid dysfunction related to psychoneurotic complaints, as these patients were treated with surgery, radio-iodine treatment, or neither.

Helen Sargent was working on the potentialities of her "Insight Test," uniquely suited to exploring the mental and physical capacities of the blind.

A followup study of all patients cared for in the Modlin section within an eighteen-month period, was being carried on by Herbert Modlin in two hours of work per week.

Grace Heider was giving half time to follow the children who had been in Escalona's infancy project.

Basic research not directly connected to the clinical programs of the Foundation included a project on individuality in processes of perceiving. Originated by George S. Klein, the cognitive systems of 60 subjects were now being studied by Klein, R. Gardner, Holzman and Schlesinger with the assistance of Diana Laskin, in a new integration study. This involved an eight-hour laboratory study of each subject in order to analyze the interrelationships between different perceptual dimensions, and the relationship of those dimensions to basic personality organization.

Gardner saw his plan for a perceptual learning project as a supplement to the perception project. "The basic problem," he wrote, "is the way in which the person may come to re-learn or reorganize his way of perceiving so as to have less of illusion and self-deception in it."

Outside funds supported two projects: the United States Public Health Service financed the perception project, and the New York Foundation financed the selection project carried on by Lester Luborsky and Robert Holt; results of this study to find the best way to select candidates for psychiatric training were in the process of being written up.

Gardner soon found that he was director of a research group for which neither adequate time nor money was available and he vigorously attacked the problem. Before the end of the first year in Topeka he was exploring other sources of support needed for the psychotherapy research project. Visiting representatives of the Ford Foundation criticized "the lack of a research atmosphere" and the small fractions of time so many people spent on research. Gardner commented to Escalona,

> I can see ever more clearly why there is so much skepticism about supporting our research and specifically supporting the Psychotherapy Research Project. There is not a single medical man who is making research his chief endeavor; after a struggle, we got six hours a week for Don Watterson to serve as chairman.... Paul [Bergman] is giving perhaps eight or ten hours a week ... in a rather scattered way.... No one else is giving more than about two or three hours, except that ... Helvi Boothe and the whole social work group are, at present, very actively developing an excellent followup study ... we very urgently need at least one medical man giving at least half his time to psychotherapy research.

Gardner was going to try to get one of the psychiatrists completing his residency to do that. "That is where I intend to get as much action as I can...." He also hoped to get "at least two of the senior people to give about three hours a week," and he was going to appeal to Dr. Robbins to give something like a full day a week to research.

If more time for the psychotherapy research project could be obtained, Gardner believed that it would be possible "to make a much stronger plea" for support from outside sources. He felt that the main achievements of the first year (1952–1953) were the development of the termination interview method by Watterson, and the development of the follow-up project by the social workers. But more systematic and complete coverage was needed; he believed "that we may be on the way to get it by fall."

Some months after Gardner arrived, a committee mobilized for the purpose drafted a ten-year plan for the Foundation. It stated that

> The Menninger Foundation is a professional organization, devoted to the conduct of research and the training of professional personnel in psychiatry and related fields.... Superior programs of education and research are unthinkable without a superior hospital, a superior clinic, a superior training school.

The faculties of the Menninger School of Psychiatry and of the Topeka Psychoanalytic Institute needed to be enlarged. Emphasizing the leadership of the Foundation in the field of psychiatry the plan noted that limited salaries and excessive work pressure had made it difficult to attract persons of established stature to the Foundation, and also to keep promising young people after they reached professional maturity.

The ten-year plan looked forward to a far broader program of research than was then possible, including the participation of specialists in many related fields—physiologists, internists, pharmacologists, biochemists, anthropologists, sociologists, geneticists and others—in addition to psychiatrists and psychologists. Such a research program would include study of the causative factors in mental illness, with studies of both organic and psychological factors ... of heredity and environment, of the processes of growing and the processes of aging. There was a plea for research and teaching "beds" to permit selection of patients for specific clinical research projects. The importance of research in prevention was discussed in relation to mental health and illness in industry, in schools, and in the community.

Other aspects of the ten-year plan included training programs for marriage counselors; institutes for vocational rehabilitation, for physicians on problems of psychosomatic illness, and for ministers, social workers, teachers and other workers in fields related to mental health. Professional development of the staff included providing work conditions that would attract high caliber professional people. Opportunities were needed for educational advancement through travel funds to visit other institutions; reduction of work schedules was urgent to permit time for work on individual projects; longer vacation periods, and an improved sick leave program were also recognized as necessary.

The staff committee working on the ten-year plan thus envisioned a wide range of improvements in the conditions of work and of life of the Foundation—many of which had implications for the development of research. The difficulty in retaining mature leaders in the Foundation continued to limit the fulfillment of the vision outlined in 1953.

After the first year Gardner realized that he needed a young psychiatrist as assistant director of research; George Klein and Philip Holzman recommended Robert (Bob) Wallerstein at the Veterans Administration Hospital in Topeka. It was a happy choice, personally as well as professionally, since the whole Wallerstein family, which included his vivid wife Judith, two children, then a third, became intimate friends and accepted us virtually as members of the family. After Gardner died, the youngest, Amy, wrote, "He was always a grandfather to me. I never thought he would die." Nina wrote wonderful letters from India where she spent a year living with a family, and also visited Gardner in his last years in our home hospital. They invited us to birthday parties, to a seder, and to Michael's bar mitzvah. Along with the Holzmans, Luborskys and Hartocollises they were a major factor in making us feel at home in Topeka.

Gardner urged Wallerstein as the assistant director to define his own research areas. These included the psychotherapy research project (Paul Bergman had left the Foundation) for which Wallerstein put together a steering and planning group. Wallerstein and Lewis Robbins became leaders of the psychotherapy research project as it undertook an intensive clinical study of 42 patients. Helen Sargent provided methodological conceptualizations as the expanded research plan was being formulated in 1955. Gardner's early concern about time for the research was relieved by Wallerstein's success in obtaining the allocation of half time for Robbins' work, and time was made available for the other staff members.

In 1954 Gardner continued to be concerned about funding the psychotherapy research project and sent an application to the Foundations Fund for Research in Psychiatry (FFRP). On February 25, 1955, Sibylle Escalona, who was then on the staff, wrote "I am very pleased . . . to be able to report positive Board action . . . the group discussed this proposal with great seriousness and interest. . . . Some [directors] especially pointed to what they felt was a significant sharpening in focus and improvement in methodology. . . ." For each of three years $19,000 was contributed for the psychotherapy research project. In 1956 the Ford Foundation made a grant of $350,000 for six years which supported the project until 1962. Until NIMH developed a general support grant for research at the Foundation, each project required a grant of its own.

Of the original group, only the clinical psychologist Lester Luborsky and the social worker Mildred Faris stayed on and played an important part in the early development of the project. In 1955 it involved some fifteen people with commitments of time ranging from six hours to full time for psychologist Helen Sargent. Gardner participated regularly in the weekly planning session, offering advice at the conceptual and planning levels.

By the middle of his second year at the Menninger Foundation Gardner felt that the work was "moving along nicely" and he wrote Escalona that his own research, the perceptual learning project, "is taking a good deal of our thinking now, with Fred Snyder and Don Spence making a major contribution." Riley Gardner and Gerry Ehrenreich were planning, with George Klein's support, observations of hospital behavior "with articulation between these observations and the findings of the Perception Project and of the testing work of the clinical psychologists."

Gardner reviewed with Bob Wallerstein many research issues. He reported to Escalona that with Bob's active work they were moving into more psychiatric problems, working with Topeka State and Winter (V.A.) Hospital on a project involving thorazine and serpasil.

Even before Gardner officially took up his post at the Foundation he had begun to develop a vision not only of what was possible but also what, as he saw it, was the obligation or the duty of the hospital if "it was to make the kind of research contribution made by other major clinics." His vision of adequate research was shaped by his comprehensive understanding of personality. He considered it necessary to study both the genetic inheritance and the cultural context of the individual's development.

Although Gardner had accepted the appointment for its opportunity to carry out his own research, he quickly donned the robe of a leader committed to the support of research throughout the Foundation. At an annual meeting in the spring of his first year in Topeka (1953) he addressed the trustees, emphasizing the crucial role played by research in the advance of medicine and the fact that research had been a respected part of the Menninger program since Rapaport and his associates had begun their studies of clinical testing a dozen years earlier. He then reviewed the programs already underway, giving special attention to the study of the effectiveness of psychotherapy spearheaded by Paul Bergman. Gardner pointed out how unusual it was for an institution to turn the searchlight on itself to study its successes and its failures. While he felt that the Foundation should be proud of this undertaking he made it very clear that support was needed to increase the number of patients studied, and also to add follow-up studies which would involve contact with the patients after several years.

Turning to his own research he expressed gratitude for financial support for two assistants on the study of the dynamics of perception, or, as he put it, increasing the flexibility or reducing the inflexibility in perceiving. He also mentioned his hopes for a study of value conflicts.

In addition, Gardner noted that he and Robbins had set up an interprofessional Research Advisory Committee to conduct a survey of the research interests of the staff in order to establish some long-range goals. This committee represented social workers, nurses and adjunctive therapists as well as psychiatrists and psychologists, in line with Gardner's hope to stimulate research throughout the Foundation.

The following year, his address to the trustees spelled out six objectives designed to expand the contribution of Menninger research:

(1) Formulate feasible, financially manageable research projects;

(2) Develop a sense of the importance of research as an integral aspect of diagnosis, therapy, and training throughout the Foundation;

(3) Add to "our understanding of the processes by which medical residents are selected for psychiatric training";

(4) Coordinate existing research efforts at the Menninger Foundation, Winter V.A. Hospital and Topeka State Hospital;

(5) Communicate with others around the world working on similar problems so as to avoid wasted effort;

(6) Maintain flexibility with reference to issues which need to be investigated — for example, the use of new drugs, or new treatment methods, new types of evaluation, and so on.

Gardner also focused attention on his concern about relationships with the Topeka community and with the state of Kansas, especially in connection with problems of prevention. He reported on conferences with psychiatrists at Topeka State and Winter hospitals as well as with clinical psychologists in both institutions, and also meetings of all psychologists in the city, paying tribute to the large contributions to outside contacts made by Drs. Will and Karl Menninger and by Dr. Robbins. In this concern he exercised a sense of obligation of the Foundation to its neighbors, and unwillingness to endorse the image of a unique island of psychiatric excellence somewhat aloof from the world around that we had felt when we first came.

He urged that the research program be kept from becoming ossified or rigidly standardized, and emphasized the value in studies of etiology and of current efforts to refine procedures for evaluation, admission, and medical records, along with Karl's studies of psychiatric conceptualization, the evaluation procedures at the Children's Service, and the systematization of personality evaluation procedures in the psychotherapy research project. The projects were all "aimed at viewing in a large panorama the social and biological synthesis which constitutes the background of the patients' adaptive or maladaptive response."

Under the heading of research in diagnosis Gardner referred to "Dr. Karl's studies of the possibility of changing our view of psychotic illness to a more dynamic one," and the research use of psychological tests in differential diagnosis. In this context he mentioned that Wallerstein had initiated with Joseph Satten a new study on the psychology of the alcoholic patient. In addition, a study by Irving Kartus and Herbert Schlesinger focused on the interrelations of psychotherapist and patient connected with the administration of sedation, and a new project on thorazine treatment involving the whole hospital staff.

Left to the end of this address, with its broad sweep, its hopes, its summary of progress and of possibilities, was Gardner's discussion of "basic research into human nature." Here he referred to the contributions by George Klein and his colleagues on the "deepseated individual differences in human ways of perceiving the world, of unconscious ways of apprehending, classifying. This matter of perceptual idiosyncrasies gets to the very heart of the psychological problems as to the devices by which people cope with this challenging and confusing world." He reported Klein's transfer to New York University and the fact that Holzman and Schlesinger were continuing the trail-blazing project. He then mentioned progress on his own perceptual learning project, "a series of studies as to the ways in which the gratifications and frustrations of living consolidate the things around us into one shape or another to give a maximum of satisfaction." He added that "the wish is father not only to the thought, but even to the process of perceiving, the process of conceptualizing, interpreting, recalling, imagining. We see richer and richer linkages here between psychoanalytic theory and experimental psychology." Gardner felt that this work was contributing to the understanding of some of the processes fundamental to psychopathology. He hoped to add something "to the understanding of that basic irrationality and distorting process which plays so large a part in human misery."

That fall of 1954 a series of articles in the *Bulletin of the Menninger Clinic* presented a fuller report of the range of psychiatric studies and also aspects of my coping study. The paper by Gardner Murphy and Wallerstein emphasized, as Gardner had done in his address to the trustees, the increasing development of a "research attitude as a pervading facet of every therapeutic, educational or service function." "Research then becomes," they continued, "a way of conceptualizing the regular working data of clinical operations . . . to allow the emergence of broad hypotheses . . . and then to systematize the data" so as to throw light on the validity of these hypotheses and the direction their revision should take. The authors explained that the Menninger Foundation with its multidisciplinary group practice was especially suited to this kind of research spirit and activity. Its hospital, day hospital and outpatient settings, its large program of individual psychotherapeutic activity working with dynamic psychiatric concepts provided a volume of clinical material available for the pursuit of clinical problems.

In that fall of 1954 a research seminar was led by Mayman, with Gardner, and several small studies were carried out by residents who were taking the seminar.

From this time on, Gardner's work at the Menninger Foundation included support of those projects whose directors sought his support, advice, and assistance in funding, as well as the close work with his own assistants. He was most closely in touch with Klein, Holt, R. Gardner, Holzman, Luborsky, Mayman, and Shevrin, as well as the coping project group working with me, and he was very concerned with Escalona's progress in utilizing the intensive data she and Mary Leitch had collected.

In 1955, two long range plans for research (Plan A, Plan B) were outlined by Gardner and Robert Wallerstein. Beginning with a statement of the research challenge offered by the Hospital, they gave as an example the study of the effects of thorazine as seen in the depth psychology of patients studied intensively before, during and after thorazine treatment. They felt that such studies should be expanded as well as multiplied. "Knowledge of the determinants and the mechanisms of change will come only from longitudinal studies, correlating changes at the level of overt behavior with changes at the ideational level, in thought and affect."

In that year the psychotherapy research project involved the work of five psychiatrists, four psychologists, two social workers as well as the work of a large part of the staff of the Department of Adult Psychiatry.

The experience with the thyroid project had stimulated a hope for more studies of that kind. But at that point the reality of the inability of the Menninger Foundation to do basic research in the physical, chemical, genetic, physiological and anatomical aspects of mental disorders became apparent. A visit to Michael Reese Hospital in Chicago exposed the directors of the Research Department to a conference at which "some twenty professional associates discussed the many aspects of a personality problem" which Dr. Roy Grinker had presented. They saw "the physical and biological sciences contributing from their various viewpoints to the understanding of one specific personality syndrome, the dynamics of which may give broad insight into psychiatric issues." They realized that despite the outstanding position in psychiatry of the Menninger Foundation, it did not have funds to achieve such an integration of disciplines at that time.

Still they hoped that the thorazine and the thyroid projects would lead (must lead) within a year or two to studies involving deeper concern with problems of chemistry, pharmacology and physiology. Facilities of the Stormont-Vail Hospital in Topeka and the Biophysics Department of the University of Kansas in nearby Lawrence were already being used. The aim in further work would be to see the whole person in the light of every systematic discipline which had something to contribute. This, the directors hoped, would enlarge the perspective of the psychiatrists and would define issues in which personality study is central rather than peripheral. Gardner saw this as an application of Freud's thought in his remark that the same data can be approached through psychoanalysis and through biology. Without throwing out of balance the psychodynamic approach that is central at the Menninger Foundation, the addition of

> say, a biochemist, a physiologist and a pathologist would extend the contributions to be made in personality study. Now that the basic psychodynamic insights of Freud have begun to take hold everywhere, the next steps surely are to study the individualizing role of specific patterns of genes in relation to specific liberating or blocking factors in the individual and community pattern.

The cessation of research in clinical testing after the departure of David Rapaport was a source of both deep concern and the "belief that serious thought should be given to the question of revitalizing the attack upon the research problems which appear in clinical testing." This required substantial time allowed for research by staff members trained in the postdoctoral Fellows program.

They also recognized the importance of the cognitive studies carried on by clinicians trained by Rapaport:

> The study of perception begun in 1947 under the leadership of Dr. George Klein was slated to come to an end August 31, 1955. Dr. Philip Holzman planned to continue research in this field, and should be given assistants and research facilities which would permit him to expand the range and depth of reach in perceptive dynamics with a closer integration between a clinical program and the laboratory program.

Gardner wrote to Paul Bergman that he was in effect trying to build a research department at the Menninger Foundation worthy to stand alongside of the departments of education and therapy. The impact of Gardner's approach was not lost on the research group who had been at the Foundation several years. One of the clinical psychologists who had been working on cognitive style research before Gardner arrived noted that before Gardner came the position of research director had been a parttime, largely administrative assignment. Gardner's full time appointment was, this writer thought, defined more broadly, and this helped to make it possible for him to provide personal, intellectual and financial support. But this in itself did not account for the freedom he gave others to work in the supportive and the loving environment he brought with him.

> His spirit was so pervasive in this sense that every aspect of the work was made somehow lighter and more pleasant. Gardner was unique in these ways. . . . We [the research personnel] changed, in a way that I cherished, from a congeries to a group. We were united by being part of a broader framework and were more caring toward each other because of him. Our personalities were at least as broadened and enriched by him as our professional selves in a more technical and specialized sense.

The other aspect of his "encompassing presence" was the "broadening intellectual stimulation he provided. He seemed interested in everything in the field and had thought about kinds of things I literally had never heard of (but needed to)." Added to this were his invitations to "guest stimulators" — such as A.R. Luria and Jean Piaget, who spent many days conferring with members of the research group.

22. Gardner's Approach as a Director

At the Menninger Foundation, Gardner worked with psychologists and psychiatrists of different levels of training and experience, from the gifted Charles Snyder, who had not completed his Ph.D., to Lewis Robbins, a senior psychiatrist. Consequently, the degree of oversight exerted by Gardner varied from one person to another. Gardner encouraged members of his perceptual learning project to define their own experiments within the area under study. Thus, experiments in perceptual learning in the auditory and tactile areas were soon added at the initiative of young investigators.

At the same time Gardner not only assisted all investigators with grant applications to the National Institute of Mental Health, he also approached many foundations and other sources in his efforts to develop financial support needed to supplement grants from the government. His detailed memoranda testify to his careful critical review of preliminary and final reports of all projects: comments on the need for definition of concepts; problems of clarity; need for discussion of implications of findings; and in some instances, technical suggestions regarding techniques for analysis of data.

Gardner critiqued the written reports submitted to him from every possible angle, insisting on the highest standards and offering praise at every opportunity. To Harold Voth and Martin Mayman he wrote on December 21, 1961: "I am very much impressed with this beautiful . . . paper: A Principle of Personality Organization." After several editorial suggestions he questioned their use of the terms *ego* and *self*. "At times they seem to be identical in your treatment. Ordinarily when content is involved we use the word *self*, and when function or process is involved, we use the word *ego* . . . you need to tighten up." And later on he protested, "Page 8, line seven, don't say *this data*; I've been after you about this for about three years. . .(!)"

And despite his disclaimers of statistical competence he corrected statistical statements: "The generalization as to what you can predict at a .01

269

level is of course contingent not only upon the function, but the number of cases." He explained that the criterion can be predicted "at the .01 level ... with a hundred subjects and fail with 25, since it's an artifact depending upon n." After other comments on the use of correlations, he concluded, "I think this study is very important.... I'd like to see you, if I may, at least once every couple of months to keep in touch with what is going on."

From time to time Gardner illustrated an issue of terminology with a literary example; in a letter to McNamara and Fisch March 13, 1961, on their paper on reality testing he commented, "The term dissonance ... which I assume is used à la Festinger, seems to overlook the possibility that the situation is capable of several different kinds of perception, none of which involves conflict or dissonance with the others, as for example, in the idle reformulations of interpretation that occur as we look at clouds." Recalling Shakespeare he continued, "It doesn't bother Polonius that a cloud looks like a whale, although he has just said that it has a back like a camel." And a little later,

> ... don't assume that the choice of this innocent term ("hitch") is just a casual matter; it will commit you up to the hilt to the way in which you view this whole matter. Compare the endless arguments between Bertrand Russell and prognosticators like John Dewey. For one, there is such a thing as internal contradictions between propositions; for the other there are only hitches in the behavioral world.

At times Gardner pushed for further reflection on hypotheses. Commenting on Riley Gardner's study of "sharpening" and "leveling" cognitive styles, Gardner wrote: "I am much impressed with the qualitative observations and believe that they are worth pursuing further. What are your own hypotheses regarding the dynamics of the tendency to try to notice a lot of differences ... versus the tendency to take things more casually and use a coarse grouping?" He also suggested that quite different dynamics may lie behind the same general form of response from one person to another. "That is one reason I would like to see the scatter diagrams...." He added that he hoped R. Gardner would make more use of the qualitative material in his published report.

An authoritative editor, Gardner was not an authoritarian director of research. He was just as hospitable to comments and criticisms from the research group as he was generous in his comments on the work of both the members of his own perceptual learning team and the clinicians who were carrying on studies of perception, cognitive styles, and other investigations.

Gardner encouraged mutual help and collaboration between those working on different projects. There was no formal link between those who were working on the perceptual learning project and those who had been and still were involved in the perception project developed by George Klein. But after a few years, collaboration on certain studies developed between members of the two groups. In addition to exchanges recorded in memoranda, private meetings and letters, there were coffee-break discussions in which members of the research group exchanged suggestions for research projects and techniques, and discussed their reports on research and Gardner's papers. There was much cross-fertilization, although the research projects were generally carried on by small teams of two or three members of the group.

Various members of the research staff have written that Gardner "encouraged cooperation and collaboration between us and actively discouraged competition or rivalry. He trusted us to do good work," and that he "created a supportive climate" in which the objectives were clear: to find out information about human misperception so that such misperceptions might be corrected. He pointed out goals and offered advice, inspiration and support for reaching them. He did not demand nor exhort but indicated, pointed, represented, exemplified. "It is a leadership style that I have not encountered since . . . based heavily on mutual respect," wrote Robert Sommer. It gave the opportunity for each one to make a maximal investment in his own creative additions to the solution of the problem of perceptual learning.

Charles Solley, who was Gardner's closest collaborator in perception research at the Menninger Foundation, wrote that the two of them would meet almost every Monday afternoon for a couple of hours to discuss the perceptual learning project. "What we were doing research-wise was always intertwined with social issues, historical issues, clinical issues, and so on. He would say that he knew very little about experimental design and that he knew absolutely nothing about statistics." (However, he insisted on the most rigorous control and analysis, and he sometimes gave specific suggestions both about experimental techniques and about statistical analyses.)

"Part of Gardner's genius as an administrator," Solley commented, "was to see important ideas in odd places, to stimulate his research associates to create new experimental procedures," and to "create a whole for understanding when we barely grasped the parts." He had a way of "making the assistants grow without pushing them, without driving them and even without telling them what to do," and of treating each person he was with "as if he were the most important person on earth."

Solley added that he never felt out of touch when Gardner was away from Topeka. "A drawer full of letters, cards, dictabelts" testify to his constant responsiveness; "he was continuously inquiring about various projects," and answering Solley's letters within a day or two of the time he received them, with endless attention to detail; "he was worried about how we had described one of I. Kohler's studies and whether we or Wallach was right." "Gardner himself was the vital link between research topics" — "he was the hub of an enormous wheel." Gardner knew about the family of each staff member. His style was personal and direct, but also very professional, "in which we were all colleagues. His style had an ineffable quality and did not fall into one of the stereotypes, authoritarian or laissez-faire."

Harold McNamara, who had begun to work with Ted Ayllon and Robert Sommer in 1955 on a project published as "Autisms Emphasis and Figure-Ground Perception," felt that his discussions with Gardner over several years constituted "an unbelievable learning experience that was unique because of the breadth of Gardner's interests and scope of his knowledge."

Joseph Kovach contrasted Gardner's humanity with the hardnosed quality of psychologists in some universities:

> Gardner had a fantastic talent for evoking . . . ideas — it was stimulating, not just nurturing, . . . but you couldn't find out how he did it. . . . There is no idea he would not be interested in . . . pause, and consider it, explore around it or sometimes leave it, and then come back to it. In seminars when there were wild disagreements, he could calm things down in his gentle way.

Many of the younger clinical people at the Menninger Foundation loved Gardner as had his students, appreciating "the personal warmth and support which all of us felt from him." "I am so grateful that some of his 'light did shine upon me,'" Lester Luborsky wrote. "He was a benign presence for all of us working on this large and tension-filled project (the Psychotherapy Research Project). But most of all he brought a breadth of vision and perspective which we needed . . . ," wrote Leonard Horwitz. Herbert Spohn commented, "Gardner was an extraordinary human being, . . . [and] he will be remembered not only as an enormously gifted and influential psychologist, but also as a very warm, empathic and selfless human being. Many of his students and surely I as well, owe their professional careers to Gardner's warm encouragement and wise counsel." Several of the Menninger group have told me that they continue to keep Gardner's picture on their desks and in some way felt him to be a father.

Donald Spence feels that "Gardner is still an unseen presence" among the Menninger group of the fifties and that "we all maintain an image of his encouraging ways and his enthusiasm for new ideas."

> He has often been compared with William James, and I think this part of him gave us a sense of being rooted in a deepseated American tradition in which philosophy is mixed with experimentation and in which even outlandish ideas (and James certainly had his share) were worth careful investigation. . . . Gardner was remarkable in his humility and in his need to let the evidence do the convincing.

23. Gardner's Research : Perceivers and Their Feelings

At City College Gardner's studies of perception had been first stimulated by Nevitt Sanford's study of the effect of deprivation of food on perception and by our acquaintance with the Rorschach and thematic apperception methods of exploring personality through perception. Gardner's commitment to the necessity of understanding the evolution of any psychological events led to the next step, the study of how people learn to perceive as they do. In therapy or psychoanalysis we find patients distorting, scotomatizing (not seeing, shutting out), exaggerating or confusing objects or events in ways that prevent a realistic perception of reality.

How does this come about? The answer must be, he thought, that laws of learning must be operating to shape perception as well as memory. Thorndike's "law of effect" states that pleasure or pain — reward or punishment — influences what we remember, as do the "recency, frequency and vividness" of a given stimulus. It was on the hypothesis that reward and punishment also influence the selectivity and patterning of perception, that Gardner had extended the series of experiments on the influence of affect on perception with his honors students at City College.

He had reflected deeply on concepts developed by psychologists to whom he had listened carefully: to Dewey's, to Köhler's description that learning "is a function of the transformation of perceptual responses," to Tolman's emphasis on cognition as central in the process of learning, and to Razran's description of *levels* of learning from the "conditioned reflex" up to complex semantic and symbolic levels. From discussions with Razran, and with others including Rapaport and George Klein, Gardner developed the theory which provided the frame of reference for his studies. He summarized it briefly in five points that describe the processes which interact in an individual's perception of the environment:

(1) the impact of energies upon the sense-organs which put us in touch with the outer world, and the transmission of impulses to cortical centers;
(2) the integration of these fresh sensory impacts with others from sources inside the body which assist in eliciting an integrated response in the brain;
(3) direction and focus to these integrative processes by goals;
(4) the association of the resulting central integrations with traces left in the brain from earlier stimulation;
(5) progressive changes in perceptual response during successive encounters with a given stimulus situation, so that perceptual learning occurs.

Affect influences perception in steps 3 and 4. The first task at the Foundation was to replicate and to demonstrate the validity of his City College studies of the influence of affect, need, reward and punishment on perception.

His aim was to build a more adequate theory of perception on the foundation of the experimental work. If a replication of the original study with new subjects and new experimenters confirmed the original results it would be safe to proceed to further studies of the perceptual learning process. He was not disappointed; as before at City College, in the early experiments at Menninger the subjects responded selectively to rewarded visual stimuli. The experimenters went on to test responses to sound and to touch, with similar results. This made it reasonable to generalize the principle that affect influences perceptual learning. Solley and Santos demonstrated further that perception could be conditioned *against* the experimental subject's initial preference, and they also found that a perceptive pattern could be trained to persist rigidly. When rapport had been developed with the subject, even a trivial reinforcement such as "Uh-huh" was effective.

Another step was taken by McNamara, who demonstrated that individuals could be influenced to make incorrect judgments on simple tasks by rewarding them for similar incorrect judgments on related tasks. Further studies focused on the role of expectancy or "set" in determining subsequent perceptions after reinforcement in a learning situation. A study of the relationship of expectancy to the direction of attention showed that differential rewards during the act of paying attention to a given animal figure were followed by eye movements of the subject toward the predominantly rewarded figure when it was shown as one of several concomitant displays of animal figures.

Scotoma, or not perceiving, was studied in the context of perceptual response competition, a situation in which certain competing stimuli are so attractive that attention is directed toward them at the expense of other equally available stimuli. In more complex situations, when stimuli associated with pain might be avoided, accurate perception would provide information or cues that would help to avoid the pain.

Other inquiries into the development of perceptual patterns had included identifying the organizing or disorganizing effects of affect at different points in the perceptual process; autonomic activity and proprioceptive (or muscle) stimulation may produce distortions in perception of even simple stimuli. Braatøy's observations of painful memories held in check by increased muscle tension suggested that perception could be influenced by the same tension. This led to the question whether awareness of muscle tensions could be useful in overcoming perceptual distortions, inadequacies or scotomas.

In an article with the understated title of "Learning to Perceive as We Wish to Perceive," Gardner and his senior assistant Charles Solley reviewed the work carried out through 1956 with the support of a United States Public Health Service grant. Beginning with their assumption that perception "is to some extent molded by specific affective experiences which set the stamp of a personal life history upon each act of perceiving," they proceeded to describe a series of studies which foreshadow work carried out during the following decade.

Granting that sense organs, nervous systems and muscles function in a fairly uniform way, Murphy and Solley believed that "cultural and personal vicissitudes lead in many instances to failure in making adequate contact with external reality"; as in *A Midsummer Night's Dream* when Theseus exclaims, "How easy is a bush supposed a bear."

They did not think that perception, memory and imagination could be sharply separated from one another, but since perception of controlled stimuli is possible in a laboratory situation, they argued that perception could be studied experimentally to better advantage than memory. They agreed that the influence of affect is enhanced in memory and imagination; when a person is not sure of what he has seen, he elaborates imaginatively. In their view the psychological process involved in perception while the impact of the stimulus material is clearly present needed to be explored experimentally.

In a variety of experiments with materials that were observed visually, listened to, or touched, different members of the perceptual learning project demonstrated that both adults and children organize figure-ground relationships in terms of rewards or avoidance of punishment. Further work demonstrated vigilant avoidance of painful or threatening stimuli. When rewarding and punishing stimuli were compared with neutral situations, the rewarded stimuli were dominant over the neutral and the punished. Whether neutral stimuli dominate over painful or disagreeable stimuli depends on the intensity of the disagreeable stimulus as experienced by the person and the possibility for escape from the unpleasant stimulus. Stimuli associated with unpleasant electric shock were seen by male subjects as clearer, but by female subjects as fainter. This difference between "vigilant" or intensified perception contrasting with "defensive" or weakened perception was studied further.

Not seeing at all, or scotoma, was also observed in some subjects in the original Schafer-Murphy experiment in which faces fit into each other; the face that had elicited punishment was so completely rejected that some children did not believe it was there. In certain experiments children not only demonstrated scotoma for punished stimuli, they also manifested perceptual distortion or affectively toned misperception. These children called the punished face a goof or idiot while the "rewarded" faces were seen as sweet and kind. These findings led to furiher efforts to study the processes of development of and correction of misperception. One plan involved the study of simultaneous tachistoscopic exposures to images each of which had positive or negative associations, in order to determine the process of organizing the perceptual field. The image that is perceived will dominate the field.

The roles of expectancy—as a result of past experience—and of the scanning process which shapes the cognitive act were also under study. These studies showed that feelings governed the attentional aspect of perception and led to a study of the conditioning of attention. This offered a possibility of exploring cross-relationships between the cognitive style studies of Holzman and Riley Gardner and the perceptual learning studies.

In view of the fact that the stimuli were innocuous and also that the rewards and punishments were trivial it may be surprising to the uninitiated that clearcut results could be obtained. But Gardner had such confidence in the principle of isomorphism that he was sure the principle that perception was shaped by affect could be and should be demonstated at the most elementary level. That is, laws governing functions at an elementary level apply to higher levels.

Although the research focused on specific narrow experiments in order to document firmly the contribution of learning to perception and errors in perception, Gardner continued from the first to provide a historical, cross-disciplinary and cross-cultural perspective to the thinking of his group, keeping the group up-to-date on relevant modern work in the field as well. From the early years of Greek philosophy through nineteenth and twentieth century experimentation there was no dearth of research on and speculation about the nature of perception and the processes leading to its development.

Charles Solley's notes on the seminars in which Gardner carried on these discussions were the basis for the 1960 book *Development of the Perceptual World*. Solley presented findings from the experiments of the years 1953 to 1959; Gardner's historical and speculative chapters extended from the past to the future of efforts to understand perception.

In this book, Solley and Murphy consistently emphasized that perceiving is an active process, not merely a passive sensory experience. In his "final look at perceptual learning," Gardner stated,

> we believe that nearly every act of perception has nativistic characteristics as well as the earmarks of prior experience; the major problem is to understand the interaction of the two factors. . . . While we have admitted that there must be primitive perceptual acts which "exist" prior to learning, we have stressed . . .

the molding, the modification, the differentiation, and the integration of these basic, unlearned perceptual acts. The level of maturation apparently governs the nature of the perceptual act at the beginning of a learning experience and the efficiency of various types of motives and reinforcers.

They described the process of perceiving as including the following sequence: expectation of stimulation $\longrightarrow$ attending $\longrightarrow$ reception $\longrightarrow$ trial and checks, along with autonomic and proprioceptive arousal and feedback $\longrightarrow$ final structuring. A percept that is clear and well-structured reinforces its own act. (We do not need a pat on the back when we recognize the uniquely symmetrical grace of a pin oak but reinforcement may help us to perceive a red pine as different from a white pine.) External, positive reinforcers are most effective when percepts are poorly defined.

The intensity of pain and individual differences in coping with it are among many factors influencing the effect of pain on the structure of the percept. Painful reinforcers change the affective context of the learning situation, the expectancy patterns, and the foci of attention. If there is a chance to escape or avoid, the percept is more highly structured; we know exactly how a mosquito or a wasp differs from a fly.

Perceptions include the products of both outward-looking (or, for instance listening) attending, and inward-oriented attention focused on muscles and viscera.

> The act of perceiving, then, is an organismic response whose fundamental dynamics—including the dynamics of learning—should be comparable with, perhaps identical with, the acquisition of overt behavior acts. . . . There is motor learning because perceptual learning is going on, defining the possibilities and instigating the changing motor responses.

Moreover, the acts of seeking, scanning, attending have to be included in the family of motor acts studied over the years by the psychologists of learning such as Thorndike, Hull, and Skinner.

The last chapter, with its illustrations from some of Gardner's favorite philosophers, composers, artists, and writers, is more than a coda or integration of themes; it looks ahead to issues that need further exploration. Gardner commented that the traditional boundaries between perception, judgment, thought and imagination are fluid and evanescent. Perceptual responses may involve memories, and they may lead into thought and imagination which influence or create expectancies of new perceptions.

These reflections evoked Gardner's effort to show that traditional association theory can include the dynamic processes of active searching and connecting. In addition, situations newly perceived become connected with old response tendencies by conditioning, and some portions of a perceptual response system may become connected with other parts. Finally, associative networks can provide connections between sensory stimulation and affective (pleasurable or frustrating) responses, resulting in repetition of or shutting out of the new experiences.

Constantly aware of the *organism* (with its active living cells) that is perceiving, Gardner stated that a relatively complex network of nerve cells established through the evolutionary process is required if complex associations are to take place. And with his perennial need to emphasize the isomorphism of inner and outer structure he also emphasized the capacity of the inner system to mirror the outer system.

Clinical thinking was being integrated with that of classical psychologists, along with the findings of recent research, in the effort to make progress toward an adequate understanding of the nature of, and processes involved in, the development of percepts. This was the goal of the "basic research" to which Gardner was committed. The assumption was that we cannot adequately understand the development of distorted perception involved in much mental illness unless we thoroughly understand the developmental processes — those of both maturation and of learning — involved in all perception. The roles of motivation and of reinforcement, of practice and of reward and punishment, were studied by analyzing mechanisms involved in perceptual learning. It was assumed from the beginning that the infant is equipped to perceive from birth (and now we can add, even before birth) and that maturation improves the refinement and scope of perception.

Gardner's researchers believed that changes in the perceptual act are related to the development of expectancy, of the conditioning of the act of attending, the development of trial and checking skills, of signals and feedback patterns, and of figure-ground relations. The place of consciousness and of conscious meaning as these are related to memories, ideas and language was seen in relation both to action and to the neurological picture of interchange of impulses between the cortex, the hypothalamus and the reticular systems of the brainstem. In other words, Gardner shared with his research group his life-long preoccupation with the overlap of biological and environmental factors in all aspects of human functioning.

"The symmetries in the thought of the child or the man are to some extent derived from the initial symmetries in the universe and to some extent the symmetries built into the child or the man impose symmetries upon the environment, the ecology to which the life adaptation can best be made." At the same time, as he recognized, there is a law of dominance as well as a law of equality. In critical phases, one kind of stimulation is more important than others. A long friendship and extensive correspondence with Gregory Razran reinforced Gardner's interest in the law of dominance and its application to problems in perceptual learning. Gardner was also deeply influenced by Ashby's Design for a Brain, especially his law of economy in nature: any *part* may take over the functional significance of the *system* which has been controlling behavior.

In moving from perception to thought he concluded that purpose is born of experience and action; that experience, influenced by tensions and modes of contact with the environment which reduce the tensions, leads to more efficient ways of escaping from the tension situation. Further, modern evidence regarding pleasure centers implies that tension reduction is only part of the pattern of factors contributing to increasing pleasure and reducing pain; it contributes then to motivation and to value systems, and to the symbolic life. The inner orchestration developed in the quest for order "comes to terms with a complex outer orchestration given both by the culture and by the human habitat in which the culture has slowly grown."

Gardner's evolutionary approach was not focused solely on the progressive development of concepts—he was always interested in the extent to which classical formulations could meet present needs in theory. We see an example of this tendency in his reconciliation of association psychology both with the complexities of thought and with the principle of pressure toward the highest integration of which the organism is capable. He believed that three levels were involved, the first level reexpressing itself in the others, and the second level also expressed in the third.

At the same time he saw jumps or quantum principles between simple cell connections and the individual's ability to arrive at simultaneous solutions of many problems. No simple principle can be adequate to explain the orchestration process:

> ... at a certain level of complexity we have to have formal laws ... or structural requirements based on isomorphism with the environment. In Rembrandt's perception of the meaning of the human face, or Schubert's and Beethoven's grasp of the possibility of transforming a simple melodic line into a breathtaking new vision of life by adding alterations in tonality or rhythm, we have sudden transitions to a higher plane, ... in which a richer isomorphism with cosmic structure is achieved. . . .

Gardner sought to demonstrate that normal and pathological cognitive functioning are governed by the same basic laws of perceptual learning. Therapists use this principle daily when they reinforce healthy perceptions and help patients to understand and to change distortions.

Gardner and Santos were interested in the differences in the degree of structuredness of different stimulus situations: in ambiguous or unstructured situations it should be easy to influence perceptual experience, and the impact of need is stronger. In studies of perception of the Necker Cube (an outlined cube which can be seen alternately facing left or right) the effects of several different reinforcing strategies were examined, such as recency of reinforcement. The psychophysiological aspects of Necker Cube reversal were also studied through a variety of techniques; these studies led to studies of attention in schizophrenics.

Efforts to condition attention in children led to the recognition that rapport with the experimenter influenced the effect of the reinforcement on the children's response. Also, open-mindedness versus dogmatism of belief systems was found to be related to "amenability to social reinforcement." Moreover, when certain objects were given "value," these objects were more sharply differentiated from their ground. When processes of attending were analyzed, experimenters identified scanning processes which extend or restrict the availability of a variety of cues. As an outcome of the many studies of attention, interesting differences in searching and scanning strategies were found to be related to the level of difficulty of the task; a strategy that was useful at one level could interfere with effectiveness at another level.

By 1959 Gardner's view of what was needed in studies of *reality testing* was broadened. In a proposal "for research on processes which aid or impair the testing of reality" he discussed the need for an integration of clinical, experimental and ethnological methods of studying the control of thought by feeling: "the bias, evasion and distortion that enter into the testing of reality, whether on the part of the scientist, the medical man and the scholar — or the statesman, the business man, the leader." This development in his thinking was influenced by his concern with peace efforts and international relations. "Field studies, comparing our own special biases and irrationalities with those obtained in other societies" could contribute dimensions which clinical and experimental studies are likely to overlook. He felt that hypotheses needed to be formulated and systematically tested.

Gardner had long been interested in roots of curiosity and found the process of searching for cues as part of reality testing described by Berlyne especially stimulating. The studies by Hebb, Harlow and others describing a kind of cognitive hunger added to this interest and led to a study of the question whether a general curiosity tendency could be increased. Preliminary results were positive and indicated the need for further study of whether a general information-seeking tendency can be developed through reinforcement and by what kinds of reinforcement. In addition, emphasis was given to studies of experimental production of sensitization to reality cues and of motivation to follow such cues. Obviously this is important for educators.

Since it appeared probable that the act of attending is significantly related to perceptual learning, new developments included experiments in controlling the act of attending to a particular stimulus or to a particular portion of space. The new studies of attentional processes included subliminal learning experiments and studies of the effect of reinforcement on later perception of autokinetic movement (the subject's report that he saw a tiny light in a dark area moving when in reality the light is static).

Experiments in subliminal learning were initiated in order to show that subjects could use information about stimuli of which they were not consciously aware. These and also the experiments in autokinesis were stimulated by earlier studies of subliminal perception and of autokinesis by clinicians at Menninger. Although possible clinical applications were not discussed in the reports, their potential contribution to psychotherapy processes and techniques is important.

The work on perceptual learning was part of a range of studies of perception that Gardner related to others' work on both innate and experientially determined perception. While "wishful thinking" is a cliché common in everyday conversation, the idea that sense perception itself is influenced by wishes, drives, fears or antipathies is not easily accepted. Even Freud said, sometimes "a cigar is just a cigar." And a chair is a chair. But much of the world is not so simple, not so definitively structured; we find ourselves confronting ambiguous situations and objects which are not reliably identifiable, or which permit interpretations shaped by the interests, needs or fears of the viewer. This is most conspicuous in our perception of new people, places such as towns, or country and wilderness areas. A city-bred two-year-old taken to the country for his health looked at the meadow and the hills beyond, and said unhappily, "No cars, no taxis, no busses, no trucks, no trains, no wheels!" While some people listening to the singing of Marian Anderson or Paul Robeson heard magnificent voices and saw great personalities, others saw only black skin. Prejudice is the most blatant example of perceptual learning. "Beauty is in the eye of the beholder," to be sure, but the eye can *learn* to perceive certain qualities and not others.

In a lecture in India, Gardner reviewed several different approaches in perception research but although *The Development of the Perceptual World* makes use of some of George Klein's and Riley Gardner's work, the work of Luborsky and Shevrin on subception and the Menninger work on autokinesis, for example, is not adequately discussed. If Gardner had not become ill and if his experience in the last years at Menninger had not been so stressful he would surely have achieved an integration of all of the studies on perception.

After he retired as director of research he was preoccupied with the problem of integrating issues involved in the understanding of inner reality and its relation to outer reality. He developed his basic theoretical synthesis in *Encounter with Reality* (1968), with Herbert Spohn's collaboration, and his application of that understanding was presented in *Outgrowing Self-Deception* (1975) with the assistance of Morton Leeds. Both books are enriched by his multidisciplinary and historical perspectives and his own observations of people of all ages.

24. New Developments in the 1960s

Gardner reached the age of 65 in July 1960, a transition generally marked by retirement. But Gardner reflected no decline of energy, purpose or zest. His birthday was honored by the publication of the Festschrift mentioned earlier, a volume containing scientific papers in both psychology and parapsychology by 25 of his distinguished students, an article on Gardner by Eugene Hartley, and another on alumni of the City College Psychology Department by John Peatman, his successor as chairman of the department. Otto Klineberg, one of the contributors, quoted a paragraph from Gardner's 1958 *Human Potentialities,*

> Others can write a great deal better about the architecture of the future, atomic energy and its uses, automation, basic English, city planning, cybernetics, diplomacy, the increasing life span, interplanetary travel, the managerial revolution, Marxism, the new pharmacology, psychoanalysis, world government, and a thousand other valuable themes. It is the human stuff that concerns me. I have believed for a long time that human nature is a reciprocity of what is inside the skin and what is outside . . . our way of being one with our fellows and our world.

With this selection Otto threw his spotlight on the essential humanity of Gardner's contribution to psychology.

In the summer of 1960 Gardner was one of a group sent by the American Psychological Association to explore the work of psychologists in the Soviet Union. On the way he taught a class in social psychology at the University of Hawaii. Stanley Krippner, a young student who was inspired by Gardner's *Personality* to become a psychologist, was his teaching assistant. His help to Gardner in that summer course and their mutual interest in parapsychology led to a lifelong friendship. At the 1963 meeting of the Parapsychology Association Gardner introduced Krippner to Montague Ullman, who was pioneering a major study of dream telepathy at the Maimonides Medical Center in Brooklyn;

this led to the appointment of Krippner as senior research associate there. Grants from the Scaife and the Ittleson family foundations made it possible to expand the research into a study of the relation between creativity and the paranormal. The studies directed by Ullman were among Gardner's favorite investigations—he contributed substantially to their funding and visited the laboratory whenever he was in New York. Both Ullman and Krippner were devoted to Gardner and visited him in his last, bedridden years.

The visit to the Soviet Union renewed contact with Professor A.R. Luria who had recently visited us at the Menninger Foundation. (He had asked me to drive him around the town and remarked "The joy of America is in its family homes.") In Moscow he arranged visits to an experimental school and to the Institute of Defectology with its remarkably creative inventions to help blind, deaf, and blind-deaf children as well as paraplegics. For instance, blind-deaf children were helped to develop knowledge of the world by systematic use of touch and by creating clay models of objects they explored.

At the University of Moscow we met Dr. E.N. Sokolov who was working on the orienting reflex. I found his discussion especially stimulating to my thinking about children's coping.

The psychologists we met discussed cognitive functioning chiefly; although they were warm and friendly, we heard no theoretical discussion of affect or conflicts until we ourselves raised the question of emotional reactions to stress in the very small apartments typical in larger cities; they were frank to recognize that this was a source of conflicts. In Leningrad our major contact was with Dr. Miasishchev at the Bechterev Institute where therapy with the mentally ill relied chiefly on drugs. Dr. Miasishchev asked me whether we "used Freud's ideas in therapy in the United States" and when I said that some of us do, he remarked sadly, "We cannot do that here."

Both in Tashkent and in Moscow we found provisions for children generous and creative—with children's parks equipped for many kinds of activities in beautiful natural settings, with magnificent posters illustrating different vocations and advertising *peace* (not soft drinks, for example). Noticing the warmth of those who worked with children we asked, "How are these workers selected?" The answer was, "We try out applicants and we select those who are good with children."

The dedication of the Gardner Murphy Research Building at the Menninger Foundation took place in 1970. Over the years between, important new developments broadened the range of research activities as chance and the prepared mind added new projects to the ongoing studies in psychotherapy research, perception, reality testing and coping. The new ones included several community studies, studies leading to the work in biofeedback, studies of schizophrenia in relation to its social context, and studies in genetics. Gardner's role in the development of all of these had roots in his biosocial approach to personality which he believed was as relevant to mental illness as to healthy personality; in addition, his interest in certain studies of the twenties and thirties contributed to the prepared mind. A brief summary of the background of each of these developments will illustrate the continuity of these aspects of his drive to humanize psychology, beyond his focus on perception seen as the activity of a perceiving person.

Gardner had been deeply interested in community studies since his visit in 1923 to the Middletown study conducted by Robert and Helen Lynd. He had maintained contact with the West End study in Boston carried out by his former student Mark Fried and Dr. Erich Lindemann and also with the work of Leo Srole in the "Yorkville Project" in New York. When Gardner was a UNESCO consultant in India in 1950, his most intense experience was his study of community tensions.

In the fall of 1960 Gardner was consultant to the Topeka Urban Renewal Project. One day when he was lunching with the sociologist William Key of Washburn University (director of the Project) a social worker, Richard Benson and a psychiatrist, Edward Greenwood, of the Menninger Foundation who had been working on that committee, Bill Key talked about his dream of a study of the effects of forced relocation on families. Topeka families were being relocated from deteriorated housing in the Urban Renewal Project, and also from an area through which a new federal highway was to be constructed. Although the new housing was, on the whole, more sanitary and attractive than the old, Bill still realized that many families would have difficulty adjusting.

Since Gardner had long wished to develop closer ties between the Foundation and the city the group agreed that they would take advantage of this remarkable opportunity for research. Studies of relocation had already revealed the dismal failure to develop a better level of functioning when families were assigned to highrise apartments in federal housing developments in major cities. Could Topeka handle relocation more successfully in an urban renewal program directed and staffed by the Menninger Foundation?

Gardner met weekly with Bill Key discussing a research design and methods of data analysis: since counselling was provided for the Urban Renewal families but not for those displaced by the new highway there was an opportunity to compare the experience of the two groups, each of which included Hispanic, black and white families of a similar range of economic and social status, age levels and ethnic cultures.

Gardner suggested that a model he had developed for research at another hospital would be appropriate: to compare the experience of one group with A impact — that is, forced relocation — along with the group experiencing A plus B impacts — that is, relocation with counselling. The counselling included every sort of help in finding a new home, dealing with the real estate broker, handling finances, obtaining needed equipment and help in dealing with family problems as well. Both groups would be interviewed in a follow-up.

Gardner was co-director of the urban renewal study and as part of his sharing of its work he visited some of the desolate spots in areas from which people
were being relocated, including a little street with eight houses that had dirt
floors, no plumbing, one cold-water spigot at the end of the road to supply
all the houses—conditions as bad as what he had seen in India.

Although most families in both groups were satisfied with their new locations, black families tended to be happier with their improved home settings
than Chicanos, who missed the extended family type of minicommunities in
which they carried on their social life. Children and elderly people, who were
less able to develop satisfying new friendships and support systems, found the
moves more stressful.

The basic support for a sense of satisfaction in the Topeka Urban Renewal
Project was the fact that the *choices* of individuals were respected; people were
not arbitrarily assigned to a new location. In certain cases black families moved
into integrated neighborhoods as the NAACP urged, in other cases they chose
not to do so. In other words, relocation took place with the maintenance of
autonomy of, and respect for, the individual as the fundamental principle.
Moreover, the new locations represented a step up the social ladder, without
exposing the relocated families to the gross contrasts to which metropolitan
families were exposed when they were relocated in highrise public housing
around the corner from luxurious apartment buildings. Topeka was, on the
whole, a middle-class town with relatively little conspicuous expenditure to
dramatize a contrast with poverty.

When the team found unemployed adults in the urban renewal group—
sometimes because of too limited a range of skills, sometimes because of
negative attitudes—the research group wanted to add professional therapeutic
help aimed to assist these people to become self-supporting. Through the good
offices of Mary Switzer, director of the Vocational Rehabilitation Agency (VRA)
of the federal government and also a Menninger Foundation trustee, the VRA
office agreed to fund therapy, with the proviso that a new director of this project on emotional aspects of vocational rehabilitation should be appointed. This
led to the recruitment of James Taylor, and it meant that there were now two
projects: the relocation project as originally planned and the vocational
rehabilitation project.

When the vocational rehabilitation project began, the people to be relocated were interviewed in order to select those who needed professional help
to deal with work problems; some were marked to receive help and the others
were regarded as a control group. Actually those in the control group improved
in their work situations about as much as those to whom help was given. I
believe that two factors could have been important in this result: the stimulus
of moving, often to a better house could have spurred them to greater effort;
beyond this, the initial interview itself, although not therapeutically oriented,
could have contributed to a constructive appraisal of themselves and their own

potentialities. (In final interviews of our children in the "coping studies" in which no therapy was offered, they told us that the interviews had been helpful — that they were stimulated to think about themselves and their plans.)

The needs of the families and the experience gained by the team led to a Community Service Center from which a psychiatrist and social worker went to the homes of families who were not using the resources of the community despite their desperate needs. These workers helped the city agencies to understand the needs of the most suffering families in addition to providing direct help to the families themselves.

In 1964 Gardner designated Key the director of the Social Science Division of Research, which, by 1966 added two new community projects: Louis Zurcher's research on the development of relationships between the leaders of Economic Opportunity Act (OEO "War Against Poverty") units and their constituents, and a study of community responses to the devastating tornado of June 1966.

The perceptual learning and reality testing studies were seen as basic to the understanding of mental health and pathology. The community studies were all concerned with problems of adjustment to change and improved functioning of the people involved. In the early sixties two new areas of research directly concerned with illness were added to the research program; although Gardner was not a therapist, a long series of influences had led to Gardner's quick response to a new approach to healing. His father's long illness had stirred young Gardner's concern with healing processes; at the age of fifteen he pushed his father's wheelchair in Bad Nauheim. At the age of seventeen he thought of studying medicine in order to help his father. Some days off duty from the Yale Mobile Hospital in World War I had been used for a visit to Lourdes, the famous faith-healing center in France. And he was deeply impressed by William James' account of his recovery after reading Renouvier's discussion of the healing power of the will. In 1938 E. Jacobson's program for muscle relaxation stimulated Gardner's interest to the point of trying it for a limited time; I think he was impatient about the time required to move relaxation from toes to neck and he did not continue the technique. But his interest in the potentialities of muscle relaxation and voluntary control of physiological processes had been aroused.

His 1947 *Personality* foreshadowed what developed as autogenic training and biofeedback methods of controlling physical symptoms. Thus Gardner responded eagerly to Bjorn Christianson's application for postdoctoral study at the Menninger Foundation; Christianson was working on Braatøy's problem of the way in which relaxation of muscle tension in the arms may release unwelcome memories; after his two-year sojourn in Topeka Christianson went home to Norway. Further work on relaxation began when Elmer and Alyce Green responded to Gardner's invitation to join the staff. Elmer Green was a biomedical engineer with a Ph.D. in biopsychology and was interested in mind-body relationships as was his wife, a psychologist. Their creative work—including success in control of blood pressure, migraine headaches and other problems— is described in a series of articles in journal symposia, and in their book, *Beyond Biofeedback* (1973). That work, supported by a series of grants from NIMH and several foundations, became a permanent addition to the therapy resources of the Menninger Foundation.

Elmer Green was committed not only to research but to an effort "to synthesize the concepts and data of psychology and neuroanatomy and at the same time demonstrate that the human potential has been seriously underestimated." He believed that obvious parapsychological data should be interpreted "in terms of neuropsychological control of bioenergies rather than as evidence for the existence of mind apart from brain."

Another permanent addition in 1964 was a clinical psychologist, Herbert Spohn, who had carried on studies of schizophrenia in relation to the social context in which it developed. Gardner's interest in psychosis had a long history. His doctoral dissertation had been a study of types of word-association in dementia praecox, manic-depressive and normal persons; he had taught abnormal psychology and had published *An Outline of Abnormal Psychology* in 1932; a second edition with Arthur Bachrach was published in 1954. These projects with psychotic patients, his teaching and writing had led to his hope for the addition of research on such patients, and to his interest in Herbert Spohn's research on schizophrenia. Spohn also worked with Gardner on an integration of the studies of reality-testing in his 1968 *Encounter with Reality* and in 1981 he became director of research in the Menninger Foundation, continuing his clinical research.

Parallel to Gardner's interest in social factors in both normal and mentally ill persons was his interest in genetics. From the early 1950s he had been consulting, and visiting the laboratories of, geneticists such as Professor Dobzhansky at Columbia University and Herbert Muller, who also visited the Foundation as a Sloan Professor. Especially after our visit to the Jackson Memorial Laboratory at Bar Harbor in 1945 he kept in touch with the geneticists John Fuller, J.F. Scott and Daniel Freedman, who were demonstrating impressive differences in dogs' responses to discipline and socialization processes. But Gardner did not find a geneticist for the Research Department. However, when Robert Wallerstein invited Joseph Kovach to speak and then to accept an appointment in 1966 he became an honored member of the Menninger staff.

During that decade these new areas of study were paralleled by continuing work on the Psychotherapy Research Project, by that time carried on by over 20 clinicians (chiefly psychoanalysts) and reported in nearly 70 articles, monographs and books discussing the design, the variables outlined, methods of study, predictions and their outcomes, and the assessment of change in patients (including change in I.Q.), evaluations of clinicians ratings on the health–sickness scale developed for use in the research, challenges or second thoughts about the importance of insight, and detailed discussions of processes and outcomes for the 42 patients in treatment. Gardner had always considered this clinical study the most important research project at the Foundation; after his early efforts to fund the project, and his consultations with the staff during the fifties, he was less involved; PRP developed its own momentum. Gardner had urged increasing the original number of patients and he had also urged that outcomes of therapy be studied in follow-up interviews. In the sixties, NIMH funded the study and Otto Kernberg became the director of that stage of data-analysis.

As I recounted earlier most of these severely ill patients came from a distance after failing to get help elsewhere, hoping to get help from the famous Menninger Clinic. After intensive examination, they were assigned to psychoanalysts for classic psychoanalysis, or for supportive-expressive psychoanalytically oriented psychotherapy. Neither their doctors nor the patients knew that they would be subjects for research; in this way the possibility was avoided that the psychotherapy process would be influenced by the study.

Reports by Horwitz and by Wallerstein agreed that greater psychotherapeutic success was achieved with supportive therapy, in contrast to the original hypothesis that success depends on the resolution of conflict (and concomitant achievement of insight); changes were "substantially in excess of the insights" in a large group of patients (nineteen). Sixteen of the nineteen were in psychotherapy. Eight patients had good analyses with good outcomes; with these patients changes and resolution of conflicts were "proportional." Another study, by S. Appelbaum, concluded that "structural change is associated with resolution of conflict, *and* that structural change can come about in the absence of conflict resolution ... conflict resolution cannot be considered essential to structural change...." In addition, in the follow-up studies, changes brought about with supportive treatment were maintained and consolidated in contrast to the expectation that they would be less stable, and "less able to weather the stresses of life." In some instances more appropriate marriages resulted from the patients' better understanding of their needs and often the positive feedback from more adaptive behavior contributed to the stability of change.

Because of the sample of extremely ill patients in this study it may not be sound to infer that classical psychoanalysis should not be the preferred treatment for mental illness; rather, it may be fair to infer that the sicker the patient, the greater the need for a supportive approach, within a psychoanalytic orientation. Wallerstein's discussions of patients in terms of their symptoms and character structure, the recommendations for treatment, the process of treatment, factors involved in change, and in overall results provide unique material for the trainee in clinical work, for the psychotherapist and for the instructor in clinical and specifically psychoanalytic courses.

Gardner was always interested in and helpful to my research and considered it another of the major studies. In 1952, when I inherited the data on 128 infants recorded by psychologist Sibylle Escalona, pediatrician Mary Leitch, Grace Heider and others, I was able to set in motion a longitudinal effort to discover, in effect, how normal children stay normal—how they cope with the ordinary and extraordinary stresses of growing up. The Coping Study was financed from 1953 to 1969 by NIMH with additional help from the Neumeyer Foundation and basic support from the Menninger Foundation. Thirty-one children at the preschool level were studied intensively; later a total of 65 children at latency, prepuberty and adolescent levels were followed by a team including psychiatrists (the experienced child psychiatrist Povl Toussieng examined the children at three levels), psychologists, a pediatrician, a home visitor, speech specialist, statisticians. Children's responses to tests, play sessions, interviews, parties, and family events such as birth of a sibling, divorce or death of parent or grandparent, moving to a new home, school or town and the 1966 tornado were recorded to provide records of coping with life challenges and threats. I guided the study, carried on Miniature Life Toy play sessions and served as parallel observer in some other sessions; I conceptualized coping techniques, strategies and styles, consulted with the members of our staff and with additional psychiatrists and others who worked on specific portions of the data; and I wrote reports on the study, both for the *Bulletin of the Menninger Clinic* and for other periodicals.

After symposia at American Psychological Association conferences in 1954 and 1955, and a presentation at the International Psychological Association in 1957, Escalona and Heider published *Prediction and Outcome* in 1959. This compared children as they were observed at the time of the infancy study with their behavior during the preschool study. My *Widening World of Childhood* followed in 1962. Other studies by members of our team included Alice Moriarty's analysis with Clyde Rousey, *Diagnostic Implications of Speech Sounds* (1965) and Grace Heider's *Vulnerability in Infants and Young Children* (1966). The concept of vulnerability had been brought into focus by our pediatrician, Patricia Schloesser, who noted zones of tension during her pediatric examinations (muscle tension, changes in pulse, blanching or flushing, tears, and so on). Then came Charles Stewart's *Adolescent Religion* (1967), Riley Gardner and Alice Moriarty's *Personality Development at Preadolescence* (1968), and Toussieng and Moriarty's *Adolescent Coping* (1976). The latter reported that contrary to our expectation of senior high school anxiety based on the prepuberty findings, the children were in better mental health at graduation from high school.

A study by Alice Moriarty and others of children's reactions to President Kennedy's assassination and many other analyses of specific problems, such as changes in I.Q. from infancy to adolescence, were reported in journal articles by Moriarty, by Toussieng, by Heider, by myself, and by three psychiatrists on the Menninger Foundation staff who made analyses of selected children.

Because I became involved in working on Head Start and Parent-Child Centers in the 1960s, and in writing 10 booklets for a series, "Caring for Children," published by the Office of Child Development, my own final report on our long study was delayed. *Vulnerability, Coping and Growth,* with Alice Moriarty, finally appeared in 1976. An intensive case study of "Helen," a resilient girl who had been a vulnerable baby, was enriched by comments of several analysts including Anna Freud. When I placed the first copy of *Vulnerability, Coping and Growth* in Gardner's hands in 1976, he sighed, "Now I feel that my life has been fulfilled." And Dr. Karl wrote "We love your book and we love you and Gardner." Later, he remarked to me "You were the only one who used my contribution" (of disintegrative reactions to stress), a concept basic to the development of my thinking about vulnerability.

In the spring of 1967, Gardner's last year at the Menninger Foundation, Dr. Roy Menninger planned a large Foundation-wide staff meeting for which he requested a program highlighting some of the Research Department activities. For this meeting Gardner succinctly reviewed the development of research during his time at the Menninger Foundation and he presented a chart listing projects within four main areas: clinical, experimental, longitudinal, and sociocultural.

He briefly described the psychophysiological and the statistical laboratories crucial to the research program as a whole, and also the financial support from USPHS and many foundations in addition to the Menninger Foundation, which had made the research possible. Asserting that research training was also part of the task of the research department he noted the future potential of the postdoctoral clinical research program in psychology, the postresidency research training program for psychiatrists and other new efforts. He felt that the area of prevention might be the "greatest area of usefulness in the era which we see coming now."

He arranged for one investigator in each of the four project areas to describe some aspects of the research under way; these included Philip Holzman to describe an experimental project; Otto Kernberg to describe the Psychotherapy Research Project; and William Key to describe the sociocultural studies. I was asked to give highlights of our longitudinal "coping project."

In his 1966–67 interviews with Montague Ullman, authorized by the American Psychiatric Association, Gardner expressed satisfaction in having built up the department; it was, in fact, his nurturing and integrative inspiration that was most effective. He himself commented that he was not as good an experimenter as he thought he was, and there was general agreement among the research group that he was not a technician. His presence as a leader who was quick to appreciate the potentialities in work carried out by teams of investigators resulted in a high level of productivity and in both stimulation of further research elsewhere and in important developments in the work of the Menninger Foundation.

In the decade of the sixties the nation as a whole was more disturbed than at any time since World War II. The discovery and shooting down over the Soviet Union of an American U2 spy plane in 1960 renewed tension between the USSR and the United States, and the failure of the Bay of Pigs invasion of Cuba by Cuban exiles trained in the United States escalated American fears of Communist dangers in Central America. President Kennedy's assassination in 1963 was followed by Lyndon Johnson's presidency and the escalation of war in Vietnam, which did not end until 1973.

Gardner participated in a conference of the Center for Research on Conflict Resolution; he corresponded with Senator Hubert Humphrey, and met with senators Carlson and Pearson in addition to corresponding with them hoping "that now, even more than before, emphasis be placed on every step leading to a test-ban treaty." Senator Carlson invited Gardner for a consultation in his Washington office. Gardner urged federal support for nonmilitary research efforts in Kansas, notably in biochemistry, genetics, agronomy, animal husbandry, medicine and the social sciences, and in 1964 urged Senator Carlson to support Bill 2274, which would establish a National Economic Conversion Commission. Senator Carlson replied assuring Gardner of his support of that bill. As the Vietnam War continued, Gardner protested "the failure to protect villages, and the use of lethal gas which *shock* the deepest human sense, with the revolting terrible image of America which we continue to foster."

Changes in Gardner's responsibility for research came about as Robert Wallerstein was appointed director of research in 1965 when Gardner reached the age of 70, but Wallerstein stayed only one year and Gardner was asked to carry on as acting director until a new director was found. Since Gardner had taught courses in the Topeka Psychoanalytic Institute during six of the years he had been at the Menninger Foundation and had also taught courses in the School of Psychiatric Education of the Menninger Foundation, he was appointed to the Henry March Pfeiffer Chair of Psychiatry and he retained this title until 1967. Following his resignation and our move to Washington, D.C., he was invited to return as consultant and lecturer, and was given the title of Henry March Pfeiffer Professor Emeritus.

The years from 1965 to 1967 were troubled years for the Foundation and for Gardner. President William C. Menninger developed cancer of the lung and after repeated hospitalizations, died on September 6, 1966. It was "Dr. Will" who had invited us to come and who had given Gardner his warm support over the years; his death was a deep loss to Gardner.

The year after Dr. Will's death was inevitably a period of confusion in the Foundation. Will Menninger and the Trustees had not made a plan for a smooth transition to a successor; in the gap a few members of the staff had dreams of taking over the administration. This would involve steps to enhance their status and to get rid of certain leading members of the staff. One of them attacked Gardner verbally so severely that Gardner told me that he had to leave. Dr. Reginald Lourie in Washington, D.C., who wanted me to work with an infancy project there, contacted George Washington University; the Psychology Department immediately invited Gardner to teach a personality course and seminar there. He also accepted an invitation to give a course in social psychology at City College in New York one day a week. And he accompanied me for a few days of the fortnight each month when I went to Topeka to complete my commitments on my final NIMH grant; Gardner was asked to return to Topeka for consultations with the research group. Herbert Spohn helped him complete *Encounter with Reality* (1968) and Joseph Kovach joined him for the third edition of his *Historical Introduction to Modern Psychology* (1972). With the assistance of consultants we finished *Asian Psychology* (1968) and *Western Psychology* (1969). With the help of a psychologist friend, Dr. Morton Leeds, Gardner completed a final book on his Menninger research, *Outgrowing Self-Deception* (1975).

In time, Roy Menninger, a psychiatrist and eldest son of Will, was appointed president of the Menninger Foundation by the trustees. Roy was well acquainted with Gardner's history and appreciated him so deeply that he initiated a plan to honor him by naming the research building, dedicated in 1970, the Gardner Murphy Research Building.

Karl and Jeannetta Menninger, as editors of the *Bulletin of the Menninger Clinic,* invited Gardner to join their editorial staff. But the Parkinsonism that developed in 1969–70 interfered with that activity.

In 1972 the American Psychological Foundation gave Gardner its Gold Medal Award.

A look at Gardner's Menninger years in the perspective of his New York years, shows that the studies of perceptual learning and reality tesing are a consolidation and extension of the studies of affect and perception in 1940–1943, and his support of the studies of biofeedback are an extension of his thinking about proprioceptive and enteroceptive perception. The community studies under William Key brought Gardner's social psychology thinking into the area of application to human problems while my longitudinal studies of vulnerability, coping and growth were experienced by him as a further development in the understanding of personality. In his lectures, conferences and writing, beyond the integration of thinking about the relation of need and affect to man's perception and conception of reality, he was applying his reflections on the nature of man to problems of peace, education, mental health and human potentialities, always within his faith in the isomorphism of man and the universe in which he grows and lives. Evolution continues, man evolves along with the rest of the universe, as does man's knowledge of himself and of the universe.

V / And Beyond

25. The Death of a Humanist

The extreme stress of the late sixties took a toll on Gardner's health. In the spring of 1966 a ruptured appendix with massive peritonitis was treated by his surgeon "by filling him up with an antibiotic"; he recovered in a few weeks from the weakness that followed but he developed cardiac problems, with angina, and orthostatic hypotension, that is, sudden drops in blood pressure that could cause him to collapse. The doctor said that he should not go out unaccompanied; so from that time on I stayed with him whenever he left the house until he developed a pattern of sitting down when he felt weak. Climbing and canoeing in New Hampshire summers were at an end; he could walk, with stops to sit on a rock, or a step, when pain from the angina flared up. But verses continued to bubble up from his irrepressibly playful mind during the rest of his fragile years—his gift to all of us who took care of him. And in the hospital he dictated:

COUGH, PLEASE
The man who can not cough nor sneeze
Gives quite suspicious E.E.G.'s;
His E.E.G.'s, with many a spike,
Cause punctures on Columbia Pike.
His E.K.G.'s and C.B.C.'s
Though oft repeated, cannot please,
The puffed-up cuff we need but mention
As evidence of hypotension.
The rhythm of his life is frozen;
He should have coughed, he should have snozen.

G.M.   (George Washington Hospital June, 1970)

During those early years in Washington we spent long happy summers in New Hampshire, and winter weeks in the Caribbean, Key West, or Flamingo

at the tip of the Everglades. In Florida there were fascinating new birds—
anhingas, and purple gallinules. Gardner wrote verses to announce our com-
ings and goings:

TO THE DAFFODILS OF TIMES SQUARE
On reading an account of the argument between
Lindsay and Ribicoff as to whether Bridgeport
is as dirty as New York

I wandered lonely in the crowd
Where silent thoughts are not allowed,
And traffic screams from all directions
Through crammed and writhing intersections.
I try, as country bumpkins do,
To breathe the smoggy smoggy dew
Well planned and skillful execution
Leads to magnificent pollution.
And then my heart with pleasure fills
To join New Hampshire's Jacks and Jills.

G.M. (Ashland, N.H., after June 15, 1969)

In 1969 he developed Parkinson tremors that interfered with his ability
to write. For the next three years, his neurologist tried different combinations
of L-Dopa and other drugs such as amantadine. But the combinations brought
disorientation and confusion. His friend David Shakow, of the neurological
division of the National Institutes of Health, supported his acceptance into an
experimental program oriented to the treatment of Parkinsonism; he went
there in December 1972. Optimistic and spirited as always, Gardner dictated
a Christmas poem for the nurses:

CHRISTMAS SONG FOR TWO WEST
by Gardner Murphy, 1972

Oh say, can you see, at the 6 A.M. waking
What so dimly we heard through the snoring and quaking
While thermometers click and the blood-pressure cuff
Gave proof through the dark that we've slept long enough.
Soon the trays will be sliding and gently colliding
The holiday atmosphere's full of confiding
You can tell at a glance that the nurses' white pants
Will carry them off to a Christmas Eve dance.
Oh say, nurses dear, forgive us our fancy
If the time and the place turn our thoughts a bit prancy

Would you give Santa Claus a couple of hints
Plum puddings for guys and for each gal a prince . .
And for everyone here a magic recovery
Would be the New Year's very nicest discovery.
MERRY   CHRISTMAS   TO   ALL

After some weeks of tests he wrote the following:

THE SPECIALISTS

They take infinite pains to get blood from your veins
With a girl and a needle each veinlet to wheedle.
Such specialized skill is pursued with a will;
Each vein has its doctoral quota to fill.
They have a machine to examine your spleen—
That is, a computer and personal tutor—
To tell if you're crabby in style à la Lucy
Or your system's just Kansan and naturally juicy.
For each of our 81 well hidden organs
There's a sphygmomanometer's eye, like a gorgon's
With their caps and their stripes showing every degree
From the technical freshman to lofty M.D.

After four months of spinal taps, and experimenting with drugs, progress was unsatisfactory, and Gardner became very depressed. I told the social worker that I felt the situation was not right for Gardner and asked that he be transferred to out-patient status. The staff felt that would be dangerous because of the likelihood of a fall, but I persuaded them that he was always alert to his condition and could find something to sit on when he felt the need to do so. To prepare for the change he was allowed to go out for short periods; the balmy spring air, azaleas, dogwoods, Japanese cherry trees and magnolias along with the birds gave him new zest and dispelled the depression. After a month he came home as an out-patient, returning weekly. Then after a couple of months of further trials he was discharged with a combination of medications that reduced the tremors but interfered seriously with speech. After some weeks, he decided that he could not endure that, and he stopped taking the medication; communication was the most urgent need. We continued our New Hampshire summers and had longer winter respites—at Tortola in the winter of 1973–4 where the Newcombs visited us, and Key West again in 1974–75. Gardner's former student and devoted friend Mort Leeds worked with him to complete the little book *Outgrowing Self-Deception* and they began work on the book that became *The Paranormal and the Normal*. I was working on the much interrupted *Vulnerability, Coping and Growth*, begun in the 1960s and finally published in 1976. At home in Washington and in

New Hampshire there was always music, reading, visits from children, grand-children and friends. Everywhere there were little walks, and Gardner once remarked, "Isn't it wonderful how much beauty we can see just walking around the block!" The "more beyond" had come to include what was near but not formerly noticed.

A catastrophic fall March 5, 1975, ended this quiet plan of living; Gardner slipped one evening in our Key West motel. His hip was fractured and with the surgery to repair it with a pin he developed pneumonia. In the intensive care unit (ICU) for three weeks, suffering intense pain, disoriented from drugs and then slipping into an "ICU psychosis," diagnosed as chronic brain syndrome, doctors and nurses did not expect him to survive, or if he survived, they felt that he would not be normal. But the chief of staff, who wrote to me later, had known of Gardner's reputation and allowed me to stay in the ICU with him "if it would help him." Keeping out of the nurses' way when they worked with him, I stayed close to him when they were away; I held him and sang to him songs we had sung together when we were first married. Nurses varied in their reactions: one nurse said, "You are helping him more than we can," but another protested, "What's this, necking in the hospital!" Loving support from Bob and Judy Wallerstein, who flew down from a conference in New York, and from Monte Ullman, who took the first plane to Florida upon disembarking from a plane returning him from Sweden, as well as week long visits from my brother Gordon, my sister Gwen, and our daughter Midge, bolstered my morale as did Dr. Ramzy's call from Topeka. In the hospital I was calm and firm — "We're going to have our 50th wedding anniversary in 1976," I insisted, when the nurses tried, so kindly and gently, to prepare me for his death. I cried myself to sleep every night.

Soon after leaving the ICU Gardner had to have a tracheotomy; a tube was inserted for suctioning his congested lungs. After that was done, it was discovered that he had been aspirating some of his food and this was causing the recurrence of pneumonia. A feeding tube was inserted into his stomach to prevent this. For the next four years he lived with tubes in his throat and stomach, replaced from time to time as problems arose.

After four more weeks in a private room, with special nurses afternoon and night while I had the morning care, the review committee decided, against the surgeon's wishes, that Gardner should be discharged, to go to the National Orthopedic and Rehabilitation Hospital near Washington. We flew up in a Lear jet. A crisis arose when a sympathetic doctor mistakenly thought Gardner could do without the trach and removed it. By 2 A.M. he was breathing with such great difficulty that he became panicky; a young resident gave him a large shot of valium which left him unconscious for 48 hours and out of contact 95 percent of the time for two weeks. When Al came down from New York to visit him in the hospital and sang a favorite Gilbert and Sullivan song, Gardner opened his eyes and was alert for a few moments. The neurologist summoned for assessment insisted that he was deteriorating into dementia. The review committee recommended that he be taken to a nursing home. But I could not accept that solution. With the help of the private nurse in the hospital I set up a "home hospital" in our living room, with all of the equipment the hospital room had had — oxygen, suction machine, and so on.

After getting home, seeing his familiar Rembrandt, Botticelli and Leonardo prints on the wall and the bookcases near his bed, Gardner's disorientation disappeared; two days later our Doctor Silver visited and observed, "His concepts are perfectly clear. He just has difficulty talking with the trach." Dr. Silver kept in close touch from then on and responded quickly whenever we had a problem; his unfailing concern made Gardner's survival possible. With the help of superb nurses he was able to walk "the grand rounds" around the first floor of our house, sit up for an hour and go out on the porch in a wheelchair.

Gardner never complained although pain was at times intense, especially from diverticulitis. He was endlessly concerned about the nurses; when one of them told us about repairs needed on her car, he asked me to give her a check to help pay for them (we were paying medical bills with help from family and friends). When I was tired and spoke irritably to a negligent young male nurse Gardner said, "Be gentle with young men, Loki — they need support."

In August we took him up to New Hampshire in another Lear jet for a month at his beloved Birchlea. He gained strength and lived nearly four years enjoying the superb symphonies, operas, and ballet on television during those years and also Steve Allen's stimulating program "Meeting of Minds" and baseball and nature programs.

At moments of threat of discouragement, he asked for Leo Rosten's *Rome Wasn't Burned in a Day,* works of Edward Lear and Phyllis McGinley, as well as Ogden Nash. The endless frustration of advanced Parkinsonism never trapped him: "Except for not being able to get around much, I'm living quite a normal life!" (Dictating comments on manuscripts sent by colleagues, consulting with some former students, enjoying television, following closely and critically my reading of scientific reports, finishing his book with Morton Leeds — *The Paranormal and the Normal* — giving me sage advice on my writing.)

We flew again to New Hampshire in the summers of 1976, 1977 and 1978. During that last summer Gardner said wistfully that he longed to see a mountain again. His Yale roommate Malcolm Baber had sent a check for $75 "for something to give Gardner pleasure." Since he could not be driven in a car or even a vehicle for the disabled, I arranged with our local ambulance to drive him, with me and our nurse, to Lake Chocorua on a late afternoon. The litter on which he lay was lifted out to the beach. Purple shadows on the mountain, reflected on the lake beneath, were broken by golden sunlight from the west. Gardner sighed, "It's more wonderful than I could have believed possible." His joie de vivre, his delight in nature, music and friends was never lost.

An honorary doctorate was awarded by the City University of New York in 1975 and another by the University of Hamburg (Germany) in 1976.

He dictated three limericks for my birthday; one of these integrated his feelings of our life:

VERSATILITY
My darling of mountains and lakes
Of Wordsworths and Shelleys and Blakes,
    With a turn of the tides
    In our little insides
Cares for gastros and elegant trachs.

In his last weeks, he looked forward to another summer in New Hampshire, planned to dictate an autobiography more complete that those he had written, and revise *Human Potentialities,* as well as help me with my book. He had professional conferences in the last days, and enjoyed Bernstein's Tchaikovsky's sixth symphony. On the morning of March 18, 1979, Mort Leeds told Gardner that his last book, *The Paranormal and the Normal,* was in galley proofs. At 8 o'clock that evening while we were watching a Balanchine ballet he drooped gently, calling "Lois!" and his heart stopped, with a coronary occlusion. As Lester Luborsky predicted, he "died with his boots on" and with a transcendent spirit.

26. Gardner's Legacy
"Say Not the Struggle Naught Availeth"

This quotation from Arthur Hugh Clough—not William Ernest Henley's "I am the master of my fate"—is from one of Gardner's favorite poems. The sensitive, impressionable, intense, enthusiastic, loving little boy who felt isolated at times, rejected by his big brother's gang, struggled to be "one of the boys," and longed in World War I to "do the part of a man." He became the awesome and inspiring teacher, the playful companion of children, the psychologist of vision who continued to explore "the more beyond" and who believed that human nature itself continues to evolve. Beneath his passionate commitment to supporting human rights was his hope to do something important that might somehow carry on his gentle reformer father's great work, or accomplish something equally important for humanity.

But toward the end of his life he was aware that his most cherished goals had evaded him. He succeeded in helping to bring psychical research into the fold of serious scientific work in America but he produced neither the definitive repeatable experiment nor the acceptable theory that would illuminate the relation of mind to body. He boldly brought psychoanalysis into the world of psychology in an era when Freud was not mentionable in that world. And with his understanding of the relation of affect and thought he demonstrated that perception as well as memory was shaped by needs and feelings. But he did not live long enough to integrate all of the studies of unconscious dynamics of perception and perceptual learning.

What then, is his legacy? In part, it is his courageous, creative struggle itself. But there is much more. With his broad orientation to the range of scientific contributions to human life he consistently defended the responsibility of psychology to work toward solutions of human problems such as racial, national and labor conflicts, mental illness, retardation, and psychogenic illnesses among others. An enduring legacy is his passionate and successful support of the inclusion in the constitution of the American Psychological Association the phrase (that its object shall be) "a means of promoting human welfare" after the phrase "to advance psychology as a science and profession."

His legacy includes his effective integration of the old and the new, the dominant and the neglected insights of a psychology woefully fragmented at the mid-century; the prescient inclusion of the forgotten self in a theory of personality preoccupied with traits and needs; his mountain top view of the field in which behavior develops as that field includes all of ecology, culture, the immediate situation and the organism with its conscious and unconscious responses. His legacy is intrinsic in the now large field of empirical social psychology, which expanded so vigorously after his 1931 vision of experimental social psychology, then matured in the 1937 edition. His support of studies at Columbia of the effect on black children of racial prejudice contributed to major social change in the direction of equality in education and in public life, and also a recognition of social factors in the development of aspects of intelligence measured by the I.Q.

His legacy expands in the greater acceptance of scientists' right to study anomalous events long dismissed as taboo; by his early anticipation of and support for biofeedback with its potential for healing; by his hospitality to contributions from the East including those of Indian yogi with their understanding of control of involuntary physiological functions.

These supportive efforts were an expression of his commitment to inclusiveness in his response to ideas and problems. His inclusiveness extended to methods as well, as he recognized both the importance and the limitations of experimental work, the necessity for field studies and for the development of new methods to attack new problems. A third illustration of his inclusiveness is his sensitivity to the contribution of insights in literature and the arts, and the importance for the psychologist of cultivating alertness to this source of understanding.

Closely related to his commitment to inclusiveness is his persistent alertness to "the more beyond"—the *plus ultra* that so fired him in his Yale Professor Chauncey Tinker's description of that legend at the time of Columbus' discovery of the new world. "New worlds" were there to be explored, in psychology as well as geography. Parallel with this commitment were the expansion of world horizons and the development of space exploration, both of which stimulated the use of psychology to explore for instance, the mind of the Soviets, and of the Japanese, and psychological problems of man in space. Gardner supported psychologists who were exploring these new worlds, which need much more research.

Another group of legacies is seen in the enduring contribution he made to institutionalized psychology; his creation of a distinguished department of psychology at the City College of New York where none had existed; his vigorous participation in founding the Society for the Psychological Study of Social Issues—an organization which has helped to develop a climate of concern for human rights; his development of a coherent department of research at Menninger; his courageous and creative dedication to making the American Society for Psychical Research an organization respected for its unassailable scientific standards. These institutions are alive and effective today.

That legend "plus ultra" which he used as a title for his autobiography in *The Psychologists* compresses his endless outreaching—for more of the world with its many cultures, its magnificent landscapes, its varied people; for more ideas and meanings in history, literature, philosophy, art, music; and into the sciences of physiology, biology, biochemistry, anthropology, for their contributions to understanding the person in the world. His students were amazed at Gardner's way of pushing them to go beyond the conventional boundaries of psychology, to explore related sciences, to attack new problems.

Related to this drive to reach out is his persistent tendency to integrate the old with the new—not to discard old loves in the world of the intellect or everyday life—work or play. The songs sung at Yale and in World War I were still fun to sing. He played old games of his childhood with our children, and invented new ones as when he used his felt hat for a frisbee before frisbees were invented. He read his own boyhood King Arthur books to little Al and newer books like *Swallowdale* to Midge; and he made up long stories to entertain our children and grandchildren.

Along with his conscious inclusiveness, reaching out, hospitality to the old, the new, the disdained and tabooed, Gardner had an unconscious persistent capacity to turn negative experience into positive responses. Sensitive to childhood rejections, he gave empathic support to the young as a teacher, a father, and a friend. Sensitive to unfair discipline at times in his boyhood he gave financial support to victims of injustice. Feeling that adults did not respect his ideas as a child, he always listened carefully to the ideas of his children and his students, and took them seriously. This unfailing respect for them earned him the love and gratitude of the young and gave them confidence.

I find another legacy in Gardner's capacity to dig deeply in his quest for reality while he also allowed scope for his dreams and his vision of potentialities. And we experienced another balance when his warmth made criticism feel like appreciation and generated creativity. And still another was his capacity to balance intense work with playfulness—in playing with words, in making love, and in his music making.

He reached for energy generating sensory experiences which delighted him in color, tone, and rhythm; and he even said that sensory experience is the basis of psychology. With the harmonica that was always in his pocket to be pulled out on a hike or when stopping to rest on a climb, music was part of him, life-giving in his final catastrophic illness. I include this as part of his legacy precisely because he did not regard sensory delights as luxuries or the dessert to the main course of life: sensory experience nurtured his vitality.

His *élan vital,* fed by a bottomless well of humor, delight and love, helped him to transcend pain.

Love, delight, and warmth were deep in Gardner's nature. His passionate concern with truth, rooted as it probably was in very early curiosity, fired by the intensity of his conflict between theology and science — and perhaps also by a dim awareness of certain ways of shutting out some aspects of reality, both in people and in nature — made him a seeker. The quest for reality led to the conviction that reality is inside of us as well as outside of us, and also to his support of and intellectual integration of ways of overcoming self-deception. He may have felt that his final conquest of self-deception was the ability to face the unlikelihood of his survival after death. His legacy is more than that of a professional psychologist; it is the legacy of a man who loved life and lived it with a creative courage and gentle warmth that inspires younger generations.

Notes

The following abbreviations are used for frequently cited names:

ASPR — American Society for Psychical Research

Bailey — *Edgar Gardner Murphy, Gentle Progressive* (Biography)

CCNY — City College of New York

Columbia — Columbia University

DB — DuBose, GM's brother

EGM — Edgar Gardner Murphy, GM's father

EGM by MKM — Biography of EGM by his wife, privately printed

GAK — George Augustus King, GM's grandfather

GM — Gardner Murphy

HPA V — *History of Psychology in Autobiography,* volume V

Kra II — *The Psychologists,* volume II, edited by P. Krawiec

LBM — Lois Barclay Murphy, GM's wife

MKM — Maud King Murphy, GM's mother

MU — Montague Ullman's 1966–67 interviews with GM include memories of his life after his 14–15 years of working in a clinical setting

Rec. — *Recollections* by L. Nyman

SLC — Sarah Lawrence College

SM — "Study of Myself"(written at Harvard at age 21; autobiography)

SPSSI — Society for the Psychological Study of Social Issues

The archival sources consulted for this book were:

American Academy of Arts and Sciences Library
American Society of Psychical Research Archives (ASPR Archives)
British Museum
City College of New York Archives
Columbia University Library Archives
Concord, Massachusetts, Free Library Archives
Ford Foundation Archives
George Washington University Archives
Harvard University Archives
Library of Congress
Menninger Foundation Archives, especially Gardner Murphy Research Archives Annual Reports to the Trustees, TPR, Menninger Perspectives

National Library of Medicine Archives
New School of Social Research Archives
Sarah Lawrence College Archives
Syracuse University Archives
Union Theological Seminary Archives
University of Akron (Ohio) Archives on the History of Psychology
University of California at Berkeley Archives
University of California at Los Angeles Archives
University of Colorado Archives
University of North Carolina Archives on Southern History
Vassar College Archives
Yale University Library Archives

Preface

x   Robert Gittings, *The Nature of Biography;* note, 19. "Biography begins, then, in one sense or another, in praise." That is, a sense of the value of the life of the person discussed by the biographer. With examples, Gittings discusses strengths such as use of direct observation and quotation, dangers of over-interpretation, the variability of the degree of participation by the subject in the life of the time. He does not discuss the evolution of a subject's contribution to the science or art of his time, as I have reviewed it in this biography.

Chapter 1

3   In a letter to LBM dated 3-6-84, Calvin Hall discussed the generation that received its training "at a time when there were acknowledged leaders ... Edward Tolman, Gordon Allport, Kurt Lewin, Clark Hull, Henry Murray, Edwin Guthrie and Gardner Murphy ... men of ideas, of vision, of quality, of human values."

3   E.R. Hilgard's perspective was developed from his own status as an APA president, council member, chairman of SPSSI, student of the history of American psychology, and widely respected author. He felt (letter to LBM 8-23-83) that "Gardner's many contributions ... make him one of the major figures of 20th century psychology. The amazing influence he had at CCNY ... is a great testimony to him as the Festschrift in his honor shows. His willingness to espouse unpopular causes — especially para-psychology — isolated him somewhat from the elitist power structure, which is part of the unfairness that the politics of science leads to. Subsequently, Hilgard referred to Gardner as "a psychologist without a peer."

5   Gardner lectured at Cooper Union, New School for Social Research, and in response to many invitations from colleges, educational groups, annual conferences and special meetings to honor distinguished professional colleagues.

5   Much of this discussion of GM's contribution to psychology draws on Ross Stagner's 1988 correspondence with me.

8   *America's Psychologists: A Survey of a Growing Profession,* Kenneth E. Clark (1957), American Psychological Association, Inc., 1333 16th St. N.W., Washington, D.C.

Chapter 2

Sources include E. Hartley's chapter in the Festschrift, 1960; GM's Freeing Intelligence Through Teaching *and* The Teacher's Craft; *GM comments on teaching in autobiographies (HPA V, Kra II, SM); letters from former students, colleagues, former president of Columbia University William McGill, John Gardner (who launched Common Cause), discussions with me, and comments about our joint interest in teaching, in* Dyadic Thought and Work *(unpublished).*

9   The Festschrift was edited by Eugene Hartley and John Peatman. Four paragraphs are quoted from Hartley's description of Gardner as a teacher. Eugene Hartley was Gardner's student as an undergraduate and a graduate, and became with his family a lifelong friend as well. His sensitive obituary of Gardner was published in *American Psychologist*, January 1980.

10   Jules Eisenbud, J. ASPR 74, 1980, 119. This issue of the J. ASPR, January 1980, contains an insightful 14-page biography of Gardner by Gertrude Schmeidler, a detailed (11 pages) tribute by his deeply perceptive colleague Montague Ullman, another (14 pages) sensitive analysis by S. David Kahn, Gardner's own *Notes for a Parapsychological Autobiography* (reprinted), half a dozen extended descriptions of his personality and work from colleagues in parapsychology and additional tributes from 20 other professionals.

11   Ernest Taves, *ibid.,* 122f.

11   Lucien Hanks to LBM, undated, c. 1984.

12   Herbert Krugman to LBM, 3-17-82 and 3-25-82.

13   Warren Blanding, J. ASPR, 74, 1980, 103f, and to LBM, 12-22-70.

14   Meyer Rabban to LBM, 7-31-79.

15   Sarnoff Mednick, J. ASPR, 74, 1980, 132f, University of Southern California.

15   S. David Kahn, *ibid.*

15   W. McIver to GM.

16   Gertrude Schmeidler, "Some Lines About Gardner Murphy, The Psychologists' Parapsychologist," *Parapsychology Review*, July–August 1976, 7. Schmeidler was a student of Gardner's in the summer of 1942 at Harvard, and subsequently became a colleague at City College of New York and a collaborator in research. Her sensitive account is based on many years of observation of Gardner in different settings.

16   Robert Holt to LBM, 3-18-82.

17   Gerald Ledford to LBM, 1980.

18   Heinz Ansbacher to LBM, 7-21-82.

18   Gertrude Schmeidler *J. Parapsychology* 43, June 1970, 90.

18   Morton Leeds, J. ASPR, 74, 1980, 128.

19   Jerome Singer and mother, letters to LBM, 1986.

19   Craig Cleaves to LBM.

20   Georgene Seward to LBM.

20   H. Proshansky in APA Memorial 1979, Akron Archives.

20   Solomon Diamond to LBM, 7-1-79, and in APA Memorial, 1979.

20   Margaret Brenman to LBM, 12-24-80.

21   E. Hartley, "Profile of a Professor," Festschrift, 8f.

22   Kra II, 325.

22   Elliott Joseph from GM, 6-15-64.

24   *Teacher's Craft*, manuscript in Akron Archives. In this manuscript, Gardner gave a more extensive account of his ideas about teaching.

25   Kra II, 326.

27   "The Service Man's Tomorrow."
27   John Gardner, who launched Common Cause, wrote me that Gardner Murphy
      was liberating while other teachers were restricting.

Chapter 3

Sources for George Augustus King and Maud King Murphy include Gardner Murphy's "Study of Myself" written for Yerkes' ontology course at Harvard; Maud King
Murphy's genealogical notes; the biography of George Augustus King in Memoirs of
the Social Circle of Concord, series V; archives in the Concord Free Library, Concord,
Massachusetts; archives of Edgar Gardner Murphy at the University of North Carolina;
a memorial booklet for Maud King Murphy written by her sons, DuBose and Gardner
Murphy, in Concord Free Library Archives. Maud's biography of Edgar Gardner Murphy and her unpublished memories of DuBose as a small child; Bailey's biography of
Edgar Gardner Murphy; interviews with, autobiographies and notes by Gardner Murphy; letters from Concord residents surviving in the 1980s who knew the Kings; and
my visits to Concord between 1926 and 1929 and again in 1957. Memories of Maud King
Murphy and other relatives of Gardner Murphy and Gardner's own memories told to
me provide material on Maud, Gardner's mother.
       Sources for Edgar Gardner Murphy, EGM, Gardner's father, include the
biographies by Bailey and by Maud; some letters in the University of North Carolina
Archives on Southern History; Gardner's letters to Daniel Levine; Gardner's references
to EGM in SM; interviews with Montague Ullman 1966–67; Gardner's autobiographies
in HPA V and Kra II; correspondence with Leonard Murphy and his correspondence
with Fort Smith, Arkansas, archives.
       The sources for Gardner's maternal grandfather, George Augustus King, included
"George Augustus King," 1940, by Hon. F.H. Chase, in Memoirs of Members of the
Social Circle in Concord, fifth series, 1909 to 1939, 148–200. SM, HPA V, GM, Kra
II, MV.
       Sources for Gardner's mother, Maud King Murphy: LBM met her in 1925, visited
her in 1926, 1927, 1928; MKM joined GM and DB on a trip to Europe in the summer
of 1929 and lived in Butler Hall, an apartment-hotel a block away from us until we
moved to Westchester in 1935. After that I saw her weekly; Gardner had lunch with
her three times a week, and we frequently took the children, Al and Midge, to visit
her from 1935 on. A memorial booklet was written by Gardner and his brother after
she died in 1957. Comments from neighbors described her in younger years and a comment from her classmate Margaret Story Washburn described her impression of Maud
King at Vassar (class of 1888). Some letters from her to GM and to me and to Cousin
Catharine survive. Impressions from Gardner's friends Frank Lorimer and Leonard
Beadle and from a neighbor who was a young boy when Gardner was at college give
additional views of her. Thelma Babbitt, wife of the son of Maud's older sister ("Minnie," Mary Brewster King) recounted his feelings about her.

31   Kra II, GM, 323; SM.
32   The picture of grandfather King's mother, Cynthia Pride King, daughter of
      a sea captain, wife of a country doctor, mother of 11 vigorous, ambitious
      children, is signed with the tribute "Wisdom, courage, patience, humor"
      (Concord Library Archives).
      Gardner did not know his great-grandmother King, but her personality was
      said to be like that of other New England relatives, a strong fine character.
34   GM conversations with LBM and Al Murphy.

34   GM interview, by MU.

35   LBM memories.

36   Father's base in Montgomery, Bailey 148; Mother with GM and DB in Concord, HPA V, 256.

36   "... My youth, long ago was spent by the little river in Concord, Massachusetts, which had been made famous, first, by the historic fight at the North Bridge, initiating the Revolutionary War and later by the writing of Emerson and Thoreau. In my time it was a quiet little stream, where young people enjoyed themselves, with no great thought of history or literature, important in our daily life and very dear to us all. When—being 25 years old, and inclined to wander a little from the old haunt—I found myself in San Antonio, Texas. "One of the wonders of that wonderful place was its turbulent, unpredictable river. No canoe would have floated on its surface nor could my arms hold steady oars against it, but it in its turn became dear to me. So that I enjoyed putting the two rivers together in my verse..." (undated note by MKM).

36   MKM comments to LBM.

36   DB letter to MKM.

36   *Approaches to Personality.*

37   MKM memorial.

37   Thelma Babbitt to LBM.

37   Frank Lorimer to LBM.

37   Alice Murphy, DuBose's wife, to LBM, 1935.

38   MKM's account of DB's early years.

38   GM in SM.

39   Rigid puritanical attitudes toward sex: Frank Lorimer to LBM, 1981.

39   MKM's friends, observed by LBM on visits to Concord, 1926.

39   MKM's poems, *Harper's* monthly magazine, October 1896.

39   Edgar Gardner Murphy, MKM, privately printed.

39   Sold house in 1919. Letter to LBM from Mrs. H. Miller, buyer.

39   DB athletic superiority, SM.

40   GM's view of MKM, SM.

40   Louisa May Alcott, author of *Little Women* and other novels.

40   GM never saw any evidence of an oedipal problem, MU.

40   The later interviews with Monte Ullman are changed in tone. Gone is the dryness of the "Study of Myself"—there is much more color and variety.

40   GM mentions MKM's put-downs to the extent of not acknowledging the greatness of many of Concord's literary celebrities. He said, "If you didn't make the Emersonian level, you were tossed off ... even Thoreau was tossed off" by her. However, this is easy to see in terms of MKM's attitude toward a respectable living style. Once GM quoted MKM to me as saying, "Thoreau was just a man who didn't pay his taxes." Strangely, of all the Concord "celebrities," the only one I never heard spoken of as a *person* independent of his literary achievements was Hawthorne. GM loved the *Wonder Book* and *Tanglewood Tales* as *literature,* but there was discussion *about* the Alcotts, *about* Thoreau, *about* Emerson. And so far as I know, Hawthorne existed only as literature for him. (AGM for GM biography, 1983.)

40   The following biographical sketch of Gardner's mother, undated and unsigned, appears to be his draft of an obituary for her. Found in GM's papers, it may have been written by him.

"Maud King Murphy, born in Barnstable, Massachusetts, April 29, 1865; died in New York, May 10, 1957.

"Daughter of George Augustus and Martha Brigham King, and sister of Mary King Babbitt, Vassar '82, she grew up in Concord, Massachusetts, and knew the Emersons and the Alcotts. She went to Vassar as a sophomore in '83, where she became a devoted admirer of President Taylor. Needing to stay out two years to earn expenses, she graduated with '88 rather than '86. In 1890 she went to teach in the San Antonio, Texas, High School. The following year she married the Reverend Edgar Gardner Murphy of San Antonio, who later became Secretary of the Southern Education Board, and organizer of the National Child Labor Committee. His *Problems of the Present South* (1904) and *The Basis of Ascendancy* (1909) represented a southern voice vigorously pleading for education for both races. Returning to the North with their two sons, she continued to share in all his work, and after his health failed she contributed much to his *A Beginner's Star Book* (1912), which after his death in 1913 she kept up to date through four editions. Under her own name she wrote *A Beginner's Guide to the Stars* (1924), and (in 1943) a biographical sketch of her husband: *Edgar Gardner Murphy: From Records and Memories*.

"After her husband's death, she had moved to Concord to care for her parents; later, to New York, where she had many devoted friends in the Columbia University neighborhood.

"She is survived by her sons, the Reverend DuBose Murphy, Rector of the Christ Episcopal Church, Tuscaloosa, Alabama, and Gardner Murphy, Research Director, Menninger Foundation, Topeka, Kansas; four grandchildren; and three great-grandchildren."

41   Younger son he adored, MKM to LBM.
42   Plantation: Fort Smith, Arkansas, archives.
42   EGM's father left the family, SM.
42   EGM in San Antonio, Bailey, 2.
42   EGM at Sewanee, etc., Bailey, 2.
42   MKM and EGM meet and marry, Bailey, 5–6.
42   EGM shocked by lynching, Bailey, 9. Mobilizing a protest.
42   The fact that EGM had such ready access to both the Northern and Southern press reflects the acceptability of efforts at reform and increasing awareness of social injustice and inequality. Robber barons capitalizing on the nation's natural resources, and the enormous profits from industry and commerce were giving big business a bad name, while Vanderbilts, Morgans and Astors were at the zenith of their power. William Jennings Bryan was the spokesman for many who felt they had no voice and the Progressive Era was ushered in with the McKinley-Bryan presidential campaign. Northern reformers such as Jane Addams warmly appreciated Edgar Gardner Murphy's efforts in the South to develop state laws to correct child labor abuses. Despite the wide acceptance of need for reform, EGM's efforts on behalf of Negroes were controversial.
43   Moves north and south, Bailey; see Montgomery.
44   Southern Society, Bailey, 30.
44   1900 Conference on Race Relations, *ibid*.
44   Tuskegee Speech, Bailey.
44   Contact with Booker T. Washington, Bailey, 32; see Bailey index.
45   Resignation from Montgomery Church, Bailey, 147.
45   Initiated National Child Labor Committee, Bailey, 87f.
45   Appointed executive secretary of the Southern Education Board, Bailey, 76.
46   Ill at Old Point Comfort, Virginia, Bailey, 179; resignation from the Board.

47   EGM's death, Bailey, 214.

48   DuBose (Gardner's brother) sources: SM, MKM's account of DB's early years;
     LBM's visits to DB's family and DB's visits to GM's family; GM's comments;
     Yale friends' letter to LBM; records in Yale 1915 Yearbook; Obituary, March
     27, 1960.

48   Little DuBose with baby Gardner playing drunken men. DB imaginative play,
     MKM.

48   GM and DB playing with cousins and hunting mountain lions, SM.

49   GM feeling rejected by DB. Compare young William and Henry James —
     William James: "I play with boys who curse and swear!" Henry James: *The
     Untried Years,* Leon Edel, New York: J.B. Lippincott, 1953, Avon/Discus,
     1978, 63.

49   DuBose's skills, SM, Yale 1915 Yearbook. Letter to LBM from DB classmate
     and from Frank Lorimer, Akron.

49   Conflicting religious views, GM letter to DB, 1916, Akron Archives.

50   Gardner's comparison of himself and DuBose, SM. Relationship as adults,
     observed by AGM and LBM.

50   With the help of Gardner's nephew, Leonard Murphy, a little more informa-
     tion on Gardner's Southern forebears was obtained from Fort Smith, Arkan-
     sas, Archives. John Gardner was born in Thetford, Vermont, and died in
     1964 at Fort Smith, Arkansas. He married Eliza Pearse Palmer, born in
     Woodstock, Vermont, April 12, 1808. She died in 1870 at Fort Smith,
     Arkansas. Anne Jane Gardner ("Janie," "Grandy Murphy") was born Octo-
     ber 12, 1844, in Fort Smith, Arkansas; she died March 24, 1910, in San An-
     tonio. Samuel Murphy, born 1841 in London, Ontario, Canada, married
     Anne Jane Gardner on June 3, 1868, in Fort Smith, Arkansas. The exact date
     of his departure from his family is not given. He died in June 1897 in Aspen,
     Colorado.
     Although Gardner seems to have been unaware of this, his heritage was from
     New England on *both* sides of his family; on his father's side the Southern
     aspect was only from the mid–19th century on.

50   The Booker T. Washington Papers, **5**, 493. EGM to BTW, 5-3-00 (GM 4 yrs.,
     10 mos.): "Mrs. Murphy and Mrs. King [GM's grandma] very much enjoyed
     their day in Tuskegee and they came back full of enthusiasm about the work
     of your noble institution."

50   Murphy received an honorary M.A. degree from Yale at its commencement in
     June 1904 and an honorary Ll.D. from the University of the South in 1911.
     (Bailey, *Edgar Gardner Murphy, Gentle Progressive,* 129, 212.)

50   The Booker T. Washington Papers, edited by L. Harlan, include a letter to
     BJW from EGM (Jan. 1, 1902) in which EGM describes the lynching of a
     Negro and his successful effort at the age of 23 to enlist the support of the
     best men in Laredo for a formal protest. "I foresaw that it would be taken
     as a precedent for many spectacles."

50   Funeral and memorial services: Bailey, 214; Maud King Murphy, *Edgar Gard-
     ner Murphy,* 211f.

50   Gardner's father was considered the "father" of the National Child Labor Com-
     mittee, since it was his idea; but he resigned when the committee as a whole
     was determined to work for a *federal* law limiting the ages and hours of
     child labor in factories; he felt deeply that laws should be made by the
     states individually. By the time Gardner had become professionally estab-
     lished he favored the efforts of the Committee and became a Trustee,

supporting the Committee with some financial help as well. The General
Secretary of the Committee, Gertrude Folks Zimand, daughter of Homer
Folks—one of the original founders of the committee—was a close friend of
ours. As a Vassar graduate of the class of 1916 she had been interested in me
in Cincinnati and tried to pressure me to leave Sarah Lawrence College and
"get to work at the national level."

Chapter 4

*Sources include Gardner to LBM; SM and other unpublished autobiographical
papers; Gardner Murphy in HPA V and in Kra II; his mother's biography of his father
and her notes on DuBose's earliest years; Bailey's biography of Edgar Gardner Murphy
and archives of Edgar Gardner Murphy at the University of North Carolina; MKM accounts of GM to LBM; photos; Larry P. Schofield letter to LBM and records from St.
Paul's Parish in Chillicothe, Ohio. Consult the index of Bailey's biography of Edgar
Gardner Murphy. Gardner enjoyed reminiscing about his early delight in the sunlight
through trees, playing with anchor blocks, etc. He also told about his feelings regarding
unfair punishment. There were no accounts of playful times with his parents, in early
years. Note variations in emphasis in GM's memories of his early childhood as these
were recalled at different times: sometimes he remembers chiefly happy times—
"golden sunlight" and other sensory delights; at other times he remembers "terrors in
Montgomery" and being "alone" in San Antonio.*

*Such variations also occur later in his comments about Menninger; at times he
mentions the opportunity, and his satisfaction in building a research department, while
in 1956–59 he was eager to leave when the prospect of a Research Institute at City College was discussed, and in 1960, he nostalgically wrote to Frank Lorimer that his New
England roots needed to be watered.*

*He never summarized, "sometimes I feel...," but simply reported his feelings as
of the moment of writing or being interviewed.*

51   According to Larry P. Schofield, Ph.D. of Chillicothe, the town is located in
      the Appalachian foothills with rather sizable hills to the east of town and
      many trees along the Scioto River which runs around the edge of town. No
      doubt there were many trees around the turn of the century. (Letter to LBM,
      2/8/85.)
51   Gardner was born on July 8 and baptized on July 23, 1895, at St. Paul's Parish
      in Chillicothe, Ohio. His grandmother Janie Gardner Murphy was a sponsor
      according to the parish register.
52   For Gardner, there is nothing like their mother's charming story of DuBose's
      early days; nor do we find her descriptions of DuBose shadowed by the
      negative phrases we encounter in her fragmentary notes on Gardner's first
      18 months: at four months of age, he "does not yet surely recognize his
      bottle, but seems to know some objects and people." At four and a half
      months: "Knows his bottle, but cannot get his hands on it." At five and
      three-quarters months: "Has been able to sit up with pillows for several
      weeks." At six and three-quarters months: "A little *uneasy with* strangers,
      not really frightened."
53   His vocabulary at that time included "seven proper names: Papa, Mamma,
      Brother, Mamie (nurse-helper), Tiny, Edgar, Doodles." "Common names
      32" included some unusual words for a toddler of that age: Hammer, plow,

scissors, horn, knife, paper, fire, stick—along with baby, boy, bed, hat, door, lamp, bread, bottle, horse, table, kitty, block, box, didy, chair, shoe, stocking, dress, ball, brush, soap. She counted seven exclamations: All right, no, how do, hello, bye-bye, oh dear, more. Two adjectives: wet, high; three adverbs: up, down, outdoors; and four verbs: hide, pull, drop, walk. His mother added, "imitative sounds of dog and cat," and, at the end of the list, as a summary comment "*No* original combinations."

55   There are many unanswered questions—questions I could not answer with the evidence available to me. For instance, was Gardner's sensitivity to scoldings and to punishment a consequence of the fact that they were rare and contrasted sharply with a prevalent devoted care and freedom from punitive confrontations with his parents; or was it due to a quality of irritability or anger that accompanied them, a quality that felt threatening. Or was it due to punishment administered for behavior which he did not feel justified it (this is implied in his complaint "taint fair" which his mother mentioned to me). His generous adult support of victims of injustice suggests that his empathy may have had roots in his own experience, and his own comments on his impulsiveness as a child suggest that his intentions were innocent when he did things his mother disapproved—like spilling food accidentally (as when our baby spilled a bit of oatmeal and she slapped him). His consistent gentleness with his own children and his students, his intense appreciation of Lewin, Lippitt and White's study of the relative absence of aggression with democratic (not authoritarian) leadership, and his own nonauthoritarian professional attitudes all seem to be related to his early feelings about and protests against aggressive authority.

55   Sense of self, Montgomery; SM terrors in Montgomery, MU.
55   Tooting of whistle at January 1, 1900, MU.
57   MKM's trip to Tuskegee, B.T. Washington.
57   1900 Conference, Bailey; Jane Addams, Bailey.
59   Happy boy smile, MGM on DB.
59   EGM withdrew, Bailey; MKM biography of EGM.

Chapter 5

Sources: Between 1926 and 1929, and also later, I visited Concord several times with Gardner; during these visits Gardner talked about his grandparents, his life in Concord from the age of seven to nine, his love of the town; he took me to Walden Pond, to 88 Main Street—his grandfather's home on the Concord River—and to the old North Bridge, the Minute Man, and Sleepy Hollow Cemetery, where the Kings and the Concord authors are buried, as is Gardner's father, Edgar Gardner Murphy. Gardner's love for Concord as a town was as deep as his love for his grandparents (cf. 1.4 MU, interview 1). Sources also include his autobiographies in HPA V, Kra II, Notes for a Parapsychology Autobiography, *SM, MU, biographies of his grandfather King, Edward Waldo Emerson, and Frederick Alcott Pratt in* Memoirs of the Social Circle of Concord, Series V; *Thoreau's* Walden; The Wayside *by Margaret Lothrop.*

62   Feeling of really belonging, HPA V.
63   Identity conflict, HPA, 255f; MU, 8, 9; GM to LBM.
64   Letter to LBM from Gladys R. Clark of Concord. Frederick Alcott Pratt: *Memoirs of the Social Circle.* Edward Waldo Emerson, *ibid.*
66   Perry Miller.

68   Entered school, SM.
68   Sense of change at seven, MU, SM.
69   Conscious of good and evil, SM.
69   The New England childhood of GM had little in common with the New
        England childhoods of some other writers such as Burges Johnson in *As
        Much As I Dare* (1944), New York: Ives Washburn. Born in Rutland, Ver-
        mont, in 1877, Johnson moved with his family to New London, Con-
        necticut, at the age of seven. There he and his playmates explored, camped,
        fished, crabbed, "fought and made up," and "engaged in youthful
        mischief." His pets included garter snakes, baby crows, a "dearly beloved
        white rat," flying squirrels and successive batches of kittens, in contrast to
        Gardner's one little dog. But his mother read to him as Gardner's mother
        did—*Back of the North Wind,* "the Alice books," Frank Stockton's tales,
        and ultimately he too became a professor (at Vassar).
69   At that time children were considered "innocent," that is, completely ignorant
        of sexual matters. I never heard the words sex, penis, vagina, or intercourse
        until my child psychology course in my sophomore year at Vassar; Miriam
        Gould, the teacher, included sex education in that course. My brother's
        penis was called his "dee-dee." Although I knew that babies came from the
        mother's body, I did not know how they got there. Taboos were so strict that
        I did not dare to ask questions. Gardner's childhood experience with these
        taboos was not unusual at that time, although the intensity of his mother's
        reaction—consistent with her punitive attitude—was probably extreme.
        Thoughts about sex were "impure," even "evil."

Chapter 6

*Sources: SM; his interviews with Montague Ullman, his own memories and his
mother's memories shared with me; my observations on visits to New Haven; letters to
me from Robert Oliver, Yale '16, who knew Gardner as a young teenager in New
Haven; letters from "Cousin Catharine," in Akron Archives.*

74   I met "Cousin Will" and "Cousin Catharine" on visits to New Haven in 1926
        and later. Cousin Will was morose though caring. With no children of their
        own, he gave us $1000 for our 1929 summer in Europe and some years after
        he died in 1933, Cousin Catharine gave Gardner $11,000 from his estate,
        which we used to buy a house on Colonial Heights in Westchester. Cousin
        Catharine was an affectionate, sensitive little old lady; when we took Al and
        Midge to visit, she delighted them with little paper Japanese flowers that
        blossomed when dropped in water. Her gifts to the children were always
        thoughtful about what children would enjoy.
74   Gardner's football prohibited by father, MU, 17.
74   Isolation at Branford, beginning to be overcome, MU, 18.
74   Camp Algonquin: MKM remarks to LBM; GM to LBM.
75   Burgee's gang, GM to LBM; Robert Oliver, New Haven playmate and Yale
        classmate, letter to LBM, 1983; MU, 23. "I doubt that any of us gave a
        thought to the feeling you say Gardner had that he 'had not been one of
        the boys.' This would have been over sensitive on his part.... I have no
        recollection whatever that playmates considered him a 'sissy.'"
75   East Rock: GM took me there on one visit to New Haven.

75   Fanatically religious, MU, 20–21.
75   Father's illness, MU, 24, SM.
76   Father gave him *Scientific American;* Gardner was fascinated with stars, MU,
      23; GM to LBM and AGM.
76   GM began Latin and French, MU, 22, but he also studied Greek.
76   EGM took the family to Bad Nauheim: MU, 26, MKM, Bailey.
77   Revivalist religion: Moody and Sankey evangelistic revivals were emotionally
      intense in their emphasis on personal salvation. My father prohibited me
      from going to them. I am sure that Gardner's intellectual mother would not
      have sympathized with that extreme and exciting type of religious ex-
      perience, but she was preoccupied with caring for her seriously ill husband.
      In MU, 19–21, GM gives a rather clinical account of this phase.

Chapter 7

*Here again SM and MU are the chief sources; GM does not discuss Hotchkiss at
length in either HPA V or Kra II; he does describe Ralph Theller's superb training in
writing in* The Teacher's Craft *(manuscript in Akron Archives), and briefly in Kra II,
327. The notice of Gardner's brilliant achievement in Latin and Greek college entrance
examinations is preserved. Letters from his father reflect both his father's deep love for
him and his stimulus to achieve excellence.*

77   When Gardner and DuBose went to Hotchkiss, Maud and Edgar moved to
      New York, first to the Chelsea, then in 1911 to the Turin, 333 Central Park
      West (change of address card).

Chapter 8

Sources: SM, Kra II, HPA Vol. V; Notes for a Parapsychological Autobiography, *interviews with MU; letters from Yale friends, especially Frank Lorimer and Malcolm Baber,
and other Yale contemporaries; MKM's biography of Edgar Gardner Murphy and my
visits to New Haven and to Concord; Yale 1916 Yearbook. Letters from faculty members
supporting Gardner's application for a Rhodes Scholarship. Letters to his family. Papers
written at Yale include his biography of Jeanne d'Arc and Yale Archives include Yerkes'
correspondence with Gardner and the original outline for the "Study of Myself" assigned
at Harvard. Frank Lorimer's letters to me and a conversation after Gardner's death.*

81   From the yearbook of the class of 1915 we learn that Gardner's brother DuBose
      in the class of 1915 won similar prizes. He was chairman of the Executive
      Committee of the Yale Hope Mission, 1914; Freshman Religious Commit-
      tee, 1911–12; Dwight Hall Executive Committee, 1914–15; director of the
      Yale Chapter of the Brotherhood of St. Andrew; vice president of the
      Berkeley Association, 1914–15; treasurer junior year, and president, senior
      year, of the Society for the Study of Socialism; and undergraduate secretary
      of Phi Beta Kappa.
      This series of elected offices held by his brother DuBose reinforced Gardner's
      feeling of social inferiority to his brother.
81   The yearbook for the class of 1916 mentions Gardner's nicknames as "Murph,"
      "Gard," and "Speed." It also mentions that he held a Woolsey Scholar-
      ship and a Waterman Scholarship, and recounts a series of prizes: the

Chamberlain Entrance Prize in Greek, a first grade Berkeley premium in Latin, the Winthrop Prize and second Thacher Prize.

He was president of the University Debating Association, vice-president of Delta Sigma Rho, and a member of Phi Beta Kappa and Sigma Xi. In his junior year he was awarded first division honors, and a philosophical oration appointment.

His address was listed as 88 Main St., Concord, Massachusetts, his grand-parents' home. His parents were living in their Central Park apartment in New York.

82   Despite the fact that Gardner's grades fell in the fall after his father's death, he received Phi Beta Kappa and Sigma Xi awards. In order to clarify this picture I asked the Yale Archives for his college grades. Their policy is to keep all records of Yale alumni locked for 75 years and they twice refused to give me the details to clarify Gardner's statements.

86   When Gardner asked his teachers for letters to support his application for a Rhodes Scholarship, their appraisals of him varied. Chauncey Brewster Tinker, the professor of English from whom Gardner learned so much, wrote: "His marks by no means indicate the peculiar quality of Murphy's mind, which is characterized by the most unusual independence and curiosity. For keenness of original thinking I am quite disposed to say that there is not his equal in the senior class; but in this characteristic there is nothing of that superficial cleverness which many mistake for depth in the youthful mind. There is nothing youthful about Murphy's thinking. He has a habit, unusual in one of his age, of basing his opinions both deeply and soundly. . . ." John Chester Adams, another member of the English department wrote more personally: "Mr. Gardner Murphy . . . is a man whom I have had an unusual opportunity to know very well. I have taught him in class, I have worked with him in debating, I have entertained him at my house, and I have sailed with him in the summer; and I can say with assurance that he is a man of unexceptionably solid character and incorrigible industry. His intellectual capacity is sufficiently indicated by his honors in scholarship and his success as a debater. My only criticism of him would be that he devotes himself too intensely to the things that are most seriously worthwhile. Only I should not wish this remark to be taken too seriously, for he is a good companion, and a very interesting talker. As a representative of the University he will be a credit to Yale and the State; in his present capacity I am sure that he will make the absolute most out of the opportunities that come within his reach. I know few men of whom I could say that without qualification, or to whom the opportunities would mean so much." The psychologist Angier commented, "His temperament and character appear to me to be remarkably well poised, his sense of values sanely balanced . . . he is quick to grasp a situation as a whole and gets distinctions clearly. He can, too, express his thoughts with precision and is alert in himself avoiding or in detecting in others, elements that would confuse the main issue. His ingenuity in laboratory manipulations and in working out the significance of his results is much above the average but I should not class him among the brilliant. It is his all-round sanity of mind that has impressed me—and his instinct for essentials. . . . He is distinctly the type of man that I am accustomed to think of as a fitting Rhodes scholar." Other members of the faculty also commented on his high level of work but emphasized what they considered his excessive seriousness. He did not receive the Rhodes Scholarship.

86   Conspicuous in Gardner's own writings from college years and from the comments by his faculty is the absence of any reference to or evidence of the
humor, gaiety, spontaneity, as we knew him in the family. This "sober as
a judge" man had within himself qualities or potentialities of qualities that
apparently were completely submerged during Hotchkiss and Yale years. To
what extent this was due to his sense of responsibility as a scholarship student, or to the stress of his father's illness and death, or simply to the achievement pressures from his parents, is hard to say.
It is interesting to note that none of his teachers at Yale commented on a "lack
of good judgment" that he himself mentioned in his "Study of Myself" and
which certain friends criticized. I rarely saw examples of this.

87   An address given at Hotchkiss had been written in a formal style presenting
an improved plan for the school paper. Gardner's papers written at Yale include a carefully documented account of his own mental imagery following
a questionnaire given in an experimental section of a psychology course. This
is an interesting report of the vividness of Gardner's imagery in all modalities
except that of motor imagery. He described the relative ease of control of
images and the synaesthesia he typically experienced: a tone may seem like
a yellow streak or a dark grey blot, etc. His imagery for numbers was so sharp
that he could square six-digit numbers in his head. Visual and tactual images
were most vivid and auditory; gustatory and thermal images followed close
after them. It was hardly possible — with the limits of an assignment — for
Gardner to convey the enormous importance of vivid imagery, and its
related sensory experience, in his everyday experience, his memories, his
delight in nature, his lively inner life. Sensory experience and vivid imagery
sustained the enthusiasm and joie de vivre that were Gardner as we knew
him in the family. Even when Parkinsonism made mountain climbing impossible after the age of 70 and when he could no longer walk great
distances, he remarked, "Isn't it wonderful how much beauty we can see just
walking around the block?" This was when azaleas, dogwoods, tulips and
other spring blossoms were making our neighborhood colorful.
Another freshman paper, almost unique among all of Gardner's writing, is his
vivid, sympathetic — one could almost say loving — account of Joan of Arc.
Still deeply religious himself, he appreciated her devotion to the Lord. He
accepted her voices and her visions while at the same time emphasizing her
sanity, her girlish play, friendship, helpfulness. He noted the probable opportunities for her to hear about the threat to France and to the Dauphin.
In short, the paper reflects a special integration of his own deep feeling with
a reasonable, thoughtful, critical evaluation of Joan's experience before she
left Domremy. That Jeanne d'Arc had been on his heart and mind for some
time is evident from the description of the little statue of her which is over
the door of her home at Domremy, and paintings of her in the Louvre in
Paris and in the Metropolitan Museum in New York. He could have seen
this last one when he was 15 or 16 years old after his parents moved to New
York. "I first saw the painting when I hardly knew who Jeanne was; it seemed
to me the most beautiful picture in the Metropolitan Museum. And everything I have learned of her and the spirit of her life seems wonderfully experienced in that painting. The plainness of her dress and her cottage in the
little orchard, and the sense of saintly loveliness which pervades the whole
spirit of the painting, tell better than any words can do what Jeanne was . . .
to understand that picture would be to understand the mystery of all her

greatness." The intensity of this response makes it all the more remarkable that Gardner was able to maintain such an objective—however emphatic—approach to his account of her. His response to the painting of Jeanne d'Arc also reflects the emotional depth, the perceptual sensitivity and the religious intensity of the adolescent Gardner in his Hotchkiss years and his freshman year at Yale.

Chapter 9

Sources: Harvard Archives was most cooperative, providing names of courses, faculty, grades obtained by GM in his work for the M.A. in Psychology in 1916–17. Other sources include autobiographies in HPA V, Kra II, MU, letters to his brother and to Frank Lorimer, his closest friend (in Akron Archives). Gardner's paper on Confucius and Christianity: memories told to LBM. Harry Helson's autobiography in HPA is also cited.

Gardner was at Harvard in the academic year 1916–17, Robert M. Yerkes' last year there as associate professor of comparative psychology; I have no record from Gardner of any experiences in the animal laboratory, but the detailed outline Yerkes developed for an ontological study of the self was conscientiously followed by Gardner in his "Study of Myself," a major source for this chapter. Yerkes kept in touch with this earnest student.

92–93   Harvard Archives sent me two final examinations which illustrate the range of subject matter of Gardner's work there for an M.A. in psychology:

PHILOSOPHY 18:

(1)   Discuss the relations of science and religion in the nineteenth century, and show how their relation affected the development of philosophy.

(2)   Summarize the criticisms of Spencer, Karl Pearson and Poincaré in "Present Philosophical Tendencies."

(3)   What is meant by the "descriptive method" in science, or by the "analytical interpretation" of scientific concepts? Why is scientific description supposed to afford inadequate knowledge?

(4)   How is modern idealism connected with Descartes, Berkeley and Kant?

(5)   Summarize the religious implications of either naturalism or idealism (choose one).

(6)   Summarize and compare James's and Bergson's views of freedom.

(7)   What is Bergson's view of "instinct"?

(8)   Expound Hegel's philosophy of history and show its bearing on present events.

Final. 1917.

PHILOSOPHY 10:

(1)   Describe the three divisions of aesthetics illustrating the treatment of the subject under each.

(2)   Discuss the relation of pleasure to beauty.

(3)   Trace the origin of the art impulse and its relation to the play impulse both in the individual and the race.

(4)   Describe the aesthetic attitude and include the three concepts, "Isolation and Detachment," "Foreground and Background" and "Psychical Distance."

(5)   Describe fully and criticize the theory of empathy and illustrate from the field of fine arts.

(6)   a. What was the development of the theory of imitation in the Greek Philosophy?; b. What is your idea of the imitation theory?

(7)   Describe the relation of form to content in literature.

(8)   How is the Freudian theory applied in literature and the drama?

Final. 1917.

93   The liberal humanistic approach to psychology at Harvard as Gardner experienced it in his year of working for his M.A. never left him.

Chapter 10

Because of the lack of Gardner's letters to his mother from 1917 to 1919 our knowledge of his experience of that period is skimpy. The chief sources are letters to his closest friend Frank Lorimer and to his Yale roommate Malcolm Baber, and notes to me in the '80s from Gardner's Yale Mobile Hospital friend Leonard Beadle. The Yale Alumni Magazine for June 1979 contains descriptions of the Yale Mobile Hospital's trip across the Atlantic in the early summer of 1917 but Gardner never mentioned the maggots in the breakfast oatmeal, or the horse meat and hard tack. In fact, he did not talk about the war with us.

Gardner did not talk about the war but he enjoyed singing World War I songs and taught me some that I had not known, such as "Lili Marlene." The experience of the war is reflected in his efforts for peace; his article, "The Service Man's Tomorrow," and his references to servicemen carrying cherished books in their pockets.

"World War I began in August 1914. In March 1917 German U Boats sank four American ships, and on April second President Wilson appealed to an assembly of both houses of Congress. The United States entered April 6, 1917. An Armistice was declared November 11, 1918" (A.J.P. Taylor, History of World War I. *London: Octopus Books n.d.).*

94   "The Yale Mobile Hospital left New Haven by train for New York and boarded
        the *S.S. Baltic* for the trip across the Atlantic in early summer of 1917. The
        Baltic sailed to Halifax to join a convoy there. Life aboard for the officers and
        nurses was comfortable in first-class accommodations. But not so for the
        enlisted men who were put in the steerage. Their meals were bad. Breakfast
        of dried apples or apricots, oatmeal with plenty of maggots cooked in it,
        hard tack, jam and tea. Lunch of horse meat, potatoes, hard tack, and tea.
        And supper of rice, hard tack and tea. In the evenings, stewards from first
        class sneaked down and sold us roasted chickens, ducks, and turkeys at exor-
        bitant prices. That helped out.
        "After several days, the convoy was made up and steamed out from Halifax
        Harbor, zigzagging all the way across the Atlantic. Finally, as we neared
        Lands End but couldn't see it, several destroyers approached us, signaling
        back and forth with their bright lights. It was a dramatic sight. Then the
        convoy separated, a destroyer accompanying one or two ships. The *Baltic*
        went on toward the Irish Sea with a destroyer escort. Toward evening, those
        of us in the steerage felt a tremendous shock. Later we learned it was a
        torpedo and that it caused no major damage. We rushed to our life-boat
        stations in time to see the destroyer laying a pattern of depth charges on the
        port side. The next morning we docked at Liverpool. That afternoon we
        boarded a train which took us across England, arriving at Southampton
        about 3:00 a.m. The day was spent at an English rest camp with more hard
        tack, jam, and tea. Then at night, we boarded a small, crowded channel
        steamer, arriving at Le Havre, France in the morning. A couple of days there
        in another dismal rest camp and we started the last leg of our long journey.
        It was on a slow freight train, one passenger car for officers and nurses and
        box cars for the enlisted men. Our cars had the famous sign in black letters:
        "Huit chevaux ou quarante hommes." En route we were sidetracked at long
        intervals in the cities. At those times, many of us climbed a fence, rushed
        to a wine shop, and bought bottles of red wine. This enlivened our spirits
        and made the trip almost enjoyable. At last we arrived in Limoges where we
        were greeted by a squad of poilus, commanded by a small, cocky major. The
        squad led us through the city to Mas L'Oucier, an empty Haviland porcelain
        factory building. This was to be our home for the next six months" (*Yale
        Alumni Magazine,* June 1979).
95   GM to M. Baber, to Frank Lorimer.
95   GM to M. Baber, Marsh Williams; GM to M. Baber.
95   Leonard Beadle to LBM.
95   GM to M. Baber.
95   Army records in GM Archives at Akron.
95   The most open, confiding letter was sent to me by Frank Lorimer and here
        Gardner pours out his anguish in a way I never experienced:

        "War Work Council, Nov. 7, 1917
        "Dearest of dear friends,
                "I want to talk to you tonight because I am lonesome and weak and weary
        and burdened with the ghastly horror and blindness and futility of it all. It
        seems worse to me now than when I first spoke of it to you in August 1914.
        Mostly I try not to grasp it, not to feel it deeply, not to let it into my heart.
        But when I do, as I did this afternoon, it breaks down my resistance and op-
        presses me. And the worst of it is that I cannot play a man's part to banish

the horrible thing from the world, but must sit here idle waiting and wondering when—if even—we shall be given work to do that can be said to help the cause. We are all wretchedly useless here. Naturally I am giving money to war-relief, buyi ıg a bond, and trying to be of use in such ways. If I was sure that the war will end in a definite promise of future peace I could be pretty patient. But how uncertain that all seems now after Russia's collapse,—can the seething uncontrolled antagonized masses of humanity organize themselves into anything that will last? Perhaps Wilson can do it."

It is this letter which helps us to understand the intense feeling supporting Gardner's peace efforts from 1940 through the Vietnam War in the 1960s.

96   See *Public Opinion and the Individual*, GM and R. Likert, 1938; *Human Nature and Enduring Peace*, GM, 1945. Correspondence.

Chapter 11

Sources include GM's autobiographies, books, articles, correspondence, unpublished papers and notes; my records and memories; letters to me in the 1980s from his former students, friends, colleagues and other psychologists; reviews; Encyclopedia of Social Science *and* Who's Who *biographies; and family letters. Harvard Archives contain extensive correspondence with Gordon Allport and with E.G. Boring. Archives at Columbia, City College of New York, University of California at Berkeley and at Los Angeles, University of Colorado, and Syracuse University contain records of summer courses taught by Gardner. FBI records are available under the Freedom of Information Act. Biographies of E.L. Thorndike, Paul Robeson and other academic and nonacademic people of the time provide relevant historical data.*

The Columbia University Library contains catalogues of the 1920s and '30s and also volumes of Archives of Psychology *which include many dissertations of psychology doctoral candidates. The psychology department discarded records of those years in a housecleaning operation, according to a report to me by former president William McGill. Consequently records of faculty meetings, planning sessions, and activities of the department for that time are not available.*

In addition to GM's biographies and obituaries, his discussions of teaching and his descriptions of Woodworth in an obituary, and GM's students', friends' and colleagues' letters to me after his death are available in the History of Psychology Archives at the University of Akron. Especially important are those of Eugene Hartley, S. Stansfeld Sargent, Joan Criswell, Theodore Newcomb, Otto Klineberg, Georgene Seward, Rensis and Jane Likert, Philip DuBois, Saul Sells, and Mary Cover Jones.

Letters from and conversations with surviving friends of that period provided a picture of GM's social life in the 1920s; those from Margaret ("Bunch") Alexander Marsh, Louise de Schweinitz, Ruth Bachwig, Frank Lorimer and Joseph Chassell were most illuminating. Autobiographical notes by GM and our letters to each other give personal data. Ross Stagner's February 1983 single-spaced letters to me, along with the long series of letters from Eugene Hartley, S. Stansfeld Sargent and Ernest (Jack) Hilgard, are a gold mine for future historians of psychology. All of these and other correspondence are in the Akron Archives.

101   Gardner's 7-11-62 autobiographical notes describe his encounter with Woodworth and courses he took at Columbia, Union Theological Seminary. This also contains his first draft of his description of Woodworth as a teacher.

101   The beginning of the twenties was marked by the official adoption of the Nine-
           teenth Amendment to the United States Constitution—giving women the
           right to vote. This was the climax of years of struggle in the women's suffrage
           movement and the beginning of the struggle for an equal-rights amend-
           ment. See Klingaman, William, *1919: The Year Our World Began,* New
           York: St. Martin's Press/Thomas Dunn, 1987.

101   "Discussions not light-hearted"; "Gardner did not have much joie de vivre,"
           letter to LBM from Margaret Marsh after GM's death; Akron Archives.
           Teenage girls and those in their early twenties wore short skirts, smoked
           cigarettes, drank, kissed boys promiscuously and even allowed boys to fondle
           their breasts, as Perrett describes (p. 151). They were called flappers and this
           led to the view of the twenties as the decade of the flappers. But although
           many graduate students smoked and drank a little, they were earnestly con-
           cerned about race problems and international issues.

101   And, although at that time the discussions merely led to more talk, seeds of
           the "sexual revolution" after World War II had been planted, just as seeds
           of the era of "women's liberation" were planted by the suffragists' marches
           demanding voting privileges for women; that effort led to the 1919 achieve-
           ment.
           As the members of the gang paired off and married, most of the women took
           their husbands' names and few, indeed, experimented with free love.
           Women with graduate degrees, in medicine, economics, and psychology,
           did pursue their careers part or full time while they raised their families,
           usually with the help of a full time housekeeper. (In the twenties and thirties
           excellent maids, cooks, and housekeepers were easily affordable since few oc-
           cupations were available for women until World War II pressed women into
           factories and other kinds of "war work.")

101   Era of dramatic social change after World War I: soldiers and nurses bred in
           the puritan standards of the Midwest and New England returned from
           Europe with images of different life-styles. Even for those of us who were not
           "flappers" nor of this "lost generation," our orientation was more free, and
           at odds with the life-style and standards of our still Victorian parents.
           Frederick Lewis Allan's *The Big Change,* 1952, reviews a long list of changes
           in the first half of the 20th century—in foreign relations, the arts, medicine
           and public health, science and technology, the waning of puritanism,
           loosening of family ties and parental authority and other areas. But nowhere
           does he mention research precursors of the powerful change in race relations
           symbolized by the 1954 Supreme Court ruling in the *Brown vs. the Topeka
           Board of Education* decision. Nor does he note the contributions of students
           like those at Columbia who provided the evidence leading to that decision.
           In fact, he does not recognize the influence of colleges and universities on
           many of the trends in religion, family life, and other areas of social change.

101   Membership in the KKK grew rapidly in the early 1900s to more than two
           million throughout the U.S. by the mid–1920s. Though the KKK is known
           for its violent politics of hate, most members during the '20s and '30s used
           peaceful means to show their anger against foes. Local Klan groups in the
           South remained strong throughout the '30s, but their representation
           weakened in the North and the Western states, and Klan membership took
           a sharp downturn in the '40s, even in the South.
           The revival of Ku Klux Klan violence paralleled the emergence of gifted Negro
           writers, singers, and other performers whose talents aroused deep interest,

especially among white intellectuals. This, as well as Gardner's boyhood during the years of his father's intense effort to improve race relations, contributed to the Zeitgeist in which psychology students were living and studying.

101   The Sacco-Vanzetti case was a celebrated murder trial in Massachusetts, extending over seven years (1920–27) and resulting in the execution of the defendants, Nicola Sacco and Bartolomeo Vanzetti, who were accused of murdering the paymaster of a shoe factory. Many believe to this day that the two were killed for their political beliefs and national origins.

102   Gardner's experience in the contrasting cultures of the North and South as well as France, Germany and England must have sensitized him to the importance of cultural differences as did my own experiences in rural and city life, Yankee and Southern towns.

102   Ruth talked about their discussions of Kant, who was not among my favorite thinkers at that time.

102   "Somewhat sardonic Gardner": 1980 Christmas card from Joseph Chassell.

102   Margaret Mead, 1930 (1975), *Growing Up in New Guinea: A Comparative Study of Primitive Education,* New York: William Morrow.

102   "Gang," "Bunch" letter to LBM from Margaret Marsh, 5-6-82.

103   "A new kind of world," HPA V, 259.

103   I had studied enough Greek at Union Theological Seminary to resonate to Gardner's reciting Greek verse.

103   The graduate student friends in the "gang" at that time were students of economics, philosophy and premedical courses. While I shared their concern about labor problems I took for granted the poetry and music which excited Gardner; evidently none of that group shared these deep interests of his although my own Vassar friends knew more than I did. I did not consider my literary and musical culture unusual in any way. What was unusual was my interest in F.W.H. Myers, Walter Prince, and Freud. In the last years of his life GM told nurses that I was the "only one." He had loved other women but no one else shared his values and interests as I did.

104   Helen Poffenberger to LBM, 1979.

106   Woodworth's warmth, RSW to H.E. Jones, 10-30-27; Akron Archives.

107   Gardner's doctoral dissertation: Types of Word Association in Dementia Praecox, Manic Depression and Normal Persons. *American Journal of Psychiatry* (April 1923), 1–33.

107   Gardner educating himself (James, H.E. Barnes, Fosdick, Scott); conversations with me; HPA V, 250.

107   Gardner's first seminar presentation, Kra II, 327.

107   Developing the history of psychology, HPA V, 258.

107   Hollingworth remarked, *ibid.*

108   "HIMP," 1929. *The Historical Introduction to Modern Psychology* was first published in London by Kegan Paul Trench Trubner.

108   Boring stated in the preface to his *History of Experimental Psychology,* 1929, that "Murphy's *Historical Introduction to Modern Psychology* appeared two weeks before I wrote the last word of my last chapter. I have referred to him in my Notes, but I did not have the advantage of his book while I was writing." Boring acknowledges "a real debt" to his seminar at Clark University in 1921–22 and to his seminar at Harvard in 1928. In that preface he also states that it was due to Titchener's influence that he "gained the conviction that the gift of professional maturity comes only to the psychologist who

knows the history of his science. In experimental psychology Titchener was the historian par excellence." The introduction by the editor of the Century Psychology Series, Richard M. Elliott, implies that he, Elliott, initiated this volume by Boring.

108 Gardner's historical view was not limited to the past—for him man's history and that of psychology extended from the past through the present into the future—he was "on the cutting edge," the edge that carves new trails of experiment and understanding. This long view did not permit him to be captured by current trends—he transcended, while he included, new developments. He did not identify himself with any "ism," humanism, behaviorism or Freudianism. Rather, he believed that psychology, like biology, or geology or chemistry was a science, one science. Psychology must include all valid contributions.

108 Gardner's illustrations and metaphors came from ancient Greek, Latin, Hebrew writing, the ancient literature from India as well as from the philosophy, literature, music and art of western civilization. The index of the 1972 *Historical Introduction to Modern Psychology* includes as many names from cultural history as from the history of psychology: Bergson, the philosopher Berkeley, and Ruth Benedict share the same column of the index with Binet; Carlyle and Catherine the Great we find near S. McKeen Cattell; Cicero and Claparede are bedfellows preceding Coleridge, Christopher Columbus, Comenius, President Conant of Harvard, Confucius, Copernicus, Coué and the social psychologist R. Crutchfield. The philosopher John Dewey has more references than anyone on that page except Descartes and Erik Erikson, while Gandhi looks out at us from the same column that includes Gesell. No wonder that some students remarked that they "got more education from Gardner Murphy's course than from all the rest of their college work together." The *Historical Introduction to Modern Psychology* remained in print (with three editions) for over 50 years—a "bible" for graduate students in psychology.

108 In the spring of 1928 he spent several months in Texas, in Tucson, Arizona, and at the Mayo Clinic consulting a series of specialists, undergoing seemingly endless tests, x-rays, and bacterial cultures to find an adequate diagnosis of his health problem, much later diagnosed as a sequel to the encephalitic flu in the spring of 1925. In 1934, at the suggestion of a friend of mine, Gardner spent a month at the sanitarium of Dr. William Hay. With a combination of detoxification, and a special diet which focused on producing a predominantly alkaline residue, Gardner's health was amazingly restored. With new energy, he was able to spend uninterrupted time at the University as well as hike and climb mountains in the summer. Meantime he had produced four more books. (See Bibliography.)

108 The weakness following Gardner's 1925 flu prevented vigorous activity and probably made it possible for him to do a great deal of thinking about both his lectures in class and also books he could write. David Leary to LBM.
Gardner's productivity was also made possible in part by eliminating trivia and simplifying necessary routines of life. He enjoyed his "George Washington coffee," Shredded Wheat and bananas, and his Prince Albert pipe tobacco in its red can. He ordered shirts, underwear and socks by the half dozen from a mail order company, thus eliminating time-consuming shopping. He did not select bright or distinctive ties but enjoyed the Gunn and Latchford silk ones that I gave him because I enjoyed them.

108 Our son, Al (Alpen Gardner), was born June 24, 1930. We brought home a

five-month-old baby girl from a Cologne orphanage in August 1932, and named her Margaret. We later nicknamed her "Midge."

109 Woodworth offered GM the social psychology, HPA V, 262.

110 Gardner's introductory course was revolutionary in its use of accounts of adult lives and its emphasis on the relation between psychology and the social sciences.

110 This account of development in the Columbia College psychology department is taken from college catalogues of the thirties.

110 Harold and Mary Cover Jones were Gardner's good friends as long as they were in New York; then after their move to Berkeley Harold invited us to the summer session at the University of California in 1938 and 1947 and we corresponded from time to time. Mary remembered that in the 1938 visit our eight-year-old son remarked, "I wish my father was Harold Jones and my mother was Sonja Henie" (the champion ice skater).

Woodworth and Poffenberger were friendly but Gardner had no close friends in the department after Harold Jones left until the mid-thirties when some of his students, notably Otto Klineberg, were given appointments. Robert Lynd in sociology, Horace Friess in philosophy and Goodwin Watson at Teachers' College were his closest friends in other departments at Columbia — intellectually and politically congenial.

Henry Garrett, who taught statistics, was no liberal — and he was openly negative to Jews and blacks, saying for instance that it was not sound to accept Jewish students — they would never get a job. The comparative psychologist, Carl Warden, was rather isolated with his rats and monkeys. John Peatman of the City College faculty wrote that Warden had warned him against Gardner's course in social psychology, that it wasn't worthwhile.

111 In 1934–35 Otto Klineberg (who became one of the few international psychologists) handled social psychology and psychology of personality in the undergraduate department and continued to do so through 1940 when Gardner left Columbia. Gardner taught social psychology and history in the graduate session, and also a course in research in social psychology that year. A new course in neurophysiology of behavior was added to the program, along with a course in Gestalt theory taught by Max Wertheimer, Klineberg's new courses in psychology and ethnology, and his problems in racial psychology. In 1935–36 three other new courses were added to the graduate program for that year: John Seward's psychology of feeling, Dr. John Levy's behavior problems of children — the first course given by a psychoanalyst, and Myrtle McGraw's psychology of infant behavior. In the summer of 1936 Gardner gave two courses: abnormal psychology, and social psychology. In 1936–37 three other new courses were offered, again for one year only: a course in ethics by Klineberg, a course in child guidance by another psychoanalyst, Caroline Zachry, and Ross McFarland's physiological approach to psychology. Of these the physiological course was the only one to be continued the next year, while the rest of the program continued as before. John Volkman, another graduate in the department, succeeded Seward in 1938–39 and taught a new course in psychology of judgment; still another graduate of the department, Dwight Chapman, taught advanced experimental and psychology of perception. In 1939 Fred Keller took the place of Dwight Chapman, and in 1940 he was appointed to take Gardner's place. Gardner began parttime teaching in the Extension division at

Columbia University in 1920; first an introductory course and then abnormal
psychology while he was working toward his Ph.D. in psychology. In 1923
he was asked to teach the history of psychology. "After collecting the doctorate in 1923 I was considered eligible to teach in Columbia College along
with Harold E. Jones." Woodworth gave up his social psychology course in
1924 and offered that evening graduate course to Gardner; accepting this
course led to the development of his identity as a social psychologist in the
'30s. He accepted a full time appointment in 1925–26 as an instructor
teaching general psychology, the introductory course, in addition to the
history. "From 1925 to 1940 I carried a full load, about three-fifths of which
was in the College and two-fifths in the Graduate School." His closest friend
in the department at that time was Harold E. Jones, who taught
developmental, and experimental psychology. In the two years, 1926–27 and
1927–28 with Jones as the departmental representative for the undergraduate work, Gardner continued to teach the introductory course and the
history of psychology.

111   Eugene Hartley, a brilliant, observant undergraduate, then graduate stu-
       dent, provided this account of Gardner's work during those years. Letter to
       LBM.

111   This account of the prejudice at Columbia was supplied by Al Murphy.

112   "The Nicholas Murray Butler Medal is awarded quinquennially in gold....
       The medal is awarded in silver or bronze to the graduate of Columbia
       University ... who has during the year preceding, shown the most com-
       petence in philosophy or educational theory, practice or administration or
       who has during that time made the most important contribution to any of
       them." In 1918 the medal was awarded to Woodworth, in 1921 to Holling-
       worth. When Gardner received it in 1932 he was the third psychologist with
       a Columbia degree to receive the Butler Medal.

112   In 1938 he was first elected to the Council of the APA, along with Gordon
       Allport, Leonard Carmichael, Harold Jones, Mark May and J.A. McGeoch;
       his three-year team overlapped those of K.F. Muenzinger, Horace English
       and Edna Heibreder among others. These years placed him at the center of
       policy and planning in the APA.

112   President William J. McGill to LBM 9-18-1979: "Considering Gardner's
       competence and his extraordinary impact on students, it is easy to imagine
       why some of them may have thought that the explanation of Columbia's
       failure to act on his promotion might involve radical politics or para-
       psychology. I am quite sure they are wrong and I believe I know the real
       story. I talked to [eight current and former members of the psychology
       department]. ... [I]n the '30s and '40s the three wings of the department
       (clinical, social, experimental) were in constant struggle with one another
       for ascendancy. The budget was rigidly controlled. ... Very simply, the
       experimentalists won. They were able ... to deprecate Gardner's work
       in relation to competitive figures in experimental psychology.... When
       [the experimentalist Clarence] Graham came in 1948 he remade the depart-
       ment as an experimental one ... deprecated the work of Wordworth ...
       and all the old guard.... The decision was political, but the politics were
       petty departmental politics with no relation to issues of national
       significance."

113   Among the psychologists whose dissertations were sponsored or cosponsored
       by Gardner were:

Muzafer Sherif, "A Study of Some Social Factors in Perception" (GM and
G.W. Allport), 1935; Eli Marks, "Individual Differences in Work Curves"
(GM, Poffenberger, Hotelling, O. Klineberg), 1935; Gregory Razran, "Con-
ditional Responses in an Experimental Study and a Theoretical Analysis"
(Poffenberger, sponsor; Woodworth, GM et al.), 1935; Solomon Asch, "A
Study of Change in Mental Organization of Information in the School
Years," 1936; Solomon Diamond, "A Study of the Influence of Political
Radicalism on Personality Development" (GM, supervisor), 1936; Lucien M.
Hanks, "Predictions from Case Material to Psychological Test Data: A
Methodological Study of Types" (GM, supervisor), 1936; Walter H. Wilke,
"An Experimental Comparison of the Speech, the Radio, and the Printed
Page in Propaganda Devices," (GM, sponsor; Likert et al.); Joseph E. Bar-
mack, "Boredom and Other Factors in the Psychology of Mental Effort"
(Poffenberger and Rounds, chairmen; GM on the committee, 1937; Philip
Eisenberg, "Expressive Movements Related to Feelings of Dominance" (GM
and committee), 1937; Christine Morgan, "The Attitudes and Adjustments
of Recipients of Old Age Assistance in Upstate and Metropolitan New York"
(GM and J.K. Folsom of Vassar for supervision), 1937; B.S. Breslaw,
"Development of a Socioeconomic Attitude," 1938; F.J. Gaudet, "In-
dividual Differences in Sentencing Tendencies of Judges" (GM, Karl N.
Llewellyn, A.T. Poffenberger, cosponsors) 1938; Joan H. Criswell, "A
Sociometic Study of Race Cleavage in a Classroom" (GM, Otto Klineberg,
Moreno, cosponsors) 1939; Stansfeld Sargent, "Thinking Processes at
Various Levels of Difficulty" (Hollingworth supervising, Woodworth and
GM cooperating), 1940; Louis Granich, "A Qualitative Analysis of Concepts
in Mentally Deficient Schoolboys" (Carney Landis supervising; Woodworth,
GM, Klineberg on the committee), 1940.

Chapter 12

*Major sources include Kra II, HPA V, 262–63 and my own recollections of the years
1925 and thereafter, including conversations with Helen and Robert Lynd, graduate
students at Columbia and faculty members at Teachers' College, Columbia; Lawrence
K. Frank; my work on experimental social psychology (1931 and 1937), my research on
sympathy in young children, and close friendship with social psychology students including Theodore Newcomb, Otto Klineberg, the Horowitzs (later Hartleys) and
others; letters from former assistants, dissertation students, colleagues in other universities, especially Robert Sömmer, Ross Stagner, S.S. Sargent, E.R. Hilgard; unpublished lectures; reviews of GM's books, biographical accounts in books on the development of social psychology such as Richard Evans' interview with GM in* The Making of
Social Psychology; *GM's chapter in Klineberg and Christie's* Perspectives in Social
Psychology *and comments on that by authors of other chapters in that book. My
perspective and excitement about GM's pioneer conception was a product of my reading
in my 1922 course in social psychology at Vassar College, with Margaret Floy Washburn.*

114   Helen and Robert Lynd: Helen Lynd was on the faculty of Sarah Lawrence Col-
       lege from 1928 to her retirement in 1964 and Robert Lynd was professor of
       sociology at Columbia from the '30s to the '60s.

114   Factory where I worked: Gruen watch factory in Cincinnati, New York Train-
        ing School at Hudson, New York.
115   Floyd Allport, HPA V, 261f.
115   "Armchair theorizing" and the lack of empirical research; Chapter 18, "Social
        Psychology and the Psychology of Religion" in GM's 1929 *Historical In-
        troduction to Modern Psychology* reviews the writings of Tarde, *The Laws
        of Imitation,* LeBon, *The Crowd,* and other social theorists, as well as the
        Theoretical Discussions of Social Psychology by Ross and McDougall. This
        chapter provides an overview of "armchair psychology" as we were exposed
        to it in the 1920s after the discussions of the previous quarter century. Much
        of the insight and observations of the early thirties has been outmoded by
        the empirical work focussed on social problems and conflicts. But the laws
        of imitation are still at work as we can see any day in looking at fashions in
        clothes, houses, cars, and other everyday aspects of life.
115   When Gardner lifted social psychology out of the armchair he wanted to
        bring it to life, as Robert Sömmer wrote me (10-28-87). His vision was
        realized in studies of prejudice and conflict and studies carried on by
        members of SPSSI.
116   Gardner's own feeling about the 1931 *Experimental Social Psychology* varied;
        according to Ross Stagner, Gardner felt that the 1937 edition was superior
        to that first volume, and many other people agreed. But in a 1954 letter to
        Calvin Hall he wrote, "Many aspects of personality theory in which I am in-
        terested, for example, the conceptual place of social attitudes in the total
        structure, problems of specificity and generality of attitude, are considered
        in the first edition of *Experimental Social Psychology.*" He said further that
        he doubted that *Personality* had "any great influence." He thought "that
        those who were sensitive to these ways of thinking had picked them up dur-
        ing the mid-forties before the book appeared." He did not want to be
        regarded as the author of one particular book on personality—but rather as
        a person "making a lot of different pokes into the dark."
116   It has not been possible for me to attempt a history of the developments in
        social psychology after our two editions of *Experimental Social Psychology*
        in the 1930s. Letters to me in the 1980s from S.S. Sargent, Ross Stagner, and
        others in the Akron Archives of the History of Psychology provide important
        data on these developments.
116   Relation between the organism and the environment: *Experimental Social
        Psychology* (1931), 43: "Certain inborn human traits, though obviously
        never detached from environmental influences, may be mathematically
        isolated." Gardner was defending the scientific process of isolating traits for
        study while he acknowledged the simultaneous impact of heredity and en-
        vironment. Later he insisted that everything is biological and at the same
        time social. Chapter III, "Nature and Nurture," reviews the evidence avail-
        able up to 1930.
116   Robert Sömmer asked urgently, what was the process of writing *Experimental
        Social Psychology*—were there 3 × 5 cards all over the floor, did we write
        till midnight? At that time, Gardner and I both had excellent memories for
        content and bibliographical references. He dictated to a stenographer and
        I wrote longhand; we paid his best students to check and complete the
        bibliography. (He used royalties from previous books to pay for the
        assistance on the next ones.) We *never* "burned midnight oil"—both of us
        wrote easily, whenever we had some time.

116   The impact of Gardner's emphasis on empirical studies in social psychology was demonstrated in a series of *Readings in Social Psychology* initiated in 1947 by two of Gardner's students, Theodore Newcomb and Eugene Hartley. In their preface to the first edition they noted that social psychologists, despite the centrifugal expansion of research, had become increasingly clear about their role and task as a discipline. With echoes of Gardner's view, they stated that, "It is the peculiar province of the social psychologist to bring to bear upon his study of the behaving organism all relevant factors—from whatever sources and by whatever methods—which inhere in the fact of association with other members of the species." Illustrations of ways in which social conditions influenced psychological processes were presented. The third edition of *Readings in Social Psychology* in 1958 attempted to represent examples of research in the entire field of social psychology as it had expanded, with special attention to studies relevant to theory. This range is indicated by some of the topical headings for groups of papers, including Perception of Persons, Communication and Opinion Change, Interpersonal Influence, The Socialization of the Child, Leadership, Group Structure and Process, Intergroup Tension, Prejudice. Sixty-two representative reports of research in these and other areas were included. Social psychology had indeed outgrown the armchair.

117   What foreshadowed in 1931 Gardner's biosocial field theory was his awareness of "the new emphasis upon the dynamic aspects of both individual and social psychology" (*Experimental Social Psychology,* p. 7). He noted that several psychologists had "taken over the concept of a highly human nature shaped almost entirely by the culture which acts upon it. . . . They grant, of course, that the only way that culture can shape individuals . . . is by modifying their original nature" (p. 8). He insisted that "psychologists would no longer think of the individual man as a biologically self-sufficient unit, but as a bundle of attitudes and habits which are a part of a historical process" (p. 9). He protested the biologically centered instinct theory which had dominated social psychology into the 1920s.

117   Canalization is Gardner's term, adapted from Janet, to refer to the massive acquisition of tastes and preferences which are intrinsically satisfying, and are not conditioned through their connections with associated satisfiers. See the chapter on canalization in Gardner's 1947 *Personality.*

117   The assumption that the IQ is a reliable measure of inherited intelligence still persists in evaluations of school children and assignments to classes for the retarded or for institutions. But much more refined evaluations of specific aspects of language such as auditory processing, word retrieval, etc., have facilitated corrective efforts with children who have difficulties.

118   GM formulated his biosocial concept in different ways at different times. All those events which may be described as cultural may be described from a different point of view as the activities of organisms. Further, "even at the level of unicellular organisms a social factor is present" (p. 11). "The interaction between organisms is one of the most fundamental of biological facts. If chasing and being pursued among human beings is a social fact, why is it not when it occurs among the amoeba? . . . The social is literally an aspect of the biological."

118   "Instinct Trend": that is, the tendency to regard instincts as basic determiners of behavior, in contrast to the behavioristic trend which emphasized conditioning as the major determinant.

119   Ross Stagner: letter to LBM.

119   In a concluding section on methodology, especially "concrete problems of research and investigation," Karpf's footnote states, "The first step in the survey of social psychology from this standpoint has already been taken in Murphy & Murphy's *Experimental Social Psychology*. Other treatments of the subject from this standpoint are bound to follow."

120   In view of the fact that after World War II, prewar research was largely ignored if not forgotten—as if scientific psychology had begun only after the war—it is worthwhile to look at the response to Gardner's work in social psychology in the '30s. Murchison's 1935 *Handbook of Social Psychology* contained 2000 names in the index; we were among the 1 percent who had ten or more references, along with Allport, Freud, Goodenough, Jung, Thorndike and Thurstone. The *Handbook* also contained our chapter "The Influence of Social Situations upon the Behavior of Children"; this was based upon 60 experimental and observational studies of infants and children. Still, Gardner's status was ambiguous—social psychological research was considered "soft," and although Woodworth, Poffenberger and Hollingworth supported Gardner warmly, his work was not regarded highly by the experimentalists. When he left Columbia, an experimentalist in the "hard data" tradition was appointed.

121   In C. Murchison's 1935 *Handbook of Social Psychology,* Gordon Allport's chapter on attitudes quoted Gardner's concept of attitude among his five references to our book; F.L. Wells, also from Harvard, referred to Experimental Social Psychology three times, while J.F. Dashiell, then from the University of North Carolina, included a reference to our book in his chapter on the influence of Social Situations on the Behavior of Individual Human Adults.

121   In Gardner's emphasis on the importance of autobiographical data in the study of attitudes we see his early awareness of the importance of an ideographic approach to the study of personality. This appreciation of the importance of study of the individual was also evident in his support and participation in my pioneer study of sympathy.

122   My research on sympathy in young children (published as *Social Behavior and Child Personality: An Exploratory Study of Sympathy*) developed from a remark by Gardner's friend Harold Coffman. He told us that the Josiah Macy, Jr., Foundation was looking for some new ideas for research. When I mentioned that someone ought to study the neglected area of sympathy in children, he urged me to talk to the president of the Foundation, Dr. Ludwig Kast. After I had explained my ideas to Dr. Kast, he said, "You do the study and send me the bills."

122   My study of sympathetic behavior in children from two to four years of age was carried out in 1932–34 in Speyer Nursery School. I recorded episodes of behavior which I considered to be expressions of sympathy for another child in distress: defending, helping, warning, etc.—with the assistance of Mary Fite and Eugene Horowitz and Gardner, as statistical consultant. He showed me how to make a scale of the kinds of items and test its validity by the use of an odd-even correlation. This was at a time when Watson's popular behavioristic emphasis on conditioning was undermining instinct theories while hereditarians were defending inborn traits.

122   The appreciations of Otto Klineberg's several careers, presented at the 1989 SPSSI conference (during the APA convention), are being published in a book.

122 Tests to Yakima Indian children.

123 Skeels, H.M.; Updegraff, R.; Wellman, B.L.; and Williams, H.M., "A Study of Environmental Stimulation; An Orphanage Preschool Project," *Studies in Child Welfare*, vol. 15, no. 4. University of Iowa, 1938; Skodak, M., and Skeels, H.M., "A Follow-up Study of Children in Adoptive Homes," *Pedagogical Seminary and Journal of Genetic Psychology*, 66:21–58 (1945).

123 In his response to the Colley-Mead Award, Ted Newcomb wrote, "I fell into the category of 'social psychology' at the ripe age of 30. Gardner Murphy asked me — very much as if I were choosing a necktie — if I would join him and Lois Murphy in a revision of their previous book: *Experimental Social Psychology*. Of course, I didn't know how little I knew, but of course that did not influence my determination to participate in the book-to-be" (*Experimental Social Psychology*, 1937).

124 Horowitz, E.L., "The Development of Attitude Toward the Negro," *Archives of Psychology*, 1936, 194; Criswell, J.H., "Racial Cleavage in Negro White Groups," *Sociometry*, 1936, 1, 81–89; Horowitz, R.E., "Racial Aspects of Self-Identification in Nursery School Children," *Journal of Psychology*, 1939, 7, 91–99.

124 K.B. and M.K. Clark's studies of skin color: "Racial Identification and Preference in Negro Children." In T.M. Newcomb, E.L. Hartley and others, *Readings in Social Psychology*. New York: Henry Holt, 1947, 169–78. Gunnar Myrdal, *An American Dilemma*.

124 Gardner launched Sherif's career by including his first book in the *Harper Psychology* series, writing introductions to subsequent ones. Sherif: "Robber's Cave Experiment," 301, Sherif, M., and Sherif, C., *An Outline of Social Psychology*, New York: Harper, 1956.

128 My memories tend to emphasize the respectability that developed for social psychology after the war, the affluence for the society (SPSSI) that came with the royalties of the SPSSI Readings, the growing dominance of the research organizations and the near-monopoly that Ann Arbor became (E. Hartley to LBM, 7-24-83).

128 Hilgard wrote me (2-18-85): "Perhaps you have overestimated the influence of J.F. Brown's *Psychology and the Social Order*. Those of us who knew him felt that he was a little mixed up, as a Gestalt psychologist who had just been analyzed by Franz Alexander, and albeit a man of some pretensions who used to stroll about New Haven with gloves and a cane and a kind of affectation, when neither the weather nor his health called for them. I'm not sure how deep his Marxism was."

128 The first six pages of our article on the influence of situational variations (Chapter 22, C. Murchison, *Handbook of Social Psychology*, 1935) were written by Gardner and contain an early statement of the relation between the organism and the environment, his field theory. In this paper he was concerned with "the organism error" and "the situation error." "In the unceasing interplay of genetic and environmental factors in the growth of the organism, it is of course impossible to mark off sharply the influence of social factors . . ." (p. 1035). He illustrated as an "organism error" this statement: "Behavior traits are fixed attributes of organisms; they maintain a degree of stability comparable to that shown by a finger-print or a well-defined birthmark. . . . The organism error is *always* present when we compare individuals with regard to their possession of traits *if the traits are*

defined without reference to the stimulus situation.... There are no traits which can be defined *solely* in terms of characteristic ways of responding."

128   In July 1963 G. Lindzey consulted GM about a revision of the *Handbook of Social Psychology*. GM (7-26-63) commented, "Social psychology is moving almost like the wind" and he urged that Lindzey pay attention "to the really big ideas that are appearing on the horizon and also to try to foresee big events of three, five or ten years from now." He urged that more emphasis be given to the response of social psychology, to new cultural trends, to new ways of thinking about man, to the current radical preoccupation with the nature of creative thinking, information and communication theory. He felt that more non–English, especially Soviet work, should be represented, that nationalism, economic-political competition and the matrix in which modern wars arise should be included. He felt that the relation of the power structure to economic, political, military and religious problems needed attention. GM was still a social psychologist.

130   Harlow, H.F., "The Development of Affectional Patterns in Infant Monkeys," in B.M. Foss, ed., *Development of Infant Behavior*, New York: Wiley, 1961; Woodworth, "Mechanism May Become a Drive": see *Dynamic Psychology*, New York: Columbia University Press, 1918. G.W. Allport's "Functional Autonomy": see G.W.A., *Personality: A Psychological Interpretation*, New York: Holt, 1937.

131   In the 1930s and '40s a stream of texts and other books on social psychology by those who had worked with Gardner included: Klineberg, O., *Race Differences* (Harper, 1935); Klineberg, O., *Social Psychology* (Holt, 1940); Sherif, M., *An Outline of Social Psychology* (Harper, 1948); Newcomb, T.M., and Hartley, E.L., eds., *Readings in Social Psychology* (Holt, 1947); Newcomb, T.M., *Social Psychology* (Dryden, 1950); Sargent, S.S., *Social Psychology* (Ronald, 1950).

131   *Perspectives in Social Psychology* represented the 1961 celebration of the opening of the Columbia Department of Psychology. The original sessions included a good illustration of the limited perspectives of the postwar "hot shots" in social psychology in the Schachter-Hartley material (E. Hartley to LBM, 9-3-83).

131   The Institute of Human Relations was established at Yale in 1929, and both the University of Michigan and Harvard had interdisciplinary programs involving social psychology, but the Columbia Department of Social Psychology was, nevertheless, unique.

132   Klineberg, O., and Christie, R., eds., *Perspectives in Social Psychology*, 1965. GM: *The Future of Social Psychology in Historical Perspective*, 21.

Chapter 13

Sources include autobiographical accounts in the 50th anniversary edition of the Journal of Social Issues, *1976; my correspondence with and interviews with early members of SPSSI, especially Ralph K. White, Ross Stagner, Ernest Hilgard, Daniel Katz, Theodore Newcomb; and Gardner's extensive correspondence with Gordon Allport which is in the Harvard Archives.*

Also see Finison, L.J., "The Early History of the Society for the Psychological Study of Social Issues": Journal of the History of the Behavioral Sciences, *15, 29–37.*

See articles on the history of SPSSI in the Journal of Social Issues, *1986, Vol. 42, no. 1: Benjamin Harris, "Reviewing 50 Years of the Psychology of Social Issues"; Lorenz J. Finison, "The Psychological Insurgency, 1936–1945"; Ross Stagner, "Reminiscences About the Founding of SPSSI."*

135   Russian Revolution 1917: The onset of the Great Depression was marked by the stock market crash of October 24, 1929, when speculators rushed to sell at any price and found no buyers. (See André Maurois, *From the New Freedom to the New Frontier.* New York: David McKay, 1963, 128.)

135   In a comment on the history of the SPSSI written for the 50th anniversary of its origin, the editors comment on omissions; these include work on topics of religion, the personal qualities of its leaders, its changing organizational structure, its work on race and its contribution to the Supreme Court decision which led to school desegregation.

Because of the frequent emphasis on the leftist biases of early SPSSI members it is important to recognize that Gardner repeatedly described himself as a "Jeffersonian democrat." He usually voted a Democratic ticket but more than that he was color-blind, ethnic-blind, and nation-blind. I never heard him say "we ought to appoint a Jew, or a black, or a Pole, or a Chinese psychologist." Appointments were made on the basis of merit and availability.

His sensitivity to the needs of the underdog, of minorities, of the poor, of the vulnerable, of children, of the elderly was not rooted in ideology – it was rooted in his empathic nature supported by his father's concern for exploited children, and for abuse of blacks.

Similarly the liberalism of his good friends Gordon Allport, Edward Tolman and Theodore Newcomb had roots in the ethical-religious background of their families. Neither Gardner nor any of the above (and other early SPSSI leaders such as E.R. Hilgard) were "leftists"; they did not think in Marxist terms. Their drive to turn the light of science – psychology – on the social problems of America was supported by their commitment to the Constitution of the United States, their belief that "all men are created equal" and their concern about injustices in this nation.

136   Progressive schools. Judeo-Christian values: see *This Is My Faith,* 1956. Stewart Cole edited chapters on the personal faith of 25 "representative Americans."

136   Religious families: see HPA IV, V, VI, for autobiographies of G. Allport, E. Tolman, and T. Newcomb.

136   "...during the early years of the movement, [the term 'Social Gospel'] meant that Christianity had implications for the social whole, as well as for individuals. The later Social Gospelers sought the establishment of 'social' Christianity. . . . The kingdom of God would come on earth when social institutions were Christianized." Fishburn, Janet, *The Fatherhood of God and the Victorian Family: The Social Gospel in America.* Philadelphia: Fortress Press, 1981, 99–100.

136   A good introduction to the Social Gospel and Progressivism is: Crunden, Robert M., *Ministers of Reform: The Progressives' Achievement in American Civilization, 1889–1920.* New York: Basic Books, 1982. See especially 8, 40–41, 45–46.

137   In the fall of 1989 I received a letter from a Sarah Lawrence student of 1934 who wrote about her memory of that visit to the unemployed men's club.

One of the men was a highly educated professional. She remarked, "You made me into a liberal Democrat," and enclosed a list of activities in which she had been engaged.

137 "In Chicago. . ." This account of the role of David Krech, New America, et al., is based on accounts by Lorenz Finison.

137 Ross Stagner in SPSSI 50th. Poffenberger: Finison. Hilgard: letter to LBM.

138 Daniel Katz: letter to LBM.

138 Ross Stagner was chairman of the Hanover, N.H., 1936 meeting when SPSSI was created. Stagner to LBM, 2-10-83.

138 Some of the same leaders we mentioned in the founding of SPSSI were also on the Committee for National Morale — Gordon Allport, Gardner Murphy, Goodwin Watson, Kurt Lewin, Leonard Doob, Leonard Carmichael, Hadley Cantril, Walter V. Bingham and Floyd Ruch helped to define roles for social psychologists in the campaign for war preparedness.

138 Hitler's *Mein Kampf* was published in 1925 and appeared in English translation in 1943. His plans to eliminate Jews are discussed on pages 310–11, 327, 453, 624, 640, 662, and 679 of the latter. We read the book but Americans could not take his plans seriously and in effect did not realize that the genocide of 6,000,000 Jews was actually under way.

139 Early plans for yearbooks: Ross Stagner to LBM, 2-21-83; conflict regarding the first peace and war book: *ibid.* The Council invited Gardner to become chairman of an editorial group to develop a substitute: *ibid.* Gardner was drafted — he did all the work on what became *Human Nature and Enduring Peace:* letters to LBM from Ross Stagner; Akron Archives.

139 Represent the mainstream. Hilgard: letter to LBM. SPSSI also sponsored *Psychology and the Prevention of Nuclear War,* edited by Ralph White.

139 The intensity of Gardner's and Gordon Allport's commitment to contributing to the World War II effort after the December 7 Japanese bombing of Pearl Harbor and German bombing of London is expressed in their correspondence of the 1940s (Harvard Archives). These letters document the work of a number of SPSSI members both in participating in government activities related to the war, and in undertaking efforts to stimulate American morale and commitment to the war.

139 Gardner and Gordon Allport were both on the APA and the Social Science research councils in the late '30s, and they collaborated on a memorandum on Cooperation and Competition for the SSRC and on activities of the APA Council. They met in New York when they could and Allport invited Gardner to teach in the 1939 summer session at Harvard, but Gardner had other plans.

With the Nazi bombing of London, concern in this country escalated. Gordon wrote to Gardner on September 21, 1940, "I have never seen anything like the fireworks that are bursting in connection with morale. I am already a member of at least three morale committees: Harvard, Arthur Upham Pope's and a group meeting last Tuesday in New York under the sponsorship of Bernays (and others). Now you come along with your attractive ideas. . . . I want very much to know your views." Allport thought the activity ought to gravitate toward the National Research Council and he hoped soon to assemble something pointing toward a blueprint of the morale problem. "Your ideas will be of great significance." Gardner sent a memorandum which Allport acknowledged October 3, and he asked Gardner for 25 copies to be distributed to the National Research Council. Gardner, along with his former student Rensis Likert and his former Yale teacher Horace English were invited to the National Research Council conference. Gardner reported October 17 that he had "sat in on the Pope conference which he wanted to discuss with Gordon," who wrote that he hoped to see Gardner at the time of a meeting of the Emergency Committee in New York.

SPSSI also took hold of the morale problem and *Civilian Morale,* edited by Goodwin, contained a chapter by Gardner.

139   On November 27, 1940, Allport vigorously urged Gardner to attend a meeting at Yerkes' office at the Institute to discuss a follow-up on morale. Because of Yerkes' conservatism Allport felt that he needed Gardner's support, or if Gardner could not come, Allport hoped that Gardner could persuade Goodwin Watson to come.

By April 2 Gardner reported to A.V. Pope's Committee for National Morale that Gordon Allport was at work to obtain funding from the Carnegie Corporation and that a plan was under discussion to develop an intersociety committee for morale research. The plan was for the committee to be responsible to the National Research Council, Social Science Research Council, American Council of Learned Societies, and American Council on Education. If the government assigned a research job with funding, that job should have priority.

Gordon Allport sent a report to the membership of SPSSI through Gardner as chairman of the Committee on Morale, asking for Gardner's advice on a statement he had prepared. He also felt that psychologists should help the War Department with the development of its brief program for training military psychologists.

139   Within a week after the Japanese attack on the American fleet at Pearl Harbor, Gardner wrote to Gordon Allport for suggestions as to how SPSSI or the Eastern Psychological Association could contribute to defense. With the help of Harry Helson, a psychologist at Brooklyn College, Gardner was mobilizing speakers on morale for the New York area.

He asked whether an intersociety morale program could be developed, using sociologists, historians and political scientists along with psychologists, and he asked Gordon to send him any available pamphlets describing the work of the Harvard Defense Council.

In 1941 and 1942 Gordon Allport and Gardner were consulting frequently regarding the various committees on morale. Gordon sought Gardner's support for distributing Al Zander's newsletter from the SPSSI Committee on Research, Leadership and Morale, and for steering Newcomb away from appointing Allport as chairman of that committee since, Gordon felt, duplication should be avoided and he would be glad to cooperate with Zander. Exchanges like these illustrate the cooperation of Gordon Allport and Gardner in the effort to smooth the way of the wartime efforts of SPSSI.

In the fall of 1942 Gordon Allport offered to help Gardner in any way he could with the war and peace book Gardner had agreed to prepare. He suggested that Tolman, Ross Stagner, and Hartman, as "peace-minded psychologists," should be put to work. Allport felt that the book was "bound to have some significant results 'in boldly educating' psychologists."

139   In June 1943, in a letter to Gordon Allport, Gardner reported on his exciting visit to the Division of Political Studies of the State Department. Sumner Welles had referred Gardner to the chief of that division, H.A. Notter, and Notter's righthand man, "a Mr. Harris." Both men were "humane, wise,

thoughtful and alert" and had already read studies (by Arnheim, Bondy, and Freed) and were "eager for all the research material as well as for all the seasoned judgments that they could get from psychologists or any other social scientists." After Gardner outlined the available research, the manifesto, books, and journal articles, "they were interested in each and all." Notter asked to see Gardner again in about a month to discuss suggestions for further research. "The cooperation is 1000%," added Gardner. He asked Gordon Allport to send additional copies of the journal article with the postwar symposium and said that he felt they should proceed full speed and "funnel in all the studies that are good enough." Notter had said, "If you wait for formal publication you will find that decisions were made one hour before the critical facts came to hand."

139   Gardner was also chairman of the Peace Action Committee, and Gordon Allport reported to him that C. Bondy and J. Bruner had accepted membership on the committee and Bruner would succeed Gardner as chairman. That fall, Gardner was "giving all the fragments of time that I have to the Yearbook" and he wrote Allport that Houston Peterson and Lyman Bryson were being very helpful.

Gardner wanted a multidisciplinary approach to the peace discussion and was deeply gratified to have the cooperation of other scientists and writers in addition to psychologists. In another multidisciplinary venture, he discussed his plan for a conference to be sponsored by the American Association for the Advancement of Science; in a letter of November 12, 1943, F.R. Moulton, its permanent secretary, suggested that the conference might include papers by scientists in various fields on the importance of international cooperation and ways of improving it. Proposals were formulated for investigations of questions that give rise to conflicts and also for the establishment of ethical principles for interrelationships among human beings of different racial, religious, or economic groups. Gardner agreed to contact leaders in psychology, education, psychiatry, sociology and anthropology, leaving the other fields to Dr. Moulton, and he asked Gordon Allport for recommendations of people in his area of specialization, and also asked whether Allport himself would participate.

Allport responded eagerly that such a stirring of scientists might lead to a World Association of Scientists (of which the AAAs could be a branch) devoted to the advancement of science, peace and the public welfare. Gardner and Gordon Allport were of one mind in their hope that science could help in the preservation of peace. The enthusiasm for the project was generated by the crisis of the war, and for the senior scientists, from their memories of the disastrous consequences of the Versailles Treaty after World War I.

Soon Gardner urged Allport to send his magnificent paper, "Restoring Morale in Occupied Territory" to the State Department and other government agencies. Allport was afraid that it would be love's labor lost.

140   Daniel Katz re the lack of hassles: letter to LBM; Akron Archives.
140   Manifesto: G. Allport to GM; Harvard Archives.
142   GM comments, SPSSI Bulletin of January 1938.
142   When the SPSSI yearbook was under way, Gardner wrote suggesting that Allport's seminar could help by (1) organizing, documenting and streamlining (in government report form) the paper on which Allport and Schmeidler worked; (2) making a first draft of the psychological manifesto

which he thought of as "shorter, with heavy emphasis, staccato almost choppy, in its insistence on a few basic things, but giving proof of the points made"; (3) psychologizing the Millspaugh book, *Peace Plans and American Choices,* a gorgeous job that could be stated in terms of psychological postulates and problems; (4) gathering two types of research material— a) psychological survey material as it related to historical issues and b) a survey of experimental matters bearing on peace planning. Gardner suggested that S.H. Duvall of George Williams College, Chicago, had material that would help. He also thought the seminar could consider how Gardner's yearbook plan could be articulated with the psychological kind of yearbook Gordon had suggested.

142 All along, from his 1943 article, "Psychology in the Making of Peace" (*Journal of Abnormal and Social Psychology* 38, No. 1, April 1943), he wrote articles dealing with peace issues—the cold war, atomic fears and others.

During the 1950s and the Vietnam War in the 1960s Gardner continued to lecture and to write on war and peace issues. He also wrote to and interviewed senators McGovern, Muskie and others committed to efforts toward peace, and contributed financially to support their re-election. See folders of peace correspondence in Akron Archives. In addition to his commitment to peace efforts, Gardner supported civil rights struggles; e.g., in the spring of 1941 he chaired the Employer-Employee Conference of the Eastern Psychological Association.

142 In 1986 the *Journal of Social Issues* published J.H. Capshew's study "Networks of Leadership: A Quantitative Study of SPSSI Presidents, 1936–1986." In addition to the fact that Gardner was the second SPSSI president ("chairman" in the first years), nine presidents had been his graduate or undergraduate students. Capshew summarized, "The influence of significant individuals such as Gordon Allport, Kurt Lewin and Gardner Murphy . . . helps explain the formation and continuation of the SPSSI presidential elite." Of the eight SPSSI presidents who, as well as Gardner, had served as presidents of the APA, Tolman, Allport, Hilgard, Newcomb and Clark were friends of Gardner and worked with him in other roles; three recipients of the Award for Distinguished Contributions to Psychology in the Public Interest had been students of Gardner (Clark, Klineberg, Chein). Capshew added, "Gordon Allport, Kurt Lewin and Gardner Murphy can be singled out as especially effective mentors for succeeding SPSSI presidents, who in turn aided the careers of their own students." During World War II this trio also served as consultants to the Department of Agriculture's Division of Program Surveys, directed by Rensis Likert. Three of Gardner's students, Hartley, Klineberg and Newcomb, were employed by the Office of War Information, and Newcomb, Klineberg and Chein worked with the analysis division of the Foreign Broadcast Intelligence Service. In addition, the Strategic Bombing Survey's analysis of civilian morale in Germany and Japan was headed by Rensis Likert, Gardner's student, and that group included his students Eugene Hartley, Otto Klineberg and Theodore Newcomb. Krech commented that the study seemed to be entirely an SPSSI operation. Evenings at Darmstadt and Bad Nauheim were spent in planning the future of social psychology in America, and SPSSI's potential role. That these discussions bore fruit is evident in developments soon after the war. Under Newcomb's direction, a Ph.D. program in social psychology was set up at the University of Michigan in 1947; this program produced 226 Ph.D.s during the next 20

years. By 1947, moreover, Rensis Likert was directing the Institute of Social Research, which included the Survey Research Center and the Research Center for Group Dynamics.

We see from Capshew's and other analyses that Gardner's influence flowed on through many of his students into their various creative undertakings, some of which have continued into the present, although Gardner was no longer "the conscience" of SPSSI in person. As SPSSI grew, factions developed; these did not destroy the organization, but led to new groups that undertook to focus on activist issues beyond the scientific commitment of SPSSI.

142   "The *Human Nature and Enduring Peace* and *In the Minds of Men* books wouldn't have made Gardner seem less a social psychologist. They did not fall into what later could be discerned as the mainstream, but they certainly didn't lead to his being seen as an outsider" (Brewster Smith to LBM, 9-7-83).

143   Re *Human Nature and Enduring Peace*. In the '30s and early '40s when SPSSI was concerned with the psychology of war and its prevention, American imperialism was not far in the past—the acquisition of the Philippines, Puerto Rico, and Pacific territories like American Samoa and Hawaii had been sources of pride. Even though the trend was now in the direction of granting independence to the Philippines and Puerto Rico, the motives of "gain, power and prestige" seemed to have been of major importance not only in the colonial expansion of 19th century Britain, France, Holland, and Italy, but also in that of the United States. Not sufficiently recognized was the German need for "Lebensraum," the need to make conquests that would forever overcome the sense of insecurity and weakness that Germany felt after World War I.

143   Dan Katz letter to LBM. GM chairman, later called president.

144   In concluding his address on SPSSI and race relations, Klineberg acknowledged those who contributed to SPSSI's work on race or international relations. "I start with the name of Gardner Murphy, my very dear friend and teacher, and my Rock of Gibraltar when we were both at Columbia; Gordon Allport, who with Gardner was one of the true builders of social psychology, ... Ted Newcomb, my partner in so many undertakings...."

144   SPSSI continued to work on peace; as late as 1988, the second issue in volume 44 was titled *Psychology and the Promotion of Peace*. It contained ten articles dealing with both strategies and the development of caring people and societies committed to peace. By 1973 a *Journal of Peace Science* was published in collaboration with the Wharton School, University of Pennsylvania and the International Peace Science Society. This was 30 years after Gardner's article asking whether science could prevent war.

144   Erik Erikson, William Stern, and Max Wertheimer all came to New York in 1933. Sigmund Freud and his daughter Anna did not leave Austria until 1938 and David Rapaport came to the United States the same year.

144   Refugees: Allport and GM correspondence; Akron Archives.

144   Hilgard letter to LBM; Akron Archives.

144   Goodwin Watson, *Civilian Morale*, Allport introduction.

145   Hilgard letter to LBM re suspicious organizations.

145   Ross Stagner letter to LBM, 2-10-83, in Akron Archives.

145   Dallenbach letter to Newcomb 3-28-44 regarding failure of continuation of clearance for GM.

146   GM letter re people denied clearance, in Akron Archives.

146 Senator Joseph McCarthy shamed on television December 2, 1954.

146 Freedom of Information Act, FBI report to LBM in Akron Archives. See Schlesinger, Arthur M., Jr., *Freedom of Information Act: The Imperial Presidency,* Boston: Houghton Mifflin, 1973, 349–50. (Act was passed in 1966.)

147 In 1943 or 1944, two men came to our door. They were representatives of the American Labor Party and they were soliciting GM's political endorsement of their platform. Upon hearing of their platform, GM said politely but unequivocally, "That sounds like the Communist party line, and I will have none of it." (This was at the time that Communist participation in the ALP led to the formation of the Liberal Party.) (Al Murphy, 12-11-83.)

147 Daniel Katz letter to LBM; Akron Archives.

148 GM's Kurt Lewin Memorial Award, 1953.

148 In HPA V, 264, Gardner reviews briefly his concern with the use of psychology in international relations and his involvement in peace activities over the years. He saw this concern as taking shape in his Yale years during World War I; his 1915 address in an oratorical competition, "A Larger Neutrality," is in the Akron Archives. He supported the Fellowship of Reconciliation, and in addition to supporting the American Friends Service Committee participated in its Ceylon conference for young diplomats (1955). He saw his book *Human Nature and Enduring Peace* and his work as a UNESCO consultant to the government of India as part of this commitment. After the escalation of nuclear armaments he participated in scientific groups working to reduce nuclear arms.

150 Ralph K. White to LBM re GM's plea for empathy for Russians.

151 Ted Newcomb letter to WBM: Newcomb was describing the climax of a long process. See Gardner's long letter (12-18-42) to Yerkes, and Alice Bryan's letter to me (ca. 1985) for evidence regarding Gardner's early efforts to influence the outcome of the argument about the constitution (Akron Archives). I have no record of the discussions between Gardner and other APA members which I assume had taken place in the days before the meeting.

151 The Yerkes committee included R.M. Elliott, E.G. Boring, E.A. Doll, C.P. Stone, and those who may still be alive are Alice I. Bryan, Carl R. Rogers, and I. (E.L. Hilgard to LBM, 9-6-83.) Among these, in addition to Yerkes, Gardner had friendly relationships with Elliott and Boring.

151 In August 1954, Kenneth B. Clark sought Gardner's assistance. On May 17th the Supreme Court had established the legal principle that state laws which required segregated schools violated the equal protection clause of the Fourteenth Amendment of the United States Constitution. It had postponed the specific decree for the implementation of this decision until after a further discussion of Questions 4 and 5. Question 4 was as follows: a) Would a decree necessarily follow, providing that, within the limitations set by normal school districting, Negro children should forthwith be admitted to schools of their choice, or b) May this court, in the exercise of its equity powers, permit an effective gradual adjustment to be brought about from existing segregated systems to a system not based on color distinctions? The NAACP had asked Kenneth Clark to collect and analyze all of the available evidence on how a change from a segregated to a nonsegregated situation could be smoothly accomplished. Clark expressed his appreciation for Gardner's previous help and counsel, and enclosed the "Social Science Consensus," a statement of social science opinion relevant to Question 4. As he later

stated in an article on "Current Trends in Desegregation" (*American Child*, November 1954), Clark had no illusions about the speed of the process of desegregation. Gardner sent detailed comments on the long memorandum—for example, "I think the argument presented on foot of page 9 and top of page 10 is slippery. The real question, I think, is not whether Southerners are less capable of changing ... but whether they are less capable of changing with respect to the *specific* issue of Negro equality. If the question had been asked: 'Is social change more difficult to expect when there is both ego involvement and group involvement against it?' the answer would be self-evident." He continued to say he thought wishful thinking was preventing the liberals from facing the true obstacles that have to be studied, understood and removed. "Surely everyone knows that it is the social structure of the South, especially its political structure, that makes the problem so massive." Although as a child Gardner knew very little about his father's specific efforts in working for social change in the South, he knew enough to be realistic about the problems involved.

152   It was organizations like SPSSI as they continued to emerge (e.g., the organizations Psychology for Social Responsibility; Consortium on Peace Research, Education and Development; Center for Nonviolent Conflict Resolution; The Fund for Peace; Peace Research Institute; Scientists on Survival; Peace Education Division of the American Friends Service Committee; Council for a Livable World; American Professors for Peace in the Middle East) that contributed to a national climate demanding control and reduction of armaments. Gardner was involved with all of these efforts, giving speeches at conferences, corresponding with scientists and senators, into the early 1970s.

Chapter 14

Sources include L. Nyman's interviews in Recollections, *City College Archives. This collection of 11 extended interviews with former chairmen of the psychology department and veteran members of the department is a rich source of information about Gardner Murphy's years at City College as seen by some of his colleagues as well as by himself; it is also a source of information about American psychology in the 20th century. The foreword to the second edition (revised for the 50th anniversary) adds important reflections on Gardner's contribution: "...his almost religious devotion to the importance of each person's worth set the tone of the department."* Recollections [Rec.], *2nd edition, XI. Henrietta Boettinger's Christmas 1989 letter to LBM regarding the 50th anniversary of the founding of the psychology department and the many memories of Gardner recalled on that occasion was consulted. Sources also included* Reminiscences of City College Days, City Psychology at Fifty, October 20, 1989: *Section on reminiscences of Gardner from 1940 to 1952 by alumni. In City College Archives and Akron Archives. These differ from memories of Columbia students in the '20s and '30s in two respects— the excitement about his personality course and the help he gave to students who were drafted in World War II, giving not only advice but strong recommendations which in some cases led to appointments to such areas as the adjutant general's office and other places in which they could use their psychological training (and at the same time not be involved in military action).*

153   Rec. iii, 20.
154   Rec. 19 re Bertrand Russell. Lawrence Nyman, Rec. 2nd ed., xi: "The Russell

appointment set off a firestorm of controversy over issues of ideology and academic freedom. Murphy's arrival acted as a steadying counterbalance. He nurtured people. Lois Murphy ... described this quality: 'he doesn't derogate, attack or assault other people's ideas ... he presents ... his perspectives like someone showing you his garden.' Murphy brought to the department a genius for encouraging each person to find his/her strengths and then providing an atmosphere [of] opportunities to examine the new discoveries."

154   "Appointed professor of philosophy at the City College of the University of New York: denounced by clergy and religious organizations; City Council condemns him as 'an enemy of religion and morality.' A taxpayer's suit brought by a Brooklyn housewife resulted in a judicial order to rescind the appointment on March 30; appeal was denied and the appointment remained invalidated." Russell was appointed William James Lecturer at Harvard in 1940, after the events at City College. Source: Paul Grimly Kuntz, *Bertrand Russell,* Boston: G.K. Hall & Co., Twayne Publishers, 1986.

154   The program was expanded, new courses were added. Peatman commented that the psychology department at City College became virtually a satellite of Columbia, since many of the members of the department had Columbia Ph.D.s; these included Peatman, Barmack, Mintz, Smith, K.B. Clark, E. Hartley, L. Plotkin, M. Blum, A. Fromme, J. Orlansky, C. Seitz, M. Smith, during Gardner's tenure at City College. Of these, Smith, Clark, Hartley, and Fromme had worked with Gardner at Columbia. Counting the 23rd Street branch at Baruch School and the evening session faculty, the department grew to about 25 members. Rec. Peatman.

154   According to a formula implemented by the dean, the expansion in number of faculty took into account the size of a class, the hours of the class and recognition that some advanced courses required more preparation. For an advanced course, the ratio of students to teachers was between 20 and 30 to one; for specialized courses like experimental and statistics, a small class load was usual. Rec. G.M.

154   Improved status of CCNY: Ross Stagner to LBM.

155   10,000 Rec. 3; GM research, Rec. 4.

156   M.A. program, Rec. 22, 36–37; Barmack administration, Rec. 38, 6: City College was awarded the clinical psychology doctoral program by the City University in 1964 because Gardner started a clinical M.A. in 1943. This program which Joe Barmack administered under Gardner's overall leadership was years ahead of its time. After Gardner left in 1952, some senior professors objected to the Freudian orientation of the old program and, while it remained clinical, it became more eclectic. Nevertheless, Gardner's foresight gave the psychology department the edge in strong competition with Brooklyn, Queens, Hunter, etc.

156   "I [Plotkin] can recount an anecdote about our M.A. program which illustrates its national reputation right after World War II. I attended an APA meeting with a classmate of mine at City College who had his graduate work with Carl Rogers at Ohio State. We went to lunch with a group of western psychologists where the discussion at the table turned to graduate programs. The consensus was that the City College had the best M.A. program in clinical psychology in the country" (L. Plotkin to LBM, 6-19-84).

156   In the following year Ruth Munroe began to alternate the Rorschach course

with Bruno Klopfer and Bela Mittelmann. In the second semester of 1948 Ruth Munroe and Bela Mittelmann brought in as guest lecturers Lauretta Bender (a child psychiatrist working with severely disturbed children), David Rapaport, known for his theoretical writings in clinical psychology, Molly Harrower, another Rorschach psychologist, and Roy Schafer. In the late '40s, the two analysts left. René Spitz went to Colorado and Ernst Kris became deeply involved in research at the Yale Child Study Center. David Beres, another friend of ours who was a member of the New York Psychoanalytic Institute, took over Kris' theory course, and the Spitz course on the psychoanalytic study of the child was covered first by Katherine Wolf and later by Martha Wolfenstein.

156   Number of Ph.D.s had undergraduate training at CCNY; special situation of CCNY, Rec. 39.

157   Milton Smith, Rec. 24f, 99. Kenneth B. Clark, Rec. MO.

158   Schmeidler re Harvard summer 1942, Rec. 134; Henrietta Boettinger, 52f.

159   Wartime decisions, Rapp-Coudert investigations, Rec. 2 regarding support from Dean Gottschall.

159   Larry Plotkin's 6-19-84 letter to LBM stated: "My memory of the Rapp-Coudert Committee is that testimony by two former members of the City College Communist Party cell was the basis for the discharge of many people at City College. I believe that Walter Neff was the only member of the department of psychology to be fired. Max Hertzman was identified as a party member by one informant but was not fired. In the McCarthy years, he was called in for questioning but, again, was not fired. Max never was permitted by the board of higher education to be promoted to full professor. Bishop Manning had nothing to do with Rapp—but was, I believe, an opponent of the appointment of Bertrand Russell."

159   For Rapp-Coudert Committee (New York State Legislature) see: Schrecker, Ellen W., *No Ivory Tower: McCarthyism and the Universities.* New York and Oxford: Oxford University Press, 1986: "[In 1940, the committee] ... was to identify as Communists dozens of New York City College teachers and to initiate what was, until the height of the McCarthy era ... by far the largest purge of politically undesirable professors ever."

160   Larry Plotkin to LBM 6-14-84: "Gardner ... set a precedent for civility in the department which lasted many years after his departure.... No psychologist trained between 1940 and 1970 was uninfluenced by Gardner's contributions."

160   I do not know of any studies of the relation of an institutional atmosphere of enthusiasm to the productivity of the staff, but from the examples of the Harvard department of social relations, the Chicago Committee on Human Development, and the City College department of psychology it looks as if a warmly supportive atmosphere contributes to creativity. With the opposite influence—when hostile pressures, demands, and criticism dominate the atmosphere—creativity can be stifled; I felt this was true at Berkeley in the '40s when the very gifted Jean Macfarlane failed to produce an integrated volume built out of her prodigious experience and insights. A negative effect on productivity can be seen in a hierarchical organization in which the executive is not only dominating but, out of a craving for maximum power, does not provide the kind of support given by President Wright and Dean Gottschall at City College.

Chapter 15

Sources include notes by GM entitled Filter paper; an interview with A. Marrow in which GM discussed Kurt Lewin at length; LBM's memories of our joint contacts with many of the people discussed here, along with memories of the state of psychology in the '20s and '30s and of the activities of psychologists and psychoanalysts we knew. Publications of some of the psychologists mentioned are listed in the bibliography.

162   Heimich Klüver, Filter paper.
163   Charlotte Bühler, Filter paper and my recollections; report of C.B.'s clinical work in L.A. by Georgene Seward to me. She also worked vigorously in Los Angeles to develop a new organization, Humanistic Psychology, which Gardner joined belatedly in the late sixties. He had repeatedly said in conversation that he did *not* believe in a "third force," which this organization proposed to be, especially as A. Maslow urged.
163   Kurt Lewin: Filter paper, personal discussions with GM and LBM, interview with Alfred Marrow; LBM and GM at "Topology" meetings, 1936.
166   William Stern: LBM and GM discussion with him and with Max Wertheimer at Kings' Crown Hotel; Filter paper.
166   Wolfgang Köhler: Filter paper.
167   Rudolf Arnheim: LBM and GM visits with him in New York, New Hampshire, at Harvard.
167   Jean Piaget: Filter paper and visits with LBM and GM in Topeka.
167   Anna Hartoch: LBM collaboration with her.
168   Klopfer: LBM Rorschach session with him, and appointment by him to the board of the *Journal of Projective Techniques.*
168   Ernst Schachtel: LBM and GM visits with him.
168   Erik Erikson and Joan Erikson: Filter paper and many visits.
169   Peter Blos: Many visits in New Hampshire.
170   Erich Fromm and Fritz Redl: LBM attendance at seminars in the Zachry study of adolescents.
170   René Spitz: joined the City College Clinical M.A. program and we saw him personally from time to time.
170   David Rapaport: Filter paper and our joint visits with him.
171   Ruth Munroe, my Vassar friend and graduate school roommate: Filter paper and very many visits.

Chapter 16

Sources include family letters, including our letters to MKM when we were away, letters from Cousin Catharine, my letters to my family, and Gardner's letters to me before and after we were married. My recollections of those years were the major source for the development of our relationship, our work together on Experimental Social Psychology, *my research and teaching, our family life in New York, Bronxville, New Hampshire, and our travels.*

177   "Electrical" conversations: "The Psychologists," Kra. II, 331.
177   *Dyadic Thought and Work,* unpublished, Akron Archives.
177   *A New Kind of World,* HPA V, 259.
178   LBM to GM, July 1925 from Chicago; in Akron Archives.

178   GM letter to LBM, summer 1925; in Akron Archives.
179   Margaret Alexander (Bunch) letter to LBM in Akron Archives. Yonghy-
        Bonghy Bo, *Walrus and the Carpenter,* Masefield.
179   Yonghy-Bonghy Bo, Edward Lear: Holbrook Jackson, *The Complete Nonsense
        of Edward Lear.* Dover: 1951, 257.
181   Sensory delights, GM and Herbert Spohn, *Encounter with Reality,* 1968.
181   Czecho-Slovak dance song, "Tansui, Tansui."
182   Birds in New Hampshire through the 1960s included over 40 species around
        our own house; they diminished in the following decades due to the destruc-
        tion of winter habitats in South America by ranchers destroying forests in
        order to develop grazing areas.
183   Cousin Will Elkin; see his biography.
183   Birchlea is the early form of my family name, Barclay, and the acres on which
        we built our house had many birch trees.
183   *Beginners' Star Book,* Kelvin McCready (pseudonym for EGM).
184   Mary (Frank) Perry, school psychologist (coauthor with L.K. Frank) as a
        20-year-old.
187   King Arthur books, Oz books.
187   Al Murphy, memories at the 1979 APA Memorial Service: "Gardner Murphy
        was my father. And one of his favorite stories was about a Grecian named
        Aristides the Just. And all the time he was known as Aristides the Just. And
        finally somebody said, I think Aristides should be banished from Greece.
        They said, 'Why?' He said, 'I'm tired of hearing him called "the Just."' Well,
        we have been talking about a person who is regarded as a saint but he was
        also a person who was capable of being annoyed and being irritated at an-
        noying and irritating things. And he would respond in quite the proper an-
        noyed and irritated way. One of the favorite memories that I have of Dad
        was that across the street from us, when I was young, was a man who was
        a stockbroker. Every day he would greet Dad at the bus station and would
        say, 'Good morning, Professor.' Well, Dad was very, very patient about this.
        And one day Dad said to me, 'One of my fondest wishes would be ... to
        get up the courage as he says, "Good morning, Professor," to return with
        "Good morning, Dealer in Stocks and Bonds."' Dad had a very trenchant
        humor which was saved for the appropriate moments. I also, as a kid, had
        difficulty finding out exactly what the nature of his work was. Psychology is
        not the kind of thing you can put in your pocket and take out. Everybody
        else's parents were teachers or businessmen or newspapermen. And he said,
        "I'm a psychologist." At that time I was very much into Sherlock Holmes,
        and I read this thing in which Dr. Watson was trying to figure out what
        Sherlock Holmes did. So he wrote a catalog of all the things that Sherlock
        Holmes did, hoping it would come out to some sort of intelligible total. And
        so I wrote, 'Goes out at 9:00 in the morning, comes back at 5:00 in the after-
        noon. Loves Beethoven's Seventh, is very fond of reading Popeye, interested
        in current affairs, but does not become overawed by political trends.' This
        was at about age ten when I tried to figure out what was going on. And one
        day I asked him, 'What exactly do you do? What really do you stand for?'
        And he said, 'Let me think about it for a minute. What we should do is sit
        down and talk.' And I said, 'All right.' And so we had a discussion in which
        he explained that which I had assumed to be the unexplainable. And twenty
        years after that, I saw a movie called *Twelve Angry Men* in which there
        were eleven jurors who wanted to convict and one who just wanted to sit

down and talk because he thought the fellow deserved a chance. Dad saw the movie with me, and he said, 'Yes, that's what I was trying to tell you when you were ten years old.' So if you ever want to remember Dad, just say, 'Let's sit down and talk and keep the door open.'"

187   He loved *Gulliver's Travels* more than anything from the 16th to the 19th centuries; he loved the names of the Lilliputians and the Brobdingnagians, etc., and the wordplay. He enjoyed words with a little bump in them. When someone asked him how a genius like Swift conceived of *Gulliver's Travels,* Gardner answered, "Once you think of big people and little people, the rest is easy." Other kinds of wordplay he enjoyed included those in *Jabberwocky, Alice in Wonderland, Nize Baby,* the limerick writers, and most of Edward Lear.

189   Comment by LBM: Conspicuous in Gardner's college writings and the comments by his faculty is the absence of any evidence of his humor, or spontaneity, as we knew him in the family. The "sober as a judge" Yale man had within himself potentialities that apparently were submerged during Hotchkiss and Yale years. Was this due to his sense of responsibility as a scholarship student, or to the stress of his father's illness and death, or simply to the achievement pressures from his parents? It is hard to say.

None of the Yale teachers commented on a "lack of good judgment" that he himself mentioned in his "Study of Myself" and which certain friends criticized. I rarely saw examples of this.

Chapter 17

In addition to the book Personality: Biosocial Approaches, *sources for this chapter include* Origins and Structures, *previous discussions of personality in* Approaches to Personality, *1932,* General Psychology, *1933,* Outline of Abnormal Psychology, *and* Public Opinion and the Individual, *with Rensis Likert, 1938.*

Since Gardner always made a complete outline for an article or a book from which he dictated or wrote, it makes sense for us to review the table of contents of Personality: A Biosocial Approach to Origins and Structure *before discussing some of its important contributions. The outline itself tells a story and reveals the architecture of his system.*

Gardner's wide range of allusions to writers and artists will not be referenced here; to do so would take another chapter.

In his 1947 foreword, Gardner concluded, "This is an attempt to formulate hypotheses which my wife and I have studied, applied, and redefined in teaching, and in research with young children and young adults, for some fifteen years." Along with his study with Rensis Likert of public opinion and the development of individual students, and his supervision of Columbia graduate students' researches, he had carried on a series of studies at City College with senior honors students. During this same period, I had completed my study of sympathy and its relation to other behavior of preschool children, and followed this with a study of personality in young children. I participated in the Bank Street College study of seven- to eight-year-old children and worked with a Sarah Lawrence College group of faculty on a study of freshmen students. We shared the findings from all of these with each other, and especially Gardner's sections on the Self, Wholeness, and the Individual and the Group, including vignettes and extended quotations from these studies. It is true that there are no complete case studies and Gardner made it clear that he could not attempt a thorough clinical assessment of a personality; he wanted to show the range of questions that would need to be answered in order to accomplish that.

193   Nomothetic: dealing with principles, not individual persons.
193   My research on personality of young children began in 1937 at the Sarah
            Lawrence College Nursery School.

194   Eclectic as *Approaches to Personality* was, it contained no hint of the far wider and deeper scope of his thinking about personality as it evolved through the next decade. A subtle hint, however, can be seen in the statement he made repeatedly about a moment of consolidation of a deep commitment to personality study at the end of that summer.

194   *Approaches to Personality* was not Gardner's first integrative project since it came on the heels of the *Historical Introduction to Modern Psychology* and *Experimental Social Psychology*. But I think it was the boldest conception, and led in time to his magnum opus, *Personality: A Biosocial Approach*. To trace antecedents of modern psychological concepts in Aristotle and Pythagoras was not very far from the analyses of relationships between Greek and modern philosophy. To lift social psychology out of the armchair and establish its scientific credibility with *Experimental Social Psychology* was a grand extension of Floyd Allport's beginning.

194   Gardner's early respect for Freud's contribution to psychology was recognized by an invitation from the Division of Clinical Psychology to give an address honoring the centenary of Freud's birth at the American Psychological Association conference, August 30, 1956. Gardner believed that a dynamic psychology aware of unconscious conflicts could not have developed without Freud's contribution. This lecture was first published in *American Psychologist*, vol. 11, no. 12, December 1956, 663–72, and reprinted in L.B. Murphy's *There Is More Beyond: Selected Papers by Gardner Murphy*, Jefferson, N.C.: McFarland, 1989.

196   Eugene Lerner had studied with Piaget in Geneva and with the psychiatrist James Plant after receiving a Ph.D. in sociology. His approach used simple experimental procedures for evoking the child's response to blocking; influenced by Piaget he was, although warm, still critical of my Miniature Toy Play approach, in which I merely said, "You may do anything you like with the toys." I was interested in the child's spontaneous way of revealing his experience, anxieties, and way of structuring his life.

196   Variability in a child's behavior: this was studied from charts of behavior recorded in my sympathy study of Betsy; in *Social Behavior and Child Personality*, 1937.

197   Gardner used the term "man" as equivalent to "human beings" including women and children. There was no conflict between this usage and his warm feminist position as illustrated in his support of female students, colleagues and relatives.

197   "William James on the Will": in *There Is More Beyond: Selected Papers by Gardner Murphy*, Jefferson, N.C.: McFarland, 1989.

197   Gardner read widely in the James literature. In addition to Perry, R.B., *The Thought and Character of William James*, 2 vols., 1935, he read *The Letters of William James*, 1920, edited by his son Henry James. And of course, William James' *Principles of Psychology*, 2 vols., 1890; among other books by James, Gardner treasured *The Varieties of Religious Experience*, 1902, *The Will to Believe, and Other Essays in Popular Philosophy*, new imprint, 1912. Gardner's presidential address, "William James on the Will," was delivered to the American Psychological Association's Division on the History of Psychology, September 1, 1968.

197   He never felt, as James felt: "What an awful trade that of professor is—paid to talk, talk, talk! ... It would be an awful universe if *everything* could be converted into words, words, words!" William James Letters I, 337–38;

letter to Grace Norton, 12-28-1892. As an adult Gardner was always interested in words, what you could do with them or play with them, what correct usage was. He was upset when people treated "data" as a singular noun
instead of the plural that it is, and when they used the expression "different
than" when "different from" was correct. While he was not a purist — he
could use informal off-the-street phrases — he enjoyed good form in writing,
prose or poetry, as well as vivid expressions.

203   "Canalization" was the term Gardner used to try to rescue the vast array of
tastes, preferences, values, interests, and attachments from the term "conditioning." As a term it does not seem more burdensome than conditioning
but it has not been adopted as widely as the need for it demands. Most sensory delights, most pleasures of every kind are *not* conditioned; they are
canalized as a consequence of their direct ability to satisfy.

205   In addition to canalization and conditioning, Gardner had already been aware
of the importance of perceptual learning in his *Briefer General Psychology*,
1933, and after Sherif he emphasized perceptual learning "in contradistinc-
tion to behavior learning."

212   Gardner deals only with the positive contributions of the family to society. The
complexities, conflicts, traumas of family life which contribute to the personality disturbances clinics struggle to alleviate are not discussed in this
chapter, despite his earlier experiences at McLean Hospital, and his *Outline
of Abnormal Psychology*. He compared his approach to that of discovering
what makes a tree (not what makes a diseased tree). Only in his discussion
of cultural liabilities does he offer a glimpse of insecurities and other aspects
of American culture which can distort personalities.

213   Century of Progress Exposition (Chicago) 1933. See "The WPA Guide to
Illinois" in *The Federal Writers' Project Guide to 1930's Illinois*, New York:
Pantheon Books, 1983, reprint, 45.

214   Generativity is the term introduced by the Eriksons in their discussion of the
life cycle; it expresses the caring, giving, constructive, creative contribution
of a fully mature person. GM to Riley Gardner: "I have learned so much
from Erikson."

215   H.A. Murray, whose pioneer *Explorations in Personality* won worldwide acclaim,
wrote in the *Survey Graphic:* "The sweep of Professor Murphy's masterpiece
reveals that psychology is not a heap of inarticulated bones, an arsenal of
brass instruments, . . . it is a measureless expanse of fertile fields, and forests
teeming with progeny . . . a responsible fellowship . . . of spacious well-
furnished minds that reach through time, backward and forward. . . .
Murphy, in short, is wholly mindful of the whole of man. This *is*
'Psychology.' The word 'biosocial' in the subtitle merely hints of its great
range, from the smallest chemical to the largest societal elements and forms.
Considering the complexity of the subject matter . . . this is an architectural
feat of the first magnitude, which was accomplished . . . mostly by em-
bracing contraries and relegating each to a different level of determinism.
Modestly he calls his Mont Blanc merely an 'approach' but, in truth, the
more confident books on personality when placed around it, look like little
peaks of arrogant sectarianism."

215   When he protested in a 1954 letter to Calvin Hall, who based his discussion
of Gardner's biosocial theory solely on *Personality*, Gardner stated that,
"Many aspects of personality theory in which I am interested, for example
the conceptual place of social attitudes in the total structure, problems of

specificity and generality of attitude, are considered in the first edition of *Experimental Social*—and a good deal of this still remains in the second edition." In addition, the first edition of *Experimental Social Psychology* contained an account of "brain drives," in which he "developed the notion that the central nervous system is itself a source of motivation"; later with Hochberg, he presented his position that "this abolished all basic cleavages between cognitive and affective processes." "Also, some of the psychical research articles developed dimensions of personality which I mistakenly felt could not be put into the 1947 book"—e.g., his discussion of field theory in his presidential address to the SPR (London) in 1949, and his 1953 paper in the *Proceedings* of the London SPR.

Although I (LBM) thought that in 1947 he regarded *Personality* as his major contribution, he contradicted this in his 1954 letter to Calvin Hall: "The original work that I have been able to stimulate in parapsychology is really beginning to make a lot of dents now, and a great many of the empirical studies I was able to sponsor at Columbia, at City College and here at Menninger's are likely to outlive by far any formulation I could make in a literary manner. I certainly do not think my theory is either definitive or comprehensive" (as he said in his last chapter).

215   Although Gardner was accused of seeing "only the good" in others, he was sensitive and open to derogations of himself. He wrote (1954) that he was "not admitted in good society"; "dozens of my particular ideas are viewed with considerable eyebrow-lifting. I am classified with the tender-minded.... My interest in parapsychology shows how uncritical I am. I'm an 'encyclopedist' rather than a 'research man' ... I am regarded as a forgivable eccentric." To this, Hall replied (1954), "I do not think you are an off-beat eccentric and I do not think other psychologists think so either. Of course, you are classified as one of the tender-minded but all decent people are.... Your humanism and engaging style may annoy some of our hard-boiled brethren ... but they are ... a noisy obstreperous neo-fascist minority who seem to scare some people by their authoritarian pronouncements.... You are the finest representative of the grass roots of psychology in this country ... your ideas permeate all of contemporary psychology ... your books are widely used and read and many of us feel that you are one of our most illustrious representatives in the larger world of affairs."

215   S.S. Stagner wrote, "The profound effect of GM's *Personality* is noted not only in articles and books" on personality but also "Social psychologists in the '50s and '60s were markedly influenced by it." Undated, probably 1987.

Chapter 18

Sources: From our earliest encounter, Gardner discussed psychical research with me, read to me records which he later included in The Challenge of Psychical Research *and in the 1920s included me in some experiments. My memories of these discussions and of remarks by some of his friends, especially Frank Lorimer, Faith Williams, and Helen Lynd, oriented me to his situation in New York. Recollections of that period shaped my approach to this chapter.*

Gardner's autobiographies in HPA V, Kra II, and Notes for a Parapsychological Autobiography *review some of his early work and its importance to him in terms of both its potential implications for humanity and the scientific problem it presented. The discussions of Gardner's colleagues in psychical research in the* Journal of the American Society for Psychical Research *(J. ASPR), January 1980, are rich in details both about specific undertakings, such events as the 1936 confrontation in an APA symposium, and sensitive observations of Gardner's relationships to young scientists.*

Karlis Osis' account of the years 1941–84 provides an historical context for Gardner's work at the ASPR. See Osis, K., "The American Society for Psychical Research 1941–1985: A Personal View," J. ASPR 79, 1985, 501–29.

As a developmental psychologist and reader of biographies, I reflected on aspects of his early experiences which I felt were important in the evolution of Gardner's deep commitment to the search for answers to questions raised by spontaneous psychical events. My approach is shaped by total respect for that search, and a belief that in time, an interdisciplinary effort bridging physics and neuropsychology will bring understanding.

Gardner's extensive writings on psychical research are included in the chronological bibliography of his works in There Is More Beyond: Selected Papers by Gardner Murphy, *published by McFarland, 1989. These are the most important sources for study of his work. Correspondence regarding psychical research, especially during his years as president of the ASPR, are in archives there, and in the Gardner Murphy Archives at Menninger.*

While I totally supported Gardner's work in psychical research, my own contributions were limited to two series of experiments in 1926–27 and 1948, along with brief trials with the Rhine cards and some informal experiments. I found that as wife, mother, homemaker, and teacher I could not give a major block of time to parapsychology. Research on nursery school children could be fitted into an hour a day, in the morning, after my children were in school and before my teaching schedule began. I followed Gardner's work and some of the developments in psychical research sufficiently to keep updated with Gardner's thinking. My reflections on his commitment to psychical research were first published as "The Evolution of Gardner Murphy's Thinking in Psychology and Psychical Research," J. ASPR, 82, no. 2, April 1988, 101–14. This is a revision of my lecture April 10, 1987, at the Cosmos Club, Washington, D.C.

216   Parapsychology (psychical research) includes telepathy, clairvoyance and precognition as mental experiences not involving sensory activity. It also includes physical events, such as poltergeists, which refer to movement of objects with no physical force apparent, and in addition mental control of objects (psychokinesis).

216   See my paper, "The Evolution of Gardner Murphy's Thinking in Psychology and Psychical Research," J. ASPR, 82, no. 2, April 1988, 101–14, for a more extended discussion of Gardner's childhood concern about souls.

217   "Modern liberal religion" did not focus on salvation or assurance of getting to heaven. The "social gospel" emphasized the social concerns of Deuteronomy, the Old Testament prophets and the New Testament writers: "faith, hope and love — and *love* (caritas, caring) is the greatest of these." This did not provide the emotional release of the old evangelical religion, which recovered influence in the last quarter of the twentieth century.

218   "Finally demolished": See Gardner's long intense 1916 letter to his brother DuBose, regarding his struggle for truth (Akron Archives).

219   Harry Helson, famous for his adaptation level theory, described in an autobiographical account (HPA V, 103+) his childhood encounters with spiritualists and some of the phenomena of parapsychology, especially

poltergeist experiences—for instance, the violent shaking of a hod of coal in the kitchen, although no one was near it. In his third year of graduate work at Harvard he became an assistant to Gardner who was then commuting from New York to carry on psychical research studies as the Hodgson Psychical Research Fellow. During that year they investigated the Margery mediumship and Helson found pieces of string which Margery's confederate in the basement was using to pull a piano stool six or seven feet away from its place. Helson's presence at the seances was then no longer desired. Helson and Gardner remained good friends throughout their lives.

219   The stipend from the Richard Hodgson Fund was referred to as a Fellowship by McDougall and in some letters from Gordon Allport and from Boring although in another letter, Boring states, "There never was a Fellowship." Evidently the stipend was treated like a Fellowship. See my correspondence in 1989 with James Matlock and with Rhea White, editor of J. ASPR, in 1989, in ASPR Archives.

219   In a typical Warcollier experiment, the agent (or the telepathic sender) would concentrate upon a drawing, and the percipient (or receiver) would draw the impression occurring to him while in a relaxed state of reverie. What distinguishes Warcollier's approach is that he considered as evidence of telepathy correspondences which were not literal or exact; indeed, he considered it typical of telepathy as a "primary process" that transformations and alterations in imagery should occur.

Listening to him explain Warcollier's conceptions, I was also exposed to the thinking of Bergson on the nature of time, Jaensch on imagery, Janet on dissociation, Levy-Bruhl on primitive thinking, and Goldstein and Klüver on perception. Donald Cook, J. ASPR, January 1980, 95–96.

221   The Taves Machine was a multicompartmented motor-driven rotating tray with a glass cover, permitting the contents to be photographed. Objects such as dice and coins were placed in the tray, one in each compartment. When the tray was in use it was in a closed and locked room. Both the tray and overhead camera were operated by remote control. A mercury commutator switch was so arranged that the tray was stopped in a horizontal position, glass top up. The solenoid-controlled camera photographed the contents when the tray had stopped rotating. Subjects in a distant room recorded their guesses or predictions regarding the contents. These data sheets were later checked against the photographic record and the results analyzed. I don't recall that our results were very exciting, but it was a good experimental setup, not susceptible either in cheating by subjects or the (witnessed) experimenter. Ernest Taves' letter to LBM, 1987.

From 1941, he was a leader in the activities of the American Society for Psychical Research, guiding its policies and encouraging its research, and holding various offices in it, including the presidency from 1962 to 1970. As must by now be clear, the thrust of his efforts was always to make it better than it was, not in competition but in cooperation with any other laboratory or society or foundation (Gertrude Schmeidler, *Parapsychology Review,* July–August 1976, 9).

After 1941, the *Journal of the American Society for Psychical Research* contained one or more contributions from Gardner in nearly every issue, and after 1950 he published papers in the *Journal of Parapsychology* and the *International Journal of Parapsychology* as well. See Bibliography in L.B. Murphy, *There Is More Beyond,* McFarland, 1989.

222   Karlis Osis' tribute to GM in J. ASPR 74, January 1980.
222   He gave Maimonides a grant which was used for "Gardner Murphy
       Fellowships." S. Krippner, J. ASPR 74, January 1980, 59.
222   Eileen Coly, J. ASPR 74, January 1980.
223   "It says much for the determination and devotion of both Eileen Garrett and
       Gardner Murphy that they harnessed together so well her extroverted and
       somewhat theatrical personality with his rather introverted, scholarly at-
       titude toward nearly everything that attracted his attention." Ian Stevenson,
       J. ASPR 74, January 1980, 81.
224   Kidd estate: see correspondence in ASPR Archives.
225   Newcomers to parapsychology in future years will encounter Gardner Murphy's
       contributions. One influence is the example Murphy provides of persistence
       in the pursuit of science in this field, undistracted by dogma of any kind,
       willing to suspend judgment, responding to frustration and minor successes
       with his continued quest from which alone could come future major suc-
       cesses. Irvin Child, J. ASPR 74, January 1980, 126.
225   See Irvin Child's tribute in J. ASPR 74, January 1980.
226   F.W.H. Myers lecture, published in 1971, "Frederick Myers and the Subliminal
       Self," J. ASPR 65, 130–43.
229   "I linger . . .," The Challenge of Psychical Research, 273.
230   "First Steps," ibid., 285.
231   J.B. Conant, On Understanding Science, 1951.

Chapter 19

Sources include Gardner's correspondence in preparation for and following
his UNESCO assignment, which are kept at the History of Psychology Archives at
Akron. My notes on the opening conference in New Delhi are also there. Gardner's
book In the Minds of Men, Basic Books, 1953, presents a distillation of the steps
followed and major findings of the studies; reports to UNESCO and correspondence
with UNESCO individuals in the Akron Archives provide more detail. Observations of
villages in India and descriptions of experiences there draw on my own extensive
recollections. Also see Kaegl, Adolf, The Rig-Veda: The Oldest Literature of the
Indians, translated by R. Arrowsmith, Boston: Ginn, 1886, and Hume, Robert E.
(translator), The Thirteen Principal Upanishads, New York: Charles Scribner's Sons,
1932.
      The Bhagavad Gita, the best known book in Hindu religion, was very useful. It
is available in many editions.

239   It has often been said that Gardner and I were given a UNESCO appointment
       for the work in India in 1950. Actually, the UNESCO appointment was
       Gardner's. I was simultaneously invited by the Sarabhais to help plan an in-
       stitute that would contribute to the welfare of children. It evolved into an
       Institute of Mental Health.
       I accompanied Gardner to the universities of Aligarh, Lucknow, Patna, Cal-
       cutta and Bombay, participating in observations and discussions and giving
       talks in each of those areas; but I did not go with him to the South Indian
       cities of Madras, Bangalore and Poona.
239   Gautam Sarabhai, owner of the Calico Mill, was administrator of a large

bequest from an aunt who wished that it be used to benefit children. Gautam's wife, Kamalini Khatau, had established a small school for young children (of all social classes) and had visited the creative Bank Street College in New York City, a center of progressive thinking about education. Gautam had wide contacts with artists in New York; one of these was Kurt Roesch, a colleague of mine at Sarah Lawrence. They were both gifted, cultivated, creative people who worked toward improvement of resources to meet needs in Ahmedabad. Gautam, for instance, developed model houses for mill workers and introduced improvements in working conditions in the Calico Mill. He also developed a subsidiary of Squibb Pharmaceutical Company and was a member of the board of Air India.

239   The urgency to explore reasons for tensions grew in part from conditions after the partition of Pakistan and India, when Hindus and other non–Moslems in Pakistan were bitter about their plight as objects of hostility there, and when they sought refuge in India, resented the severe deprivation and savage attacks they met. Other sources of tension of longer standing came into the awareness of the government as attention was stimulated by the religious conflicts. See 242, 247f.

Gardner saw his UNESCO project as the impetus to discussions of international relations and to contacts with other groups such as the Center for Conflict Resolution at the University of Michigan where a leading member of SPSSI was located and to Donald Michael's work at the Institute for Policy Studies. He wrote that "a tiny dent on the war problem is being made by psychology" and he found that deeply gratifying.

We were together at several dinners given by governors or vice-chancellors, and Zakir Hussein — later president of India — visited us in New York. Because of my extensive observations of children with the Sarabhais, Gardner asked me to write a chapter on child development in India for his book *In the Minds of Men.*

The Constitution of UNESCO states that "since wars begin in the minds of men, it is in the minds of men that the defenses of peace must be constructed." This was the source of Gardner's title for his book on the UNESCO tensions project in India: *In the Minds of Men.*

240   "Immediacy of relating": we found no communication problems at all. From the highest social level to the simplest, the people were spontaneously expressive. I sat next to a policeman on a trip from Calcutta to Santiniketan — an educated, intelligent man. When I commented to a village headman who displayed his daughter's dowry — an array of gold jewelry, and one gold embroidered sari — that I had never seen so much gold in my life, he laughed and said, "You Americans hide it in those vaults in Kentucky."

Bearers are multipurpose assistants who do errands, get travel tickets, carry suitcases and handle many chores that our secretaries generally disdain to handle.

241   The government leaders involved in the UNESCO project were highly intelligent, sophisticated men, warm, gracious, congenial to work with.

242   *Mother India,* a book devastatingly critical of India, focused on the poverty, disease, illiteracy and other problems of India.

244   At Wardha, the upper border of a meeting room included a series of portraits of religious leaders — Moses, Buddha, Mohammed, Jesus — illustrating the tolerance and respect which had contributed to the long persistence of India which survived through absorbing new ideologies and faith.

249   Mahasabha is a political group.
251   We returned for two weeks in 1955 and again in 1960, consulting with the BM
      Institute in Ahmedabad and some of the universities.
251   The publication and reviews of *In the Minds of Men* in 1953 were followed by
      an increase in invitations to participate in international conferences and in
      conferences dealing with international problems. There were invitations to
      address other meetings as well but Gardner had to refuse most of those in
      order to protect time for research; conferences dealing with international
      relationships and strategies to work toward peace had a high priority
      throughout his active life. One of the meetings in which he was especially
      interested was the American Friends Service Committee conference of junior
      diplomats and social scientists in 1955 in Sri Lanka, which he combined with
      another visit to India.

Chapter 20

*Sources include letters between Sibylle Escalona and GM 1951–1959, letters from
David Rapaport and Paul Bergman regarding research before 1954, Gardner's letters to
Eastern friends regarding his experience in the early '50s and '60s, and GM correspondence accepting or rejecting speaking invitations, to Kansas U.S. Senators regarding nuclear arms control, and with scientists concerning issues in psychology and
plans for conferences.*

*Also of use were LBM memories of discussions related to the move to Kansas and
work at the Menninger Foundation.*

Menninger Foundation reports in publications for staff and trustees are cited.

*Other sources include letters to LBM after the death of GM re his work at Men-
ninger Foundation — especially from Robert Wallerstein, Robert Sommer, Leonard
Horwitz, Robert Holt, Herbert Spohn, Joseph Kovach, and Cotter Hirschberg. Of value
were LBM discussions with William Key, Lester Roach, T. Dolgoff, I. Sheffel, Dr. Karl,
and others.*

*Manuscripts recording early plans and unpublished lectures and notes regarding
research or concepts being developed were also used.*

*Photographs of GM during those years, all of which are in the GM section of the
Menninger Archives, William Key's records of the community projects, reprints of
research reports, books by research staff and GM, and letters from Karl Menninger after
GM left the Foundation were also of use.*

252   During our years at the Menninger Foundation there were overtures from other
      universities in locations to which Gardner did not want to move. He did not
      consider leaving until 1956, when City College developed plans for a
      Research Institute to be headed by Gardner—a plan approved at all levels
      until it was rejected by the state authority on the grounds that it would not
      be fair to the other colleges in the New York City University system.
252   The *Menninger Bulletin* contains articles reporting on some of the work in the
      '40s. Until 1946–47, when Dr. Will returned from the Army, the Founda-
      tion was organized in four sections: clinical services, administrative services,
      educational services, and research services; with Robert Knight, John Stone,
      Karl Menninger, and David Rapaport as directors and Dr. Will Menninger
      as overall coordinator.
252   In a memorandum dated January 22, 1953, David Rapaport reviewed the

history of psychology in the Menninger Foundation. Steady growth was noted from the days of psychological testing at Southard School in the '30s to combined training and research in the '40s under Rapaport. After studying with Kurt Lewin in Germany for a year, Rapaport came to the University of Kansas where he studied psychological testing and held seminars for Menninger interns in the Children's Service. He then entered analysis with the intention of making psychoanalysis into a "respectable science."

At this time Karl Menninger was completing his training at Harvard, under Dr. Southard. Rapaport felt that Menninger "was a man of imagination and a flair for new things and liking for science," but at the same time was fearful of Menninger's "irascible moods" and "unreliability." Though he hesitated to accept an appointment at the Menninger Clinic for these reasons, he finally decided to go and found his "worst fears justified." Still, Karl Menninger was a major support to him until 1947, as Rapaport was developing his landmark book on *Diagnostic Testing*.

Despite Menninger's help, Rapaport felt that Karl "was never interested" in what he "was actually doing." In addition, Rapaport had doubts about finding colleagues who wanted to do serious science. He attempted a seminar for psychiatric residents that "proved worthless," but a seminar for Southard School interns brought Margaret Brenman. Research on hypnosis was then undertaken and in 1943 a research committee was organized with Rapaport as chairman, and Robert Knight and Merton Gill as members.

Sibylle Escalona arrived in 1943 as a psychologist and therapist. She conducted research along Lewinian lines and later began infant testing which led to her unique 1948–52 infancy study with Dr. Mary Leitch. Through these early years, Rapaport wrote, "somebody either present in the group or joining for a particular purpose slowly shift[ed] under attentive eyes with the help of those who have some say-so about arrangements." One of those who joined the group, Paul Bergman, was interested in a variety of problems, including experimentation in therapies. Since the Menninger Clinic was committed to a psychoanalytic approach, Bergman was seen as a rebel.

252   "Although Gardner was not a psychiatrist...." An example of GM's status among psychiatrists and psychoanalysts is the invitation he received to give the Sandor Rudo lectures in 1964 at the New York Academy of Medicine. Previously, this honor had gone only to psychoanalysts: M. Balint, John Bowelsy, David M. Levy, Franz Alexander, Abram Kardiner, Thomas French, and Edith Wergirt. The lectureship was sponsored by the Psychoanalytic Clinic of the Columbia University College of Physicians and Surgeons and its Alumni Association. GM's topic for the Rudo lectures was "A Cross-Cultural View of Ego Dynamics."

252   Gardner protested the idea that he initiated the "new look" approach to experiments on perception. In a letter to Calvin Hall in November 1954 he wrote: "Bruner was never a student of mine. Postman was . . . but I think he moved rapidly away from the view which I was developing. Sherif had his own ideas. . . ." "I think the two great landmarks are first, Rorschach in the early twenties and second, Murray in the mid-thirties. Murray and his students were working on experimental formulations in autism (guided, of course, somewhat by Bleuler but by others too). . . . I think I drew somewhat later than they did upon sources which were largely similar, including Rorschach research. The idea of the structural reorganization of a perceptual

field as a result of affective factors came to me, I think, in '37 or '38.... [At] City College in 1940, I was determined to do something in this field and all the five experiments ... along these lines were formulated in the first three years I was there."

252   In my conversation with Escalona and George Klein in 1951, Escalona said that there was so much material on the infants that our respective studies of it could not present conflicts. The observations by my research group of the same children at the preschool stage led to further studies at latency, puberty and senior year of high school stages. See Bibliography.

252   Dr. Karl had written three well-known books in the early Menninger years: *Man Against Himself*, New York: Harcourt Brace, and World, 1938; *Love Against Hate*, New York: Harcourt Brace, 1942, with the collaboration of Jeanetta Lyle Menninger; and *The Human Mind*, New York: A.A. Knopf, 1930. In 1963 his creative *The Vital Balance*, New York: Viking Press, was cowritten with Martin Mayman and Paul Pruyser.

David Rapaport had developed widely recognized diagnostic procedures and had trained clinical psychologists in diagnosis of mental illness and character disorders. His work had led to a training program for clinical psychologists.

253   In the early 1950s the Menninger Foundation buildings included a modest clinic building adapted from a large farmhouse with pleasant grounds, trees, a pond and walkways for patients; a hospital which also contained the dining room for patients and staff; another building for clinicians with a house nearby adapted for the use of the Topeka Psychoanalytic Institute. A little distance east of this group was a large house for the in-patient residence of the Children's Service with a small building to the rear of that for the Southard School. Across the street was another large house for the clinicians working with the children. My office, and that of Alice Moriarty, was on the third floor of that house. Gardner's office was in a little house across the street. At first I had to carry on the research sessions for the coping project in a rented house a few blocks away.

Over the years we were in Topeka, all this was changed; three small houses were acquired for the research staff; one of these generously provided office space for my secretary Marie Smith, for Alice Moriarty, for two typists and for our statisticians as well as for me. Two other small houses provided space for Gardner's research group.

Early in the 1960s a group of buildings was constructed for the Children's Service providing residences, an excellent school with an arts area and gymnasium, and a building for the clinical staff. A nearby house was adapted for a therapeutic preschool center.

A major change in facilities in the early sixties involved the move of some adult services to a large building on what became the West Campus; research staff were moved to one large building; administration and some clinicians were moved to another. With Dr. Roy's administration a new group of buildings designed for in-patient housing, dining and other uses, were added to the impressive resources of the enlarged Foundation. The Menninger Foundation also expanded to include services for infants at risk, for the elderly, and for homeless boys, and it developed branch centers in Kansas City and Phoenix, Arizona.

While initially our work settings were extremely modest, over time they became spacious. Gardner enjoyed his excellent office with its large conference table where he could have meetings of several members of the research group; the building contained offices and technical facilities for the research staff.

From the beginning secretarial assistance was superb and made possible the productivity of both of our research groups (see our bibliographies for those years, and my bibliography for the coping studies in *Vulnerability, Coping and Growth*). Marie Smith's warmth was an important support to the children.

253 Currently, there is much discussion of the "sacrifices" women make in supporting their husbands' work (see *Models of Achievement*, Russo and McConnell, Basic Books, 1985). In feeling that it "was Gardner's turn," I recognized the endless support he had given me for my work at Sarah Lawrence College and Bank Street College in New York. I did not feel that I was making a sacrifice; I was balancing the support. Actually in some ways the Topeka move was better for me than it was for Gardner, as he wrote a friend.

253 Gardner's memorandum of 1951–52 and subsequent memoranda are in the Murphy Archives at the Menninger Foundation.

254 Research on value conflicts: Gardner's concern about the poor and ideas of living with or like the poor conflicted with my needs for health and limited stress as a prerequisite for effective work and care of our family. He himself had other values as well; in more than one statement he declared his belief that life in a small town like Concord was best for children and leaving the dirt and noise of New York for Westchester County was important for them, although inconvenient for him. His wish to do research on value conflicts had this background. Another conflict was concerned with money, which he felt should be "used to help people, not to be saved"; belatedly in his sixties did he realize the need to provide for retirement and old age, too late to provide adequately for the expense of his own last illness.

254 Gardner and I did not know that Dr. Karl was considered "the real boss" and since Escalona repeatedly emphasized to Gardner that he should take all questions to Dr. Will, I assume that she did not consider that Karl had authority over Dr. Will (see Escalona's letters to GM in Menninger Archives). Since the Children's Service and my offices were at a considerable distance from Gardner's I had no direct evidence of the stress (as others told me after his death) Gardner experienced with Dr. Karl's pressures, and I felt no strain in my relationship with him. I was stimulated by his thinking about disintegrative reactions to stress, which was relevant to my research on coping. Dr. Karl was always cordial to our son, Al, during his time in Topeka. After we left, Dr. Karl wrote warm letters to us.

254 Satisfying home setting: we were leaving the beautiful wooded suburbs of Bronxville, N.Y., with its magnificent trees, wood thrushes, gardens and the Bronx River.

256 Along with lectures, GM was writing on problems of war and peace. His lifelong concern for peace and war found expression in "Nuclear Dementia" in *The Nation* (1950); "Face Those Atomic Fears" (1958); "Psychological Aspects of the Cold War" (1962); "A Psychologist Views the Nuclear Crisis" (1962); and "Political Invention as a Strategy Against War" (1965).

Gardner was also one of 25 "representative Americans" who were invited to "state the fundamental convictions that support your life, the basis of your religious convictions that support your life, the basis of your religious faith." This varied group included scientists like Einstein, philosophers such as Ernest Hocking, and educators such as William H. Kilpatrick.

Gardner's statement began: "The basic religious values in the Judeo-Christian tradition are to me two, and they are closely related. The first is the value of love, both given and received. . . . I think that love is an absolutely fundamental central experience rooted in human tissues."

He went further, asserting that man finds other things "profoundly worthy of love." He urged that followers of the Judeo-Christian tradition, such as St. Francis preaching to the birds and the Anti-Steel Trap league trying to put an end to the torture and destruction of the animals of the Arctic tundra, all have their place somehow in a Jesus-like, or Whitman-like love.

Following are examples of GM papers written in the'60s (and two from the '70s):

1961, John F. Santos and GM, "Perceptual Learning and Reality Testing," *Perceptual and Motor Skills,* 13, 130.

1962, GM, "A Scientist Views the Nuclear Crisis," *Toward a Science and a Program for Human Survival,* 1st Int. Congress of SOS (pub. 1965).

1963–64, GM, "Research Trends Today and Tomorrow," *Menninger Quarterly,* winter.

1964, GM and H.J. McNamara, "Curiosity and Reality Contact: A Preliminary Report," *Perceptual and Motor Skills,* 18, 976.

1966, GM and Lois Barclay Murphy, "Human Nature and Human Potentialities: Imagination and the Imaginary," in *Explorations in Human Potentialities,* ed. by Herbert A. Otto; Charles C. Thomas.

1967, Alice E. Moriarty and GM, "An Experimental Study of ESP Potential and Its Relationship to Creativity in a Group of Normal Children," *Journal of the American Society for Psychical Research,* 61 (4), October.

1968, GM, John F. Santos, Charles M. Solley, "Development and Transfer of Attentional Habits," *Perceptual and Motor Skills,* 26, 515–19.

1971, GM, "On the State of Psychology," *Annals of the New York Academy of Sciences,* 184, 289–96.

1976, GM, "Experiments in Overcoming Self-Deception," *Schweizerische Zeitschrift für Psychologie und ihre Anwendungen/Revue Suisse de Psychologie Pure et Appliquée,* Bern und Stuttgart: Hans Huber.

256   Our son, Al, was drafted for the Korean war and left for boot camp in 1951. After two years as company clerk, he completed work for an AB at Columbia, then continued graduate work. While studying he also participated in Gilbert and Sullivan operettas at Barnard, at times singing, acting, and directing. After a bout with pneumonia, he came to Topeka for a rest and did some part-time work. The Topeka Civic Theatre, needing another director, signed him on and Gardner was able to fit into a role on one occasion. In January 1957, Al directed a reading of Steinbeck's *Of Mice and Men,* but was unable to adequately fill the role of Lennie, the feeble-minded laborer. Al shifted his best young actor, originally cast as the Boss, to the role of Lennie, but this left open the Boss role. On a hunch, Al asked Gardner if he would give it a try and soon Gardner was cast in the role. He made a crusty, wizened, weather-beaten Boss, somewhat cynical and skeptical about hiring two itinerant laborers.

256   My therapy with a brain-damaged girl: see *Robin,* New York: Basic Books, 1982. Cotter Hirschberg was an extraordinarily supportive, sensitive supervisor, appreciating the effective steps I took with my patient and very gently questioning unwise responses by me. This rewarding experience contrasted with a devastating "disintegrative" experience I had with another very aggressive supervisor. Hirschberg was able to release the therapist's creativity and was generally considered a remarkable guide in psychotherapy.

256 Several members of the superb Children's Service staff became warm friends, notably Cotter Hirschberg, Povl Toussieng, Walter Kass and Arthur Mandelbaum.

I was very much impressed with child care workers who have the hour-to-hour task of helping the children learn to live together, to take responsibility for themselves, and to cope with the frustrations of everyday life. My observations of the sensitive work of the staff there led to a book, *Growing Up in Garden Court.*

The Southard School provided small classes of four or five children; a "time-out place" where a child oversensitive to stimulation could have peace and quiet; individual learning aimed to help each child with his or her particular problems; and sensitive, creative teachers with unusual understanding.

257 My analyst, Ishak Ramzy, was flexible, supportive, creative, and stimulating. I had entered analysis with some awareness of infants' feelings about separation from their mothers, approaches of strangers and other situations; but I came to realize that babies have feelings about *everything* they experience.

Chapter 21

Sources include correspondence with Escalona, Paul Bergman, George Klein, Lester Luborsky, Robert Holt, Robert Wallerstein, et al. Also included are annual reports to trustees, T.P.R.'s, a 1954 article by Gardner Murphy and Robert Wallerstein, "Perspectives of the Research Department of the Menninger Foundation," in the Bulletin of the Menninger Clinic, *vol. 18, 1954, unpublished papers by Paul Bergman on early work on the psychotherapy research project, and by committees (authors not listed) on Plan A and Plan B for the Foundation. Records of research under way and staff interests in research, and other correspondence in the Murphy Archives at Menninger were also valuable sources.*

259 The small psychotherapy project initiated by Paul Bergman led to the famous Psychotherapy Research Project (PFP) with its millions of dollars of financial support over nearly 20 years. Gardner's efforts and prestige were crucial in the early efforts to receive the funds needed to expand the project.

259 The survey of ongoing studies is available in manuscript in the Murphy Archives at the Menninger Foundation. Paul Bergman's role in initiating the psychotherapy research project was forgotten as the project was enlarged, becoming PRP, the Psychotherapy Research Project, with more subjects and increased staffing.

259 Although Bergman left the Psychotherapy Research Project, a comparison of his April 4, 1954, report with the final formulation of the project reveals the seeds of its subsequent development:

"This study aims firstly to arrive at tentative hypotheses about how and how well this method may work. Those who participate hope also that this particular task will make them see more clearly what is needed in order to arrive at a usable evaluation of outcome of treatment.

"The group uses, wherever possible, the following sources of information:
    Data of the initial psychiatric examination,
    Initial psychological tests,
    Observations by staff members, e.g., hospital staff,

> Progress notes,
> Therapy process notes,
> Recordings of therapy sessions,
> Interviews with the therapist towards or after the end of treatment,
> Interviews with the patient towards or after the end of treatment,
> Final or followup psychological tests.

"Each member of the group studies all the available evidence by himself. He then rates the patient's state before therapy and after (or at the end of) therapy, using the scales provided by the Psychotherapy Project. He rates the general impression of psychiatric health as well as the seven 'dimensions' noted above. The group then compares and discusses the ratings, but does not try to bring about a higher degree of conformity in impressions than has spontaneously emerged. In these ratings, as well as in the subsequent formulation of hypotheses, each member of the group has the choice of agreeing with any of the others or of expressing and recording his own opinion."

At the time Paul Bergman left, he had worked on a pilot project, studying nine cases, and Lester Luborsky had developed a Health-Sickness scale.

260   Grace Heider's follow-up of the children in Escalona and Leitch's infancy project were useful in her work on the coping study and her collaboration with Escalona in their book, *Prediction and Outcome* (Basic Books, 1959), comparing infancy and preschool records, and in her study of vulnerability in infants and young children.

261   Ten year plan. Unsigned, undated. (In Murphy Archives at Menninger.)

263   Work was "moving along nicely": letter to Escalona.

263   The Psychotherapy Research Project suffered from the changes in staff beginning with the early departure of Paul Bergman and Donald Watterson. Robert Wallerstein, who joined Gardner early in 1954, recalled that the only concrete accomplishment before he arrived was the Health-Sickness Rating Scale developed by Lester Luborsky, a psychoanalytically trained psychologist. From the time of his arrival, Wallerstein devoted most of his half-time commitment to research for the Psychotherapy Research Project, and he convinced Lewis Robbins, one of the leading analysts at the Foundation, to commit a quarter of his time—along with his prestige—to the Project. He then recruited Helen Sargent, a senior psychologist, who played the largest part in creating its design and methods. Of the original group, only Lester Luborsky and the social worker Mildred Faris stayed on and played an important part in the development of the project. By 1955 it involved some 15 people with commitments of time ranging from six hours to full time for Helen Sargent, and a steering committee of which Gardner was a member; he participated regularly in the weekly planning sessions, and was involved in soliciting funds to finance the project, as well as the other research activities that he was supporting at the Foundation. (Until NIMH developed a general support grant for research at the Foundation, each project required a grant of its own.)

264   Manuscript of address to trustees in Murphy Archives, Menninger Foundation.

266   Plan A, Plan B: manuscript in Murphy Archives at Menninger, undated, unsigned; identified by internal evidence.

267   Murphy and Wallerstein, "Perspectives of the Research Department of the Menninger Foundation," *Bulletin of the Menninger Clinic,* vol. 18, no. 6, November 1954.

268   Riley Gardner letter to LBM.
268   As a member of the committee to administer the funds from the Sloan Foundation assigned to finance visiting lecturers, Gardner was able to persuade a number of distinguished psychologists to give seminars and lectures at the Menninger Foundation.

Chapter 22

Sources include GM memos and research staff letters to LBM.

269   Although Wallerstein, Sömmer and Holtzman agree that GM did not direct research in the usual sense of assigning specific projects to individuals, his great care in appreciating and critiquing reports is documented in memoranda in the Murphy Research Archives.
269   Gardner was acutely aware of the fact that the statistical training of young experimenters went far beyond what he had acquired at Yale or Columbia or later, but he used the statistical principles he had absorbed very effectively.
270   Holtzman and Wallerstein both commented that his approach worked well at that time, but that when funds were less available a more directive approach would be needed. Lolafaye Coyne felt that he should have held a tighter rein. I think that the many demands made on him from inside and outside of the Foundation may have made it hard for him to concentrate on his research as well as he did at City College.
270   For example, Riley Gardner, D. Jackson and S. Messick studied personality organization in cognitive control principles and intellectual abilities, and Solley and Long worked together on perceptual learning in response set learning. Riley Gardner and Alice Moriarty (of the coping team) collaborated on a study of adolescents. Samuel Messick worked with both GM's team and with Phil Holzman and R. Gardner's team. R. Gardner assisted H. Voth and M. Mayman in planning the study of the autokinetic phenomenon; this was followed later by further work carried on by Gardner Murphy's reality-testing team. R. Gardner also assisted H. Schlesinger and others in the thyroid team to develop a useful rating scale for patients' behavior. He also attended meetings of the perceptual learning team when GM was away. In relation to techniques, hypotheses and direct work on projects, there was a degree of mutal aid between members of different teams.
271   Robert Sömmer wrote (8-31-83) that "He was neither directive nor non-directive—but rather pointed out the goals and offered us advice, inspiration, and support for reaching it. He did not demand nor exhort but indicated, pointed, represented, exemplified. It is a leadership style that I have not encountered since. It was based heavily on mutual respect.
"In terms of write-ups and criticisms, he would wait until we sent him drafts and then he would react promptly and supportively. The comments usually contained an explicit or implied invitation to visit him afterwards in his office to discuss the paper/experiment.
"He did not spend time observing us conduct our experiments, training us, or otherwise engage in direct supervision. The project was organized on a democratic basis with no hierarchy among research assistants, associates, or post-docs. There was no intermediary between the lowest paid research staff and Gardner. Everyone felt that if there were problems, they should go to him directly. I had the distinct impression that he did not like hierarchies.

"He tried to know each of us on a personal basis. When my father's business in Stroudsburg, Pennsylvania, was destroyed by a flood in 1955, he was extremely solicitous and inquired about the state of the business various times after that. Again if I had to characterize his administrative style it would be personal and direct rather than bureaucratic. However, it was also very professional, in which we were all colleagues with similar objectives."

271   Letters to LBM from Robert Sömmer, 8-31-83, and from Charles Solley.

272   Letters to LBM from Harold McNamara, Joseph Kovach, Lester Luborsky, and Donald Spence.

272   Gardner continued to keep a sharp eye on the budgetary needs of members of the Psychotherapy Research Project who applied for grants after they left Topeka. He shared his experience where it was relevant to their needs. For instance, after Lester Luborsky left the Foundation, but continued to work on that project, Gardner commented:

"I think it would be worthwhile to get a statistical assistant at a fairly high level who would give you as much as a third of his time, thus raising this amount from $1000 to something over $2000. I also doubt if you are asking enough for consultant services. I think you should allow more than one round trip to Topeka and more for fees for subjects. All these things together will only increase your total budget by a small amount. On page 3, the footnote, the phrase 'continues part of these projects' seems to me not quite right; parts or portions of some of these projects would seem to be closer to what you mean."

"I think that the terms *one-quarter* and *one-half* should be spelled out in full on the middle of page 4."

". . . On page 10 it is not clear to me whether the rebus technique is to be used in Philadelphia as well as in Topeka. If it is to be used in both places, the degree of independence, the problem of replication and the problem of pilot studies being cross-validated later are all of some interest in this kind of work. Will the two investigators or two groups of investigators even work somewhat independently, not knowing each other's hypotheses, until data are available? . . ."

In addition he served as an editor to make the grant applications as correct in every detail as possible.

272   While many people compared Gardner with William James, the comparison needs a close look. They were similar in the breadth of their interests and in the quality of their writing, but Gardner's involvement in issues of peace, justice, and his cross-cultural concerns made him a uniquely humanitarian psychologist.

272   LBM comment: "Gardner's modest and gentle way was legendary; it grew out of his dislike of 'stuffed shirts,' autocratic, pretentious, overbearing, bossy people, as well as identification with the gentle men of Concord, Massachusetts, whom he had known as a child, and the modesty of Woodworth, his major supporter at Columbia. He was never aggressive or irritable, and was always considerate of the feelings of others. The young people at the Menninger Foundation found him approachable and warm; they felt that he exaggerated his limitations. Some clinicians recognized his gifts; they consulted with him, and joined seminars he carried out with visiting scientists, clinicians and writers such as the author Aldous Huxley and the noted Swiss psychologist Jean Piaget."

Chapter 23

Sources include notes regarding further topics to be studied, Gardner's statement about his plans for research at Menninger, his papers coauthored with members of his research team, papers authored by them, and books using his research. His comments in correspondence with former students, colleagues, and friends—in the Gardner Murphy Archives at Menninger—were also of importance.

273   Although members of the research team were not already there as they had been at City College, they came. Robert Sömmer wrote, "He was so well known, and had so many contacts in the field that people wrote to him seeking positions. . . . I was doing graduate work (at Penn State) when I read some of Gardner's papers, noted that he was director of a research unit at a psychiatric clinic, which was the right combination of a type of person I respected doing a type of research that I wanted to do. . . . Students at Kansas heard of the interesting work going on at Menninger's and wrote to him. . . . Some of the research assistants were friends of earlier assistants—for example, Teodoro Ayllon . . . had been a friend of mine. Gardner had a lot of confidence in people and they tended in the main to rise to the occasion. Actually, the research assistants were mobilized in different ways: Donald Spence wrote me that he heard Gardner speak at the University in Wichita; '[I] nerved myself up to . . . ask if he might have an opening.' . . . Then when all the interns at the Guidance Center where he was working visited Topeka, he arranged to stay with Gardner, who then accepted him as a research assistant. (Spence was invited by George Klein and Robert Holt, after a year, to go to New York University where he stayed for twenty years.) Other assistants were recommended by colleagues to whom Gardner wrote for suggestions, and some were invited by members of Gardner's team as they were completing graduate work at the University of Kansas. A few were already at work in research on perception—for example, John Santos at Tulane University."

273   As the perceptual learning studies of the '50s were being extended, discussions and challenges between members of the team, and also other investigators, were encouraged by Gardner. Bob Holt was especially generous in sharing reactions—for instance, to Gardner's discussion of aspects of learning, as in "Affect and Perceptual Learning," in an attempt to reduce the increase of perceptual differentiation and integration to various shifts of figure and ground. Holt said he did not find Gardner's use of figure-ground shifts clear. Gardner replied by acknowledging that the definition of figure and ground was so difficult he thought he would use *emphasis* as Tolman did, or *figural dominance* as George Klein suggested. They also discussed self-destructive tendencies, Gardner feeling that people with that tendency derive pleasure from punishment. Holt also urged Gardner to rethink his use of the terms "autism" and "need," and suggested corrections in his statements about the pleasure and reality principles, which Gardner accepted. Later, Holt read Gardner's article "Toward a Dynamic Trace Theory" with great interest and felt that in the hands of Hartmann and Rapaport, psychoanalysis could move in the direction of Gardner's thought.

   These brief glimpses offer a look at Gardner's receptiveness to criticism and questions, and his handling of information from interested colleagues. The development of his thinking about perceptual learning did not take place in a closed room.

273   From the beginning of his experimental work Gardner had been concerned
        with the problem of correcting errors in judgment, including errors in
        perception. In his Harvard "Study of Myself" he commented that his im-
        pulsive judgments were often unsound, but that when he took time to think
        about an issue his conclusion was sound. He was not yet aware of the
        scotomatizing that characterizes our perceptions when reality conflicts with
        our wish or need to shut out unpleasant aspects of a cherished person. His
        studies of the influence of affect on perception led to the next step, studying
        reality- testing.

273   As was consistent with his broad view of psychology, GM appreciated R.S.
        Woodworth's concept of perception. In 1957 Gardner responded to an in-
        vitation to contribute a chapter to *Current Psychological Issues* in honor of
        Robert S. Woodworth's 90th birthday. Gardner's chapter, "Some Relations
        of Perception to Motivation," outlined the implications of Woodworth's
        achievements in showing that the organism's separation of motivation from
        perception, from learning, from thinking, were inadequate. Woodworth's
        vision, Gardner said, showed us ways of getting back to the integrity of the
        living system, which led to the idea that motivation can spring from any
        system of the body and even from forces external to the body.
        Another development brought the recognition that perception was not merely
        the registration of an impression on something like a photographic plate;
        scanning, searching operations and complicated integrative activities made
        perception far more than a passive acceptance of an outer reality. When at
        Columbia, Woodworth was sensitive to the motor components in the re-
        ceptor functions and took an organismic view of perception. Gardner, who
        usually thought in evolutionary terms, saw Woodworth's organismic views
        as revolutionary in contrast to the faculty psychology taught before World
        War I and even later.
        Gardner continued with Woodworth's 1947 paper on the reinforcement of
        perception, which criticized the assumption that reinforcement strengthens
        only overt responses. Gardner saw an isomorphic relationship between
        perceptual and motivational phenomena, and between these and the world
        of stimuli as "field theory makes clear." Motivation and perception express
        synthetic organismic activity flowing through time. Thus, life becomes a
        continuous moving web through the feedback processes and self-stimulation
        devices of the organism; motives and perceptions are abstractions reacting
        to the flow of many intersecting events.
        Though Gardner's research focused on specific perceptual acts and the effects
        of reward and punishment on perceptual learning, he never lost sight of the
        fact that isolated laboratory experiments cannot adequately reflect this com-
        plex flow of real life perceptual experiences.

273   GM's article, "Affect and Perceptual Learning" (1956), also reprinted in *There
        Is More Beyond: Selected Papers of Gardner Murphy* (McFarland, 1989), is
        a basic summary of his hypotheses about perceptual learning as he for-
        mulated them during and after his City College research in the '40s. This
        provided the orientation for his research in the '50s at the Menninger
        Foundation. This article was preceded by GM's papers at City College with
        his honors students in 1940–43, by his discussions in his 1947 *Personality,*
        by a presentation in 1949 to the British Psychological Society in London, and
        by his article with Julian Hochberg, "Perceptual Development, Some Tenta-
        tive Hypotheses," 1951, *Psychological Review,* 58:332–347.

276   *Development of the Perceptual World,* C. Solley and G. Murphy, New York: Basic Books, 1960.

276   "We believe that...," *ibid.,* 319.

278   "symmetries in the thought of the child...," *ibid.,* 328.

279   "at a certain level of complexity...," *ibid.,* 332.

279   A card file of the papers produced by Gardner's research group is available in the Murphy Archives at the Menninger Foundation.

Chapter 24

Sources include Gardner's memoranda, letters to research personnel, correspondence with colleagues outside of the Menninger Foundation, correspondence with Robert Wallerstein, and books by Leonard Horwitz, Otto Kernberg, and Robert Wallerstein on the outcomes of the Psychotherapy Research Project. Letters to LBM from Louis Zurcher, William Key, Richard Benson and James Taylor regarding the community studies, William Key's files and his papers on those studies and books reporting on them, letters from Robert Wallerstein to LBM about the new appointments of Joseph Kovach, and Elmer and Alyce Green and publications of the latter, were also used. Annual Reports and TPR reports of new developments and records of the 1967 annual meeting with Gardner's summary of 31 studies in clinical, experimental, longitudinal and community areas, and Dr. Roy Menninger's dedication of the Gardner Murphy Research Building, all in the Gardner Murphy Archives at Menninger, were of great importance. Dr. Montague Ullman's 1966–67 interviews with GM for the American Psychiatric Association are in the archives of that organization.

Unfortunately, a file drawer containing the grant applications of Gardner's years at Menninger was lost in moving his files from the Tower Building to the Neiswanger Building which houses the archives. Replacements which I requested from research personnel are incomplete. My file of grant applications from 1953 to 1966 is complete, however.

282   See "Soviet Life and Soviet Psychology," Gardner Murphy and Lois Barclay Murphy, Chapter 8, in *Some Views on Soviet Psychology,* Washington, D.C., APA.

283   The inpatient settings for children at the Bechterew Institute at the time we visited them were bare and unstimulating, and there was little evidence of the creative approach we saw in Moscow at the Institute of Defectology, and the stimulating settings for children in Moscow and Tashkent—both in children's parks and the activities for the Young Pioneers.

283   Dr. Roy Menninger's tribute to Gardner and Gardner's response at the dedication of the Gardner Murphy Research Building are in the Gardner Murphy Archives at the Menninger Foundation.

283   A natural sequence following the perceptual learning studies was the exploration of approaches to reality-testing. Here curiosity and creativity, parapsychological studies—with their interrelations—found a place, in addition to studies of attention and factors influencing attention in the direction of heightened vigilance or defensive non-seeing.

283   Undated John F. Santos and GM: "A project of interrelated studies in perceptual learning has been underway at the Menninger Foundation since 1952 (USPHS Research Grant M 715) and was recently expanded into a more broadly conceived Program in Reality Testing (USPHS Research Grant

M 3924); this will investigate the means by which 'veridical' contacts with the environment may best be used in overcoming misperceptions and misconceptions." Conditioning procedures which have been effective in perceptual learning series "will be utilized in further studies dealing with judgment, memory, conceptual thinking and other cognitive functions. Further work is being contemplated with the experimentation which has succeeded in conditioning *attention* so as to influence the direction and efficiency of perception."

283   In the subception studies, psychiatric interviews and autokinetic records were used to evaluate sensitivity to inner or outer sources of stimulation, and then predictions were made regarding the subject's subception performance. These predictions succeeded in 17 out of 21 cases and led to the feeling that further studies of autokinesis in relation to reality testing were needed. Improvement in performance resulted not from practice alone but from a combination of practice accompanied by incentives and immediate knowledge of results. Thus it was felt that autokinesis might probe underlying predispositions not easily demonstrated in more structured situations. Some of these expectations, but not all, were fulfilled. While the pattern of autokinetic movement remained stable in a control group, experiments demonstrated that positive reinforcement increased the proportion of movement in a given spatial region.

Further experiments were carried out in order to discover factors influencing autokinetic perception: patterns for individuals not exposed to experimental reinforcement remained stable for six months to a year, indicating stable personality patterns. In addition, after six weeks subjects reliably recalled their autokinetic experiences. Autokinesis was used in many other investigations dealing with curiosity, subception, personality, psychopathology, body awareness and school achievement, as well as in cross-cultural studies.

Similarities were found across different cultures along with subtle differences in the testing pattern. The cross-cultural studies, by John Santos, required special planning to provide acceptable testing conditions, and to decrease stress for subjects not accustomed to testing and experimentation. In addition, it was necessary to develop translations and adaptations of tests to collect normative data on personality and adjustment.

The aim of the cross-cultural studies was to develop methods by which predictions of behavior can be tested. Characteristics such as perceptual flexibility or rigidity, the degree of openness or closedness to external or internal sources of stimulation might influence the efficiency with which persons from different cultures can handle tasks where these characteristics help or hinder their performance.

284   The Economic Opportunity Act of 1964 established the Office of Economic Opportunity (O.E.O.) and declared a "War Against Poverty." The Act provided for the creation of local poverty intervention organizations with the task to stimulate changes which would meet the needs of and improve the level of functioning of the poor. Among the 700 poverty intervention organizations funded by O.E.O. was the Topeka Office of Economic Opportunity (O.E.O.) which was established May 1, 1965; it was managed by a director and assistant director who located ten target neighborhoods distinguished by poverty and blight. Each of these was represented by a neighborhood group which elected its chairman, vice-chairman and secretary and met monthly to formulate community action proposals. Dr. Louis

Zurcher, a sociologist in the Menninger Foundation Research group, followed the projects that developed in these neighborhoods, keeping a record of the vicissitudes suffered by the new organizations; his findings were published in his books *Poverty Warriors* and *The Leader and the Lost,* and in several papers.

Unaccustomed mixtures of middle-class and poor people, and urgent pressure by the poor who wanted immediate changes in contrast to the traditional bureaucratic pattern of planning for long term change, contributed to conflict and frustration. Zurcher also undertook a study of changes in achievement orientation, activism, anomie isolation powerlessness, alienation, and "particularism" (obligations of friendship). As expected, there were significant differences in points of view between the representatives of the poor and the middle-class representatives of city agencies. But even the short period of seven months between two adminstrations of the evaluation scales produced significant increases in achievement orientation and activism among the representatives of the poor (Zurcher, 1970).

One group succeeded in achieving agreement that an urgent need was a day care center for young children in poor families. With the support of the Head Start program funded by the Office of Child Development, a Center was established in a poor neighborhood in North Topeka; the staff included black and Chicano aides from the neighborhood. It flourished from the beginning and developed into a larger center whose director is now a regional supervisor. The National Institute of Mental Health funded my time as a consultant to the Center. On the basis of my records, I prepared ten booklets for a series "Caring for Children" published by O.E.O. No analysis of changes in staff, parents or children was made at the time, but an informal follow-up revealed dramatic changes in some of the staff; one woman who had not completed high school at the time she was first employed completed her high school equivalency, then completed the four-year course in the local college, and continued to an M.A. in special education. She then taught in a Topeka public school.

284 Some mothers — initially disorganized and unkempt, with a different father for each of several children — were stimulated by membership on a committee. With a new self-respect, they said, "Now I can *be* somebody — I think I'll settle down." Statistics are not adequate to evaluate the importance of such major changes. When even a small proportion of such a group "get off welfare," the costs of that program are significantly reduced.

I reported on my observations of personality development in children and their mothers at a hearing of a congressional committee in June 1969. Largely as a result of broad popular support, recognizing the importance of the work in Head Start for deprived children, this program survived the cuts in social programs during the '70s and '80s. Gardner visited the North Topeka Head Start group and was interested in the development of the children, their parents, and the staff.

He also accompanied me to the Northern Vermont Parent-Child Center which I visited twice as consultant in the late '60s. Lyndon Johnson had sent a mandate "to take priority over all other programs" to psychologists who were now required to develop a plan for help to infants and young children in their family settings; this led to the Parent-Child Centers, staffed chiefly by residents of the rural and small town areas in which they were located.

284   William Key's records of the Relocation Study are available in the Gardner
        Murphy Research Archives. There are also unpublished monographs in the
        archives, including: "When People Are Forced to Move: A Study of Forced
        Relocation," May 1967 (GM as codirector), and "Doorstep Psychiatry in the
        Low Income Ghetto," James Taylor with Beth Sheppel and Alvin Green. A
        "Final Report" and other papers by William Key, records of seminars on
        helping people move, and correspondence related to the research are also
        available.
            In June 1966, when the most destructive tornado that had hit any town in the
        United States struck Topeka, demolishing houses over a 12-mile stretch from
        the southwest to the poorest northeast corners of the city, the Menninger
        Foundation set up relief centers and another community study focused on
        that experience. Again, families were relocated where homes had been
        demolished. Nearby towns responded to the disaster, in one instance closing
        all business for a day so that all available trucks could go to Topeka to help
        with the moving and with the transportation of furniture which was offered
        by residents who had not been harmed. The record of that experience made
        the book *Tornado*.

286   Gardner had been excited by E. Jacobson's *Progressive Relaxation* (1929) when
        it first appeared, but as far as I recall, he did not at that time connect that
        discussion of the possiblity of control of muscle tension with perception. In
        any case, Braatoy's work on the treatment of arm neuroses, reported in 1952,
        stimulated Gardner's conviction that perception should be studied in the
        proprioceptive and also the interoceptive modalities as well as in the ex-
        teroceptive senses of sight, hearing, touch and smell. But he needed staff
        members competent to undertake research in proprioceptive avenues to
        reality-testing. In the late '50s he discussed these issues with his perceptual
        learning project team and then with the reality testing team. Progress in
        psychophysiology and improved instruments led to new studies which
        generated new ideas—e.g., the need for a system of concepts relating to the
        dynamics of a process of inhibition by which muscle tension can be involved
        in shutting out certain types of information. In the spring of 1964, Elmer
        Green was added to the staff; as a senior engineer who added a Ph.D. in
        psychology to his training, he became a pioneer in the study of proprioce-
        tive feedback (a form of "biofeedback"). In addition, with the development
        of a well-equipped psychophysiological laboratory it became possible to
        study autonomic functions (pulse and galvanic skin potential) in relation to
        visual and auditory perception as well as to proprioceptive feedback.
            Gardner believed that systematic supplying of cues from one's own body can,
        to a considerable degree, eliminate cognitive errors, and that the develop-
        ment of this capacity could lead to a "general reduction of one's own self-
        deceptions in the whole perceptual-cognitive sphere." These studies led to
        Gardner's book with Herbert Spohn, *Encounter with Reality* (1968).
            Elmer Green and his wife Alyce soon developed useful applications of their
        biofeedback techniques to treatment of migraine headaches, high blood
        pressure and other physical problems. As work on biofeedback developed in
        different centers, a biofeedback society was formed; at one meeting those
        who attended suggested organizing the group under the name The Gardner
        Murphy Biofeedback Society but he adamantly refused the honor.

287   From studies of perceptual learning, research into reality testing developed,
        which included the study of control and attention, subliminal learning, the

relation between reinforcement and autokinetic movement and even curiosity. Cross-cultural studies in Mexico, Brazil, and Guatemala compared results of experiments there with those in the United States.

Analysis of results of many experiments demonstrated that when there is clear-cut structure, perceptual changes may arise through alteration in the selection of external cues or shifts of attention in the individual. When objects in a field are vaguely structured, perception is influenced by factors within the person which override the external factors.

Studies of attention, growing out of a long series of studies of Necker Cube reversal, led to studies of schizophrenia by Herbert Spohn and Paul Thetford. Studies of autokinesis in relation to personality, curiosity, subception, body awareness and psychopathology produced variable results, but still encouraged continued study of the autokinetic process in relation to rigidity and flexibility of cognitive processes and personality functioning.

The research group discussed the role of proprioceptive and autonomic feedback in the perceptual shifts they studied, and felt a need for a system of ideas relating to the dynamics of a process of inhibition by which muscle tension could shut out certain types of information. This led to the development of a psychophysiological laboratory with Elmer Green, an experienced electronics engineer with a Ph.D. in psychology. Gardner and John Santos saw the proprioceptive feedback research as organically related to the sequence in perceptual learning and reality testing.

287   When Gardner arrived at the Menninger Foundation, he brought more than his desire to carry on his own research on perception and to contribute to the Menninger research programs. His orientation was rooted in his deep commitment to his biosocial approach to both normal and disturbed personality; the biological part included the organism as seen by Kurt Goldstein the neurologist, and genetic contributions to individuality as seen by geneticists. The social part of his biosocial approach included not only family influences but neighborhood and school experiences as these were studied by Hartshorne and May and others. His approach included studies of the larger settings of the community as seen by the Lynds in their *Middletown* research on an average town, and by Leo Srole in his study of mental illness in Midtown Manhattan, as well as the Boston study of which his former student Marc Fried worked with the psychiatyrist Dr. E. Lindemann. Earlier interests in mental illness were expressed in his 1923 dissertation at Columbia and his 1932 *Outline of Abnormal Psychology*. Neither he, nor those involved in bringing him to the Foundation were fully conscious at the time he was appointed, of the influence these deeply rooted commitments would have on his work at the Menninger Foundation.

But his efforts in the first few years reflected his comprehensive approach, and the developments of the last decade, the 1960s, marked the extent to which his vision of a genetic and community oriented research department was realized, as well as his initial commitment to the study of the dynamics of perception, and the emergence of more beyond that early vision.

287   The success of the Greens' biofeedback therapy led to a permanent program for this treatment, which left little time for futher research on the processes involved. Herbert Spohn stated to me that this limitation of research on biofeedback disappointed Gardner.

287   See Robert S. Wallerstein, *Forty-two Lives in Treatment* (1986), for the bibliography of reports on the Psychotherapy Research Project.

GM's chart for 1967 annual meeting.

Personality Organization

Autogenic Training

Psychotherapy

Psychosomatics (Diabetes)

Thyroid

Identity

Neuropsychology

Self-Confrontation

Association and Abstraction

Lobotomy

Cognition (E)

Preconscious Perception

Hearing and Respiration

Development of the Self-Concept

Proprioceptive Feedback

Altered Ego States (E)

Experimental Psychopathology (Attentional Deficit in Schizophrenia)

Ethology

Residential Treatment of Children *(E)

Urban Renewal

Emotional Correlates of Rehabilitation

Poverty Intervention Organization

Vulnerability

Disaster Dynamics

Aged in Disaster

Aging and Memory (E)

Activities Manual

Evaluation Manual

Adolescent Testing

S
O
C
I
O
-
C
U
L
T
U
R
A
L

E
X
P
E
R
I
M
E
N
T
A
L

LONGITUDINAL

288 Since the 1950s, when these patients were first studied, much more has been and continues to be learned about organic factors in personality integration, such as disorders with the central nervous system, autonomic nervous system, hormones, and the visceral, sensory and motor systems. Problems in any of these areas can contribute to difficulties in managing stress and can threaten psychic structure — ego strength and self-image.

Gardner was incapacitated by Parkinsonism and unable to read Horwitz's *Clinical Predictions in Psychotherapy* when he received it in 1974, and he did not survive to know of Wallerstein's monumental *Forty-two Lives*. Both of these books and other reports appearing after Gardner became very ill would have been profoundly gratifying to him since he had worked hard in the 1950s to make such studies possible.

288 See L.B. Murphy and Moriarty, *Vulnerability, Coping and Growth* (1976), for a bibliography of the coping studies.

290 The concepts of coping, vulnerability and resilience which arose during our study of children's development have stimulated research by others and such discussions as can be found in E.J. Anthony and B. Cohler's *The Invulnerable Child* (1987) and in G. Coelho, D. Hamburg and J. Adams' *Coping and Adaptation* (1974). The time was ripe for a study of positive responses to the stresses of life. I was extraordinarily lucky to have the devoted work of a team of senior clinicians: Alice Moriarty throughout the study; Povl Toussieng at three levels; Patricia Schloesser and Grace Heider at two levels.

290 Gardner's relation to these many different research areas varied: he was a supportive critic to many investigators without being personally involved. He was deeply interested in, and actively responsive to and involved in, the work of investigators like Christianson and Elmer Green who were working on problems in an area of Gardner's interest. He had also been concerned throughout his professional life with the relation of environmental forces to personality development and adjustment; this made the community studies deeply gratifying to him. When NIMH and President Johnson mandated work on Head Start and Parent-Child Centers, Gardner kept in touch with my work as well, joining me in consultations with a center in northern Vermont, for example. He was personally most involved in the group of reality-testing studies on attention, curiosity and creativity, following the perceptual learning studies.

His two books, *Encounter with Reality,* with Herbert Spahn, and *Outgrowing Self-Deception,* with Morton Leeds, integrated his thinking about perception of the outside world and the inside world and discussed the contribution of a range of methods — including biofeedback — to self-understanding and control.

291 See GM's correspondence in the Gardner Murphy Research Archives at the Menninger Foundation.

291 Wallerstein told me that he left after a confrontation with Dr. Karl; he and his family went to California and made a home in Belvedere while he accepted a position at Mt. Zion Hospital in San Francisco.

292 Dr. Reginald Lourie, a child psychiatrist, was a pioneer in research and treatment of infants at risk in the 1960s. Conferences of a multidisciplinary group assembled for an NIMH Task Force led to a book on early child care after which an intensive study of treatment was financed by NIMH in the 1970s. This led to the Regional Center for Infants and Children in Rockville,

Maryland, and the National Center for Clinical Infant Programs. The former focused on treatment of infants and children with problems, the latter promoted workshops and study groups nationwide with biennial conferences in Washington, D.C. These organizations stimulated new efforts to diagnose and treat medical and developmental problems in infants and young children—an important development at a time of increasing problems, especially in babies of teenage and working mothers.

292 Gardner's use of "man" should be considered the equivalent of "human being of either sex." At that time the term "man" was a shortcut. It lost acceptance after the women's movement in the 1970s.

292 The Humanistic Psychology group considered Gardner to be one of them, and he joined the group after he received a letter in 1966 from Charlotte Bühler urging him to join. But I remember his frequent protests—in conversations—against the idea of a "third force" in psychology (the other two being behaviorism and psychoanalysis). He wanted psychology to be an integrated science, with room for all useful methods and concepts.

Willard Frick interviewed GM, Abraham Maslow and Carl Rogers in 1969 for his 1971 book *Humanistic Psychology*. Gardner challenged the idea of self-actualization: "every individual represents many potential selves and self-actualization implies that there's just *one* potential self." He said that "the stuff of human nature . . . is very rich in open potentialities for movement in many possible directions. . . . I hope the time will come when we talk about the realization of potentials."

Gardner also discussed with Frick his concept of isomorphism in relation to mysticism, Maslow's peak experiences, yoga and Zen Buddhism, psychedelic drugs and hypnosis, and Wordsworth's "Tintern Abbey" and "Ode on Intimations of Immortality"—experiencing something that transcends the competitive individual. These thoughts were not new; in the early months of our acquaintance he had asked me whether I believed that mysticism— that is, mystical experiences—contributed new knowledge. I had done a great deal of reading on mysticism for papers at Vassar and at Union Theological Seminary. In answer to his question, I said no, that I felt from my own experience that mystical experience was emotional, that it intensified or deepened insights or beliefs that one already had, but it did not add new knowledge.

Gardner's interest had persisted through our reading of Eastern thought (which led to our book *Asian Psychology*), his responsiveness to others' experiments with psychedelic drugs, and a visit to the Esalen center for expansion of the self. He insisted that he did not understand these experiences, or Maslow's "peak experience." He even related these to my work with students, stimulating their appreciation of children, saying, "Hardly anything in human life could be more beautiful." He also said to some of his students at George Washington Universtiy, "Lois gets high on fall leaves; I don't see why people have to use drugs to get high."

Actually, Gardner was endlessly enthusiastic; he did not suffer from the severe depression Maslow had at times, nor did he suffer from a lack of closeness to people as do many people who seek "highs" from special group experiences. I think he did not need "peak experiences" because he was usually joyous, as all of us in our family experienced him. And friends typically remarked, "He is a happy man."

Beyond this, he felt deeply that LSD-25 and Mescaline should be studied on a scientific basis under supervision. He was concerned about the hazards in drug use and also warned about letting students get into radical methods of self-examination through unusual types of experience, especially when isolation was involved. Gardner kept the door open for exploration of new mind-stretching experiences under supervision, while he also gave warnings about the risks. He believed in trying to understand all of human experience.

292   Gardner's intramural work at the Menninger Foundation can be summarized in the following group of activities:

1. He became involved in the long term psychotherapy research project begun by staff members at the Foundation before he arrived. Gardner was instrumental in backing and helping to carry it to completion. He faithfully attended all meetings and helped in design issues and generally lent his knowledge and support to the work. He also initiated and supported major efforts to fund the research.

2. He maintained an advisory relationship with other studies already under way when he arrived, such as Riley Gardner's studies of cognitive styles and Voth and Mayman's autokinetic studies. This often included detailed editorial reading of manuscripts, as well as advising and facilitating publication arrangements.

3. He supported biochemical studies carried on by members of the Menninger staff.

4. He began a long series of investigations into problems in perceptual learning, his initial focus in his own research. For this he mobilized pre- and post-doctoral students as staff members, made applications for grants to support them, and consulted with them in different time patterns according to their needs.

5. He taught courses in the Menninger School of Psychiatry and the Psychoanalytic Institute, and gave lectures open to the entire Menninger community, such as the series published in *Pythagoras to Freud* (1968).

6. He attended conferences at the National Institute of Mental Health related to research he was carrying on or supervising.

7. He developed cooperative relationships with the University of Kansas and Kansas State University; his chief interest was to facilitate the completion of work for the doctorate by research assistants who had not yet obtained their Ph.D.s and also to facilitate training for other members of the Menninger staff and for students at those universities. As a department chairman, he was also a member of certain administrative committees.

292   An invitation for GM to present a paper to the Wayne State University Centennial Symposium in Detroit, May 19, 1968, published in *American Psychologist,* vol. 24, no. 5, May 1969, led to his prescient forecast: *Psychology in the Year 2000.* His predictions of development of psychophysiology, internal scanning, confrontation of the unconscious world, the development of voluntary control over the inner world, new study of the relation of psychology to biological sciences especially genetics, and also to social sciences, have already been confirmed to a degree. His broad vision profited from his exposure to more and more aspects of functioning he had barely glimpsed in his biosocial concept developed in the '30s.

292   GM memberships in the 1960s: American Academy of Arts and Sciences (Fellow), American Association for the Advancement of Science (Fellow), American Orthopsychiatric Association (Fellow), American Psychological

Association Council Fellow (President 1943–44), American Society for Psychical Research, (President 1962–71), Menninger Monograph Committee, Menninger School of Psychiatry (Lecturer), Menninger School of Psychiatry Alumni Association (Honorary Member), National Association for Mental Health, National Jewish Committee (Consultant), New York Academy of Science (Fellow), Sloan Professorship Committee of the Menninger Foundation, and the Topeka Institute for Psychoanalysis (Lecturer).

Bibliography

Ackerknecht, E.H. White Indians. *Bulletin of the History of Medicine.* 15(1944):35–46.

Adams, Henry. *Mont St. Michel and Chartres.* Boston: Houghton Mifflin, 1913.

Adorno, T.W., et al. *The Authoritarian Personality.* New York: Harper, 1950.

Aeschylus. Persians. In *Plays of Aeschylus,* 4th ed., trans. by Robert Potter. London: Routledge, 1895.

Alcott, Louisa May. *Little Men.* Boston: Roberts Brothers, 1871.

_____. *Little Women.* Boston: Roberts Brothers, 1868–69.

Allen, Frederick Lewis. *The Big Change: America Transforms Itself: 1900–1950.* New York: Harper, 1952.

_____. *Only Yesterday.* New York: Harper, 1931.

Allport, Floyd H. *Social Psychology.* Boston: Houghton Mifflin, 1924.

_____. *Theories of Perception and the Concept of Structure.* New York: Wiley, 1955.

Allport, Gordon W. *Personality: A Psychological Interpretation.* New York: Holt, 1937.

_____. Prejudice: A Problem in Psychological and Social Causation. *J. Social Issues.* Supplement Series, No. 4, November, 1950.

_____. What Is a Trait of Personality? *Proc. 1st Intern. Cong. Psychol.* Princeton: Psychological Review. 1930, pp. 57–58.

_____, and Vernon, P.E. *Studies of Expressive Movement.* New York: Macmillan, 1933.

Ames, A., Jr. Visual Perception and the Rotating Trapezoidal Window. *Psychol. Monog.* No. 324; 7(1951):65.

Amory, Cleveland. *The Proper Bostonians.* Orleans, Mass.: Parnassus Imprints, 1984.

Anastasi, A., and Foley, J.H., Jr. *Differential Psychology.* New York, Macmillan, 1949.

Appelbaum, Stephen A.; Coyne, Lolafaye; and Siegal, Richard S. Change in I.Q. During and After Long-term Psychotherapy. *J. Projective Techniques.* 33(1969):290–297.

Arnheim, Rudolf. *Art and Visual Perception.* Berkeley: University of California Press, 1964.

Asch, Solomon E. *Social Psychology.* New York: Prentice-Hall, 1952.

Ashby, W.R. *Design for a Brain.* New York: Wiley, 1952.

Ayllon, T., and Sommer, R. Autism, Emphasis and Figure-Ground Perception. *J. Psychol.* 41(1956):163–176.

Bacon, Francis. "Novum Organum." Various editions, including that in *The World's Great Thinkers,* edited by Saxe Commins and Robert N. Linscott. New York: Random House, 1947.

Bailey, H.C. *Edgar Gardner Murphy: Gentle Progressive.* Coral Gables, Fla.: University of Miami Press, 1968.

Bakewell, C.M. *Source Book in Ancient Philosophy,* rev. ed. New York: Scribner, 1939.

Baldwin, James M. *Mental Development in the Child and the Race.* New York: Macmillan, 1895.

Bambrough, Renford, ed. *The Philosophy of Aristotle,* trans. by J.L. Creed and A.E. Wardman. New York: New American Library, Mentor Books, 1963.

Barrett, W.F. *Psychical Research.* New York: Holt, 1911.

Barron, Frank. *Creative Person and Creative Process.* New York: Holt, Rinehart and Winston, 1969.

Bateson, G. *Naven,* 2nd ed. Stanford, Calif.: Stanford University Press, 1958.

Bayley, Nancy. Consistency and Variability in the Growth of Intelligence from Birth to Eighteen Years. *J. Genet. Psychol.* 75(1949):165–196.

Beard, Charles A. *History of Civilization.* Boston: Ginn, 1937.

Bell, Margaret. *Margaret Fuller: A Biography.* New York: Charles Boni Paperbooks, 1930.

Benedict, Ruth. *Patterns of Culture.* Boston: Houghton Mifflin, 1934.

Bergman, Paul, and Escalona, Sibylle K. *Unusual Sensitivities in Very Young Children. Psychoanalytic Study of the Child 3 and 4.* New York: International Universities Press, 1949.

Bergson, Henri. *Creative Evolution,* trans. by Arthur Mitchell. London: Macmillan, 1911.

_____. *Matter and Memory,* trans. by Nancy Margaret Paul and W. Scott Palmer. Garden City, N.Y.: Doubleday, Anchor Books, 1959.

_____. *The Two Sources of Morality and Religion.* Garden City, N.Y.: Doubleday, 1935.

Berlyne, D.E. *Conflict, Arousal and Curiosity.* New York: McGraw-Hill Book Co., 1960.

_____. A Theory of Human Curiosity. *Brit. J. Psych.* 45(1954):180–191.

Bleuler, E. Autistic Thinking. In *Organization and Pathology of Thought,* edited by D. Rapaport. New York: Columbia University Press, 1951.

Blos, Peter. *The Adolescent Passage: Developmental Issues.* New York: International Universities Press, 1979.

_____. *The Adolescent Personality.* New York: D. Appleton Century, 1941.

Blum, John Morton. *The Republican Roosevelt,* 2nd ed. Cambridge, Mass.: Harvard University Press, 1954.

Boas, Franz. *The Mind of Primitive Man.* New York: Macmillan, 1911.

Boguslavsky, G.W. Vigilance as a Factor in Reinforcement. *J. Genet. Psychol.* 91(1957):109–113.

Bohr, Niels. *Atomic Physics and Human Knowledge.* New York: Wiley, 1958.

Boring, Edwin G. *History of Experimental Psychology.* New York: Appleton-Century-Crofts, 1929. 2nd ed., Appleton-Century-Crofts, 1950.

_____ and Lindzey, Gardner, eds. *A History of Psychology in Autobiography.* Vol. V. New York: Appleton-Century-Crofts, 1967. See autobiographies by G.W. Allport, K. Goldstein, H.A. Murray, B.F. Skinner, as well as Gardner Murphy.

Boyle, R. *The Skeptical Chymist.* London: J. Crooke, 1661.

Brett, G.S. *History of Psychology.* London: G. Allen, 1921. 3 vols.

Bridges, K.M.B. *The Social and Emotional Development of the Preschool Child.* London: Routledge, 1931.

Broad, C.D. *The Mind and Its Place in Nature.* London: Kegan Paul; New York: Harcourt, 1925.

Brooks, Van Wyck. *The Flowering of New England.* New York: E.P. Dutton, 1936.

_____. *New England: Indian Summer.* New York: E.P. Dutton, 1940.

Brown, Frederick Augustus. *Margaret Fuller and Goethe.* New York: Holt, 1910.

Brown, Harrison. *The Challenge of Man's Future.* New York: Viking, 1954.

Brown, J.F. *Psychology and the Social Order.* New York: McGraw-Hill, 1936.

Bruner, Jerome S. *In Search of Mind: Essays in Autobiography.* New York: Harper and Row, 1983.

_____, and Postman, Leo. Tension and Tension-Release as Organizing Factors in Perception. *J. Pers.* 15(1947):300–308.

Bucke, R.M. *Cosmic Consciousness.* Philadelphia: Dutton, 1906.

Carington, Whately. *Thought Transference.* New York: Creative Age, 1946.

Carmichael, L. Heredity and Environment: Are They Antithetical? *J. Abnorm. & Soc. Psychol.* 20(1925):245–260.

Carroll, Lewis. *Alice in Wonderland—Through the Looking Glass.* New York: Macmillan, 1883.

Cassirer, Ernst. *An Essay on Man: An Introduction to a Philosophy of Human Culture.* New Haven: Yale University Press, 1944.

Charcot, J.-M. *Oeuvres Complètes.* Paris: Bureaux de Progrès Medical. 1888–94.

Child, I.L. Tribute Honoring the Memory of Gardner Murphy. *J. Am. Soc. Psych. Res.* 74:125–127.

Clark, K.B., and Clark, M.K. Skin Color as a Factor in Racial Identification of Negro Preschool Children. *J. Soc. Psychol.* 11(1940):159–169.

Clark, K.E. *America's Psychologists. A Survey of a Growing Profession.* Washington, D.C.: American Psychological Association, 1957.

Clifford, Geraldine Joncich. *Edward L. Thorndike: The Sane Positivist.* Middletown, Conn.: Wesleyan University Press, 1968.

Clifford, W.K. On the Nature of Things in Themselves. In *Lectures and Essays.* London: Macmillan, 1879.

Clough, A.H. "Say Not the Struggle Naught Availeth." In *Poems of A.H. Clough,* edited by H.S. Milford. London: Henry Frowde, 1910.

Cobb, Edith. The Ecology of Imagination in Childhood. *Daedalus.* 88(1959):537–548.

Cobb, Stanley. *Borderlands of Psychiatry.* Cambridge, Mass.: Harvard University Press, 1943.

Coghill, G.E. *Anatomy and the Problem of Behavior: Lectures Delivered at University College, London.* New York: Hafner Pub. Co., 1964. (Originally published 1929.)

Coleridge, Samuel T. "Kubla Khan." In various sources.

Conant, J.B. *On Understanding Science: An Historical Approach.* New Haven: Yale University Press, 1947.

Craig, W. Male Doves Reared in Isolation. *J. Animal Behav.* 4(1914):121–133.

Criswell, Joan. A Sociometric Study of Race Cleavage in the Classroom. *Archives of Psychology,* No. 235, 1939.

Crombie, A.C. *Medieval and Early Modern Science.* Garden City, N.Y.: Doubleday, 1959.

Cummings, E.E. *Complete Poems: 1913–1962.* New York: Harcourt, Brace, 1972.

Dallenbach, Karl M. The Emergency Committee of Psychology, National Research Council. *Am. J. Psychol.* 59(1946):496–587.

Darwin, Charles. *On the Origin of the Species.* London: Murray, 1859.

Dashiell, J.F. *Fundamentals of General Psychology.* Boston: Houghton Mifflin, 1937.

Davidson, Elizabeth H. *Child Labor Legislation in the Southern Textile States.* Chapel Hill: University of North Carolina Press, 1939.

Day, Clarence. *This Simian World.* New York: Knopf, 1920.

De Quincey, T. *Confessions of an English Opium Eater,* 2nd ed. London: Taylor and Hassey, 1923.

Descartes, R. *Les Passions de l'Âme. (The Passions of the Soul.)* 1650. Various editions.

Dewey, John. *Democracy and Education: An Introduction to the Philosophy of Education.* New York: Macmillan, 1916.

————. *Interest and Effort in Education.* New York: Houghton Mifflin, 1913.

————. *The School and Society.* Chicago: University of Chicago Press, 1899.

The Dial: A Magazine for Literature, Philosophy, and Religion. Boston: Weeks, Jordan and Co., 1840–1844.

Diamond, Solomon. *Personality and Temperament.* New York: Harper, 1957.

Dickens, Charles. *Great Expectations.* Various editions.

Dobzhansky, Theodosius. *Genetics and the Origins of the Species.* New York: Columbia University Press, 1937, 1941, 1951.

————. *Mankind Evolving.* New York: Bantam, 1970.

Drabek, Thomas E., and Key, William H. *Conquering Disaster: Family Recovery and Long-Term Consequences.* New York: Irvington, 1984.

Duberman, Martin B. *Paul Robeson*. New York: Knopf, 1988.
Dubos, René. *The Torch of Life: Continuity in Living Experience*. New York: Simon and Schuster, 1962.
Dunlap, Knight. Are There Instincts? *J. Abnorm. & Soc. Psychol.* 14(1919):307–311.
Eddington, Sir Arthur. *The Nature of the Physical World*. Ann Arbor: University of Michigan Press, 1958.
————. *The Philosophy of Physical Science*. New York: Macmillan, 1939.
Edel, Leon. *Henry James: The Untried Years*. New York: Avon/ Discus, 1978.
Eiseley, Loren. *The Firmament of Time*. New York: Athenaeum, 1975.
Emerson, Ralph Waldo. *Essays*. Boston: Ticknor and Fields, 1865.
Erikson, Erik. *Childhood and Society*. New York: Norton, 1950.
————. *Gandhi's Truth*. New York: Norton, 1969.
————. *Identity: Youth and Crisis*. New York: Norton, 1968.
Erikson, Joan. *Wisdom and the Senses*. New York: Norton, 1988.
Escalona, Sibylle, and Heider, Grace. *Prediction and Outcome*. New York: Basic Books, 1959.
————; Leitch, Mary; et al. Early Phases of Personality Development: A Non-Normative Study of Infant Behavior. *Monograph for Research in Child Development 17*. 54(1), 1952.
Estabrooks, G.H. A Contribution to Experimental Telepathy. *Bulletin of the Boston Society for Psychical Research*. 5(1927):1–28.
————. The Enigma of Telepathy. *North American Review*. 227(1929):201–211.
Evans, Richard I. *The Making of Social Psychology: Discussions with Creative Contributors*. New York: Gardner Press, 1980. Chapter 1. Gardner Murphy.
Farrow, B.J.; Santos, J.F.; Haines, J.R.; and Solley, C.M. Influence of Repeated Experience of Latency and Extent of Autokinetic Movements. *Perception and Motor Skills*. 20(1965):1113–1120.
Fernald, Mabel R. The Diagnosis of Mental Imagery. *Psychol. Rev.: Monograph Supplement*. 14(58)(1912).
Finison, Lorenz J. The Psychological Insurgency—1936–1945. *J. Social Issues*. 42(1)(1986):21–34.
Fisher, R.A. *The Design of Experiments*. Edinburgh: Oliver and Boyd, 1935.
Frank, L.K. Projective Methods for the Study of Personality. *J. Psychol.* 8(1939):389–413.
————. *Society as the Patient: Essays on Culture and Personality*. New Brunswick, N.J.: Rutgers University Press, 1948.
————. Tactile Communication. *Genet. Psych. Monograph*. 56(1967):209–255.
Freud, Sigmund. *Group Psychology and the Analysis of the Ego*. London: Hogarth, 1922.
————. *New Introductory Lectures on Psychoanalysis*. New York: Norton, 1932.
————. *An Outline of Psychoanalysis*. New York: Norton, 1949.
Fromm, Erich. *Escape from Freedom*. New York: Farrar and Rinehart, 1941.
Fuller, J.S., and Thompson, W.R. *Behavior Genetics*. New York: Wiley, 1960.
Gandhi, Mohandas Karamchand. *An Autobiography: The Story of My Experiments with Truth*, trans. by M. Desai. Washington: Public Affairs Press, 1948.
Gardner, R.W. Cognitive Control Principles and Perceptual Behavior. *Bull. Menninger Clin.* 23(1959):241–248.
————; Jackson, D.N.; and Messick, S. Personality Organization in Cognitive Control Principles and Intellectual Abilities. *Psychol. Issues* 2, 1960.
Gerard, R.W.; Kluckhohn, C.; and Rapaport, A. Biological and Cultural Evolution. *Behavioral Science*. 5(1956):101–111.
Gesell, Arnold, and Thompson, Helen. *Infant Behavior: Its Genesis and Growth*. New York: McGraw-Hill, 1934.
Gibran, Kahlil. *The Prophet*. New York: Knopf, 1925.
Gibson, J.J. *The Perception of the Visual World*. Boston: Houghton Mifflin, 1950.
Gittings, Robert. *The Nature of Biography*. Seattle: University of Washington Press, 1978.

Glass, B. The Hazards of Atomic Radiation to Man—British and American Report. *Bull. Atomic Scientist.* 12(1956):312–317.

Going, A.J. The Reverend Edgar Gardner Murphy: His Ideas and Influence. *Historical Magazine of the Protestant Episcopal Church.* December, 1956.

Goldstein, Kurt. *The Organism.* New York: American Book Co., 1939.

Green, Elmer E.; Green, A.M.; and Walters, E.D. Voluntary Control of Internal States: Psychological and Physiological. *Transpersonal Psychology.* 2(1970):1–26.

Hall, C.S., and Lindzey, G. *Theories of Personality.* New York: Wiley, 1957.

Harlan, Louis, and Smock, Raymond W., eds. *Booker T. Washington Papers.* Urbana: University of Illinois Press, 1972–.

Harlow, H.F. The Development of Affectional Patterns in Infant Monkeys. In *Determinants of Infant Behavior,* edited by B.M. Foss. New York: Wiley, 1961.

Hartmann, Heinz. *Ego Psychology and the Problem of Adaptation,* trans. by David Rapaport. New York: International Universities Press, 1958.

_____. The Mutual Influences in the Development of the Ego and the Id. In *Psychoanalytic Study of the Child, Vol. 7.* New York: International Universities Press, 1952.

_____; Kris, Ernst; and Lowenstein, Rudolph M. *Papers on Psychoanalytic Psychology. Psychol. Issues.* (Vol. IV, No. 2. Monograph 14.) New York: International Universities Press, 1964.

Hartshorne, H., and May, M.A. *Studies in Deceit.* New York: Macmillan, 1928.

_____; _____; and Maller, J.B. *Studies in Service and Self Control.* New York: Macmillan, 1929.

_____; _____; and Shuttleworth, F.K. *Studies in the Organization of Character.* New York: Macmillan, 1930.

Hawthorne, N. *Tanglewood Tales.* Boston: Ticknor, Reed, and Fields, 1853.

Hebb, D.O. *The Organization of Behavior.* New York: Wiley, 1949.

_____. The Role of Neurological Ideas in Psychology. *J. Pers.* 20(1951):39–55.

Hefferline, R.F. The Role of Proprioception in the Control of Behavior. *Transactions of the N.Y. Academy of Science.* 20(1958):739–764.

Heider, Grace. Vulnerability in Infants and Young Children. A Pilot Study. *Genet. Psychol. Monographs.* 73(1)(1966):1–216.

Helson, H. *Adaptation Level Theory.* New York: Harper, 1964.

Henley, William Ernest. "Invictus." In *Works of W.E. Henley.* London: D. Nutt, 1908.

Herbart, J.F. *A Textbook in Psychology: An Attempt to Found the Science of Psychology on Experience, Metaphysics and Mathematics,* 2nd ed., edited by W.T. Harris and trans. by M.K. Smith. New York: Appleton, 1891. (Originally published 1816.)

Hess, E.H. Imprinting. *Science.* 130(1959):133–141.

Hilgard, E.R. From the Social Gospel to the Psychology of Social Issues: A Reminiscence. *J. Social Issues.* 42(1)(1986): 107–110.

_____. *Theories of Learning.* New York: Appleton-Century-Crofts, 1948. (For 5th ed., see Bower and Hilgard, 1981.)

Hitler, Adolf. *Mein Kampf,* trans. by Ralph Mannheim. Boston: Houghton Mifflin, 1943.

Hobbes, Thomas. *Human Nature* (1651). Various editions, e.g. London: Bowman, 1960.

_____. *Leviathan* (1651). Various editions, e.g. that edited by M. Oakeshott. New York: Collier, 1962.

Hodgson, Richard. A Record of Observations of Certain Phenomena of Trance. *Proceedings of the Society for Psychical Research.* 8(1892):1–168.

Hoffman, Edward. *The Right to Be Human: A Biography of Abraham Maslow.* Los Angeles: Jeremy P. Tarcher, Inc., 1988.

Hofstadter, Richard. *The Age of Reform.* New York: Knopf, 1955.

Holt, E.B. *Animal Drive and the Learning Process.* New York: Holt, 1931.

Holzman, P.S., and Rousey, C. The Voice as Percept. *J. Pers. & Soc. Psychol.* 4(1966): 79–86.

Horney, Karen. *The Neurotic Personality of Our Time.* New York: Norton, 1937.
Horowitz, E.L. The Development of Attitude Toward Negroes. *Arch. Psychol.* No. 194, 1936.
Horowitz, R.E. Racial Aspects of Self-Identification in Nursery School Children. *J. Psychol.* 7(1939):91–99.
_____, and Murphy, L.B. Projective Methods in the Psychological Study of Children. *J. Experimental Education.* 7(1938):133–146.
Horwitz, Leonard. *Clinical Prediction in Psychotherapy.* New York: Jacob Aronson, 1974.
Hume, D. "An Inquiry Concerning Human Understanding." In *Essays and Treatises,* vol. 3. Basel: J.S. Tourneisen, 1793.
Hume, R.E. *The Thirteen Principal Upanishads,* trans. from the Sanskrit. 2nd ed., revised by George C.O. Haas. Madras: India Branch, Oxford University Press, 1949.
Hunt, J. McV., ed. *Personality and the Behavior Disorders: A Handbook Based on Experimental and Clinical Research.* New York: Ronald Press, 1944.
Huxley, Aldous. *Brave New World.* London: Chatto and Windus, 1932.
Huxley, Julian. *Man in the Modern World.* New York: Universal, 1947.
Huxley, T.H. *Evolution and Ethics, and Other Essays.* New York: D. Appleton, 1897.
Hyslop, J.H. Psychic Research in Harvard University. *J.A.S.P.R.* 13(1919):355–360.
Isaacs, Susan. *Social Development in Young Children.* London: Routledge, 1933.
Jackson, D.N. A Further Examination of the Role of Autism in a Visual Figure-Ground Relationship. *J. Psychol.* 38(1954):339–357.
Jacobson, E. *Progressive Relaxation,* 2nd ed. Chicago: University of Chicago Press, 1938.
James, William. *Principles of Psychology,* vols. 1 and 2. New York: Holt, 1890.
_____. Report on Mrs. Piper's Hodgson-Control. *Proceedings of the Society for Psychical Research.* 28(1909):1–121.
_____. *The Varieties of Religious Experience.* New York: Longmans, 1902.
_____. *The Will to Believe and Other Essays in Popular Philosophy.* New York: Longmans, 1903.
Janet, P. *Psychological Healing: A Historical and Clinical Study,* trans. by Eden and Cedar Paul. London: G. Allen and Unwin, 1925.
Johnson, Burges. *As Much as I Dare.* New York: Ives Washburn, Inc., 1944.
Jones, Harold E. *Development in Adolescence: Approaches to the Study of the Individual.* New York: Appleton-Century, 1943.
_____. The Galvanic Skin Inflex in Infancy. *Child Development.* 1(1930):106–110.
Jones, Mary Cover. The Elimination of Children's Fears. *J. Exper. Psychol.* 7(1924):382–390.
Kallman, F.J. *Heredity in Health and Mental Disorder.* New York: Norton, 1942.
Kant, I. *The Critique of Pure Reason.* Riga: Hartknoch, 1781.
Kardiner, A.H. *The Individual and His Society: The Psychodynamics of Primitive Social Organization.* New York: Columbia University Press, 1939.
Keats, John. "Ode on a Grecian Urn." In *The Oxford Book of English Verse,* edited by Arthur Quiller-Couch. Oxford: Clarendon Press, 1930.
Kempf, E.J. Autonomic Functions and the Personality. *Nervous and Mental Disease Monographs,* No. 28, 1918.
Kernberg, Otto. Summary and Conclusions of "Psychotherapy and Psychoanalysis: Final Report on the Menninger Foundation's Psychotherapy Research Project." *Int. J. of Psychiatry.* 11(1973):62–77.
Key, William H. "When People Are Forced to Move." Final Report on a Study on Forced Relocation. Unpublished. 1967. Research Archives of the Menninger Foundation.
Kipling, Rudyard. *The Jungle Book.* London: Macmillan, 1894.
_____. *Just So Stories.* New York: Macmillan, 1982. (Original, London: Macmillan, 1902).
_____. *The Second Jungle Book.* London: Macmillan, 1895.
Klein, G.A. Adaptive Properties of Sensory Functioning. *Bull. of Menninger Clin.* 13(1949):16–23.

_____. Need and Regulation. In *Nebraska Symposium on Motivation,* edited by M.R. Jones. Lincoln: University of Nebraska Press, 1954.

Klineberg, Otto. *Negro Intelligence and Selective Migration.* New York: Columbia University Press, 1935.

_____. *Race Differences.* New York: Harper, 1935.

_____, and Christie, Richard, eds. *Perspectives in Social Psychology.* New York: Holt, Rinehart and Winston, 1965. See Gardner Murphy, "The Future of Social Psychology."

Kluger, Richard. *Simple Justice: The History of Brown v. Board of Education and Black America's Struggle for Equality.* New York: Vintage Books, 1977.

Klüver, Heinrich. Contemporary German Psychology. In *Historical Introduction to Modern Psychology,* by Gardner Murphy. New York: Harcourt, Brace, 1929, 1938.

Koffka, K. *The Growth of the Mind,* trans. by R.M. Ogden. New York: Harcourt, Brace, 1931.

_____. *Principles of Gestalt Psychology.* New York: Harcourt, Brace, 1935.

Köhler, Wolfgang. *The Mentality of Apes,* trans. by E. Winter. New York: Harcourt, Brace, 1925. (Originally published 1917.)

Kovach, J.K., and Gardner Murphy. *Historical Introduction to Modern Psychology,* 3rd ed. New York: Harcourt Brace Jovanovich, 1972.

Krantz, David L., ed. *Schools of Psychology: A Symposium of Papers by David L. Krantz, E.G. Boring, Edna Heidbreder, R.J. Herrnstein, Wolfgang Köhler, David Shakow, Gardner Murphy, on the Occasion of the Seventy-Fifth Anniversary of the Founding of the American Psychological Association.* New York: Appleton-Century-Crofts, 1969.

Krech, David. Dynamic Systems as Open Neurological Systems. *Psychol. Rev.* 57(1950): 345–361.

Kretschmer, E. *Physique and Character: An Investigation of the Nature of Constitution and of the Theory of Temperament.* London: Kegan Paul Trench Trubner, 1925.

Kuhn, T.S. *The Structure of Scientific Revolutions.* Chicago: University of Chicago Press, 1962.

Kuo, Z.Y. The Genesis of the Cat's Responses Toward the Rat. *J. Comp. Physio. Psychol.* 11(1930):1–35.

_____. Giving Up Instincts in Psychology. *J. Philosophy.* 18(1921):645–666.

Lacey, John I., and Van Lehn, Ruth. Differential Emphases in Somatic Response to Stress. *Psychosomatic Medicine 14,* No. 2, 1952.

Ladd, G.T., and Woodworth, R.S. *Elements of Physiological Psychology,* rev. ed. New York: Scribners, 1911.

Lamarck, J.B. de. *Système des Animaux Sans Vertébrés.* Brussels: Culture et Civilisation, 1969. (Originally published 1801.)

Langer, Susanne. *Philosophy in a New Key.* Cambridge, Mass.: Harvard University Press, 1951.

Leakey, Richard E. *One Life: An Autobiography.* Salem, N.H.: Salem House, 1964.

Lear, Edward. *The Complete Nonsense of Edward Lear,* edited and introduced by H. Jackson. New York: Dover, 1959.

LeBon, G. *The Crowd: A Study of the Popular Mind.* New York: Viking Press, 1960. (Originally published 1895.)

Leeds, Morton, and Murphy, Gardner. *The Paranormal and the Normal.* Metuchen, N.J.: Scarecrow Press, 1980.

Levine, Daniel. *Varieties of Reform Thought.* Madison: State Historical Society of Wisconsin, 1964.

Levine, J.M., and Murphy, G. The Learning and Forgetting of Controversial Material. *J. Abnorm. & Soc. Psychol.* 38(1943):507–517.

Levine, R.; Chein, I.; and Murphy, G. The Relation of the Intensity of a Need to the Amount of Perceptual Distortion: A Preliminary Report. *J. Psychol.* 13(1942):282–293.

Levy, David M. *Maternal Overprotection.* New York: Columbia University Press, 1943.

_____. *Studies in Sibling Rivalry.* New York: Columbia University Press, 1937.

Lewin, Kurt. *A Dynamic Theory of Personality: Selected Papers.* New York: McGraw-Hill, 1935.

_____. *Principles of Topological Psychology.* New York: McGraw-Hill, 1936.

_____; Lippitt, R.; and White, R.K. Patterns of Aggressive Behavior in Experimentally Created Social Climates. *J. Social Psychol.* 10(1939):271–299.

Likert, Rensis. *A Technique for the Measurement of Attitudes.* Archives of Psychology. No. 140, 1932.

Lindzey, Gardner. *Handbook of Social Psychology.* Vols. 1–2. Cambridge, Mass.: Addison-Wesley, 1954. See Gardner Murphy, "Social Motivation."

_____, ed. *A History of Psychology in Autobiography,* Vol. VI. Englewood Cliffs, New Jersey: Prentice-Hall, 1974. See autobiographies by Floyd H. Allport, Ernest R. Hilgard, Otto Klineberg, David Krech, A.R. Luria, Margaret Mead, Theodore M. Newcomb, friends of Gardner and Lois Murphy.

Locke, J. *Essay Concerning Human Understanding.* London: Basset, 1690.

Lodge, Oliver. Evidence of Classical Scholarship and of Cross-Correspondence in Some New Automatic Writings. *Proceedings of the Society for Psychical Research.* 25(1911):113–175.

London, Jack. *Star Rover,* epilogue by Gardner Murphy. New York: Grosset and Dunlap, 1963.

Lorenz, K. *King Solomon's Ring.* New York: Crowell, 1952.

Lothrop, Margaret. *The Wayside: House of Authors.* New York: American Book Co., 1940.

Lowes, J.L. *The Road to Xanadu.* Boston: Houghton Mifflin, 1927.

Luborsky, Lester. Clinicians' Judgments of Mental Health: A Proposed Scale. *Archives of General Psychiatry.* 7(1962):407–417.

Lucretius. *On the Nature of Things,* trans. by William Ellery Leonard. New York: E.P. Dutton, 1952.

Luria, A.R. *The Role of Speech in the Regulation of Normal and Abnormal Behavior.* London: Pergamon Press, 1966.

Lynd, R.S., and Lynd, H.M. *Middletown: A Study in Contemporary American Culture.* New York: Harcourt, Brace, 1929.

MacDonald, George. *At the Back of the North Wind.* London: Strahan, 1871.

McDougall, W. *Introduction to Social Psychology,* 15th ed. Boston: T.W. Luce & Co., 1923.

Macfarlane, Jean. From Infancy to Adulthood. *Childhood Education.* 39(1963):336–342.

McGinley, Phyllis. *Times Three.* New York: Viking Press, 1968.

McNamara, Harold J. Non-Veridical Perception as a Function of Rewards and Punishments. *Percept. & Motor Skills.* 9(1959):67–80.

_____, and Fisch, R.I. Personal Space and Laterality in Perception. *Percept. & Motor Skills.* 10(1960):70–123.

_____; Solley, C.M.; and Long, J. Effects of Punishment (Electric Shock) Upon Perceptual Learning. *J. Abnorm. & Soc. Psychol.* 57(1958):91–98.

Mannheim, Karl. *Ideology and Utopia.* New York: Harcourt, 1936.

Margenau, Henry. *Integrative Principles of Modern Thought.* New York: Gordon and Breach, 1972.

Marks, E. Skin Color Judgments of Negro College Students. *J. Abnorm. & Soc. Psychol.* 22(1940):3–14.

Marrow, Alfred. *Living Without Hate: Scientific Approaches to Human Relations.* New York: Harper, 1951.

_____. *The Practical Theorist: The Life and Work of Kurt Lewin.* New York: Basic Books, 1969.

Marx, Karl. "Communist Manifesto." Various editions.

Masefield, J. *Poems.* New York: Macmillan, 1955.

Maslow, A.H. *The Psychology of Science.* New York: Harper and Row, 1966.

Mauskopf, Seymour H. The History of the American Society for Psychical Research: An Interpretation. *J.A.S.P.R.* 83(1989):7–29.

Mead, G.H. *Mind, Self, and Society.* Chicago: University of Chicago Press, 1934.

Mead, Margaret. *Coming of Age in Samoa.* New York: Morrow, 1928.

————, ed. *Cooperation and Competition Among Primitive Peoples.* New York: McGraw-Hill, 1937.

————. *New Worlds for Old.* New York: Morrow, 1956.

Menninger, Karl. *The Vital Balance.* New York: Viking, 1963.

Menninger, William C. *A Psychiatrist for a Troubled World: Selected Papers,* edited by Bernard H. Hall. New York: Viking Press, 1967.

Messick, S.J., and Solley, C.M. Probability Learning in Children: Some Exploratory Studies. *J. Genet. Psychol.* 90(1957):23–32.

————; ————; and Jackson, D.N. "Autism, Distraction and Attention." Unpublished, 1956. Research Archives of the Menninger Foundation.

Miller, Perry. *The Puritans,* rev. ed. New York: Harper and Row, 1963.

————. *The Transcendentalists.* Cambridge, Mass.: Harvard University Press, 1960.

Mittelmann, B. Motility in Infants, Children and Adults. In *Psychoanalytic Study of the Child,* vol. 9. New York: International Universities Press, 1954.

More, Thomas. *Utopia.* London: A. Vele, 1551.

Moreno, J.L. *Who Shall Survive?* Washington, D.C.: Nervous and Mental Disease Publ. Co., 1934.

Moriarty, Alice E. *Constancy and I.Q. Change: A Clinical View of Relationships Between Tested Intelligence and Personality.* Springfield, Ill.: Charles C. Thomas, 1966.

Mortleer, John. *Ralph Waldo Emerson: Days of Encounter.* Boston: Little, Brown, 1984.

Muller, H.J. *Out of the Night: A Biologist's View of the Future.* New York: Vanguard, 1935.

————. *Uses of the Past: Profiles of Former Societies.* New York: Oxford, 1952.

Mumford, Lewis. *The Story of Utopias.* New York: Boni and Liveright, 1922.

Munnor, Ruth. *Schools of Psychoanalytic Thought.* Boston: Dryden Press, 1965.

Murchison, Carl, ed. *Handbook of Social Psychology.* Worcester, Mass.: Clark University Press, 1935.

Murphy, Edgar Gardner. *The Basis of Ascendancy.* New York: Longmans, Green, 1909.

———— [under pseudonym Kelvin McKready]. *A Beginner's Guide to the Stars,* arranged by Maud King Murphy. New York and London: G.P. Putnam's Sons, 1924.

———— [under pseudonym Kelvin McKready]. *A Beginner's Star Book.* New York and London: G.P. Putnam's Sons, 1912.

————. *The Larger Life.* New York: Longmans, Green, 1897.

————. *Problems of the Present South.* New York: Macmillan, 1904.

————. *Words for the Church.* New York: Whittaker, 1897.

Murphy, Gardner. A.S.P.R. Forum on Extrasensory Perception. *J.A.S.P.R.* 60(1966): 198–201, 212–213.

————. The Abilities of Man: A Summing Up. In *Higher Education and the Abilities of Man.* Third Annual California Conference on Higher Education. Burlingame: California Teachers Association, May 1964, pp. 55–68.

————. Affect and Perceptual Learning. *Psychol. Rev.* 63(Jan. 1956):1–15.

————. The American Eugenics Movement. *Eugenical News.* 37(1952):35–37.

————. Answer to Boring. Letter in *Contemp. Psychol.* 1962, pp. 357–358.

————. The Boundaries Between the Person and the World. *Brit. J. Psychol.* 47(May 1956):88–94.

————. *A Briefer General Psychology.* New York: Harper, 1935.

————. *The Challenge of Psychical Research.* New York: Harper, 1961.

————. A Comparison of India and the West in Viewpoints Regarding Psychical Phenomena. *J.A.S.P.R.* 53(1959):43–49.

————. A Cosmic Christmas Carol. *Saturday Review.* 41:45–48, December 13, 1958.

————. Creativity and Its Relation to Extrasensory Perception. *J.A.S.P.R.* 57(Oct. 1963):203–214.

————. A Cross-Cultural View of Ego Dynamics. *Bull. New York Acad. Med.* (two parts). 41(March 1965):268–285; 41(April 1965):335–346.

_____. The Current Impact of Freud upon Psychology. *Am. Psychologist.* 11(Dec. 1956):663–672.

_____. Education and the Creative Reconstruction of Society. In *That All May Learn to Read.* Proceedings of the 1959 Annual Reading Conference. Syracuse, N.Y.: Syracuse University Press, 1960, pp. 62–69.

_____. Education of the Will. *Quest.* (Monograph IV.) April 1965, pp. 1–9.

_____. Education: Transition or Challenge. In *The Danforth Lectures 1957–1960.* Muncie, Indiana: Ball State Teachers College, 1962, pp. 77–78.

_____. The Enigma of Human Nature. *Main Currents in Modern Thought.* 13 (Sept. 1956): 11–15.

_____. Evolution: Charles Darwin. *Bull. Menninger Clin.* 32(March 1968):86–101.

_____. An Experimental Study of Literary vs. Scientific Types. *Am. J. Psychol.* 28(April 1917):238–262.

_____. Face Those Atomic Fears! *Christian Century.* 75:250–251, February 26, 1958.

_____. Facing the Realities of the Space Age. *SPSSI Newsletter,* 3, November 1959.

_____. Foreword. In *Psychology: Briefer Course,* by William James. New York: Collier, 1962, pp. 5–7.

_____. Four Conceptions of Research in Clinical Psychology. *Bull. Menninger Clin.* 25(Nov. 1961):290–295.

_____. Freedom Through Order: A Persisting Paradox. In *Higher Education and the Abilities of Man.* Third Annual California Conference on Higher Education. Burlingame: California Teachers Association, May 1964, pp. 6–22.

_____. *Freeing Intelligence Through Teaching: A Dialectic of the Rational and the Personal.* New York: Harper, 1961.

_____. The Freeing of Intelligence. *Psychol. Bull.* 42(1945):1–19.

_____. The Future of Social Psychology in Historical Perspective. In *Perspectives in Social Psychology,* edited by Otto Klineberg and R. Christie. New York: Holt, Rinehart and Winston, 1965, pp. 21–34.

_____. Future Research in Precognition. *International J. Parapsychol.* 2(1960):5–20.

_____. Gardner Murphy. In *A History of Psychology in Autobiography,* vol. V., edited by E.G. Boring and Gardner Lindzey. New York: Appleton-Century-Crofts, 1967.

_____. *General Psychology.* New York: Harper, 1933.

_____. *Historical Introduction to Modern Psychology.* New York: Harcourt, Brace, 1929, 1949, 1972.

_____. *Historical Introduction to Modern Psychology,* rev. ed. New York: Harcourt, Brace, 1949.

_____, ed. *Human Nature and Enduring Peace.* Boston: Houghton Mifflin, 1945.

_____. Human Potentialities. *J. Social Issues.* Suppl. Series, No. 7, Kurt Lewin Memorial Award Issue, 1953, 19 pp.

_____. *Human Potentialities.* New York: Basic Books, 1958.

_____. Human Psychology in the Context of the New Knowledge. *Main Currents in Modern Thought.* 21(March-April 1965):75–81.

_____. *In the Minds of Men: A UNESCO Study of Social Tensions in India.* New York: Basic Books, 1953.

_____. Interrelationships Between Perception and Personality: A Symposium, Part I. *J. Personality.* 18(1949):51–55.

_____. Introduction. To *Biochemistry and Behavior,* by Samuel Eiduson, Edward Geller et al. Princeton, N.J.: Van Nostrand, 1964.

_____. Introductory Aspects of Modern Parapsychological Research. *Transactions of the N.Y. Academy of Science.* Series II; 2(30)(Dec. 1967):256–260.

_____. Karl Bühler and the Psychology of Thought. In "Symposium on Karl Bühler's Contributions to Psychology," edited by James F.T. Bugental, et al. *J. Gen. Psychol.* (75:181–219)75(Oct. 1966):188–195.

_____. Kurt Lewin and Field Theory. *Bull. Menninger Clin.* 30(Nov. 1966):358–367.

_____. Lawfulness versus Caprice: Is There a Law of Psychic Phenomena? *J.A.S.P.R.* 58(Oct. 1964):238–249.

_____. The Life Work of Frederic W.H. Myers. *Tomorrow.* 2(Winter 1954):33–39.

_____. Modern Views Regarding the Survival Problem. *Physics International.* 1(May 1964):47–49.

_____. Motivation: The Key to Changing Educational Times. In *Curriculum Research Institutes,* edited by Vergil Ort. Columbus: Ohio Association for Supervision and Curriculum Development, 1964, pp. 55–69.

_____. The Natural, the Mystical, and the Paranormal. *J.A.S.P.R.* 46(1952):125–142.

_____. The Nature of Man. In *Stephanos: Studies in Psychology Presented to Cyril Burt,* edited by Charlotte Banks and P.L. Broadhurst. London: University of London Press, 1965, pp. 91–108.

_____. Notes for a Parapsychological Autobiography. *J. Parapsychol.* 21(Sept. 1957):165–178. Reprinted in *Pastoral Psychology.* 18(Nov. 1967):45–54.

_____. Notes on Instinct Theory. *Darshana.* 1(August 1961):67–69.

_____. Nuclear Dementia. *The Nation.* May 20, 1950, pp. 484–485.

_____. Organism and Quantity: A Study of Organic Structure as a Quantitative Problem. In *Perspectives in Psychological Theory,* edited by Seymour Wapner and Bernard Kaplan. New York: International Universities Press, 1960, pp. 179–224.

_____. Our Pioneers III: William James. *J. Soc. Psychical Res.* (London). 39(1958):309–313.

_____, ed. *An Outline of Abnormal Psychology.* New York: Modern Library, 1929.

_____. Parapsychology. In *Encyclopedia of Psychology,* edited by P.L. Harriman. New York: Philosophical Library, 1947, pp. 417–436.

_____. Parapsychology. In *Taboo Topics,* edited by Norman L. Farberow. New York: Atherton, 1963, pp. 56–63.

_____. Personal Impressions of Kurt Goldstein. In *The Reach of Mind: Essays in Memory of Kurt Goldstein,* edited by Marianne Simmel. New York: Springer, 1968, pp. 31–34.

_____. Personal Maturation Through Education: Possibilities and Risks. In *Förderungen an die Psychologie,* edited by F. Hardesty and K. Eyferth. Verlag Hans Huber: Bern und Stuttgart, 1965, pp. 68–82.

_____. *Personality: A Biosocial Approach to Origins and Structure.* New York: Harper, 1947.

_____. The Place of Parapsychology Among the Sciences. In Symposium [1948] of the [Washington, D.C.] Society for Parapsychology. *J. Parapsychol.* 13(March 1949):62–71.

_____. Plans for Research on Spontaneous Cases. *J.A.S.P.R.* 49(1955):85–98.

_____. Political Invention as a Strategy Against War. In *Psychology and International Relations,* edited by Gerald Sperrazzo. Washington, D.C.: Georgetown University Press, 1965, pp. 93–102.

_____. Potentiation: A Clue to Integration in the Living System. The First Annual Lecture of the Samuel H. Flowerman Memorial Lectures. New York Society of Clinical Psychologists. New York City, December 1959.

_____. The Prevention of Mental Disorder: Some Research Suggestions. *J. Hillside Hospital.* 9(July 1960): 131–146.

_____. Progress in Parapsychology. *J. Parapsychol.* 22(1958):229–236. (Reprinted *J.A.S.P.R.* 53[Jan. 1959]:16–22.)

_____. Psychical Phenomena and Human Needs. *J.A.S.P.R.* 37(1943):163–191.

_____. Psychical Research and the Mind-Body Relation. *J.A.S.P.R.* 40(Oct. 1945):189–207.

_____. Psychoanalysis as a Unified Theory of Social Behavior. In *Psychoanalysis and Human Values,* edited by Jules Masserman. New York: Grune & Stratton. 1960. See also *Psychiatry.* 23 (Nov. 1960):341–346.

_____. Psychological Aspects of the Cold War. Mimeographed lecture, Veterans

Administration–Universities Semi-Annual Conference. Catholic University of America, Washington, D.C., December 5, 1962.

_____. *Psychological Thought from Pythagoras to Freud.* New York: Harcourt, Brace & World, 1968.

_____. Psychological Views of Personality and Contributions to Its Study. In *The Study of Personality: An Interdisciplinary Appraisal,* edited by Edward Norbeck et al. New York: Holt, Rinehart and Winston, 1968, pp. 15–40.

_____. A Psychologist Views the Nuclear Crisis. Excerpted in *Toward a Science and a Program for Human Survival.* Proceedings of First National Conference, 1962, Congress of Scientists on Survival. New York: Scientists on Survival, 1965, pp. 11–13.

_____. Psychology and Psychical Research. *Proc. Soc. Psychical Res.* 50(Jan. 1953):26–49.

_____. Psychology and the Knowledge of Man. In *The Unity of Knowledge,* edited by Lewis Leary. (Columbia University Bicentennial Conference Series.) Garden City, N.Y.: Doubleday, 1955, pp. 98–124.

_____. Psychology and the Post-War World. *Psychol. Rev.* 49(1942):298–318.

_____. Psychology: New Ways to Self-Discovery. In *The Frontiers of Knowledge,* edited by Lynn White, Jr. New York: Harper, 1956, pp. 19–32.

_____. The Psychology of Freedom. *Challenge.* January, 1960, pp. 27–33.

_____. The Psychology of 1975: An Extrapolation. *Am. Psychologist.* 18(Nov. 1963): 689–695.

_____. Psychology Serving Society. *Survey Graphic.* 37(Jan. 1948):3–14.

_____. Pythagorean Number Theory and Its Implications for Psychology. *Am. Psychologist.* 22(June 1967):423–431.

_____. A Qualitative Study of Telepathic Phenomena. *J.A.S.P.R.* 56(April 1962): 63–79. Reprinted in *Neue Wissenschaft,* January 1964, pp. 1–13.

_____. The Relationships of Culture and Personality. In *Culture and Personality,* edited by S.S. Sargent. New York: Viking Fund, 1949, pp. 13–30.

_____. The Research Task of Social Psychology. *J. Social Psychol.* 10(1939):107–120.

_____. Review of Gordon W. Allport: *The Person in Psychology:* Main selection by the Behavioral Science Books Service, December 1967.

_____. Review of *The Mind of a Mnemonist: A Little Book About a Vast Memory,* by A.R. Luria. New York: Basic Books, 1968. In *Science.* 161:349–350, July 26, 1968.

_____. Review of William McDougall: *Explorers of the Mind: Studies in Psychical Research,* edited by Raymond Van Over and Laura Oteri. New York: Helix Press (Garrett Publications), 1967. In *International Journal of Parapsychology.* 10(Summer 1968):217–218.

_____. Robert Sessions Woodworth, 1869–1962. *Am. Psychologist.* 18(1963):131–133.

_____. Roles, Nomos and Midtown Misery. Review of *Mental Health in the Metropolis: The Midtown Manhattan Study* (Vol. I), by Leo Srole, Thomas S. Langer et al. New York, McGraw–Hill, 1962. *Contemp. Psychol.* 1963, pp. 35–37.

_____. The Service Man's Tomorrow. *Tomorrow.* April 1945, pp. 5–8.

_____. Social Motivation. In *Handbook of Social Psychology,* edited by Gardner Lindzey. Cambridge, Mass.: Addison-Wesley Press, 1954 (Chapter 16, pp. 601–633).

_____. Social Psychology. In *American Handbook of Psychiatry,* edited by S. Arieti. New York: Basic Books, 1959.

_____. Some Needed Research into Personality Structure. In *Centennial Papers Saint Elizabeth's Hospital 1855–1955,* edited by Winfred Overholser. Washington, D.C.: 1956, pp. 179–192.

_____. Some Obscure Relations of Organism and Environment. *Scient. Month.* 53(Sept. 1941):267–272.

_____. Some Reflections on John Dewey's Psychology. *University of Colorado Studies Series in Philosophy,* No. 2, August, 1961, pp. 26–34.

_____. Some Relations of Perception to Motivation. In *Current Psychological Issues,* edited by Georgene S. Seward and John P. Seward. New York: Holt, 1958 (Chapter 2, pp. 23–38).

_____. Statement in Honor of Piaget. *Revue Suisse de Psychologie Pure et Appliquée.* 25(1966):194–196.

_____. The Statue with a Sense of Smell. *J. Psychol. Res.* 7(1963):1–3.

_____. Telepathy as an Experimental Problem. In *The Case For and Against Psychical Belief,* edited by C. Murchison. Worcester, Mass.: Clark University Press, 1927.

_____. Testing the Limits of Man. *J. Social Issues.* 17(1961):5–14. Adaptation reprinted in *Menninger Quart.* 15(Winter 1961):1–6.

_____. The Third Human Nature. *J. Ind. Psychol.* 13(Nov. 1957):125–133.

_____. *Three Papers on the Survival Problem.* New York: American Society for Psychical Research, 1955. (First published in 1945 in *J.A.S.P.R.*) See also: An Outline of Survival Evidence (January 1945); Difficulties Confronting the Survival Hypothesis (April 1945); Field Theory and Survival (October 1945.)

_____. To Connaître, to Savoir. *Contemp. Psychol.* 12(May 1967): 241–242. (Review of Maslow, *The Psychology of Science,* New York: Harper, 1966.)

_____. Toward a Dynamic Trace-Theory. *Bull. Menninger Clin.* 20(May 1956):125–134.

_____. Toward a Field Theory of Communication. *J. Communication* 11(Dec. 1961): 196–210. (Symposium on Foundations of Communication Theory. Dr. Bess Sondel, symposium editor.)

_____. Trends in the Study of Extrasensory Perception. *Am. Psychologist.* 13(Feb. 1958):69–76. (Also under title: Psychological Aspects of Studies in Extrasensory Perception. *International J. Parapsychol.* 3[1961]:37–55.)

_____. Types of Word-Association in Dementia Praecox, Manic-Depressives, and Normal Persons. *Am. J. Psychiat.* 11(April 1923):1–33.

_____. A Visit to the S.P.R. in London. *J.A.S.P.R.* 43(Oct. 1949):137–142.

_____. Where Is the Human Race Going? Report No. 2, Western Behavioral Sciences Institute, LaJolla, Calif., 1961. (Reprinted in *Science and Human Affairs.* [Lucile P. Morrison Lectures, Western Behavioral Sciences Institute], edited by Richard R. Farson. Palo Alto, Calif.: Science and Behavior Books, 1966, pp. 7–17.)

_____. William James and Psychical Research. *J.A.S.P.R.* 43(July 1949):85–93.

_____. William James on the Will. *J. Hist. Behav. Sci* VII, 3, 249–260

_____, and Bachrach, A.J., eds. *An Outline of Abnormal Psychology,* rev. ed. New York: Modern Library, 1954.

_____, and Ballou, R.O. *William James on Psychical Research.* New York: Viking Press, 1960.

_____; Chein, Isidor; Levine, Robert; Proshansky, Harold; and Schafer, Roy. Need as a Determinant of Perception: A Reply to Pastore. *J. Psychol.* 31(1951):129–136.

_____, and Cohen, Sidney. The Search for Person-World Isomorphism. *Main Currents in Modern Thought.* 22(Nov.-Dec. 1965):31–34.

_____; Harrell, Samuel; and McNamara, H.J. Curiosity and Reality Contact: A Preliminary Report. *Percept. & Motor Skills.* 18(1964):976.

_____, and Hochberg, Julian. Perceptual Development: Some Tentative Hypotheses. *Psychol. Rev.* 58(1951):332–349.

_____, and Jensen, F. *Approaches to Personality.* New York: Harper, 1932.

_____, and Klemme, Herbert L. Unfinished Business. *J.A.S.P.R.* 60(Oct. 1966):306–320.

_____, and Kovach, J.K. *Historical Introduction to Modern Psychology,* 3rd ed. New York: Harcourt Brace Jovanovich, 1972.

_____, and Leeds, M. *Outgrowing Self-Deception.* New York: Basic Books, 1975.

_____ and _____. *The Paranormal and the Normal.* Metuchen, N.J.: Scarecrow Press, 1980.

_____, and Levine, J.M. The Learning and Forgetting of Controversial Material. *J. Abnorm. & Social Psychol.* 38(1943):507–517.

_____; Levine, Robert; and Chein, Isidor. The Relation of the Intensity of a Need to the Amount of Perceptual Distortion: A Preliminary Report. *J. Psychol.* 13(1942):283–293.

———, and Likert, R. *Public Opinion and the Individual.* New York: Harper, 1938.

———, and Moriarty, Alice E. An Experimental Study of ESP Potential and Its Relationship to Creativity in a Group of Normal Children. *J.A.S.P.R.* 61(Oct. 1967):326–338.

———, and Murphy, Lois Barclay, eds. *Asian Psychology.* New York: Basic Books, 1968.

———, and ———. *Experimental Social Psychology.* New York: Harper, 1931.

——— and ———. Hermann Rorschach and Personality Research. In *Rorschach Psychology,* edited by Maria Rickers-Ovsiankina. New York: Wiley, 1960, pp. 341–357.

——— and ———. Human Nature and Human Potentialities: Imagination and the Imaginary. In *Explorations in Human Potentialities,* edited by Herbert A. Otto. Springfield, Ill.: Charles C. Thomas, 1966, pp. 5–18.

——— and ———. A Richness of Experience. *Psychiatry & Soc. Sci. Review.* 1(Nov. 1967):7–11. (Review of Allen, *William James.* New York: Viking, 1967) Also in *J.A.S.P.R.* 62(Jan. 1968):87–94.

——— and ———. Soviet Life and Soviet Psychology. In *Some Views on Soviet Psychology.* Washington, D.C.: American Psychological Association, 1962. (Chapter 8, pp. 253–276.)

——— and ———. *Western Psychology.* New York: Basic Books, 1969.

———; ———; and Newcomb, T. *Experimental Social Psychology,* rev. ed. New York: Harper, 1937.

———, and Postman, Leo. The Factor of Attitude in Associative Memory. *J. Exper. Psychol.* 33(1943):228–238.

———, and Proshansky, Harold. The Effects of Reward and Punishment on Perception. *J. Psychol.* 13(1942):295–305.

———, and Santos, John F. Perceptual Learning and Reality Testing. *Percep. & Motor Skills.* 13(Oct. 1961):130.

——— and ———. An Odyssey in Perceptual Learning. *Bull. Menninger Clin.* 24(1960):6–17.

———, and Schafer, Roy. The Role of Autism in a Visual Figure-Ground Relationship. *J. Exper. Psychol.* 32(1943):335–343.

———, and Schmeidler, G.R. The Influence of Belief and Disbelief in ESP upon Individual Scoring Levels. *J. Exp. Psychol.* 36(1946):271–276.

———, and Solley, Charles M. *Development of the Perceptual World.* New York: Basic Books, 1960.

——— and ———. Learning to Perceive as We Wish to Perceive. *Bull. Menninger Clin.* 21(1957):225–237.

———, and Spohn, H. *Encounter with Reality.* Boston: Houghton Mifflin, 1968.

———; Taves, Ernest; and Dale, L.A. American Experiments on the Paranormal Cognition of Drawings. *J.A.S.P.R.* 39(July 1945):144–150.

———; ———; and ———. A Further Report on the Midas Touch. *J.A.S.P.R.* 37(July 1943):111–118.

———, and Wallerstein, Robert S. Perspectives of the Research Department of the Menninger Foundation. *Bull. Menninger Clin.* 18(1954):223–231.

———, and Woodruff, J.L. Effect of Incentives on ESP and Visual Perception. *J. Parapsychol.* 7(Sept. 1943):144–157.

Murphy, Lois Barclay. *The Home Hospital.* New York: Basic Books, 1982.

———. *Personality in Young Children,* 2 vols. New York: Basic Books, 1956.

———. *Social Behavior and Child Personality.* New York: Columbia University Press, 1937.

———. *Widening World of Childhood.* New York: Basic Books, 1962.

———, and Hirschberg, J. Cotter. *Robin: Comprehensive Treatment of a Vulnerable Adolescent.* New York: Basic Books, 1982.

_____, and Ladd, Henry. *Emotional Factors in Learning.* New York: Columbia University Press, 1944.

_____, and Leeper, Ethel. *Caring for Children.* (Ten booklets for Head Start.) Washington, D.C. U.S. Department of Health, Education and Welfare, Office of Child Development. U.S. Government Printing Office. DHEW Publication No. (OHDS)78-31026-31030; (OCD)77-31031; 76-31032; 74-1033; 74-1035.

_____, and Moriarty, Alice E. *Vulnerability, Coping and Growth.* New Haven: Yale University Press, 1976.

Murphy, Maud King. *Edgar Gardner Murphy: From Records and Memories.* New York: privately printed, 1943. In History of Psychology Archives. University of Akron, Ohio.

_____. My Two Rivers. *Harper's Monthly Magazine,* October, 1896.

Murray, H.A. *Explorations in Personality.* New York: Oxford University Press, 1938.

Myers, F.W.H. *Human Personality and Its Survival of Bodily Death,* vols. 1–2. London, Longmans Green, 1903.

Myrdal, Gunnar. *An American Dilemma: The Negro Problem and Modern Democracy.* New York: Harper, 1944.

Nelson, Raymond. *Van Wyck Brooks: A Writer's Life.* New York: E.P. Dutton, 1981.

Newcomb, Theodore. *Personality and Social Change: Attitude Formation in a Social Community.* New York: Holt, 1943.

_____. *Social Psychology.* New York: Dryden, 1950.

_____. Theodore M. Newcomb. In *A History of Psychology in Autobiography* (Vol. VI), edited by Gardner Lindzey. Englewood Cliffs, N.J.: Prentice-Hall, 1974.

Nietzsche, Friedrich. *The Birth of Tragedy,* trans. by Francis Golffing. Garden City, N.Y.: Doubleday, 1956.

Northrup, F.S.C. *Science and First Principles.* New York: Macmillan, 1931.

Nyman, Lawrence. "Recollections. An Oral History of the Psychology Department of the City College of the City University of New York." City College Archives. 1976.

Ogden, C.K., and Richards, I.A. *The Meaning of Meaning.* London: Kegan Paul, 1923.

Osborn, Frederick H. *Preface to Eugenics.* New York: Harper, 1957.

Oshinsky, David. *A Conspiracy So Immense: The World of Joe McCarthy.* New York: Free Press, 1983.

Osis, K. The American Society for Psychical Research 1941–1985: A Personal View. *J.A.S.P.R.* 79(1985):501–529.

Owen, Robert. *The Life of Robert Owen, Written by Himself.* London: E. Wilson, 1857–1858.

Pachter, Marc, ed. *Telling Lives: The Biographer's Art.* By Leon Edel, Justin Kaplan, Alfred Kazin, Doris Kearns, Theodore Rosengarten, Barbara Tuchman, Geoffrey Wolff. Washington, D.C.: New Republic Books, 1979.

Parrington, V.L. *Main Currents in American Thought.* New York: Harcourt, Brace, 1927.

Peatman, J., and Hartley, E.L., eds. *Festschrift for Gardner Murphy.* New York: Harper and Row, 1960.

Perry, R.B. *The Thought and Character of William James,* vols. 1–2. Boston: Little, Brown, 1935.

Piaget, Jean. *The Child's Conception of Physical Causality.* London: Kegan Paul, 1930.

_____. *The Child's Conception of the World.* New York: Harcourt, Brace, 1929.

_____. *The Construction of Reality in the Child.* New York: Basic Books, 1954.

_____. Jean Piaget. In *A History of Psychology in Autobiography* (Vol. IV), edited by E.G. Boring, H.S. Langfeld, et al. Worcester, Mass.: Clark University Press, 1952.

_____. *Judgment and Reasoning in the Child.* New York: Harcourt, Brace, 1928.

_____. *The Language and Thought of the Child.* London: Routledge, 1932.

_____. *The Moral Judgment of the Child.* London: Kegan Paul, 1932.

_____. *The Origins of Intelligence in Children.* New York: International Universities Press, 1952.

Plato. *The Republic.* Various editions, especially that trans. by Benjamin Jowett (1881).
_____. *The Symposium.* Various editions.
Postman, Leo. The Experimental Analysis of Motivational Factors in Perception. *Current Theory and Research in Motivation: A Symposium.* Lincoln: University of Nebraska Press, 1953.
_____. Toward a General Theory of Cognition. In *Social Psychology at the Crossroads,* edited by J.H. Rohrer and M. Sheridan. New York: Harper, 1951, pp. 242–272.
_____, and Murphy, Gardner. The Factor of Attitude in Associative Memory. *J. Exper. Psychol.* 33(1943):228–238.
Pratt, J.G. *Gaither Pratt: A Life for Parapsychology,* edited by Jürgen Keil. Jefferson, N.C.: McFarland, 1987.
_____. William McDougall and Present-Day Psychical Research. *J.A.S.P.R.* 64(4)(1970):385–403.
Proshansky, H.M. Reflections on Some SPSSI Issues. *J. Social Issues.* 42(1986):133–136.
_____, and Murphy, Gardner. The Effects of Reward and Punishment on Perception. *J. Psychol.* 13(1942):295–305.
Pyle, Howard. *The Story of King Arthur and His Knights.* (Reproduction of 1903 ed.) New York: Macmillan, 1984.
Quénetain, Tanneguy de. Origines et aboutissements du pouvoir de la musique. *Réalités.* 141(1957):80–117.
Ram, Pars. A UNESCO Study of Social Tensions in Aligarh, 1951–2. History of Psychology Archives in Akron, Ohio, 1952.
_____, and Murphy, Gardner. Recent Investigations of Hindu-Muslim Relations in India. *Human Organization.* 11(1952):13–16.
Rapaport, David. *Organization and Pathology of Thought.* New York: Columbia University Press, 1951.
_____; Gill, Merton; and Schafer, Roy. *Diagnostic Psychological Testing,* edited by Robert R. Holt, rev. ed. New York: International Universities Press, 1968.
Razran, G. Conditioning and Perception. *Psychol. Rev.* 62(1955):83–95.
_____. Russian Physiologists' Psychology and American Experimental Psychology: A Historical and a Systematic Collation and a Look into the Future. *Psychol. Bull.* 62(1965):42–64.
Reisman, David. *Individualism Reconsidered.* Glencoe, Ill.: Free Press, 1954.
_____. *The Lonely Crowd.* New Haven: Yale University Press, 1950.
Rhine, J.B. *Extra-Sensory Perception.* Boston: Bruce Humphries, 1934.
Robinson, James Harvey. *The Mind in the Making.* New York: Harper, 1921.
Ross, E.A. *Social Psychology: An Outline and Source Book.* New York: Macmillan, 1908.
Rossman, J. *The Psychology of the Inventor.* Washington, D.C.: Inventors' Publishing Co., 1931.
Rosten, Leo. *Rome Wasn't Burned in a Day.* Garden City, N.Y.: Doubleday, 1972.
Rourke, Constance. *The Roots of American Culture,* edited by Van Wyck Brooks. New York: Harcourt, Brace & World, 1942.
Rousey, Clyde, and Moriarty, Alice E. *Diagnostic Implications of Speech Sounds.* Springfield, Ill.: Charles C. Thomas, 1965.
Russell, Bertrand. *The Free Man's Worship.* Portland, Maine: Mosher, 1923.
_____. *Marriage and Morals.* New York: Liveright, 1929.
Salinger, J.D. *The Catcher in the Rye.* Boston: Little, Brown, 1951.
Samelson, Franz. Struggle for Scientific Authority: The Reception of Watson's Behaviorism, 1913–1920. *J. History of the Behavioral Sciences.* 17(1981):399–425.
Sanford, R.N. The Effects of Abstinence from Food Upon the Imaginal Processes. A Preliminary Experiment. *J. Psychol.* 2(1936):129–136.
Sargent, Helen D. Intrapsychic Change: Methodological Problems in Psychotherapy Research. *Psychiatry.* 24(1961):93–108.

Schachtel, Ernst. *Metamorphosis: On the Development of Affect, Perception, Attention and Memory*. New York: Basic Books, 1959.

Schafer, Roy, and Murphy, Gardner. The Role of Autism in Figure-Ground Relationships. *J. Exp. Psychol.* 32(1943):335–343.

Scheerer, M. Spheres of Meaning: An Analysis of Stages from Perception to Abstract Thinking. *J. Ind. Psychol.* 15(1959):50–61.

Schilder, Paul. *Image and Appearance of the Human Body*. London: Psyche Monographs, 1936.

_____. *Mind: Perception and Thought in Their Constructive Aspects*. New York: Columbia University Press, 1942, Chapter XX.

Schlesinger, Frank. *William Lewis Elkin, 1855–1933*. Washington, D.C.: National Academy of Sciences, 1937.

Schmeidler, Gertrude R., and McConnell, R.A. *ESP and Personality Patterns*. New Haven: Yale University Press, 1958.

Schrödinger, Erwin. *What Is Life? The Physical Aspect of the Living Cell*. New York: Macmillan, 1945.

Scott, John Paul. *Animal Behavior*. Chicago: University of Chicago Press, 1958.

Sears, R. Motivational Factors in Aptitude Testing. *Am. J. Ortho.* 13(1943):465–493.

Seidenberg, Roderick. *Posthistoric Man: An Inquiry*. Chapel Hill: University of North Carolina Press, 1950.

Seton, Ernest Thompson. *Two Little Savages*. New York: Doubleday, 1903.

Seward, John P. The Effect of Practice on the Visual Perception of Form. *Arch. Psychol.* 130(1931):20.

Sherif, M. The Psychology of Social Norms. New York: Harper, 1936.

_____, et al. *Experimental Study of Positive and Negative Intergroup Attitudes Between Experimentally Produced Groups. Robbers' Cave Study*. Norman: University of Oklahoma, 1954.

Sherringon, C.S. *The Integrative Action of the Nervous System*. London: Constable, 1906.

Shevrin, H., and Fritzler, D.E. Visually Evoked Response Correlates of Unconscious Mental Processes. *Science*. 161(1968):295–98.

Shils, E. Tradition, Ecology and Institution in the History of Sociology. In "The Making of Modern Science." *Daedalus*. Cambridge, Mass.: American Academy of Arts and Sciences, 1970.

Shoben, Edward J. *Lionel Trilling*. New York: Ungar, 1981.

Simpson, G.G. *The Meaning of Evolution: A Study of the History of Life, and of Its Significance for Man*. New Haven: Yale University Pres, 1949.

Simpson, J.E. The Influence of Auditory Stimulation on Aniseikonic Perception: A Preliminary Study. *J. Psychol.* 41(1956):235–241.

Skinner, B.F. *The Behavior of Organisms*. New York: Appleton-Century, 1938.

Smith, G. Visual Perception: An Event Over Time. *Psychol. Rev.* 64(1957):306–313.

Smith, M. Brewster. *Social Psychology and Human Values*. Chicago: Aldine, 1969.

Smith, Page. *The Rise of Industrial America*, vol. VI. New York: McGraw-Hill, 1984.

Snyder, F.W., and Snyder, C.W. The Effects of Reward and Punishment on Auditory Perception. *J. Psychol.* 31(1956):177–184.

Sokolov, E.N., ed. *The Orienting Reflex and Problems of Higher Nervous Activity*. Moscow: APN-RSFSR, 1959.

Solley, Charles M. Affect, Fantasy and Figure-Ground Organization. *J. Genet. Psychol.* 62(1960):75–82.

_____, and Engel, Mary. Perceptual Autism in Children: The Effects of Reward, Punishment and Neutral Conditions upon Perception Learning. *J. Genet. Psychol.* 97(1960):77–91.

_____; Jackson, D.N.; and Messick, S.J. Guessing Behavior and Autism. *J. Abnorm. & Soc. Psychol.* 54(1957):32–36.

————, and Long, J. Perceptual Learning Versus Response Set Learning. *Percept. & Motor Skills.* 8(1958):235–240.

————. Reduction of Error with Practice in Perception of the Postural Vertical. *J. Exp. Psychol.* 52(1956):329–333.

————, and Santos, John. Perceptual Learning with Partial Verbal Reinforcement. *Percept. & Motor Skills.* 8(1958):183–193.

————, and Sommer, R. Perceptual Autism in Children. *J. Gen. Psychol.* 56(1957):3–11.

Sommer, R. The Effects of Rewards and Punishments during Perceptual Organization. *J. Pers.* 25(1957):550–558.

Sontag, Lester W.; Baker, C.T.; and Nelson, V.L. Mental Growth and Personality Development: A Longitudinal Study. *Monographs of the Society for Research in Child Development 23* (Serial No. 68), 1958.

Spencer, H. *First Principles.* New York: Appleton, 1900.

Spinoza, B. *Ethica (The Ethics)* (1677). Malibu, Calif.: J. Simon Publishing Co., 1981.

Stagner, Ross. *A History of Psychology Theories.* New York: Macmillan, 1988.

————. *Psychology of Personality.* New York: McGraw-Hill, 1936.

————. Reminiscences About the Founding of SPSSI. *J. Social Issues.* 42(1986).

Spitz, René. *Anaclitic Depression: An Inquiry into the Genesis of Psychiatric Conditions in Early Childhood. Psychoanalytic Study of the Child,* vol. 2. New York: International Universities Press, 1946.

Stapledon, W.O. *To the End of Time,* edited by Basil Davenport. New York: Doubleday, 1953.

Steig, William. *Persistent Faces.* New York: Duell, Sloan & Pearce, 1945.

Steinbeck, John. "Of Mice and Men." In *Twenty Best Plays of the Modern American Theatre,* edited by John Gassner. New York: Modern Library, 1958.

Stekel, Wilhelm. *The Interpretation of Dreams: New Developments and Techniques,* trans. by Eden and Cedar Paul. New York: Liveright, 1943.

Stern, W. *General Psychology from the Personalistic Standpoint,* trans. by H.D. Spoerl. New York: Macmillan, 1938.

Stevenson, Ian. *Twenty Cases Suggestive of Reincarnation,* 2nd ed., revised and enlarged. Charlottesville: University of Virginia Press, 1974.

Stewart, Charles W. *Adolescent Religion: A Developmental Study of the Religion of Youth.* Nashville: Abingdon Press, 1967.

Stoddard, W.O. *Two Arrows.* New York: Harper, 1886.

Sullivan, Harry S. *Conceptions of Modern Psychiatry.* Washington, D.C.: William Alanson White Foundation, 1947.

————. *The Interpersonal Theory of Psychiatry.* New York: Norton, 1953.

Sullivan, J.W.N. *The Limitations of Science.* New York: Viking Press, 1940.

Sumner, W.G. *Folkways.* Boston: Ginn, 1906.

Swift, Jonathan. *Gulliver's Travels* (1726). Various editions.

Szilard, Leo. Disarmament and the Problem of Peace. *Bulletin of the Atomic Scientists.* 11(1955):297–357.

Tarde, G. *The Laws of Imitation,* trans. by E.C. Parsons. New York: Holt, 1903. (Originally published 1890).

Tart, C.T., ed. *Altered States of Consciousness.* New York: Wiley, 1969.

Taves, E.; Dale, L.A.; and Murphy, Gardner. A Further Report on the Midas Touch. *J.A.S.P.R.* 37(1943):111–118.

Tawney, R.H. *Religion and the Rise of Capitalism: A Historical Study.* New York: Harcourt, 1926.

Taylor, James B. "Doorstep Psychiatry: In the Low Income Ghetto." Unpublished, 1971. Research Archives of the Menninger Foundation.

————; Zurcher, L.A.; and Key, W.H. *Tornado: A Community Response to Disaster.* Seattle: University of Washington Press, 1970.

Teilhard de Chardin, Pierre. *The Phenomenon of Man.* New York: Harper and Row, 1961.

Thomas, W.I., and Znaniecki, F. *The Polish Peasant in America,* vols. 1–5. Boston: Badger, 1918–1920.

Thompson, W.R. Traits, Factors and Genes. *Eugenics Quart.* 4(1957):8–16.

Thoreau, Henry D. *Walden.* Boston: Ticknor and Fields, 1854.

Thorndike, Edward Lee. *Educational Psychology. Vol. I: Original Nature of Man.* New York: Teachers College, Columbia University, 1913.

Tietze, T.R. The "Margery" Affair. *J.A.S.P.R.* 79(1985):339–379.

Tinburgen, N. *The Study of Instinct.* London: Oxford University Press, 1951.

Titchener, E.B. *A Textbook of Psychology.* New York: Macmillan, 1910.

Tolman, Edward C. Cognitive Maps in Rats and Men. *Psychol. Rev.* 55(1948):189–208.

————. *Drives Toward War.* New York: Appleton-Century, 1942.

————. Edward Chase Tolman. In *A History of Psychology in Autobiography,* vol. IV, edited by E.G. Boring et al. Worcester, Mass.: Clark University Press, 1952.

————. *Purposive Behavior in Animals and Men.* New York: Appleton-Century, 1932.

Toynbee, Arnold. *A Study of History.* New York: Oxford, 1949.

Train, Arthur Cheney. *Puritan's Progress.* New York: Scribner, 1931.

Troland, L.T. "A Technique for the Experimental Study of Telepathy and Other Alleged Clairvoyant Processes." Unpublished, Albany, N.Y., 1917.

Trotter, W. *Instincts of the Herd in Peace and War.* London: Unwin, 1916.

Ullman, M.; Krippner, S.; and Feldstein, S. Experimentally Induced Telepathic Dreams: Two Studies Using EEG-REM Techniques. *Int. S. Neuropsychiat.* 2(1966):420–37.

————; ————; and Vaughan, A. *Dream Telepathy.* New York: Macmillan, 1973. (2nd ed., Jefferson, N.C.: McFarland, 1989.)

Veblen, Thorstein. *The Theory of the Leisure Class: An Economic Study of Institutions.* New York: B.W. Huebsch, 1924.

Velde, Theodor Henrick van de. *Ideal Marriage.* London: W. Heinemann, 1928.

Voth, Harold M., and Mayman, M. A Dimension of Personality Organization. *Archives of General Psychiatry.* 8(1963):366–380.

Wallerstein, Robert S. *Forty-Two Lives in Treatment: A Study of Psychoanalysis and Psychotherapy.* New York: Guilford Press, 1986.

Walters, R.H. Conditioning of Attention as a Source of Autistic Effects in Perception. *J. Abnorm. & Soc. Psychol.* 57(1958):197–201.

Warcollier, René. *Experimental Telepathy,* trans. by J. Gridley; edited with foreword by Gardner Murphy. Boston: Boston Society for Psychical Research, 1938.

Warner, L.W., and Lunt, P.S. *The Social Life of a Modern Community.* (Yankee City Series, vol. 1.) New Haven: Yale University Press, 1941.

Washburn, Margaret Floy. *Movement and Mental Imagery.* Boston: Houghton Mifflin, 1916.

Washington, Booker T. *Up from Slavery.* New York: Doubleday, 1901.

Watson, Goodwin. *Civilian Morale.* (Yearbook of the Society for the Psychological Study of Social Issues.) Boston: Houghton Mifflin, 1942.

Watson, J.B. *Behaviorism,* rev. ed. New York: Norton, 1930. (Originally published 1924.)

————. *Psychological Care of Infant and Child.* New York: Norton, 1928.

Webb, W.P. *The Great Plains.* Boston: Houghton Mifflin, 1936.

Weiner, M. Effects of Training in Space Orientation on Perception of the Upright. *J. Exp. Psychol.* 49(1955):367–373.

Wells, Carolyn. *Nonsense Anthology.* New York: Dover Publications, 1958. (Originally published by Ayer, 1902.)

Wells, H.G. *Outline of History.* London: G. Newnes, 1920.

Werner, H. *Comparative Psychology of Mental Development,* trans. by E.B. Garside. New York: Harper, 1940.

Wertheimer, Max. *Productive Thinking,* edited by Michael Wertheimer. Enlarged. New York: Harper, 1969. (Original English edition published 1945.)

White, Lynn, Jr., ed. *Frontiers of Knowledge in the Study of Man.* New York: Harper, 1956.

White, Ralph K. *Fearful Warriors: A Psychological Profile of U.S.-Soviet Relations.* New York: Macmillan, Free Press, 1974.

White, R.W., ed. *The Study of Lives: Essays on Personality in Honor of Henry A. Murray.* New York: Atherton, 1963.

Whitman, Walt. *Leaves of Grass.* New York: Modern Library, 1944 and many other editions.

Whyte, Lancelot W. *The Next Development in Man.* New York: Holt, 1948.

Whyte, William H., Jr. *The Organization Man.* New York: Simon and Schuster, 1956.

Wiener, Norbert. *Cybernetics.* New York: Wiley, 1948.

_____. *The Human Use of Human Beings: Cybernetics and Society.* Garden City, N.Y.: Doubleday, 1951.

Wilder, Thornton. *The Skin of Our Teeth.* New York: Harper, 1942.

Witkin, H.A. *Personality and Perception.* New York: Harper, 1954.

Wolman, B.B., ed. *Handbook of Parapsychology.* New York: Van Nostrand, Reinhold, 1977. See chapter on Gardner Murphy. (Reprinted, Jefferson, N.C.: McFarland, 1986.)

Woodworth, R.S. *Dynamic Psychology.* New York: Columbia University Press, 1918.

_____. *Experimental Psychology.* New York: Holt, 1938.

Woolley, Helen T., Personality Study of Three-Year-Olds. *J. Exp. Psychol.* 5(1922): 381–391.

Wundt, W. *Outlines of Psychology,* trans. by C.H. Judd. Leipzig: Wilhelm Engelmann, 1897.

Yerkes, R.M., and LaRue, D.W. *Outline of a Study of the Self.* Cambridge, Mass.: Harvard University Press, 1913.

Young, P.T. Studies of Food Preference, Appetite and Dietary Habit. *J. Comp Psychol.* 39(1946):139–176.

Zachry, C. *Emotion and Conduct in Adolescence.* New York: Appleton-Century, 1940.

Zimmer, Heinrich. *Philosophies of India.* New York: Meridian Books, 1956.

Zurcher, Louis A. *Poverty Warriors.* Austin: University of Texas Press, 1970.

_____, and Bonjean, C.M., eds. *Planned Social Intervention: An Interdisciplinary Anthology.* Scranton, Pa.: Chandler, 1970.

Index

Blos, Peter, xi, 169, 170 183
Boardman, Ruth, 102
Boas, Franz, 14, 122, 130, 174, 198
"Boche psychology," 95
body/mind dualism, 287
Boehme, Jacob 206
Boettinger, Henrietta, 158
Bombay, 241, 242, 246, 247, 249
Boothe, Helvi, 261
Boring, E.G., 13, 108, 146, 234
Boston Society for Psychical Research, 227
Boston West End Community Study, 284
Botticelli, 299
Boyle, Robert, 213
Braatøy, Trygve, 275, 286
Brahmin Hindus, 240
brain, relation to mind/body dualism, 217;
   damage, 256
Brain and Personality, by Dr. Thompson, 86
Braly, Kenneth 149
Brandeis university, 175
Brenman, Margaret, xi, 20
Brett, G.S., 90, 107, 108
Brewster, Huldah, 32
Brewster, Elder William, 31, 32
Brewsters, ancestors of G. Murphy, 31
Bridges, K.M.B. 125
Briefer General Psychology, by G.
   Murphy, 112
Brighams, ancestors of G. Murphy, 31
Bronxville, N.Y., ix, 3, 21, 104, 188
Brooklyn College, 160, 174
Brooks, the Reverend Phillips, 42
Brown, J.F., 128, 138, 139
Brown, Norman W., 241
Brown vs. the Board of Education, 4, 150, 151
Bruner, Jerome, xi, 155, 156
Brussels International Congress of
   Psychologists, 166
Bryan, Alice, xi
Bryant, Keith, 260
Bühler, Charlotte, 163, 164
Bulletin of the Menninger Clinic, 265, 289, 292
Bunyan, Paul, 206, 207
"Burgee's Gang," 75
Burgess, Gelett, 179
Burks, Barbara, 144, 167, 175
Burns, Robert, 33, 180
Butler, Nicholas Murray, 112, 116

C

Cadbury, Dr., 178
Calcutta, 214, 242, 244, 250

California, University of, 106
Calvinism, 65, 67, 131
Cambodia, 249
Cambridge University, England, 244
Cambridge University, Peterhaus, 4
Camp Algonquin, 53, 74, 199
canalization, 127, 129, 199, 204, 210, 212
Cape Cod, 33, 37
capitalism, 97
Caribbean, 295
Caring for Children, by L.B. Murphy, 144
Carlson, Sen. Frank, 291
Carmichael, Leonard, 91, 116, 117, 118
Carnegie, Andrew, 39, 44, 57
Carraway, Dr. Robert xi
Carroll, Lewis, 179
Carter, R.L., 151
Cartwright, D., 137
Caruso, Enrico, 33
case study of a resilient child by L.B.
   Murphy, 256
cathexis, 129, 205
Catholic ethics, 131
Center for International Studies at Massa-
   chusetts Institute of Technology, 97
Center for Research in Conflict Resolution, 291
Central America, 291
Challenge of Psychical Research, The,
   by G. Murphy with L.A. Dale, 220, 229
Chand, Tara, 241
Charcot, J.M., 197
Chari, M., xi
Chassell, Joseph, xi, 102
Chein, Dr. Isador, 149, 150
Chicago, University of, 4, 172
Child, Irvin, xi, 224, 233
child development, in India, 241
childbirth, and psychical research, 230
Childhood and Society, by E.H.
   Erikson, 27, 168
children, perceptions of figure-ground rela-
   tionship, 275; and personality, 214;
   responses to stress, 289; and JFK's assassi-
   nation, 289
Children's Services, Menninger
   Foundation, 256
Chillicothe, Ohio, 35, 43, 51, 66
Chisholm, George Brock, 144
Chowdry, Kamla, 241, 250
Christians, in India, 249
Christianson, Bjorn, 286
Chrysanthemum and the Sword, The, by R.
   Benedict, 174